design

THE DEFINITIVE VISUAL GUIDE

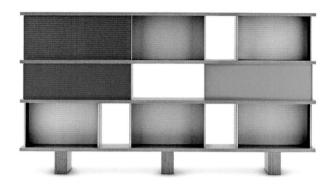

design

THE DEFINITIVE VISUAL GUIDE

DK

DK Penguin Random House

Senior Editor	Angela Wilkes
Senior Art Editors	Gadi Farfour, Jane Ewart
Project Editor	Hugo Wilkinson
Editors	Anna Fischel, Sammy Kennedy, Stuart Neilson
US Editor	Jennette ElNaggar
Designers	Stephen Bere, Phil Gamble
Picture Researchers	Sarah Smithies, Liz Moore
Managing Editor	Gareth Jones
Senior Managing Art Editor	Lee Griffiths
Producer, Pre-production	Nikoleta Parasaki
Senior Producer	Mandy Inness
Jacket Designer	Mark Cavanagh
Design Development Manager	Sophia M.T.T.
Publishing Director	Jonathan Metcalf
Associate Publishing Director	Liz Wheeler
Art Director	Phil Ormerod
Deputy Art Director	Karen Self
Consultants	Keith Baker, Professor Jonathan Woodham
Writers	Alexandra Black, R. G. Grant, Ann Kay, Philip Wilkinson, Iain Zaczek

Delhi Team

Senior Editor	Sreshtha Bhattacharya
Senior Art Editor	Anjana Nair
Assistant Editor	Ira Pundeer
Project Art Editor	Neha Sharma
Art Editor	Akanksha Gupta, Namita
Assistant Art Editors	Meenal Goel, Priyansha Tuli
Managing Editor	Pakshalika Jayaprakash
Managing Art Editor	Arunesh Talapatra
Production Manager	Pankaj Sharma
Pre-production Manager	Balwant Singh
Senior DTP Designer	Sachin Singh, Vishal Bhatia
DTP Designers	Syed Md Farhan
Picture Researcher	Surya Sankash Sarangi

Smithsonian Enterprises

President	Christopher A. Liedel
Senior Vice President	Carol LeBlanc
Vice President	Brigid Ferraro
Licensing Manager	Ellen Nanney
Key Accounts Manager	Cheryl Stepanek
Product Development Manager	Kealy Gordon

This American Edition, 2021
First American Edition, 2015
Published in the United States by DK Publishing
1450 Broadway, Suite 801, New York, NY 10018

Copyright © 2015, 2021 Dorling Kindersley Limited
DK, a Division of Penguin Random House LLC
21 22 23 24 25 10 9 8 7 6 5 4 3 2 1
001–316696–March/2021

A catalog record for this book is available from the Library of Congress.
ISBN 978-1-4654-9137-4

DK books are available at special discounts when purchased in bulk for sales promotions, premiums, fund-raising, or educational use. For details, contact: DK Publishing Special Markets, 1450 Broadway, Suite 801, New York, NY 10018
SpecialSales@dk.com

Printed and bound in China

For the curious
www.dk.com

MIX
Paper from responsible sources
FSC™ C018179

This book was made with Forest Stewardship Council ™ certified paper—one small step in DK's commitment to a sustainable future. For more information go to www.dk.com/our-green-pledge

Contents

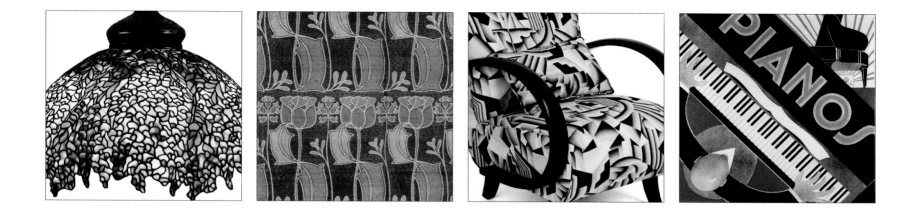

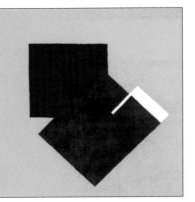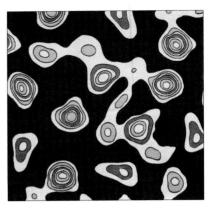

POSTMODERN & CONTEMPORARY
1980s onward

314

✸ Smithsonian

Established in 1846, the Smithsonian—the world's largest museum and research complex—includes 19 museums and galleries and the National Zoological Park. The Smithsonian is a renowned research center, dedicated to public education, national service, and scholarship in the arts, sciences, and history.

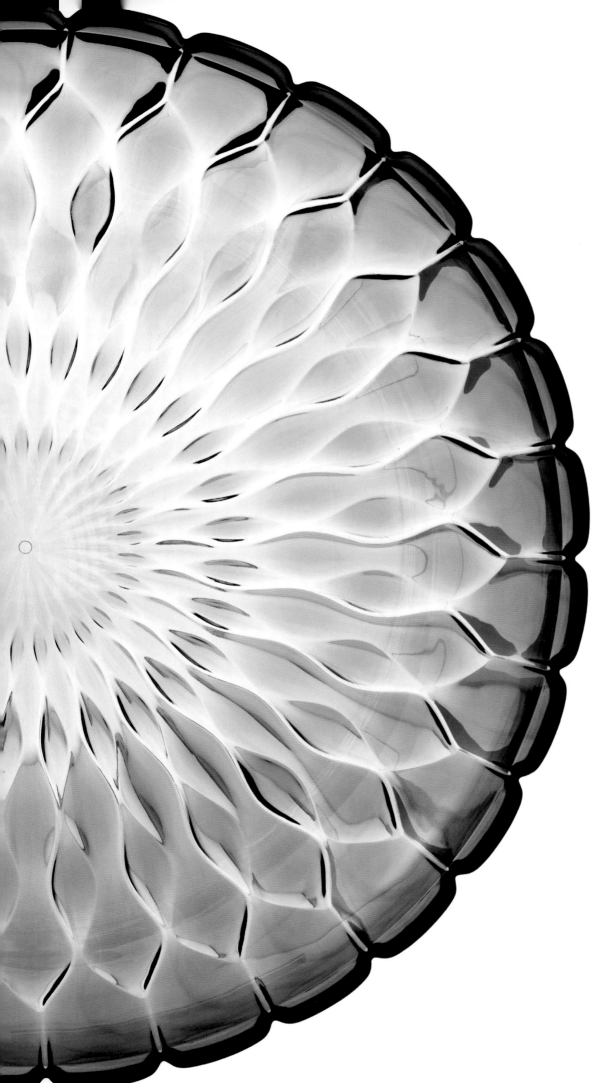

**Industry,
invading like
a river that rolls
to its destiny,
brings us
new tools.**

Le **Corbusier**

Man loves everything that satisfies his comfort.

Adolf **Loos**
Furniture designer

WHAT IS DESIGN?

Design is an attitude.

ROGER TALLON, INDUSTRIAL DESIGNER

Origins

Although design is essentially a 20th-century term, objects have been designed for more than a million years. Paleolithic hand tools are perhaps the world's oldest designed things: the first tools had been found, rather than made, but humans eventually realized that they could create a better tool by designing it. Strategic chipping away at a piece of rock resulted in a shaped tool with a vastly superior cutting edge. This early act of design was an important step in the transition of Stone Age people to modern society.

Aesthetics

Design progressed from its initial, single goal—functionality—to a process in which an object's appearance and its cost were just as important, if not more so, than its usefulness. The classical civilizations of ancient Greece and Rome elevated the aesthetics of design, establishing principles of balance, harmony, and symmetry that have held sway ever since, notably during the Renaissance and the classical revivals of the late 18th and 19th centuries. Ancient Greek currency is one example of the classical emphasis on graceful form and ornamentation, and the elegantly decorated coins of Athens set the standard for modern money design.

Developing typography

The notion that an object's appearance was intertwined with its function also became embodied in the printed word. Around 1439, Johannes Gutenberg invented the printing press, using a movable typeface he had designed, and as print technology developed over subsequent decades, people became interested in typography. Frenchman Claude Garamond created a Roman typeface that combined readability with style rather than simply mimicking handwriting as previous fonts had done. As the first designer to develop and sell typefaces to printers, Garamond was a pioneer of graphic design, a field that came into its own from the late 1800s, spurred by the fledgling advertising industry.

The meaning of design

A century after the printing revolution, "design" entered the languages of Europe. According to etymologists, the word came from the Latin *designare*, meaning to mark out or devise. The root of the word, *signum* (sign), conveys the original intention: to design meant to translate an idea into a written or drawn plan and then sign your name to it. Like the designer, an artist also signs their work, but what sets design apart from art is the purpose: functionality is not essential to art, but it is crucial to design. American designer Charles Eames defined design as "a plan for arranging elements in such a way as best to accomplish a particular purpose." He also believed that design, unlike art, possesses constraints: "… of price, of size, of strength, of balance, of surface, of time …"

From craft to design

Until the 18th century, objects were usually made by craftsmen in a workshop. In the late 1700s, however, the production of goods became increasingly mechanized and the designer became removed from the hands-on process of creation. To produce objects in a factory setting efficiently, it was essential for the designer to devise a comprehensive master plan for workers to follow. At the same time, the growth of towns and cities, and a rising middle class, fueled demand for products.

Eager to win a share of this lucrative market, manufacturers had to pay careful attention to their costs. Price, materials, and production technology became critical to the success of a product, indeed sometimes more so than its

Anglepoise® lamp | George Carwardine, 1934, UK.
This lamp's elegant appearance is derived from its versatile functionality. It is a classic design that has given rise to many variants over the years.

Chandelier | Gio Ponti, 1946, Italy. In this hand-blown chandelier, Ponti takes a classic lighting form and gives it a modern twist with vibrant colors.

usefulness or appearance. During the 20th century, mass-production techniques made design an even more complex task. A designer working in industry now had to collaborate closely with engineers, technologists, and managers to come up with products that would suit the demands of a company's particular market and satisfy expectations regarding quality, visual appeal, and cost.

Rising standards

The spread of industrialization, and the establishment of laws to regulate quality control and safety, brought design to the fore in the second half of the 20th century, and it became a subject that was studied and debated.

Some designers, including Dieter Rams and Terence Conran, have therefore come up with guidelines as to what constitutes good design: the criteria vary a little from one person to another, but most generally agree that good design means something that works well and is easy to use, is pleasing in appearance, and is good value for money. Good design should also be innovative and create objects that last.

Design is now big business, because everything people use has been designed. This focus on design has led to a revival of the designer as craftsperson— someone who is able to produce objects that not only work well and are beautiful to look at but also meet customer expectations.

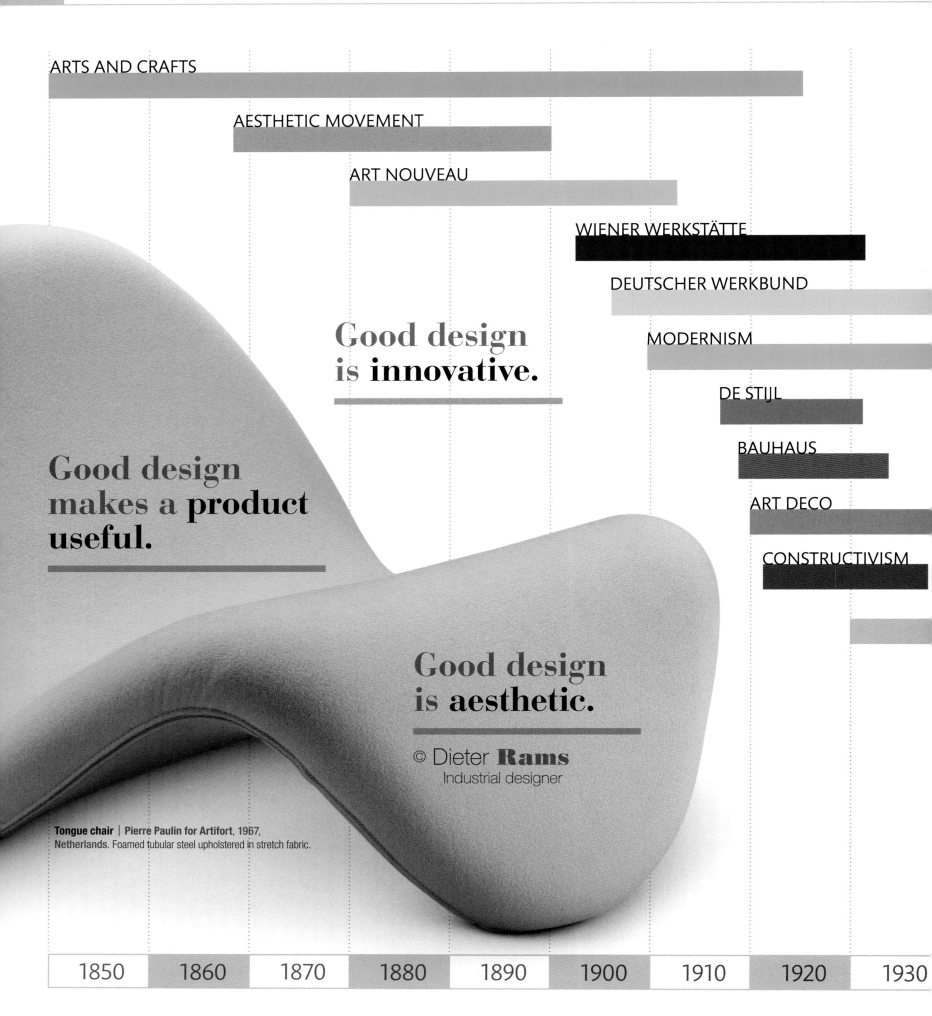

ARTS AND CRAFTS

AESTHETIC MOVEMENT

ART NOUVEAU

WIENER WERKSTÄTTE

DEUTSCHER WERKBUND

MODERNISM

DE STIJL

BAUHAUS

ART DECO

CONSTRUCTIVISM

Good design
is **innovative.**

Good design
makes a **product
useful.**

Good design
is **aesthetic.**

© Dieter **Rams**
Industrial designer

Tongue chair | **Pierre Paulin for Artifort, 1967,**
Netherlands. Foamed tubular steel upholstered in stretch fabric.

| 1850 | 1860 | 1870 | 1880 | 1890 | 1900 | 1910 | 1920 | 1930 |

Chronology

Design as we know it started around the mid-19th century when industrialization made it possible to mass-produce household goods. Then, as now, objects designed for the same purpose could differ widely in appearance, depending on the market for which they were created. Often, however, there was a prevailing style that defined an era, something that is especially clear in hindsight. Sometimes, several styles were in fashion concurrently—

for example, the Aesthetic Movement took place within the Arts and Crafts era and streamlining is associated with Art Deco. Most styles developed in one place and gradually spread to other countries, giving them a regional flavor. Some styles were named after a publication, group, workshop, or cultural shift that gave rise to them; other titles were affixed retrospectively or called by different names in different languages.

Arts and Crafts Influence and ideology spread from the UK to the rest of Europe, especially Austria and Germany, and to the US, where the movement had real strengths

Aesthetic Movement Notion that beauty need serve no purpose; popular in the UK

Art Nouveau Sinuous style in France, Belgium, and UK spread to Central and Eastern Europe and Scandinavia; known as Jugendstil in Germany and Austria, Stile Liberty in Italy, and Modernisme in Spain

Wiener Werkstätte Vienna Workshops in Austria, inspired by William Morris and the Arts and Crafts movement

Deutscher Werkbund German Association of Craftsmen, also inspired by Arts and Crafts, founded in Munich, closed by the Nazis in 1938, and reestablished after World War II

Modernism International, particularly after World War II: Europe, Scandinavia, North America, and Asia. Before World War II, Modernism was associated with social utopianism; after World War II, it became the style of multinational corporations

De Stijl First issue of avant-garde art review *De Stijl* published in the Netherlands in 1917. One of its leaders, Theo van Doesburg, died in 1931, and the magazine ceased publication

The Bauhaus Began in 1919; many teachers and ex-students from this German educational institution emigrated with the rise of the Nazis in Germany, spreading its influence

Art Deco Swept across Europe, the US, China, India, New Zealand, Australia, and South America, with many aspects of it tracing roots back to the 1910s

Constructivism Term conceived in early 1921 in Russia, taken up internationally in the 1920s, for instance, in Poland where the Blok group was set up in 1924, and in the UK and other European countries, as well as South America

Streamlining Fluid aerodynamics applied to product design in the US and Europe

Space Age Characterized by decorative features inspired by the space race between the US and Russia and the moon landing

Pop Art Subject matter featured everyday objects, sometimes physically incorporated, in art in the US and UK

Minimalism Extreme simplicity of form and objective approach taken up in the US, Europe, Japan, and elsewhere

Postmodernism New use of decorative elements and modern materials, inspired by dissatisfaction with Modernism

Contemporary Worldwide

STREAMLINING

SPACE AGE

POP ART

MINIMALISM

POSTMODERNISM

CONTEMPORARY

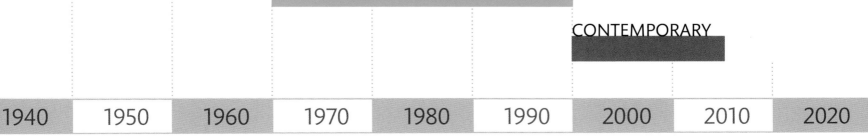

| 1940 | 1950 | 1960 | 1970 | 1980 | 1990 | 2000 | 2010 | 2020 |

Color

Because it creates an instant impact, color is one of the most powerful elements of any design. It is also a critical commercial consideration, attracting or repelling buyers and often overriding other criteria such as materials, shape, and proportion. When choosing colors, designers consider three factors: the hue itself, such as red, yellow, or green; how light or dark the hue is; and its saturation or intensity. Artist Wassily Kandinksy was instrumental in developing modern color theory, assigning particular emotional and psychological attributes to each color. Teaching at the Bauhaus in the 1920s, Kandinsky influenced generations of designers—his ideas about color were expanded by the De Stijl movement and became part of architectural and industrial design practice. From the mid-20th century, designers and manufacturers also began to use colors as branding for their products.

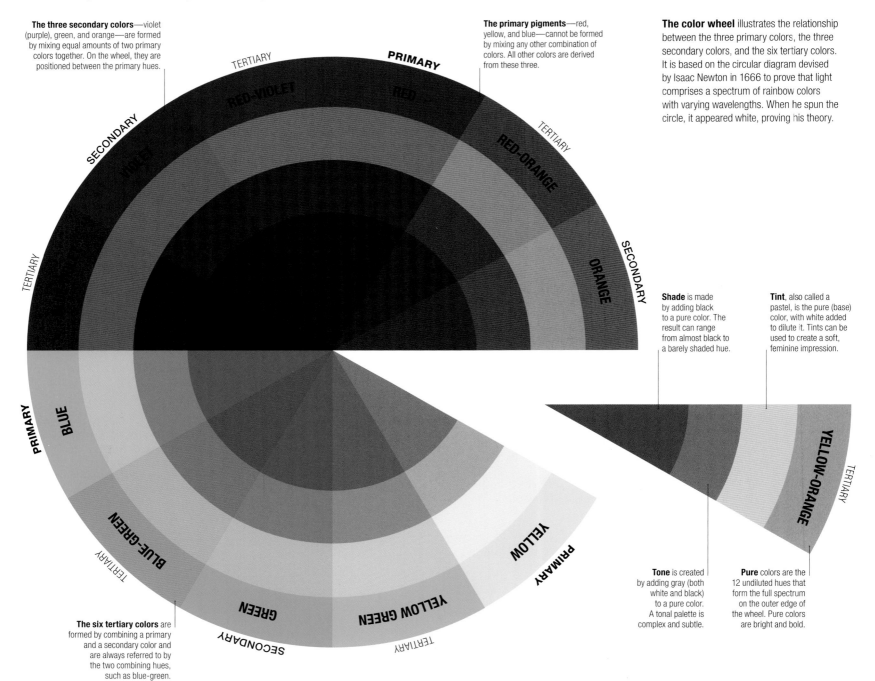

The three secondary colors—violet (purple), green, and orange—are formed by mixing equal amounts of two primary colors together. On the wheel, they are positioned between the primary hues.

The primary pigments—red, yellow, and blue—cannot be formed by mixing any other combination of colors. All other colors are derived from these three.

The color wheel illustrates the relationship between the three primary colors, the three secondary colors, and the six tertiary colors. It is based on the circular diagram devised by Isaac Newton in 1666 to prove that light comprises a spectrum of rainbow colors with varying wavelengths. When he spun the circle, it appeared white, proving his theory.

Shade is made by adding black to a pure color. The result can range from almost black to a barely shaded hue.

Tint, also called a pastel, is the pure (base) color, with white added to dilute it. Tints can be used to create a soft, feminine impression.

Tone is created by adding gray (both white and black) to a pure color. A tonal palette is complex and subtle.

Pure colors are the 12 undiluted hues that form the full spectrum on the outer edge of the wheel. Pure colors are bright and bold.

The six tertiary colors are formed by combining a primary and a secondary color and are always referred to by the two combining hues, such as blue-green.

TERTIARY • PRIMARY • RED-VIOLET • RED • SECONDARY • VIOLET • RED-ORANGE • TERTIARY • TERTIARY • SECONDARY • ORANGE • PRIMARY • BLUE • YELLOW-ORANGE • TERTIARY • BLUE-GREEN • TERTIARY • GREEN • YELLOW GREEN • YELLOW • PRIMARY • SECONDARY • TERTIARY

Primary

Artists and designers use a theory called subtractive color, which starts with the idea that light is white and that the three primary pigments appear that way because they absorb or subtract the wavelengths of other colors. In design, the primary hues are considered the boldest and are often used sparingly as accent colors. Of the three primaries, red has the highest visibility. It can indicate danger, positive energy, strength, love, and war. Yellow is linked to happiness, creativity, and sunshine, while blue is perceived as conservative, tranquil, and trustworthy.

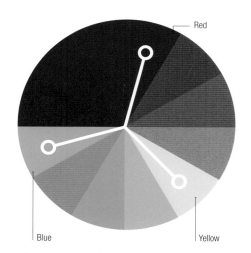

Red

Blue

Yellow

Designers of De Stijl, active during the 1910s and 1920s, used only primary colors. Gerrit Rietveld's chair is a classic example.

Constructivist artist Alexander Rodchenko believed that by using primary colors he could distill art and graphic design into their purest forms.

Complementary

Hues on opposite sides of the color wheel complement each other and can be used to create a dramatic, bold scheme. Complementary pairings always include a primary and a secondary color, one warm and one cool, for maximum contrast—for example, red and green, yellow and violet, blue and orange. Because of the high contrast between complementary colors, they are used for products requiring high visibility, such as an orange lifeboat on a blue-tinted sea, and for designs intended to generate visual tension.

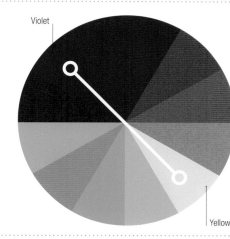

Violet

Yellow

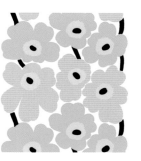

Marco Zanini's ceramic uses violet and yellow as its main color scheme, conveying vibrancy and energy.

Red dominates Yoichi Ohira's glass vase, layered thickly over its opposing green to undercut the heat.

Analogous

Positioned next to each other on the color wheel, analogous colors are also referred to as harmonious because there is little contrast between them and they tend to be either cool or warm, not mixed. Designers often use analogous colors in groups of three, with one color more dominant than the other two. Although they are not as eye-catching as a complementary color scheme, analogous combinations can appear elegant and project an image of richness.

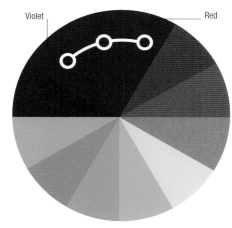

Violet

Red

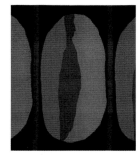

This classic Unikko print for Marimekko is mainly yellow, paired soothingly with its neighbor, yellow-green.

Flavio Poli creates depth with blue-green and blue in different intensities framing a blue-violet center in this vase.

Monochrome

A monochrome color scheme takes a slice from the color wheel from one hue and uses some or all of the tints, tones, and shades within that hue. Because of its simplicity, a monochrome palette is well suited to streamlined design. It allows for high contrast—using the lightest tint and darkest shade together, for example—and is especially useful in graphic design, where legibility is the most important factor. The minimalist design trend of the 1960s and 1970s, which recurred in the 1990s and 2000s, made wide use of monochrome schemes, especially in interiors.

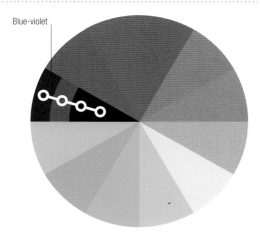

Blue-violet

Shirley Craven designed this fabric in the 1960s for UK manufacturer Hull Traders. She balanced bold shapes with a monochrome palette.

Finnish designer Kaj Franck highlighted the form of his 1958 glass decanter by strategically using monochrome coloring.

Proportion

Although proportion and scale are not always the first elements to catch the eye, they are integral to the overall impression a design conveys. They are separate but interrelated concepts: proportion refers to the position of each component in a design, and the relationship between all of its constituent parts, while scale is the relative size of each component in a design. It is also the size of the design in its entirety compared to the size of the viewer.

Leonardo da Vinci is credited with defining what the "ideal" proportions were, and his ideas provide the basis of modern design practice. Applying the ancient Greek mathematical principle of *phi* to the human figure, Leonardo proposed that the height from foot to navel should be 1.6 times that of navel to head. He applied the same calculations to art and architecture, setting the ideal ratio of height to width as 1.6. This is known as the golden ratio.

The golden ratio demonstrates that when a line is divided into two parts, the longer part divided by the smaller part is equal to the whole length divided by the longer part.

$$\frac{a+b}{a} = \frac{a}{b} = \varphi = 1.61803$$

The architects of ancient Greece used *phi*, which became known as the mathematical divine proportion or golden ratio, to design the Parthenon.

Leonardo da Vinci drew a figure, known as Vitruvian Man, to apply his theory to human physical proportions. In his ideal person, the main intersecting line created by applying the golden ratio falls on the navel.

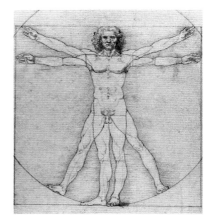

Symmetry

Symmetrical designs have order, stability, and harmony. The simplest type of symmetry is bilateral, in which elements are positioned on either side of an imaginary axis to mirror each other—the axis can have any orientation: vertical, horizontal, diagonal. A love of symmetry is often thought to be ingrained in human nature and forms the basis of conventional notions of beauty.

Marcel Wanders's Tulip armchair (2010) is symmetrical along a vertical axis, with each half a mirror image of the other.

Symmetrically arranged objects tend to have the greatest appeal, since the human body is broadly designed this way.

Scaling up

One of the most dramatic design techniques available is to exaggerate the scale of an object in relation to the person viewing it. This was a common device of the 17th-century Baroque period, with architectural decoration and interior objects scaled up to create a sense of power and awe. Experiments in size were also a feature of design in the 1960s, inspired by the Pop art movement.

The supersized Joe armchair accurately scales up a baseball glove to seat a person.

A simple visual trick, scaling up can heighten the impact of a design by giving it an element of surprise.

Radial symmetry

Derived from circular arrangements found in nature, such as the sun, dandelions, and sea anemones, radial symmetry (also called rotational symmetry) is achieved when design elements radiate out from a central core. Radial symmetry can be used to give a sense of speed and motion and guide the eye in- or outward from the middle.

Patricia Urquiola applies the principle of radial symmetry to bring unity and balance to her Jelly plate for Kartell.

With radial symmetry, viewers focus on the center of the circle and then move their gaze to the outer edge.

Playing with scale

Design is generally expected to adhere to human scale, but when designers alter the relative size of elements they can create unexpected effects, such as distortion, that grab the viewer's attention. The size of a design can be varied in relation to the user or the environment around it. Alternatively, individual parts of the design can be scaled up or down for visual tension.

Graphic designer Josef Müller-Brockmann exaggerates one element to grab the viewer's attention.

The scale and placement of each component can indicate importance within the overall design scheme.

Asymmetry

The opposite of symmetry, asymmetry can interrupt an otherwise symmetrical design to create a visual hierarchy that directs attention to a specific point. Unlike a symmetrical arrangement with its mirror imagery and formal harmony, asymmetrical balance is informal and relaxed, relying on elements that are different but have the same visual weight. While repetition is important to symmetry, contrast is integral to asymmetrical design.

This poster by Kasimir Malevich uses asymmetry to create movement and draw the viewer's eye toward the typography.

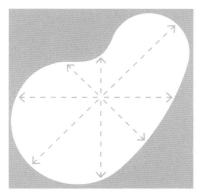

In an asymmetrical design, harmony can be achieved by placing elements off-center but giving each part an equal visual importance.

Ergonomics

Design is ergonomic when it is based on the principle that objects should be suited to the physical needs of the human user. Ergonomics takes into consideration the height, limb length, hand grip, lumbar construction, strength, sensory perception, and movement patterns of the user. The intention of ergonomics is to make products easier to use, safer, and more comfortable, and centers on the points of contact between the designed object and the user.

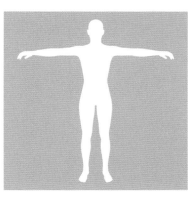

The Aeron chair of 1994 was designed to be fully adjustable in order to fit varied body types.

The science of ergonomic design began with a focus on the workplace but has since spread to other areas of product design.

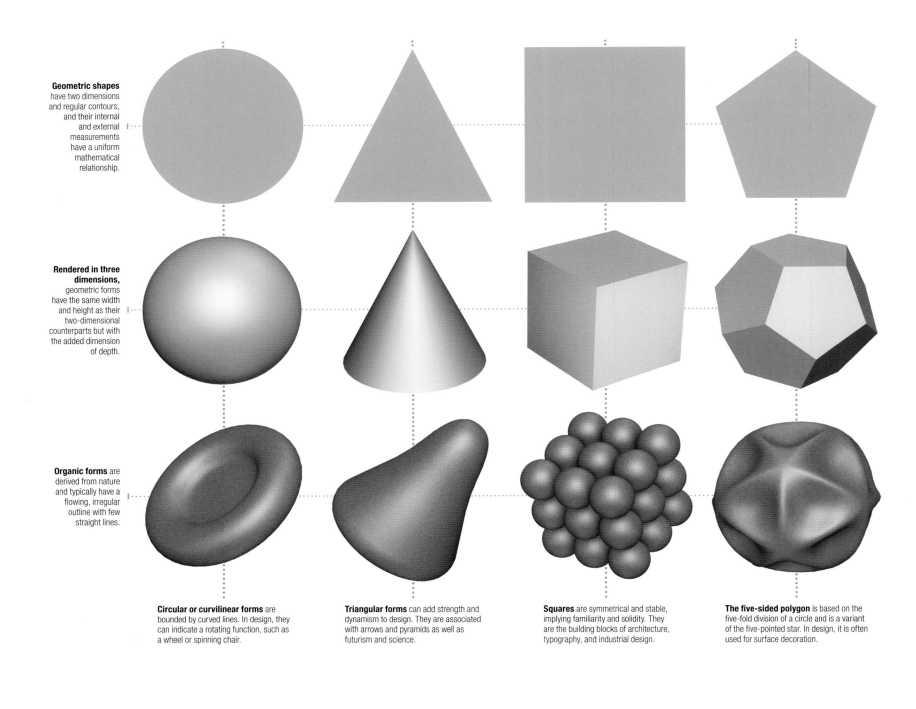

Geometric shapes have two dimensions and regular contours, and their internal and external measurements have a uniform mathematical relationship.

Rendered in three dimensions, geometric forms have the same width and height as their two-dimensional counterparts but with the added dimension of depth.

Organic forms are derived from nature and typically have a flowing, irregular outline with few straight lines.

Circular or curvilinear forms are bounded by curved lines. In design, they can indicate a rotating function, such as a wheel or spinning chair.

Triangular forms can add strength and dynamism to design. They are associated with arrows and pyramids as well as futurism and science.

Squares are symmetrical and stable, implying familiarity and solidity. They are the building blocks of architecture, typography, and industrial design.

The five-sided polygon is based on the five-fold division of a circle and is a variant of the five-pointed star. In design, it is often used for surface decoration.

Shape and Form

The starting points for any design are shape and form: shape is two-dimensional—the outline of an object; form is three-dimensional—the volume that fills out a shape. The brain processes the shape first and then the form, in an attempt to recognize it, drawing on past experience. For this reason, shape is the design variable most closely connected to the end use of an object. Shape can immediately convey the function of an object based on convention and expectation, and designers can play with presumptions of how an object should be shaped for humorous or shocking effects. Designers may innovate by making products that require new processes or that use materials not previously associated with a particular form or shape. But in mass manufacture, logistics and costing generally demand that shape and form are compatible with existing production processes and materials.

Geometric

The most common types of shape and form in the design world, geometric objects and structures have been made since the earliest times. They generate symmetry and a sense of order—a visual attempt to eliminate the randomness and irregularity that is found in nature. Circles, polygons, and lines are the building blocks. Geometric designs are linked with the classical, neoclassical, Art Deco, and Modernist styles and movements.

Bauhaus designers used geometry for clean, simple lines, as in Wilhelm Wagenfeld's lamp.

The polygon is a basic geometric unit, comprising squares and triangles. Its name derives from Greek, meaning "many angles."

Organic

Derived from nature, organic shapes are suited to crafted designs, in which production is largely carried out by hand. Ceramics and glass, for example, lend themselves to the fluid, free-form lines that are typical of organic structures. However, some organic forms are also geometric, such as a snowflake, starfish, or crystal structure.

Panasonic's Toot-a-Loop radio is made from two swiveling sections loosely based on a teardrop outline. They form an "S"-shape when twisted open.

The teardrop or raindrop is instantly recognizable as an organic shape. It can be found in designs as varied as jewelry, cars, ceramics, and furniture.

Isometric

An isometric design creates a pleasing sense of symmetry because all of its dimensions are the same. The classic isometric shapes are the triangle and square, notably used in design patterns from the 1960s and 1970s to create the optical illusion of three dimensions on a two-dimensional surface, such as wallpaper or fabric.

Aldo Rossi turned a humble kettle into a sleek designer object with an isometric form.

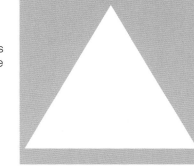

An isometric shape is defined as having equal dimensions on each side, whether in a flat format such as a triangle or its three-dimensional counterpart, the pyramid.

Zoomorphic

Shapes that resemble animals bring humor and playfulness to design, and zoomorphism is a recurring motif in postmodernism, with the intention of challenging accepted ideas about taste and the role of design itself. A greater environmental awareness in design since the 1980s has inspired furniture and home wares that connect with the animal world.

Ettore Sottsass's Tahiti lamp from 1981 is an example of postmodern zoomorphic design.

Just as zoomophorism is used in literature to compare humans and animals, so it is applied in design to contrast the natural world with the human-made.

Combined

Mixing organic and geometric forms together in one design generates a sense of energy. The juxtaposition of the two different shape categories creates visual tension to make a design more dynamic and interesting. Flowing organic elements can soften the crisp lines of a geometric design, and a sense of geometry can order an otherwise organic scheme.

Poul Henningson's 1931 Snake Chair merges a swirling frame with circular forms for the base, seat, and chair back.

Individual geometric elements are concentrically arranged to create the impression of an organic floral structure found in the natural world.

Biomorphic

Abstract and organic, biomorphic forms and shapes are drawn or designed in a free-form style to resemble a living organism. The concept of biomorphism was developed in the 1930s by the surrealists and particularly celebrated spontaneous and irrational design. With irregular outlines, rounded forms, and asymmetry, biomorphic design looks comfortable yet unconventional.

This glass form by Marvin Lipofsky is organic and abstract, inspired by human organs and the volatility of nature.

Biomorphic designs are often based on the outline of an amoeba, the single-cell organism that randomly changes shape.

Pattern and Texture

Texture and pattern are both vital considerations in creating the look and feel of a design. Pattern is the most flexible element, capable of transforming any object through surface decoration. Used to add interest to the mundane and to express individual beliefs or taste, patterns have historically been applied to household objects, textiles, domestic interiors, and public buildings. In modern times, printing techniques have expanded the possibilities for the use of pattern, from wallpaper to high-tech plastics. Texture can be integral to the design structure itself: for example, a wooden spoon is hard to the touch and displays the grain of the wood; or it can applied on the surface, regardless of the underlying material. A sofa covered in velvet upholstery is one such example.

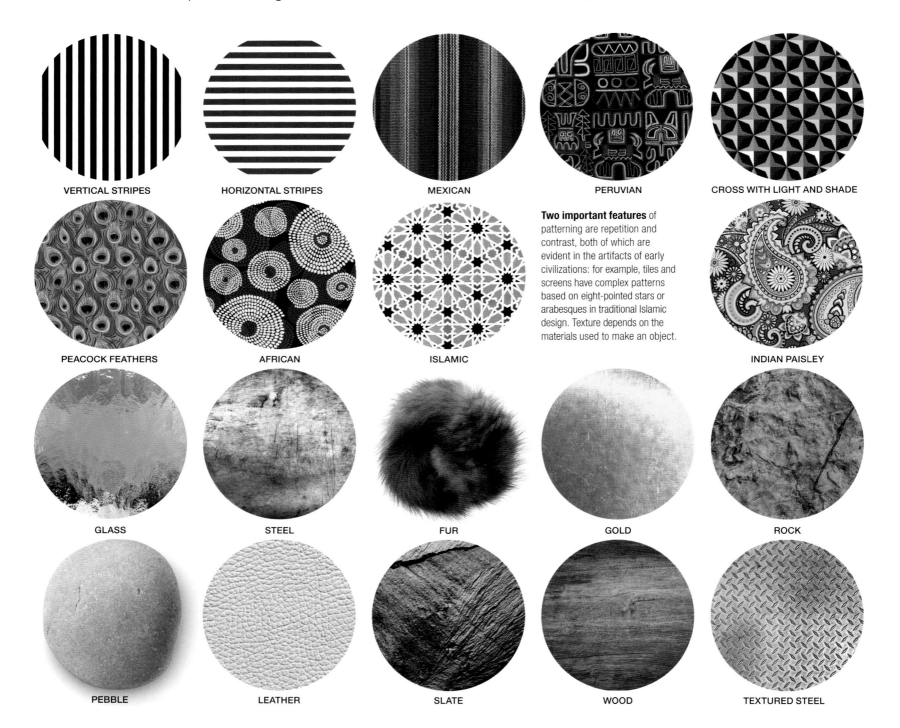

VERTICAL STRIPES

HORIZONTAL STRIPES

MEXICAN

PERUVIAN

CROSS WITH LIGHT AND SHADE

PEACOCK FEATHERS

AFRICAN

ISLAMIC

Two important features of patterning are repetition and contrast, both of which are evident in the artifacts of early civilizations: for example, tiles and screens have complex patterns based on eight-pointed stars or arabesques in traditional Islamic design. Texture depends on the materials used to make an object.

INDIAN PAISLEY

GLASS

STEEL

FUR

GOLD

ROCK

PEBBLE

LEATHER

SLATE

WOOD

TEXTURED STEEL

Regular

The human brain is attuned from an early age to detect patterns—it is adept at recognizing repetition in a sequence of visual or audio cues. Repetition has therefore been a commonly recurring artistic device since prehistoric times, is visible in early ceramic decoration, and still remains one of the main techniques used by designers to create objects with symmetry and order.

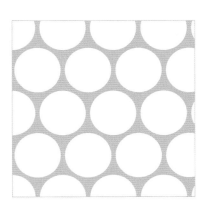

When a motif is repeated at the same intervals, the resulting pattern looks pleasingly symmetrical, evident in Lucienne Day's Isosceles textile design.

Graphics that display an even, symmetrical placement of repeated elements provide familiarity and visual stability.

Texture

A key point of interaction with a design is how its surface feels to the touch. This element can be communicated in two ways: first, through the textural appearance, which tells potential users of an object what to expect when they come into contact with it; and, second, through the actual texture—how it feels to drink from or sit on, for example.

Tapio Wirkkala's glass vase from 1950 mimics the appearance of ice, with a texture that is cool, hard, and smooth to the touch.

Texture can be conveyed purely by how an object looks on the surface, though this is not always how it feels to the touch.

Irregular

Patterns that follow asymmetrical lines are irregular. They lack the predictability of symmetrically ordered graphics, but irregular patterns can be used to focus the eye, create a sense of movement, and differentiate the points of a design. One of the most important uses of asymmetrical patterning is to make a visual hierarchy, drawing attention to specific design features.

Random patterning in the Campana brothers' Harumaki chair gives it a strong sense of spontaneity.

Irregular or asymmetric patterning is often found in nature, making it a useful device for designs with an organic feel.

Hardness

The softness of a design is visible from a distance by the amount of light that reflects on the surface or is absorbed by it. A highly reflective surface is hard, while a surface with no highlights and a visible pile is soft. Designers can choose hard materials to evoke masculinity or soft ones to create a sense of femininity.

Masanori Umeda's velvet-covered chair looks welcoming and comfortable because of its layers of soft upholstery.

When deciding which materials to use, a designer must take into consideration how hard or soft they feel, something that is often closely allied to their texture.

Contrast

By highlighting differences in materials, color, or shape, designers can create visual dynamism. They juxtapose opposing elements to establish order and invigorate both the surface and structure of a design. Examples of contrasting design components include light and dark, soft and hard, small and large, plain and patterned, and organic and human-made.

By contrasting a hat in natural straw with a base in metal, this Philippe Starck piece offers a playful twist on the table lamp.

Contrasting light and dark colors or light and dark shades of the same color adds energy to flat designs.

Sheen

In past centuries, the glittering surface of precious metals often indicated the value of an object and the wealth of its owner. Fine metals such as gold and silver had a lustrous sheen, as did expensive fabrics such as silk and satin. Modern production processes can give a rich sheen to even the most inexpensive object.

An Iranian ewer from the 17th to 19th centuries combines a high gloss glaze with a burnished metal lid and spout, the sheen suggesting wealth.

A shiny or polished surface can communicate a feeling of luxury. It is also associated with cleanliness, modernity, and technological mastery.

ARTS & CRAFTS
1850–1920

The designer is in essence an artist.

GEORGE NELSON, INDUSTRIAL DESIGNER

ARTS AND CRAFTS
Introduction

The Arts and Crafts movement promoted traditional craftsmanship, the use of locally available materials, and integrity in the way things were made. It began in late 19th-century Britain, when writers such as John Ruskin and William Morris rejected mass production and the often poor-quality, machine-made items that were found in many stores and homes. Morris, in particular, believed in the importance of the individual craftsman and advocated a return to hand craftsmanship, which, he argued, would not only produce better furniture, pottery, textiles, and other items but also help people lead better, more fulfilling lives. Mass production, he maintained, was responsible for a decline in values.

Followers

Morris found many followers in Britain, from craftsman-designers such as William de Morgan to architects like C. F. A. Voysey, who designed houses and their contents according to Arts and Crafts principles. Soon, Morris's writings and designs, and the work of these followers, became known in Europe, and the movement spread there. Morris's visionary ideals were also embraced in North America and were adapted to create an American version of the Arts and Crafts style. French chairs by Léon Jallot and Arts Furniture by Americans such as Gustav Stickley look subtly different from pieces made in Britain but remain true to Arts and Crafts values.

STAINED GLASS

William Morris trained as an architect and was passionate about medieval stained glass. Arts and Crafts designers revived the craft, using colored glass in domestic windows, light fixtures, and churches.

CELTIC MOTIFS

Knots, swirls, Celtic crosses, and entrelac (interlaced designs) inspired by ancient Celtic art featured in the work of many Arts and Crafts designers, notably Archibald Knox, especially on metalwork.

ISLAMIC ORNAMENT

Some Arts and Crafts designers were admirers of Islamic art, with its huge variety of richly colored patterns, and borrowed motifs from Islamic tiles and ceramics, as well as Moorish architectural features.

Nothing should be made by man's labor which is not worth making, or which must be made by labor degrading to the makers.

William **Morris**

Influences

Many Arts and Crafts designers drew on the influence of medieval craftsmanship, and their objects and interiors exploited the distinctive qualities of natural materials, from beautifully finished oak to hand-woven tapestries. Others, however, looked farther afield for inspiration, incorporating vivid colors inspired by Middle Eastern art or Egyptian motifs in their work. Decoration was used sparingly, however, as Arts and Crafts designers rejected the ornate, cluttered interiors that were typical of Victorian middle-class homes. Arts and Crafts rooms, by contrast, were sparingly furnished,and carefully designed so that every piece of furniture, ceramics, metalwork, and floor covering formed part of a harmonious whole—the perfect setting, in fact, for the simple life that Morris and Ruskin advocated and that was so central to their ideals.

Truth to materials

Although William Morris wanted Arts and Crafts design to be accessible to everyone, many of the objects produced were too expensive for those on low incomes. However, the movement had a strong influence, creating a craft revival that lasted throughout the 20th century and encouraged designers to see their work in terms of "truth to materials." This notion inspired later design movements such as the Modernism of the 1920s.

HANDCRAFTSMANSHIP

The Arts and Crafts movement held that work crafted by hand, using traditional techniques, had a special virtue and integrity. Furniture was therefore plain, with features of the joinery clearly visible.

MEDIEVAL INFLUENCE

Morris harbored a romanticized vision of the medieval period as a golden age of craftsmanship. The influence of Gothic architecture and medieval paintings and tapestries is evident in much Arts and Crafts work.

NEEDLEWORK

William Morris sparked a revival of handweaving and needlework, in reaction against the mass-produced cloth of the Industrial Revolution. Arts and Crafts fabric designs were inspired by the natural world.

Female mask mount in ormolu (a gold-colored alloy)

Shaped apron with floral marquetry

Floral carved apron

Frame carved with clusters of grapes

Cabriole leg

Louis XV revival center table | *c.* 1860, **UK**. Rich marquetry in a number of colored woods, metal decorative mounts on the legs, and a curvaceous serpentine form mark this Victorian table as a piece in the Louis XV revival style.

Renaissance revival sofa | *c.* 1865, **US**. Renaissance-revival furniture could be highly opulent, combining very decorative carving with striking shapes. The three-section back of this sofa, with its distinctive silhouette and carved mask crest, shows the contemporary taste for elaborate ornamentation.

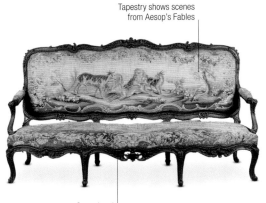

Tapestry shows scenes from Aesop's Fables

Carved and molded frame

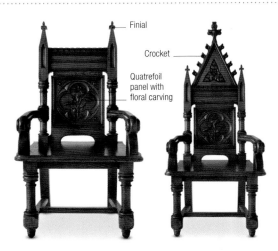

Finial

Crocket

Quatrefoil panel with floral carving

Rococo revival sofa | *c.* 1875, **France**. The 18th-century rococo style was known for lightness and elegance and the use of scrolls, curves, and floral carving. This 19th-century sofa is upholstered with 18th-century tapestry.

Gothic revival dining chairs | *c.* 1880, **UK**. Inspired by details of medieval architecture, the pinnacles, crockets, and decorative finials on these pitch-pine chairs are derived from the Decorated Gothic style of the 14th century.

Sheraton revival commode | *c.* 1890, **UK**. British cabinetmaker Thomas Sheraton (1751–1806) made light and elegant neoclassical furniture, often with painted decoration. His style is replicated in this Victorian satinwood commode.

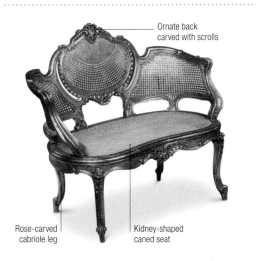

Ornate back carved with scrolls

Rose-carved cabriole leg

Kidney-shaped caned seat

Carved multifoil arch from the Islamic tradition

Shaped back

Lion-head terminal

Foot in the form of a dolphin

Louis XV revival love seat | 1905, **UK**. Many Louis XV–style pieces, such as this Edwardian love seat, are entirely made up of curves—even the caned back panel is a sweeping curve. The gilding gives the piece an opulent feel.

Spanish Renaissance revival bedstead | *c.* 1910, **Spain**. Although pieces such as this are usually labeled "Renaissance revival," they often drew on several past styles, using carving, painted decoration, and gilding to sumptuous effect.

Italian Renaissance revival chair | *c.* 1910, **Italy**. With a richly carved walnut frame and shaped, padded back, this chair was designed to imitate the furniture seen in the palace of an Italian Renaissance prince.

THE AGE OF REVIVALS

From furniture to architecture, the 19th century was a period of historical revivals. Architects and designers looked to the past for inspiration, and much furniture was based on the work of the neoclassical cabinetmakers of the 18th century, on the lighter, more ornate rococo designs of the same period, and on earlier Renaissance styles. There was also a long-standing fashion for reviving the highly ornamental Gothic manner of the Middle Ages. Since little medieval furniture had survived, cabinetmakers and designers drew on the architectural details of Gothic churches and cathedrals, incorporating pointed arches, pinnacles, and even window tracery into their work. Revival pieces satisfied the 19th-century appetite for lavish decoration and a connection with the past, and cabinetmakers, gilders, and painters were kept busy producing some of the most elaborate furniture in the history of design.

Cast putti

Leather-fronted drawers

Kingwood body with marquetry in lighter woods

Ormolu mount

Louis XV revival desk and cartonnier | **Unattributed**, early 20th century, France. This flat-topped desk and cartonnier (drawer unit) is made in the Louis XV style of the mid-18th century. The features of this ornate style include the desk's distinctive inward-curving and outward-bulging *bombé* shape and its ornate marquetry and ormolu (gold-colored metal) decoration.

GLASS AND IRON

I n 1851, London's Hyde Park was home to the Great Exhibition, an all-embracing international showcase of industry and manufacturing. The exhibition was housed in the Crystal Palace, a massive building conceived by engineer Joseph Paxton, a specialist in designing huge greenhouses. With its iron frame and hundreds of thousands of glass panes, the Crystal Palace was a pioneering example of industrial prefabrication and a typical piece of Victorian ingenuity. The glass and iron parts were made in distant factories, then brought to Hyde Park, where an army of workers assembled them into a cathedral-like structure.

The building's modular construction meant that it could be erected quickly: 80 men could install 8,000 panes of glass in a week. At the end of the exhibition, it was equally easy to take the palace apart and move it, in pieces, to South London.

The vast, light building was ideal for showcasing displays from around the world. Cossack cavalry armor was exhibited in the same space as jewel-encrusted Indian costumes, the latest reaping machines, and the huge Koh-i-noor diamond.

> **It is a wonderful place—vast, strange, new, and impossible to describe.**
>
> Charlotte **Brontë,** 1851

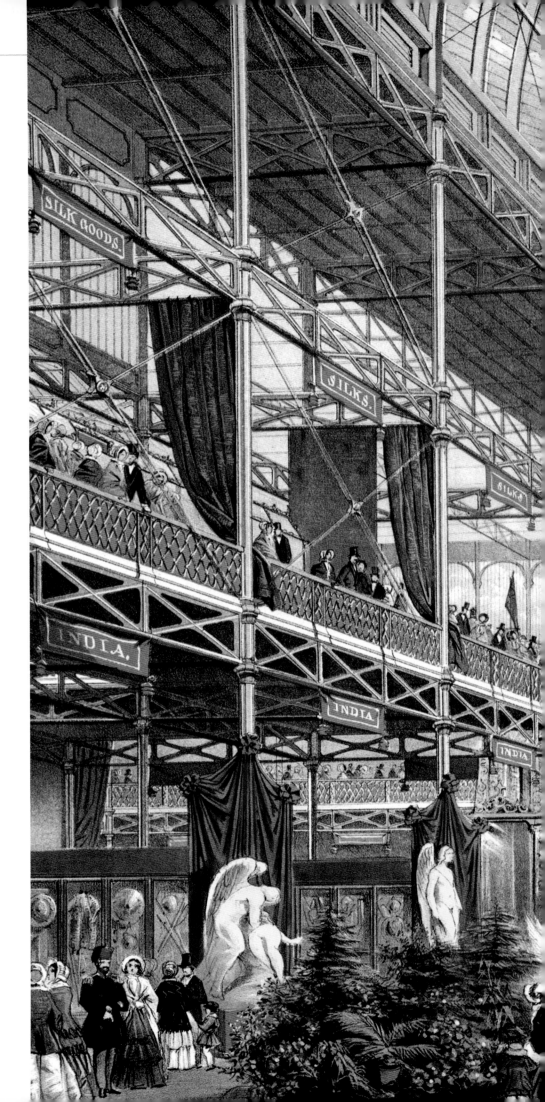

Transept of the Crystal Palace, London, UK, Joseph Nash, 1851
The cavernous interior of the Crystal Palace resembled a cathedral built from glass and iron. Packed with around 100,000 exhibits, the building was large enough to accommodate two tall trees that were already growing on the site.

△ **The beautiful curving stems,** swirling leaves, and finely drawn flowers make Loddon (1884) one of the most enduring of Morris's fabric designs.

William Morris

British writer, designer, and socialist William Morris was one of the most influential figures of the 19th century. He was especially known for his vibrant wallpaper and fabric patterns, often based on observation of real plants and birds, and hand-printed with wooden blocks. Morris was fascinated by traditional art and craft techniques and the medieval artisan's vision of design as a holistic process. He therefore championed the idea of the designer-craftsman, a creator who could actually produce the objects.

Morris revived traditional techniques, learning to weave, embroider, and dye using plant-based pigments. In 1861, he and a group of friends founded a business (originally called Morris, Marshall, Faulkner & Co., later Morris & Co.) to produce Morris's fabrics and wallpapers, alongside items that Morris lacked the skill to make, such as furniture and stained glass. The company's furniture, which was often brightly decorated, drew on medieval designs, and its stained glass on Pre-Raphaelite paintings. William Morris had a deep influence on the Arts and Crafts movement but, despite his "art for all" philosophy, his hand-printed wallpapers were expensive and far from accessible to everyone. However, his knowledge of traditional crafts, together with his comprehensive approach to design, was admired by teachers and students at the Bauhaus in the 1920s, and many of his designs are still produced today.

Life

1834–1896

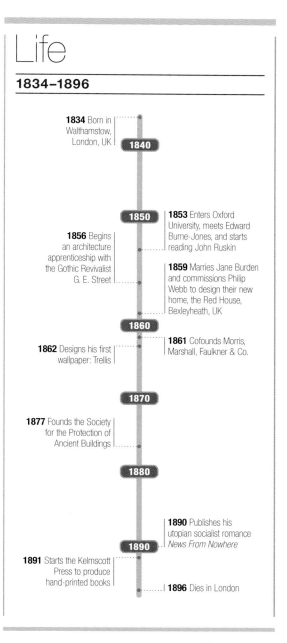

1834 Born in Walthamstow, London, UK

1840

1850

1853 Enters Oxford University, meets Edward Burne-Jones, and starts reading John Ruskin

1856 Begins an architecture apprenticeship with the Gothic Revivalist G. E. Street

1859 Marries Jane Burden and commissions Philip Webb to design their new home, the Red House, Bexleyheath, UK

1860

1862 Designs his first wallpaper: Trellis

1861 Cofounds Morris, Marshall, Faulkner & Co.

1870

1877 Founds the Society for the Protection of Ancient Buildings

1880

1890 Publishes his utopian socialist romance *News From Nowhere*

1890

1891 Starts the Kelmscott Press to produce hand-printed books

1896 Dies in London

Artichoke tile | *c.* 1870. Morris produced a number of tile designs in delicate blues and grays. The strong, clear outline of the stylized flowers and leaves creates a series of organic curves.

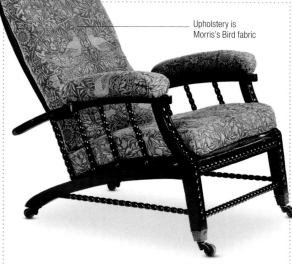

Upholstery is Morris's Bird fabric

Adjustable armchair | **Philip Webb**, *c.* 1870. British architect Philip Webb based this ebonized wood-framed chair on an old English design. Morris's firm made it from 1869 to 1890.

Evenlode | 1883. This fabric design, named after a tributary of the Thames River, features stylized roses, sunflowers, and carnations entwining with Persian-style flower heads.

HANDCRAFTED FURNITURE

The Arts and Crafts movement, spearheaded in Great Britain by William Morris and his followers, promoted handcrafted furniture that was solidly built and functional. Many of their pieces were unornamented and based on vernacular designs—designers relied on the appeal of woods, such as oak and elm, and traditional form. Other items were one-of-a-kind pieces made of more costly woods, with ornament drawn from nature, sometimes inlaid or with elaborate metalwork hardware. The Arts and Crafts values of good workmanship and truth to materials spread widely, both to Europe, where designers were also inspired by the Jugendstil movement, and to the US, where a plainer style prevailed. Although Morris rejected machine-made work, some designers did use machinery to produce furniture more cheaply, making it available to a wider market.

Swan-neck terminal
for side support

Back splat
with pair of
swan necks

Flat board seat

Curving legs harmonize
with swan-neck form

Swan chair | C. F. A. Voysey, *c.* 1905, UK.
Architect-designer Voysey designed his original oak Swan chair in the 1880s, but this is a later variation. He exploited the arched form of the bird's neck in both the side supports and the back, with its pair of symmetrical swans.

C. F. A. Voysey

1857–1941

In 1892, Charles Voysey stated: "Begin by casting out all the useless ornaments … Eschew all imitations. Strive to produce an effect of repose and simplicity." Influenced by William Morris, Voysey strove to use natural motifs and honest materials in his work. His furniture emphasized the innate beauty of fine pieces of lumber, especially unpolished oak, and it often had tapered legs and restrained pierced decoration. Birds and plants inspired both the motifs on his furniture and his wallpaper and fabric designs. Voysey also worked as an architect, and he is best remembered for the elegant vernacular style of buildings such as Dixcot House, which set the tone for many British suburban homes.

Dixcot House, Wandsworth, southwest London, designed in 1897.

Oak lamp table | **Roycroft**, 1880–1920, US. The solid construction is typical of furniture by the Roycroft community of East Aurora, New York. The table has a molded apron and feet based on a design by British architect A. H. Mackmurdo.

Carved brackets in flowing Art Nouveau style

Settee | **Charles Rohlfs**, 1900, US. Rohlfs specialized in individual pieces, usually in richly colored oak, that drew on both medieval and modern sources for inspiration. This dark-stained oak piece has Art Nouveau–style carving.

Flare side with scalloped top

Demi-lune cutout

Oak magazine stand | **Charles Limbert**, 1905–1910, US. The demi-lune cutouts in the sides of the stand show the influence of Mackintosh and the Vienna Secession, evident in much of Michigan-based Limbert's furniture.

Slightly curved rail

Square-section tapered and splayed leg

Draft screen | **Morris & Co.**, c. 1890, UK. The mahogany frame has ball finials at the top and a pierced section at the bottom. The fabric panels are worked with flowers in the Morris tradition, possibly by the textile artist J. H. Dearle.

Curve-ended stretchers

Table | **M. H. Baillie Scott**, c. 1900, UK. Baillie Scott favored plain wooden furniture based on vernacular pieces. Several of his tables had three legs with diagonal, curved stretchers that added strength and created a subtle visual rhythm.

Side chair | **Harry Napper**, c. 1905, UK. Known mainly as a textile designer, Napper also designed some furniture. The strong, linear style of this beech and elm chair, with its rows of spindles at the back, is similar in style to his fabrics.

Nickel-plated pull

Gentleman's pine commode | **Richard Riemerschmid**, c. 1905, Germany. Riemerschmid made simple pieces in inexpensive materials featuring straight lines, sometimes with ornamental metal or mother-of-pearl inlays.

△ **The living room** of Stickley's house in New Jersey typifies his approach to interiors—integrating textiles, ceramics, and metalware, and combining the furniture's natural browns with other earth tones.

Gustav Stickley

American furniture manufacturer Gustav (originally Gustave—the "e" was dropped in 1903) Stickley was one of the most important figures in the craft revival in North America in the early 20th century. After a number of short-lived business ventures making typical 19th-century revivalist furniture, he set up the Gustave Stickley Company in Eastwood, New York, and started to produce items influenced by the Arts and Crafts movement.

Stickley was attracted to the movement's ideals of truth to materials, its stress on fine workmanship, and its use of local woods for furniture. His chairs, tables, and cupboards were made of oak and other native woods, colored so as not to obscure the natural grain, and had joints in which dowels and dovetails were exposed. The furniture also featured beautifully crafted hardware (often in patinated copper) and chair coverings that were mostly simple leather or canvas. To promote his work and values, Stickley published *The Craftsman* magazine, named after his workshop. Stickley's work proved successful, particularly after May 1903, when he employed the talented architect Harvey Ellis to produce new furniture designs. Ellis died a few months later, but his influence was profound and his furniture sold well. In spite of this, Stickley went bankrupt in 1915, but his designs spawned imitators, who continued to produce furniture in his American Craftsman style.

Life

1858–1942

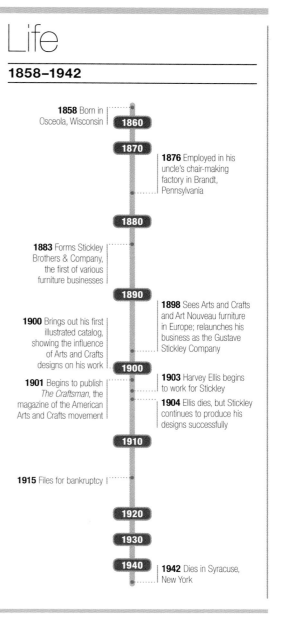

1858 Born in Osceola, Wisconsin

1876 Employed in his uncle's chair-making factory in Brandt, Pennsylvania

1883 Forms Stickley Brothers & Company, the first of various furniture businesses

1898 Sees Arts and Crafts and Art Nouveau furniture in Europe; relaunches his business as the Gustave Stickley Company

1900 Brings out his first illustrated catalog, showing the influence of Arts and Crafts designs on his work

1901 Begins to publish *The Craftsman*, the magazine of the American Arts and Crafts movement

1903 Harvey Ellis begins to work for Stickley

1904 Ellis dies, but Stickley continues to produce his designs successfully

1915 Files for bankruptcy

1942 Dies in Syracuse, New York

Chest of drawers | Harvey Ellis for The Craftsman Workshop, *c.* 1903. The overhanging top is typical of Harvey Ellis. Tapering sides and fine handles give the piece a fluid feel.

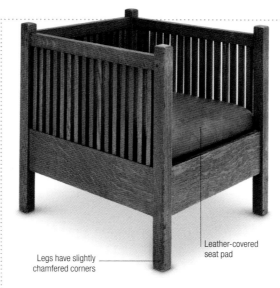

Legs have slightly chamfered corners

Leather-covered seat pad

Cube chair | 1907. Stickley used oak slats to form the sides and backs of many of his chairs. This example is made of light oak and its narrow vertical slats create a strong linear design.

Pierced pattern creates an effect of lightness

Tabouret table | *c.* 1910. The stylized organic form of this mahogany table's legs and the curvaceous outline of the tabletop and stretcher show Art Nouveau's influence on Stickley.

△ **The Arab Hall of Leighton House,** London, UK, was based on a room in La Zima, a 12th-century Sicilian palace. The sumptuous blue tiles recall the feathers of the peacock, a popular Aesthetic motif.

The Aesthetic **Movement**

△ **Oscar Wilde** | 1854–1900

The Aesthetic Movement began in Great Britain in the 1870s, both as a reaction to the stiffness and poor quality of contemporary Victorian design and to celebrate the pleasure that can be found in beautiful everyday objects. It was an informal movement, inspired in part by the idea of "art for art's sake," a phrase popularized in English by the speeches and writings of Oscar Wilde. The movement inspired designers, such as E. W. Godwin and William de Morgan, and artists, including the British Lord Leighton and James McNeill Whistler.

Favorite Aesthetic motifs included the peacock, valued for its rich blue-green feathers, and the sunflower, which appeared in realistic depictions on ceramics and in terra-cotta panels on exterior walls. The predominant colors were strong: bright blues, greens, and yellows were favored, often in combination with ebonized furniture. Styles from around the world were adopted and combined in new and original ways, so it was not uncommon for an Aesthetic vase to have a Persian shape and be decorated with Japanese or Egyptian patterns.

The initial impact of Aestheticism was felt mainly in Great Britain. However, the desire to elevate an everyday object to a work of art through quality craftsmanship and design influenced other movements, including both Arts and Crafts and Art Nouveau, which helped carry Aesthetic ideas around the globe.

Key dates

1818–1894

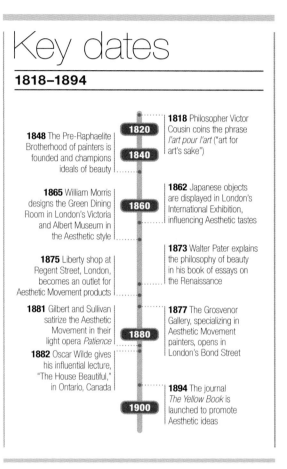

1818 Philosopher Victor Cousin coins the phrase *l'art pour l'art* ("art for art's sake")

1848 The Pre-Raphaelite Brotherhood of painters is founded and champions ideals of beauty

1862 Japanese objects are displayed in London's International Exhibition, influencing Aesthetic tastes

1865 William Morris designs the Green Dining Room in London's Victoria and Albert Museum in the Aesthetic style

1873 Walter Pater explains the philosophy of beauty in his book of essays on the Renaissance

1875 Liberty shop at Regent Street, London, becomes an outlet for Aesthetic Movement products

1877 The Grosvenor Gallery, specializing in Aesthetic Movement painters, opens in London's Bond Street

1881 Gilbert and Sullivan satirize the Aesthetic Movement in their light opera *Patience*

1882 Oscar Wilde gives his influential lecture, "The House Beautiful," in Ontario, Canada

1894 The journal *The Yellow Book* is launched to promote Aesthetic ideas

Moon flask | **Ming Dynasty, early 15th century**. East Asian art was very fashionable among aesthetes, especially Japanese prints and blue-and-white porcelain from China.

Circular spout

Scroll decoration on the handle

Flat base

Plated metal pitcher | *c*. **1880**. The organic, twisted, branchlike handles of this pitcher contrast with its more formal rounded shape and its delicate, engraved garlands.

Engraved banding

Tile | **William de Morgan, *c*. 1890**. The vibrant designs of William de Morgan's handcrafted tiles were lighter and more subtle than the prevailing elaborate Victorian style.

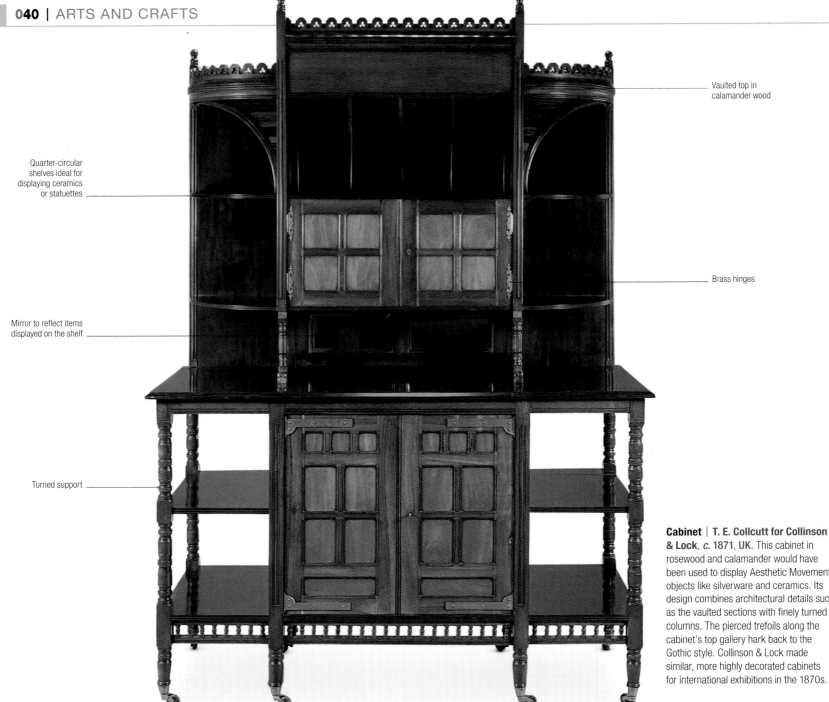

Vaulted top in calamander wood

Quarter-circular shelves ideal for displaying ceramics or statuettes

Brass hinges

Mirror to reflect items displayed on the shelf

Turned support

Cabinet | **T. E. Collcutt for Collinson & Lock**, *c.* 1871, UK. This cabinet in rosewood and calamander would have been used to display Aesthetic Movement objects like silverware and ceramics. Its design combines architectural details such as the vaulted sections with finely turned columns. The pierced trefoils along the cabinet's top gallery hark back to the Gothic style. Collinson & Lock made similar, more highly decorated cabinets for international exhibitions in the 1870s.

AESTHETIC MOVEMENT FURNITURE

The Aesthetic Movement of the 1870s and 1880s drew its inspiration from the doctrine of "art for art's sake." Aesthetic Movement designers, such as the architect E. W. Godwin, wanted to create interiors that were beautiful in their own right and full of objects that were pleasing to the eye. Their most costly pieces of furniture often featured striking woods such as calamander, although a more common choice was ebonized (black-painted or stained) wood, often with turned legs or stretchers. This ebonized furniture was sometimes enlivened with gilding or decoration featuring motifs such as stylized flowers (especially sunflowers), peacock feathers, or fan shapes. There was a strong Japanese influence on this movement, manifested in dominant rectangular shapes and in openwork features, such as galleries, designed like a series of rectangles.

Corner cabinet | **Bruce Talbert for Gillows**, *c.* 1875, UK. The decorative panels on the central door of this rosewood cabinet are made of gilt-tooled leather. Stylized flower motifs were especially popular among Aesthetic Movement designers.

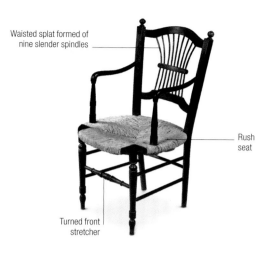

Waisted splat formed of nine slender spindles

Rush seat

Turned front stretcher

Armchair | **Dante Gabriel Rossetti (attributed) for Morris & Co.**, *c.* 1875, UK. This chair, based on vernacular French styles, may have been refined by the British artist Dante Gabriel Rossetti for the company of his friend William Morris.

Lacquer panel set in embossed leather paper

Sideboard | **E. W. Godwin for William Watt**, *c.* 1878, UK. Details such as the openwork gallery, upturned finials, and lacquer panels show both the Japanese influence on this mahogany sideboard and Godwin's considerable craftsmanship.

Molded edge of ebonized wood

Column comprising a cluster of turned uprights

Turned and splayed feet

Tripod table | *c.* 1880, US. *Pietra dura* is an inlay technique using colored stone. It works especially well with the floral designs popular in the late 19th century, such as the spray on this table that is set into a black background of ebonized wood.

Octagonal calamander top

Stretchers radiate like the spokes of a wheel

Octagonal-topped table | *c.* 1880, UK. Aesthetic Movement cabinetmakers prized the beautiful striped grain of calamander wood. This table also has striking curved legs in ebonized wood that match the molded edge of the tabletop.

Leather lion head decoration

Rocking chair | *c.* 1880, UK. Tooled leather was widely used in the 19th century, and the leather decoration is the outstanding feature of this rocking chair. It has panels arranged in a striking checkerboard pattern featuring floral designs.

Turned bobbin

Front leg with turned banding

Side chair | **Bruce Talbert for Gillows**, *c.* 1880, UK. Ebonized wood was often used to set off the rich colors of decorations and upholstery fabrics. Dark wood also displays the art of the turner—this chair has several ornate turned details.

Upholstered top rail

Lower rails separate from the chair legs as in Japanese furniture

Lattice sides

Parlor chair | *c.* 1880, UK. This chair's proportions, with uprights that are close together near the corners and farther apart in the center, creates a pattern typical of the Japanese-influenced furniture that was popular in this period.

Bright colors contrast with the rich, dark wood

Walnut and parcel gilt jardinière stands | *c.* 1890. The birds and flowers on the foliate-painted, mirrored, and silkwork patterns of these jardinière stands were popular motifs of the Aesthetic Movement.

△ **Takamizawa woodblock print** of Mount Fuji, Japan. Prints from Japan showing landscape scenes with asymmetric trees and branches were especially popular in Europe.

Japonisme

△ **Mirrored panel** | **Aubrey Beardsley**, 1930s

The French word *Japonisme* is widely used to refer to the fashion for Japanese art and design that spread across Europe and North America in the late 19th century. It began after Japan, which had been closed to international trade, opened its ports to western ships in the 1850s. Japanese prints, pottery, lacquerware, and fans flooded onto the European market and were soon being shown in major exhibitions and sold in expensive shops such as Siegfried Bing's Maison de l'Art Nouveau in Paris and Liberty in London. Some of the prints from less scrupulous dealers were fakes, or faded, older examples touched up with modern paints. Inlays of lacquer and ivory, known as Shibayama, were also popular.

Artists from Whistler and Beardsley to Gauguin fell in love with Japanese prints, admiring their strong lines, asymmetrical composition, and striking colors. Some western painters and designers also began to depict Japanese subjects—the popularity of cherry blossoms, water lilies, and dragonflies in Art Nouveau ornament is largely due to this Japanese influence. Some European glassworkers, including Daum and Gallé, and potters such as Dammouse began to make or decorate their wares in the Japanese style, and numerous cabinetmakers created lacquered furniture. Some of the best work was by designers such as Christopher Dresser, who did not imitate eastern models but were inspired by Japanese art and created items with clean lines, asymmetrical designs, and simple shapes.

Key dates

1854–1890

1854 The Tokugawa Shogunate opens its seaports to trade with the West — **1850**

1858 The US and Japan sign a major trade treaty

1862 London's International Exhibition features an extensive Japanese section; La Porte Chinoise, a shop for Oriental items, opens in Paris — **1860**

1867 The Japanese stand at the Paris Exposition Universelle proves extremely popular

1875 Claude Monet paints a portrait of his wife wearing a Japanese costume — **1870**

1876 British designer Christopher Dresser visits Japan as a government guest

1880

1885 *The Mikado*, Gilbert and Sullivan's comic opera set in Japan, is premiered

1888 Art dealer Siegfried Bing begins to publish his journal *Le Japon Artistique*

1890 A major exhibition of ukiyo-e prints is held at the École des Beaux Arts, Paris — **1890**

Inlaid cabinet | **Koike Art Shop**, *c.* 1875–1900. This cabinet features ivory inlaid with various colored and asymmetrically composed relief images in the Shibayama style.

Shibayama style inlaid panel

Inlaid panel

Bracketed support

Writing cabinet | **Gillows**, 1880s. The bracketed supports of this cabinet's stretchers and legs give it a Japanese appearance, reinforced by the Shibayama lacquer and ivory panels.

Distinctive, beaklike spout

Tea service | **Raoul Lachenal**, *c.* 1920. The striking shapes, black butterfly handles and finials, and asymmetrical eucalyptus leaf patterns on these pieces show a Japanese influence.

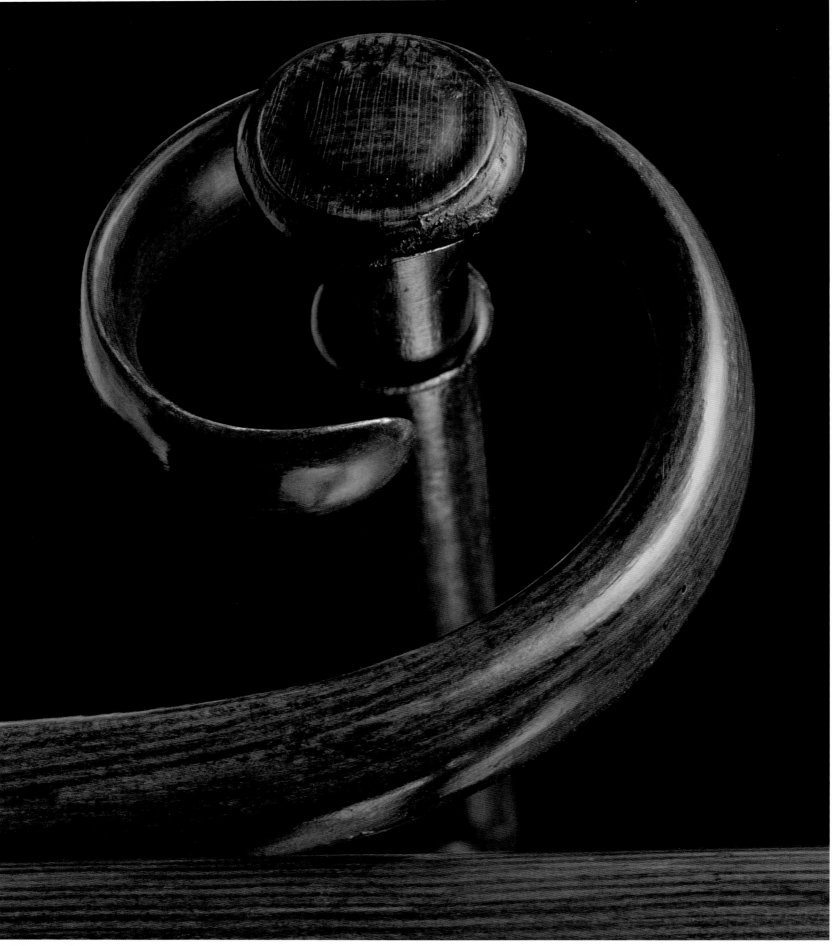

△ **This detail of a bentwood chair** shows the elegant curves made possible by Thonet's revolutionary process.

Thonet

Michael Thonet was a Prussian furniture maker who created the bentwood chair. Trained as a cabinetmaker, he began experimenting with bentwood furniture in 1830. His breakthrough came when he devised a method of shaping solid beechwood by steaming it and then bending it to the required curve with metal molds and tools that he had designed himself. Using this method, Thonet discovered that he could make a chair cheaply out of bentwood components that could then be assembled using screws. The resulting furniture was lightweight, strong, inexpensive, and unornamented—its beauty came from its attractive curves and simple, balanced shapes.

In 1853, Thonet set up as a manufacturer, Gebrüder Thonet, with his five sons. They developed a range of bentwood furniture—dining chairs, armchairs, rockers, sofas, stools, tables, even cradles for babies—and established a factory in Moravia (now in the Czech Republic), where local beechwood provided much of the raw material. In the same decade, the company exhibited its furniture widely, expanding steadily and producing millions of items per year by the early 20th century. The secret of Thonet's success was in the elegance, low cost, and portability of its designs: the parts of chairs could be shipped around the world and assembled with ease by distributors. Today, the company is still owned by the Thonet family.

Key dates

1796–1930

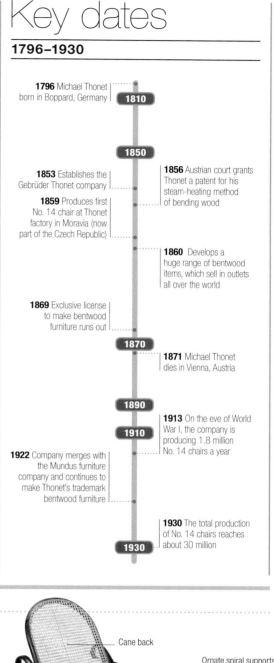

1796 Michael Thonet born in Boppard, Germany

1810

1850

1853 Establishes the Gebrüder Thonet company

1856 Austrian court grants Thonet a patent for his steam-heating method of bending wood

1859 Produces first No. 14 chair at Thonet factory in Moravia (now part of the Czech Republic)

1860 Develops a huge range of bentwood items, which sell in outlets all over the world

1869 Exclusive license to make bentwood furniture runs out

1870

1871 Michael Thonet dies in Vienna, Austria

1890

1913 On the eve of World War I, the company is producing 1.8 million No. 14 chairs a year

1910

1922 Company merges with the Mundus furniture company and continues to make Thonet's trademark bentwood furniture

1930 The total production of No. 14 chairs reaches about 30 million

1930

Cane seat is both light and comfortable

Components are put together using screws

No. 14 chair | **For Gebrüder Thonet**, 1859. Simple, light, and inexpensive, the No. 14 chair was the most successful of all Thonet's designs, used in cafés and homes all over the world.

Pattern of three pierced holes above three slats, a typical Secessionist motif

Leather seat lightens effect of ebonized wood

Ebonized beechwood chair | **For Gebrüder Thonet**, *c.* 1905. The curved supports of this Secessionist-style chair sweep elegantly upward to create a U-shaped back.

Cane back

Ornate spiral supports strengthen seat

Rocking chair | **For Gebrüder Thonet**, *c.* 1890. Bent beechwood was an ideal material to form this rocking chair, which features side elements that curve to form the rockers.

EVOLUTION OF CHAIRS

The chair is one of the most familiar objects in the world, and one that is used by everyone, every day. Chairs have to be comfortable, have to fit in with any decorative scheme and trend, and should preferably be straightforward to manufacture and store. Designing a chair therefore poses a major challenge, one that most designers have taken on. The results of their experiments have varied. They have exploited new materials and techniques, such as bent wood, tubular steel, or plastic at some point during their career, and have found different ways to make seats comfortable, affordable, and attractive. The chair is an emblem of its era, reflecting contemporary tastes and concerns, and therefore the story of the chair is the history of design itself.

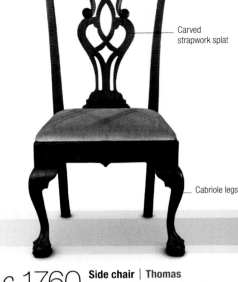

Carved strapwork splat

Cabriole legs

c. 1760 **Side chair** | **Thomas Chippendale, US**. Chairs such as this example with symmetrical scrollwork appeared in *The Gentleman and Cabinet-Maker's Director*, Chippendale's pattern book for furniture makers.

Flexible plywood uprights

Leather cover fits over the frame at each corner

1934 **Standard Chair** | **Jean Prouvé for Vitra, France**. Prouvé used hollow-section steel for this chair's weight-bearing rear legs. The chair was light, strong, and easy to assemble, unlike earlier metal furniture, which had to be shaped by hand.

1935 **Artek 69** | **Alvar Aalto for Artek, Finland**. Aalto was one of the pioneers of bent plywood. With his wife, Aino (also a designer), Aalto founded Artek to sell pieces like this chair and to promote interest in plywood as a material.

1938 **BKF chair** | **Antonio Bonet, Jorge Ferrari Hardoy, and Juan Kurchan for Artek-Pascoe, Argentina**. The BKF's innovative structure, based on two bent steel rods, inspired other designers to use rods to create dramatic new chair shapes.

Splayed armrests resemble bird wings

Form-molded laminated wooden seat

Clean lines typical of midcentury modernism

1952 **The Bird Chair** | **Harry Bertoia for Knoll, US**. This chair is one of the most striking results of Bertoia's experiments with industrial materials. The bent metal rods supporting the foam upholstery give the piece a sculptural grace.

1952–1955 **The Ant** | **Arne Jacobsen for Fritz Hansen, Denmark**. This lightweight, stackable, bent-plywood chair was named for the shape of its back, which resembles an ant's body. It was an influence on later biomorphic designs.

1956 **Tulip armchair** | **Eero Saarinen for Knoll, US**. Rejecting "the slum of legs," Saarinen designed Tulip in a revolutionary pedestal form. He combined an aluminum base and a fiberglass seat to produce a comfortable chair with a futuristic design.

Chair back and rear legs made of one piece of bent wood

Horizontal elements increase in size toward the top

Turned uprights

Leather upholstery

Bent steel frame

1859 | **No. 14 chair** | **Michael Thonet, Austria**. The essence of simplicity, this design exploits Thonet's process for bending wood. Its lightness, prefabricated construction, and elegance ensured its popularity.

1900 | **Ladderback armchair** | **Ernest Gimson, UK**. This Arts and Crafts chair, made of unadorned ash, has spindle stretchers, a ladder back, and a seat of woven rushes, all of which recall traditional English forms.

c. **1900** | **Side Chair** | **Hector Guimard, France**. With its sinuous lines, floral carving, and unusually shaped leather panel, this pearwood Art Nouveau chair was typical of the style.

1926–1927 | **B5 Side chair** | **Marcel Breuer for Standard-Möbel, Germany**. Breuer was inspired by his bicycle handlebars to create this, the first tubular steel chair.

Flat planes cushion sitter's shoulders

Surface consists of woven wire covered with tough kraft paper

Zigzag shape gives chair a soft, toylike appearance

1947 | **Peacock Chair** | **Hans Wegner for PP Møbler, Denmark**. Named for the way its dramatic, sweeping uprights resemble the feathers of a peacock, this chair was a midcentury modern interpretation of the traditional British Windsor chair.

1940s–1950s | **Lloyd Loom armchair** | **William Lusty, UK**. Made from wire wound with paper and woven like a basket, the Lloyd Loom's arms softly curved into the large, comfortable seat.

Fiberglass tubes made with silicone molds

1965 | **Ball chair** | **Eero Aarnio for Asko, Finland**. Ball is perhaps the best example of experimentation with the chair's form. With an acrylic frame and soft cushion upholstery, Aarnio created a chair that was at once cozy, comfortable, and excitingly new.

1971 | **Stack chair** | **Rodney Kinsman for OMK, UK**. A 1970s approach to the stacking chair, this steel piece's flowing lines and decorative holes make it gentler than its Modernist forerunners. The cutout in the back functions as a carrying handle.

2015 | **3-D-printed fiberglass chair** | **Markus Johansson, Sweden**. Johansson exploited the 3-D printer to unlock new forms, creating this piece that copies the form of a traditional chair but looks as if it has been squeezed from a tube.

ART POTTERY

In the late 19th century, individually decorated ceramics became increasingly popular with middle-class buyers, who wanted to furnish their homes with everyday objects that had the qualities of unique works of art. Some of this art pottery was designed by prominent figures, such as the illustrator Walter Crane or the tile specialist William de Morgan. More frequently, the decorators were artists—often women—working in the studios of manufacturers such as Doulton or Newcomb College. They worked in a variety of styles, from designs influenced by the Gothic Revival to flower and leaf patterns, sometimes with animals and birds, favored by the Aesthetic and Art Nouveau movements. Most of the pots are colorful, and many have vibrant or luster glazes.

William **de Morgan**

1839–1917

In 1872, after working for Morris & Co., William de Morgan set up his own studio in London to decorate tiles and pottery. He experimented with luster glazes and enamel techniques, frequently emulating ceramics from Persia (now Iran). From 1882, he specialized in handmade tiles, deftly adapting motifs from nature and fantasy, such as plants, fish, birds, and mythical animals, to the flat square surface of tiles with colorful and gleaming exuberance.

A Persian-style tile panel in which each three-tile frieze depicts a peacock above a vase of flowers.

Vase interior is richly colored

Pink carnations stand out against the turquoise background

Vase | **Joe Juster for William de Morgan,** 1888–1898, UK. The strong coloring of this design, including the deep blue of the tall framing leaves, shows the influence of Middle Eastern ceramics and is typical of de Morgan's Persian style.

Tapering baluster form

Design combines transfer printing and hand decoration

Intarsio vase | **Frederick Alfred Rhead for Foley Pottery,** c. 1890–1900, UK. This example of Rhead's popular boldly painted and printed Intarsio line features glowing poppies and foliage picked out in bright colors.

Gilt detailing

Moon vase | **Doulton,** c. 1900, UK. The palette and printed design of this Aesthetic Movement vase copies Japanese ceramic decoration. Many Doulton pieces are unique: designers from the nearby Lambeth School of Art were given a free rein.

Stylized ferns show Art Nouveau influence

Crisp surface molding

Vase | **Newcomb College,** 1902, US. Painted by female students, early vases such as this one often had stylized flower patterns with incised outlines. Inspiration for the decoration came from the local Louisiana flora and fauna.

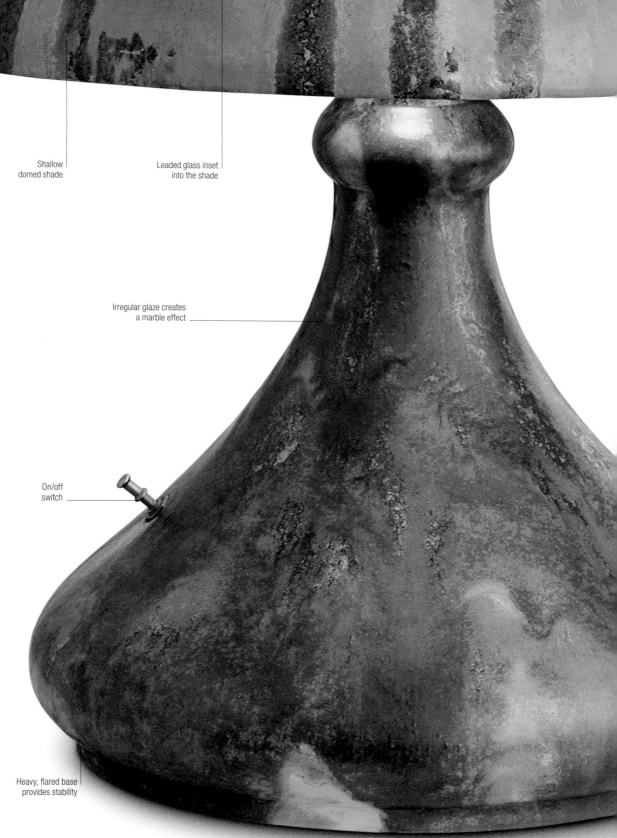

Table lamp | **Fulper**, *c.* 1910, **US**. From around 1910, after producing utilitarian wares for decades, the Fulper factory of Flemington, New Jersey, began to produce art pottery. The company was best known for its mushroom-shaped lamps decorated with glowing, irregular glazes.

Shallow domed shade

Leaded glass inset into the shade

Irregular glaze creates a marble effect

On/off switch

Heavy, flared base provides stability

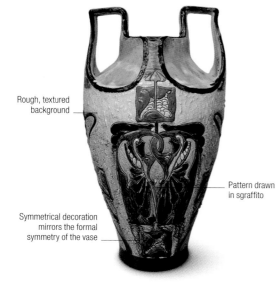

Rough, textured background

Pattern drawn in sgraffito

Symmetrical decoration mirrors the formal symmetry of the vase

Vase | **Frederick Braddon for Brannam,** 1904, **UK**. Braddon used slip—watered-down colored clay—to paint the complex pattern. In some places, he scraped away the slip to reveal the clay beneath, a technique called sgraffito.

Copper luster glaze depicts foliage

Ruby luster background

Lancastrian vase | **Richard Joyce for Pilkington,** 1918, **UK**. The Burton Brothers developed the Lancastrian range for Pilkington in 1892. It was famous for its luster glazes—glowing reds or golds created by adding materials such as copper oxide.

△ **The application of a Vellum glaze** on this 1920s landscape plaque by Lenore Asbury enhances the hazy, atmospheric charm of the landscape scene.

Rookwood

△ **Aqua Matte–glazed vase** | **Albert R. Valentien**

One of the most highly regarded American art potteries, Rookwood is famous for the distinctively glazed and beautifully painted pots that it produced in the decades after it was founded in 1880, which span the Japonisme, American Arts and Crafts, and Art Nouveau styles. Rookwood's founder was Maria Longworth Nichols of Cincinnati, Ohio, who had a strong amateur interest in pottery and wanted to turn this enthusiasm into a business. The studio produced wares, particularly jugs and vases, that were intended to be purely ornamental, in a multitude of shapes. Production increased rapidly during the business's heyday of the 1890s and early 1900s.

Rookwood became famous for a number of versatile glazes, such as the rich, golden Tiger Eye, Sea Green, Aerial Blue, clear Iris, and matte Vellum. The glaze matched the subject matter—Sea Green gave the underglaze decoration a blue-green depth good for aquatic themes, while hazy Vellum suited landscapes and flowers. A particular success for Rookwood was a series of vases bearing images of Native Americans—all portraits of real people painted in stunning detail. For these vases, Rookwood set off the portraits with their Standard glaze to give a high-gloss finish warmly tinted with yellow. Although production continued until the 1960s, Rookwood pottery is still best known for items like these from the 1890s.

Key dates

1880–1967

1880 Founded in Cincinnati by Maria Longworth Nichols — **1880**

1881 The painter Albert R. Valentien becomes the first regular employee and helps set high standards

1886 Painter Artus Van Briggle becomes one of Rookwood's chief designers

1887 The Japanese painter Kataro Shirayamadani starts work; he becomes one of their most successful artists

1889 The pottery's work is awarded a gold medal at the Paris Exposition Universelle

1890 William Watts Taylor, who had been manager, takes over the company, and Rookwood's financial success increases

1900

1902 Expands into architectural ceramics, producing flat plaques for home decoration

1920 Continues to be commercially successful, employing about 200 people — **1920**

1930

1934 Makes a loss for the first time as a result of the Great Depression

1960

1967 Ceases production

Flared rim

Incised inscription

Figure carved in relief

Cylindrical vase | 1882. Early in its history, Rookwood responded to the fashion for Japanese art with Oriental-style vases. The figures are balanced by an inscription on the top half.

Ground graduates from dark to light, to highlight the portrait

Indian vase | **Matthew A. Daly,** 1900. This vase shows the fine detail achieved in these realistic portraits. Strands of the subject's hair are painted individually.

Sea Green glaze

Iris glaze

Vases | **Timothy Hurley**, 1901; **Kataro Shirayamadani,** 1907. A fish painted amid foaming waves and a hazy mountain landscape demonstrate both artists' versatile use of glazes.

EVOLUTION OF
BICYCLES

The history of the bicycle stretches over more than 150 years, but many of today's bikes look very similar to those made at the end of the 19th century. The main design changes to the standard road bicycle have been to improve the safety, handling, and comfort of the ride, but numerous features, from pneumatic tires and other necessities to sophisticated gear systems and lightweight frames, have been added over the years. The bicycle has also become increasingly specialized, as designers and engineers have created models for specific uses, such as off-roading or track racing, and these have, in turn, influenced the design of the road bike.

Thick wooden spokes

1818 **Hobby Horse** | **Karl Von Drais, France.** Described as a "pedestrian curricle" when it first appeared in London, the Hobby Horse was powered by riders pushing their feet against the ground. The ornate gilt and leather hardware did little to improve speed or stability.

Downward-sweeping crossbar

1920s **Women's bicycle** | **Humber, UK.** The elegantly downward-sweeping crossbar on this bicycle was designed to allow women in long dresses to cycle. However, this weakened the frame, a fault this model compensated for with strong seat suspension.

Drop handlebars

Mudguards in accent color

1928 **Road Racer** | **Sunbeam, UK.** This bicycle, which Sunbeam marketed directly to the club cyclist, reflected the growing popularity of cycling as a pastime. With its drop handlebars and the addition of a clip-on pump, it was designed for both touring and racing.

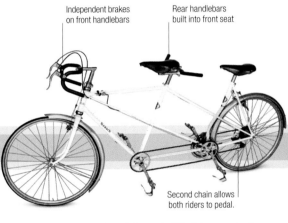

Independent brakes on front handlebars

Rear handlebars built into front seat

Second chain allows both riders to pedal.

1948 **Tandem** | **Rensch, UK.** This example of a two-person tandem bike was originally intended for long-distance touring, so it had an exceptionally lightweight frame. It was also equipped with independent calliper rim brakes and a 12-speed derailleur gear.

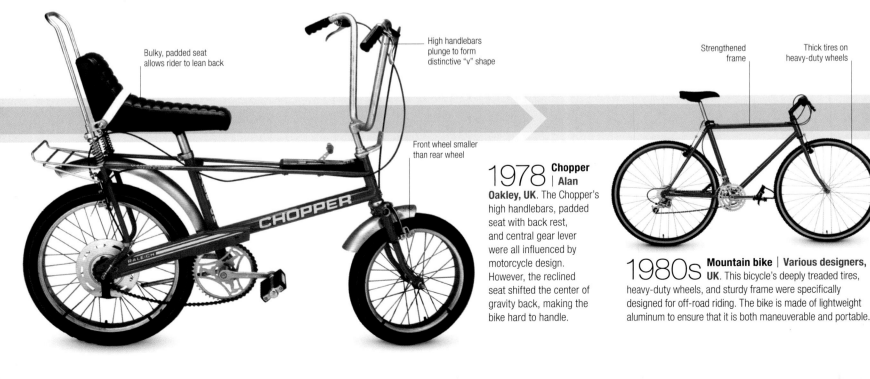

Bulky, padded seat allows rider to lean back

High handlebars plunge to form distinctive "v" shape

Front wheel smaller than rear wheel

1978 **Chopper** | **Alan Oakley, UK.** The Chopper's high handlebars, padded seat with back rest, and central gear lever were all influenced by motorcycle design. However, the reclined seat shifted the center of gravity back, making the bike hard to handle.

Strengthened frame

Thick tires on heavy-duty wheels

1980s **Mountain bike** | **Various designers, UK.** This bicycle's deeply treaded tires, heavy-duty wheels, and sturdy frame were specifically designed for off-road riding. The bike is made of lightweight aluminum to ensure that it is both maneuverable and portable.

Pedals drive front wheel directly

c. 1870 **Penny-farthing** | **Eugène Meyer and James Starley, France, UK**. The rider of a penny-farthing (also called an ordinary or high-wheel bicycle) sat above the huge front wheel. The wire spokes and solid rubber tires helped make the ride smoother.

Chain links pedals to rear wheel

1880s **Rover Safety Bicycle** | **James Starley, UK**. Marketed as less dangerous than the penny-farthing, the Rover had smaller wheels and a lower saddle than its predecessor and also featured a chain drive. It is the ancestor of modern cycles.

Strip provides extra grip

1890s **Bicycle with pneumatic tires** | **Édouard Michelin, France**. This bicycle was equipped with pneumatic tires, which improved the ride dramatically. This model also had rudimentary suspension on the seat to cushion the rider against bumps.

Brake cables

Leather-bound brake levers

Derailleur gear

Strap-in pedals

1951 **Paris-Roubaix** | **Bianchi, Italy**. This bicycle featured a revolutionary cable-operated "parallelogram derailleur" gear system. It was named after a one-day race in northern France and Belgium, which was won on a model much like this.

Belongings can be strapped on back

Rubber suspension improves ride

1962 **Moulton small-wheel bicycle** | **Alex Moulton, UK**. With its tiny wheels and step-through F-shaped frame, the Moulton was the first radically different bicycle design in many years. The bicycle was compact, had little drag, and was easy to steer. Its modern appearance made it a commercial success.

Padded rubber seat

Hinged frame

1981 **Brompton folding bike** | **Andrew Ritchie, UK**. An iconic city bike, the Brompton's specially designed features, including a hinged main tube, a pivoting rear triangle, and a hinged handlebar stem, make it easy to fold up.

Rear wheel attaches to one side of the frame, without a rear fork

Handlebars force rider into most aerodynamic position

1987–1992 **Lotus 108** | **Mike Burrows, Richard Hill, UK**. From its airfoil profile to its carbon-fiber composite frame (made as a monocoque, with the outer skin providing the strength) everything about the Lotus 108 was designed for speed.

Frame, fork, and seatpost are designed to minimize drag

2019 **SystemSix Carbon Ultegra** | **Cannondale, US**. This lightweight 11-speed carbon road bike is built entirely for speed and generates less drag than any other current road bike. It has wireless electronic gear shifting and powerful disc brakes.

METAL TABLEWARE

Arts and Crafts metalware is varied but has cleaner lines and more restrained ornament than much other Victorian work. It was produced both by individual designers and artisans, who often belonged to guilds, and by groups such as the Keswick School of Industrial Arts in Cumbria, the Guild of Handicraft (see p.59), the Birmingham Guild, and the Artificer's Guild in London. These groups were well known for producing tableware made from traditional, affordable metals such as pewter and copper, crafted in artistic ways—with a hand-hammered finish, for example. They also used silver and gold with great flair, in pieces ranging from the detailed work of C. R. Ashbee and other members of the Guild of Handicraft, who worked by hand and were often influenced by medieval models, to the Celtic-inspired but modern-looking, machine-made designs of Archibald Knox for Liberty.

Spiral wirework handle

Beadwork edging

Silver toast rack | C. R. Ashbee, c. 1899, UK. With ornate end panels pierced in a stylized foliate pattern and simpler dividers consisting of silver wirework rings, this toast rack is made up of a pleasing series of scrolling curves.

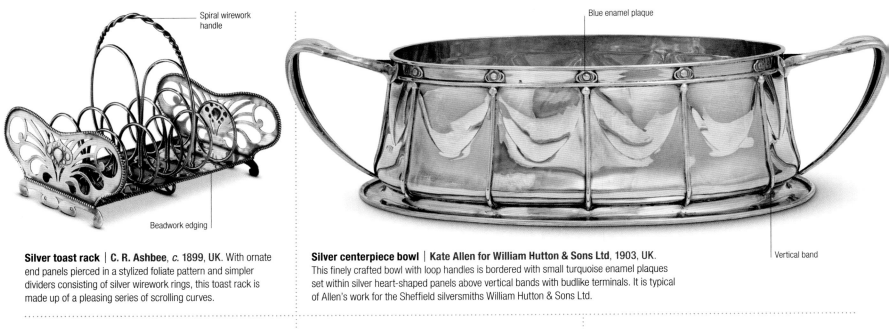

Blue enamel plaque

Vertical band

Silver centerpiece bowl | Kate Allen for William Hutton & Sons Ltd, 1903, UK. This finely crafted bowl with loop handles is bordered with small turquoise enamel plaques set within silver heart-shaped panels above vertical bands with budlike terminals. It is typical of Allen's work for the Sheffield silversmiths William Hutton & Sons Ltd.

Silver mounts

Copper pedestal

Copper and silver tazza | Edward Spencer, c. 1900, UK. This simple-shaped tazza by the chief designer of the Artificer's Guild has intricate ornamentation. The base is mounted with silver rose motifs and inset with mother-of-pearl plaques.

Copper tea caddy | Newlyn School, c. 1905, UK. Metalworkers in the Cornish village of Newlyn were known for their copper repoussé (hammered decoration in low relief). Their designs were inspired by sea creatures and the fishing industry.

Ice bucket | Archibald Knox for Liberty & Co., c. 1905, UK. Liberty's affordable Tudric range of pewter included numerous items by Knox. This ice bucket is embellished in relief with interlaced Celtic-inspired plant stems or tendrils.

Low-relief
decoration

Tea kettle and stand | **Archibald Knox for Liberty**, 1905,
UK. Many of Knox's teapots and tea kettles are circular or
elliptical in shape. This example, adorned with Celtic motifs,
is complemented by the sweeping curve of the bone handle.

Ebonized
wood base

Silver centerpiece bowl | **A. E. Jones**, *c.* 1905, **UK**. Here,
Jones, formerly of the Birmingham Guild of Handicraft, combines
simple form with subtle decoration—a floral motif against
banding and a base studded with Ruskin pottery plaques.

Rosewater dish | **Robert Hilton**, *c.* 1907, **UK**. One of the
main designers for the Keswick School, Hilton conceived this
copper dish with a central rose boss and hammered decoration
showing stags and hounds among oak leaves.

Claret jug | **Archibald Knox
for Liberty**, 1902, **UK**. This
silver-mounted glass claret jug
was part of Liberty's Cymric
range. The intertwining bands
of silver are typical of Knox's
Celtic-inspired designs, but the
jug has a purity of line that also
anticipates Modernism.

Interlacing
silver bands

CHARLES ROBERT ASHBEE

Silver Footed Bowl

YEAR 1903 | **MANUFACTURER** Guild of Handicraft | **DIMENSIONS** *Height* 2¾ in (7 cm), *Width* 9¾ in (25 cm), *Diameter* 4 in (10.5 cm) | **MATERIALS** Silver, set with cabochons, glass liner

The British architect and designer Charles Robert Ashbee founded the Guild of Handicraft in 1888 to bring artisans together in a cooperative, with the aim of reviving traditional crafts. The Guild specialized in furniture, jewelry, and various kinds of metalwork, from wrought iron to fine tableware. Ashbee's designs for silver jam and butter dishes, with their dramatically looping handles, were among his most successful and influential objects.

With pieces like this bowl, Ashbee wanted to emphasize the special qualities silver can have when it is traditionally crafted—its gleaming, pale surface, its potential for striking shapes, and the way in which it complements beautifully colored gemstones. This silver footed bowl's blend of traditional craft skills and visual flair typified the high standards of design and workmanship fostered by the Arts and Crafts movement.

> **Good honest craftsmanship is better done the nearer people get into touch with the elemental things of life.**
>
> C. R. **Ashbee**
> Article in *Art Journal,* 1903

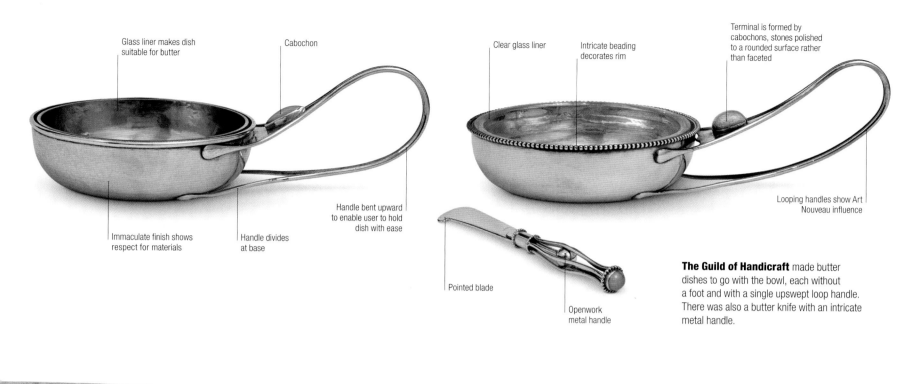

Glass liner makes dish suitable for butter

Cabochon

Immaculate finish shows respect for materials

Handle divides at base

Handle bent upward to enable user to hold dish with ease

Clear glass liner

Intricate beading decorates rim

Terminal is formed by cabochons, stones polished to a rounded surface rather than faceted

Looping handles show Art Nouveau influence

Pointed blade

Openwork metal handle

The Guild of Handicraft made butter dishes to go with the bowl, each without a foot and with a single upswept loop handle. There was also a butter knife with an intricate metal handle.

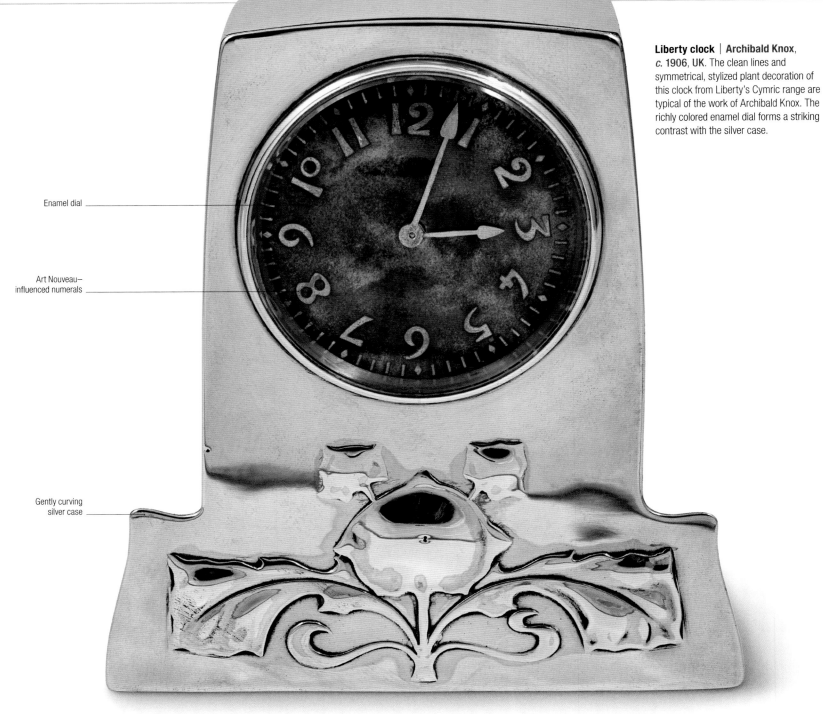

Liberty clock | **Archibald Knox,**
c. 1906, UK. The clean lines and
symmetrical, stylized plant decoration of
this clock from Liberty's Cymric range are
typical of the work of Archibald Knox. The
richly colored enamel dial forms a striking
contrast with the silver case.

Enamel dial

Art Nouveau–
influenced numerals

Gently curving
silver case

METAL
HOMEWARE

From the Cotswolds to California, Arts and Crafts
metalworkers applied their skills to all kinds of products,
including both traditional household objects such as
candlesticks or more modern items such as electric lamps that were new to the market. The metalworkers were
accomplished decorators, incorporating relief ornament and brightly colored enamels into many of their pieces. They also
paid great attention to the overall form and design of their products, whether giving a satisfying rounded shape to a plain
vase or creating a candelabra in the organic form of a flower or a branch. Whichever approach they took, their work
embodied the doctrine of truth to materials. It is always obvious which metal was used—whether shining silver or glowing
copper, its qualities were emphasized—and the artist rarely concealed how an object was made.

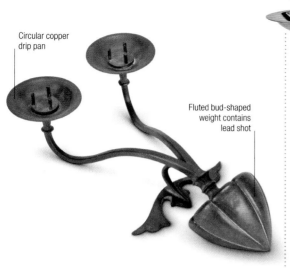

Circular copper drip pan

Fluted bud-shaped weight contains lead shot

Copper and brass candlestick | **W. A. S Benson**, *c*. 1900, UK. The foot, branches, and bud-shaped counterweight of this piece are all based on plant forms. Benson treated many of his ingenious designs with a special lacquer to prevent tarnishing.

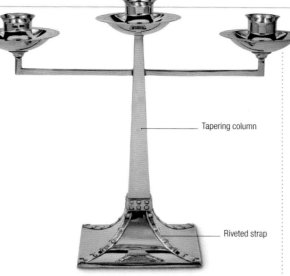

Tapering column

Riveted strap

Silver candelabra | **James Dixon & Sons**, *c*. 1900, UK. The visible straps and rivets of this candelabra show how Arts and Crafts designers, such as those working for this established firm of silversmiths, liked to display details of construction.

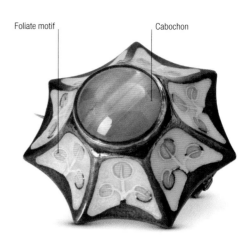

Foliate motif

Cabochon

Heptagonal silver brooch | **C. R. Ashbee**, *c*. 1902, UK. The central agate cabochon is surrounded by seven enameled sections, each with a leaf pattern. Motifs inspired by nature and semiprecious stones are typical of Ashbee's work.

Mica panel

Table lamp | **Dirk van Erp**, *c*. 1910, US. California-based coppersmith van Erp was especially well known for his lamps made from hand-hammered copper and mica (a lustrous natural material resistant to heat and electricity).

Trumpet-shaped neck

Squat oviform body

American Beauty vase | **Roycroft**, *c*. 1910, US. The artisans of the Roycroft Copper Shop in East Aurora, New York, produced much Arts and Crafts hand-hammered copperware like this. It was a strong tradition in the US.

The Guild of Handicraft

1888–1907

Founded in London by C. R. Ashbee in 1888 and based in Chipping Campden in England's Cotswold hills from 1902, the Guild of Handicraft Ltd. was renowned for its metalwork. This ranged from fine silver and jewelry to items made of beaten copper or wrought iron.

Ashbee promoted the Arts and Crafts idea that the value of a jewel was determined by the integrity of its design and the way in which it was treated rather than by the value of the stone itself. Although the Guild was disbanded in 1907, its high standards of workmanship and its appreciation of the status of the craftsman and the importance of the good, simple life continued, attracting like-minded people to the Cotswolds and making the area a center of excellence for those interested in arts and crafts.

Enameled plaques   Knop   Beaded band

Rich foliate decoration

Silver box | **Omar Ramsden and Alwyn Carr**, 1912, UK. In contrast to the plain silver base, the lid of this box has a mass of finely worked detail, including flower and leaf decoration, beaded banding, and ornate supports to the knop.

Geometric stamped decoration

Polished steel surface

Cotswolds candlestick | **Ernest Gimson**, *c*. 1930, UK. The fine craftsmanship of this steel candlestick shows how the Arts and Crafts traditions lived on in the Cotswolds. The piece was probably made by metalworkers Alfred or Norman Bucknell.

The cover of a Guild of Handicraft Ltd. catalog, *c*. **1900,** showing the silversmithing shop.

△ **"Sailing Around the Bathroom,"** designed by Christopher Dresser and produced by Streiner and Co., *c.* 1898, was printed on cotton and featured tall ships surrounded by dolphins amid waves.

Christopher
Dresser

British-born Christopher Dresser, creator of striking and original metalware, ceramics, and other objects, is sometimes known as the first industrial designer. He started his career as a botanist and botanical artist, and in his twenties wrote articles on the use of botany in decorative art. He did not advocate copying plant forms, but understood the underlying geometry of plant structures and used this knowledge to devise geometrically balanced forms and harmonious decoration. Dresser also took inspiration from Gothic Revival designers such as A. W. N. Pugin, and from Japanese art, on which he became an expert, traveling to Japan and collecting objects on behalf of the Tiffany Company (see pp.102–103).

A prolific designer, he created carpet designs for Brinton and Lewis, colorful ceramics for manufacturers such as the Linthorpe Pottery, and glassware for James Couper & Sons of Glasgow. Unlike other designers of the time, he embraced industrialization. Some of his best-known, and most revolutionary, designs, are for metalwork, which show Dresser rethinking household objects in striking new ways. His items for companies such as James Dixon & Sons have strong, very modern-looking, geometric designs, often with undecorated surfaces, and sometimes with exposed rivets. These objects were far ahead of their time, prefiguring the work of Bauhaus designers and other 20th-century Modernists.

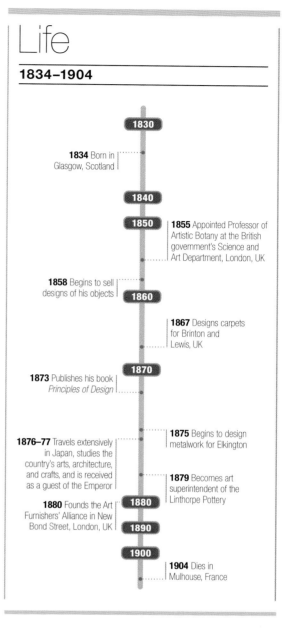

Life

1834–1904

1830

1834 Born in Glasgow, Scotland

1840

1850

1855 Appointed Professor of Artistic Botany at the British government's Science and Art Department, London, UK

1858 Begins to sell designs of his objects

1860

1867 Designs carpets for Brinton and Lewis, UK

1870

1873 Publishes his book *Principles of Design*

1875 Begins to design metalwork for Elkington

1876–77 Travels extensively in Japan, studies the country's arts, architecture, and crafts, and is received as a guest of the Emperor

1879 Becomes art superintendent of the Linthorpe Pottery

1880 Founds the Art Furnishers' Alliance in New Bond Street, London, UK

1880

1890

1900

1904 Dies in Mulhouse, France

Lid integrated into square of the body

Teapot | **For James Dixon & Sons**, *c.* 1880. Dresser's teapots show how he could radically rethink an object, producing a totally unexpected design based on strong geometrical shapes.

Sparrow-beak spout

Angled handle accommodates the user's hand and thumb

Wine jug | **For James Dixon & Sons**, 1881. Dresser made use of an unusual and effective combination of straight lines and curves in this electroplated wine jug.

Articulated divisions

Rivets secure the dividers to the base

Letter rack | **For Hukin & Heath**, 1881. Exposed rivets and joints are typical of Dresser's approach to metalwork, while the rounded bun feet mirror the shape of the divider joints.

Symmetrically
arranged rushes

Swans portrayed
in profile

**Swan, Rush, and Iris
wallpaper | Walter Crane**, *c.* 1875,
UK. This pattern was one of Walter
Crane's first wallpaper designs. Its use
of black outlines, plain blocks of color,
and profile views suggests the influence
of ancient Greek vase paintings. Jeffrey
& Co. began to produce the wallpaper
in 1877. The border indicates that the
paper was designed for use on a dado
(the lower part of a wall).

FABRIC AND WALLPAPER

Reacting against the mechanization of the Industrial Revolution,
the Arts and Crafts movement revived handweaving and embroidery.
William Morris was a leader in this field, mastering both of these techniques
and designing many fabrics and wallpapers. The textiles sold by his firm had flat, complex patterns featuring plants and animals and
were dyed in natural colors such as madder red, peacock blue, and sage green. Morris's work inspired others, such as the designers
of the Silver Studio and architects including C. F. A. Voysey. In the US, there was also a resurgence in hand-produced textiles, largely
thanks to the work of textile designer Candace Wheeler. In Europe, the Wiener Werkstätte in Austria had a textile section by 1910.
Wallpapers took inspiration from similar sources to textiles, and together the wallpapers and fabrics of the Arts and Crafts movement
helped people create lighter, less fussy interiors than had been the norm in the mid-19th century.

Floral design | **Owen Jones**, 1863, UK. Jones produced hundreds of textile and wallpaper patterns, many based on floral motifs. His inspiration came from nature and the architecture he saw during the travels of his Grand Tour of Europe.

Naturalistic flowers

Donegal rug | **Gavin Morton**, *c.* 1900, Ireland. Morton was a prominent designer of rugs and carpets woven in Ireland and Scotland. This example combines stylized plant forms with more realistic, delicate, trailing flowers against a rich, deep ground.

Bold floral elements stand out against a pale ivory border

Strawberry Thief fabric | **William Morris**, *c.* 1883, UK. This famous design was inspired by Morris's observation of birds among the strawberries in his kitchen garden at Kelmscott Manor. Although formal, the pattern is full of naturalistic details.

The Grammar of Ornament

1856

British designer and theorist Owen Jones collected thousands of examples of flat patterns from different cultures and time periods for his book *The Grammar of Ornament*, which was a summary of his design theories. Many of the patterns came from the Alhambra Palace in Spain; Jones was entranced by the colors and geometry of the Islamic decoration. The book is still in print and is used as a sourcebook today.

Original drawing for *The Grammar of Ornament*, Persian No. 1, Plate XLIV.

Embroidery | *c.* 1900, Scotland. In this design, two women in idealized medieval dress are linked by garlands of roses and daffodils. The shapes of the trees in the background show the influence of Scottish artists such as Charles Rennie Mackintosh.

Swallows in flight

Floral garland

Metallic thread provides highlights

Pillow cover | **Candace Wheeler**, *c.* 1876–1877, US. Wheeler promoted objects designed and made by women by founding the New York Society of Decorative Art and the Women's Exchange. Much of her work had strongly delineated floral subjects.

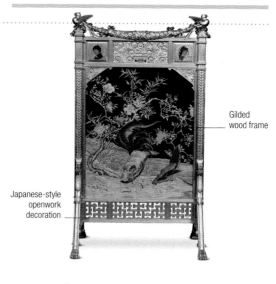

Fire screen | **Herter Brothers**, 1878–1880, US. The centerpiece of this screen is an embroidered, painted, and gilded panel depicting birds and flowers, which was probably made in Japan. Herter Brothers designed the frame specifically for it.

Gilded wood frame

Japanese-style openwork decoration

△ **Hera was one of the colorful fabrics** designed by Arthur Silver for Liberty. It was produced commercially by roller printing from 1887.

△ **Silver clock** | Archibald Knox, *c.* 1905

The British retailer Liberty has a well-established reputation for selling and promoting the best in design and workmanship across a range of goods, from clocks to carpets. Arthur Lasenby Liberty began by specializing in Oriental, especially Japanese, design but was increasingly influenced by the Arts and Crafts movement, employing, among others, C. F. A. Voysey for carpet and textile designs and Archibald Knox for metalwork. Knox designed many pieces of silverware for Liberty's Cymric line as well as pewter items for its Tudric line. Most were in a Celtic style that stood out from the Art Nouveau designs sold by other retailers. In the 1890s, the company concentrated on Art Nouveau pieces.

As a result of Liberty's close relationships with many key designers and studios, the company became known for high-quality design in a variety of fields, including finely crafted silverware, furniture with distinctive metal handles and hinges, and colorful fabrics patterned with flowers or peacock feathers. Although many of the objects it stocked were handmade, the company also exploited technology, which enabled it to bring good design to a wider market. Liberty's fame spread across Europe, to the extent that in Italy, Art Nouveau became known as *Stile Liberty*. The company still trades today, commissioning new designs and reviving old ones, such as Arthur Silver's ever-popular peacock-feather fabric called Hera.

Key dates
1875–

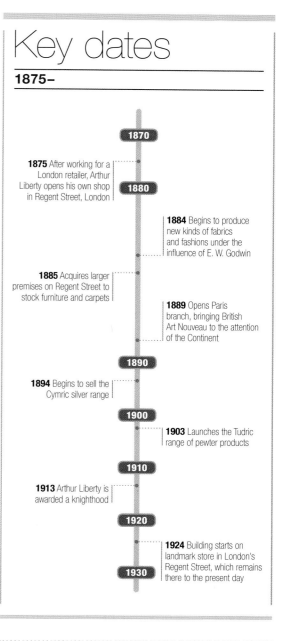

1870

1875 After working for a London retailer, Arthur Liberty opens his own shop in Regent Street, London

1880

1884 Begins to produce new kinds of fabrics and fashions under the influence of E. W. Godwin

1885 Acquires larger premises on Regent Street to stock furniture and carpets

1889 Opens Paris branch, bringing British Art Nouveau to the attention of the Continent

1890

1894 Begins to sell the Cymric silver range

1900

1903 Launches the Tudric range of pewter products

1910

1913 Arthur Liberty is awarded a knighthood

1920

1924 Building starts on landmark store in London's Regent Street, which remains there to the present day

1930

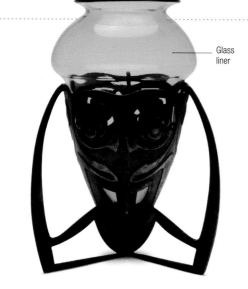

Glass liner

Pewter vase | **Archibald Knox**, glass liner by Whitefriars Glass, *c.* 1900. The supports resemble plant stems, and the low-relief decoration is of stylized honesty seedpods.

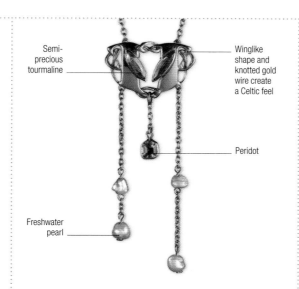

Semi-precious tourmaline

Winglike shape and knotted gold wire create a Celtic feel

Peridot

Freshwater pearl

Gold necklace | **Archibald Knox**, 1900. Known mainly for his silver and pewter pieces, Archibald Knox also designed gold and silver jewelry with the Celtic look for which he was famous.

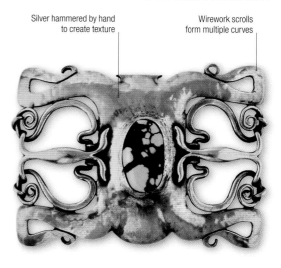

Silver hammered by hand to create texture

Wirework scrolls form multiple curves

Silver buckle | **Oliver Baker**, 1900. Baker designed buckles and clasps in silver adorned with semiprecious stones such as turquoise. He also made tableware.

ART NOUVEAU

1880–1910

The endless continuity of line
and spring of curve.

SIGNAL MAGAZINE

ART NOUVEAU
Introduction

Art Nouveau is the name of the style of architecture and design that developed around 1890 and remained fashionable until the beginning of World War I. The style was triggered by a reaction against the historicist revivals of the 19th century and appealed to a wide range of people. The designers of the 1890s, anticipating the dawn of a new century, turned their back on the past, refusing to copy old ideas, and strove to forge a new style of art that was suited to their own time. Instead of designs based on past styles, therefore, they drew on nature or abstract motifs for inspiration, producing work that seems much freer than what had gone before it, both because it is often asymmetrical and also because it has

great variety. Art Nouveau design embraced many fields, including decorative, inlaid furniture by Louis Majorelle, jewelry incorporating semiprecious stones by designers such as Lalique, and striking posters featuring dreamy females and lavish lettering by artists such as Alphonse Mucha. Technical expertise and quality craftsmanship were matched by imagination, creativity, and vision.

France, Belgium, and beyond

The new movement was international, but the results varied from one place to another, reflecting the character of each country. In France and Belgium, for example, designers drew inspiration from natural forms and

WHIPLASH MOTIFS

The sinuous double curve, known as the whiplash curve, was the key linear motif in French and Belgian Art Nouveau. Based on the shape of swirling plant roots, it was similar in appearance to an unfurling whip.

ASYMMETRY

A characteristic feature of Art Nouveau, asymmetry was influenced by Japanese art and the 18th-century Rococo style. Asymmetrical forms and decoration were usually based on the organic forms found in nature.

FEMALE FIGURES

Typically French Art Nouveau, the image of a maiden with flowing hair, much loved by Symbolist poets and artists, was often entwined with swirling plant tendrils and was sometimes half woman and half flower.

Color is to the eye what music is to the ear.

Louis Comfort **Tiffany**

arranged these in flowing, asymmetric designs, linked by sinuous lines. Irises, tulips, leaf tendrils, dragonflies, and butterflies appeared as decorative motifs on furniture, glass, metalware, and jewelry. Brussels and Paris were major centers of Art Nouveau. In Paris, where its influence can still be seen in the swirling cast-iron Métro station entrances designed by Hector Guimard, dealer Siegfried Bing opened a gallery called Maison de l'Art Nouveau. There, he sold contemporary art objects with a Japanese influence, in a style that came to be known as Art Nouveau, after the gallery. Among Bing's products were items made by the American company Tiffany, a link that helped spread the new style around the world.

Jugendstil

In Germany and Austria, Art Nouveau was more geometric and symmetrical in style, relying on rectilinear patterns and a graphic sense of light and shade. It also had different names—it was called Jugendstil in Germany and Secessionist in Austria—and the Secessionists, in particular, spread their ideas farther afield, both across the Austro-Hungarian empire and via links with designers overseas, such as the great Scottish architect Charles Rennie Mackintosh. Although cut short by World War I, Art Nouveau had a powerful impact, and the rectilinear work of the German and Austrian designers later had a great influence on Modernism.

IRIDESCENT GLASS

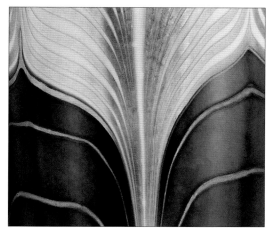

Inspired by the sheen on ancient Roman glass that had recently been excavated, Art Nouveau glassmakers tried to recreate the effect themselves and used metal oxides when firing glass, to create an iridescent effect.

CAMEO GLASS

The cameo effect is created by using several layers of colored glass and carving or etching parts of the top layer away to create an image in relief. The technique was adopted by many Art Nouveau glassmakers.

INSECTS AND PLANTS

Art Nouveau designers were deeply inspired by nature and strove to recreate the striking forms and diaphanous beauty of plants and insects with great precision, notably in furniture, glassware, and jewelry.

CURVED FURNITURE

During the 1890s, cabinetmakers in France and Belgium turned their backs on revivalist styles and began producing highly sculptural pieces with curved, sinuous lines. Often, in the case of designers such as Hector Guimard, these pieces had little additional ornamentation. However, some cabinetmakers, such as Louis Majorelle and Émile Gallé, used rich, tendril-like carving and created marquetry decoration—images built up by combining different colored woods—that depicted subjects from the natural world. Door handles and relief panels could also represent popular Art Nouveau themes, from flowers to young women in flowing dresses. This style of Art Nouveau furniture, stimulated by the work of craftsmen in Nancy, France, and Brussels, Belgium, was marketed by businesses such as Siegfried Bing's famous gallery in Paris and promoted at a number of major exhibitions. Designers continued to work in this style until the eve of World War I.

Dragonfly handle

Wheel-segment support

Desk | **Carlo Bugatti**, *c.* 1900, Italy. The bronze, brass, and pewter inlays and the Oriental motifs are typical of Bugatti's furniture, as are circular elements, such as the wheel-segment supports of this small desk.

Mahogany frame

Inlay of enameled lava stone

Hall Stand | **Hector Guimard**, *c.* 1900, France. Famous for his Paris Métro entrances, architect and designer Guimard developed a distinctive style, using sinuous curves, as in this hall stand, and juxtaposing materials in innovative ways.

Marquetry leaf inlay

Desk | **Léon Benouville**, *c.* 1900, France. Benouville's furniture, with its intricate woodwork and delicate marquetry, epitomizes French Art Nouveau. This desk's leaf decoration is rendered in immaculate marquetry.

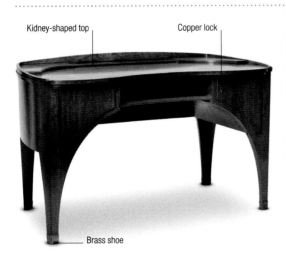

Kidney-shaped top

Copper lock

Brass shoe

Scheidemantel writing desk | **Henry van de Velde**, *c.* 1903, **Belgium**. This kidney-shaped writing desk in mahogany has curved front supports that make a strong visual statement as well as provide a space for the user to sit.

Steeply arched back

Armchair | **Bruno Paul**, *c.* 1900, Germany. The curved uprights and tightly arched top rail are the most striking features of this mahogany-framed chair. Paul was an important figure in the German Jugendstil movement.

Arched apron

Stylized animal-paw foot

Occasional table | **Henry van de Velde**, *c.* 1916, Belgium. The gentle curves of this walnut table show the more restrained side of Art Nouveau. It was one of several designs van de Velde created for German theater director Kurt von Mutzenbecher.

Encoignure | **Louis Majorelle**, *c.* 1900, **France**. Nancy-based designer Louis Majorelle became famous for his elaborate Art Nouveau furniture decorated with marquetry. Flowers, leaves, insects, and animals were among the subjects he depicted most often in marquetry, as seen here in the lower panels.

Mahogany side panels

You have … unity achieved by infinite variety.

Hector **Guimard**
Designer and architect

Paris Exposition

1900

The Paris Exposition Universelle of 1900 was a major exhibition intended to celebrate the achievements of the past century and to look forward to those of the next. Art Nouveau was the dominant style, from the architecture of many of the exhibition buildings to the items on display, including jewelry by René Lalique and interiors by Georges de Feure. More than 50 million visitors came to the exhibition, which covered 296 acres (120 hectares) around the Eiffel Tower, and 58 countries participated, ensuring that Art Nouveau became the best-known style in the coming years.

This lithograph advertising the Exposition by French artist Luigi Loir features Art Nouveau–style female figures.

△ **The dining room of Villa Majorelle** in Nancy showcases tables and chairs designed by Majorelle himself.

Louis Majorelle

French decorator and cabinetmaker Louis Majorelle was one of the greatest furniture producers of the late 19th and early 20th centuries, celebrated for his finely crafted works. His rich, polished wooden pieces have soft, flowing lines and are often decorated with intricate inlays depicting plants, leaves, or dragonflies. Majorelle began by making furniture based on earlier revivalist styles, but while living and working in Nancy, he was inspired by the Art Nouveau designers based there and soon began to make similar work. He became a leading member of the School of Nancy (see p.94) and collaborated with other members of the group, including the glassmakers Daum.

As a highly skilled craftsman, Majorelle always had a great respect for work produced by hand, but he also used machines in his factory so that he could increase production, lower the prices of some ranges, and sell his furniture more widely. In order to meet increasing demand, Majorelle established multiple workshops and started his own metalwork department to make handles, mounts, and other hardware that matched his woodwork. His immaculately produced furniture, usually made in dark hardwoods and often inlaid with a combination of pewter, brass, or mother-of-pearl, is still highly prized by collectors today.

Life
1859–1926

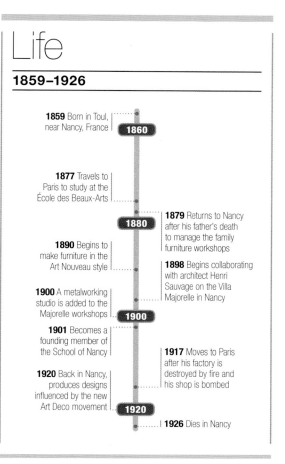

1859 Born in Toul, near Nancy, France

1860

1877 Travels to Paris to study at the École des Beaux-Arts

1879 Returns to Nancy after his father's death to manage the family furniture workshops

1880

1890 Begins to make furniture in the Art Nouveau style

1898 Begins collaborating with architect Henri Sauvage on the Villa Majorelle in Nancy

1900 A metalworking studio is added to the Majorelle workshops

1900

1901 Becomes a founding member of the School of Nancy

1917 Moves to Paris after his factory is destroyed by fire and his shop is bombed

1920 Back in Nancy, produces designs influenced by the new Art Deco movement

1920

1926 Dies in Nancy

Carved central post

Floral marquetry

Cabinet | *c.* 1900. There are several hallmarks of Majorelle's work in this piece: tapering straight lines; an organic, flowing shape; intricate floral marquetry; and rich decorative carving.

Tapering leg

Chair | *c.* 1900. One of Majorelle's simpler pieces, this elegant walnut chair combines naturally inspired, sweeping lines with a plain aesthetic.

Gilt bronze leaf and berry handle

Writing desk | *c.* 1910. Although the overall shape of this piece is more traditional than most of Majorelle's work, the carving on the legs and gilt handles displays the influence of Art Nouveau.

Panel featuring a
lyre player, based
on a figure in the
Beethoven Frieze

Maple inlay

Oak figuring arranged
in a geometric pattern

Panel depicting
a knight

**Display cabinet | Georg
and Gustav Klimt**, *c.* 1905–1910,
Austria. This display cabinet,
combining elongated rectangles
of oak with inlaid squares of maple,
is typical of the Vienna Secession.
The brass panels are based
on figures from Gustav Klimt's
Beethoven Frieze, displayed in
the Secession Building in Vienna.

SECESSIONIST
FURNITURE

The artists and designers of the Vienna Secession, who left the Austrian art establishment in 1897, created a new style of furniture. Rejecting both the simple, traditional forms of 19th-century Biedermeier design and the sinuous curves of Art Nouveau, designers such as Josef Hoffmann and Joseph Maria Olbrich took a more linear approach. Their furniture was often made from nontraditional materials, such as bent beechwood or aluminum, and created a strong, almost graphic impression with ebonized wood. Although some designers rejected ornament altogether, Secessionist furniture did feature restrained decoration, often involving geometrical patterns of squares or rectangles, and some pieces have outstanding metalwork, in the form of high-quality door detailing or embossed panels in brass or bronze. There are often pronounced linear elements, such as repeated slats or uprights, creating a geometry that reflects the influence of the great Scottish designer Charles Rennie Mackintosh (see pp.80–81).

Armchair | Joseph Maria Olbrich for Niedermoser, *c.* 1898–1899, **Austria.** Olbrich was famed for designs with a pronounced linear quality—the patterns made by the stretchers and uprights in this black-varnished maple armchair are typical.

Brass terminal

Turned carrying handles

Nest of tables | Josef Hoffmann for J. & J. Kohn, *c.* 1905, **Austria.** The Viennese Kohn company produced several of Hoffmann's designs, including this nest of tables in mahogany-stained beech. The grid pattern of uprights and horizontals on the sides of the large table is a recurring Secessionist motif.

The Vienna Secession

1897–1939

With the aim of revitalizing the conservative attitude of Austrian academic art, a group of 19 artists and designers, including Gustav Klimt and Joseph Maria Olbrich, broke away from the existing Austrian art societies in 1897. Calling themselves the Secessionists, the artists were not unified by a single style but shared a desire for creative freedom and a rejection of historicism. The motto above the entrance of the Secession building in Vienna read: "To every age its art. To art its freedom." Secession exhibitions attracted artists from across Europe, introducing Viennese artists to French Impressionism, and designers to the furniture of Charles Rennie Mackintosh.

Cover for *Ver Sacrum (Sacred Spring),* Koloman Moser, 1897 *Ver Sacrum* was a Secessionist magazine.

Beech frame stained to resemble mahogany

Armchair | Marcel Kammerer for Thonet, *c.* 1910, **Austria.** Based on a bent beechwood frame, this chair by Viennese architect and designer Marcel Kammerer combines its back and arms into one continuous curve.

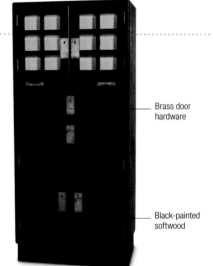

Brass door hardware

Black-painted softwood

Cabinet | Adolf Loos, 1908, **Austria.** The furniture of architect Adolf Loos features a balanced combination of lines and planes. A critic of the Secession, Loos later rejected ornament completely in his famous essay *Ornament and Crime.*

Back rail made using Thonet's bentwood techniques

Ebony ball bracket

Cabaret Fledermaus chair | Josef Hoffmann for Thonet, *c.* 1907, **Austria.** Hoffmann created this beechwood chair for the Cabaret Fledermaus, which was decorated by the Wiener Werkstätte, the craft workshops allied to the Secession.

Rounded corners harmonize with circular legs beneath

Splayed bentwood leg

Table | *c.* 1910, **Austria.** The ball brackets beneath the shelves of this table recall those used by Hoffmann for his Fledermaus chair. But this table has bentwood legs that curve outward, lending it stability and recalling Thonet bentwood furniture.

△ **Casa Batlló, Barcelona, 1904,** features Gaudí's typical flowing stonework, asymmetrical carving, and stained glass.

Antoni Gaudí

The Catalan Antoni Gaudí was one of the most original architects in the entire history of building. Although he was influenced by past styles, including the Gothic of the Middle Ages and various forms of Oriental architecture, Gaudí forged a unique style of his own, featuring undulating, organic facades, columns that look like bones, unusually shaped arches, and surfaces covered with carving or brightly colored mosaics. "Anything created by human beings is already in the great book of nature," he said.

Gaudí's work includes houses, apartment buildings, a college, garden structures and statuary, and churches. Nearly all of these buildings are in the city of Barcelona in northeastern Spain, where he was based. Barcelona is also home to the most famous of all his buildings—the still-unfinished church of the Sagrada Família. Gaudí designed furniture, too, and these pieces show the same traits as his buildings—a multitude of curves and few straight lines or flat surfaces. As well as looking extraordinary, his work is structurally inventive, and his buildings sometimes feature non-load-bearing walls, sloping columns, or parabolic arches. Although his radical and sometimes eccentric approach to design meant that he had no obvious followers, his originality and talent for lateral thinking make him a favorite with designers and architects alike.

Life

1852–1926

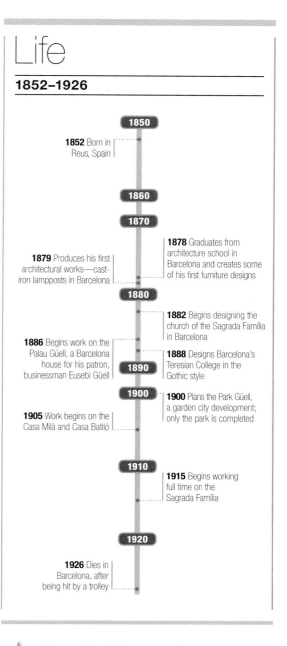

1850

1852 Born in Reus, Spain

1860

1870

1878 Graduates from architecture school in Barcelona and creates some of his first furniture designs

1879 Produces his first architectural works—cast-iron lampposts in Barcelona

1880

1882 Begins designing the church of the Sagrada Família in Barcelona

1886 Begins work on the Palau Güell, a Barcelona house for his patron, businessman Eusebi Güell

1888 Designs Barcelona's Teresian College in the Gothic style

1890

1900

1900 Plans the Park Güell, a garden city development; only the park is completed

1905 Work begins on the Casa Milà and Casa Batlló

1910

1915 Begins working full time on the Sagrada Família

1920

1926 Dies in Barcelona, after being hit by a trolley

Back conceals a shelf for prayer books

Rear feet have attachments for a wooden kneeler

Prayer bench | 1898–1914. Supported on a wrought-iron frame, the rich Spanish oak of the seat and back is carved in a series of comfortable curves.

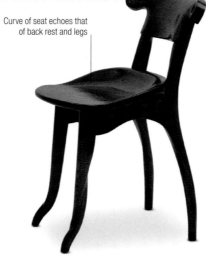

Curve of seat echoes that of back rest and legs

Side chair | **For Casa Ribas Seva, Barcelona**, 1905–1907. Smoothly curving lines give this polished oak chair the fluid, organic appearance that is typical of Gaudí's work.

Smoke can exit through the eyeholes

Chimney pots | 1900–1914. The Casa Milà in Barcelona is famous for its undulating walls and its roof, which includes these chimneys with cowls shaped like helmets or masks.

BALTIC PEARL

The building at 8 Smilšu Street, which occupies a corner lot near the center of Riga, is a highly decorative example of early 20th century Art Nouveau architecture. After a major exhibition of industry and crafts in 1901, the rapidly growing city of Riga became famous for its new buildings in the Art Nouveau style. The 8 Smilšu Street building was designed and built by German-born architects Heinrich Scheel and Friedrich Scheffel, who were both pioneers of Art Nouveau in the Baltic.

The building has shops on the ground floor, with apartments above them. The facade has elaborate bay windows and balconies decorated with plasterwork and sculpture by Sigismund Otto and Oswald Wassil. Set amid the standard Art Nouveau motifs of plant forms and hybrid creatures are faces and masks. The most prominent of these, by the building's entrances, depict a number of melancholy women with closed eyes, which show the influence of *fin-de-siècle* symbolism on Latvian architecture. These faces demonstrate the flair of Riga's little-known architects and sculptors, who rebuilt more than a third of the city's core to create the greatest concentration of Art Nouveau buildings in Europe.

The terrifying and edible beauty of Art Nouveau architecture

Salvador **Dalí,** 1935

8 Smilšu Street, Riga, Latvia, Heinrich Scheel & Friedrich Scheffel, 1902
The face, with its closed eyes, serene expression, and stylized hair ornaments, is a small detail in the rich facade at 8 Smilšu Street. The city became a major center for ornamental plasterwork and sculpture around 1900.

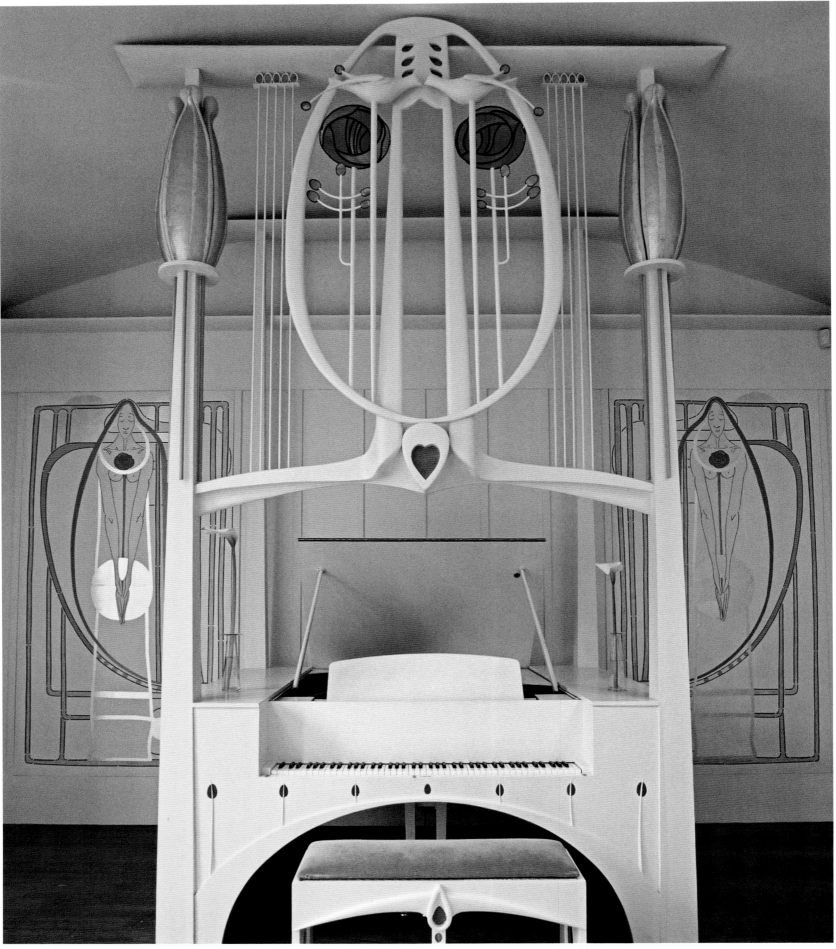

△ **Mackintosh's House for an Art Lover** was designed in 1901 but built from 1989 to 1996. It includes this piano in the music room, which combines strong, geometric lines with the rose's soft organic curves.

Charles Rennie
Mackintosh

Charles Rennie Mackintosh was one of Europe's most celebrated architects and designers, famous for groundbreaking buildings such as the Glasgow School of Art and for his striking furniture designs. He developed a distinctive, rectilinear form of Art Nouveau in his architectural work and his many designs for furniture, lighting, metalwork, and other items. This style—typified by chairs with multiple slats, usually in plain ebonized or white-painted wood—combined strong, straight lines with restrained, gentle curves.

Mackintosh widened his scope by collaborating with his wife, Margaret MacDonald, her sister, Frances, and Frances's husband, J. H. MacNair, in a group that came to be known as "The Four," to design pieces from posters to metalware. This work greatly impressed and influenced the designers of central Europe, especially after Mackintosh exhibited at the 8th Vienna Secession exhibition in 1900.

In the years that followed, Mackintosh created a number of outstanding buildings, including tea rooms, schools, a church, and several houses, mostly in Scotland. However, due to economic troubles and an unfounded accusation, in 1915, that he was spying for the Germans, his career was cut short and he designed little in his later years, though he produced some extraordinary watercolors. Despite this, his reputation lives on, and his work is still collected and copied by admirers.

Life

1868–1928

1868 Born in Glasgow, Scotland **1870**

1889 Joins the architectural firm of Honeyman and Keppie

1892 Meets his future wife, fellow designer Margaret MacDonald, in evening classes at Glasgow School of Art **1890**

1896 Undertakes his first project for Glasgow tea-shop owner Kate Cranston: a stenciled interior wall decoration

1896 Designs a successful competition entry to build the new Glasgow School of Art

1903 Designs the building, interiors, and furniture for Kate Cranston's Willow Tea Rooms, Glasgow **1900**

1900 Marries MacDonald, and they collaborate on various interior designs

1904 Completes the Hill House, Helensburgh, Scotland, including the interior with its famous tall slatted chairs

1914 Leaves Honeyman and Keppie and moves to Suffolk, England **1910**

1928 Dies in London

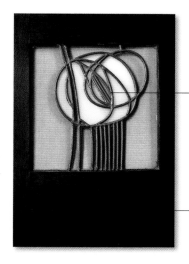

Rose stained glass door | 1901. One of Mackintosh's most complete designs was his House for an Art Lover. The rose, here in stained glass as part of a door, was one of his favorite motifs.

Intersecting cames (grooved lead strips) suggest the folds of the rose's petals

Ebonized wooden door

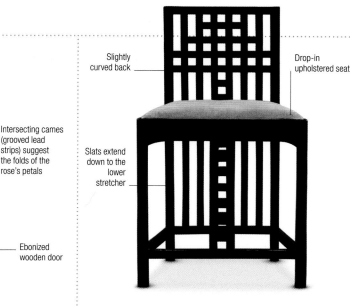

Slightly curved back

Drop-in upholstered seat

Slats extend down to the lower stretcher

Chair | **For Hous'hill, Glasgow, 1904.** This chair's pattern of dark, intersecting slats, designed to contrast with the white fixtures of the house's bedroom, suggests a stylized tree.

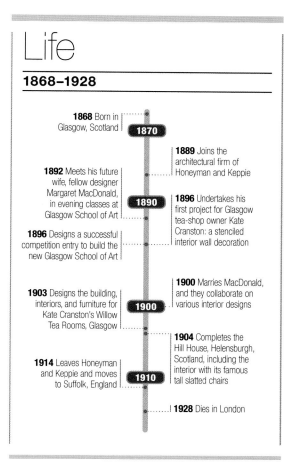

Inlay of erinoid, an early type of colored plastic

Domino clock | 1917. Mackintosh devised domino-like panels for this clock, each with a different number of spots. It was made for one of his main patrons, the toy maker W. J. Bassett-Lowke.

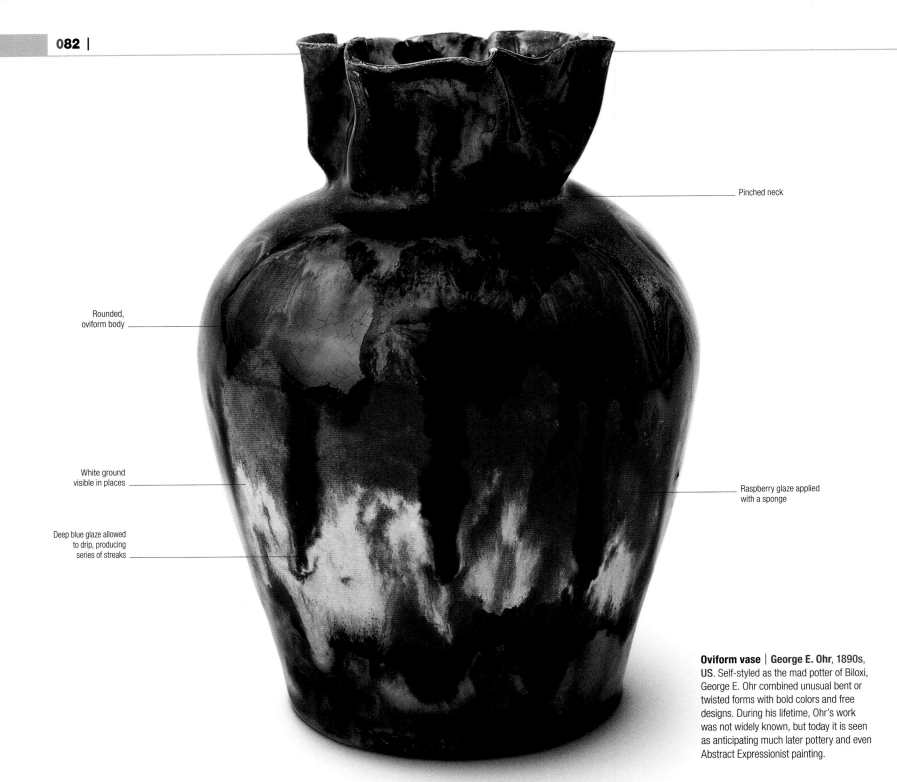

Pinched neck

Rounded, oviform body

White ground visible in places

Raspberry glaze applied with a sponge

Deep blue glaze allowed to drip, producing series of streaks

Oviform vase | George E. Ohr, 1890s, **US**. Self-styled as the mad potter of Biloxi, George E. Ohr combined unusual bent or twisted forms with bold colors and free designs. During his lifetime, Ohr's work was not widely known, but today it is seen as anticipating much later pottery and even Abstract Expressionist painting.

COLORFUL
CERAMICS

Most Art Nouveau ceramics were curvaceous and made a bold impact. The form of the pot and the painted decoration were often closely related and, in the work of potters such as George E. Ohr and Clément Massier, could also be vividly colored. Some skilled modelers, notably Artus Van Briggle, broke free of the rigid symmetry of pots thrown on the wheel, producing sculptural vessels, vases, and jugs that seem to be transforming into favorite Art Nouveau subjects—attractive young women or beautiful flowers. Many designers brought their objects—decorative sculptures rather than practical vessels—to life in dazzling iridescent colors. There were also more restrained designs, in which the color palette was toned down or the decoration became more formal or symmetrical, influenced in part by the more ordered and disciplined decorative style of much of the work of the Vienna Secession (see pp.74–75).

Stylized leaf ribs picked out in darker color

Dark key makes flowers stand out

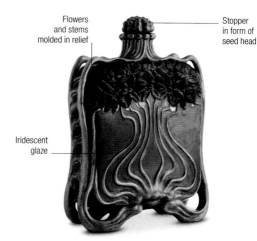

Flowers and stems molded in relief

Stopper in form of seed head

Iridescent glaze

Iridescent vase | **Clément Massier**, *c.* 1900, France. This oviform earthenware vase is shaped with spiraling dimples and decorated with honeysuckle blooms and tendrils over luster glazes that gleam like metal.

Porcelain vase | **L. Mimard for Sèvres**, 1897, France. Carefully painted leaves and flowers trail down the sides of this vase. The formal, symmetrical design shows the influence of the Vienna Secession.

Flask with stopper | **Zsolnay**, *c.* 1900, Hungary. The sinuous stems, bright colors, and double-curve shape of this vessel are unmistakably Art Nouveau. The stopper and unusual form indicate that it was designed to be purely decorative.

Twigs and branches painted in fine detail

Hair flows into body of vase

Luster glazes

In 1887, Clément Massier, who had a pottery studio near Cannes in southern France, started to collaborate with the French artist Lucien Lévy-Dhurmer. Lévy-Dhurmer had been collecting earthenware from Moorish Spain that was decorated with glazes containing compounds of metals such as copper, silver, and gold, and the two men began to make their own pots using a similar technique. The metallic iridescence of the luster glazes that they created were both widely admired and imitated.

Lorelei vase | **Artus Van Briggle**, *c.* 1900, US. The asymmetric shape and flowing lines of the Lorelei—the most famous of Van Briggle's vases—are typical of Art Nouveau. The girl's hair and robes seem to emerge from the clay.

Finely delineated details

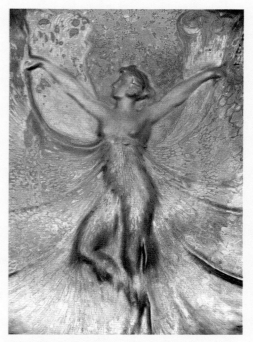

This iridescent glaze on a ceramic by Clément Massier was made by spraying metal oxides into the kiln.

Vase | **Arnold Krog and Anna Smidth for Royal Copenhagen**, 1900, Denmark. The strength of this design comes from the muted palette, distinctive lines and shapes, the quality of the painting, and the fineness of the porcelain.

Vellum glaze vase | **Carl Schmidt for Rookwood**, 1906, US. Vellum was the bridge between Rookwood's gloss and matte glazes. Wild mushroom species decorate the ground, which is graduated to suggest the sky and grass.

SINUOUS METALWARE

Many Art Nouveau craftsmen took to metalwork, and the period is renowned for beautiful metal objects designed to adorn the dining table. The followers of the Art Nouveau movement especially liked silver for its luxury and the ways in which it could be shaped or embossed into curvaceous designs. Lavish items such as bowls could be displayed as table centerpieces, and silversmiths could test their skills giving new form and ornament to a range of products, from candlesticks to claret jugs.

However, less costly metals were also popular, particularly pewter, as it can be easily cast. Secessionist designers such as Austrian architect Joseph Maria Olbrich were especially successful at embossing metal, ornamenting it in low relief to produce designs of great subtlety, and often combining geometric forms with graceful curves or floral motifs.

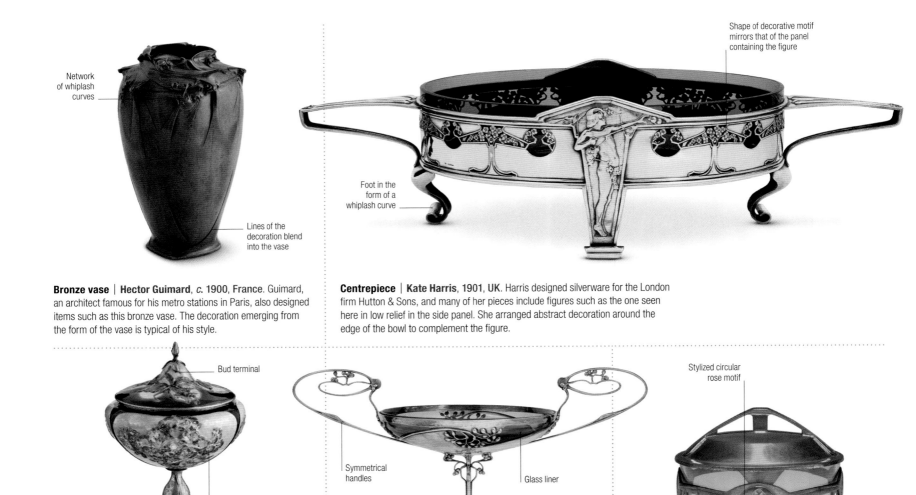

Network of whiplash curves

Lines of the decoration blend into the vase

Shape of decorative motif mirrors that of the panel containing the figure

Foot in the form of a whiplash curve

Bud terminal

Azalea decoration

Pedestal foot

Symmetrical handles

Glass liner

Stylized circular rose motif

Bronze vase | **Hector Guimard**, c. 1900, France. Guimard, an architect famous for his metro stations in Paris, also designed items such as this bronze vase. The decoration emerging from the form of the vase is typical of his style.

Centrepiece | **Kate Harris**, 1901, UK. Harris designed silverware for the London firm Hutton & Sons, and many of her pieces include figures such as the one seen here in low relief in the side panel. She arranged abstract decoration around the edge of the bowl to complement the figure.

Pedestal cup and cover | **Eugène Feuillâtre**, 1901, France. Feuillâtre was an enameler who had previously worked for René Lalique. This enameled silver cup and cover combine attractive floral decoration with a unifying pale green hue.

Footed bowl | **Kate Harris**, 1902, UK. Decorative silver cups and bowls were among Harris's specialties: this example, intended as a table centerpiece, has particularly fine handles and stylized leaf decoration.

Preserve pot and tray | **Joseph Maria Olbrich**, 1903, Austria. Secessionist designer Olbrich created this pewter-mounted pot and matching tray. The effectiveness of the design comes from the strong geometry of the metalwork.

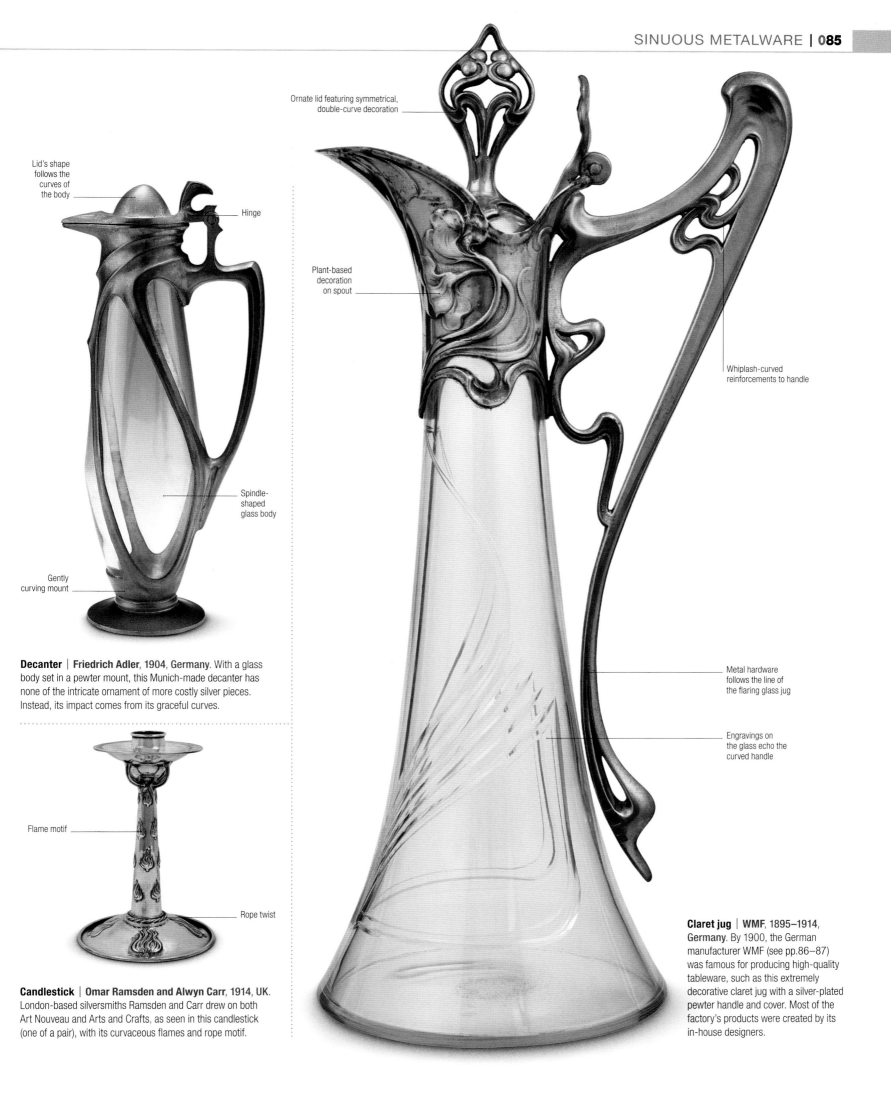

Lid's shape
follows the
curves of
the body

Hinge

Ornate lid featuring symmetrical,
double-curve decoration

Plant-based
decoration
on spout

Whiplash-curved
reinforcements to handle

Spindle-
shaped
glass body

Gently
curving mount

Metal hardware
follows the line of
the flaring glass jug

Engravings on
the glass echo the
curved handle

Decanter | **Friedrich Adler**, 1904, **Germany**. With a glass
body set in a pewter mount, this Munich-made decanter has
none of the intricate ornament of more costly silver pieces.
Instead, its impact comes from its graceful curves.

Flame motif

Rope twist

Candlestick | **Omar Ramsden and Alwyn Carr**, 1914, **UK**.
London-based silversmiths Ramsden and Carr drew on both
Art Nouveau and Arts and Crafts, as seen in this candlestick
(one of a pair), with its curvaceous flames and rope motif.

Claret jug | **WMF**, 1895–1914,
Germany. By 1900, the German
manufacturer WMF (see pp.86–87)
was famous for producing high-quality
tableware, such as this extremely
decorative claret jug with a silver-plated
pewter handle and cover. Most of the
factory's products were created by its
in-house designers.

△ **This typical Art Nouveau–style dish** from around 1900 depicts a young woman's profile and flowing hair.

△ **Table casket** | *c.* 1900

Founded in the mid-19th century, the German manufacturer WMF (Württembergische Metallwarenfabrik) was a prolific producer of fine metalware. It is still in operation today but is known particularly for its work from the 1890s and early 1900s. In this period, under the leadership of German sculptor Albert Mayer, it ran a large studio, employing numerous designers, sculptors, modelers, and craftsmen to create objects based on the latest fashions in the decorative arts.

Although WMF is most famous for its tableware, it has also produced a huge range of other items, including card trays, mirrors, candlesticks, and clocks. The company works in many different design styles but is best known for its curvaceous Art Nouveau pieces, often featuring the female form, and for its more restrained, geometric Jugendstil designs. These products were immaculately made in pewter or silver plate, and the manufacturer advertised them in elegantly designed, multilingual catalogs. WMF sold decorative items, tableware, and kitchen utensils widely all over Europe, and the firm's success made its name a byword for quality and elegance. These virtues are still prized by collectors of WMF metalwares today.

Key dates

1853–1945

1853 Württemberg Electroplate Company founded in Geislingen, Germany

1860

1870

1880 The electroplate company and several other firms amalgamate and form WMF

1880

1884 Albert Mayer becomes director of the WMF studio

1890

1890 Acquires a German electrotyping company and becomes a successful manufacturer of statues for buildings and monuments

1895 Its designs begin to be strongly influenced by the flowing, asymmetrical lines of Art Nouveau

1900

1900 WMF becomes the world's largest producer of tableware

1910

1914 Expands further and employs around 6,000 people

1920

1927 Opens a new Handicrafts department producing designs by well-known architects

1930

1930 Becomes the first company to produce stainless steel household items commercially

1940

1945 Continues modernization of its factories after World War II

Whiplash handle

Openwork side panels with foliate decoration

Jardinière | *c.* 1900. The handles of this silver-plated jardinière (plant stand) are based on curved botanical forms, in typical Art Nouveau manner. The side panels are adorned with butterflies.

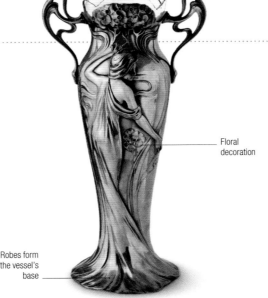

Floral decoration

Robes form the vessel's base

Pewter vase | *c.* 1900. *Femme-fleurs*, female figures with long robes and flowing hair, are featured on many WMF items, as seen here in this polished pewter vase.

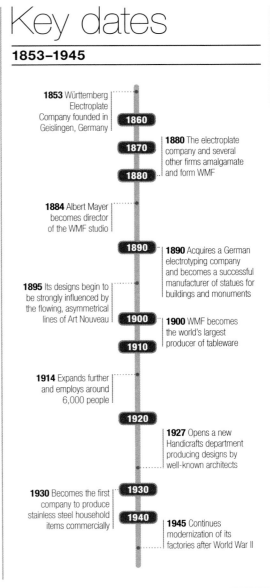

Crystal glass liner

Flower dish | *c.* 1900. This flower dish in silver plate takes the form of a boat set on breaking waves, with a finely modeled, cormorant-like bird sitting on the prow.

ART NOUVEAU
JEWELRY

The typical subjects of Art Nouveau decoration—flowers and leaves, young women, and various kinds of creatures—were well suited to the jeweler's craft, and as Art Nouveau took hold, French jewelers were soon making insect or flower brooches studded with precious stones. However, by about 1900, jewelers had begun to use other, less costly materials such as enamel, semiprecious stones, horn, or glass to create beautifully crafted and highly naturalistic pieces. The great designers, such as French jeweler René Lalique, influenced followers who created brooches, pendants, and other objects in the forms of creatures, such as dragonflies and butterflies, and flowers, including irises and daffodils. Other jewelers, especially those from Central Europe, worked in the Jugendstil manner, using the stylized, flowerlike designs and more linear style associated with it.

Enamel background

Pearl, a symbol of purity and loyalty

Stylized leaf in blue enamel

Emerald

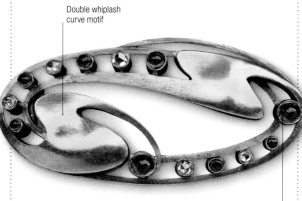

Double whiplash curve motif

A ruby forms a terminal to the curve

Stickpin | Jean Auguste Dampt for Charles Rivaud, *c.* **1898, France.** The finely detailed modeling of the head and slightly enigmatic expression on the figure's face suggest this design was influenced by the Symbolist movement in the arts.

Gold brooch | Henry van de Velde, *c.* **1898, Belgium.** This strikingly shaped and linear brooch is composed of two whiplash curves in gold, which extend to form the setting for eight rubies and five diamonds.

Pendant | Lluís Masriera, *c.* **1900, Spain.** The beautifully modeled main figure of this pendant stands out in relief against a landscape background in enamel. At the end of the figure's long dress, a single pearl is suspended.

Delicate silver swirls

Green-stained chalcedony cabochon

Enamel decoration

Belt buckle | Max Joseph Gradl for Theodor Fahrner, *c.* **1900, Germany.** This silver buckle is set with stylized enamel flowers and a pair of chalcedony cabochons. The swirls of silver that loop their way around the stones are typical of a number of pieces that Gradl designed for Theodor Fahrner, a prolific jewelry maker.

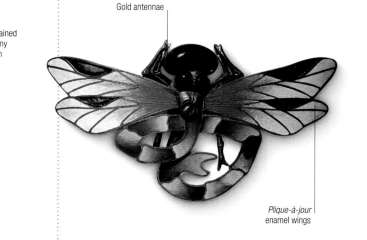

Gold antennae

Plique-à-jour enamel wings

Dragonfly brooch | *c.* **1900.** The twisting body and fine wings of this dragonfly brooch are formed from a fine network of gold and enamel. The use of *plique-à-jour* (transparent enamel) makes the insect's wings convincingly delicate.

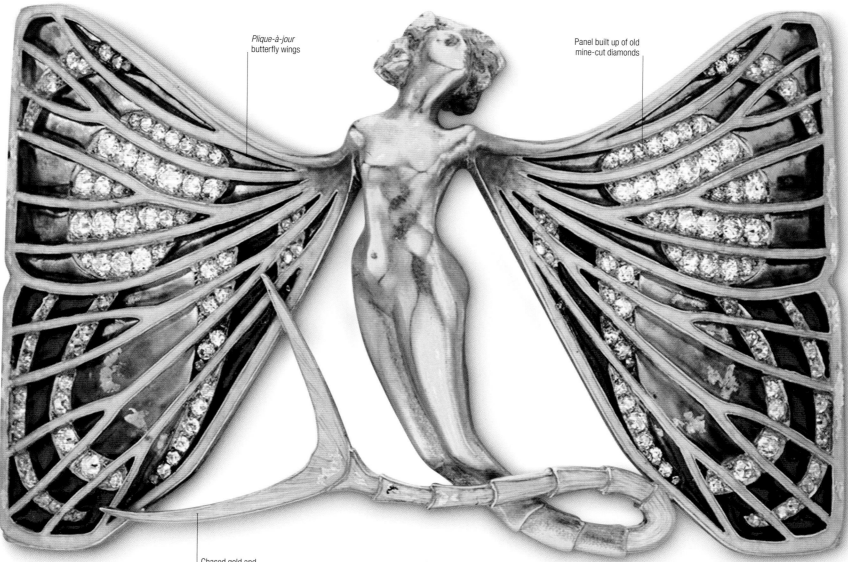

Plique-à-jour butterfly wings

Panel built up of old mine-cut diamonds

Chased gold and enamel fish tail

Sylph dog collar | **René Lalique**, *c.* 1900, **France**. Art Nouveau designers were fascinated by figures that changed shape. The arms of this Lalique sylph (mythological spirit of air) are transforming into butterfly wings, and its legs are turning into a fish's tail. The central figure is modeled in gold in high relief.

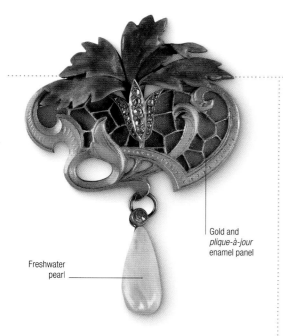

Freshwater pearl

Gold and *plique-à-jour* enamel panel

Brooch | **Georges Fouquet**, *c.* 1900. This brooch has a delicate central carnation of red enamel, set with old-cut diamonds, and is mounted against a honeycomb panel of *plique-à-jour* enamel with an elegant freshwater pearl drop.

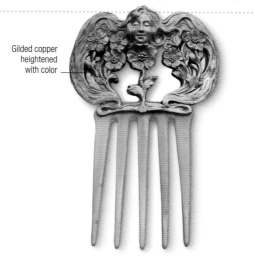

Gilded copper heightened with color

Comb | *c.* 1900, **France**. The top of this comb combines exquisitely sculpted floral elements with stylized flowing female hair to create a sinuous outline. It is made of horn and gilded copper with added color.

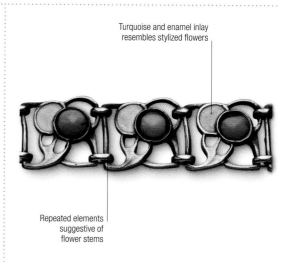

Turquoise and enamel inlay resembles stylized flowers

Repeated elements suggestive of flower stems

Bracelet (detail) | **Theodor Fahrner**, *c.* 1904, **Germany**. This bracelet is made up of repeated elements reminiscent of stylized stems, a typical Secessionist motif, combined with simple floral elements of circular turquoise cabochons and enamel inlay.

△ **The entrance hall** to the 13th exhibition of the Vienna Secession, designed by Hoffmann in 1903.

Josef Hoffmann

Josef Hoffmann was one of the most versatile architects and designers of the Vienna Secession (see p.75), producing stunningly modern, highly geometric buildings, furniture, tableware, glass, and textiles. He worked for much of his life in the Austrian capital, where he was at the heart of the city's artistic life as a founding member of the Secession and other influential groups of craftsmen and designers such as the Wiener Werkstätte (Vienna Workshops). He came to prominence in the 1890s and early 1900s as he developed a simple but striking geometric aesthetic that came to be known locally as Quadratstil (square style). This can be seen in Hoffmann's dazzling black-and-white interiors for the Secession exhibition of 1903, in the stylish tableware and plant stands he designed for the Wiener Werkstätte, and in his radically modern furniture.

In his architecture, Hoffmann perfected a style typified by strong cubic proportions and geometric decoration, and his strong grids and frames owed much to Charles Rennie Mackintosh (see pp.80–81). Later, Hoffmann moved toward more luxurious interiors for his famous Palais Stoclet in Brussels, Belgium, and he continued to design furniture, textiles, and exhibition pavilions throughout the early decades of the 20th century. Like Mackintosh, he has had an enduring influence, and some of his pieces are still produced by Italian manufacturer Alessi today.

Life

1870–1956

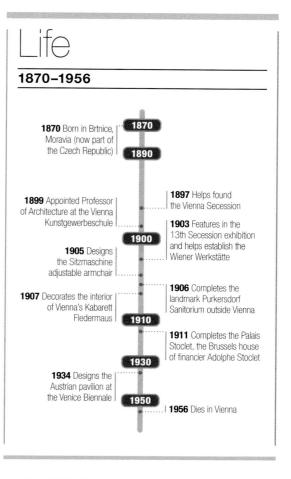

1870 Born in Brtnice, Moravia (now part of the Czech Republic)

1897 Helps found the Vienna Secession

1899 Appointed Professor of Architecture at the Vienna Kunstgewerbeschule

1903 Features in the 13th Secession exhibition and helps establish the Wiener Werkstätte

1905 Designs the Sitzmaschine adjustable armchair

1906 Completes the landmark Purkersdorf Sanitorium outside Vienna

1907 Decorates the interior of Vienna's Kabarett Fledermaus

1911 Completes the Palais Stoclet, the Brussels house of financier Adolphe Stoclet

1934 Designs the Austrian pavilion at the Venice Biennale

1956 Dies in Vienna

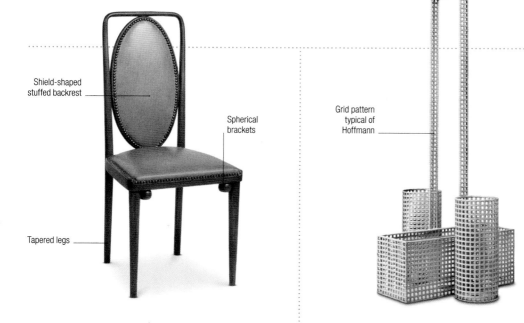

Shield-shaped stuffed backrest

Spherical brackets

Tapered legs

Stained beechwood chair | **For J. & J. Kohn**, *c.* 1890s. The strong lines of this side chair prefigure the stark geometric style that would come to characterize Hoffman's later work.

Grid pattern typical of Hoffmann

Flower basket | **For the Wiener Werkstätte**, *c.* 1905. Hoffmann designed painted metal items, such as trays, plant stands, boxes, and baskets, to be made at the Wiener Werkstätte.

Black enamel decoration shows the influence of Charles Rennie Mackintosh

Glasses | **For J. & L. Lobmeyr**, 1914. These glasses with a striking linear decoration resulted from a collaboration between Hoffmann, the Werkstätte, and Lobmeyr that had begun in 1910.

GUARDIAN ANGELS

The church of St. Leopold is the Roman Catholic oratory of Vienna's Steinhof Psychiatric Hospital. Completed in 1907, this dazzling Art Nouveau building is the work of the Viennese architect Otto Wagner. Wagner was a pioneer of Jugendstil (the Central European version of Art Nouveau) and an early member of the Secession, the group of Viennese artists who broke away from the establishment.

In his book *Moderne Architektur* (republished posthumously in 1985), Wagner encouraged architects to abandon historical styles and adopt new architecture and ornament, and the Steinhof Church embodies these ideas. It is topped with a gilded copper dome, and its walls are covered in white marble attached with exposed rivets that form patterns across the surface. The building's rich decoration draws on the skills of Secessionist artists and includes wreaths, crosses, and angels in gilded copper. The interior, which is designed to suit the needs of the hospital's patients, features gilded stylized flowers and abstract swirls, as well as mosaics and stained glass by the Viennese designer Koloman Moser, all of which make the building a glittering example of Jugendstil and stunningly modern for its time.

Modern art must yield for us modern ideas.

Otto **Wagner**

Steinhof Church, Vienna, Austria, Otto Wagner, 1907 The front entrance of the church is dominated by four columns topped with copper angels made by the sculptor Othmar Schimkowitz. The angels' wings are gilded and their costumes decorated with swirling patterns and gold ornaments similar to those of the figures in paintings by Secessionist artist Gustav Klimt. The image of God in Koloman Moser's stained-glass window is visible in the center.

DECORATED
VASES

The decorative Art Nouveau style suited glass well. Glassmakers could mold or modify vases to create swirling, organic shapes and use a number of special effects to produce vibrant, jewel-like decoration. Many glassmakers created cameo glass, in which one or more layers of different colored glass were overlaid onto a vessel and then partially wheel-cut or acid-etched away to reveal the different shades of glass beneath. Émile Gallé, the best known of many glassmakers working in and around the French city of Nancy, was a master of this technique. Other makers, inspired by recent excavations of Roman glass with lustrous surfaces, created iridescent glass or made *pâte-de-verre* objects from glass paste that was molded and then fired.

Full-bloom body with iridescent glaze

Flared base

The School of Nancy

1890–1904

Many of the prominent French Art Nouveau designers, including the Daum brothers, Victor Prouvé, Louis Majorelle, and Émile Gallé, worked in Nancy in eastern France. Under Gallé's leadership, they formed a group or "school" with the aim of collaborating to produce fine, handmade pieces and increase the prestige of the Alsace-Lorraine region.

These craftsmen and designers produced much of the best French Art Nouveau work in glassware and furniture and specialized in imaginative figurative and floral decoration. Their work, particularly the glass produced in the period before Gallé's death in 1904, is still highly regarded today.

Dimpled walls

Combed decoration

Combed vase | **Loetz**, *c.* 1900, Bohemia. The iridescent, bright colors and unusual form of this vase make it a typical example of Loetz work. A combing technique was used to create the parallel marks on the golden surface.

Jack in the Pulpit vase | **Quezal**, *c.* 1905–1915, US. This flaring lily vase is one of the most famous produced by Quezal. One of the company's founders had worked for Tiffany, and the iridescent finishes show the famous glassmaker's influence.

Masson dining room, Musée de l'École de Nancy, designed by Charles Masson and Eugène Vallin, *c.* 1904.

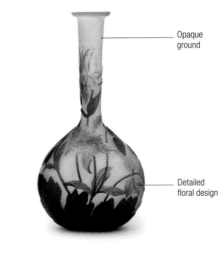

Opaque ground

Detailed floral design

Cameo vase | **Émile Gallé**, *c.* 1905, France. This vase demonstrates the virtuosity of Gallé's cameo technique, with its elegant botanical design featuring delicate and detailed acid-etched lilies and leaves over an opaque ground.

Leaf pattern

Cameo vase | **Müller Frères**, *c.* 1900, France. This unusual piece by the Müller Frères features an intricate leaf pattern and distinctively bulbous shape. Its opalescent finish was achieved by fire-polishing in a kiln.

Etched, botanical decoration

Cabinet vase | **Émile Gallé**, *c.* 1908, **France**. This is a very basic example of Gallé cameo glass. The vase is simply decorated with acid-etched leaves and branches on a green and frosted yellow ground.

> **Our roots are in the depths of the woods—on the banks of streams and among the mosses.**

Émile **Gallé**
Glassmaker

Acid-etched enameled leaves

Translucent orange ground

Cameo vase | **Hans Bolek for Loetz**, *c.* 1913, **Bohemia**. Bolek produced many pieces for Loetz with decoration in black, often featuring stylized leaves and tendrils. In this vase, the leaves stand out against a vibrant burnt orange background.

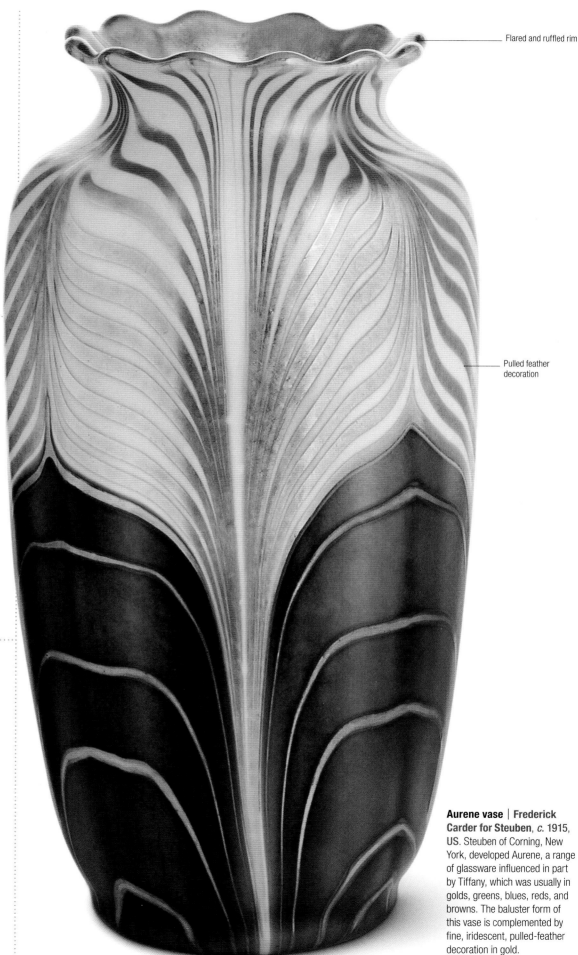

Flared and ruffled rim

Pulled feather decoration

Aurene vase | **Frederick Carder for Steuben**, *c.* 1915, **US**. Steuben of Corning, New York, developed Aurene, a range of glassware influenced in part by Tiffany, which was usually in golds, greens, blues, reds, and browns. The baluster form of this vase is complemented by fine, iridescent, pulled-feather decoration in gold.

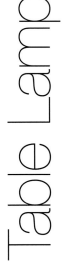

LOUIS MAJORELLE / DAUM FRÈRES

Table Lamp

YEAR 1903 | **MANUFACTURER** Louis Majorelle and Daum Frères, Nancy, France | **DIMENSIONS** *Height* 16½in (419mm), *Width* 9in (229mm) | **MATERIALS** Bronze (stand); glass (shade)

The brothers Jean-Louis Auguste and Jean-Antonin Daum were successful glassmakers in Nancy, France, who began their career making glass tableware. After seeing an exhibition of glass by Émile Gallé in the early 1890s, they began to produce art glass in the newly fashionable Art Nouveau style.

Among their most striking works were lamps, produced in collaboration with Nancy cabinetmaker and metalworker Louis Majorelle, who became interested in Art Nouveau at about the same time. The Daum brothers produced their richly colored lampshades using a range of decorative techniques, such as cameo glass, in which the craftsman cuts away layers of glass—either by acid-etching or using a wheel—to reveal its different hues. Their lamps often had sinuous metal stands in the form of plant stems or leaves and decorated, flowerlike glass shades. As the use of electric lighting spread and people realized what a huge effect lamps—especially those with colored and decorated shades—could have on the atmosphere of a room, the lamps created by Daum and Majorelle became increasingly popular. They are still highly sought after today.

... with nature as their repertoire, the Daum brothers experimented in order to be able to produce breathtaking works...

Sotheby's
Concise Encyclopedia of Glass

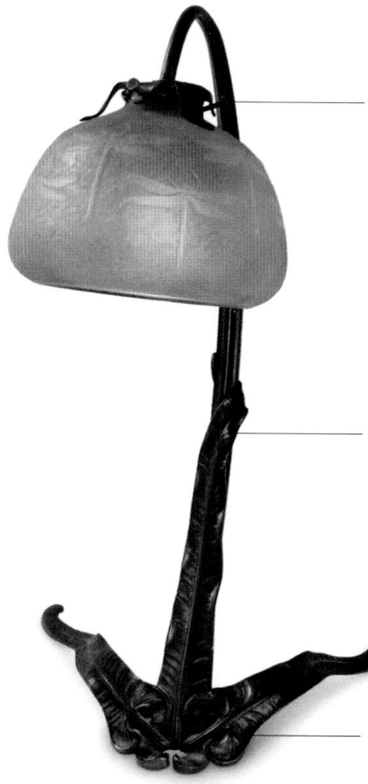

Screw fixture makes it possible to remove shade

Upper part of stand curves like a plant stem

Leaf's veins depicted in strong, vigorous relief

△ **Front**

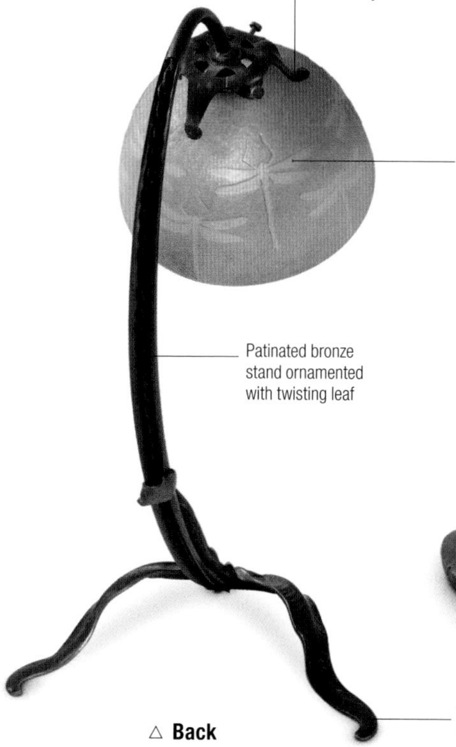

Metal shade attachment shaped like the calyx of a flower

Wheel-carved dragonfly

Patinated bronze stand ornamented with twisting leaf

Leaf design flattens at its tip to form a stable foot

△ **Back**

ELECTRIC LIGHTING

The arrival of electric lighting in the late 19th century opened up a new opportunity for designers, and, with their love of rich colors and flowing forms, it is not surprising that Art Nouveau craftsmen and women produced outstanding lamps. Unlike the utilitarian chimneys of oil lamps, glass shades for electric lamps could have highly decorative, expressive shapes and were even more effective when combined with a sculptural or colorful base. Artists such as the Belgian sculptor Victor Rousseau excelled at richly detailed cast figures that made perfect lamp bases, and manufacturers such as Daum created fine glass shades. Daum, like the American company Tiffany, also produced entire lamps from colored glass, achieving internal polychrome effects and overlays that produced a mottled color. When illuminated, these lamps could fill a room with rich colors.

Lampshade in the form of a veil

Gilded bronze figure

Shade in the form of a Japanese paper lantern

Figural lamp | **Antoine Bofill**, *c.* 1900, **France**. Sculptor Antoine Bofill created this gilded bronze lamp depicting a woman whose long gown seems to float above the ground. The red glass shade was by the glassmakers Daum Frères of Nancy.

Rim is trimmed with bronze beads

Stylized flowers

Patinated copper framework

Relief decoration features a dragon

Stem joins leaf with a looping curve

Figural lamp | **Victor Rousseau**, *c.* 1900, **Belgium**. Sculptor Victor Rousseau may have modeled this lamp on the celebrated American dancer Loie Fuller, who often danced with flowing veils and dresses and was a favorite subject of artists.

Slag glass lamp | **Charles Parker Co.**, *c.* 1900, **US**. Charles Parker was famous for its metalware and also made lamps with shades of slag glass—a mold-made glass that used additives such as slag from iron furnaces for a streaked or marbled effect.

Nautilus shell lamp | *c.* 1900, **US**. Translucent nautilus shells made popular lampshades in the Art Nouveau period. Here, the shell forms a flowerlike shade, mounted on a bronze stem with a base in the form of a leaf.

Hanging shade | **Clara Driscoll for Tiffany & Co**, *c.* 1905, **US**. Although most famous for table lamps, Tiffany also made hanging lampshades like this one. Contrasting colored glass is used to form a design of nasturtiums and a trellis with a blue-gray ground.

Rectangular pieces of glass represent trellis

Wheel-carved glass shade

Heavy base

Multilayered glass shade

Shades are attached using wrought-iron mounts

Shade has a stylized Art Nouveau motif

Cast bronze figure

Onyx base

Daum table lamp | **Louis Majorelle**, *c.* 1902, **France**. The lamp's bronze body curves toward the shade, which is carved in the form of a lily. Although it is not modeled as a realistic stem, it is organic in form, in keeping with the flower shade.

Les Copins lamp | **Émile Gallé**, 1904, **France**. By using overlays and working glass on the wheel, Gallé added an element of realism to this lamp, designed in the shape of a group of mushrooms. All three mushrooms light up.

Figural lamp | **Marcel Bouraine**, *c.* 1914, **France**. Bouraine became well known for sculpture in the Art Deco style in the 1920s. This lamp combines an Art Nouveau stained-glass shade with a figure that anticipates Deco confidence.

EVOLUTION OF
LIGHTING

With electricity becoming more widespread as the 20th century progressed, designers discovered the potential of lighting. They used their ingenuity to devise effective desk and work lamps casting directional light, to provide ambient lighting, and to create decorative effects. Architects and designers soon realized that lamps and light fittings could transform the atmosphere of a room and responded with a range of designs, from the elaborate stained-glass lampshades sold by Tiffany to the elegant, functional lamps created at the Bauhaus. Lighting today, often quirky and sculptural, still varies between these extremes.

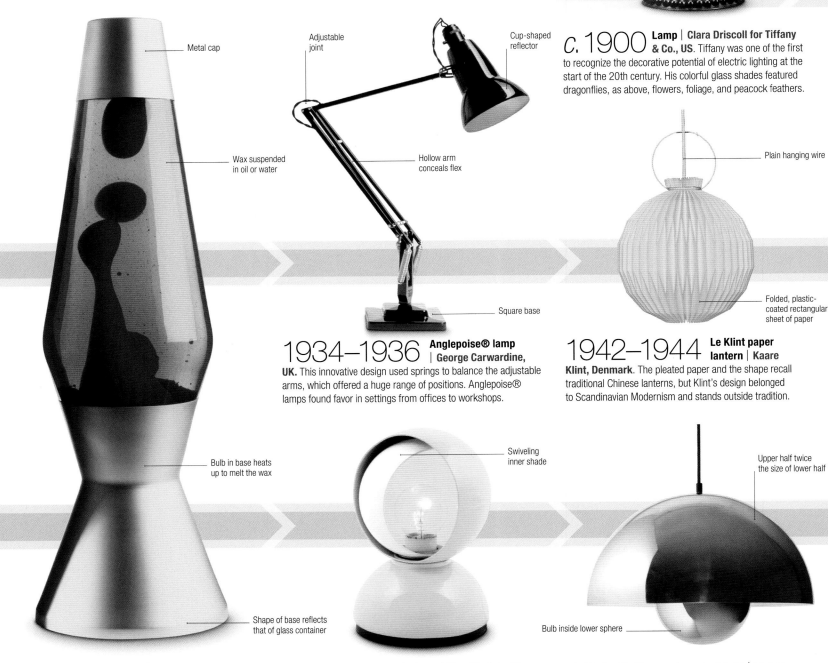

Pieces of glass are joined using copper foil and solder

Dragonflies typical of Tiffany and Art Nouveau

Metal cap

Wax suspended in oil or water

Adjustable joint

Cup-shaped reflector

Hollow arm conceals flex

Square base

Plain hanging wire

Folded, plastic-coated rectangular sheet of paper

Bulb in base heats up to melt the wax

Swiveling inner shade

Upper half twice the size of lower half

Shape of base reflects that of glass container

Bulb inside lower sphere

c. 1900 Lamp | Clara Driscoll for Tiffany & Co., US. Tiffany was one of the first to recognize the decorative potential of electric lighting at the start of the 20th century. His colorful glass shades featured dragonflies, as above, flowers, foliage, and peacock feathers.

1934–1936 Anglepoise® lamp | George Carwardine, UK. This innovative design used springs to balance the adjustable arms, which offered a huge range of positions. Anglepoise® lamps found favor in settings from offices to workshops.

1942–1944 Le Klint paper lantern | Kaare Klint, Denmark. The pleated paper and the shape recall traditional Chinese lanterns, but Klint's design belonged to Scandinavian Modernism and stands outside tradition.

1963 Astro Lava lamp | Edward Craven Walker, UK. The lava lamp was an icon of the 1960s. Inside its glass container, a lump of colored wax moved and changed shape as the lamp heated up and cooled down. The wax globules create a mesmerizing sight.

1966 Eclisse table lamp | Vico Magistretti for Artemide, Italy. The ingenious Eclisse (Eclipse) is made of enameled metal. When turned, the bulb is "eclipsed," which reduces the amount of light emitted. Hinges in the base allow the lamp to be mounted on a wall.

1968 Flowerpot pendant light | Verner Panton, Denmark. Simple in concept, two half spheres both hide and reflect the bulb, beaming the light downward. The surface is undecorated, maximizing the reflective sheen of the polished steel.

Brass fittings

Glass "Emeralite" shade

Decorative horizontal banding

Anthemion motif based on honeysuckle flower

Cast bronze figure

Stepped onyx base

Cup-shaped reflector

Adjustable joint

Wedge-shaped base

1909 **Banker's lamp** | **H. D. McFaddin, US**. With their brass bases made in New York and their glass shades from Moravia, banker's lamps were among the most widely sold early desk lamps. They fitted well into traditional interiors and provided good task lighting.

1914 **Figural lamp** | **Marcel Bouraine, France**. The female nude supports a leaded glass globe with a stylized Art Nouveau floral motif made out of mottled amber and fuchsia segments. The stepped base anticipates a typical Art Deco feature.

1927 **Kandem bedside light** | **Marianne Brandt for Körting & Mathiesen, Germany**. Brandt designed this simple steel light, with its adjustable head, at the Bauhaus. The shape of the lamp influenced countless other lighting designers.

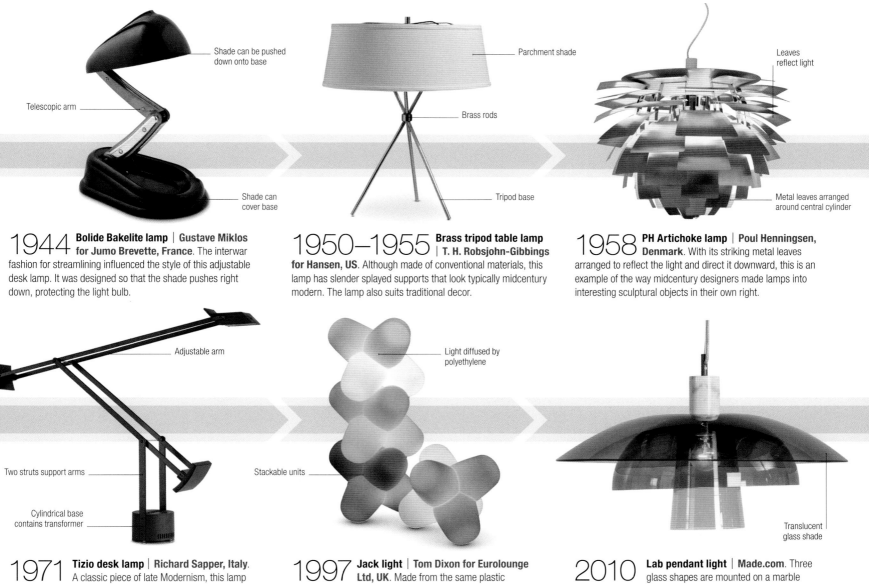

Shade can be pushed down onto base

Telescopic arm

Shade can cover base

Parchment shade

Brass rods

Tripod base

Leaves reflect light

Metal leaves arranged around central cylinder

1944 **Bolide Bakelite lamp** | **Gustave Miklos for Jumo Brevette, France**. The interwar fashion for streamlining influenced the style of this adjustable desk lamp. It was designed so that the shade pushes right down, protecting the light bulb.

1950–1955 **Brass tripod table lamp** | **T. H. Robsjohn-Gibbings for Hansen, US**. Although made of conventional materials, this lamp has slender splayed supports that look typically midcentury modern. The lamp also suits traditional decor.

1958 **PH Artichoke lamp** | **Poul Henningsen, Denmark**. With its striking metal leaves arranged to reflect the light and direct it downward, this is an example of the way midcentury designers made lamps into interesting sculptural objects in their own right.

Adjustable arm

Two struts support arms

Cylindrical base contains transformer

Light diffused by polyethylene

Stackable units

Translucent glass shade

1971 **Tizio desk lamp** | **Richard Sapper, Italy**. A classic piece of late Modernism, this lamp displays beautiful geometry and is perfectly balanced. The electric current passes along the arms, so there is no need for internal wiring and it can be tilted at different angles.

1997 **Jack light** | **Tom Dixon for Eurolounge Ltd, UK**. Made from the same plastic as traffic bollards, this light can be customized: the lightweight, rounded-edge crosses can be stacked vertically or horizontally, or both, and come in a range of colors.

2010 **Lab pendant light** | **Made.com**. Three glass shapes are mounted on a marble drop cap to make a sculptural statement. Every glass piece is hand molded and individually blown, so each example has unique air bubbles visible through the colored layers.

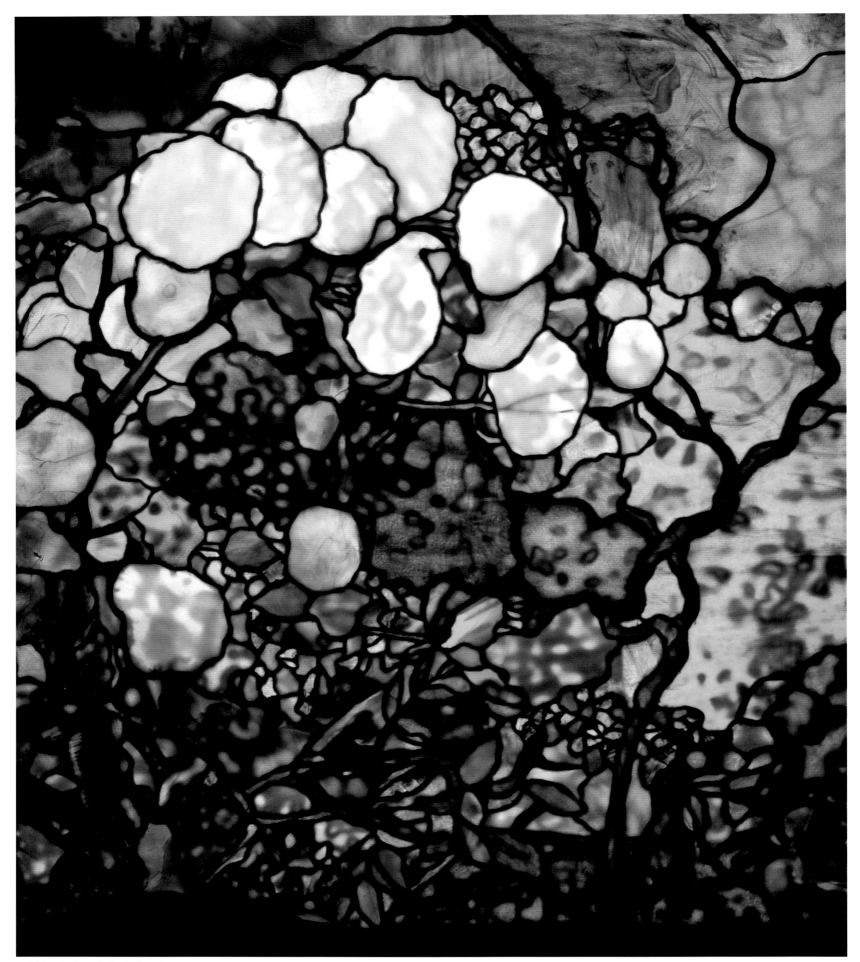

△ **Tiffany's Snowball window** of *c.* 1900 depicts the snowball rose, also known as the guelder rose.

Louis Comfort Tiffany

American designer Louis Comfort Tiffany is celebrated for his unique work in colored glassware. He invented a type of handblown iridescent glass, which he patented under the name of Favrile (handcrafted), founding his own glassworks in 1892 to produce vases, bowls, and goblets in typical, curvaceous Art Nouveau forms. He also gained a reputation for stained glass, much of which was featured in the windows and panels of interiors he designed for prominent New Yorkers. The two sides of Tiffany's career came together when he began to produce his famous handmade, leaded-glass lamps depicting natural subjects such as poppies, lilies, and dragonflies. The lamps were made individually until 1899, when stained-glass techniques were adapted to produce multiple copies.

Tiffany lamps owe their unique qualities to two people. The first was the American designer Clara Driscoll, who worked for Tiffany for more than 20 years and was head of a team of women glass cutters. The other was Arthur J. Nash, Tiffany's glass furnace manager, who experimented with different chemicals to produce a variety of colors and effects. The color and pattern choices, and the quality of the glass used in Tiffany's products, ensured their widespread popularity and led to many imitations by manufacturers on both sides of the Atlantic, but the quality of Tiffany's originals has remained unmatched.

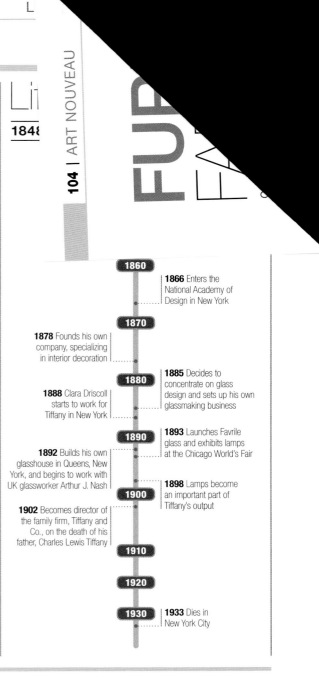

1848

1860

1866 Enters the National Academy of Design in New York

1870

1878 Founds his own company, specializing in interior decoration

1880

1885 Decides to concentrate on glass design and sets up his own glassmaking business

1888 Clara Driscoll starts to work for Tiffany in New York

1890

1893 Launches Favrile glass and exhibits lamps at the Chicago World's Fair

1892 Builds his own glasshouse in Queens, New York, and begins to work with UK glassworker Arthur J. Nash

1898 Lamps become an important part of Tiffany's output

1900

1902 Becomes director of the family firm, Tiffany and Co., on the death of his father, Charles Lewis Tiffany

1910

1920

1930

1933 Dies in New York City

Agate vase | c. 1900. In Tiffany's agate vases, glass canes cut in cross section imitate the striking banded colors of agate. The faceted surface looks as if it is made of stone.

Mottled glass tiles known as turtlebacks

Grueby lamp base

Table lamp | **Clara Driscoll**, c. 1905. Tiffany made this mottled, floral-patterned glass shade to go with the ceramic lamp base produced by the American Grueby Faience Company.

Wisteria blossom

Thin sections of glass portray the plant's stem

Wisteria blossom glass chandelier | **Clara Driscoll**, c. 1910. Made of hundreds of pieces of mottled glass, the bottom of this lampshade suggests fringes of hanging blossoms.

FURNISHING FABRICS

Textiles for curtains, furniture covers, cushions, wall hangings, and carpets became increasingly important in homes in the Art Nouveau period, and designers responded to the demand with what are now considered typical turn-of-the-century motifs—especially floral patterns and abstract designs with expressive, sinuous lines. One such textile—an embroidered panel by Hermann Obrist—became one of the iconic expressions of Art Nouveau. Manufacturers produced fabrics with either woven or printed patterns, and some craftsmen and women embroidered pieces by hand, so a huge variety of designs was available. These ranged from the flattened and abstracted patterns produced by Austrian designers such as Koloman Moser to those that used light and shade to create greater depth. Marketed by retailers such as Siegfried Bing in Paris and Liberty in London, Art Nouveau fabrics were sold widely and acquired an international appeal.

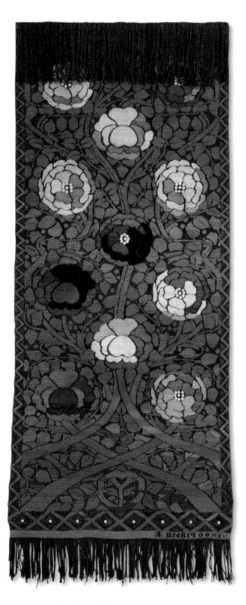

Tapestry door hanging | **Frida Hansen for Det Norske Billedvoeveri**, *c.* 1900, **Norway**. This hanging is semitransparent, woven from hand-spun and hand-dyed wool, and features an innovative design of semiabstract flowers.

Silk upholstery fabric | **Edward Colonna**, *c.* 1900, France. Interlaced lines and whiplash curves combine to create complex, abstract, geometric forms. Colonna designed fabrics, jewelry, and furniture for Bing's Art Nouveau shop in Paris around 1900.

Scylla fabric hanging | **Koloman Moser**, 1901, Austria. This interlocking design for a wall hanging is typical of Moser's work, which was usually based on stylized plant forms. The letterforms are characteristic of the Vienna Secession.

Furnishing fabric | **Harry Napper for J. W. & C. Ward**, *c.* 1900, UK. The rows of tulips and bellflowers show Napper's talent for stylized floral motifs, recalling similar repeating patterns in the work of Austrian Secessionist designers.

Floral textile | **Dagobert Peche for Backhausen**, 1912, **Austria**. Peche initially favored realistic floral motifs but then turned to more abstract designs. This pattern was designed for both furnishing fabrics and carpets.

Whiplash panel | **Hermann Obrist**, 1896, Germany. A visitor to the 1896 exhibition in Munich, where this woolen wall panel was originally shown, compared the curving cyclamen flower stem to a lashing whip. The name "whiplash" has been used for this kind of hairpin Art Nouveau curve ever since. Berthe Ruchet, the manager of Obrist's workshop, embroidered the hanging, delicately shading the stems using rich gold- and warm-colored threads that stood out against the neutral background.

Embroidery in
several shades
of gold silk thread

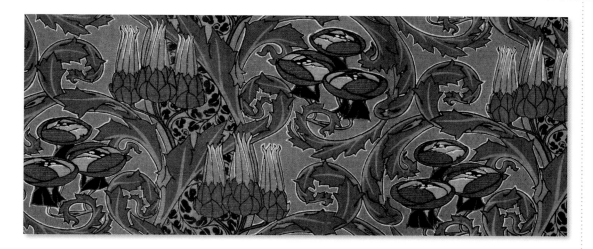

Liberty thistle fabric | **Harry Napper for GP & J Baker**, *c.* 1900, UK. The stylized floral pattern of this block-printed cotton-and-linen fabric was designed to appeal to Liberty's fashion-conscious customers. Many of Napper's designs had repeated motifs of wild flowers—here, he interpreted the traditional image of the thistle in the undulating forms of Art Nouveau. He was influenced by contemporary French, Belgian, German, and Austrian textiles, so his designs became popular in France.

Hermann
Obrist

1862–1927

Swiss-born Obrist designed furniture and ceramics as well as textiles and made fantastical organic sculptures akin to the work of his Catalan contemporary Antoni Gaudí. Obrist based his model of design on nature—a trait that was shared by the German Jugendstil movement, which also believed in simplicity of construction. Abstract natural forms bursting with energy characterize his work, which can best be seen in the flicking stems and leaves of his whiplash embroidery (above).

ART NOUVEAU
POSTERS

During the 1880s, advances in print technology finally made it possible to produce colored images in long runs. Artists and advertisers seized on this opportunity, and the poster was born. The first posters were created in France, by artists such as Jules Chéret and Eugène Grasset. They developed a style in which images of elegant young women were combined with colorful, ornate lettering to sell products that ranged from cabaret performances to stationery. Czech-born Alphonse Mucha made his posters more elaborate, and his floral backgrounds, swirling borders, and glamorous, languid women became the epitome of Art Nouveau. The style spread, particularly to the US, and posters became so popular that they were considered collectible works of art in their own right.

Cat's body conveyed with a simple outline and a block of color

Informal lettering

Cloud forms

Winglike pattern on dress

Voltaire poster | **Jules Chéret**, *c.* 1877, France. Chéret, "the father of the poster," used bold colors, strong lettering, and clear, graphic imagery in hundreds of posters to advertise everything from concerts to stores, as in this example for a tailor.

Marquet poster | **Eugène Grasset**, 1892, France. Grasset designed this poster of a woman holding a quill pen for a French ink manufacturer. Several details, such as the clouds and the harp on which she leans, suggest a dream or reverie.

Cabaret Chat Noir poster | **Théophile-Alexandre Steinlen**, 1896, France. Steinlen produced this poster for the cabaret Chat Noir. Its strong, almost cartoonlike imagery contrasts with Steinlen's more realistic posters for other clients.

Background of stylized lilies

Finely delineated hair

Hourglass symbolizes passing time

Scrolls frame the lettering

Lithograph | **Louis John Rhead**, *c.* 1897, US. British-born Rhead took French Art Nouveau to the US after visiting Paris in 1891. His work, like this lithograph for the magazine *L'Estampe Moderne*, often features figures against a background of flowers.

Automobile Club de France poster | **Henri Privat-Livemont**, 1902, France/Belgium. In contrast to the many Art Nouveau posters that show figures in profile, the driver in this motor show poster is shown full face, strikingly lit from above.

Calendar advertisement | **Koloman Moser**, 1903, Austria. Moser's posters show the disciplined side of Secessionist graphics, with simplified images, large areas of flat color, and letterforms that are elaborate but legible.

Floral headdress

Whiplash stems and branches

Lefèvre-Utile calendar | **Alphonse Mucha**, 1897, **France/Czech Republic.** Mucha's graphic work often features glamorous young women drawn in pastel shades, framed by flowing lines and plants. Ornate, flowing letterforms, as on this promotional calendar for a cookie company, were another Mucha specialty.

EVOLUTION OF
CAMERAS

Photography has developed rapidly over the last 150 years, culminating in the major breakthrough move from film to digital photography. Cameras of the 20th century accommodated different film formats and had better viewing systems, such as the SLR (Single Lens Reflex), which enable photographers to see exactly what the camera will record. Manufacturers added ever more features, from in-camera metering to autofocus, making it easier to take better pictures. From digital SLRs to tiny automatic compacts, and a host of designs in between, manufacturers continue to produce cameras for photographers at every level.

Cable release

Lens on front panel

1880s **Plate camera** | UK. Early cameras were made of wood, with leather bellows so the photographer could move the front panel, using brass sliders and screws to focus the lens. The shutter was controlled with a cable release, to prevent camera shake.

Lens panel moves back and forth for focusing

1947 **Pacemaker Speed Graphic** | **Graflex Inc., US**. A sophisticated and robust version of the early plate cameras with bellows, press photographers favored the Speed Graphic. It took sheet film, offered a range of adjustments, and produced high-quality images.

Pentaprism housing

1949 **Contax S** | **Wilhelm Winzenberg, Germany**. The Contax S was the first true SLR camera. Its key innovation was the pentaprism, a piece of glass that directed the image in the lens to the viewfinder, allowing the photographer to see the subject exactly as it would appear on the film.

Hand grip contains battery pack

1988 **Nikon F4** | **Giorgetto Giugiaro, Japan**. The first professional autofocus camera from Nikon accepted manual-focus lenses, too, for a huge choice of optics. It also had an LCD viewfinder display, programmed auto exposure, and a sophisticated exposure meter.

Retracting lens

2000 **Digital IXUS** | **Canon, Japan**. Canon produced small digital cameras that combined good looks with high image quality. The Digital IXUS, with its distinctive flat-sided metal body, fitted easily into a user's pocket or handbag.

Shutter release set in hand grip

2005 **Canon 5D** | **Canon, Japan**. Soon after its launch, the Canon 5D became the industry standard professional digital SLR. Although it is a highly specified full-frame digital SLR, its body is relatively compact and easy to hold.

Viewfinder

Lens

Viewing lens

Film winder

Picture-taking lens

Rangefinder for focusing

Folding case

1925 **Leica I | Oskar Barnack for Ernst Leitz**, Germany. The Leica was the first practical 35mm camera. Its high-quality lens and beautifully engineered shutter made pin-sharp images possible with small film. It became the benchmark for portable cameras.

1929 **Rolleiflex | Franke & Heidecke**, Germany. The first medium-format roll-film camera, the Rolleiflex has one lens for viewing and another for taking the picture. A viewfinder in the top plate lets the user look down the camera.

1935 **Kodak Bantam Special | Walter Dorwin Teague**, US. The enameled, streamlined case of this Art Deco camera conceals a high-quality lens mounted on a small bellows, featuring an impressive range of controls.

Viewfinder Shutter release

Prism unit also incorporates through-the-lens metering

Pop-up viewfinder housing

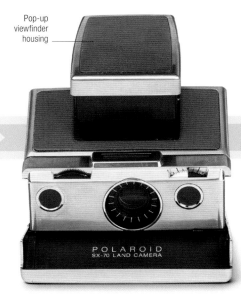

1963 **Kodak Instamatic | Dean M. Peterson**, US. Kodak designed the Instamatic line around the 126 film cartridge, which the user dropped straight into the camera without the need to thread or wind it. The cameras were very simple to use, with few controls.

1965 **Nikon F | Nippon Kogaku Company**, Japan. With a full range of interchangeable lenses and focusing screens, a motor-drive option, and lens apertures that reset automatically after each exposure, the Nikon F was the first SLR widely used by professionals.

1972 **Polaroid SX-70 | Polaroid Corporation**, US. Using Polaroid's self-developing instant-picture film, the SX-70 has an ingenious design. The pop-up viewfinder, lens panel, and body fold down flat, taking up virtually no space when the camera is not in use.

Different body colors introduced

Vintage-style looks

2005 **Fuji Finepix S9500 | Fuji**, Japan. A landmark "bridge" camera, the S9500 offered professional-grade features—such as wide-angle capability and fully manual controls—in a compact, easy-to-use form.

2012 **Nikon 1 J1 | Nippon G**, Japan. Offering the versatility of interchangeable lenses with the speed and ease of use of a compact camera, the Nikon 1 J1 is excellent for both still and movie photography.

2019 **Lumix DC-G95/90 | Panasonic**, Japan. This classic-looking, midrange compact camera is designed to be used for both stills and video. It offers an extensive degree of direct control, has a flip-out touchscreen, and includes in-body stabilization.

ART DECO

1919–1940

Pleasure was the
color of the time.

HAROLD CLURMAN, THEATER DIRECTOR

ART DECO
Introduction

In the 1920s and 1930s, designers left behind the sinuous curves of Art Nouveau and developed a new decorative style that was angular, geometric, and confidently, self-consciously modern. Many of the style's pioneers were French, or worked in Paris, where the landmark Exposition Internationale des Arts Décoratifs et Industriels Modernes was held in 1925. This exhibition, at which 34 countries (although not the United States) exhibited, promoted the new style and encouraged designers all over the world to interpret it in their own way. Most of them knew it as the modern style, but later, historians dubbed it Art Deco, recalling the name of the exhibition. The style evolved over three decades, up until the start of World War II.

Sources and symbols

Art Deco's sources were as eclectic as the movement itself. The style was partly triggered by the passionate interest in ancient civilizations that followed the discovery of Tutankhamun's tomb in 1922. Art Deco designers borrowed motifs from ancient civilizations, such as the Egyptians, the Aztecs, and Classical antiquity, but they used them in a modern way, sometimes combining them with geometric shapes influenced by Cubist paintings, or with typical Art Deco abstract motifs, such as chevrons, zigzags, or broad bands of color. Whether these patterns adorned buildings or carpets, furniture or ceramics, they were generally used in bold, sometimes clashing colors.

SUNBURST

A classic Art Deco motif, the geometric, abstract sunburst appeared everywhere, from buildings to ceramics. Representing dawn, it symbolized the excitement of the age and optimism for the future.

AFRICAN INFLUENCE

The enthusiasm for African art included decorative motifs based on imagery drawn from ancient Egyptian tombs and temples, or borrowed from African tribal art, especially masks and sculptures.

STYLIZED WOMEN

In Art Deco design, women are energetic and animated—this was the age of the flapper. Often dancing or playing sports, they have long, supple limbs, flexible, gamine bodies, and fashionably bobbed hair.

People who appreciate truly beautiful and original creations ... are not frightened by innocent tomfoolery!

Clarice **Cliff**

Many designers also adopted the imagery of modern life and were inspired by symbols of progress and the machine age, such as skyscrapers, electricity, airplanes, and streamlined trains.

Diversity

Many of the famous Art Deco designers, including furniture maker Jacques-Émile Ruhlmann and architect Louis Süe, prized high-quality materials, creating pieces and entire interiors that were the epitome of luxury. However, the period between the two world wars was also a time of technological innovation. Items such as radios, clocks, combs, and even door handles were produced in Bakelite, an early plastic that could be molded easily and inexpensively. Affordable objects like these brought Art Deco to many homes.

A worldwide movement

Art Deco's influence on the modern world was immense, and it is sometimes called the first global style of design. It affected the look of every aspect of contemporary life, injecting a combination of glamour and modernity into the design of everything from skyscrapers, movie theaters, luxury ocean liners, and cars to jewelry, domestic appliances, typography, and posters. The style finally went into decline when World War II put an end to such luxury.

CUBISM

Cubist painters painted scenes as if broken up into a series of fragments. By the mid-1920s, Art Deco design often incorporated characteristics of Cubism, such as faceted forms and geometric arrangements of shapes.

EXOTIC MATERIALS

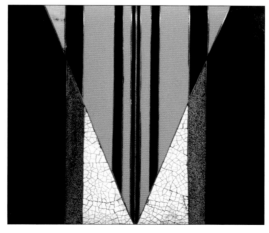

Art Deco designers loved luxurious, exotic materials such as rare mahogany, ebony, ivory, and shagreen, a type of sharkskin. They used them in a modern way, however, juxtaposing them to create dramatic effects.

JAZZ

The 1920s and 1930s were known as the Jazz Age. Textile and poster designers translated the pace and tempo of the times into rhythmic geometric motifs influenced by the Cubists and bold color combinations.

Circular drawer pulls
with faux pearl centers

Cross-hatched
mahogany parquetry

Mahogany chest | **Eugene Schoen for Schmieg, Hungate & Kotzian,** *c.* 1935, US. This chest-on-stand in solid and veneered mahogany displays a refined, 18th-century French style combined with cleverly introduced hints of clean-lined Modernism.

FUNCTIONAL FURNITURE

In marked contrast to the Art Deco furniture that looked luxurious and fluid, some pieces were sturdy and pared back, with angular, Modernist forms. Much of this second style—the work of designers such as Eugene Schoen, Gilbert Rohde, and Donald Deskey—was aimed at the US market and was mass-produced. Deskey was a pioneer of the more industrially modern, American approach, often characterized by the use of metal and Bakelite (see pp.136–137). Blonde woods such as birch also began to appear during the 1920s, providing a refreshing contrast to the rich, dark woods used in the more traditional styles of furniture. Art Deco pieces contained a fascinating mix of approaches: Jacques-Émile Ruhlmann, the masterful French cabinetmaker, often gave his pieces stunning Modernist forms, while European influences—from French refinement to German Bauhaus minimalism—appeared in the work of American designers Schoen, Rohde, and Deskey.

Fluted spindle legs taper at the top and bottom

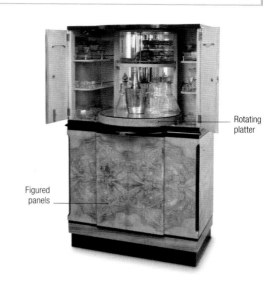

Rotating platter

Figured panels

Demi-lune cabinet | **Jacques-Émile Ruhlmann**, *c.* 1919, France. The streamlined form of this cabinet looks Modernist, but the relief carving on the drawer adds a traditional touch. It is veneered in rosewood with a striking swirl of ivory inlay work.

Low stool | 1928, France. Set in a rosewood frame with zebrawood banding, this stool's upholstered cushion features a modern geometric pattern that suggests an industrial theme of wheels and machine parts.

Cocktail cabinet | **Harry and Lou Epstein**, 1929, UK. With the emphasis on functionality, this cocktail cabinet's upper hinged double doors enclose a mirrored, illuminated interior and a revolving display.

Ebonized handles

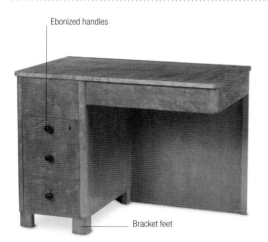

Bracket feet

Metal support linking frame and drawers

Bird's-eye (swirling-figured) maple

Dark wood contrasts with lighter drawers

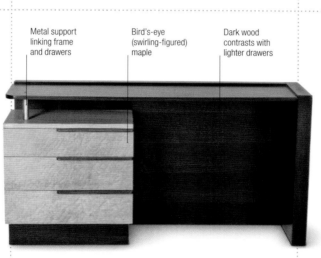

Birch dressing table/desk | Early 1920s. The rectangular top of this desk is discreetly attached with a piano hinge (a thin hinge that stretches the length of the movable part), making it easy to access the storage space beneath.

Single-pedestal desk | **Gilbert Rohde for Herman Miller Furniture Co.**, 1930s, US. Substantial yet stylish, this desk has a raised, rectangular mahogany frame and contrasting maple-veneered drawer fronts.

Long sycamore drawer pulls

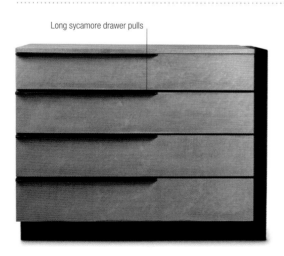

Rosewood veneer

Chrome-plated banding

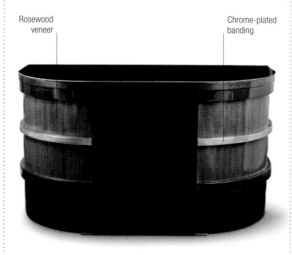

Chest of drawers | **Gilbert Rohde for Herman Miller Furniture Co.**, *c.* 1934, US. In Rohde's signature style, this piece's mahogany top and drawers form a striking contrast with the black enameling of its base and sides.

Knee-hole desk | **Donald Deskey for Widdicomb Furniture Co.**, *c.* 1935, US. This D-shaped knee-hole desk features chrome, a popular Art Deco material. The black lacquering shows the influence of Japanese style.

Filing cabinet | **Donald Deskey**, *c.* 1935, US. Typically of Art Deco, this cabinet combines a black-lacquered body with drawer fronts and overhang made of rosewood and bold, vertical drawer pulls of nickel-bronze.

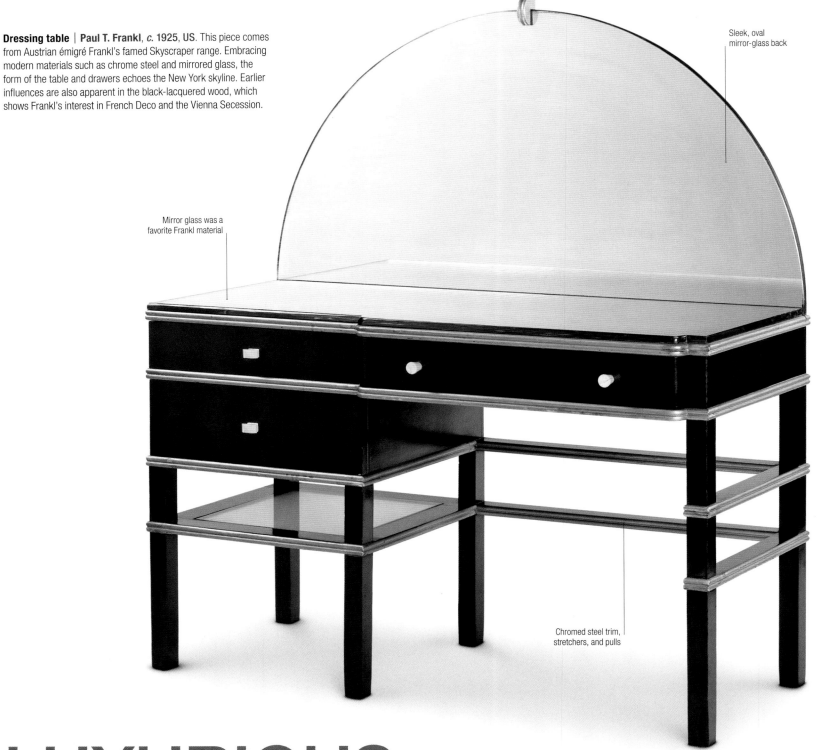

Dressing table | **Paul T. Frankl**, *c.* **1925, US**. This piece comes from Austrian émigré Frankl's famed Skyscraper range. Embracing modern materials such as chrome steel and mirrored glass, the form of the table and drawers echoes the New York skyline. Earlier influences are also apparent in the black-lacquered wood, which shows Frankl's interest in French Deco and the Vienna Secession.

Sleek, oval mirror-glass back

Mirror glass was a favorite Frankl material

Chromed steel trim, stretchers, and pulls

LUXURIOUS
CONTOURS

Much Art Deco furniture was luxurious, with sumptuously padded upholstery, sinuous shapes, and rich materials offset by elegant lines. The meticulously crafted, high-end work of Jacques-Émile Ruhlmann embodied a refined, French aesthetic, while the stark and angular pieces of Viennese-born Paul T. Frankl were inspired both by the New York skyscrapers that soared upward around his Manhattan gallery and by his European background. The furniture of other designers incorporated curves and touches of luxury such as lacquerwork—Art Deco designers, notably the Irish designer Eileen Gray, were fascinated by Japanese lacquerwork. Gray settled in Paris in 1907 and forged a highly individual path with the decorative quality of the furniture she created in the period leading up to World War I. From around 1925, however, she was increasingly influenced by the understated, minimalist work of Modernist architects such as Le Corbusier and Walter Gropius.

Mahogany frame

Ebony carvings with mother-of-pearl highlights

Coffee table | **Rosel (retailer)**, 1925, **Belgium**. The strong cubic form of this table gives the piece a functional feel, while the airy design, glass top, and prettily carved ebony flowers lend it lightness and a touch of traditional luxury.

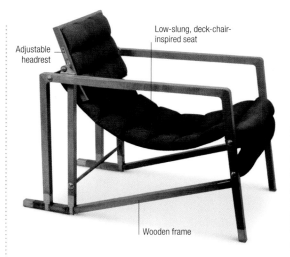

Adjustable headrest

Low-slung, deck-chair-inspired seat

Wooden frame

Transat armchair | **Eileen Gray**, 1925–1930, **France**. This chair is named after the deck chairs on the transatlantic cruisers of the day. Mixing wood, leather, and chrome, it was used in E-1027, Gray's self-designed house in Roquebrune-Cap-Martin, France.

Adjustable, foldable top

Sinuous lines

Cla-Cla table | **Jacques-Émile Ruhlmann**, c. 1926, **France**. This ebony table combines gentle curves with simple angularity typical of Ruhlmann. A rack mechanism makes it possible to tilt the tabletop between horizontal and vertical.

Nest of tables | **Harry and Lou Epstein**, c. 1930, **UK**. Made by prolific Art Deco furniture designers the Epsteins, this five-piece nest of tables is veneered in burr maple and features ebony details.

Thick, luxuriant upholstery

Softly curving lines

Her framed chair | **Gilbert Rohde for Heywood-Wakefield**, c. 1934, **US**. The "female" half of a his-and-hers pair, this chair's elegant form shows the influence of French Modernism—Rohde had visited Paris in 1927.

Ocean liners

1927–c. 1939

With its blend of engineering excellence and sumptuous style, the grand oceangoing liner became a floating embodiment of Art Deco. Rejecting the traditional styles popular before World War I, a new kind of Modernism could be seen in the design of the public spaces aboard the first great Deco liner, *Île de France*. Decorated in exotic materials, it reflected the spirit of the 1925 Paris Exhibition. Other countries soon began to build their own fashionably streamlined, elegantly contoured vessels in a race to have the fastest, most luxurious liner. Eventually, nautical styles influenced designs onshore, as porthole windows and balconies that resembled ships' bridges began to appear on buildings in the *moderne* style.

Glass top

Substantial plinth gives visual balance

Side table | late 1930s. This style of occasional table—here in maple veneer—is an Art Deco classic tackled by many designers, including Ruhlmann. Simple, functional, and delicate, the table has a side support with an unusual curved base.

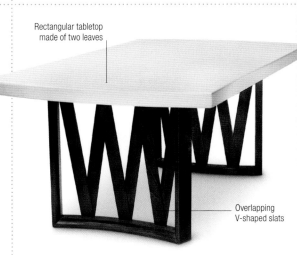

Rectangular tabletop made of two leaves

Overlapping V-shaped slats

Dining table | **Paul T. Frankl**, **US**. This extension table cleverly plays with shape, color, and material. The sleek white gesso top contrasts effectively with the mahogany legs, and its gentle bowing is echoed in the shape of the supports.

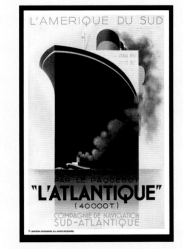

The vast size of the 40,000-ton *Atlantic* liner to South America is trumpeted in this poster by Cassandre.

△ **The Salon d'Afrique,** now in the Musée National des Arts d'Afrique et d'Océanie, included Ruhlmann's Elephant chairs. The interior was shown at the 1931 Exposition Coloniale Internationale in Paris.

Jacques-Émile
Ruhlmann

French furniture designer Ruhlmann was a leading post–World War I cabinet-maker. His exquisite pieces in exotic woods, which cleverly blend luxurious, 18th-century French traditions with a simple, smooth, and refined modernity, are considered to be among the finest examples of classic *Style Moderne*—French Art Deco. France, and specifically the 1925 Exposition Internationale des Arts Décoratifs et Industriels Modernes, held in Paris, is widely regarded as the birthplace of Art Deco. Appearing at this show made Ruhlmann an international figure, with thousands of visitors enraptured by his lavish Hôtel du Collectionneur pavilion. It also established him as one of the founders of Art Deco.

The French had a long tradition of producing luxury goods, especially furniture, and their Art Deco furniture was no exception. Ruhlmann was essentially a self-taught designer rather than a cabinetmaker. He ran a highly skilled workshop that produced beautifully crafted unique or limited-run pieces in rare, expensive, and often contrasting materials, such as veneers of Macassar ebony and amaranth, with delicate inlays of tortoiseshell or ivory. He loved to show off his pieces in grand settings, such as the offices of the French Minister of the Colonies (see left). His work is still held in great esteem today, and famous collectors have included Pop artist Andy Warhol and fashion designer Yves Saint Laurent.

Life

1879–1933

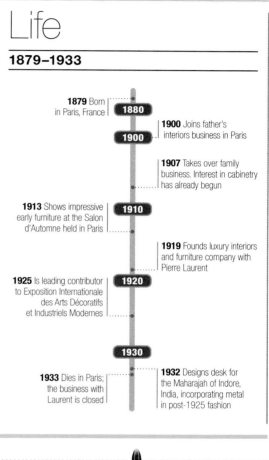

1879 Born in Paris, France | **1880**

1900 Joins father's interiors business in Paris | **1900**

1907 Takes over family business. Interest in cabinetry has already begun

1913 Shows impressive early furniture at the Salon d'Automne held in Paris | **1910**

1919 Founds luxury interiors and furniture company with Pierre Laurent

1925 Is leading contributor to Exposition Internationale des Arts Décoratifs et Industriels Modernes | **1920**

1930

1933 Dies in Paris; the business with Laurent is closed | **1932** Designs desk for the Maharajah of Indore, India, incorporating metal in post-1925 fashion

Strong, smooth, unbroken lines

Metal sabot

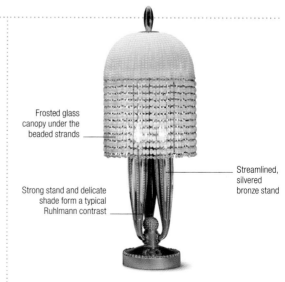

Frosted glass canopy under the beaded strands

Strong stand and delicate shade form a typical Ruhlmann contrast

Streamlined, silvered bronze stand

Armchair | *c.* 1913. Upholstered in luxurious velvet, this chair has a frame made of rare and precious amboyna burl wood, which has an unusual grain, with subtle ebony detailing.

State cabinet | *c.* 1922–1923. Ruhlmann made several similar corner cabinets—this one is veneered in amaranth wood, and its ebony and ivory floral centerpiece features complex marquetry.

Table lamp | *c.* 1925. This model of a table lamp, shimmering with clear and frosted glass beads, appeared in Ruhlmann's pavilion at the 1925 Exposition Internationale.

BOLD CERAMICS

The possibilities of color, pattern, and shape that ceramics offered were a gift to potters in the 1920s and 1930s. Some styles, such as the successful Argenta pieces from Sweden, showed Art Nouveau influences lingering on in a stylish form of Art Deco. In contrast, British ceramic designer Susie Cooper experimented with abstract Modernist patterns and combined a modern practicality with simple elegance. The figurine also came into its own, and popular styles showing high-society ladies at play kept the 1920s flapper spirit alive. Key Art Deco characteristics in ceramics included streamlined shapes, as in some of French ceramicist René Buthaud's pieces; stylized natural motifs, such as British sculptor John Skeaping's animals; and exotic colors and patterns reminiscent of China and Japan, seen regularly in Carlton Ware.

Lady's backward lean balanced by dog's upright stance

Vivid floral pattern echoes Japanese art

Vivid colors, a bright sheen, and gold give luxurious feel

Placing strong colors next to each other was a Carlton feature

Smooth, shouldered oval shape

Stylized cockerel in medallion

Ginger jar | **Carlton Ware, 1920s, UK.** This is one of many Carlton Ware jars in this shape and with similar, brightly colored decoration in exotic Eastern styles. Stylized flowers were a favorite motif.

Vase | **Boch Frères Keramis, 1925, Belgium.** Made from a compact stoneware known as *grès*, the vase has a sensual shape and curling decoration that recall Art Nouveau—a great influence on Deco work.

Figurine | **Claire Weiss-Herczeg for Goldscheider,** *c.* 1930, Austria. A young society lady strikes a stylish pose, with the folds of her gown beautifully sculpted, while walking her Russian borzoi. Such frivolous pieces were Art Deco staples.

Obvious brushmarks

Deer | **John Skeaping for Wedgwood,** *c.* 1927, UK. This stylized sculpture with a glossy glaze is one of 14 animal pieces that Skeaping designed for Wedgwood. It stands only 7 in (18 cm) tall on its chamfered pedestal.

Hand-painted plate | **Susie Cooper,** *c.* 1928, UK. This plate pulsates with color, although Cooper's work was often much more muted. The abstract Overlapping Triangles design is influenced by Cubist painting.

Color seems to radiate happiness and the spirit of modern life.

Clarice **Cliff**
1930

Plain, clean-lined oval form

Slight taper adds elegance

Child's mug | **Susie Cooper, 1933–1934, UK.** This transfer-printed Skier mug is from Cooper's range of nursery and christening ware. The simple banding on the rim and handle is typical of her nurseryware.

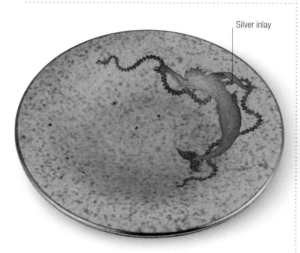

Silver inlay

Argenta stoneware plate | **Wilhelm Kåge for Gustavsberg**, *c.* 1940, **Sweden.** The mermaid figure, with her flowing Art Nouveau lines, has been inlaid with silver, mirroring the edging band of the plate.

Stoneware vase | **René Buthaud, 1928–1930, France.** The design of this crackled-glaze vase recalls African art— a great influence on Buthaud and many other Deco designers. It also reflects the geometric abstraction of Modernist art.

Painted in enamels and luster

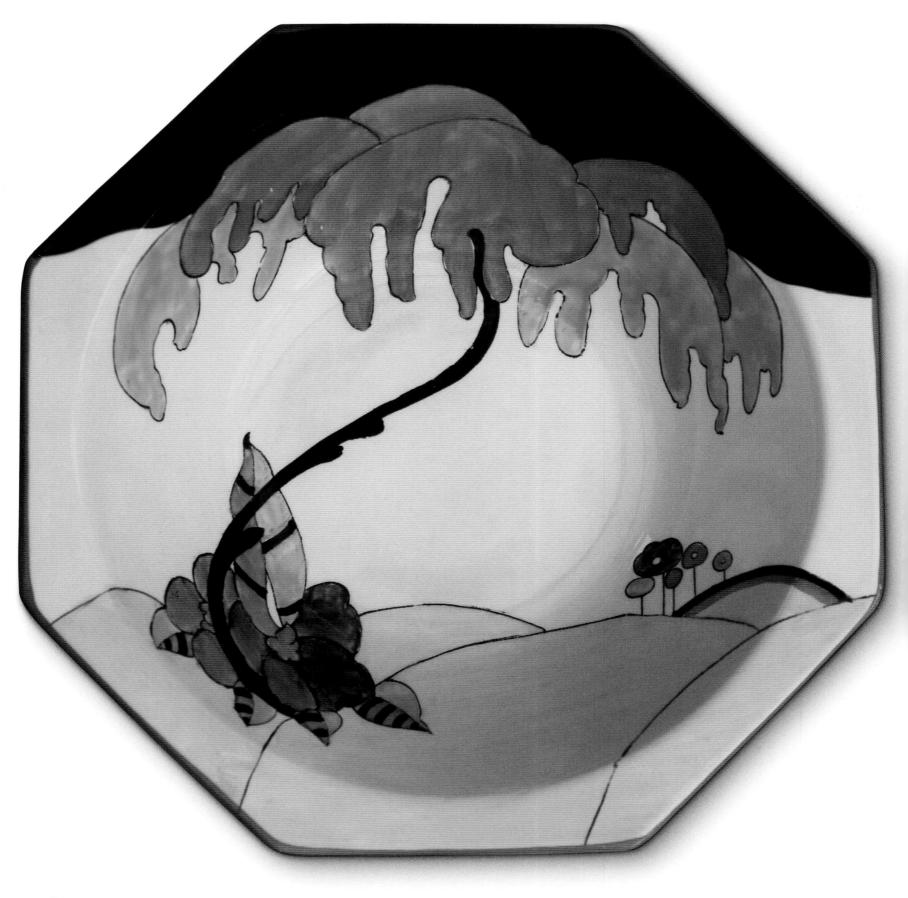

△ **This woodland bowl, from around 1931,** features the color scheme and tree, hills, and distant lollipop flowers that were characteristic of this pattern.

Clarice Cliff

Pioneering British ceramic designer Clarice Cliff started producing bestselling hand-painted tableware in often-flamboyant Art Deco designs in the late 1920s, at a time when the style was new to the UK. By the early 1930s, Cliff had produced hundreds of shapes and about 400 designs. Her daring, taste-shaping style was hugely successful until the mid-1930s. It celebrated boldly colorful, graphic patterns and geometric shapes that echoed adventurous Modernist art. Perhaps the most prolific Art Deco pottery designer, Cliff sold multiple designs under the umbrella name Bizarre. Crocus was the most popular, reflecting the public's particular love of her floral and fruit patterns. Others included Conical, Fantasque, and Appliqué, while the stylized landscapes of the Woodland pattern showed Cliff's talent with solid blocks of unconventional color.

Cliff was born into a working-class family in Staffordshire—the heart of the UK's pottery industry. At the age of 13, she began a pottery-painting apprenticeship, and by 1930, the Newport Pottery where she worked produced only her ware. Her flair lay less in original design and more in blending influences—such as work by French Art Deco metalworks Maison Desny—to inspire a wide public and seize the Jazz Age spirit. From the mid-1930s, Cliff's style, and her more conservative work that followed, failed to find great success, but collectors rediscovered her from the 1960s on.

Life

1899–1972

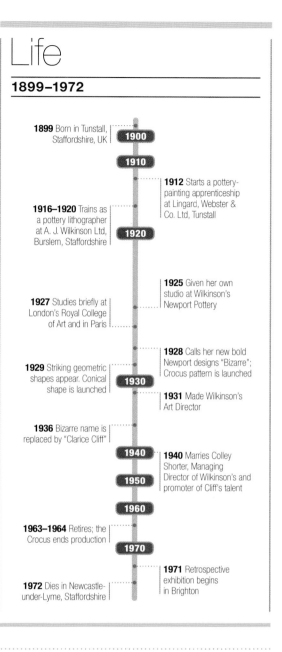

1899 Born in Tunstall, Staffordshire, UK
1900
1910
1912 Starts a pottery-painting apprenticeship at Lingard, Webster & Co. Ltd, Tunstall
1916–1920 Trains as a pottery lithographer at A. J. Wilkinson Ltd, Burslem, Staffordshire
1920
1925 Given her own studio at Wilkinson's Newport Pottery
1927 Studies briefly at London's Royal College of Art and in Paris
1928 Calls her new bold Newport designs "Bizarre"; Crocus pattern is launched
1929 Striking geometric shapes appear. Conical shape is launched
1930
1931 Made Wilkinson's Art Director
1936 Bizarre name is replaced by "Clarice Cliff"
1940
1940 Marries Colley Shorter, Managing Director of Wilkinson's and promoter of Cliff's talent
1950
1960
1963–1964 Retires; the Crocus ends production
1970
1971 Retrospective exhibition begins in Brighton
1972 Dies in Newcastle-under-Lyme, Staffordshire

Orange Autumn pattern

Stylized tree reflects Cliff's interest in Japanese art

Red Roofs pattern

Distinctive painted outlining of shapes

Bold brushstrokes give appealingly hand-painted appearance

Conical sugar shakers | **For A. J. Wilkinson,** *c.* 1935. These shakers belong to Cliff's Fantasque range, regarded by many as her most important design.

Crocus teapot | **For A. J. Wilkinson,** *c.* 1935. This globe-shaped teapot is painted in the simple but popular Crocus pattern, using the rarer blue colorway.

Red net is typical of Tennis pattern

Cauldron | **For A. J. Wilkinson,** *c.* 1931. The multicolored exterior of this piece is enamel-painted in the Tennis pattern—named after the abstract array of net, circles, and lines.

DOMESTIC METALWARE

Small, stylish metalware pieces such as candlesticks were one of the major products of Art Deco design, and they sat perfectly within the new streamlined interiors. Metalware was the ideal medium for capturing the sleek, industrial, machine-age spirit. Silver and the more affordable chromed surfaces were also ideal for creating interesting reflections that worked well with simple Modernist shapes. Many Art Deco designers were concerned with producing forms that matched their function yet were innovative, easy to use, and expressed a new kind of beauty. Ahead of the game were the Wiener Werkstätte (Vienna Workshop) artists in Austria, who in the very early 1900s were already producing the kind of radically simplified designs that would become typical of Art Deco.

> ## We will have to begin anew in everything.
>
> Josef **Frank** on Viennese design after World War I

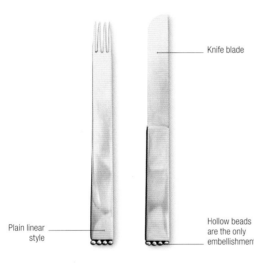

Knife blade

Plain linear style

Hollow beads are the only embellishment

Flat Model cutlery | **Josef Hoffmann for Wiener Werkstätte**, 1903, **Austria**. The starkly flat, rectangular forms of this early silver dessert fork and knife, from a larger set, were pioneering and hugely influential.

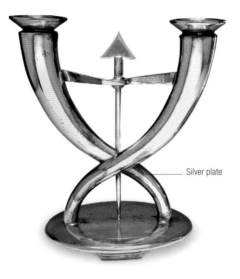

Silver plate

Candlestick | **Gio Ponti for Christofle**, 1920s, **France**. The bold, simple form of crossed cornucopias is given a dynamic upward thrust by the central arrow to which they are joined. This is one of a pair of identical two-socket candlesticks.

Angled surfaces create reflections and a sparkling appearance

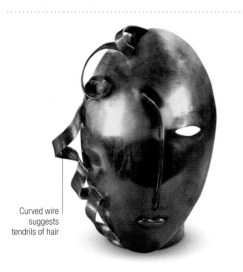

Curved wire suggests tendrils of hair

Bronze mask | **Hagenauer Werkstätte**, *c.* 1925–1930, **Austria**. This stylized female face resembles the tribal masks that influenced much early 20th-century art. The Hagenauer workshop produced many heads and masks in African styles.

Tiered finial

Matte lower section

Bulbous tea service | **Wolfers Frères**, *c.* 1927, **Belgium**. Wolfers had an Art Nouveau heritage, but this bulbous silver service is strongly Modernist. The teapot, sugar bowl, and milk jug have both horizontal and vertical segments; the handles and the tiered finials on the domed lids are in stained ebony.

Tall, angular form recalls skyscrapers

Daringly geometric shapes

Cubic coffee service | **Erik Magnussen for Gorham Manufacturing Co.**, 1927, US. Also called The Lights and Shadows of Manhattan, this service is the pinnacle of American Art Deco. Danish émigré Magnussen combined Cubism, the Jazz era, big-city life, and the machine age in a coffee set made of silver, silver gilt, oxidized silver, and ivory. The contrasting triangles of oxidized silver and gilt break up the surfaces and make the whole set shimmer.

Multiple angles echo the Cubist paintings of Pablo Picasso and Georges Braque

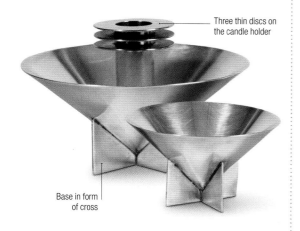

Three thin discs on the candle holder

Base in form of cross

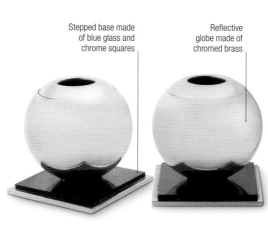

Stepped base made of blue glass and chrome squares

Reflective globe made of chromed brass

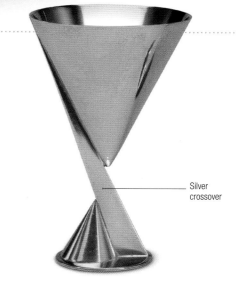

Silver crossover

Conical candlestick and bowl | **Ilonka Karasz for Paye & Baker Manufacturing Co.**, c. 1928, US. These smooth silver-plated pieces by Hungarian-born Modernist designer Karasz have distinctive cross-shaped bases.

Chromed globe candlesticks | **Chase Brass & Copper Co.**, 1930s, US. An example of the popular and affordable Chase Chrome range, this pair of candlesticks makes a typically Art Deco use of color contrast.

Cocktail goblet | **Maison Desny**, c. 1930, France. The crossover device of this silver goblet, one of a pair, uses folds and twists of metal. Desny's designers had a talent for stylish smaller objects such as this.

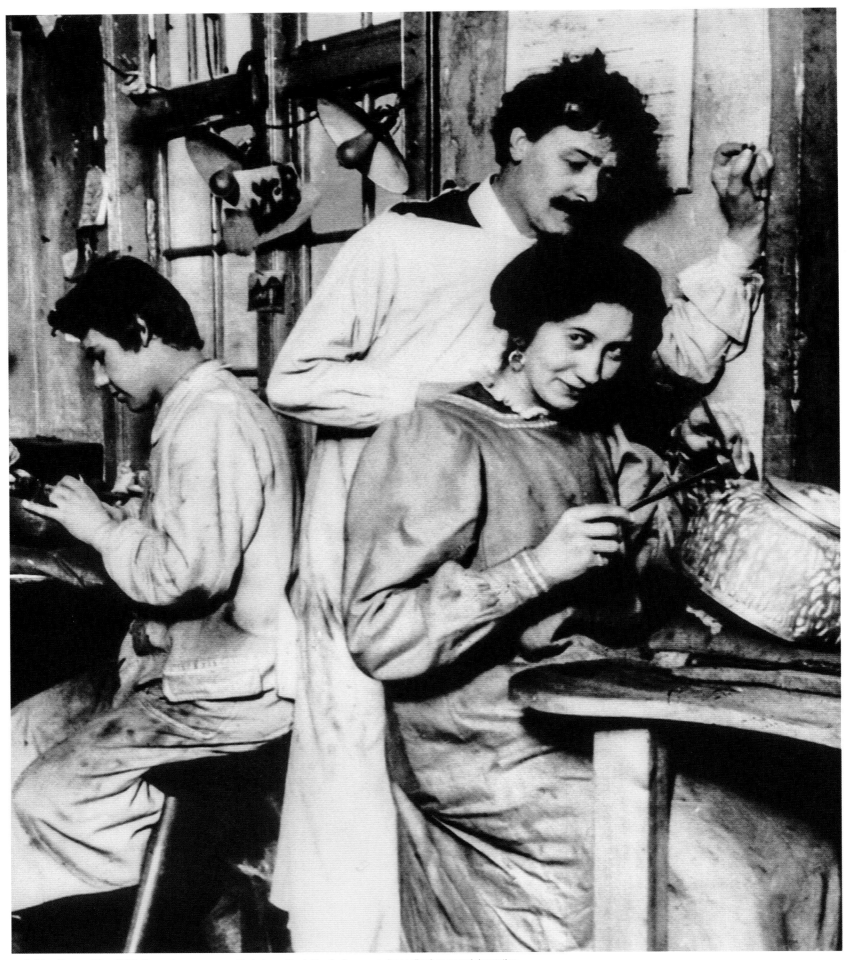

△ **In his silversmithy, 1920,** Georg Jensen oversees his trainee, Alba Lykke Andersen, as she applies hammered decoration.

Georg Jensen

The Danish silversmith Georg Jensen was internationally renowned for his sculptor's eye, his original ideas, and his exquisite craftsmanship. In 1904, he created a company that modernized metalwork with simple and refined designs. His workshop combined the strong shapes, aesthetic ideals, and honest materials of Arts and Crafts with the flowing lines and naturalistic themes of Art Nouveau and the stylish functionality of streamlined Art Deco. Jensen began his career producing Art Nouveau jewelry, but he later achieved equal success with Art Deco–style pieces.

Jensen played a pivotal role in creating the simple, elegant style of flatware (cutlery) that is still popular today, and he was perhaps the first silversmith to make money with modern designs rather than replicating traditional patterns. His flair owed much to his eclectic training: he served a goldsmithing apprenticeship before studying sculpture, then took up ceramics before finally returning to metalwork.

The 1920s was a pivotal time for Jensen, as the firm created its first line of Modernist cutlery and went into a series of fruitful collaborations with designers such as Harald Nielsen. By the time Jensen died in 1935, his company had outlets all around the world. Many of his designs are still in production today, and the Jensen company continues to flourish.

Life

1866–1935

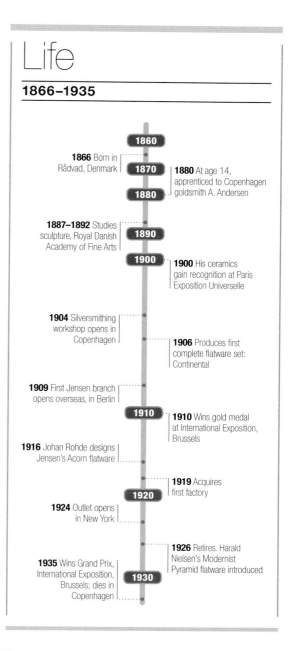

1866 Born in Rådvad, Denmark

1880 At age 14, apprenticed to Copenhagen goldsmith A. Andersen

1887–1892 Studies sculpture, Royal Danish Academy of Fine Arts

1900 His ceramics gain recognition at Paris Exposition Universelle

1904 Silversmithing workshop opens in Copenhagen

1906 Produces first complete flatware set: Continental

1909 First Jensen branch opens overseas, in Berlin

1910 Wins gold medal at International Exposition, Brussels

1916 Johan Rohde designs Jensen's Acorn flatware

1919 Acquires first factory

1924 Outlet opens in New York

1926 Retires. Harald Nielsen's Modernist Pyramid flatware introduced

1935 Wins Grand Prix, International Exposition, Brussels; dies in Copenhagen

Silver covered goblet | **Johan Rohde**, *c.* 1920s. The swelling form of this goblet is typical of many Jensen pieces. The stem's swirling lines are reminiscent of Art Nouveau ornament.

Highly stylized organic forms

Capped spout

Crosshatched pattern on body

D-shaped, banded handle

Cocktail shaker | **Sigvard Bernadotte**, *c.* 1937–1938. This modern-looking Deco cocktail shaker was by Sigvard Bernadotte, the leading Modernist designer at Jensen's company in the 1930s.

Silver brooch | **Arno Malinowski**, *c.* 1930s. Jensen and Malinowski shared a love of natural motifs. Bold, clean shapes give this openwork silver brooch a strong Art Deco feel.

△ **The bell is lowered** onto Great Britain's *Coronation Scot* train, with its racing stripes, in preparation for the 1939 New York World's Fair.

Streamlining

△ **Raymond Loewy** | 1893–1986

Characterized by smooth, rounded corners and decorative speed bands that suggest movement, streamlining (under the name Streamline Moderne) is often seen as the main form of Art Deco in 1930s America. The style was the expression of designers' interest in the velocity and dynamism of modern life—they admired aerodynamic forms with a low drag factor and regarded the teardrop as an ideal shape. Designers were greatly influenced by industry and the fast, stylish modes of transportation that were produced at the time—trains, planes, ocean liners, and cars such as Ford's famously aerodynamic 1936 Lincoln-Zephyr (see pp.146–147).

Streamline designers included Walter Dorwin Teague, Kem Weber, and, in particular, Raymond Loewy and Norman Bel Geddes. Creative crossovers meant that ideas about cars were applied to products for the home, from furniture to radios and refrigerators. Loewy created innovative, aerodynamic products, such as his Coldspot Super Six refrigerator of 1935, which spawned countless imitations. Bel Geddes's vision—and perhaps streamlining in general—reached a climax in his Futurama pavilion for General Motors at the 1939 New York World's Fair. Transportation featured prominently in the show, and the exhibits included sleek, progressive trains such as Great Britain's *Coronation Scot*.

Key dates

1870–1939

1870s Term "streamline" said to have first appeared in print — 1880

Early 1900s Car companies thought to have used "streamline" to describe sweeping shapes — 1900

1925 Exposition Internationale des Arts Décoratifs et Industriels Modernes, held in Paris, includes sleek, modern styles — 1920

1927 Bel Geddes sets up an industrial design company

1932 Bel Geddes's influential book *Horizons* promotes futuristic streamlining ideas — 1930

1934 Chrysler Airflow is launched; streamlining highlighted at conference of US automotive engineers

1935 Loewy designs Coldspot Super Six refrigerator for Sears, Roebuck & Co.

1936 Loewy designs the *3768* locomotive for the Pennsylvania Railroad

1939 Bel Geddes's pavilion at New York World's Fair imagines the future metropolis — 1940

Classic feature of three speed lines also aids grip

Open cabinet doors the same width as table

Ebonized mahogany

Four chrome glass galleries inside each door

Made from brass and Bakelite

The banded design creates an aerodynamic look

Table lighter | **Art Metal Works Inc. for Ronson**, *c.* 1925. The sloping shape of this plastic and chromium-plated steel lighter makes it look like a liner cutting through the waves.

Cocktail cabinet | **Maurice Adams**, 1933, UK. This beverage cabinet with a semicircular table support was designed as part of a modern cocktail room with a glass ceiling and silver walls.

Electric Zephyr clock | **Kem Weber (attributed) for Lawson Time Inc.**, *c.* 1934. The horizontal banding and rounded corners of this piece are typical of streamlining.

EVOLUTION OF
TRAINS

Rail travel presents a number of complex design challenges, often involving years of development and many different designers and engineers. It encapsulates many of the key principles of design on a large scale, since trains need to be affordable, efficient, comfortable, and, above all, safe. Throughout their history, locomotives for long-distance, surface-level transportation have been designed for speed—by creating more powerful engines, designing streamlined bodies, and working with track engineers to deal with gradients and curves. Underground trains and light rail, meanwhile, present a different set of priorities—how to design rugged, durable trains that are economical to run and that can carry as many passengers as possible.

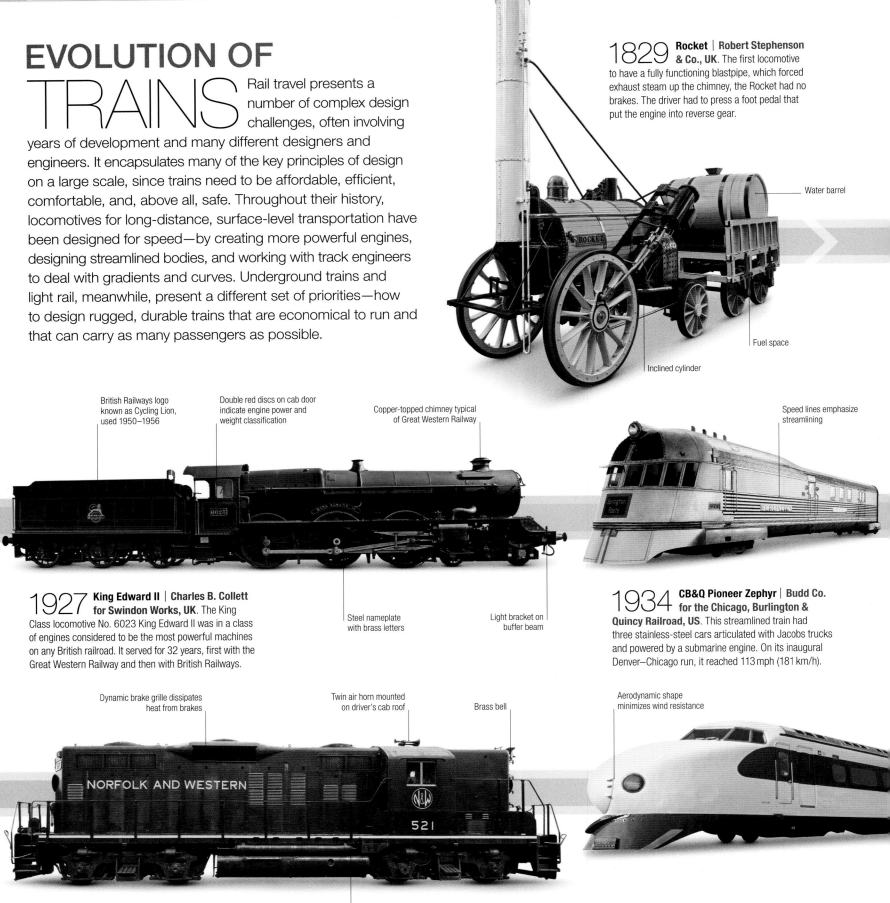

1829 **Rocket** | **Robert Stephenson & Co., UK**. The first locomotive to have a fully functioning blastpipe, which forced exhaust steam up the chimney, the Rocket had no brakes. The driver had to press a foot pedal that put the engine into reverse gear.

Water barrel

Fuel space

Inclined cylinder

British Railways logo known as Cycling Lion, used 1950–1956

Double red discs on cab door indicate engine power and weight classification

Copper-topped chimney typical of Great Western Railway

Speed lines emphasize streamlining

Steel nameplate with brass letters

Light bracket on buffer beam

1927 **King Edward II** | **Charles B. Collett for Swindon Works, UK**. The King Class locomotive No. 6023 King Edward II was in a class of engines considered to be the most powerful machines on any British railroad. It served for 32 years, first with the Great Western Railway and then with British Railways.

1934 **CB&Q Pioneer Zephyr** | **Budd Co. for the Chicago, Burlington & Quincy Railroad, US**. This streamlined train had three stainless-steel cars articulated with Jacobs trucks and powered by a submarine engine. On its inaugural Denver–Chicago run, it reached 113 mph (181 km/h).

Dynamic brake grille dissipates heat from brakes

Twin air horn mounted on driver's cab roof

Brass bell

Aerodynamic shape minimizes wind resistance

NORFOLK AND WESTERN

521

Safety railing runs the full length of locomotive

1949 **GP9 Class No. 521** | **General Motors' Electro-Motive Division for Norfolk & Western Railway (N&W), US**. The last 21 GP9s bought by the N&W for passenger trains were given a special livery of Tuscan Red with yellow lettering, earning them the nickname "the redbirds."

1964 **O series Bullet train** | **Japanese National Railways, Japan**. Built for Japan's high-speed lines in the 1960s, the lightweight, aerodynamic bullet trains were inspired in part by aircraft design. They used electric power to reach speeds of up to 130 mph (210 km/h) on special high-speed track.

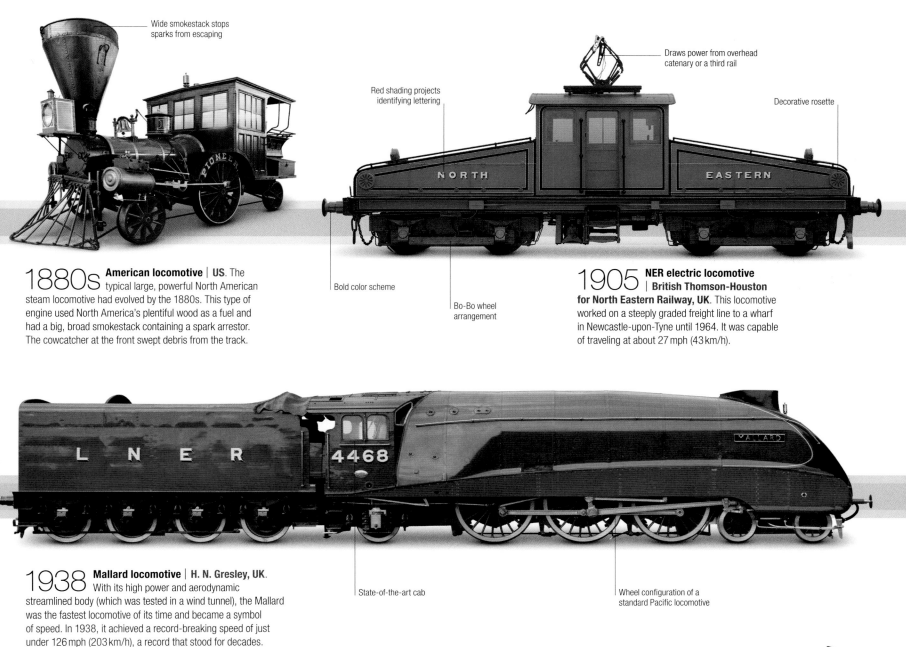

Wide smokestack stops
sparks from escaping

Draws power from overhead
catenary or a third rail

Red shading projects
identifying lettering

Decorative rosette

Bold color scheme

Bo-Bo wheel
arrangement

1880s **American locomotive | US**. The
typical large, powerful North American
steam locomotive had evolved by the 1880s. This type of
engine used North America's plentiful wood as a fuel and
had a big, broad smokestack containing a spark arrestor.
The cowcatcher at the front swept debris from the track.

1905 **NER electric locomotive
| British Thomson-Houston
for North Eastern Railway, UK**. This locomotive
worked on a steeply graded freight line to a wharf
in Newcastle-upon-Tyne until 1964. It was capable
of traveling at about 27 mph (43 km/h).

State-of-the-art cab

Wheel configuration of a
standard Pacific locomotive

1938 **Mallard locomotive | H. N. Gresley, UK**.
With its high power and aerodynamic
streamlined body (which was tested in a wind tunnel), the Mallard
was the fastest locomotive of its time and became a symbol
of speed. In 1938, it achieved a record-breaking speed of just
under 126 mph (203 km/h), a record that stood for decades.

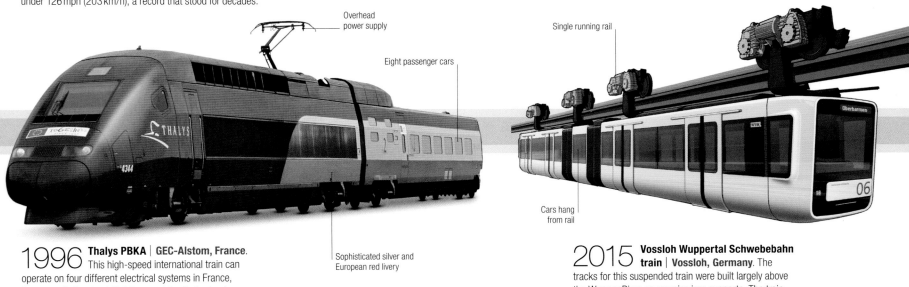

Overhead
power supply

Eight passenger cars

Single running rail

Cars hang
from rail

Sophisticated silver and
European red livery

1996 **Thalys PBKA | GEC-Alstom, France**.
This high-speed international train can
operate on four different electrical systems in France,
Germany, Switzerland, Belgium, and the Netherlands.
The 17 train sets built operate services between Paris,
Brussels, Cologne (Köln), and Amsterdam, hence PBKA.

2015 **Vossloh Wuppertal Schwebebahn
train | Vossloh, Germany**. The
tracks for this suspended train were built largely above
the Wupper River on massive iron supports. The train
is a three-section, articulated vehicle, with the power
supply coming from a rail adjacent to the running rail.

DECO DOME

The Union Terminal in Cincinnati, Ohio, was built in 1933 to bring the city's rail lines together at one convenient point: an enormous state-of-the-art station in the fashionable Art Deco style. The lead architects were Alfred T. Fellheimer (who had worked on New York's Grand Central Station) and Steward Wagner. However, the building's design was the responsibility of architect Roland Wank and French-born design consultant Paul Philippe Cret. Together, they transformed the station into one of North America's greatest Art Deco monuments.

At the front of the station is an enormous lobby containing booking facilities and leading onto the platforms. This cavernous ticket hall, roofed with what was, at the time, the world's largest semidome, is lit by a great window that forms the centerpiece of the facade. The vast limestone-clad arch that houses the window is covered with Art Deco ornamentation and forms a symbolic gateway to the city. Cincinnati Union was one of the last great railroad terminals, but its heyday was short-lived. Forty years after its opening in 1932, it was converted into a library and museum complex.

The entrance is a great arch 200 feet in diameter—the unchallenged giant of station portals.

Carroll L. V. **Meeks,** 1956

Union Terminal, Cincinnati, Ohio, Alfred T. Fellheimer and Steward Wagner, 1933 Relief sculptures by Maxfield Keck, showing stylized Art Deco figures representing Transport and Commerce, flank the vast window, modern central clock, and stepped walls of the station entrance facade.

Curled lip

Wear-ever mixing bowl | **The Aluminum Cooking Utensil Co., US.** An array of anonymously designed cooking utensils were made in aluminum in the Art Deco years. The material was used to mass-produce modern, metallic kitchenwares.

Steam valve

Moka Express coffee maker | **Alfonso Bialetti**, 1933, **Italy.** Aluminum-worker Bialetti developed the first model for this world-famous coffeepot. Designs varied over the decades, but all retain the distinctive eight-sided shape and contrast of materials.

Magnalite teakettle | **John G. Rideout for the Wagner Manufacturing Co.,** 1936, **US.** Magnalite (a magnesium-aluminum alloy) was especially energy-efficient. The sleek kettle features a contrasting handle made of lacquered wood.

Copper-bottomed stainless steel

Pressure cooker | **W. Archibald Welden for Revere Copper & Brass, Inc.,** 1938–1939, **US.** Revere Ware was chic, rustproof, durable, and light. Rounded edges aided cleaning, and the pistol-shaped plastic handles were comfortable and safe.

Enameled cover

Soda King Siphon | **Norman Bel Geddes/Worthen Paxton for the Walter Kidde Sales Co.,** 1938, **US.** With the futuristic hallmark of Bel Geddes, the conical body is in chromed metal and the dome-shaped cover is enameled.

Gap in casing reveals lens

Focus dial

Rounded corners

Riga Minox camera | **Walter Zapp for Valsts Electro-Techniska Fabrika,** 1936, **Latvia.** Zapp's tiny camera was used by intelligence agents in World War II and after. The casing extends and closes to reveal or hide the working parts.

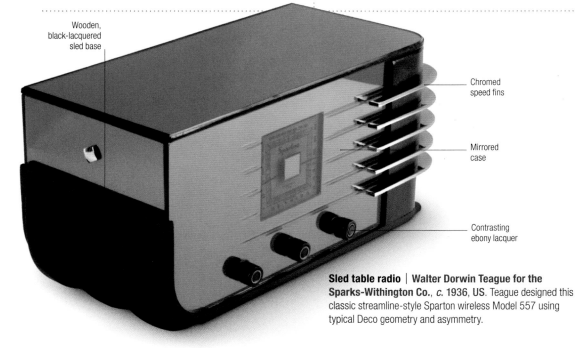

Wooden, black-lacquered sled base

Chromed speed fins

Mirrored case

Contrasting ebony lacquer

Sled table radio | **Walter Dorwin Teague for the Sparks-Withington Co.,** c. 1936, **US.** Teague designed this classic streamline-style Sparton wireless Model 557 using typical Deco geometry and asymmetry.

Norman **Bel Geddes**

1893–1958

Stage designer, author, architect, and industrial designer Bel Geddes is more famous for his vision than his designs—of which few were completed. He foresaw that "utilitarian objects will be as beautiful as what we call today 'works of art,'" and "the home will become so mechanized that handwork will be reduced to a minimum." His streamlined designs extended to urban planning, foreshadowing the US interstate highway system and bringing hope to a generation of Depression-era Americans.

PRODUCT DESIGN

Beauty and utility came together in Art Deco designs, as many product designers aimed to marry form and function while creating attractive objects. At their service were exciting new materials, thanks to advances in plastics, stainless steel, and aluminum. These materials were ideal for lightweight wares in which the clean Deco look of shiny surfaces formed a contrast with other materials. Ergonomics were key; so, for example, the tiny, round-cornered Riga Minox camera handled pleasingly and could easily be slipped into a pocket. Just as technical advances led to a greater number and variety of new products—from radical new radios to soda siphons—so too did a rise in consumerism and leisure pursuits, especially in the US. The detailing on such products—the speed fins on Walter Dorwin Teague's Sled radio, for example—often imitated the aerodynamic streamlining of contemporary cars and planes.

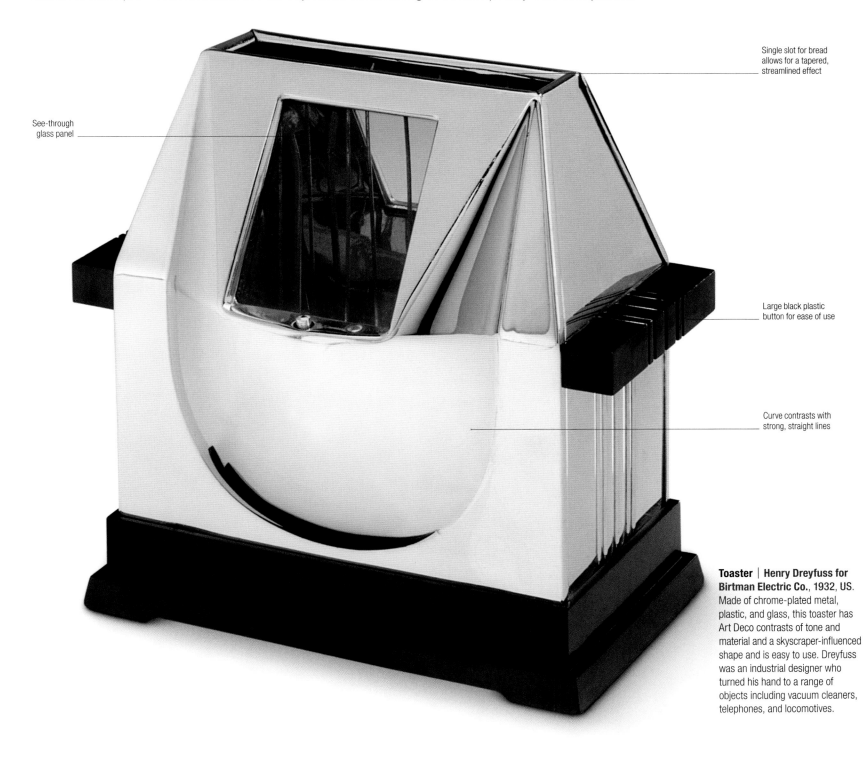

Single slot for bread allows for a tapered, streamlined effect

See-through glass panel

Large black plastic button for ease of use

Curve contrasts with strong, straight lines

Toaster | **Henry Dreyfuss for Birtman Electric Co.**, 1932, US. Made of chrome-plated metal, plastic, and glass, this toaster has Art Deco contrasts of tone and material and a skyscraper-influenced shape and is easy to use. Dreyfuss was an industrial designer who turned his hand to a range of objects including vacuum cleaners, telephones, and locomotives.

Mouthpiece

Cloth cord

Candlestick telephone | **Kellogg**, early 1900s, **US**. With the mouthpiece at the top of the stand and a separate earpiece, the candlestick telephone was a popular model. Its simple design anticipated streamlining.

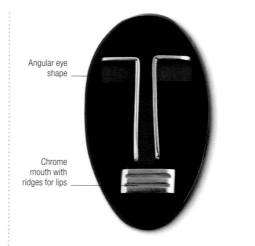

Angular eye shape

Chrome mouth with ridges for lips

Mask pin | **1920s**. This African-style mask pin in contrasting-colored Bakelite has a chromed mouth and steel eyebrows. African art was a big influence on Art Deco, bringing geometry, abstract patterns, and a taste for the exotic to everyday life.

Bakelite casing

No. 2 Hawkette Camera | **Kodak Ltd., Bakelite components by E. K. Cole**, 1930s, **UK**. This folding camera, with a speckled, compression-molded Bakelite body, was probably Kodak's first plastic-bodied camera.

The science of Bakelite

Patented 1907–1927

Marketed as a machine-age miracle in the 1930s, Bakelite is a thermosetting resin, which means that it does not melt once it has been heated and set. As a liquid, Bakelite could be poured over stacked sheets of paper to saturate them and produce a thin, hard laminate. Once cooled, this was ideal for encasing electrical devices such as telephones and radios. It could be reinforced with fillers, such as wood flour, asbestos, or powdered slate, and molded into any shape. Dark colors were necessary to conceal the filler and were generally chosen to resemble wood. When cast as a liquid, a range of colors was possible.

Molded-in speed lines

Tuning dial

Bullet radio, multicolored No.189 model | **FADA, early 1940s, US**. This sleek Art Deco classic was produced in interesting futuristic shapes and bright, modern colorways made possible by the use of Catalin plastic.

Textured grip

Pistol Lighter | **JYM**, 1940s, **France**. Black Bakelite cigarette lighters were a feature of social life in the Art Deco era and promoted a sense of fun, novelty, and frivolity. "Firing" the pistol lit the flame.

Ekco radio A 22 model by E. K. Cole, 1945, UK. The round shape of this radio's Bakelite casing is typically Deco.

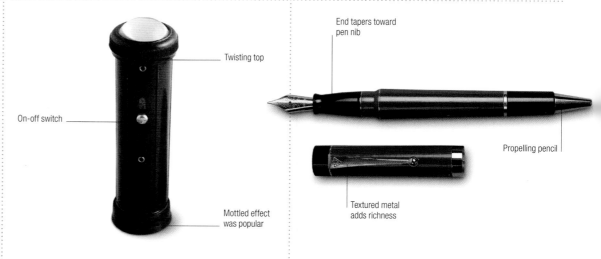

Twisting top

On-off switch

Mottled effect was popular

Flashlight | **1940s**. The simple lines of this Bakelite-cased flashlight owe much to Deco principles. Commercial designers of the Depression-era 1930s and 1940s relied on Bakelite to produce affordable consumer products such as flashlights.

End tapers toward pen nib

Propelling pencil

Textured metal adds richness

Monte Carlo fountain pen and pencil | **Visconti**, c. 1980s, **Italy**. Bakelite was still used for certain items after its heyday. The clean lines and color contrast of this combination pen show the legacy of Art Deco style.

Rotary dial

Directory of
telephone numbers

Self-contained telephone | GPO, *c.* 1930s,
UK. This Bakelite telephone has a rotary dial, a
cloth cord, and an integral drawer containing
a miniature telephone directory. Its sculpted,
curving lines, made possible by the qualities
of the plastic, established it as an early
20th-century domestic icon.

EARLY PLASTIC PIECES

Plastics were an exciting invention for Art Deco designers. Contemporary designer Peter Müller-Munk described plastic as "the hallmark of modern design … the mysterious and attractive solution for almost any application requiring eye appeal." Plastic was smooth, lightweight, modern-looking, hard-wearing—if often rather brittle early on—and easy to mass-produce. Bakelite was the first completely synthetic plastic, patented by Dr. Leo Baekeland in 1907. This was the trade name for phenol-formaldehyde or phenolic resins, but Bakelite is often used as a catch-all term for early plastics. True Bakelite's composition and production methods, especially its need for fillers and reinforcing materials, made most products dark-colored and opaque. In the late 1920s, however, new kinds of phenolic resins such as Catalin were produced. These were easier to mold and could be produced in many colors, as in FADA's Bullet radio (see opposite), paving the way for the bold, bright hues of 1950s and 1960s plastics.

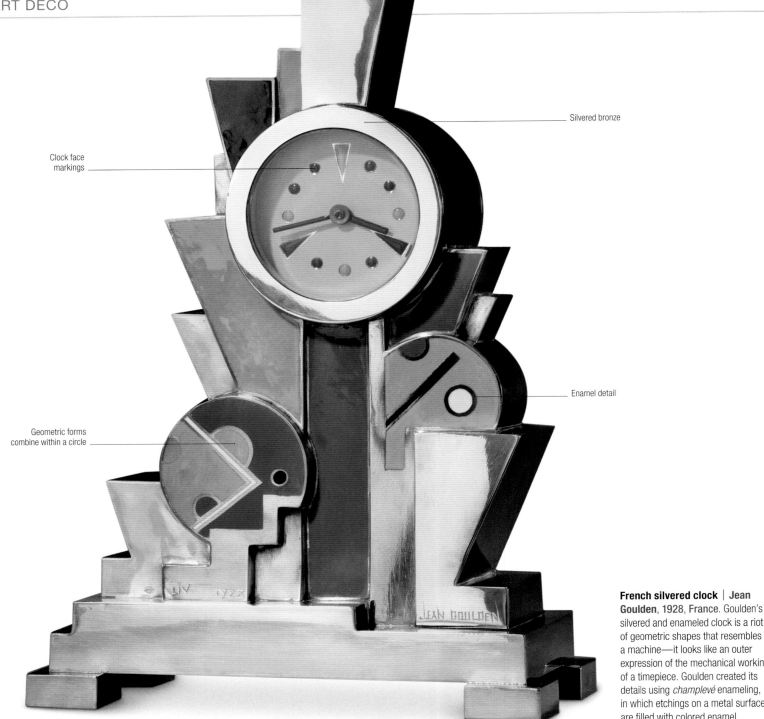

Silvered bronze

Clock face markings

Enamel detail

Geometric forms combine within a circle

JEAN GOULDEN

French silvered clock | **Jean Goulden**, 1928, France. Goulden's silvered and enameled clock is a riot of geometric shapes that resembles a machine—it looks like an outer expression of the mechanical workings of a timepiece. Goulden created its details using *champlevé* enameling, in which etchings on a metal surface are filled with colored enamel.

ELEGANT TIMEPIECES

Clock design was an area in which Art Deco artists favored an abstract, geometric style. Many of them characterized their Art Deco aesthetic as a rebellion against the flowing lines of Art Nouveau, and a number of timepieces from this era had a pronounced Modernist look. Jean Goulden produced Cubist-influenced pieces, while the purist Jean Puiforcat indulged his love of simple shapes and clean lines with a Bauhaus-like zeal (see pp.168–169). Female statuettes were also a popular feature of designs in the 1920s and 1930s: they often appeared on clocks, providing an effective contrast to the angular simplicity of the casings, a stylistic device seen in the work of artists such as Josef Lorenzl and Ferdinand Preiss. Art Deco clocks sometimes featured motifs depicting popular contemporary trends, such as Egyptomania and ancient temples.

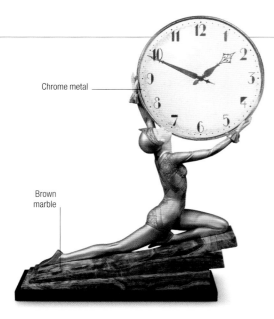

Chrome metal

Brown marble

Kneeling girl clock | **Ferdinand Preiss**, 1920s, Germany. Ivory carver Preiss made detailed figures of young women, many in active poses. He often used the fashionable Art Deco combination of ivory and bronze, as in this example.

Onyx-cased clock | 1920s. The painted bronze and ivory figure mounted on this clock is dressed in the costume of Pierrot, a character from the Commedia dell'Arte—an Italian troupe of players dating back to the 1600s.

Bronze clock face with silvered numbers

Statuette clock | **Josef Lorenzl**, c. 1930, Austria. Vienna-born sculptor Lorenzl produced many attractive Art Deco figures. This clock is supported by a nude female dancer cast in bronze with a silver patina and perched on an onyx column.

Pharaoh clock | **Albert Cheuret**, 1925, France. This famous piece made from silvered bronze and onyx was designed to look like a pharaoh's headgear, reflecting the obsession with Ancient Egyptian culture that was popular at the time. As well as its striking shape, the clock face has unusual numbers that consist entirely of straight lines and resemble Egyptian hieroglyphics.

Mantel clock | **Figure by Geo (Georges) Maxim**, c. 1930, France. Adorned with one of Maxim's many female statuettes, this clock is framed by angular, colored marble sections, adding to its geometric look.

Chiming wall clock | c. 1930–1935. This chiming clock has an interesting mix of 19th-century Arts and Crafts—in the carved roses and leaves—and geometric Modernism, as in the front panels of walnut that surround an octagonal clock face.

Modernist clock | **Jean Puiforcat for Hour-Lavigne**, 1932, France. A devoted Modernist, Puiforcat believed in distilling designs down to their functional basics. By 1932, his focus had moved from straight lines to circles, as seen here.

EVOLUTION OF CLOCKS

During the 20th century, clocks changed from being costly precision items made by hand and needing regular maintenance to affordable, mass-produced objects that kept near-perfect time. Clock designers have responded eagerly both to technological changes (including the advent of electric and battery power and the development of small electronic movements) and to fashion. Clocks have been made in every style, from ornate to minimalist, because, whether in a gilt case or made of plastic, they are not just useful but also decorative.

1877 **Carriage clock** | **Alphonse-Gustave Giroux, France**. Designed to fit into a box for traveling, clocks such as this robust gilt-brass example were extremely popular in the late 19th century. The case has restrained classical molding.

c. **1910** **Tudric clock** | **Archibald Knox for Liberty, UK**. Liberty used pewter for its Tudric line, which included many Art Nouveau and Celtic-inspired designs by Knox. Adding a little silver to the pewter alloy made the metal shine and set off the clock's decoration.

Enameled face

Pewter case

Carrying handle links bells

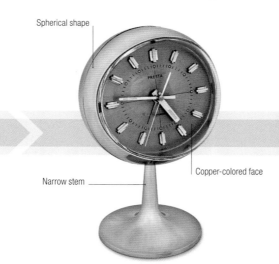

1920s **Double-bell alarm clock** | **Westclox, US**. The double-bell alarm clock probably appeared at the end of the 19th century, and Westclox made examples from the 1920s onward. A plain round dial with luminous hands in a round case is typical.

Brass inlay

Speed line

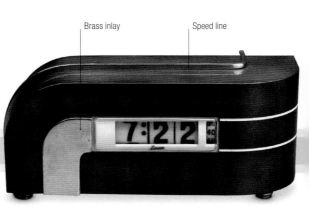

c. **1930** **Zephyr digital clock** | **Kem Weber for Lawson Time Inc., US**. The dynamic lines of this early digital clock make it a classic example of Art Deco style. Weber's heritage in industrial design is clearly visible: the piece was inspired by the streamlined "Zephyr" train.

Spherical shape

Narrow stem

Copper-colored face

1970 **Asteroid alarm clock** | **Presta, Japan**. This clock has a spherical form influenced by the Space Age, set on a pedestal base. Its hands and dial are luminous. The minutes are marked, but there are no numbers on the face.

Curves soften sleek casing

Fluorescent digital display

1976 **DN40 digital clock** | **Dieter Rams for Braun, Germany**. With the advent of LED displays, digital clocks became more practical and reliable and were common by the 1970s. This example shows Rams's trademark minimal casing.

c.1880 | **Cuckoo clock** | **Germany**. Germany's Black Forest region has been the center of cuckoo clock production for 300 years. This chalet-style wooden model, with its foliate decoration, is based on examples from Switzerland.

Stained pine case

c.1880 | **Postman's alarm clock** | **Germany**. The postman's alarm was a simple and popular clock that was usually made in Germany, in an inexpensive case. This example has a plain dial with Roman numerals.

Pendulum swings freely in an arc

1883 | **Pendulum clock** | **Galileo, Italy**. In 1641, Galileo had the idea of using a pendulum for a clock, but he died before his invention could be completed. This 19th-century model was the first realization of Galileo's original design.

c.1890 | **Mantel clock** | **Mappin & Webb, Germany**. This clock, with silvered dial and Roman numerals, has chamfered edges, a curved top, and a carrying handle; many clocks were more elaborate.

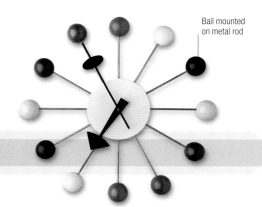

Ball mounted on metal rod

1949 | **Atomic Wall Clock** | **George Nelson for Howard Miller Clock Company, US**. The wooden balls found in models of atoms and molecules inspired this clock by George Nelson. The balls were mounted on metal rods and available in painted or wood finishes.

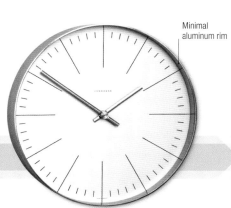

Minimal aluminum rim

1957 | **Wall clock** | **Max Bill for Junghans, Germany/Switzerland**. Bill created this clock according to the principles of good form he taught at the Ulm School of Design in Germany. Functionality and simplicity were the key aims, together with durability.

Face based on an aircraft dial

1959–1960 | **Lorenz Static clock** | **Richard Sapper, Germany**. The weighted base that contains this clock's battery ensures that it sits on its end, with its face tilted upward, always finding the correct angle. A recycled torpedo timer powers the hands' movement.

Yellow alarm hand clearly identifiable

1987 | **AB1** | **Dietrich Lubs for Braun, Germany**. The AB1 typifies Braun's goals of simplicity and good form. Its plain sans-serif numerals, clearly marked dial, elegant hands, and black case make the design a striking example of 1980s minimalism.

Full color range

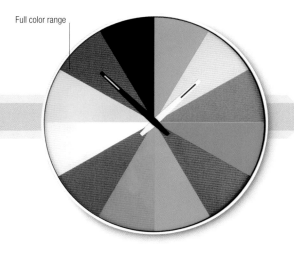

2010 | **Ultra-Flat Multicolor Wall Clock** | **Thomas Buchheim for Kikkerland, US**. This clock is made of ultra-thin plastic with a near-silent movement. It features primary and secondary colors as well as different shades of the same hue.

Drawings based on figures and nature

2015 | **Önskedröm wall clock** | **Olle Eksell for IKEA, Sweden**. Part of a series that includes kitchen tablewares, fabrics, cushions, and bed linen, the playful Önskedröm has pencil hands that point to imaginative drawings instead of numbers.

WELLS COATES

Ekco Radio AD-65

YEAR 1900 | Manufacturer E. K. Cole Ltd. (Ekco), UK | **DIMENSIONS** *Height* 16 in (40.5 cm), *Width* 15½ in (39.5 cm), *Depth* 8¼ in (21 cm) | **MATERIALS** Bakelite, stainless steel, woven cloth

Until the 1930s, radios were large units like furniture. In 1934, however, Wells Coates, a Canadian-born architect and industrial designer, created this small, round radio after winning a competition to design a plastic radio case. Influenced by Le Corbusier's minimalist work, he also produced pioneering building designs such as studio interiors for the BBC (1931).

For this radio, he molded Bakelite to create a stark, compact design made possible by the smaller electronic components that had recently become available. By the standards of the early 1930s, the radio was avant-garde. The clean, circular geometry is echoed throughout—in the round knobs and semicircular dials, for example. The AD-65 was originally finished in the typically Art Deco combination of black plastic and chrome, but it was the finish shown here—brown Bakelite in the style of walnut burl—that became the most popular. Coates produced variations on the model into the 1940s, and his designs did much to establish the blueprint for the modern radio.

He approached the problem as one of **designing** a piece of **modern machinery.**

Nikolaus **Pevsner**
Art historian

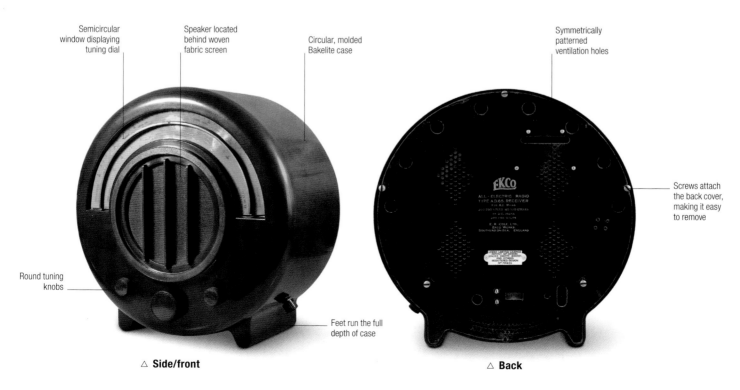

Semicircular window displaying tuning dial

Speaker located behind woven fabric screen

Circular, molded Bakelite case

Symmetrically patterned ventilation holes

Round tuning knobs

Feet run the full depth of case

Screws attach the back cover, making it easy to remove

△ **Side/front**

△ **Back**

Shiny, metal detailing
contrasts boldly with red tank

Chunky and
substantial handle

Industrial shape resembles
an outboard motor

Drinks dispenser | **Raymond Loewy for the Dole Valve Company**, 1947, France. Loewy's iconic countertop Dole Deluxe fountain dispenser shows that his pioneering streamline style was still at work after World War II. Nicknamed the "outboard motor," the fountain produces Coca-Cola drinks by simultaneously dispensing soda water and Coca-Cola syrup. This design was a huge success from the outset.

MACHINE-AGE PRODUCTS

Industrial processes and aesthetics had a greater influence on the products of the Art Deco era than they ever had before. Unprecedented numbers of affordable goods were being manufactured at the time, and designers celebrated technical progress by borrowing industrial shapes, structures, materials, and motifs. As competition increased, they used even more striking forms and technical improvements to make their products stand out, and the lean years of the Great Depression provided additional impetus to create functional designs in practical materials.

As designers moved from industrial design to products for the home, the US began to lead the way in machine-age design, but the influence of Europe remained strong, and many designers working in the US were émigrés. The US designer Raymond Loewy, for example, was born in France and brought Gallic style and flair to his smooth, clean-lined machines.

Wooden handle contrasts with metal body

Shape recalls a missile

Angled stand suggests momentum

Pencil sharpener | **Raymond Loewy**, 1933, US. Loewy's prototype pencil sharpener is a famous example of streamlined, industrial-style design. Made of chromed metal, it has clean, aerodynamic lines and a sleek, futuristic look.

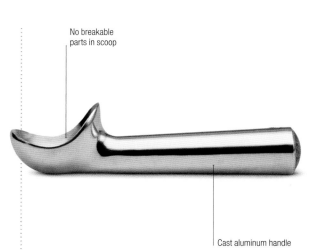

Ribbons add color

Ribbonaire fan | **W. O. Langille for the Singer Sewing Machine Company**, c. 1935, US. This small tabletop fan uses ribbons as blades, promoted as a safety feature. It has a cleanly functional Bakelite body and a three-speed electric motor.

No breakable parts in scoop

Cast aluminum handle

Ice-cream scoop | **Sherman L. Kelly for The Zeroll Co.**, 1935, US. The handle of this functionalist piece contains heat-conducting fluid to transfer warmth from the user's hand to the ice cream. It is considered the first modern ice-cream scoop.

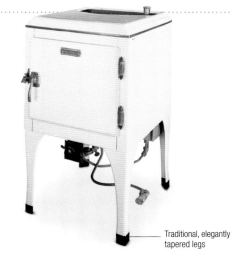

Traditional, elegantly tapered legs

Gas fridge | **Electrolux**, c. 1936. Part of the wave of new, mass-produced domestic appliances, this small refrigerator is gas-powered. Although a decidedly modern item, its square shape harks back to traditional drawing-room furniture.

Radio Nurse speaker | **Isamu Noguchi for Zenith Radio Corporation**, 1937, US. One half of a baby monitor system, the soft, elegant shape of this Bakelite speaker reflects sculptor Noguchi's Japanese American heritage.

The Chrysler Building

1930

New York City's Modernist Chrysler Building symbolizes the US's leading role in Art Deco architecture and machine-age design. It soars to 1,046 ft (319 m), its gleaming spire clad in nickel-chromed stainless steel arcs and chevron-shaped windows. Sleekly futuristic, the building's exterior and interior are dominated by geometric forms. Its shining steel decoration includes winged hubcaps, eagle gargoyles, and a pattern of streamlined cars.

Designed by William van Alen, the Chrysler Building is seen as the ultimate Art Deco skyscraper.

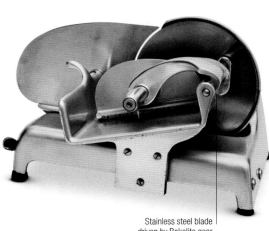

Stainless steel blade driven by Bakelite gear

Streamliner Meat slicer | **Egmont Arens for the Hobart Manufacturing Co.**, c. 1940, US. An icon of streamlining, this meat slicer's rounded surfaces are not just decorative but functional, eliminating crevices where food might get stuck.

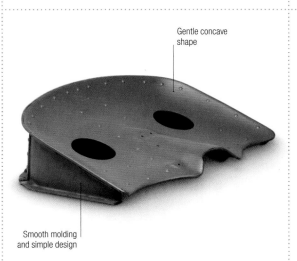

Gentle concave shape

Smooth molding and simple design

Gun-turret seat | **McDonnell Aircraft Corp.**, c. 1939–1944, US. Aeronautics provided a fund of cutting-edge ideas about design and new materials. This gun-turret mount seat is made of Structomold—laminated paper impregnated with plastic.

JOHN TJAARDA

Lincoln-Zephyr

YEAR 1936 | MANUFACTURER Lincoln assembly plant, Detroit, Michigan, for Ford Motor Company, US | DIMENSIONS *Length* 202½–210 in (514–533 cm), *Height* 69 in (175 cm) | MATERIALS Steel (frame/body combined)

The car's logo shows distinctive Art Deco styling in the lettering and bold lines. "Zephyr" was used in various product names in the Deco years to suggest speed.

Although the public was unprepared for some of the groundbreaking, streamlined car designs of the 1930s—including Chrysler's futuristic but unpopular Airflow model (1934)—Ford's Lincoln-Zephyr captured the spirit of the times with great success. This symbol of Art Deco aerodynamics set a benchmark for modern car design. Crucially, it also offered the general public a taste of luxury at a comparatively affordable price.

The Zephyr's sleek, drag-minimizing shape featured a roof and back in a long, undulating curve and teardrop arches over the wheels. It was the first Lincoln model to boast a unibody—a body and frame combined in one unit—which reduced the weight of its steel construction, and it was powered by a new kind of 12-cylinder "V" engine, whose compact form matched the car's streamlined shape. The appearance of the Zephyr owed much to the Dutch immigrant designer John Tjaarda, who was heavily influenced by aviation, but Howard Bonbright, Edsel Ford, and Bob Gregorie also contributed. There were various Zephyr designs during the 1930s and '40s, but the Zephyr name was not used after 1942. The model shown here is the three-window coupe.

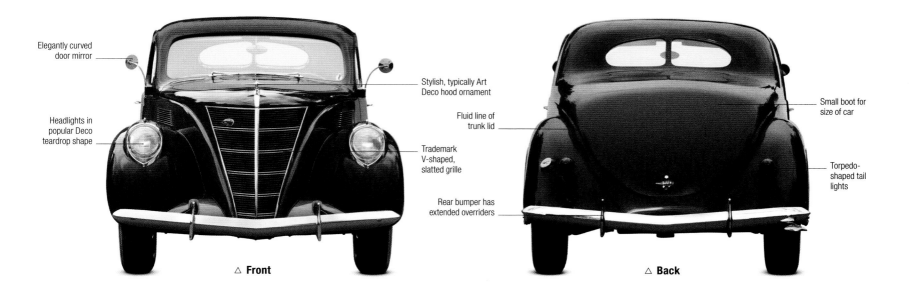

Elegantly curved
door mirror

Headlights in
popular Deco
teardrop shape

Stylish, typically Art
Deco hood ornament

Trademark
V-shaped,
slatted grille

△ **Front**

Fluid line of
trunk lid

Rear bumper has
extended overriders

Small boot for
size of car

Torpedo-
shaped tail
lights

△ **Back**

Its striking appearance expresses the most modern principles of aerodynamic design.

Car brochure, **Lincoln-Zephyr**
Lincoln Motor Company, 1936

OPULENT
GEMS

As with much Art Deco, the French took a lead in jewelry, excelling at opulent, gem-encrusted pieces—Cartier was a leading luxury brand, and although it placed its extravagant jewels on modern Deco shapes, it avoided the more extreme geometry and streamlining of jewelers such as Anders Nilsson. From the 1920s onward, Coco Chanel pioneered costume jewelry. By the 1930s, platinum had taken over from gold as the precious metal of choice, and there was a boom in affordable, mass-produced pieces. Designers made inventive use of modern, industrial materials such as Bakelite, and turned to enamels for striking, rich color. Jewelry design was widely influenced by Cubist art, the Ballets Russes's bold sets, and costume designs, Egyptomania, Mayan temples, and African art from the French colonies. As ever, jewelry also complemented contemporary fashion—the trend for sleeveless dresses, for example, made bangles a popular accessory.

Egyptomania

In 1922, archaeologist Howard Carter breached the doorway of a sealed tomb in the Valley of the Kings near Luxor, Egypt, and saw "everywhere the glint of gold." As the wondrous objects emerged from the tomb of the boy pharaoh Tutankhamun, the craze known as Tutmania erupted.

French jeweler Pierre Cartier correctly predicted in 1923 that "the discovery of the tomb will bring in some sweeping changes in fashion in jewelry." In the following years, Cartier created an Egyptian temple gate clock, while Van Cleef & Arpels depicted Ancient Egyptian–style vultures, dogs, and baboons on some of their pieces. Other jewelers produced scarab beetle, snake, and sphinx motifs.

Egyptomania fueled the imagination of designers of everything from luxury liners to retail fashion. Even British aristocrat Lady Elizabeth Bowes-Lyons (mother of Queen Elizabeth II) sported a Tut-inspired outfit on her honeymoon.

Detail of winged scarab beetle, Egyptian Theatre, Hollywood, California.

Bold openwork

Steel cabochons on wings

Scarab bangle | 1920s. This copper costume bangle is made from inexpensive materials. The centerpiece is a scarab beetle cast from Bakelite—the scarab was sacred to the Ancient Egyptians and became a popular motif for Deco designers.

Neat, compact shape

Frog brooch | **Chanel**, 1927, France. This costume brooch in the popular Deco shape of a frog is made from enamel on a lead casting. The rhinestones on the eyes and webbed feet are pavé set (placed closely together so the backing is not visible).

Silver brooch | 1920s, US. This openwork brooch has gilded and polychrome-enameled Egyptian bird, reptile, and plant forms, two ruby glass cabochons, and, at the center, a large stone scarab beetle.

Diamonds frame the sapphires

Square- and baguette-cut sapphires

Hinged platinum and gold bracelet-bangle | **Boucheron**, 1930s, France. The two bucklelike ends of this bangle have four rows of invisibly set sapphires contrasting with brilliant-cut diamonds. Boucheron also designed a hair clip to go with it.

Side pieces
stepped like
ancient temples

Sterling-silver bracelet | **Wiwen Nilsson for Anders Nilsson**, 1930s, **Sweden**. Set within angular lines typical of Modernist Deco jewelry, this bracelet's two chunks of black onyx provide the perfect foil for its faceted rock crystal.

Typical Art Deco
color contrast

Interlocking geometric
shapes—an Art Deco
and Van Cleef feature

Platinum pin | **Van Cleef & Arpels**, *c.* 1932, **France**. This pin carries five rings set with 84 six-carat, round-cut diamonds. The platinum bar is set with 14 four-carat, caliber-cut Burmese blue sapphires, with a large, round-cut diamond at its center.

Rubies set
invisibly into
channel

Platinum ring | **Van Cleef & Arpels**, 1940s, **France**. Championing the machine age, this ring has invisibly set rubies. Van Cleef introduced a method of cutting stones to slot precisely into a parallel setting so that they look unsupported.

Diamond wristwatch | **Cartier**, 1920s, **France**. Cartier became famous for its extravagant wristwatches. This ladies' timepiece has a platinum case. Typically, Cartier adopted the simple, geometric forms of Art Deco but adorned them with diamonds.

Short bands
joining elements

Square face

Roman
numerals

CARTIER
PARIS

B TA S.G.D.G

Outer acid-etched layer of vitrified glass

Etched papyrus flowers and olive branches in an Egyptian theme

Highly stylized natural forms in an intertwined pattern

Egyptian-style cameo glass vase | **Daum Frères**, **1926**, **France**. This vase is an excellent example of the fine cameo glass produced by the glassworks of the Daum brothers, Antonin and Auguste. Cameo glass features multiple, colored layers and designs that have been etched mechanically or with acid. This vase is made of a colorless glass with milky powder inclusions and a glazed blue outer layer, which has been acid-etched with stylized papyrus flowers and olive branches.

STATEMENT
GLASSWARE

Art Deco glass was extremely creative, expressive, and technically innovative. Beautiful effects were achieved by working with layers of glass and creating vivid layers of color by means of etching or enameling. Molding was explored and difficult techniques such as *pâte-de-verre* (translucent glass) and *pâte-de-cristal* (transparent glass) were utilized for wealthier clients. Fluid motifs from Art Nouveau still lingered on, but bold, modern shapes were gaining currency and substantial, thick-walled pieces were popular. French glassmakers—such as Gabriel Argy-Rousseau, François-Émile Décorchement, and the Daum brothers—dominated the field, especially with luxury work, while those in the US produced some fine Modernist pieces. Stylized motifs from nature were a major theme, as were ancient civilizations, notably in the Egyptomania craze triggered by the 1922 discovery of Tutankhamun's tomb.

Les Baigneuses | **Marcel Goupy**, *c.* 1926, France. Enameled glassware was Goupy's specialism, with decoration often featuring figures or landscapes. Here, he depicts female bathers in a rural setting.

Streaked effect suggests marble or semiprecious stones

Classical vase | **François-Émile Décorchement**, 1920s, France. Made of *pâte-de-verre* (a paste produced from powdered glass), this vase's color was created by adding metallic oxides. The marbling and face motifs are homages to ancient civilizations.

Bulb vase | **Daum Frères**, 1920s, France. This twin-handled vase demonstrates many of the Daum brothers' trademark techniques—the mottled, richly colored background; the hammered metal effect; and applied foil-backed decoration.

Handle's flowing style recalls Art Nouveau

Cigarette box | **Gabriel Argy-Rousseau**, 1923, France. This translucent *pâte-de verre* piece is entitled Ibis, as the handle recalls the shape of the sacred ancient Egyptian bird. The rich, deep colors are typical of Argy-Rousseau.

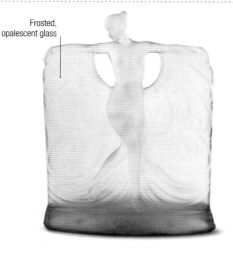

Frosted, opalescent glass

Glass figure | **Marius-Ernest Sabino**, *c.* 1923–1939, France. This lamp is a homage to René Lalique's hugely popular *Suzanne au Bain* sculpture. It could be ordered with a stand that illuminated it from beneath.

Cameo glass techniques

c. 30 BCE–present

Originally developed by gemstone engravers, the cameo technique was later adapted by glassmakers who would blow and fuse layers of differently colored glass together before acid-etching, hand-cutting, or sand-blasting away the first layer to create a surface in low relief. Later developments, such as using hydrofluoric acid to etch away background color, resulted in a great variety of stunning multilayered designs.

The cameo technique reached a pinnacle in the work of Émile Gallé, who could create elegant designs from as many as five layers of colored glass, through a combination of cutting, hand-carving, and acid-etching.

Gazelle bowl | **Sidney Waugh for Steuben**, *c.* 1939, US. The clean shapes of this bowl are Modernist, and Waugh's etched frieze of delicate gazelles is typically stylized. Gazelles had been a popular 1920s motif, readopted here by Waugh.

Glass became the most versatile and stylish of modern materials.

Ghislaine **Wood**

Four-layered cameo vase *c.* 1900, Émile Gallé. With acid-etched and wheel-carved layers in pink and amethyst.

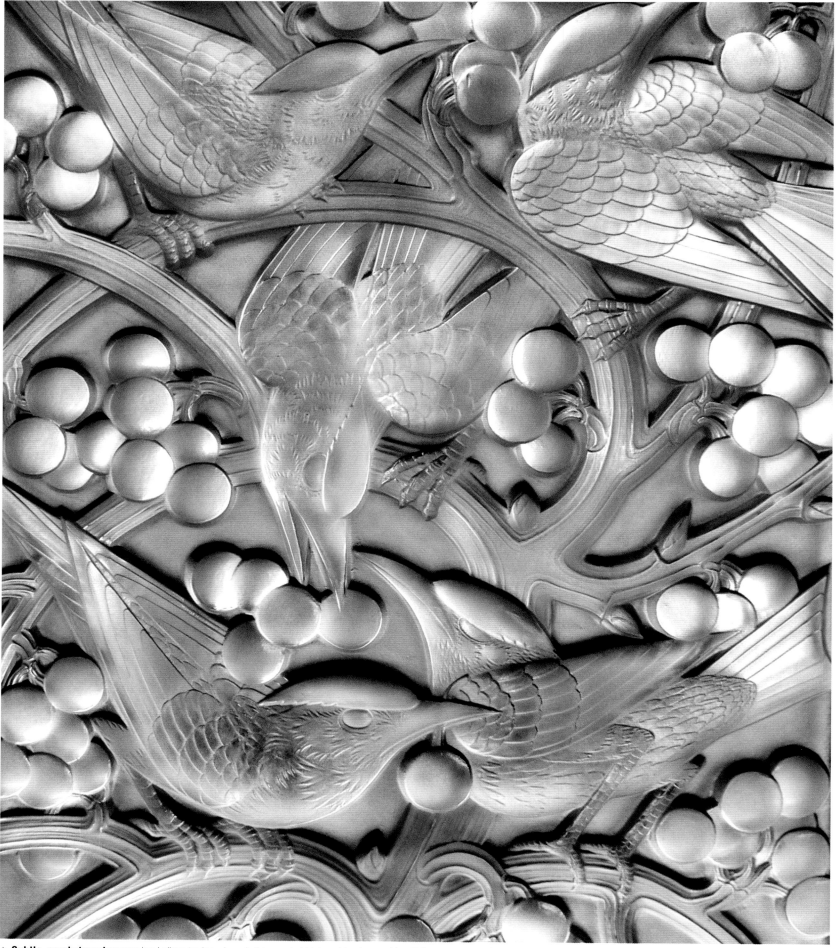

△ **Subtle, pearly translucence** is a Lalique trademark, as in this panel of birds and berries used in a Pullman car on the Orient Express train.

René Jules
Lalique

First a leading contributor to Art Nouveau style with his stunning jewelry, René Jules Lalique then forged a second successful career as a glassmaker who helped define Art Deco style. Lalique's jewelry had a sensuous style featuring exquisite dragonflies, scarabs, and flowers in combs, brooches, and pendants that combined gold and silver with subtle gemstones; unusual materials such as horn; and delicate, translucent *plique-à-jour* enameling.

In the 1890s, Lalique began to design glass perfume bottles for companies such as Coty and Worth. He was an astute businessman and a hands-on perfectionist, and by the 1920s he was heading a thriving, glass business producing everything from vases and plates to car mascots and lamps. Although a darling of the luxury, limited-edition market, Lalique also created more affordable pieces—especially during the Great Depression—and his factory at Wingen was technologically advanced in its mass-production molding methods.

Lalique used methods such as hand blowing and *cire perdue* (lost wax) to cast delicate shapes in his glass. He typically used detailed relief patterns, natural motifs, and female figures in opalescent white glass with subtle blue hints, but he also worked in stronger colors such as amber and cobalt. Lalique's glassware showcased the simpler lines of Deco style but still retained a flowing Art Nouveau element.

Life

1860–1945

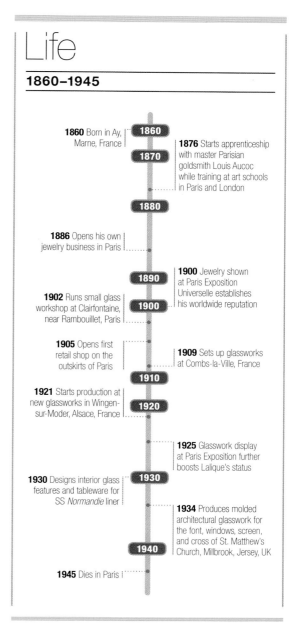

1860 Born in Ay, Marne, France

1876 Starts apprenticeship with master Parisian goldsmith Louis Aucoc while training at art schools in Paris and London

1886 Opens his own jewelry business in Paris

1900 Jewelry shown at Paris Exposition Universelle establishes his worldwide reputation

1902 Runs small glass workshop at Clairfontaine, near Rambouillet, Paris

1905 Opens first retail shop on the outskirts of Paris

1909 Sets up glassworks at Combs-la-Ville, France

1921 Starts production at new glassworks in Wingen-sur-Moder, Alsace, France

1925 Glasswork display at Paris Exposition further boosts Lalique's status

1930 Designs interior glass features and tableware for SS *Normandie* liner

1934 Produces molded architectural glasswork for the font, windows, screen, and cross of St. Matthew's Church, Millbrook, Jersey, UK

1945 Dies in Paris

Gold *cloisons* (cells) with *plique-à-jour* enameling

Stylized dragonfly heads

Globe-shaped stopper adds decorative note

Simple shape with clean lines

Dragonfly pendant | 1903–1905. The dragonfly motif, colorful enameling, and curving shapes of this delicately detailed piece are typical of Lalique's Art Nouveau jewelry.

Perfume bottle | **For Molinard**, *c.* 1928. Form was very important to Lalique, and he produced numerous perfume bottles in simple shapes, often with minimal or no color.

Flower heads highlighted by dark enameled centers

Nemours bowl | 1929. This popular Nemours bowl, created in several variations, features repeating rows of flowers, decreasing in size. It is made from thick clear and frosted glass.

Lamp angle
can be rotated

Adjustable
stand

Angled shade was one
of Dell's trademarks

Chromed
metal finish

Rondella lamp | **Christian Dell for
Schwintzer & Gräff**, 1926, Germany.
A master silversmith and metalworker, Dell
worked as a foreman in the Bauhaus metal
workshop and helped forge the Bauhaus
style, which became a major Modernist
influence on Deco design. This unadorned
Rondella lamp, made from two connecting
pieces of metal, was one of his most
important lamp designs.

ART DECO
LIGHTING

In many ways, lighting was at the forefront of Art Deco design—which is perhaps
unsurprising considering that household electricity itself was still relatively new—and
lighting pieces were therefore an adventurous product. Pared-down, "industrial,"
Modernist designs that made use of modern materials such as Bakelite proliferated, but more stylized pieces were also popular,
often decorated with cameo glass and ornate metalwork and reflecting fashionable Deco motifs, such as stylized plants.

Perhaps the best-known *moderne* example is the still-loved "poise" lamp, such as George Carwardine's famous British
Anglepoise model, which was developed in the 1930s. In the same vein, Christian Dell and Walter von Nessen were notable for their
strikingly simple, adjustable floor and table lamps—Nessen pioneered the use of materials such as fiberglass and spun aluminum.
Deco lamps were also a major showcase of chrome plating, a material that was refined in the mid-1920s.

Shimmering glass shade features oak leaves, acorns, and fluttering birds

Stand decorated like an ivy-covered tree

Floor lamp | **Daum Frères (shade)**, France. This lamp has an Art Deco cameo glass uplighter shade and a slender cast metal stand, possibly made by Louis Majorelle, with whom the Daum brothers often worked.

Lampshade finished in baked enamel

Floor lamp | **Walter von Nessen for Nessen Studio Inc.**, *c.* 1927–1935, US. A typically bold adjustable floor lamp in chrome-plated brass by the pioneering lighting designer Walter von Nessen, this piece has a Bauhaus simplicity.

Desk lamp | **Wells Coates for E. K. Cole Ltd.**, 1930s, UK. This elegantly curving desk lamp is made from one of the newly fashionable plastics available at the time. It was produced by E. K. Cole Ltd., well known for its EKCO radios.

Chrome and enamel lamp | 1930s, US. A striking blend of bold shapes and colors, the stepped base and tiered shaft of this table lamp are reminiscent of the motifs taken from ancient temples, a subject of fascination for Deco designers.

Masque lamp | **Helen Dryden (attributed) for the Revere Copper & Brass Co.**, 1930s, US. This curved mood lamp, designed for a bedside table or hallway, is reminiscent of the head sculptures of the Modernist artist Amedeo Modigliani.

Anglepoise® lamp | 1930s. The clever combination of springs and articulated parts in Anglepoise® lamps meant they could be bent into a wide range of positions. The design could also be easily adapted to desk, floor, or wall models.

Bolide desk lamp | **Gustave Miklos for Jumo/Brevete**, *c.* 1940–1945, France. This daringly Modernist articulated lamp is made from black Bakelite and folds down neatly. A switch in the base turns the lamp on automatically when it is opened.

WORDS AND IMAGES

Art Deco designers welcomed advances in technology, urbanization, and commercialization. With so many new products and services to sell, it was a great age for graphics, and posters became emblematic melting pots of everything the bold Deco style had to offer. The glamour of Hollywood movies and international travel was mirrored in campaigns promoting elegant lifestyles and high-speed train trips to enticing destinations. Many posters were influenced by modern art movements, and both the dynamism of the Italian Futurists and the geometric motifs of the Cubists can be seen in the work of artists such as Cassandre. Text was used to great effect, and designers sometimes created their own fonts, which often reflected soaring Art Deco architecture.

Vanity Fair **cover** | **Georges Lepape**, 1919, US. Influential fashion illustrator and graphic artist Lepape created this simple, uncluttered image. The design has the refined elegance typical of many French Deco commercial artists of the 1920s.

Underground poster | **Horace Taylor**, 1924, UK. Taylor's vivid colors reinforce this poster's message that the Tube is for all. A wide range of 1920s fashions and people are packed onto the escalators—from operagoers and commuters to children.

La Joie de Paris **poster** | **Zig (Louis Gaudin)**, 1927, **France**. Many posters for Josephine Baker and her Paris revues were produced during this period. Zig's vibrant color and tropical imagery hint at Baker's glamorous exoticism.

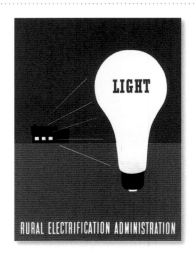

Monte Carlo poster | **Roger Broders**, *c.* 1930, France. This poster for France's PLM railroad celebrates the high life. Broders used bold color, punchy light and shadow, and a dramatic viewpoint to suggest the glamour of the destination.

Train poster | **Munetsugu Satomi**, 1937, Japan. In this Japanese railroad advertisement, Satomi's view from a train suggests thrilling speed. It shows both traditional and modern features in the landscape to convey Japan's rapid change.

Electricity poster | **Lester Beall**, 1937, US. This poster for the government agency that brought electricity to rural America has Beall's trademark bold and spare approach. It helped place him at the forefront of Modernist graphics in the US.

Serif font contrasts with the lighter background text

Cloudlike softening of the text creates a more harmonious background

Strong lines of the compass mirror the tracks to imply forward motion

Train tracks stretching into the distance suggest a sense of progress

French train poster | **Cassandre, 1929, France**. The work of the French designer Cassandre (Adolphe Jean-Marie Mouron) celebrated the limitless possibilities industrialization seemed to offer. In this poster for the French railroads, he blends the aesthetics of contemporary art with commercial appeal. The Cubist-style montage of a metallic compass with the optimistic bright blue of the sky suggests the potential promised by the march of technology.

△ **The Peninsula Hotel** on the Bund, Shanghai's central waterfront area in the International Settlement quarter, features a luxurious circular stairway in a modern interpretation of Art Deco styling.

△ **Luggage label** | Broadway Mansions hotel, Shanghai, *c.* 1930s

Shanghai

n the Art Deco years of the 1920s and 1930s, certain cities around the world became dazzling centers dedicated to the pursuit of pleasure—frivolity and decadence were important ingredients of Deco style. Shanghai was a leading example, notable for its blend of East and West. While many Western designers were inspired by traditional Chinese and Japanese styles, Shanghai itself became a playground for a Deco approach that was highly American in style.

Shanghai was the blueprint for a modern city and looked to the West for the latest architectural ideas. The most visible signs of this were the high-rise Modernist and Deco department stores, movie theaters, hotels, and apartment buildings that echoed the New York skyline and dominated the city in the 1930s. Skyscraper hotels were an important meeting point for the jet set, as the glitterati moved from cocktail bars to the racetrack and from watching American movies to dancing. The deluxe Cathay Hotel featured Deco style inside and out; the Peninsula Hotel and Park Hotel both boasted glamorous Deco interiors; and the Broadway Mansions hotel was built in the shape of a ziggurat.

One of the key figures to put a Deco stamp on the city was entrepreneur Victor Sassoon, who demolished huge numbers of old buildings to make way for new Deco ones. Much of his work was seen in the British American International Settlement quarter, a hymn of praise to Western-style capitalism and culture.

Key dates

1863–1941

1863 International Settlement quarter of Shanghai formed from US and British possessions

1860

1895 End of first Sino-Japanese War brings increased foreign investment to Shanghai

1890

1917 Great World entertainment complex opens in Shanghai

1920

1930 Great World acquires new owner, who expands the center

1932 Art Deco Cathay Hotel built by businessman Victor Sassoon

1934 Modernist/Deco Park Hotel, Shanghai, then Asia's highest building, is erected

1937 Chinese/Japanese tensions lead Japan to bomb Shanghai

1939 W. H. Auden and Christopher Isherwood's *Journey to a War* documents the decadence of 1930s Shanghai

1941 Japan takes control of Shanghai

1950

***A Great Love* cover** | Qian Juntao, *c.* 1930. This image fuses traditional Chinese characters with Art Deco styling. French cubism inspired the geometry of the two figures.

Modern face powder | Yamana Ayao for Shiseido, 1932. Ayao designed this Deco-style packaging for pioneering Japanese firm Shiseido to appeal to a sophisticated audience.

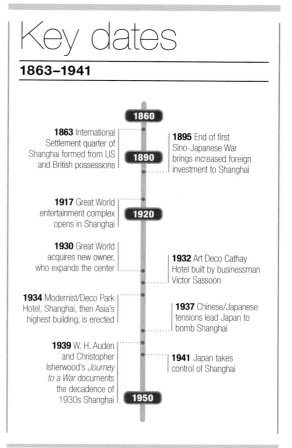

***Kuangwu* (Crazy wild dancing)** | Zhang Zhengyu, 1929. Magazines such as *Shanghai Sketch* stimulated the Chinese appetite for the high life with illustrations such as this.

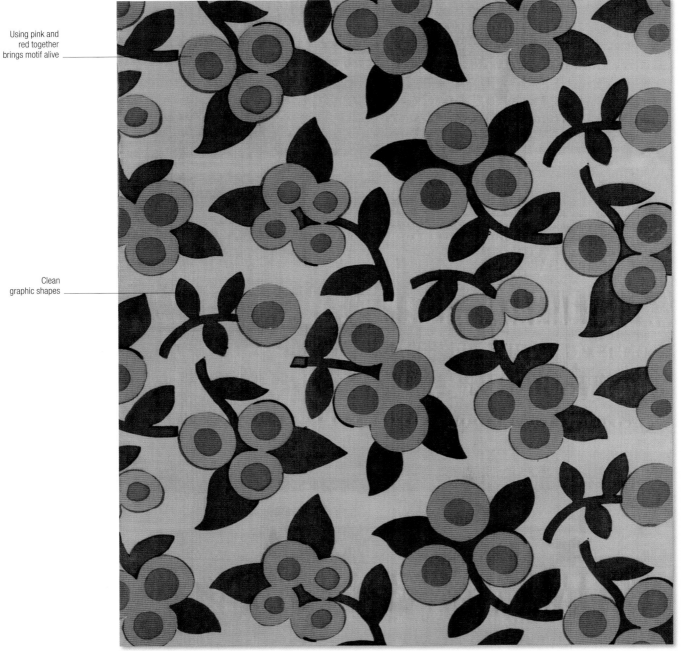

Using pink and red together brings motif alive

Clean graphic shapes

Printed Japanese silk | **Atelier Martine**, before 1913, France. Naive forms and strong colors were hallmarks of Atelier Martine fabrics, as seen in this textile featuring bold, simplified flower shapes and a vivid, contrasting color palette. Overseen by Parisian couturier Paul Poiret, the company also ran an art school for working-class girls.

ARTISTS'
FABRICS

Two major Art Deco characteristics—natural themes and bold color—were well represented by fabrics of the era. Stylized flowers and leaves were common, along with the vivid hues of early Deco: hot pinks, reds, oranges, and lavenders in unconventional combinations, as well as gold. Atelier Martine—the design studio of pioneering French couturier Paul Poiret—was producing such fabrics before World War I. France in general led the way in textiles, inspired by the bright designs of the Ballets Russes, the ballet company established in 1909 by Russian impresario Serge Diaghilev. Many artists also dabbled in textiles, including the great French colorists Henri Matisse and Raoul Dufy, and British sculptor Frank Dobson. Meanwhile, the US was home to another significant textile school, featuring American designers such as Donald Deskey and Ruth Reeves. Both were influenced by abstract, geometric painting and modern architecture, and they also worked on the famed Deco interiors of New York's Radio City Music Hall in the early 1930s.

Sonia **Delaunay**

1885–1979

The vibrant textile designs of Sonia Delaunay are an extension of her abstract painting style. In the words of her husband and fellow artist, Robert, their work "would depend only on color and its contrast but would develop over time, simultaneously perceived at a single moment." Based on color blocks, Delaunay's paintings and textile designs were a stepping stone for abstract art—the visual equivalent in many ways of the music of French jazz artist Django Reinhardt, a friend of the Delaunays' son.

Bluette design | **Atelier Martine**, *c.* 1912, France. This design was screen-printed onto a cotton and linen mix. A bold profusion of stylized flowers and leaves tumble across an earthy background.

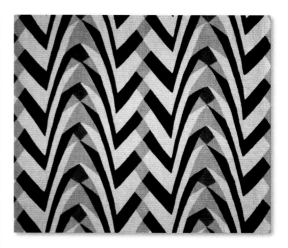

Furnishing linen | **F. Gregory Brown for William Foxton Ltd.**, *c.* 1922, UK. The avant-garde design is typical of Foxton, in a monochrome scheme often favored by Deco designers. This textile won a gold medal at the 1925 Paris Exhibition.

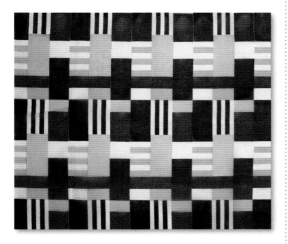

Tissu simultané Silk No. 46 | **Sonia Delaunay**, 1924, France. This strongly abstract geometric work features a stepped motif, a popular device during the Art Deco era that recalled the roofs of Mayan temples.

Floral cotton | **Raoul Dufy for Bianchini-Férier**, *c.* 1930, France. Dufy is known for his bold, colorful floral textiles in the Deco style, but this cotton print hints at his love of more traditional designs.

Screen-printed linen | **Donald Deskey**, *c.* 1930–1931, US. Deskey took a traditional fabric—woven woolen tartan—and transformed it into this print by tilting it and using an unconventional color palette.

Dancing Women lino-printed linen | **Frank Dobson**, 1938, UK. Dobson's early sculptures were influenced by Cubist painters, and the simplified, statuesque women on this fabric are reminiscent of Picasso's nudes.

Avis cotton and rayon furnishing fabric | **Marion Dorn for Edinburgh Weavers**, *c.* 1939, UK. Much sought after for her stylish Modernist carpets, Dorn also designed fabrics. This particular pattern is named after the Latin word for bird.

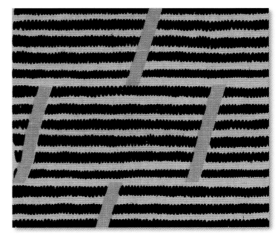

Striped linen | **Ruth Reeves for Morley Fletcher Ltd.**, 1948, US. By the early 1930s, Reeves had produced textiles that forged a radical new American style. Many pieces—such as this late one—showed a love of geometry and abstraction.

ALL THAT GLITTERS

The outstanding feature of the facade of the world-famous Folies-Bergère theater in Paris, France, is undoubtedly this large relief by sculptor and decorator Maurice Picaud (known as Pico). The sculpture, which dates from the theater's remodeling in 1926–1928, depicts the Russian dancer Lila Nikolska, who was a performer at the Folies-Bergère. Pico's sleek and glamorous depiction of the female form, together with the surrounding patterns of cloudlike curves, powerful sunbursts, and stacked rectangles that resemble stylized buildings, is the epitome of Art Deco style.

In the 1920s and 1930s, this alluring type of decoration was especially popular in theaters and cinemas that wished to project an image of glamorous modernity. Art Deco theaters the world over have similar carvings, but Pico's relief is a particularly large and prominent example. The facade was originally covered with copper foil, but this was replaced with gold leaf during a recent restoration, making the overall effect even more vibrant and eye-catching.

Art Deco architecture was an architecture of ornament, geometry, energy, retrospection, optimism, color, texture, light....

Patricia **Bayer,** 1992

Folies-Bergère theater facade, Paris, France, Maurice Picaud, 1926–1928 Although the dancer's face and hair are quite detailed, her body is highly stylized. The way that her back and limbs recede in a series of stepped-back layers is typical of Art Deco sculptural relief.

MODERNISM
1910–1939

Less is more.

LUDWIG MIES VAN DER ROHE, ARCHITECT AND BAUHAUS DIRECTOR

MODERNISM
Introduction

After World War I, many of Europe's most progressive designers wanted to make a break with the styles of the previous era. Their new approach, known today as Modernism, concentrated on simple forms, plain surfaces, and uncluttered interiors, and dispensed with ornament almost completely, based on the notion that the form of an object should depend on its function.

This change was partly a reaction to the decorative excesses of Art Nouveau, partly a longing for a new beginning after the war, and partly the result of a feeling that the machine age merited a different style of design—one that was truly modern. It was also influenced by the ideas emerging from new design schools, such as the

Bauhaus in Germany, and by new political movements, such as Communism in Russia. These blended art with ideals, preferring objects that could be standardized to suit the needs of ordinary people, and rejecting decoration as being an obstacle to mass production.

Design and architecture

Modernist designers explored the use of new materials such as plywood and tubular steel. Some products were mass-produced and others were made by hand, but they all looked strikingly new. Many of the most innovative designs were for pieces of furniture. Designers such as Eileen Gray and Charlotte Perriand produced metal-

PLYWOOD

Modernist furniture designers made the most of bent plywood. Bending wood reduced the need for so many different components of furniture, allowing fewer joints and smoother overall designs.

ABSTRACT GRAPHICS

Graphic art was influenced by Cubist paintings and the propaganda posters of the Constructivists. Designers favored strong patterns and shapes, and type was bold and often in more than one color.

GEOMETRIC FORMS

Abstract painters often based their compositions on simple but subtle patterns of squares, rectangles, circles, and other geometric forms. These had a profound influence on Modernist metalware and textile designs.

Let us together create the **new** building of the future which will be **all in one:** architecture and sculpture and painting.

Walter **Gropius**

framed tables and chairs, as did Le Corbusier and Mies van der Rohe, both of whom also designed Modernist buildings with flat roofs, white concrete walls, and large windows. The work of these designers and architects was shown in a memorable exhibition at MoMA, New York, in 1932, and from then on, critics and designers began to refer to the movement as the International Style, paying tribute to its global extent.

Fit for purpose

True to their maxim of "form follows function," Modernists went to great lengths to make their furniture comfortable, and the teachers at the Bauhaus emphasized that

everything—from pots to lamps—should be well crafted. The school's original aim had been to counter the revival of ornate historical styles by creating a new formal language of design that united the fine and applied arts. Some courses even included psychological education.

Modernism, therefore, earned its fashionable status, but it did not supplant other styles, such as Art Deco, that were in vogue at around the same time. Although the development of Modernism was halted by the rise of Nazism and the outbreak of World War II, the influence of Modernist architects and designers survived well into the postwar period, leading ultimately to a softer, less severe interpretation of the style during the 1950s.

TUBULAR STEEL

In the 1920s, designers began to make furniture from tubular steel. Affordable, flexible, durable, and lightweight, it was ideal for them, and the resulting designs were a perfect blend of form and function.

BLOCKS OF COLOR

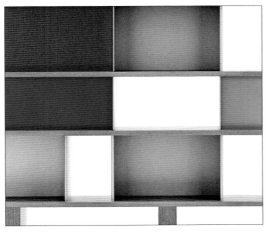

To Modernists, form was more important than ornament, so solid blocks of strong color were often used to emphasize shape and create contrast. Primary colors and black and white were preferred.

MINIMALISM

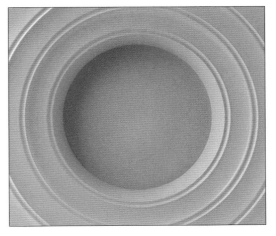

The Modernist style was minimalist, rejecting the fussiness of 19th-century decorative tradition. Forms were plain and simply adorned, but they were often made of fine materials and immaculately finished.

△ **The Bauhaus building in Dessau** was designed by Walter Gropius in 1925–1926. Later architects imitated its functional layout, concrete structure, and glass curtain walls.

The Bauhaus

△ **B3 club chair** | Marcel Breuer, 1927–1928

ounded in 1919, the Bauhaus became internationally known as a dynamic school of art and design within 10 years. The Modernist outlook it promoted—that the form of an object was determined by its function—had a lasting influence on both designers and manufacturers. The school was established by German architect Walter Gropius, who attracted some of the most innovative designers and artists to teach there, including Wassily Kandinsky, Paul Klee, and László Moholy-Nagy. Its original aim was to create a unity of all the arts and to modernize the ideas of the Arts and Crafts movement by teaching a practical knowledge of craftsmanship. Students took a preliminary course, learning subjects such as color theory and exploring the properties of different materials; then they specialized, working in fields such as metalwork, textiles, or cabinetmaking. Bauhaus designers created stunning objects, from elegant tableware to lamps, which combined a functionalist aesthetic with well-honed craftsmanship. Later, Gropius and his successors moved toward industrial design and mass production.

By the early 1930s, however, Germany's right-wing leaders were turning against the school's radical ideas and products, and the Bauhaus was forced to close. Its teachers dispersed—many leaving Germany for the US—but they took their ideas with them, spreading the influence of this seminal school of design.

Key dates

1919–1933

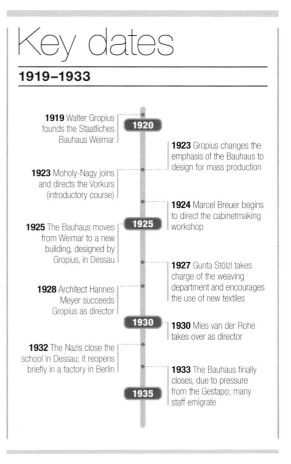

1919 Walter Gropius founds the Staatliches Bauhaus Weimar

1920

1923 Gropius changes the emphasis of the Bauhaus to design for mass production

1923 Moholy-Nagy joins and directs the Vorkurs (introductory course)

1924 Marcel Breuer begins to direct the cabinetmaking workshop

1925 The Bauhaus moves from Weimar to a new building, designed by Gropius, in Dessau

1925

1927 Gunta Stölzl takes charge of the weaving department and encourages the use of new textiles

1928 Architect Hannes Meyer succeeds Gropius as director

1930

1930 Mies van der Rohe takes over as director

1932 The Nazis close the school in Dessau; it reopens briefly in a factory in Berlin

1933 The Bauhaus finally closes, due to pressure from the Gestapo; many staff emigrate

1935

Table lamp | 1926. The Bauhaus's pared-down approach to design influenced many Modernist household items from the period, including this table lamp.

Adjustable shade

Curved support

Bauhaus poster | Joost Schmidt, 1923. This lithograph print uses modern typography, bright colors, and arresting shapes and angles to advertise a Bauhaus exhibition.

Upright supports books

Lacquered pattern

Bookends | Marianne Brandt, c. 1930. These L-shaped bookends are made of simple sheet metal lacquered with an abstract geometrical pattern.

Cantilever chair | **Mart Stam**, 1926–1927, Germany.
Directly influenced by the tubular steel chairs that Marcel
Breuer developed at the Bauhaus in 1925–1926, Mart Stam
created his first cantilevered tubular furniture for a house
in Stuttgart's Modernist Weissenhof housing exhibition.
Stam saw tubular furniture as a product that could be
made available to the masses at a low cost.

Leather seat

Polished tubular steel
frame (Stam originally used
lengths of standard piping)

TUBULAR METAL
FURNITURE

During the 1920s, designers began to see the huge potential
of tubular metal, especially steel, in furniture production. Many of
these designers were architects, including Marcel Breuer, who was
the first to adopt the material, sparking a new trend for sleek, metal-framed furniture with the designs that he produced at the
Bauhaus (see pp.168–169) in Germany during the mid-1920s.

Breuer, along with Mart Stam and Ludwig Mies van der Rohe, used tubular steel to produce chairs that were strong
yet light, simple and uncluttered in design, and visually unobtrusive—perfect for a Modernist interior. Steel furniture was
low-maintenance and easy to mass-produce, and progressive manufacturers quickly saw its potential, so although relatively
few of the many designs made it to factory production, those that did became classics and are still in demand today.

Arm attached to frame with metal piece

Seat wraps under the frame

Frame curves gracefully beneath seat

MR armchair | **Ludwig Mies van der Rohe**, 1927, **Germany**. Early examples of the MR, which first appeared at the Stuttgart Exhibition, had cane seats, but the chair was also made with a leather seat and back, as in this example.

Flexible rubber belt is hooked onto frame

Varnished tubular steel frame

Chaise Sandows | **René Herbst**, 1928–1929, **France**. In this chair, Herbst combined a simple steel frame with a seat and back made up of multiple rubber stretchers. He aimed to create a comfortable chair using minimal materials.

Dipping tubular arm

Single sheet of canvas

Curve to base provides foot

Sessel Siesta armchair | **Ladislav Žák and Antonín Kybal**, 1930, **Czechoslovakia (now Czech Republic)**. This deck chair–like design is one of the simplest tubular steel chairs, but its clean lines and shape make it sophisticated nonetheless.

Tubular steel

c. 1920–present

One of the most important discoveries in 20th-century furniture, tubular steel was apparently inspired by the handlebars of Marcel Breuer's bicycle. Breuer saw no reason why, if tubular steel could be bent into handlebars, it could not be used to make furniture, too, especially since it was cheap, malleable, and easy to mass-produce.

By the 1927 Weissenhof Exhibition in Stuttgart, Germany, several designers had tubular steel chairs to show. The exhibition also included a specially built collection of Modernist houses, all furnished in the latest fashions, and the style quickly spread beyond furniture. More and more uses were found for tubular steel, and the material became very popular for both construction and decoration.

Tubular steel frame wraps around to form back

Kindergarten table and chairs | **Giuseppe Terragni**, *c.* 1930, **Italy**. By adding thin, brightly colored plywood backs and seats to metal-framed chairs, Giuseppe Terragni was able to produce furniture that was practical, durable, and light—ideal for use by young children.

This Victorian coach house was refurbished in the 1980s with the addition of a tubular steel spiral staircase.

Chromium-plated steel frame

Leather-covered seat

Genni reclining chair | **Gabriele Mucchi**, 1935, **Italy**. Mucchi, part of the anti-fascist Corrente Italian design group, combined a steel frame with springs for this recliner with a seat that can be set in two different positions.

Pressed aluminum seat

Rubber foot

Landi armchair | **Hans Coray**, 1938–1939, **Switzerland**. This outdoor chair was designed for the Swiss National Exhibition. It is made of aluminum (a major Swiss product) and is therefore rustproof and very light, making it perfect for use outdoors.

NEW FORMS

The Modernist designers of the period after World War I had different outlooks but shared several key principles: they wanted to reduce their designs to fundamentals, stripping away ornament and old ideas; they believed that an object's function should determine its form; and they preferred to produce pieces that were transparent in design instead of concealing details of their construction or materials. A range of chairs from the interwar period demonstrate these principles. Gerrit Rietveld's revolutionary Red-Blue and Zig-Zag chairs went back to basics, using inexpensive woods to redefine their structure and form. Other designers, such as Hans and Wassili Luckhardt, studied the human body and the way in which people sat or reclined so they could create chairs in which form truly followed function. Many of these furniture designs became classics and remained in production for many years.

De Stijl

1917

The De Stijl movement began in 1917 in the Netherlands as a magazine founded by two abstract painters, Piet Mondrian and Theo van Doesburg, and grew to embrace many fields, including textiles and interiors. Several architects and designers, such as Gerrit Rietveld and J. J. P. Oud, later joined the group. The principle they shared, which they called neoplasticism, involved reducing an object (whether a painting or a design) to its essentials, using only black, white, and the primary colors and a simple geometry of straight lines and planes that did not intersect. Rietveld's Schröder House in Utrecht, his Red-Blue chair, and Mondrian's abstract paintings are among the movement's most celebrated and typical works. The group disbanded after van Doesburg's death in 1931, but De Stijl principles continued to influence generations of artists, designers, and architects for many years.

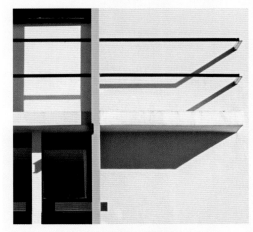

Balcony of the Rietveld Schröder House, Gerrit Rietveld, 1924, Utrecht, Netherlands.

Back is set at a 30° angle, which Rietveld believed provided optimum relaxation

Red-Blue chair | **Gerrit Rietveld,** 1917–1918, The Netherlands. With an open frame made of beech lumber and plywood, an angular form, and primary colors (as used in the paintings of Mondrian), Rietveld's Red-Blue chair overturned all notions of what an armchair should look like. The components of the frame all intersect at right angles, where they are joined with wooden pegs, while the plywood seat and back overlap and are connected with metal hardware. This chair became a signature design of De Stijl.

Parts connect side-on, so no complex joints were required

Framework made of standard cross sections of lumber

Backrest made of woven cane

Metal hardware allows chair to be folded almost flat

Rectangular elm panel

Jute bands similar to those used to secure horse saddles

Arm forms continuous curve with back and front legs

Front legs cut after chair had been molded

A triangular-section batten reinforces the joint

Deck chair | **Kaare Klint**, 1933, **Denmark**. Klint was influenced by traditional furniture, and his pieces were always carefully proportioned. The teak and cane Deck chair shows his resourceful use of meticulously crafted materials. The chair was fully collapsible and originally came with a loose cushion in natural canvas.

Vilstol (Easy chair) | **Bruno Matthsson**, 1933–1936, **Sweden**. This organically curvaceous chair has a lightweight frame of bent birch and a seat of woven jute bands. It is the result of study into human proportions and sitting positions.

Armchair | **Gerald Summers**, 1934, **UK**. This chair is made from a single sheet of plywood with no joints. The manufacturer made parallel cuts in the wood then pressed it in a mold to form the arms, legs, and seat.

Zig-Zag chair | **Gerrit Rietveld**, 1934, **The Netherlands**. Inspired by the cantilevered tubular steel of the Bauhaus designers, Rietveld's chair is made from battened Z-shaped wood. His design anticipated plastic seating of the 1950s.

Metal plates link wood sections

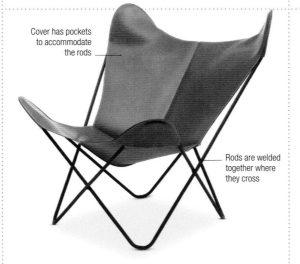

Cover has pockets to accommodate the rods

Rods are welded together where they cross

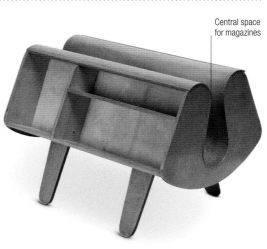

Central space for magazines

Siesta Medizinal chair | **Hans and Wassili Luckhardt**, 1936, **Germany**. This chair has a carefully balanced mechanism that enables the back, seat, and leg rest to move automatically as the sitter changes position.

BKF chair | **Antonio Bonet, Juan Kurchan, and Jorge Ferrari Hardoy**, 1938, **Argentina**. This lightweight design consists of two bent iron rods acting as legs and support for a leather or canvas cover that forms both seat and back.

Penguin Donkey bookcase | **Egon Riss and Jack Pritchard**, 1939, **UK**. This bookcase, constructed out of bent plywood by Isokon, was just the right size for the newly popular Penguin paperbacks and was marketed as the Penguin Donkey.

△ **The Wassily chair (1926)** was one of Breuer's earliest pieces in metal; he designed it so that it could be made from readily available steel tubing.

Marcel **Breuer**

Born in Hungary, Marcel Breuer worked in both Europe and North America, designing innovative furniture and buildings using modern materials in new and distinctive ways. After training at the Bauhaus, he was inspired to use tubular steel for furniture, creating his famous metal-framed chairs, which he often upholstered with tough industrial belting fabric. He also cofounded a company, Standard-Möbel, to manufacture and distribute some of his designs. His inventiveness with new materials made him an ideal designer for the British company Isokon, which pioneered the use of plywood furniture for the home.

Breuer also designed many elegant Modernist houses, favoring traditional materials, such as local stone, but also incorporating large areas of glass and concrete. He often left visible the marks of the wooden molds into which the concrete was poured, to create a distinctive, textured surface.

As a teacher, Breuer inspired several important pupils, including the industrial designer Eliot Noyes, and his designs have had a lasting influence. His famous steel and leather B3 chair (later named the Wassily chair after Wassily Kandinsky, the painter who taught at the Bauhaus), for example, remains a defining example of the Modernist aesthetic.

Life

1902–1981

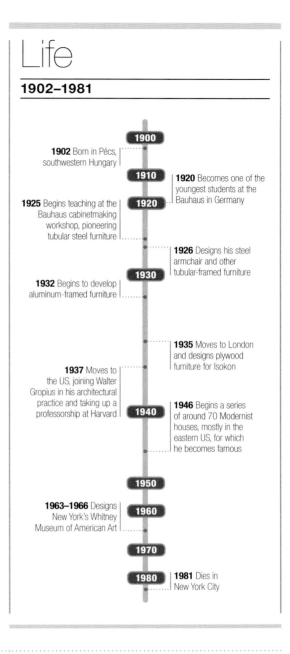

1902 Born in Pécs, southwestern Hungary

1920 Becomes one of the youngest students at the Bauhaus in Germany

1925 Begins teaching at the Bauhaus cabinetmaking workshop, pioneering tubular steel furniture

1926 Designs his steel armchair and other tubular-framed furniture

1932 Begins to develop aluminum-framed furniture

1935 Moves to London and designs plywood furniture for Isokon

1937 Moves to the US, joining Walter Gropius in his architectural practice and taking up a professorship at Harvard

1946 Begins a series of around 70 Modernist houses, mostly in the eastern US, for which he becomes famous

1963–1966 Designs New York's Whitney Museum of American Art

1981 Dies in New York City

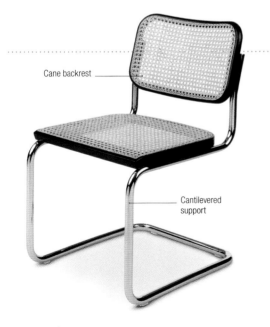

Cane backrest

Cantilevered support

B32 chair | **For Standard-Möbel**, 1928. By combining tubular steel with wood and cane, Breuer created a chair that worked in both modern and traditional settings.

Tubular steel supports join in the center

B56 stool | **For Standard-Möbel**, 1928. This stool with a cane seat was made to match the B32 chair. Its legs join at the bottom to form a stretcherlike construction for added rigidity.

Strong upright armrest

Tilted seat

Curved leg rest is comfortable for relaxing

Chaise lounge | **For Isokon**, 1939. Breuer drew on an earlier design that he had produced for a curved aluminum chaise longue to create this sinuous plywood-framed lounger.

LUDWIG MIES VAN DER ROHE / LILLY REICH

Barcelona Chair

YEAR 1929 | **DIMENSIONS** *Height* 30 in (75 cm), *Width* 30 in (75 cm), *Depth* 30 in (75 cm) | **MATERIALS** Chromium-plated steel frame; leather-covered cushions filled with PU foam

Created for the German Pavilion at the 1929 Barcelona International Exposition, the Barcelona chair is one of the best-known pieces of Modernist furniture. It is traditionally credited to the great German architect Ludwig Mies van der Rohe, who also designed the Pavilion, but Van der Rohe collaborated on the project with his colleague and companion Lilly Reich, who probably had a major share in the chair's design.

The Pavilion was a beautifully finished building that incorporated costly materials such as marble and onyx, and the designers wanted its furniture to reflect this luxury. The Barcelona chairs, in particular, were intended to be used as thrones for Spain's king and queen when they visited the exhibition and, although simple in design, the heavy steel frame and leather-covered cushions were made to the highest standards. This blend of comfort, luxury, and simplicity has ensured that the design has lasted. It works well in all kinds of settings, especially those that are Modernist or minimalist.

> ## A chair is a very difficult object. A skyscraper is almost easier. That is why Chippendale is famous.
>
> Ludwig **Mies van der Rohe**

Upholstery is buttoned, recalling luxury of traditional easy chairs

Steel frame flattens at bottom to form chair foot

△ **Front**

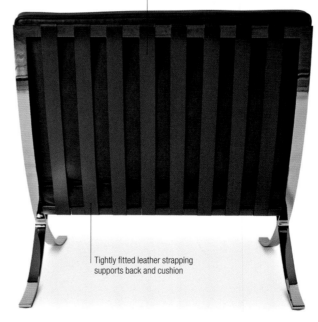

Straps match upholstery

Tightly fitted leather strapping supports back and cushion

△ **Back**

△ **The Unité d'Habitation** in Berlin, Germany. Perriand designed a prototype kitchen for the first apartment building Le Corbusier built in Marseille.

Charlotte
Perriand

French designer Charlotte Perriand's innovative, sculptural furniture, made in industrial materials like steel and glass, has earned her a reputation as one of the most important pioneers of the machine age. She is particularly famous for her work with Le Corbusier, which began after the French-Swiss architect was impressed by a Modernist rooftop bar Perriand had furnished using glass, steel, and aluminum. While working with Le Corbusier, she created a number of pieces, notably for the Maison La Roche, a Paris house that the architect designed in the late 1920s. Le Corbusier asked Perriand to produce chairs for "relaxing, holding conversations, and sleeping." She subsequently came up with a number of striking designs, including the celebrated LC4 chaise longue, a modern reinterpretation of the traditional 18th-century daybed.

After working with Le Corbusier, Perriand designed interiors for hospitals and apartments, and even the conference rooms of the United Nations office in Geneva. As well as her famous tubular steel-framed furniture, she worked in traditional materials such as wood and cane, hoping her economical, stripped-down pieces would make good design accessible to people of modest means. Although few of her items went into mass production, and her reputation was eclipsed by that of Le Corbusier, Perriand's work demonstrated the huge potential of modern materials.

Life

1903–1999

1903 Born in Paris, France

1910

1925

1927 Le Corbusier invites Perriand to join his studio, after seeing her Bar sur le Toit at the Paris Salon d'Automne

1928 Designs the LC2 and B301 chairs and LC4 chaise longue in tubular steel

1929 Designs an apartment furnished with steel and glass pieces for the Salon

1937 Leaves Le Corbusier's studio to work on a ski resort in Savoie and a pavilion for the Paris Exhibition

1939 Works on prefabricated buildings with other designers, including Jean Prouvé

1940

1950 Designs prototype kitchen fixtures for Le Corbusier's Unité d'Habitation

1955

1957 Designs conference rooms for the UN building in Geneva, Switzerland

1962 Starts work on further ski resorts in Savoie

1970

1990

1999 Dies in Paris

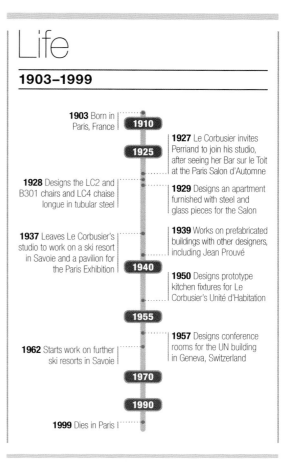

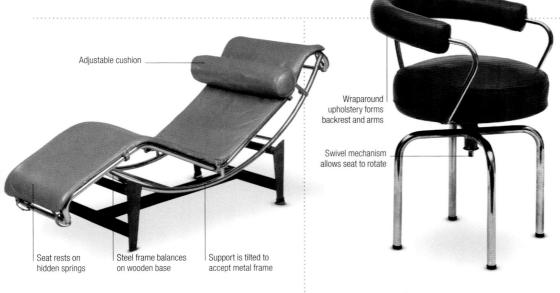

Adjustable cushion

Seat rests on hidden springs

Steel frame balances on wooden base

Support is tilted to accept metal frame

LC4 chaise longue | **Charlotte Perriand, Le Corbusier, and Pierre Jeanneret**, 1928. This tubular-steel chaise longue can easily be adjusted to the user's preferred position.

Wraparound upholstery forms backrest and arms

Swivel mechanism allows seat to rotate

B302 swivel chair | **Charlotte Perriand, Le Corbusier, and Pierre Jeanneret**, 1928–1929. Perriand aimed for flexibility with this chair, designed for use in both office and dining room.

Frame in black-finished wood

Indochine chair | **Charlotte Perriand**, 1943. Charlotte Perriand designed this wooden-framed chair with comfortable leather upholstery for her own personal use.

MODERN LIVING

One of the pivotal designs of the great Swiss-French architect Le Corbusier, the Villa Savoye on the edge of Paris is a famous example of early Modernist architecture known as the International Style. The house, with its white walls, flat roof, and cleverly positioned windows, is typical of Le Corbusier. It embodies the five key principles that he thought essential to the design of a house: the use of pilotis (slender columns) to support the structure; a free facade uninterrupted by structural elements; an open floor plan; strip windows; and a roof garden.

From the outside, the house seems to float free of the surrounding landscape. Inside, the light, airy living spaces merge into one another and the levels are linked by sloping ramps. Architects from around the world were stunned by the house's design, especially the visual balance of its facades and the free-flowing interior. Many of them have since tried to imitate the Villa, but few, if any, have been able to successfully replicate the clean lines, perfectly proportioned spaces, and elegant purity of Le Corbusier's design.

A house is a machine for living in.

Le **Corbusier,** 1923

Villa Savoye, Poissy, France, Le Corbusier, 1929 Le Corbusier's principles are visible in the Villa Savoye. Pilotis surround the service rooms and garage, and strip windows on the first floor look onto a terrace, filling the living rooms with light. The top-floor roof garden has a curved screen wall to give sunbathers privacy.

△ **At the heart of Wright's** Guggenheim Museum, New York, is a striking top-lit space with a spiral ramp leading to a vast skylight.

Frank Lloyd **Wright**

Frank Lloyd Wright was probably the greatest American architect of the 20th century, famous for the celebrated Guggenheim Museum in New York City and for the many innovative houses he produced throughout his career. Wright believed that the design of a house was about much more than just the building itself—the landscaping outside and the fixtures, lighting, furniture, and carpets inside were all essential elements, and Wright designed all of these things for his houses. This produced a unique artistic whole, with each object designed for its specific setting, a concept that Wright called "organic architecture."

Wright's furniture is equally distinctive. Like his buildings, his chairs were made with natural materials, innovative structures, striking intersecting planes, and strong lines. In the quality of their craftsmanship and the use of local materials, they reflect the influence of the Arts and Crafts movement, and sometimes of Art Nouveau designers such as Charles Rennie Mackintosh (pp.80–81), but they always retain an individual flavor and often bring out the natural color and grain of the wood.

Despite his love of traditional craftsmanship, Wright's fresh approach meant that his furniture was often far from conservative in appearance—his chairs sometimes have three rather than four legs. His skill as an architect also led him to use groups of furnishings to create distinctive, coherent spaces for his interiors.

Life

1867–1959

1867 Born in Richland Center, Wisconsin

1870

1887 Gets his first job, as a draftsman with Chicago architect Joseph Lyman Silsbee

1888 Starts work with the prominent Chicago architect Louis Sullivan

1890

1893 Sets up on his own after being fired for doing freelance work; designs houses for clients in and around Chicago

1900 Develops the Prairie style of buildings, which have a close connection between interior and exterior

1908 Completes Unity Temple in Illinois; many call it the first modern US building

1910

1910 Completes the Robie House, the greatest of his Prairie houses, in Chicago

1914 Taliesin, Wright's home and a showcase of his design principles, burned down by servant, killing his partner and several others

1923 Develops a new system of building houses using precast concrete blocks

1930

1936 Starts work on the headquarters building for S. C. Johnson & Son in Racine, Wisconsin

1937 Completes his most famous house, Fallingwater, in Bear Run, Pennsylvania

1943 Begins work on the Guggenheim Museum in New York

1950

1959 Dies in Phoenix, Arizona

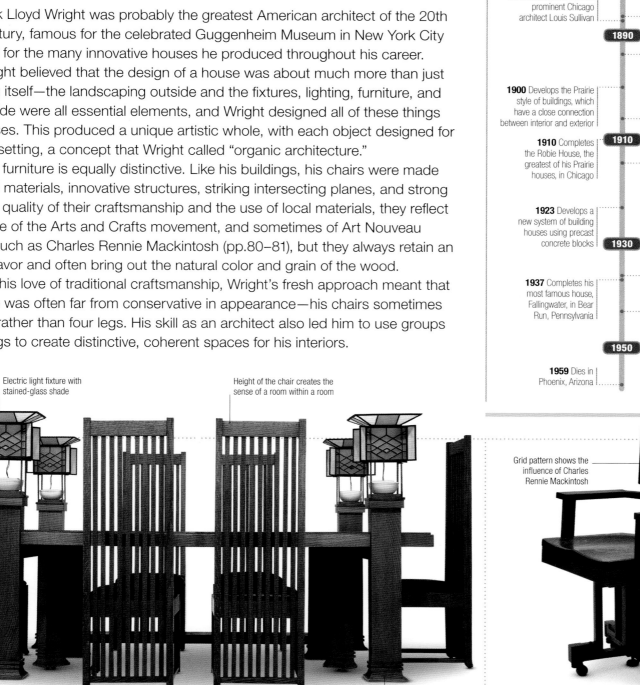

Electric light fixture with stained-glass shade

Height of the chair creates the sense of a room within a room

Pier finished with molding like a classical column

Dining room furniture | **For the Robie House**, 1910. Wright designed these pieces to create their own clearly defined space within the room. The high-back slatted chairs and the integrated light fixtures harmonize with the rest of the room.

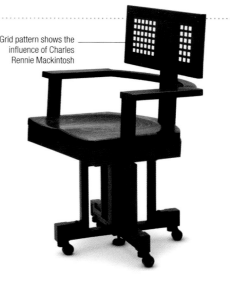

Grid pattern shows the influence of Charles Rennie Mackintosh

Office armchair | **For Van Dorn Iron Works Co.**, 1904–1906. Wright's desire to preserve and emphasize the natural color and feel of materials is clear in the rich, dark wood of this armchair.

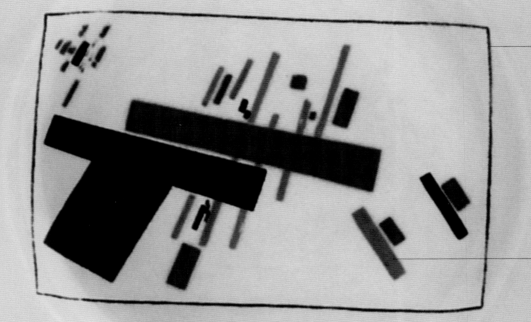

Design based on
Malevich's lithograph
In Suprematist Space

Malevich's Suprematist
designs were mainly
composed of rectangles
in restricted colors

Porcelain Suprematist plate |
**Kasimir Malevich for the Russian
State Porcelain Factory**, 1923,
Russia. Malevich saw the decorative
potential of his Suprematist canvases
and produced similar designs for use
on ceramics. His work still inspires
artists and designers today.

EARLY MODERNIST CERAMICS

The ceramicists of the 1920s and 1930s practiced their craft in a number of ways. Some responded to artistic developments such as abstraction, using similar techniques to decorate pots. Others absorbed the influence of craft and studio workers. The early Bauhaus students took this route, learning under the masters Max Krehan and Gerhard Marcks. They and other Modernist potters often worked in earthenware—a material that had previously been considered inferior. Ceramicists such as Susie Cooper in the UK produced earthenware pieces that were just as well proportioned—and more contemporary in their decoration—as the china tableware that most middle-class people had previously used. Cooper and colleagues, including Keith Murray and the Swedish ceramicist Wilhelm Kåge, all produced tableware that was both practical and beautiful—with an emphasis on purity of form rather than decoration. They helped bring elegant, modern design within the reach of ordinary consumers.

Cups are distinguished
by their straight sides

Curved handle

Horizontal ridges

Moonstone coffee set | **Keith Murray for Wedgwood**, *c.* 1933, UK. Known for his plain earthenware or basalt pieces for Wedgwood, Murray favored the use of matte surfaces and distinctive horizontal ridges. This coffee set was part of the Moonstone series, which was characterized by its simple lines and white glaze.

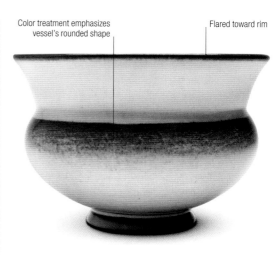

Color treatment emphasizes
vessel's rounded shape

Flared toward rim

Stoneware bowl | **Otto Lindig**, *c.* 1923, Germany. Lindig learned the craft of pottery at the Bauhaus, producing harmonious designs such as this, which combined traditional colors, forms, and techniques with new ideas.

Kasimir Severinovich
Malevich

1878–1935

The Russian artist Kasimir Malevich was influenced by the art trends of the early 20th century, especially Futurism and Cubism, before creating his own movement, Suprematism, based on abstract patterns made up of geometrical shapes on a white background. After the Russian Revolution, he played a major role in his country's art education, attracting talented students such as artists El Lissitzky and Nikolai Suetin. As well as writing, teaching, and painting numerous abstract works, such as *Black Square* (1915), he designed textiles, theater costumes, a silver tray, a teapot, and decorations for ceramics.

Dynamic Suprematism (oil on canvas), Kasimir Malevich, *c.* 1920s.

Glaze colors
inspired by
nature

Deliberately
crumpled top

Studio pot | **Frans Wildenhain**, *c.* 1925, Germany. This pot shows Wildenhain's flair for both traditional earth-colored glazes and strong forms. He studied under Krehan at the Bauhaus before working in the Netherlands and later the US.

Warm color
palette

Porcelain coffee pot | **Nicolai Suetin**, 1926, Russia. Like Malevich, Suetin was a Suprematist artist. The abstract alignment of geometric shapes on this coffee pot is typical of the movement.

Bowls stack for easy
storage in small
modern kitchens

Minimal hand-painted
decoration

Praktika tableware | **Wilhelm Kåge for Gustavsberg**, 1933, Sweden. Kåge's tableware was functional, as its name suggests, with simple forms and sparse decoration. It was designed to be easy to use, clean, and store.

Restrained
use of color

Ring handle
easy to hold

Falcon tableware | **Susie Cooper**, 1938–1942, UK. Cooper produced earthenware with transfer-printed decoration that offered customers sophisticated tableware at a lower price than bone china. The Falcon shape came in several patterns.

△ **Brick screen,** 1922, is one of Gray's most celebrated designs. Its black-lacquered wooden panels are on a steel frame and can be set at different angles.

Eileen Gray

Scots-Irish designer Eileen Gray is famous for creating ingenious furniture, beautiful rugs with abstract designs, and immaculate lacquered screens, but her work went out of fashion after World War II, and she was virtually forgotten until her designs were revived in the 1970s. Gray initially trained in lacquerwork and produced minimalist, finely crafted screens but changed direction in the 1920s: inspired by the work of Marcel Breuer at the Bauhaus, she began to make furniture from tubular steel and create functionalist interior designs. Her celebrated Bibendum armchair, the unusual E-1027 table, and many other pieces were the result. Some of these had innovative features that made it possible to adjust them in various ways. The E-1027 table, for example, can be set at different heights to suit the user and the panels of the Brick screen can be angled in several positions.

During this period, Gray also began to design buildings, with the encouragement of her partner, Romanian architect Jean Badovici. She was soon at the cutting edge of modern architecture, designing flat-roofed, white-walled houses that were admired by major architects, such as Le Corbusier. With her inventive Modernist designs, which include space-saving storage and drawer units, Eileen Gray has inspired and is celebrated by successive generations of designers.

Life

1878–1976

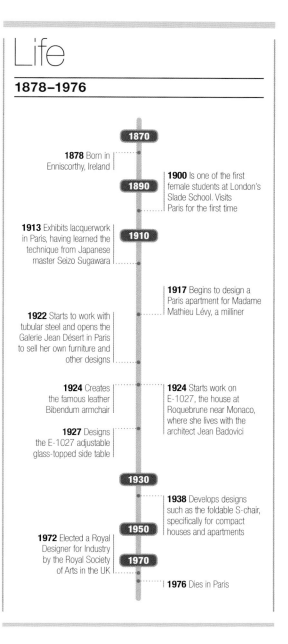

1870

1878 Born in Enniscorthy, Ireland

1900 Is one of the first female students at London's Slade School. Visits Paris for the first time

1890

1913 Exhibits lacquerwork in Paris, having learned the technique from Japanese master Seizo Sugawara

1910

1917 Begins to design a Paris apartment for Madame Mathieu Lévy, a milliner

1922 Starts to work with tubular steel and opens the Galerie Jean Désert in Paris to sell her own furniture and other designs

1924 Creates the famous leather Bibendum armchair

1924 Starts work on E-1027, the house at Roquebrune near Monaco, where she lives with the architect Jean Badovici

1927 Designs the E-1027 adjustable glass-topped side table

1930

1938 Develops designs such as the foldable S-chair, specifically for compact houses and apartments

1972 Elected a Royal Designer for Industry by the Royal Society of Arts in the UK

1950

1970

1976 Dies in Paris

Castellar Rug | *c.* 1934. As well as furniture, Gray also designed many rugs. This golden background was inspired by the sunshine at Castellar, her home in France.

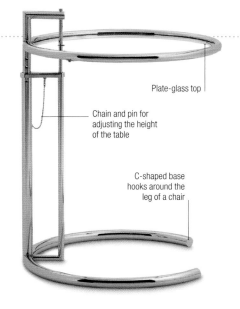

Plate-glass top

Chain and pin for adjusting the height of the table

C-shaped base hooks around the leg of a chair

E-1027 table | 1927. The tabletop of the E-1027 is supported by a chromium-plated, tubular steel frame. The table is designed so that the top can be slid into position over a chair or bed.

Tubular steel leg

Bibendum chair | 1926. The distinctive, leather-covered bulbous upholstery of this armchair was inspired by Bibendum, the Michelin man, whose body is made up of rubber tires.

GEOMETRIC METALWARE

Modernist metalworkers in the 1920s turned away from the classically inspired forms of previous generations and began to base items such as lamps, kettles, and pitchers on geometrical shapes—cubes, cylinders, and spheres. These designs could often be produced by machine (or at least made to appear as if they were machine-made) and as a consequence looked starkly new. Designers such as Marianne Brandt, Wilhelm Wagenfeld, and Hendrik Gispen all explored the Modernist idiom. The pared-down style was also associated with the Bauhaus (see pp.168–169), and designs such as Wagenfeld's Bauhaus table lamp were widely imitated, which helped the style spread internationally. German Modernists, Dutch followers of de Stijl, and Scandinavian craftsmen all adopted the machine-age look. In metalwork, as in other fields such as architecture and graphics, Modernism had become an international style.

Handle, top, and lip form continuous line

Finely beaten surface

Silver pitcher | **Johan Rohde for Georg Jensen**, 1920, **Denmark**. The simple form, flowing lines, and finely worked surface of this elegant pitcher are a far cry from the ornate classical pieces Jensen and Rohde had previously produced.

Spherical counterweight

Cylindrical cantilevered lamp directs light downward onto music stand

Heavy circular base designed to sit on top of an upright piano

Piano lamp | **J. J. P. Oud**, 1927, **Netherlands**. This lacquered brass lamp displays a strong sense of geometry. Fulfilling the Modernist idea that form should follow function, the long cylindrical lamp was intended to create a broad strip of light to illuminate an upright piano's keys and music stand. The spherical weight at the back provides a dynamic counterbalance.

Metal reflector spreads light across the room

Glass balloon shade diffuses light

Giso lamp No. 23 | **Willem Hendrik Gispen**, 1927, **Netherlands**. Manufactured by Gispen's Giso company, this lamp uses specially constructed glass to diffuse the light. Its simple style made it popular with designers and consumers.

Height adjustment

Adjustable copper shade

Table lamp | **Christian Dell**, 1928, **Germany**. Dell was a master metalworker, and this piece, with its hooded shade on an adjustable mount, set the standard for the modern desk lamp.

Ebony knob

Thumb rest

Coffee pot | **Naum Slutzky**, c. 1924, **Germany**. With its plain, geometric forms and matte-finished steel, this coffee pot shows the influence of Slutzky's time at the Bauhaus. The high standard of finish demonstrates his skill in metalwork.

Design is **not** a profession but an **attitude.**

László
Moholy-Nagy

Wear-Ever coffee pot | **Lurelle Guild**, 1934, US. Guild was a skilled metalworker as well as an industrial designer, and his creations were highly practical. The elliptical coffee pot was influenced by the fashion for streamlining.

Chrome-plated
steel lid

Powder-coated
steel body

Vipp step trash can | **Holger Nielsen**, 1939, Denmark. Originally designed for his wife's hair salon, Nielsen's trash can soon found a wider market. Customers admired its crisp mechanism, heavy base, and hygienic appearance.

Opalescent glass shade

24 Table lamp | **Wilhelm Wagenfeld**, 1924, Germany. Known as the Bauhaus table lamp, this strong, functional design went through several versions, but the key elements are the glass base and stem and the metal fixture that holds the switch. Embodying Bauhaus simplicity, the lamp is crafted from three geometric forms—a circle, a cylinder, and a half sphere. Well made and well proportioned, it became a classic and is still produced today.

Glass stem contains metal
tube to accommodate cord

Thick
glass base

△ **This lithograph** of an AEG Metal Filament lamp poster from 1907 shows the influence of the Vienna Secession on Behrens's graphic work.

Peter Behrens

German architect Peter Behrens has a unique place in the history of design, as the first individual to oversee every aspect of a major company's style. Behrens's involvement began when Walther Rathenau, managing director of the German electrical company AEG, asked him to be the firm's design consultant. A key part of Behrens's work was designing consumer products such as radiators and stoves. He restyled some items, such as electric fans, and created others that were entirely new, including his ground-breaking electric teakettles, which were the first appliances of their type.

Most of Behrens's product designs had clean, modern lines, simple shapes, and good proportions. They were intended for mass production, leading some to call Behrens the first industrial designer. Behrens did graphic work for AEG, too, creating the company's logo and corporate identity and producing numerous posters that show his visual flair. He also drew up the plans for several of AEG's factories and offices, including the celebrated Berlin Turbine Factory, a steel-framed structure that became a landmark in the history of architecture and a model for many later industrial buildings. His work had a huge influence—Le Corbusier, Mies van der Rohe, and Walter Gropius all worked in Behrens's office as young men and passed his values on to a whole generation of architects and designers.

Life

1868–1940

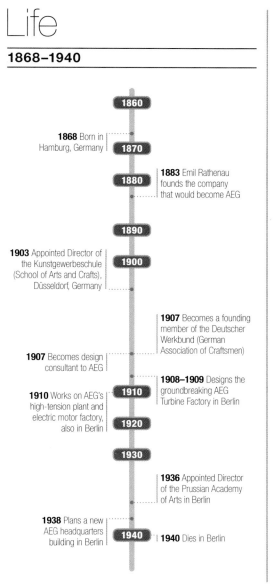

1860

1868 Born in Hamburg, Germany **1870**

1880 **1883** Emil Rathenau founds the company that would become AEG

1890

1903 Appointed Director of the Kunstgewerbeschule (School of Arts and Crafts), Düsseldorf, Germany **1900**

1907 Becomes a founding member of the Deutscher Werkbund (German Association of Craftsmen)

1907 Becomes design consultant to AEG

1908–1909 Designs the groundbreaking AEG Turbine Factory in Berlin

1910 Works on AEG's high-tension plant and electric motor factory, also in Berlin **1910**

1920

1930

1936 Appointed Director of the Prussian Academy of Arts in Berlin

1938 Plans a new AEG headquarters building in Berlin **1940** **1940** Dies in Berlin

Cane-covered, heatproof handle

Nickel-plated brass body

Electrical socket

Electric teakettle | **For AEG**, 1908. The features of Behrens's electric teakettles—heatproof handles, removable lids, and metal bodies—influenced thousands of later kettles.

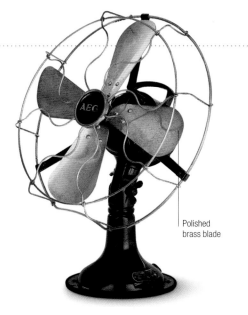

Polished brass blade

Electric fan | **For AEG**, c. 1908. Behrens's fans combined cast-iron bodies in shiny black or green paint with polished brass blades and guards, blending functionality with a beautiful finish.

Synchronous Electric Clock | **For AEG**, 1910. Behrens's skill with type is shown in the clearly legible but stylized numerals on this brass clock. The AEG logo was also designed by Behrens.

Curves help hold
flower stems in position ————————

———— Deep, fabriclike fold

Savoy vase | **Alvar Aalto and Aino Marsio**, 1938, Finland. This vase was used in Helsinki's Savoy restaurant. Its beauty lies in the deep folds of the mold-blown glass sides. One account states that Aalto, in collaboration with his wife, Aino, based his design on the leather pants worn by Inuit women; another interprets it as reminiscent of the undulating Finnish landscape, studded with lakes.

PURE AND PLAIN
GLASS

In the 1920s and 1930s, many glassmakers and designers rejected the ornate glassware of the previous generation and created plainer, more functional designs in which the beauty of pure glass and the blower's skill were revealed—closer in look to the vernacular, utilitarian, anonymously designed glassware that was and is continually manufactured. Everything—from simple drinking glasses to coffee makers—was rethought along plainer lines, influenced partly by the Bauhaus and functionalism and partly by major Modernists such as Adolf Loos and Alvar Aalto. Modernist designers used clear glass and simple, rounded or straight-sided forms and worked for mass production as well as on unique pieces. In Central Europe, Jenaer Glaswerk Schott & Gen. in Germany, Lobmeyr in Austria, and Kavalier in Czechoslovakia led the way. Modernism even influenced the glassworks of Venice, generally known for their colorful and decorative output.

Sides of pitcher form straight lines

Milk pitcher | **Marianne Brandt for Jenaer Glaswerk Schott & Gen.**, 1920s, Germany. As with Brandt's innovative metalware at the Bauhaus, the outline of this pitcher is a striking blend of curves and straight lines.

Insulated handle

Clear, heatproof glass

Tea service | **Ladislav Sutnar for Kavalier**, *c.* 1928, Czechoslovakia. Sutnar was best known as a graphic designer, but he also designed tableware, toys, textiles, and other items. In this tea service, he combined a functionalist lack of surface decoration with pure, curved shapes. The form of the cup matches that of the teapot.

Heatproof wooden handle

Rubber seal

Heat-resistant glass

Sintrax coffee maker | **Gerhard Marcks**, *c.* 1925, Germany. The shape of this coffee maker, designed for mass production, reflects Marcks's early career as a sculptor and potter. His work became more functional at the Bauhaus.

Beauty is the harmony of function and form.

Alvar **Aalto**

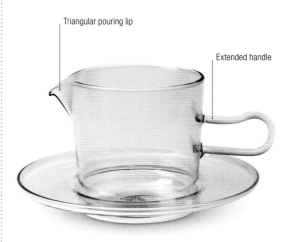

Triangular pouring lip

Extended handle

Pitcher and saucer | **Wilhelm Wagenfeld for Jenaer Glaswerk Schott & Gen.**, 1930s, Germany. Made from heat-resistant glass, this pitcher-and-saucer ensemble is part of a larger set of plain, clear glass tableware.

Satin-polished, brilliant-cut base

Service No. 248 | **Adolf Loos for Lobmeyr**, 1931, Austria. The plain, cylindrical design of these otherwise undecorated glassware pieces was much imitated. The sides of the decanter and glasses thicken toward their brilliant-cut bases.

Blown glass body

Subtle spiral decoration

Blown glass vase | **Paolo Venini for Murano**, 1938, Italy. Venini produced much plainer designs than normal for the glassworks of Venice, in response to the influence of Modernism. Here, he combines a simple shape with restrained decoration.

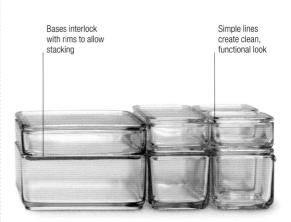

Bases interlock with rims to allow stacking

Simple lines create clean, functional look

Kubus storage containers | **Wilhelm Wagenfeld for Lausitzer Glassworks**, 1938, Germany. Wagenfeld designed these containers to fit snugly when stacked by working to a modular unit that could be scaled up or down.

△ **The light and spacious living room** of Maison Louis Carré, 1956–1959, was designed by Alvar Aalto with a slight organic curve to the ceiling.

Alvar Aalto

Finnish architect and designer Alvar Aalto was one of the leading figures in modern architecture, producing landmark Modernist buildings and creating some of the most elegant and popular furniture of the 20th century. His early architectural work in Finland included houses and public buildings such as the Paimio Sanitorium and the Viipuri Library; these light, asymmetrical, functional, and user-friendly buildings helped define modern architecture.

At the same time, seeking total control over the interiors of his buildings, Aalto turned to furniture design, developing a particular flair for pieces in bentwood, especially using plywood and birch. He recognized that wood, with its warmth and attractive grain, was still ideal for constructing furniture, and his use of it increased his reputation for softening the hard lines of modern architecture. His chairs and other items of furniture, from tables to tea carts, became famous for their simplicity—with forms reduced to a few curving components—as well as for their convenience and comfort. Aalto cofounded the company Artek to market his furniture. Often working with his wife, Aino, also an architect and designer, Aalto designed glassware—notably for Finnish company Iittala—and ingenious light fixtures. All of these items have sold all over the world, drawing attention to Aalto's brilliance and spreading his influence among consumers and designers.

Life

1898–1976

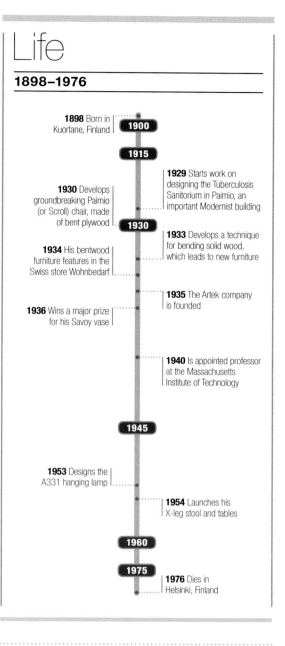

1898 Born in Kuortane, Finland

1900

1915

1929 Starts work on designing the Tuberculosis Sanitorium in Paimio, an important Modernist building

1930 Develops groundbreaking Paimio (or Scroll) chair, made of bent plywood

1930

1933 Develops a technique for bending solid wood, which leads to new furniture

1934 His bentwood furniture features in the Swiss store Wohnbedarf

1935 The Artek company is founded

1936 Wins a major prize for his Savoy vase

1940 Is appointed professor at the Massachusetts Institute of Technology

1945

1953 Designs the A331 hanging lamp

1954 Launches his X-leg stool and tables

1960

1975

1976 Dies in Helsinki, Finland

Structure of bent birch

Model 37 lounge chair | **For Artek**, 1935–1936. The broad cantilevered arms of this chair give an impression of strength, complementing Aalto's pieces in narrower wood.

Jointed sections of pine

Model 100 screen | **For Artek**, 1936. Made from lacquered pine, this screen is easily adjusted to form a variety of curves that can fit any space.

Flat plywood seat

Model 60 stool | **For Artek**, 1936–1937. This stool has legs of bent laminated birch. The seat is also made of birch and was originally produced in black, red, and blue versions.

MODERNIST PRODUCT DESIGN

In the 1930s, the profession of industrial designer became more established. Freelance consultants hired to work on specific products took into account the manufacturing costs, ease of use, hygiene, and look of a mass-produced item, often using experimental materials. With new materials came new styles. Bakelite, for example, could be molded into all kinds of shapes, from the simple Modernist radio receivers developed in Europe to the distinctive molded ridges of US Kodak cameras. A streamlined look, in which rounded corners, stripes, and chrome-plated panels created an impression of speed, was favored, especially in the US. On both sides of the Atlantic, however, it was increasingly clear that when it came to sales, making an object look new and appealing was almost as important as making it efficient.

Walter Gropius

1883–1969

Surprisingly for an architect, Walter Gropius had difficulty physically holding a pencil. But being forced away from the drawing board only gave him a keener understanding of design and construction principles.

In 1919, Gropius founded the Bauhaus to remove "the arrogant barrier between craftsmen and artists." When the school moved to Dessau in 1925, Gropius designed its buildings as a synthesis of architecture and machinery—an architectural expression of the Modernist aesthetic.

In 1928, Gropius stepped down from the directorship of the Bauhaus and returned to his architecture practice in Berlin. In 1934, the rise of Nazism forced him to emigrate first to Great Britain and then to the US, where he became professor of architecture at Harvard. He remained there until his death.

Gropius designed several limousines for the German Adler company in the early 1930s, but only a few were ever made.

Perforated windshield

Closing the cover extinguishes the flame

Plated brass body

Zippo cigarette lighter | **George G. Blaisdell**, 1932–1933, **US**. Blaisdell based his Zippo lighter on an earlier Austrian model. The smooth metal body and windshield chimney enable the lighter to stay lit in a strong wind.

> The **mind** is like an umbrella— it **functions** best when open.
>
> Walter **Gropius**
> Architect

Bakelite dial

People's radio | **Walter Maria Kersting**, 1933, Germany. Only German and Austrian stations were marked on the dial of this affordable radio, commissioned by Nazi government minister Josef Goebbels to spread propaganda to the German people.

Metal viewfinder

Fixed focus lens

Brownie camera | **Walter Dorwin Teague for Kodak**, 1934, US. In the late 1920s, Kodak hired Teague to restyle their camera range. He cased the popular Brownie in a streamlined Bakelite body with distinctive ridges in the center.

Cord protector

Ceramic body

Heat control

Electric iron | **Christian Barman for HMV**, *c.* 1936, UK. The shiny chromium-plated soleplate of this iron, shown at the 1936 London Ideal Home Exhibition, glides and conducts heat easily. The porcelain body and handle protect the user from heat.

Rubber covering

Lifting handle

Chromium-plated fittings

Glider

Vacuum cleaner | **Lurelle Guild for Electrolux**, 1937, US. Guild made the 1937 Electrolux cylinder cleaner streamlined and efficient, with its sloping end and fluted chromium-plated side panels. Steel gliders made it easy for the user to pull the vacuum cleaner across the floor. This design was produced for more than 20 years.

Base unit cradles handle securely

Numbers set inside finger holes of the dial

Unit flares at base to give room for bell

Type 302 telephone for Bell | **Henry Dreyfuss**, 1937, US. The Type 302 model for the Bell Telephone Corporation was inspired by the Swedish Eriksson company's 1930 unit. The phone was durable, an attractive shape, and simple to use. Dreyfuss had researched how people used phones in their daily lives before designing the 302.

EVOLUTION OF
AUDIO

In 1877, Thomas Edison succeeded in recording the nursery rhyme "Mary Had a Little Lamb" on a sheet of tinfoil, thereby creating the phonograph. Since then, inventors and designers have continually pushed the boundaries of what is possible in audio quality, portability, and design. Technological developments in audio recording and reproduction, from records, radio, and tape to CD and MP3, run alongside developments in the design of the appliances themselves, from streamlined Art Deco radios to the innovative Apple iPod.

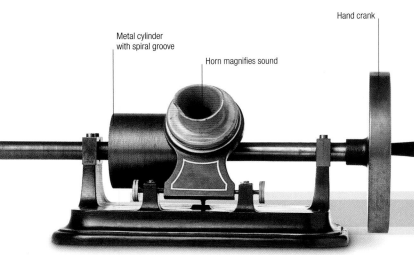

Metal cylinder with spiral groove

Horn magnifies sound

Hand crank

1877 **Phonograph** | **Thomas Edison, US**. This device was the first that could both record and reproduce sound. Sonic vibrations were engraved by the machine onto a sheet of tinfoil placed on the cylinder. These were then translated back into sounds.

1957 **TR-63** | **Sony, Japan**. The TR-63 was the first product exported by Sony to the US. One of the new wave of lightweight, portable radios, it was marketed as "pocket-sized," although in reality it was too large to fit in most pockets.

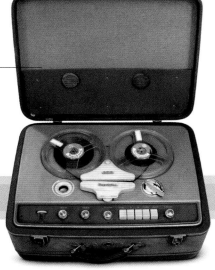

Thermoset plastic casing

"Airplane" dial

Case for secure transportation

1930s **Art Deco radio** | **FADA, US**. The Bullet radio is a classic of streamline design, with a sleek shape and dial in the style of an airplane dashboard. Made from Catalin, a polymer resin similar to Bakelite, it could be manufactured in bright colors.

1935 **Magnetophone** | **AEG, Germany** The first magnetic tape recorder was developed by AEG in Germany and displayed at the Berlin Exhibition in 1935. Early versions produced disappointing results, but later improvements led tape to largely replace records.

In-ear earplugs

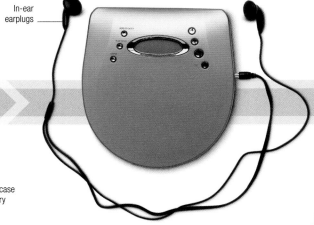

Leather case accessory

1979 **Sony Walkman TPS-L2** | **Sony, Japan** The popularity of the Walkman was a surprise to Sony—they doubted there was a market for a portable tape player. The design has since became so iconic that its name has become a synonym for portable music.

1984 **Portable CD player** | **Unknown**. Sony released the first portable CD player, in 1984, leading to many imitations, such as this aluminum-cased example. CD players were bulky and prone to audio skipping but were popular until the rise of MP3 technology.

Large single speaker

Brightly colored casing

Amplifying horn

Record

1887 **Gramophone** | **US**. The gramophone played flat discs or records, improving on the bulky cylinders of previous sound recording equipment. The technology was patented by Emile Berliner in 1887 and made cylindrical players largely obsolete.

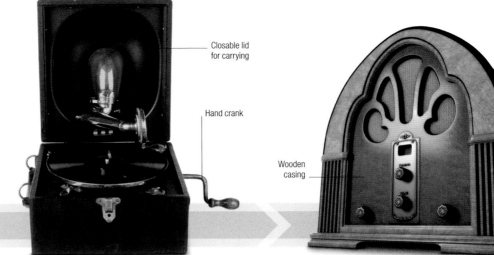

Closable lid for carrying

Hand crank

1920 **Portable record player** | **Unknown**. This record player was housed in a secure wooden box with a carrying handle on one side. The removable hand crank would be turned to wind up a spring, which would slowly provide the record player with power.

Wooden casing

1930s **Cathedral radio** | **US**. One of the iconic appliances of prewar America, the Cathedral radio (named after its resemblance to Old World cathedral facades) enjoyed a brief burst of popularity during the Depression, thanks to its low cost.

Carrying handle for portability

1959 **Bush TR82** | **Ogle design for Bush, UK**. The TR82 transistor radio was built for portability with its carrying handle and robust yet stylish Bakelite casing. It proved immensely popular, particularly with teenagers, and has since become a design classic.

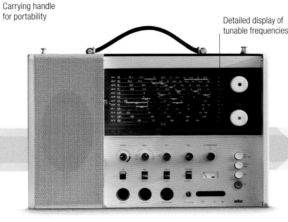

Detailed display of tunable frequencies

1962 **Braun T 1000 radio** | **Dieter Rams for Braun, Germany**. Encompassing its designer's ethos, "simple, but better," the T 1000 was not only one of the most advanced radios of its time but also one of the most stylish, with an aluminum cover and crisp design.

Aerial picks up analog radio signals

1970s **Transistor radio** | **Roberts, UK**. The portable transistor radio was marketed by Roberts as a glamorous accessory. The company experimented with refined casing designs, such as the red leatherette and teak finishes on this example.

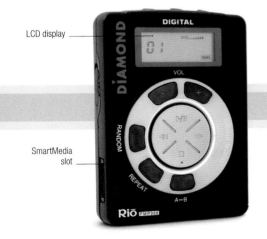

LCD display

SmartMedia slot

1998 **Portable MP3 Player** | **Diamond Multimedia, US**. The Rio was not the first portable MP3 player, but it gained notoriety as the target (and victor) of a major lawsuit by the music industry, who alleged that MP3s encouraged music piracy.

Menu-based file access

Signature click wheel

2001 **iPod** | **Apple, US**. The "Walkman of the 21st Century" was released in 2001 but did not become popular until three years later. The iPod's slimline design and intuitive user interface came to dominate the MP3 market, and it won multiple design awards.

Band lights up

2019 **Echo Smart Speaker** | **Amazon, US**. The form and function of this version of the Echo are based on those of the Echo Plus, a music speaker. It offers more powerful sound, hands-free voice control, and the intelligent personal assistant service "Alexa."

MODERNIST GRAPHICS

During the 1920s, there was a growing trend in many countries to make graphic arts simpler so that everything, from posters to magazines, was more visually arresting, less cluttered, and more legible. This change took place alongside more rigorous education for graphic designers in schools such as the Bauhaus in Germany and, influenced by Cubism, the rise of new and abstract movements, such as de Stijl in the Netherlands and Constructivism in communist Russia. Constructivist graphics spread beyond Russia. In Czechoslovakia, for example, designers copied the Constructivists' use of strong shapes and colors, photomontage, and dynamic, diagonal lines. Meanwhile, in Germany, several designers—some of whom were linked to the Bauhaus—adapted Constructivist ideas for use in commercial work, and Jan Tschichold led the drive toward a more disciplined approach to typography.

Red band striking through tickets doubles as road for car

Aero poster | **František Zelenka**, 1932, Czechoslovakia (now Czech Republic). Prolific architect and designer Zelenka produced this poster for the Prague-based car manufacturer, Aero. In a collagelike image of the freedom provided by personal transportation, the car is shown racing dramatically uphill in front of crossed-out train and streetcar tickets. The clear lines of the car contrast with the grubbiness and illegibility of the tickets, hinting at the clean, bright, and efficient future that motoring offered.

Dynamically angled lettering | Lightning bolt symbolizing power | Effective use of muted colors

BP Ethyl poster | **Edward McKnight Kauffer**, 1933, UK. The Anglo-Dutch oil company Royal Dutch Shell commissioned many high-quality posters and advertisements during this period. An American designer working in the UK, McKnight Kauffer produced this photolithograph—a technique using light-sensitive chemicals—combining strong typography with graphic imagery to create a clean but dramatic appearance.

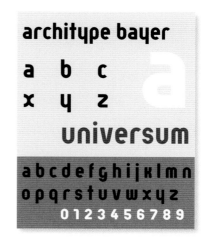

Universal Alphabet | **Herbert Bayer**, 1925, Germany. While at the Bauhaus, Bayer devised the Universal Typeface, which pared letters down to basics, with no serifs or capitals. Never cast in metal, it was later digitized as Bayer Universal.

Sans-serif capitals create bold rectangles of text | Elements all set at same angle

Poster for Kandinsky's 60th Birthday Exhibition | **Herbert Bayer**, 1926, Germany. Designed at the Bauhaus, this poster displays the Modernist love of blocks of type, rules, and patches of color. All elements contribute to a machine-made look.

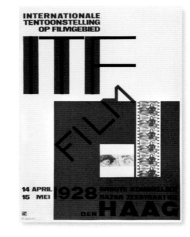

Film Exhibition poster | **Piet Swart**, 1928, Netherlands. Diagonals, primary colors, photomontage, and varied typefaces typify Swart's work. His designs were influenced by de Stijl—the blue square recalls Mondrian canvases—and Constructivism.

The New Typography

1928

In Germany, Modernist graphic design emphasized clarity and became known as the New Typography, after the definitive text on machine-age graphic design by Jan Tschichold, which was published in 1928. Following Tschichold's lead, designers limited the number of typefaces used, developed clear hierarchies of text sizes and headings, and championed plain, unadorned sans-serif fonts. As in his special issue of the trade journal *Typographische Mitteilungen* (below), Tschichold used the same size and typeface for most of the text and uniform colored bars to denote the different sections.

ReD magazine cover | **Karel Teige**, 1928, Czechoslovakia. Teige was editor and designer of the Devêtsil group's magazine, *ReD*. Among the ideas that Devêtsil championed were the use of the bold graphics and lettering seen here.

Times New Roman typeface | **Stanley Morison with Victor Lardent for the Monotype Corporation**, 1932, UK. Designed for *The Times* newspaper and still popular, this elegant, legible, space-efficient typeface balances thick and thin strokes.

Elementare Typographie, Jan Tschichold, 1925, Switzerland and Germany

EDWARD YOUNG

Penguin Paperback Covers

YEAR 1935 | **MANUFACTURER** Penguin Books Limited | **DIMENSIONS** *HEIGHT* 7 in (18 cm), *WIDTH* 4½ in (11 cm) | **MATERIALS** Printed paper

When the company Penguin Books launched its range of paperbacks in 1935, it transformed publishing. The mission of Penguin's founder, Allen Lane, was to make good books available cheaply. Their covers ensured that these mass-produced paperbacks were instantly identifiable. Edward Young designed the covers with a plain white panel between two brightly colored bands that indicated the subject category of the book (orange for general fiction, green for crime, blue for biography, purple for books of essays, and cerise for travel). The title and author's name were positioned in the center, the publisher's name at the top, and the publisher's logo, a stylized penguin, in the middle of the lower band. Young kept the typography simple, using the Gill Sans font, a typeface created by British designer Eric Gill in 1927–1928, for everything except the publisher's name.

The basic elements of the cover design remained the same until the early 1950s (although there were revisions to make the type clearer and more consistent), making a major contribution to the company's success as Penguin's rapidly expanding list stood out from the crowd in stores and on bookstalls.

> We believed in the existence ... of a vast reading public for intelligent books at a low price and staked everything on it.
>
> Allen **Lane**
> Founder of Penguin Books

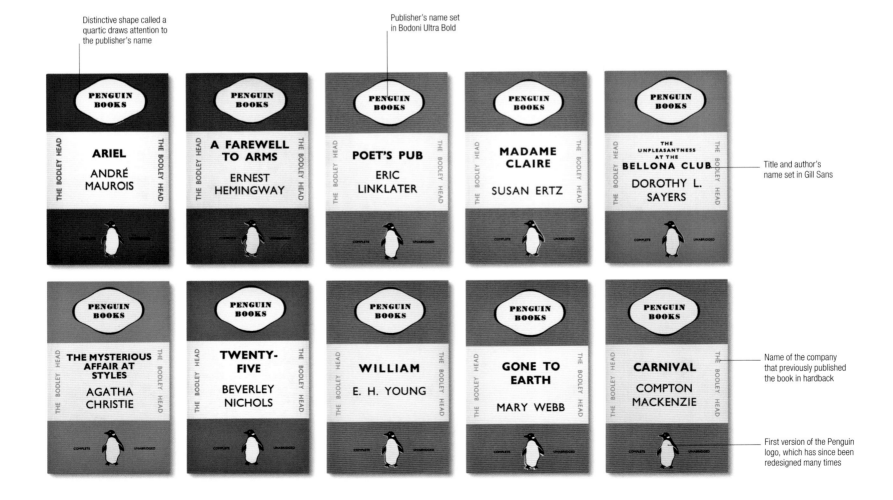

Distinctive shape called a quartic draws attention to the publisher's name

Publisher's name set in Bodoni Ultra Bold

Title and author's name set in Gill Sans

Name of the company that previously published the book in hardback

First version of the Penguin logo, which has since been redesigned many times

CONSTRUCTIVIST GRAPHICS

After the 1917 Russian Revolution, graphic design became highly valued because its blend of words and images, unfettered by the past, could support the revolutionary cause far better than "bourgeois" media, such as oil painting. Kasimir Malevich's Suprematist movement, with its abstract designs based on geometric shapes, acquired new prominence, especially with the publication of El Lissitsky's famous communist poster "Beat the Whites with the Red Wedge." Constructivism, spearheaded by Varvara Stepanova and her husband Alexander Rodchenko, was even more successful. The Constructivists focused on graphics supporting the Revolution and on practical projects, such as designing workers' clothing. Their graphic work has geometric elements, bold type often set along dynamic diagonal lines, and a striking use of imagery. It impressed Soviet leaders and Western designers alike.

Beat the Whites with the Red Wedge | **El Lissitsky**, 1919, **Russia**. In this poster, the geometric forms represent the Reds (the revolutionaries), and their opponents, the Whites. The shapes used may mirror the marks used on military maps.

***Dr. Mabuso* film poster** | **Kasimir Malevich**, 1922, Russia. As in his paintings, Malevich used geometric shapes to create this poster, combining them with stylized lettering made up mostly of circles, rectangles, and triangles.

Red typography dominates center

***Musical New Land* cover** | **Lyubov Popova**, 1924, USSR. On the cover of this periodical, Popova showed what could be achieved using only typography, simple shapes, and printing in two colors. She gave pride of place to the word *novy* (new).

Poster for Leningrad State Publishers | **Alexander Rodchenko**, 1925, USSR. This poster combines Suprematist-style geometric shapes with expressive typography and bold color. The woman is Varvara Stepanova, shouting "Books!"

Human legs mirror those of tripod

***Man with a Movie Camera* poster** | **Georgi Augustovich Sternberg**, 1929, USSR. By combining photomontage, drawn imagery, mirrored shapes, and typography, this film poster has visual unity in spite of its busy appearance.

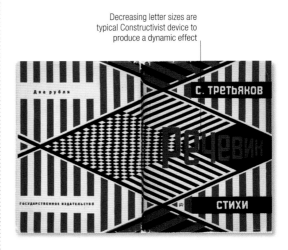

Decreasing letter sizes are typical Constructivist device to produce a dynamic effect

Book cover design | **Alexander Rodchenko**, 1929, USSR. Rodchenko assembled a dazzling array of stripes in his cover design for *Rechevik: Stikhi* (Orator: Verse). Its patterns and letterpress printing are true to the Constructivist style.

"Don't forget Giz!"

Soviet hammer-and sickle-emblem is a trademark feature

Arrow directs viewer's eye downward

Poster for Giz state publishers Varvara Stepanova, 1925, USSR. This poster relies mainly on the open book shape and the colorful typography, set in a variety of curves and stepped patterns, and in several sizes and fonts. The slogan tells the viewer: "Don't forget Giz! This trademark means a source of knowledge and enlightenment."

EVOLUTION OF
WRITING MACHINES

In the 19th century, inventors began to create mechanical typewriters to cut down the labor of producing documents, which had previously been done by clerks writing in longhand. Manufacturers in the 20th century produced ever more efficient typewriters, but a revolutionary change came about with the rise of personal computers in the 1980s. Since then, computers have been transformed from ugly boxes operated by specialists to the user-friendly devices of today. Engineers continue to cram increasing amounts of power into ever smaller machines, as the quest for improvement continues.

Four-row QWERTY keyboard

1874 Sholes and Glidden typewriter | Christopher Latham Sholes, US. Also named the Remington No 1, after its first manufacturer, this was the first successful typewriter. It pioneered the QWERTY keyboard and platen or roller, but it printed only capital letters.

Fraction keys   Capital keys

Base of carrying handle

Clearly visible ruler

c. **1910 Royal Bar-Lock | Columbia Typewriter Company, US.** This machine's layout, with separate keys for the capitals and the lower-case characters, did not catch on domestically, but some industrial printing machines used a similar design.

Case designed to harmonize with IBM's other office products

1961 IBM Selectric | Eliot Noyes, US. At the heart of this revolutionary design was an interchangeable spherical type head that led to the nickname "golfball typewriter." Unlike conventional typewriters, the type head moved along while the carriage remained still.

1969 Olivetti Valentine | Ettore Sottsass and Perry A. King, Italy. Housed in an orange-red molded plastic housing (with an integral handle), the Valentine slipped into a case of the same material. It was light and easy to carry and suggested fun rather than work.

Large, clear letterform

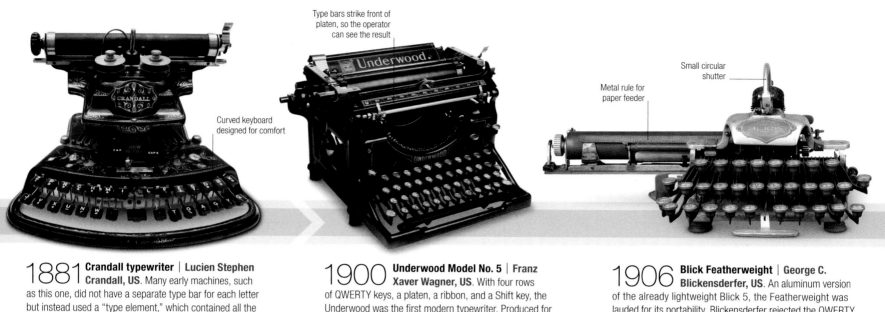

Type bars strike front of platen, so the operator can see the result

Curved keyboard designed for comfort

Metal rule for paper feeder

Small circular shutter

1881 **Crandall typewriter** | **Lucien Stephen Crandall, US**. Many early machines, such as this one, did not have a separate type bar for each letter but instead used a "type element," which contained all the letters and moved according to which key was pressed.

1900 **Underwood Model No. 5** | **Franz Xaver Wagner, US**. With four rows of QWERTY keys, a platen, a ribbon, and a Shift key, the Underwood was the first modern typewriter. Produced for about 30 years, it influenced countless later machines.

1906 **Blick Featherweight** | **George C. Blickensderfer, US**. An aluminum version of the already lightweight Blick 5, the Featherweight was lauded for its portability. Blickensderfer rejected the QWERTY keyboard and created his own "scientific" key layout.

Central "turret" contains two shuttles carrying letters and fonts

Plastic carriage guard

Casing hides moving parts

Contoured case

1913 **Multiplex** | **Hammond Typewriter Company, US**. This typewriter had an interchangeable circular shuttle. Changing the shuttle enabled one to use other fonts, or change to a font with extra symbols or accents.

1940s **Hermes Baby** | **Giuseppe Presioso, Switzerland**. Reputedly the favorite typewriter of Ernest Hemingway, the lightweight Baby had a modern design with a colorful plastic body and keys. It was compact and popular with travelers.

1949–1950 **Olivetti Lettera 22** | **Marcello Nizzoli, Italy**. The compact design, clear graphics, and housing of enameled metal set the Lettera 22 apart from the majority of typewriters, which were usually large and black.

Two-tone screen

Inner electronics partially visible through translucent casing

Exceptional display

Extremely comfortable keyboard

Colorful plastic keys

Integral tape deck

1984 **CPC 464** | **Amstrad, UK**. Following an instruction from Amstrad founder Alan Sugar to create a computer that was affordable and consumer-friendly, this was the first machine sold with all its parts, including the keyboard and monitor, bundled together.

1998 **iMac** | **Jonathan Ive and Apple design team, US**. The iMac broke with the fashion for gray, beige, or black computers. Its brightly colored plastic reflected Apple's intention to create machines that were fun and easy to use.

2020 **Dell XPS 15** | **Dell, US**. This powerful laptop performs as well as a desktop. Its streamlined design makes it light, and advanced technology makes streaming fast and smooth. A full SD slot makes it possible for photographers to import RAW images fast.

MIDCENTURY MODERN

1940–1959

More for less

RICHARD BUCKMINSTER FULLER, ARCHITECT AND DESIGNER

MIDCENTURY MODERN
Introduction

In the middle of the 20th century, and especially after World War II, modern design underwent a subtle change. Architects and designers turned away from the plain, hard-edged Modernism of the 1920s and 1930s to a gentler version of the Modernist style. Midcentury modern furniture, ceramics, homewares, glass, and textiles were more decorative than those of the previous period, even though their design was often influenced by recent scientific discoveries. They are lighter in touch, and the stark geometry of earlier Modernism was replaced by more natural, organic forms, flowing lines, clear pastel colors, and distinctive patterns with a touch of humor. The style is often referred to as soft modernism.

A welcoming environment

The change came about largely because of the urgent need to rebuild after the war. Design was seen as a crucial aid to raising living standards, creating a warm, welcoming home environment, and raising morale. The shortage of materials after the war meant that designers had to create products that were easy to manufacture from the materials available, and advances in science and technology spurred them on to innovation. The postwar rebuilding quickly gathered momentum, and people found the light touch and cheerful patterns of the new, softer Modernism uplifting. In the United Kingdom, the 1951 Festival of Britain helped promote the style.

CLEAN LINES

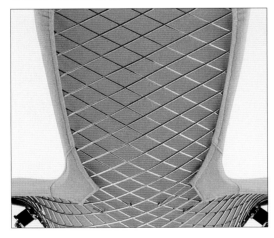

Midcentury designers learned the value of the clean line from their Modernist forebears. Simple, angular shapes dominated but were gradually replaced by a more organic aesthetic at the end of the 1950s.

EXUBERANT COLOR

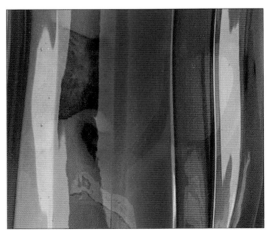

From the vibrant tones of Murano glass to the more subtle, naturalistic hues of Scandinavian wares, color was striking. Homewares were often in pastel shades, and drab colors were perceived as old-fashioned.

ORGANIC SHAPES

Biomorphic design—abstract forms based on organic shapes found in nature—was used by many designers. They eschewed surface decoration, allowing the simple shapes and clean lines to stand out.

Design is a plan for arranging elements in such a way as best to accomplish a particular purpose.

Charles **Eames**

All over the western world, Scandinavian designers such as lighting designer Poul Henningsen and silversmith Georg Jensen, both from Denmark, had a powerful influence. The work of Scandinavian architects like Alvar Aalto and Arne Jacobsen was also popular because they designed whole interiors, and their furniture, lights, and tableware were widely available. Because these designers and architects worked internationally, the style soon spread around the world. Nordic manufacturers such as the glassmaker Iittala and Aalto's own company, Artek, were perfectly placed to take advantage of the design boom. Midcentury designers enthusiastically tried out new materials, sculpting foam to make unusual-shaped chairs,

for example, but they also experimented with more traditional materials, using pale woods to create innovative modern furniture and coming up with new techniques to create textured glassware inspired by nature.

An enduring fashion

Soft Modernism proved popular, and the style remained fashionable throughout the 1950s, affecting the design of both one-of-a-kind items and mass-produced pieces. Many designers went on producing furniture, ceramics, glassware, and fabrics in a similar vein well into the 1960s. By then, however, the colorful and dramatic aesthetic of Pop Art was bringing a new and vibrant edge to design.

NATURAL INSPIRATION

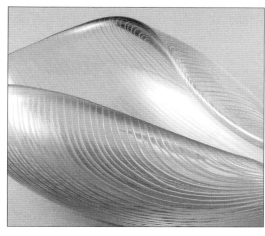

From Scandinavian glass, which emulated the textures of bark or rippling water, to the flowing shapes of chairs and light fixtures, midcentury designers drew inspiration from the landscapes around them.

QUIRKY FABRICS

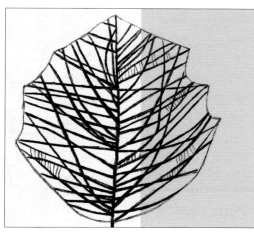

Bright, new abstract patterns enlivened textiles and homewares. The simple geometry of Modernist designs segued into two-dimensional, colorful designs often based on nature or the latest discoveries in science.

SCIENTIFIC INFLUENCES

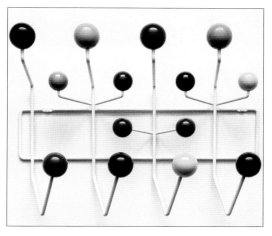

The development of atomic science and space technology gave designers a new visual vocabulary on which to draw, from microscopic forms such as atomic structures, to Sputnik and other spacecraft.

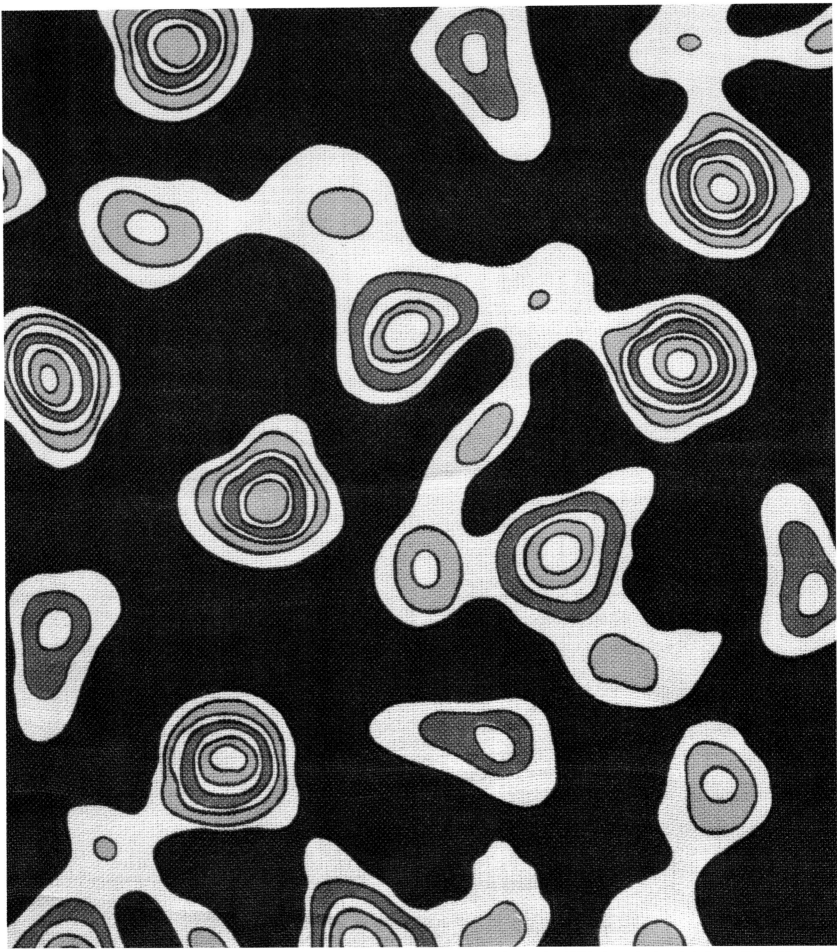

△ **This dress fabric pattern** by S. M. Slade is based on a crystallography model, Afwillite 8.45, and printed on rayon—a demonstration of British advances in science, technology, and industrial design.

Festival of Britain

△ **Festival of Britain symbol** | **Abram Games**, UK, 1948

n 1951, a nationwide festival was staged in Great Britain as a celebration of national achievements in the arts and sciences and as an entertaining diversion from post–World War II austerity. Called the Festival of Britain, it drew on the skills of some of the most talented individuals of the period, including architects such as Hugh Casson, Philip Powell, and Hidalgo Moya and designers such as Wells Coates, Robin Day, Lucienne Day, and Ernest Race.

This group developed a fresh, contemporary aesthetic that influenced design, especially in Great Britain, throughout the 1950s. It was a soft-edged but modern style, featuring bright colors, strong lines, and ornamental effects that drew heavily on Scandinavian design and appeared in everything from buildings to textiles. In a marriage of art and science, the Festival Pattern Group was also set up to draw designs based on crystallography, a type of X-ray atomic analysis, in which the UK led the world.

Contemporary style was seen at its most concentrated at the event's heart, an exhibition centered on the Festival Hall on London's South Bank, and in various nearby buildings constructed for the festival, such as the huge Dome of Discovery (designed by Powell and Moya) and the tall Skylon tower (by Ralph Tubbs).

Key dates
1943–1952

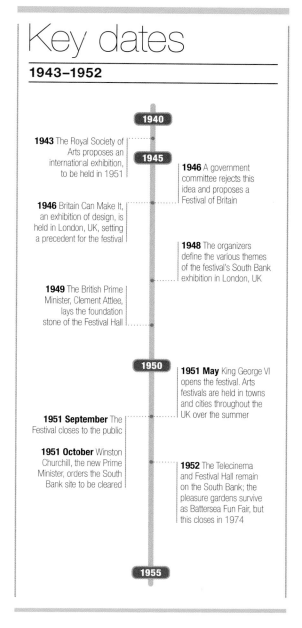

1940

1943 The Royal Society of Arts proposes an international exhibition, to be held in 1951

1945

1946 A government committee rejects this idea and proposes a Festival of Britain

1946 Britain Can Make It, an exhibition of design, is held in London, UK, setting a precedent for the festival

1948 The organizers define the various themes of the festival's South Bank exhibition in London, UK

1949 The British Prime Minister, Clement Attlee, lays the foundation stone of the Festival Hall

1950

1951 May King George VI opens the festival. Arts festivals are held in towns and cities throughout the UK over the summer

1951 September The Festival closes to the public

1951 October Winston Churchill, the new Prime Minister, orders the South Bank site to be cleared

1952 The Telecinema and Festival Hall remain on the South Bank; the pleasure gardens survive as Battersea Fun Fair, but this closes in 1974

1955

Poster | **Printed by Sanders Phillips & Co**, 1951. The advertisement for the Festival was a collaborative venture; Abram Games designed the patriotic central emblem.

Molded plywood seat

Antelope chair | **Ernest Race**, 1951. Designed to provide outdoor seating during the festival, this chair's bent steel-rod frame inspired a generation of metal-framed chairs.

Skylon cotton bale label | 1951. The Skylon is this label's main subject; behind it are other festival structures such as the Dome of Discovery, which housed an exhibition about exploration.

SOFT MODERNISM

In many parts of the world, furniture designers of the 1950s enthusiastically adopted a softer and increasingly futuristic form of Modernism. A trend common in countries from Great Britain to Japan was a return to traditional materials and techniques that were used in a new and modern way. Designers such as Robert Heritage applied meticulous craftsmanship to create softer, modern pieces that owed much to contemporary Scandinavian style. Others, such as Florence Knoll, who was taught by Mies van der Rohe, were inspired by the hard-edged Modernism of the 1930s but used more forgiving, softer upholstery fabrics. However, from George Nelson in the US to Robin Day in the UK, designers in the 1950s were unified by their willingness to try out new materials, such as plastics, and softened their work in another way: by injecting brighter colors.

¾ in (19 mm) plate-glass top

Supports linked by concealed metal rod

Coffee table | **Isamu Noguchi**, 1947, **US**. Sculptor Noguchi balanced this table on a pair of matching wooden supports that resemble the biomorphic forms seen in surrealist art. The shape of the glass top harmonizes with the curves of the supports.

Upholstery padded for comfort

Bertoia Bird Chair | **Harry Bertoia for Knoll**, 1952, **US**. Made from bent metal rods, this chair combines a modern, sculptural shape with stunning color. Rubber buffers were incorporated into the seat to make it more comfortable.

Plywood frame

Vinyl-covered seat

Pretzel chair | **George Nelson**, 1957, **US**. The continuous curve of the plywood arms and back gave this chair its name. It was inspired by the Thonet bentwood chairs in Nelson's office. Production costs were high, so few Pretzels were made.

Robin Day
1915–2010

One of Britain's most celebrated furniture designers, Robin Day came to prominence in the 1950s. He used low-cost materials, including plywood and plastic, to suit Britain's postwar austerity, creating light, compact pieces that worked well in small, modern rooms. The pieces that he designed for Hille, an established British furniture maker eager to modernize, were especially successful, ranging from his Form seating units, widely used in corporate settings, to his iconic polypropylene chairs.

Mahogany table top

Fabric-covered cushions

Black-painted steel frame

Form seating unit | **Robin Day for Hille**, 1957, **UK**. Day designed the Form system to be simple and flexible. The units (seats, backs, and tables) could be combined in different ways, including straight runs and corners, to suit the setting.

Vinyl-covered foam disk

Metal frame

Marshmallow sofa | **Irving Harper for George Nelson Associates**, 1956, US. When foam padding was developed, Irving Harper designed this sofa around the innovation of foam disks, which he covered in brightly colored vinyl, leather, or fabric. The design became a classic. "Despite its astonishing appearance, this piece is very comfortable," enthused the original catalog.

Fabric upholstered cushion

Turned brass handle set in elliptical recess

Teak door

Reeded rosewood drawer front

Tapering leg

Stool Model No. S-302 | **Isamu Kenmochi**, 1963, Japan. Kenmochi took the traditional, natural material rattan and used it to create a radically simple design. This stool is a companion piece to a chair with a similarly curved shape.

Hamilton sideboard | **Robert Heritage for Archie Shine**, 1957, UK. Heritage designed the sideboard in teak and rosewood, the manufacturer's trademark woods. With its long, low proportions, the sideboard shows that Heritage drew inspiration from Scandinavian design, an influence that lasted well into the 1960s in the UK.

△ **Danish designer Finn Juhl** created furniture with backs and seats that seem minimally supported, in white with accents of bright color.

Scandinavian Style

△ **Crinolette armchair** | Ilmari Tapiovaara, 1962

One of the most important influences on midcentury design was the work of companies and designers in Sweden, Norway, Finland, and Denmark. They used natural wood, muted colors, and curvaceous forms to soften the hard lines of 1930s Modernism (this look is sometimes called soft Modernism). Scandinavian style began before World War II, but the movement became well known in the early and mid-1950s with the establishment of the Lunning Prize for Nordic designers and the Scandinavian Way of Living, an exhibition that toured North America from 1954 to 1957.

Many of the chief designers from the region were also architects, such as Alvar Aalto from Finland, Finnish-American Eero Saarinen, and the Dane Arne Jacobsen. All of these men were prolific and took advantage of major projects such as Jacobsen's Copenhagen Air Terminal to design everything from chairs to cutlery, which could then also be sold on the open market. Key manufacturers—such as Aalto's furniture company Artek and glassmakers Iittala and Orrefors—also helped popularize Scandinavian style, and its impact was felt across many parts of the world. From North America to Japan, as well as in the UK, France, and Germany, designers of the 1950s drew on the movement's organic forms and pastel colors.

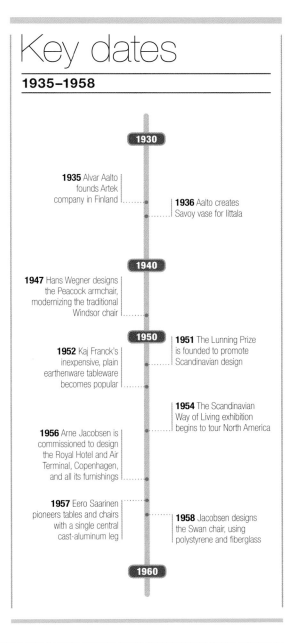

Key dates

1935–1958

1930

1935 Alvar Aalto founds Artek company in Finland

1936 Aalto creates Savoy vase for Iittala

1940

1947 Hans Wegner designs the Peacock armchair, modernizing the traditional Windsor chair

1950

1951 The Lunning Prize is founded to promote Scandinavian design

1952 Kaj Franck's inexpensive, plain earthenware tableware becomes popular

1954 The Scandinavian Way of Living exhibition begins to tour North America

1956 Arne Jacobsen is commissioned to design the Royal Hotel and Air Terminal, Copenhagen, and all its furnishings

1957 Eero Saarinen pioneers tables and chairs with a single central cast-aluminum leg

1958 Jacobsen designs the Swan chair, using polystyrene and fiberglass

1960

Pressed birch plywood seat and back

Domus lounge chair | **Ilmari Tapiovaara for Artek**, 1946. With its plywood seat bent to follow the contours of the human body, this chair typifies light, organic Scandinavian design.

Neck looks like apple stalk

Apple vase | **Ingeborg Lundin for Orrefors**, 1955. Differences in the thickness of the body and a layer of plain glass over the colored glass create the subtly varying color.

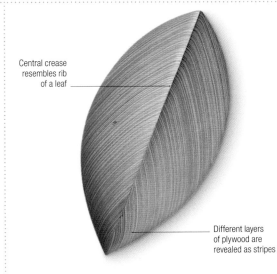

Central crease resembles rib of a leaf

Different layers of plywood are revealed as stripes

Birch platter | **Tapio Wirkkala**, 1951. Wirkkala made this platter by cutting through blocks of plywood to reveal a cross section. The smooth edge of the platter forms a leaflike curve.

SCANDINAVIA AND ITALY

European furniture designers as far apart as Finland and Italy exploited the properties of modern materials, creating items that were innovative, pleasant to use, and sculptural. One material Scandinavian and Italian designers successfully experimented with was plywood. Taking a cue from prewar designs by Charles and Ray Eames, members of the Bauhaus, and the 1930s furniture of companies such as Isokon, they bent and cut plywood into new shapes, producing work that stood out for its fluidity and innovation. Some of the resulting products, such as Arne Jacobsen's Ant chair, were made in great numbers, while others won prizes at major exhibitions. European designers thus won more attention, showing how technology could be used to make comfortable new forms and how design could bring a new lightness of touch to homes and workplaces.

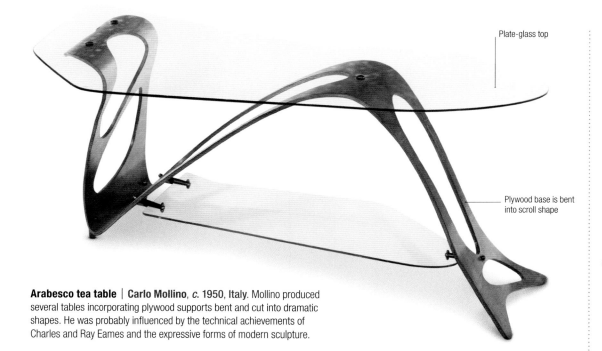

Plate-glass top

Plywood base is bent into scroll shape

Arabesco tea table | **Carlo Mollino**, *c.* 1950, **Italy**. Mollino produced several tables incorporating plywood supports bent and cut into dramatic shapes. He was probably influenced by the technical achievements of Charles and Ray Eames and the expressive forms of modern sculpture.

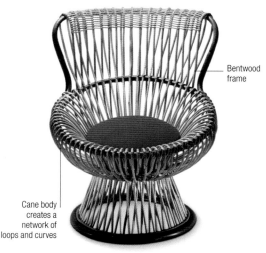

Bentwood frame

Cane body creates a network of loops and curves

Margherita wicker chair | **Franco Albini for Bonancina**, 1950, **Italy**. A winner at the Milan Triennale furniture exhibition in 1951, Albini's chair reveals the respect for traditional craft techniques still shown by many Italian designers of the 1950s.

Separate arms enable rapid factory upholstering

Splayed metal leg

Lady armchair | **Marco Zanuso for Arflex**, 1951, **Italy**. Zanuso used fabric-covered foam rubber on a concealed wooden frame for this piece, which won the gold medal at the 1951 Milan Triennale.

Horseshoe-shaped seat

Heavy teak leg

Sauna stool | **Antii Nurmesniemi**, 1952, **Finland**. With its laminated birch seat and straight teak legs, this stool combines an attractive finish with comfort and practicality. The seat shows off the different colored layers of the birch plywood.

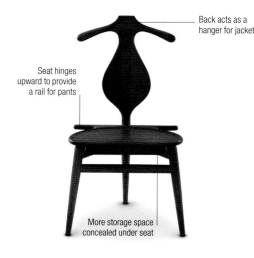

Back acts as a hanger for jacket

Seat hinges upward to provide a rail for pants

More storage space concealed under seat

Valet chair | **Hans Wegner**, 1953, **Denmark**. This wooden chair ingeniously provides hanging and storage for each item of a man's suit. As well as integrating this storage space, Wegner created a chair with a satisfying organic appearance.

A chair ... should be beautiful from all sides and angles.

Hans **Wegner**

Articulated back

Folding section beneath seat also incorporates a slide-out metal footrest

P40 lounge chair | **Osvaldo Borsani**, 1954, **Italy**. This comfortable reclining chair comprises four sections—two back elements, the seat, and a folding leg and footrest. A system of joints allows the chair to be set in different positions.

Tubular steel arm

Sloping seat

Lukki 5AR chair | **Ilmari Tapiovaara for Artek**, 1956, **Finland**. Tapiovaara met the challenge of designing lightweight stackable seating by creating this chair with a tubular-steel frame and a plywood seat and back.

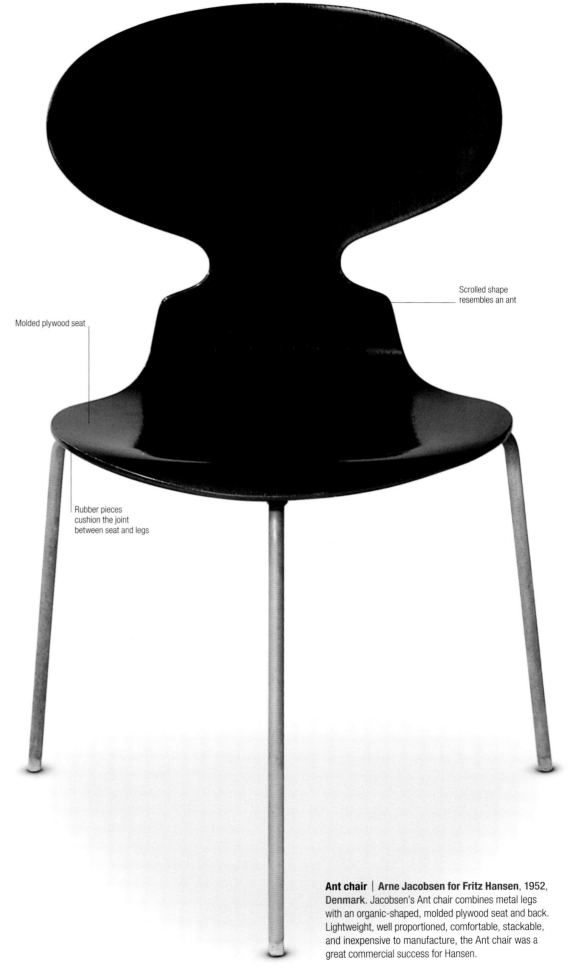

Scrolled shape resembles an ant

Molded plywood seat

Rubber pieces cushion the joint between seat and legs

Ant chair | **Arne Jacobsen for Fritz Hansen**, 1952, **Denmark**. Jacobsen's Ant chair combines metal legs with an organic-shaped, molded plywood seat and back. Lightweight, well proportioned, comfortable, stackable, and inexpensive to manufacture, the Ant chair was a great commercial success for Hansen.

HOLISTIC HOTEL

Copenhagen's SAS Royal Hotel (now the Radisson Blu Royal Hotel) is one of the masterpieces created by Arne Jacobsen, who was famous as both an architect and a designer. Jacobsen planned the hotel as a tower in the postwar Modernist style. It stands 69.6 m (228 ft) high and is set on top of an entrance building and covered completely in gray-green glass and aluminum (a picture of it is on the wall on the right of the photograph). The exterior was based on the skyscrapers in New York, and, unusually, the Danish architect had designed everything inside the building, too, from the fixtures and hardware down to the ash trays.

Among the most successful of these specially designed items were Jacobsen's Egg and Swan chairs, which combined elegant, sculptural lines with comfort and support. Their curves offset the straight lines of the custom furniture Jacobsen also included, making the SAS Royal a showcase of the design that defined the soft Modernism of 1950s Scandinavia. The Egg and Swan chairs soon became classics of modern design, and Jacobsen's fame spread, both as a designer of furniture and as a creator of complete interiors.

The **primary factor** is **proportion.**

Arne **Jacobsen,** 1971

SAS Royal Hotel, Copenhagen, Denmark, Arne Jacobsen, 1956–1960
Although the hotel's decoration has changed, one room (606) is still kept as Jacobsen intended, with pale blue Egg, Swan, and Drop chairs. Jacobsen's example of integrated interiors went on to influence countless hotel designs.

△ **Charles and Ray Eames** in their house in Pacific Palisades, California, designed by Charles Eames in 1948–1949 and assembled from prefabricated parts.

Charles and Ray
Eames

△ **Eames elephant** | **For Vitra**, 1945

Husband and wife team Charles and Ray Eames transformed interior design with pioneering furniture made from materials that reflected the forms of modern architecture. They also made influential films, such as *Glimpses of the USA* (1959) for the American National Pavilion at the Moscow World's Fair. They are best known for their curvaceous, comfortable chairs, which have colorful, molded plastic seats supported by legs made of metal rods. The Eameses also worked in wood, designing a chair consisting of two pieces of molded plywood on a metal rod frame. This metal-framed furniture was light and not costly to manufacture, and it helped popularize a soft-edged, clean look that worked well in modern buildings like those designed by the Eameses themselves. The plastic items created welcome splashes of color in midcentury interiors.

The couple also created more luxurious furniture, such as their famous lounge chair and ottoman, a Modernist interpretation of the traditional leather armchair. Like much of their work, this design was originally attributed to Charles, but both are now credited for it. Many Eames pieces are still produced, and some, such as their plastic-seated chairs, have spawned countless imitations by companies exploiting the market they created for cheap, colorful, and versatile seating.

Lives

1907–1988

1900

1907 Charles Eames is born in St. Louis, Missouri

1912 Bernice Kaiser, known as Ray, is born in Sacramento, California

1920

1938 Charles begins to study at the Cranbrook Academy of Art, subsequently becoming its head of Industrial Design

1940

1941 Charles marries Ray, his colleague at Cranbrook Academy. Eames designs win prizes at MoMA, NY Organic Design competition

1945 Charles and Ray design the DCW wooden dining chair

1946 Charles becomes consultant designer at the Herman Miller Furniture Company

1956 Charles and Ray create the celebrated Eames lounge chair

1958 The couple launches their Aluminum Group range of furniture

1960

1978 Charles Eames dies

1980

1988 Ray Eames dies

2000

2005 Are the first designers elected to the Designer Hall of Fame at Gwangju Design Biennale, South Korea

Molded fiberglass shell

Steel framework

Maple wood rocker

Rocking Armchair Rod | **For Herman Miller**, 1948. This chair came first in MoMA's Competition for Low-Cost Furniture Design. It combines elegance with ease of manufacture.

Balls do not leave creases on clothes hung over them

Wire framework

Hang-It-All coat hanger | **For Vitra**, 1953. The Eameses were interested in design for children, and these colorful balls were intended to encourage them to hang up their coats.

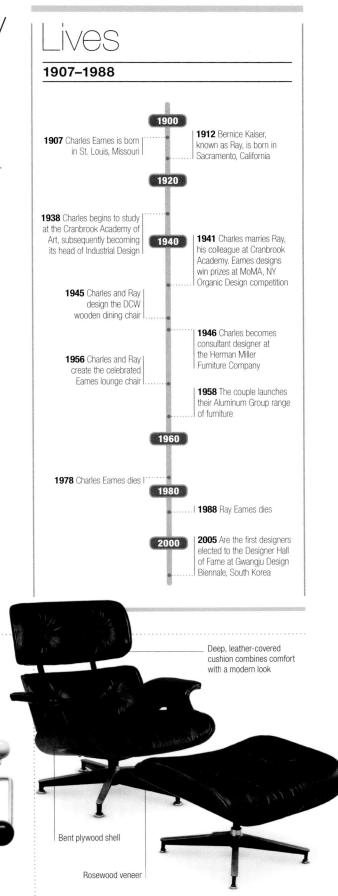

Deep, leather-covered cushion combines comfort with a modern look

Bent plywood shell

Rosewood veneer

Lounge chair 670 | **For Herman Miller**, 1956. The soft contours of this chair are designed to envelop and cushion the sitter in the way an old-fashioned club armchair might.

Supportive
wraparound back

Solid hardwood frame

Upholstery in contrasting
colorway

Sofa | Finn Juhl for Baker Furniture Inc., 1951, Denmark. Because the back of this sofa is made up of two sections, one half seems to float weightlessly above the other, creating an impression of lightness. Juhl designed a range of molded furniture with solid wooden frames like this, some of which was manufactured by the American Baker company.

MOLDED FURNITURE

Sculptural, molded seating in striking forms that followed the contours of the human body became increasingly common in midcentury furniture. Some designers, including Sori Yanagi, molded furniture from bentwood. Others, such as Bruno Mathsson, used canvas or webbing to make not just the upholstery but also the seats and backs of chairs. However, one key new material that became increasingly popular in furniture manufacture was fiberglass, a moldable plastic reinforced with glass that had been developed during World War II to construct radar domes for aircraft. Designers such as Arne Jacobsen and Eero Saarinen created fiberglass furniture with generous curves and rounded forms. The organic forms of this molded furniture led many people to compare it to sculpture—Danish designer Finn Juhl even exhibited his pieces alongside carvings by the prominent British sculptors Henry Moore and Barbara Hepworth.

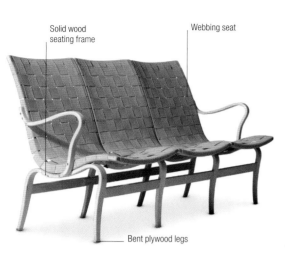

Solid wood seating frame

Webbing seat

Bent plywood legs

Pernilla three-seat sofa | **Bruno Mathsson**, *c.* 1941, **Sweden**. Molded furniture was also made using traditional materials. This sofa has an organically curved bentwood frame and is upholstered with webbing made of woven hemp.

Soft foam padding

Womb chair | **Eero Saarinen for Knoll**, 1946, **Finland**. This was the first fiberglass chair to appear on general sale. Fiberglass made it both light and resilient, and the light foam upholstery was Saarinen's answer to overstuffed club armchairs.

Florence **Knoll**

1917–2019

In 1943, architect Florence Schust joined the Knoll company, which had been founded in 1938 by German American furniture maker Hans Knoll (see pp.326–327). She developed the interior-design side of the business and began to work with architects and major designers on furniture projects. Florence and Knoll (above) were married in 1946, and the company prospered, espousing the values of the Bauhaus and Florence Knoll's mentor Mies van der Rohe. Knoll produced classic items by designers such as Harry Bertoia, Eliel Saarinen, and Mies himself. Hans Knoll died in a car crash in 1955, and Florence took over the running of the company. In the 1960s, she concentrated on design and defined the look of the typical US office. The company survives as a major manufacturer of classic Modernist furniture and new pieces.

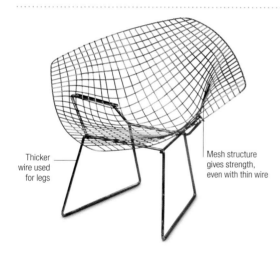

Thicker wire used for legs

Mesh structure gives strength, even with thin wire

Diamond chair | **Harry Bertoia**, 1952, **US**. Drawing on his work as a jeweler and his time with Charles and Ray Eames, Bertoia used a diamond-shaped mesh of steel wire to mold this chair with arms that come to a point, like a diamond.

Grain of two halves matches perfectly

Metal stretcher rod

Butterfly stool | **Sori Yanagi**, 1956, **Japan**. The strong curves of this stool echo those of much Japanese architecture. However, the material—bent plywood—was widely used for furniture in the West, representing a meeting of cultures.

Florence Knoll and Eero Saarinen studying the base of the Tulip table in 1957

Hammock-like canvas seat

Cantilevered tubular metal frame

Paulistano chair | **Paulo Mendes da Rocha**, 1957, **Brazil**. The slinglike seat of this chair, suspended from a tubular metal frame, molds itself to the user's body. The design echoes both campaign chairs and the BKF chair (see p.173).

Body curves to form a supportive back and wing

Chair rotates on a central spindle

Egg lounge chair | **Arne Jacobsen**, 1958, **Denmark**. One of the most famous 1950s chairs, the Egg has a molded fiberglass body with an enveloping form that is lightly covered in foam and cloth. A tilt control reclines the chair.

Rounded back

Hole can be covered by a cushion

Legless chair | **Kenji Fujimori for Tendo Mokko**, 1961, **Japan**. Made from a light plywood shell, this stackable chair can be bought as a set and topped with a cushion for comfortable floor-level dining at a low table in traditional Japanese style.

RESTRAINED
CERAMICS

The demands of World War II placed many restrictions on the manufacture of ceramics, as factories were commandeered for other uses, resulting in severely limited production in many places. After the war, however, designers such as the American Russel Wright began to create new kinds of ceramics to fit the postwar lifestyle, with simpler, more flowing and organic lines than those produced by Art Deco potters. Designers and producers in other countries followed suit, some making wares with patterns—often inspired by nature, and sometimes with abstract motifs—in a restrained range of pastel greens, blues, yellows, and pinks. Dinner and tea services were now available to buy as individual pieces so that consumers could pick and choose the specific items they wanted or build up a set gradually instead of having to buy it all at once. This flexibility helped make the new homewares accessible to more people, especially in countries dealing with austerity measures and rationing in the decade that followed the war.

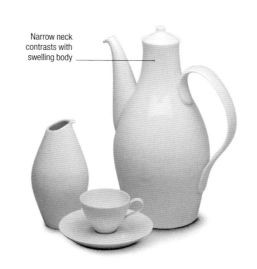

Narrow neck
contrasts with
swelling body

Museum glazed porcelain dinner service | Eva Zeisel for Castleton China, *c.* 1942–1945, **UK**. Zeisel created flowing, elegant forms, which worked well in the plain colors that were imposed by wartime restrictions.

Flush handle
with recess

Integrated
spout and lid

Plain coupe shape
(without rim)

Casual china | Russel Wright for Iroquois China Company, 1946, **US**. Wright's Casual line included stackable containers that matched the muted tones of the range's cookware. "Good design is for everyone," he said.

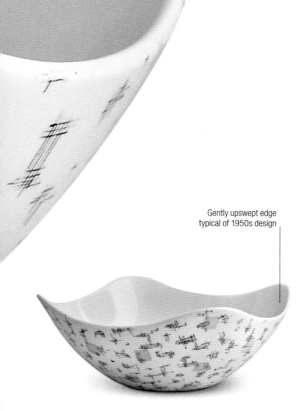

Gently upswept edge
typical of 1950s design

Savanna bowl | Jessie Tait for Midwinter, *c.* 1956, **UK**. Tait's clean, abstract designs, such as this one in which the yellow squares pick up the color of the interior, helped Midwinter transform mass-market ceramics in the UK in the 1950s.

Glaze varies subtly
in color

Stoneware pitcher | Gunnar Nylund for Rörstrand, **1950s**, **Denmark**. Nylund specialized in richly glazed stoneware, and the semi-matte glaze on this pitcher shows his flair for texture. Its more abstract form is typical of his postwar work.

Wild flowers
painted on inside
of vase's mouth

Simple repeat pattern
in pale blue with
black accents

Vase | Stig Lindberg for Gustavsberg, *c.* 1952, **Sweden**. Lindberg produced sculptural, organically shaped vases, bowls, and plates, decorating them with understated patterns in colors typical of the period, such as the pale blue used here.

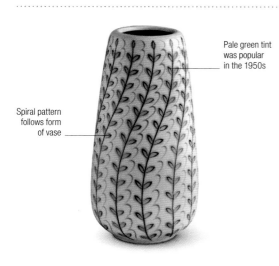

Pale green tint
was popular
in the 1950s

Spiral pattern
follows form
of vase

Contemporary vase | Alfred B. Read for Poole Pottery, *c.* 1953–1955, **UK**. Read's designs had subtle, curving patterns featuring motifs such as leaves and stripes. Decoration like this made a refreshing change from plain British wartime wares.

Triangular finial

Tapering,
spindle shape

Model 2000 coffee service | Raymond Loewy and Richard Latham for Rosenthal, 1954, **US**. This unusual, spindle-shaped form was popular in the 1950s. It came in various colorways, including some with discreet patterns.

Recessed lid

Soy sauce bottle | Masahiro Mori for Hakusan Toki, 1958, **Japan**. Mori excelled at designing simple, functional, and memorably Modernist forms for everyday tableware. This bottle was produced in several plain colors.

Water pitcher 1075 | **Henning Koppel for Georg Jensen**, 1952, **Denmark**. Koppel was a successful silversmith who worked for Georg Jensen from the late 1940s onward. He designed elegant, curvaceous forms that were intended to look beautiful from any angle. This polished steel pitcher with an exaggerated lip is one of his most famous creations.

Handle has a pronounced upward sweep

Curving silver knob

Heatproof melamine handle

Contour coffee service | **John Van Koert and Robert J. King for Towle**, 1951–1952, **US**. Designer Van Koert created this silver coffee service with metalworker King. The simple lines and forms were influenced by Danish silversmith Georg Jensen.

Meticulous hand-finished surface

AJ flatware | **Arne Jacobsen**, 1951, **Denmark**. This minimalist but immaculately finished flatware, in which the handles and fork tines merge, is a classic style still produced today, more than 60 years after it was designed.

Head of fork matches the size of spoon bowl

Diamond-shaped spoon bowl

Flatware | **Gio Ponti for Argenteria Krupp**, *c.* 1951, **Italy**. Architect Gio Ponti designed this distinctive stainless steel flatware. The diamond hole in the handles mirrors the shape of the spoon bowl, showing the designer's inventiveness.

DOMESTIC METALWARE

Although many metalworkers trained as silversmiths, producing table- and flatware using traditional techniques, in the 1950s, they were increasingly drawn to materials such as aluminum and stainless steel. These were considered ideal for well-designed, mass-produced items, since they were not only cheaper than silver but also easier to care for. Scandinavian designers, such as Arne Jacobsen, produced successful, modern-looking wares that were simple in form and easy to clean. There was also a strong group of British metalworkers, many of whom trained at the Royal College of Art in London; of these, Robert Welch, David Mellor, and Gerald Benney all established lasting reputations. Whether making one-of-a-kind pieces in silver or creating practical stainless steel items for mass production, the best metalworkers created distinctive designs that have stood the test of time.

Acetal resin handle

Brushed satin finish

Pride cutlery | **David Mellor for Walker and Hall**, 1953, **UK**. David Mellor had a long career designing cutlery. In his Pride line, he blended the proportions and fine finish of traditional cutlery with sleek forms, creating a modern classic.

Como tea and coffee service | **Lino Sabattini for L'Orfèvrerie Christofle**, 1957, **Italy/France**. The striking, asymmetrical shapes of Sabattini's silver-plated brass Como range influenced many contemporary designers.

Flatware | **Russel Wright for the John Hills Cutlery Corporation**, 1957, **US**. A prolific industrial designer, Russel Wright believed in making objects for easier living. His stainless steel flatware felt good in the hand and was easy to clean.

Slight rim

Curved sides

Pagoda-like divisions

Gently upturned handle

Tapering spout with slight flare

Wooden insulator

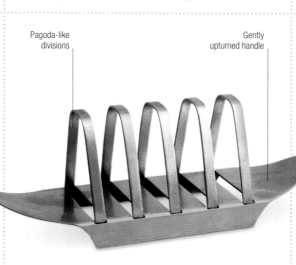

Bowl | **Sori Yanagi**, *c.* 1958, **Japan**. This stainless steel bowl shows how beautiful sheer simplicity can be. Like much 1950s metalware, it was designed for mass production, making good design accessible to ordinary working people.

Oriana toast rack | **Robert Welch**, *c.* 1958, **UK**. Influenced by the Scandinavians' use of stainless steel, Welch designed many items for mass production. This toast rack, created for the cruise liner *Oriana*, is one of his most enduring designs.

Saddleback teapot | **Gerald Benney**, 1960, **UK**. Benney favored strong, slightly quirky geometric shapes, as in this immaculately finished silver teapot. The gently concave "saddleback" lid gives the teapot its name.

△ **This 1953 Perpetua fabric** design for Heal's shows Day's artful use of strong and recessive elements.

Lucienne Day

The British designer Lucienne Day is famous for her bright, original textiles and wallpapers, which helped revitalize design in the decades after World War II. At a time when conventional floral chintzes were fashionable, she based her designs on abstracted botanical forms, simplifying them and making them more geometric. Day's palette was vibrant, often including a bright, slightly acidic yellow, but she limited it to a few colors in each design. Her patterns also drew on abstract art—especially the works of the Catalan Surrealist Joan Miró and Swiss German painter Paul Klee. Day first came to attention with her plant-based design for Heal's called Calyx, which was hung in the Homes and Gardens Pavilion of London's South Bank exhibition for the 1951 Festival of Britain.

From then on, Day had a successful career designing a huge number of fabrics. Although some of these were hand printed on linen, others were produced in bulk on newly developed, synthetic fabrics such as rayon, which made them accessible to people on modest incomes. Day also created many designs for carpets and wallpapers. Through the 1950s and 1960s, her designs evolved, becoming more linear and then more vibrant, incorporating brighter zigzags and stripes. Together with her husband, the designer Robin Day, she worked as design consultant for BOAC, and for John Lewis from 1962 to 1987, but she always kept her creative independence and had a lasting influence on the decor of British homes.

Life

1917–2010

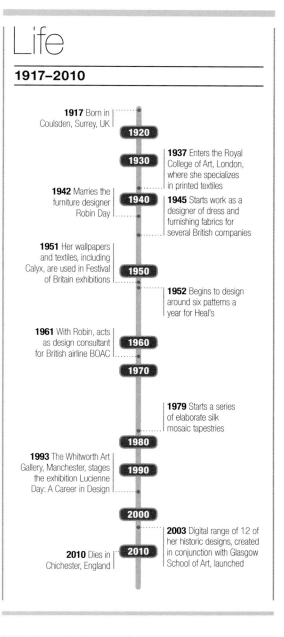

1917 Born in Coulsden, Surrey, UK

1920

1930

1937 Enters the Royal College of Art, London, where she specializes in printed textiles

1942 Marries the furniture designer Robin Day

1940

1945 Starts work as a designer of dress and furnishing fabrics for several British companies

1951 Her wallpapers and textiles, including Calyx, are used in Festival of Britain exhibitions

1950

1952 Begins to design around six patterns a year for Heal's

1961 With Robin, acts as design consultant for British airline BOAC

1960

1970

1979 Starts a series of elaborate silk mosaic tapestries

1980

1993 The Whitworth Art Gallery, Manchester, stages the exhibition Lucienne Day: A Career in Design

1990

2000

2003 Digital range of 12 of her historic designs, created in conjunction with Glasgow School of Art, launched

2010 Dies in Chichester, England

2010

Calyx furnishing fabric | **For Heal's**, 1951. Calyx was Day's breakthrough design. Its abstracted plant forms and strong but limited color palette set the style for 1950s design.

Small Hours fabric | **For Heal's**, 1952. One of Day's bolder designs, Small Hours contrasts large areas of black with abstract motifs, showing the influence of painters such as Paul Klee.

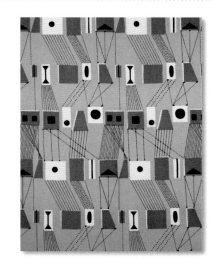

Rig fabric | **For Heal's**, 1953. The pattern of shapes connected by thin lines suggests the ropes and blocks of a ship's rigging. Heal's screen printed the design onto linen.

△ **A 1962 magazine advertisement for Tupperware** shows a woman sitting beside an Eero Saarinen Tulip table covered in plastic containers.

Plastics

△ **Cactus-shaped juicer** | Gear Atelier for Living Gear, 1995

Plastics came to the forefront of design in the late 19th century, after the discovery of Parkesine (later branded as Celluloid), the first synthetic thermoplastic—a plastic that softens when heated and hardens when cooled. Manufacturers liked thermoplastics because they could be formed in a mold and therefore offered a cheap alternative to materials such as ivory or tortoiseshell for making objects as diverse as billiard balls and combs. The first completely synthetic thermoset (hardens when heated) plastic was Bakelite, which was extensively used in the first half of the 20th century for everything from radio cabinets to jewelry. Bakelite was usually dark brown, as in early electric switches and radios, but scientists soon discovered ways to make plastics in a wide range of colors, from jade green to red, finishing them to a shiny polish.

After World War II, plastics became increasingly popular as a material for kitchenware and kitchen units, light fixtures, electrical appliances, and toys. Manufacturers also made furniture from them—plastic chairs began to appear in large numbers in the 1950s, and by the following decade, their bright colors, unusual molded shapes, and practicality had made them ubiquitous. Since then, the versatility of plastics has given designers the chance to try out ever more inventive shapes, making the world a more colorful place.

Key dates

1862–

1862 Parkesine features in the International Exhibition in London

1860

1870 The Hyatt brothers create Celluloid. It proves a commercial success.

1880

1900

1907 Belgian Leo Baekeland invents Bakelite

1920

1920s Couturier Coco Chanel uses Bakelite in her jewelry collections

1931 Bakelite telephones are mass-produced by Siemens

1933 The ICI company invents the first practical polyethylene

1935 Nylon is patented

1938 Earl Tupper develops Tupperware, using waste products from the oil industry

1940

1946 Melamine, a tough, heat-resistant resin, is developed

1963 British designer Robin Day produces the first mass-produced molded chair

1960

1963 Eero Aarnio's Ball chair makes plastic furniture synonymous with 1960s pop culture

2020

Patriot radio | **Norman Bel Geddes for Emerson**, 1940. This radio, which came in different colorways, has a curved grille, demonstrating Bel Geddes's love of streamlining.

Case made of polished Catalin

Carrying handle

Tupperware tumblers | **Tupperware Corporation** 1950s–1960s. These tall tumblers, made of injection-molded polyethylene, were sold in a range of translucent colors.

Textured plastic surface

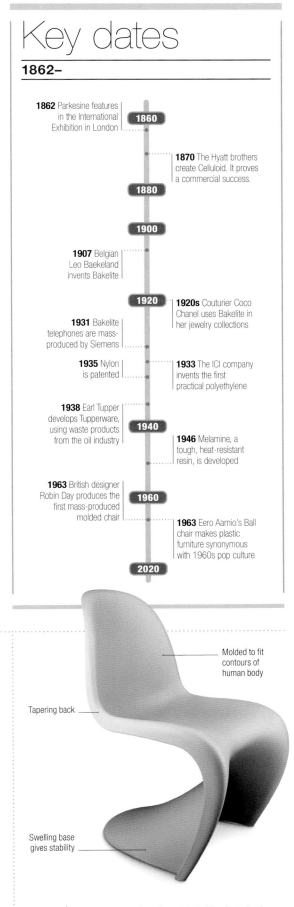

Molded to fit contours of human body

Tapering back

Swelling base gives stability

S chair | **Verner Panton for Vitra**, 1959. The first plastic chair to be made of a single component, its curved form creates a sense of lightness.

DOMESTIC APPLIANCES

In the first half of the 20th century, a range of electrical appliances was invented. At first, they were heavy and cumbersome—televisions and radios had bulky wooden cabinets to make them look like traditional pieces of furniture, and kitchen gadgets were chunky. In the 1950s, designers took advantage of new technology to reduce the size of appliances, making them neater and better suited to compact, contemporary rooms. Television sets and radios became lighter and smaller, and kitchen appliances were sleeker and easier to clean. The fashion for soft-edged, modern-looking design led to objects that were a pleasure to handle, and the best examples had clearly marked controls. Products also became simpler to use—technology was no longer something that required expertise but a part of everyday life.

Rise of home appliances

1950s

After World War II, most homes in the Western world had electricity, and television ownership burgeoned in the 1950s. This created a market for television receivers, transistor radios, stereos, and other gadgets for the home. Many more women also went out to work and had less time for housework.

The leisured modernity that machines and industry helped create was captured by British artist Richard Hamilton in his famous Pop collage below. Electrical appliances such as the vacuum cleaner, TV, and tape recorder, as well as the canned ham and giant lollipop, reference the consumerism and increasingly colorful advertising imagery of the time.

Just what is it that makes today's homes so different, so appealing? Richard Hamilton, 1956

Kenwood Chef food mixer | **Ken Wood,** *c.* 1950, UK. As well as brightening up the kitchen, this elegant processor could mix everything from dough to cocktails and had attachments for potato peeling and sausage making.

Two plastic switches operate dryer and control temperature

Bakelite hairdryer | **Ormond Engineering Company Ltd.,** 1950s, UK. The casing of this electric handheld dryer is made in two sections held together by screws. The pistol shape is geometric, based on circles and cylinders.

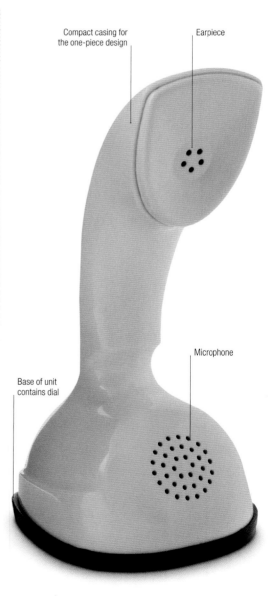

Compact casing for the one-piece design

Earpiece

Base of unit contains dial

Microphone

Ericofon | **Ralph Lysell for Ericsson,** 1954, Sweden. This phone was totally unlike the two-piece telephones of the 1950s. It came in a range of colors and was popular with hospitals since it was easy to use and comfortable to hold even when lying in bed.

Company name embossed in chrome

Ergonomic handle

Refrigerator | **Smeg design team**, *c.* 1950, **Italy**. Smeg tapped into the spirit of the age with its line of now-classic refrigerators. As dining lost formality and snacks became more popular, the refrigerator was designed to be a focal point in the kitchen. Smoothly rounded corners and fashionable color choices gave it a wide consumer appeal that lasts to this day.

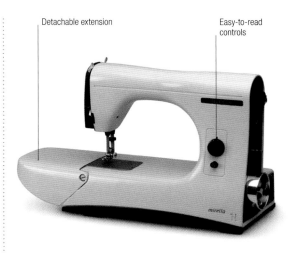

Detachable extension

Easy-to-read controls

Mirella sewing machine | **Marcello Nizzoli**, 1956–1957, **Italy**. Designed to appeal to people who wanted an electric alternative to hand-cranked or treadle machines, the Mirella had smooth lines and a needle mechanism with an integral light.

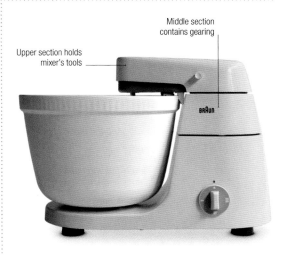

Middle section contains gearing

Upper section holds mixer's tools

KM3 food mixer | **Gerd Alfred Müller for Braun**, 1957, **Germany**. The positioning of the motor in the bottom section of this unit and the tapering design make the mixer both stable and sculptural. Its internal parts are separated by horizontal divisions.

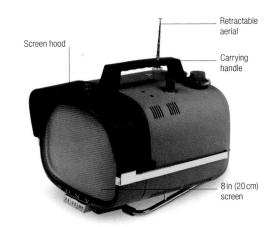

Retractable aerial

Screen hood

Carrying handle

8 in (20 cm) screen

TV-8-301 | **Sony design team**, 1959, **Japan**. The first TV to be fully transistorized, Sony's portable was much smaller than any previous model. Its metal curves follow the shape of the screen, and a protruding hood helps reduce glare.

EVOLUTION OF
VACUUM CLEANERS

The first vacuum cleaners were hand operated and were superseded by electric models only after World War I. As more and more women began working outside the home, manufacturers responded to the needs of busier households with cleaners that were lighter, more efficient, and easier to use. Designers also responded to fashion, making streamlined cylinder cleaners in the interwar period and adopting the bright colors and strong forms of postmodernism in the late 20th century. Improved suction mechanisms from manufacturers such as Dyson, and the introduction of robotic cleaners, have made this an ever-more competitive and innovative field.

1910 Vacuum cleaner | Star, UK.
Developed by the bicycle company Star, this vacuum cleaner was powered by hand. Users had to push and pull the central pump up and down, creating a vacuum that sucked air and dust in through the cleaning head.

Accordion-like drum

Cleaning head

Carrying handle made of ridged plastic

Dust bag features Hoover's iconic logo

Bakelite handle

Bag made of heavy oiled cotton

Handle ridged for grip

Colorful ABS plastic components

Dust collects in transparent cylinder

1926–1930 Dustette handheld cleaner | Hoover, US.
The Dustette was the first of Hoover's pioneering line of handheld cleaners. It was lightweight, with a dust bag attached to a small unit housing the motor, and enabled the user to clean up crumbs or pet hairs.

1936 Hoover Junior Model 375 upright cleaner | Henry Dreyfuss, US.
The influence of automobile design is evident in the streamlining that Dreyfuss applied to this vacuum cleaner. The model includes a carpet beater driven by a spindle of the fan motor.

Carrying handle

Vacuum unit separates from charger

1954 Constellation | Hoover, US.
Spherical in shape, the Constellation seemed to be a cleaner for the coming Space Age. Its unique selling point was that it floated on a cushion of air and could be pulled across a room with just a gentle tug. Its flared skirt directed exhaust downward.

1981 Dustbuster | Mark Proett and Carroll Gantz for Black and Decker, US.
Originally marketed for workshop users, these cordless vacuum cleaners were soon taken up in the home, and the Dustbuster became a success. The convenient cordless operation was popular.

1986 Dual Cyclone cleaner | James Dyson, UK.
Dyson's big innovation was to make a bagless cleaner, because vacuum cleaner bags tend to clog up, reducing suction. This machine uses a cyclone mechanism, which spins air around, removing the dust by centrifugal force.

1914 **Baby Daisy cleaner** | **France/United Kingdom**. This hand-operated cleaner worked by pumping a bellows to create a partial vacuum. One person worked the bellows, which were double-action, to create a vacuum with each movement of the pole. Another person collected dust, using the hose.

Leather bellows

Dust bag concealed inside the machine

1920 **Air-Way cleaner** | **Daniel Benson Replogle, US**. The swiveling motor of the ingenious, lightweight Air-Way made it easy to clean under furniture. The suction could also be diverted along the hollow handle, to get at dirt or cobwebs that were beyond the reach of the floor nozzle. A filter kept the exhaust air clean.

Valve allows suction to be diverted

Self-adjusting wheels made it possible to clean both hard floors and rugs

1920 **Cylinder cleaner** | **Electrolux, UK**. Electrolux successfully tapped into the popular desire for a cylindrical vacuum cleaner. The machine's cylinder contained the motor and dust bag; a flexible hose took different tools to clean all kinds of surfaces. It was easy to drag the cylinder around on its metal gliders.

Upholstery attachment

Canvas outer bag

Top section houses motor

Dust is collected in the bottom section

1936–1937 **Rexair Model A** | **T. Russ Hill, US**. The Rexair was an innovative canister cleaner. It did away with the filter and dust bag, as these tended to become clogged. Water in the bottom section trapped fine dust, preventing it from being expelled back into the room.

1937 **Vacuum cleaner** | **Raymond Loewy for Electrolux, US**. Electrolux hired the streamlining expert Raymond Loewy to create its 1937 canister model. Loewy produced a torpedo-like shape and set the cylinder on polished metal gliders.

ELECTROLUX

1950s **Junior upright** **1224** | **Hoover, US**. In the 1950s, Hoover marketed their cleaners on the basis of their light weight and convenience. These small Junior vacuum cleaners, similar in shape to the company's 1930s models, had a reusable canvas dust bag.

Powerful motor spins at up to 125,000 rpm

Wand body is light enough to lift up walls

Anthropomorphic decoration

Henry

Control buttons allow users to select room size

Roomba Robotic FloorVac

2002 **Roomba cleaner** | **iRobot Corporation, US**. The first commercially successful robotic cleaner, Roomba's sensors track its course around the room, redirecting it if it meets an obstacle. If the robot gets stuck, the motor switches off and the machine sounds an alarm.

2009 **Henry** | **Numatic, UK**. The selling point of the various Henry models, which were first released in 1980, is their smiling faces, which are reminiscent of the Thomas the Tank Engine characters. The models are robust and reliable but heavier than most cylinder vacuum cleaners.

2019 **Dyson V11 Absolute vacuum cleaner** | **Dyson, UK**. Cordless vacuum cleaners are now as efficient as plug-ins. Dyson has been at the forefront of creating cordless vacuums with lightweight "stick" bodies and no bag to empty. The V11 has a six-stage filtration system to capture the finest particles, as well as an advanced LCD screen.

△ **This recreation** of Dieter Rams's living space showcases his furniture, stereo, tiles, and rug, demonstrating characteristic clarity and simplicity.

Dieter Rams

The hugely influential German industrial designer Dieter Rams transformed the way products looked in the 1950s and 1960s. His most important work was for the German manufacturer Braun, for whom he became Design Director, creating hundreds of products such as stereo systems, alarm clocks, pocket calculators, and slide projectors. Through these products, he developed a clear and simple approach to design, rejecting the wooden casings in which many household items were hidden, and making products easier to understand and use. His designs look uncluttered and minimal but are carefully worked out down to the smallest detail. Their pleasant, rounded corners, clearly labeled, well-arranged controls, and stylish finish made them a joy to use. Above all, similarly designed modules can be used separately or together—for instance, the PC3-SV turntable unit was incorporated into other Braun stereo systems.

Dieter Rams's designs also set trends. Many manufacturers imitated Braun's black calculators, elegant stereo systems, and easy-to-use radios, but they copied their look without adopting Rams's thorough approach to design and detail, and few of the copies were as effective or as well made. However, Rams's design principles were also influential at a deeper level, and designers today, such as Jonathan Ive, Senior Vice President for Design at Apple (see pp.364–365), follow the principles he established.

Life

1932–

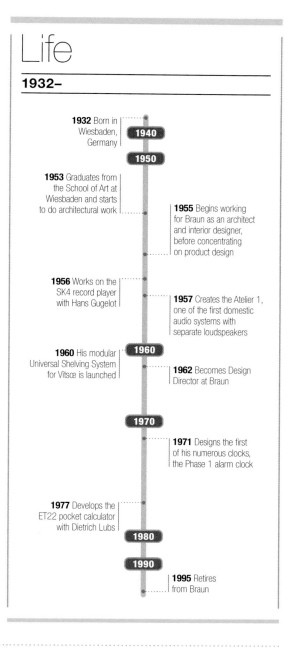

1932 Born in Wiesbaden, Germany

1940

1950

1953 Graduates from the School of Art at Wiesbaden and starts to do architectural work

1955 Begins working for Braun as an architect and interior designer, before concentrating on product design

1956 Works on the SK4 record player with Hans Gugelot

1957 Creates the Atelier 1, one of the first domestic audio systems with separate loudspeakers

1960 His modular Universal Shelving System for Vitsœ is launched

1960

1962 Becomes Design Director at Braun

1970

1971 Designs the first of his numerous clocks, the Phase 1 alarm clock

1977 Develops the ET22 pocket calculator with Dietrich Lubs

1980

1990

1995 Retires from Braun

T24 portable transistor radio | **For Braun**, 1956. Inside the slim plastic case—so different from the prevalent wooden cases—are transistors, making the radio light enough to carry.

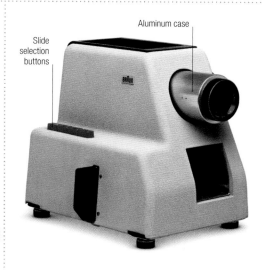

PA2 slide projector | **For Braun**, 1956. The PA2 has simply labeled controls and an automatic mechanism that loads slides from a tray. Before, the operator had to load slides one by one.

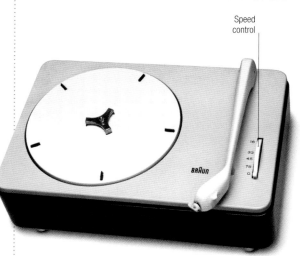

PC3-SV turntable | **For Braun**, 1957. With only one control, to regulate the speed, the motor starts when the user lifts the pickup arm and stops when the record has finished playing.

Shape of handle follows line of case

Plastics are the hallmark of modern design.

Peter **Müller-Munk**

Translucent plastic enables user to see how full container is

Lid has seal based on those used on metal paint cans

Tupperware lidded bowl | **Earl Tupper**, 1946, US. Tupper created containers using plastic made from waste from the oil refining process. The containers became successful when they were sold at Tupperware parties held in people's homes.

Bush TR82C transistor radio | **Ogle Design**, 1959, UK. In a turn away from dark Bakelite, this successful portable radio has a pale plastic molded case and vinyl sides. The large tuning dial is made from clear injection-molded polystyrene.

POSTWAR
HOMEWARES

After World War II, the US enjoyed an economic boom, which gave its citizens more spending power. Industry responded by flooding the market with homewares for this new consumer class. In Europe, the mood was more austere, but there was still an expanding market as economies picked up and homeowners restocked their houses. Designers and manufacturers responded enthusiastically, bringing modern design and technology to millions of homes for the first time. Some midcentury Modernist design followed the aesthetic austerity of the Bauhaus era or the rationality that underpinned design at the influential design school at Ulm in the late 1950s and 1960s, but there also was a prevailing mood of optimism, which encouraged postwar designers to create cheerier, more colorful, and more affordable objects to liven up people's homes.

Keyboard lacks keys for numbers 0 and 1

Bold colors and a stackable design

Atomic Wall Clock | **George Nelson**, 1949, US. Nelson's design started as a sketch made one evening with friends, the designers Isamu Noguchi, R. Buckminster Fuller, and Irving Harper, based on the balls scientists use to model molecules.

Olivetti Lettera 22 typewriter | **Marcello Nizzoli**, 1950, **Italy**. Designed to be portable, and a favorite with journalists, this sleek and functional typewriter won the inaugural Compasso d'Oro, an Italian industrial design award, in 1954.

Lemon juicers | **Gino Columbini for Kartell**, 1958, **Italy**. These juicers, along with a Kartell line of other small, low-cost, plastic household items, turned utilitarian products into something colorful and fun. They were hugely successful.

Volume control

Woven plastic speaker grille

Tuning control

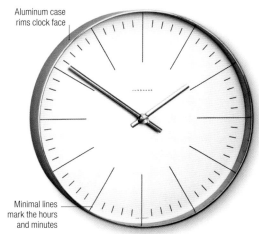

Aluminum case rims clock face

Minimal lines mark the hours and minutes

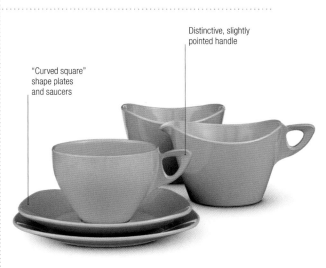

Distinctive, slightly pointed handle

"Curved square" shape plates and saucers

R786 Coronation Twin Radio | **Ultra Electric Ltd.**, 1953, **UK**. Designed to work using battery or AC power, this radio has case panels of molded phenol formaldehyde and Bakelite, including removable sections for accessing the batteries.

Wall clock | **Max Bill**, 1957, Germany/Switzerland. Bauhaus-trained Max Bill had a mathematical approach to design. He pared the clock face down to its basics to create what German designers of his era called "good form."

Modern tea service | **A. H. Woodfall and John Vale for Midwinter**, 1957, **UK**. Midwinter won awards for their tableware that combined strong shapes with plain colors or simple abstract patterns, coming after decades of floral crockery.

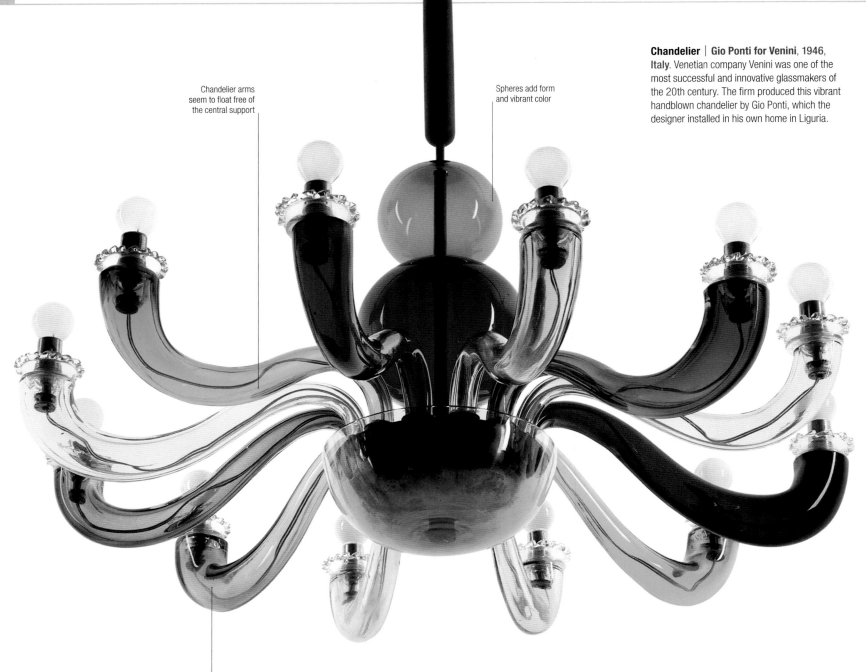

Chandelier arms
seem to float free of
the central support

Spheres add form
and vibrant color

Chandelier | Gio Ponti for Venini, 1946,
Italy. Venetian company Venini was one of the
most successful and innovative glassmakers of
the 20th century. The firm produced this vibrant
handblown chandelier by Gio Ponti, which the
designer installed in his own home in Liguria.

Arms have a generous
sweeping double curve

DECORATIVE
GLASSWARE

In the postwar years, decorative glassware became
more colorful and adventurous in form. The Venetian island
of Murano, a key center of glass production, experienced
a revival, employing many designers who were new to the world of glass. Manufacturers such as Venini, Cenedese, Vistosi,
and Seguso Vetri d'Arte produced outstanding work, much of which reinterpreted traditional techniques. Rods of glass
were used in cross section to create colored patterns called murrines, and layers of colored glass were combined to
dazzling effect. Murano and other flourishing centers of glassmaking, such as Czechoslovakia (now the Czech Republic),
known for both its cut-glass vessels and its organic-looking, sculptural molded glass, attracted the interest of consumers.
This resulted in the widespread use of colorful glassware, from vases to chandeliers, as a key element of interior design.

Transparent upper section

Lower part of body in opaque glass

Incalmo decanters | **Gio Ponti for Venini**, 1946, Italy. Both of these stoppered bottles were made using the *incalmo* technique, in which two sections of a vessel are blown separately and then joined together while still hot.

This colorway is known as "Paris"

Translucent color reveals other shades on the opposite side of the vase

Flowing, asymmetrical form

Pezzato vase | **Fulvio Bianconi for Venini**, 1950, Italy. Tesserae (colored squares of glass) are fused onto the clear glass body of this patchwork vase, recalling Bianconi's early career as an illustrator and graphic designer.

Layers of red, blue, and turquoise glass

Sommerso ashtray | **Seguso Vetri d'Arte**, 1950s, Italy. The *sommerso* technique, in which layers of colored glass are combined, was much used by Seguso Vetri d'Arte of Murano. The curvaceous form of this ashtray is typical of their work.

Shape of pouring lip mirrors dimple

V-shaped pattern made by dimple

Vase | **Jan Kotík for Borske sklo glassworks**, 1957, **Czechoslovakia**. Painter, printmaker, and glass artist Jan Kotík experimented with colored glass to create abstract designs. This jewel-toned vase was shown at the 1957 Milan Triennale.

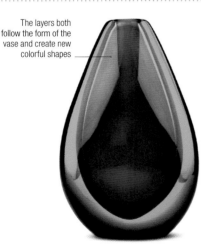

The layers both follow the form of the vase and create new colorful shapes

Sommerso vase | **Flavio Poli for Seguso Vetri d'Arte,** *c.* 1958, Italy. This vase shows the rich color effects possible when using the layered *sommerso* technique. Both blue and green glass are simultaneously visible through the clear casing.

Clear murrines are revealed when glass is cut in cross section

Neck twist distorts the square pattern

Occhi vase | **Carlo Scarpa for Venini,** *c.* 1959, Italy. Architect Scarpa was one of many outside the glassmaking industry who designed for the Murano companies. Here, he has created a striking, gridlike pattern of red lines and clear squares.

Lemonade carafe and glasses | **Adolf Matura**, 1959– 1960, Czechoslovakia. The elegance of this drinks set, combining a green carafe and clear glasses, unified by the deep dimples in their bases, won it a prize at the 1960 Milan Triennale.

DINO MARTENS

Model 5380 Oriente vase

YEAR 1954 | **MANUFACTURER** Aureliano Toso, Murano, Venice | **DIMENSIONS** *Height* 17³⁄₄ in (43.8 cm), *Diameter* 5¹⁄₂ in (14 cm) | **MATERIALS** Polychrome patchwork glass

Italian painter and designer Dino Martens was artistic director of the Aureliano Toso glassworks on the island of Murano, Venice, between 1946 and 1960. Collaborating closely with the factory's master glassworkers, he produced one-of-a-kind vases and dishes using traditional techniques in new ways to create dazzling pieces that seemed to express the optimism of the times.

The vases of his Oriente series are often asymmetrical in form, and their decoration draws on Martens's background as a painter to produce dynamic combinations of color and pattern. They typically feature techniques such as filigrana (a range of patterns made up of fine glass rods) and murrines (bundles of colored rods cut to reveal their patterned cross section), combined in innovative ways and using bright colors.

Martens also used aventurine glass, in which metals such as copper are combined with the material to produce a shimmering effect. In his Oriente vases, he employed these techniques to produce abstract compositions that were both eye-catching and, because of the technical challenges they posed, showcases of the glassworker's craft. This radical approach to both decoration and form gave the glass industry on Murano a much-needed boost.

A contemporary equivalent in glass to Abstract Expressionist painting

Sotheby's Concise Encyclopedia

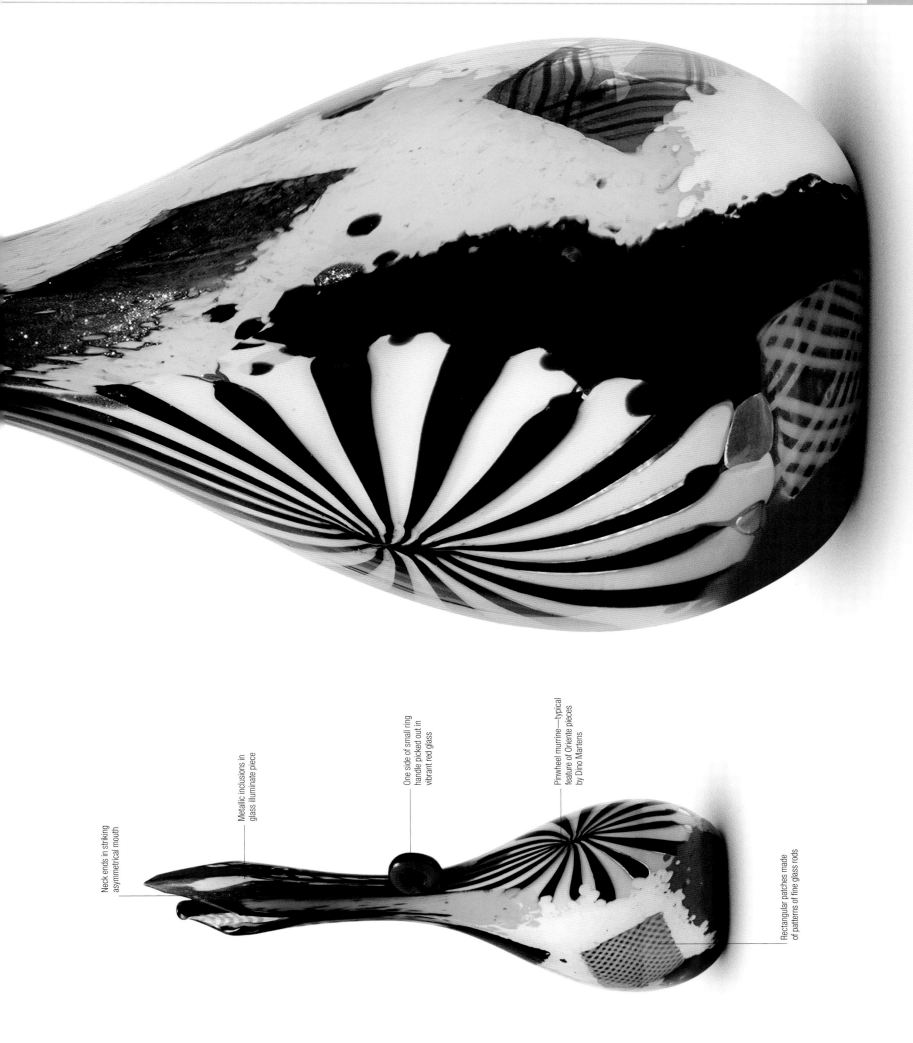

Neck ends in striking asymmetrical mouth

Metallic inclusions in glass illuminate piece

One side of small ring handle picked out in vibrant red glass

Pinwheel murrine—typical feature of Oriente pieces by Dino Martens

Rectangular patches made of patterns of fine glass rods

Clear, olive-tinged glass

Heavy base and flat bottom provide stability

Egg sculpture | **Kaj Franck for Nuutajärvi**, **1951**, **Finland**. Franck's glass is known for its simplicity and balance. This piece takes the form of a vase, with a narrow opening at the top, but is intended as a sculpture, to be admired for its purity.

Slightly tapering form

Spots on opposite sides overlap

Pantteri (Panther) vase | **Saara Hopea for Nuutajärvi**, **1954**, **Finland**. Best known for her jewelry, Hopea created pattern and texture with colored inclusions (both purple and green versions were made) and bubbles in the glass.

Facets like icicles

Jäävuori (Iceberg) vase | **Tapio Wirkkala**, **1950**, **Finland**. Wirkkala made this thick-walled, faceted vase by blowing glass into a mold. It is a good example of the inspiration he took from the natural scenery of the Nordic lands.

SCANDINAVIAN
GLASS

Europe's Nordic countries are still a major center of glass production, and after World War II, companies such as Kosta, Iittala, Orrefors, and Nuutajärvi were at the forefront of glassware design and manufacture, producing pieces that had enough sculptural presence to form the focal point of a room. These companies employed some of the greatest designers, such as Kaj Franck and Per Lütken, who favored smooth surfaces and organic forms, and Tapio Wirkkala, who was known for his use of texture. They were inspired by a wide range of influences, drawing on a mixture of pure, Modernist forms and natural themes, notably Scandinavia's scenery—its rocks and fjords, and the textures of stones, bark, and ice. The resulting cased or mold-blown glass was technically outstanding but looked more restrained than that of Italy or Czechoslovakia, with its palette of muted colors such as cool, translucent blues and greens.

Combination of clear and brown glass creates a smoky effect

Kosta bowl | **Vicke Lindstrand for Kosta**, *c.* 1955, Sweden. For this bowl, Lindstrand used the cased technique, in which a layer of clear glass is placed over the colored glass while the material is still hot.

Thick walls

Heavy base

Vase | **Per Lütken for Holmegaard**, 1958, Denmark. Lütken was especially known for his curvaceous 1950s vases in cool colors such as gray and ice blue. This example is typical of his pieces, but he also made asymmetrical designs.

Spherical upper stopper

Rounded forms like Russian onion domes

Tapered base

Lower vessel echoes forms above

Kremlin Bells decanter No. 1500 | **Kaj Franck for Nuutajärvi**, 1957, Finland. This piece is two containers in one, with the upper decanter acting as a stopper for the lower one. Both the rounded forms and ingenuity are typical of Franck.

Cross section looks like a cog wheel, with teeth and depressions

Sides thicken toward base

Cog vase | **Tapio Wirkkala**, 1950s, Finland. This acid-etched and highly polished vase was inspired by machinery rather than nature and has a hard-edged profile to match. The teeth of the "cog" reflect the light in stripes.

Straight-sided rim

Ball glass | **Timo Sarpaneva for Iittala**, 1955, Finland. Sarpaneva used this gently curving shape for clear and opaque white glasses in several sizes. This version bears out Kaj Franck's assertion that "color is the only decoration needed."

DESERT HEAT

With its walls of Utah sandstone, white interior surfaces, thin flat roofs, and huge areas of glass, the Kaufmann Desert House epitomizes postwar American Modernism. Its architect, Austrian-born Richard Neutra, designed many such houses, but this one, for businessman Edgar J. Kaufmann, is one of his best. The cool color palette, elegant rooms, and complex floor plan (with service wing, master suite, and guest wing radiating from a central living space) are all brilliantly handled.

Neutra had to be especially inventive to manage the relationship between inside and out. He wanted to include plenty of glass, and when the sliding glass panels are pushed back, the house and garden merge. However, the desert heat, wind, and sunlight posed a challenge to this approach. Neutra provided movable screen walls to give shelter from sandstorms, louvers and overhanging roofs to create shade, and an upper-level unroofed sleeping area to take advantage of the heat. Neutra's houses inspired many other architects and builders, but few achieved his sensitivity to materials, concept, and location.

I am an **eyewitness** to the ways in which **people relate** ... and my work is a way of **scooping and ladling** that experience.

Richard **Neutra**

Kaufmann Desert House, Palm Springs, California, Richard Neutra, 1946 In the seating area, sliding panes of glass with overhanging roofs create a pattern of warming light and cool shade. Full-height curtains are also part of the system that Neutra developed to regulate light and heat indoors.

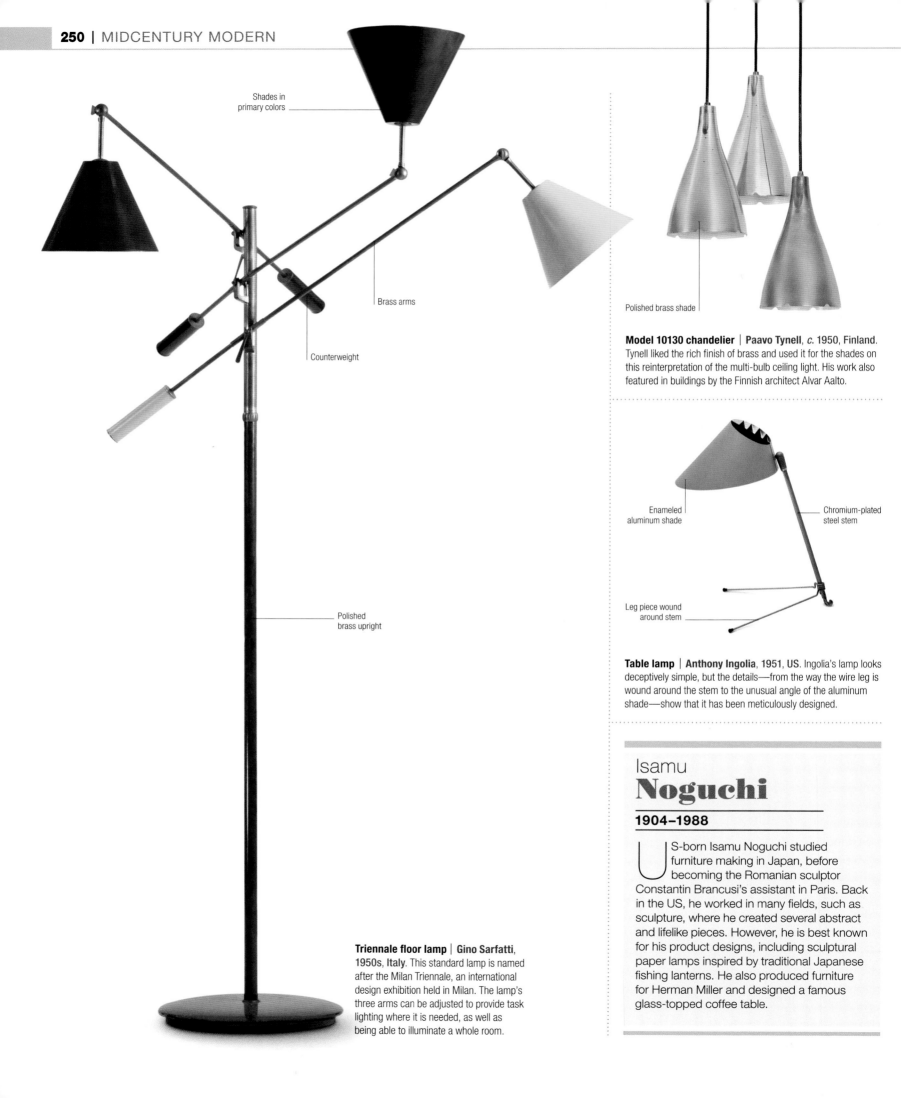

Shades in primary colors

Brass arms

Counterweight

Polished brass upright

Triennale floor lamp | **Gino Sarfatti**, **1950s, Italy**. This standard lamp is named after the Milan Triennale, an international design exhibition held in Milan. The lamp's three arms can be adjusted to provide task lighting where it is needed, as well as being able to illuminate a whole room.

Polished brass shade

Model 10130 chandelier | **Paavo Tynell**, *c.* 1950, Finland. Tynell liked the rich finish of brass and used it for the shades on this reinterpretation of the multi-bulb ceiling light. His work also featured in buildings by the Finnish architect Alvar Aalto.

Enameled aluminum shade

Chromium-plated steel stem

Leg piece wound around stem

Table lamp | **Anthony Ingolia**, 1951, US. Ingolia's lamp looks deceptively simple, but the details—from the way the wire leg is wound around the stem to the unusual angle of the aluminum shade—show that it has been meticulously designed.

Isamu
Noguchi
1904–1988

US-born Isamu Noguchi studied furniture making in Japan, before becoming the Romanian sculptor Constantin Brancusi's assistant in Paris. Back in the US, he worked in many fields, such as sculpture, where he created several abstract and lifelike pieces. However, he is best known for his product designs, including sculptural paper lamps inspired by traditional Japanese fishing lanterns. He also produced furniture for Herman Miller and designed a famous glass-topped coffee table.

SCULPTURAL LIGHTING

In the 1950s, many designers turned their attention to producing lamps for desks or dining tables, as well as more general mood lighting. Some of their lights were highly sculptural, ranging from Isamu Noguchi's paper lamps—restrained in color but generous in size—to the minimalist forms created by the Castiglioni brothers. Designers realized that they could make their lamps look modern by simply using a metal rod as a stem, for example, or by giving them conical shades. A polished silver or bronze finish could suggest luxury, while bright colors created a more contemporary and lighthearted feel.

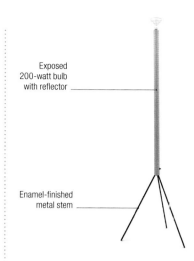

Exposed 200-watt bulb with reflector

Enamel-finished metal stem

Luminator floor lamp | **Achille and Pier Giacomo Castiglioni**, **1955, Italy**. Designed by the Castiglioni brothers, and made by Gilardi and Barzaghi, this minimalist uplighter has slender steel legs and a painted upright reflector.

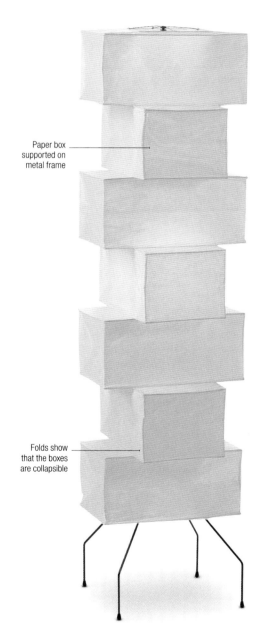

Paper box supported on metal frame

Folds show that the boxes are collapsible

Light sculpture | **Isamu Noguchi**, *c.* 1950, US. Noguchi created a whole series of lights from folded paper structures, similar to Japanese paper lanterns, supported on a metal frame. In this example, the boxes are stacked one upon the other.

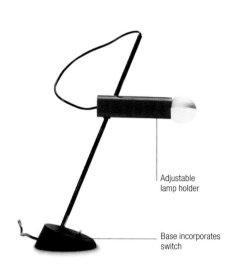

Adjustable lamp holder

Base incorporates switch

566 table lamp | **Gino Sarfatti for Arteluce**, **1956, Italy**. The 566 table lamp is typical of Arteluce's many finely crafted pieces. The heavy base keeps the upright at a constant steep angle, but the lamp holder moves up and down.

Steel shade

Space originally designed for ashtray

Desk lamp | **Arne Jacobsen**, **1956, Denmark**. This desk lamp by Jacobsen has an immaculate black-lacquered finish. The conical shade directs the beam downward, making it easy to adjust the position of the light as required.

Light made of painted spun aluminum

Shade reflects light downward

PH50 ceiling light | **Poul Henningsen**, **1958, Denmark**. This light, 20 in (50 cm) in diameter, was designed to hang low above a table and provide a glare-free light. It was produced in a range of colors, including white.

Cestita lamp | **Miguel Mila for Santa & Cole**, **1962, Spain**. This lightweight, portable lantern can be used either on a tabletop or on the floor. It combines a simple pine frame with a frosted glass lamp that produces a subtle glowing light.

MIDCENTURY POSTERS

The graphic designers of the late 1940s and 1950s produced posters that were simpler and more eye-catching than those of the interwar period. They used large, vibrant blocks of color, striking typography, and photography to recreate the strong images used in newspapers and films. This graphic work involved bold visual gestures—a logo blown up to giant size, a humorous drawing, an informally placed object or figure. Lettering itself could suggest an atmosphere or mood—a script style for informality or red type to convey a warning. Although often amusing or informal, these posters were created with great care. Typographers such as Josef Müller-Brockmann and his Swiss colleagues meticulously arranged geometric, unadorned text to look striking and clear. Designers such as Abram Games and Saul Bass produced work with equal flair and precision, and their impact is still felt today.

Subway advertising poster | **Paul Rand**, 1947, US. The concentric circles of Rand's design simultaneously suggest a face, a target, and a subway tunnel. The three-word slogan and bold use of color pull the three ideas together.

Perrier poster | **Raymond Savignac**, 1950, France. Humor is a powerful element in advertising. In this poster, Savignac combined a cartoon figure with informal layout and typography to suggest a relaxed, enjoyable lifestyle.

Olivetti poster | **Giovanni Pintori**, 1953, Italy. Pintori's explosion of colored lines linking letters—suggesting the rapid movement of a typist's fingers from key to key—created a colorful poster for a product that is mainly monochromatic.

Univers typeface | **Adrian Frutiger**, 1954, Switzerland. Clean, legible Univers is still popular today for everything from corporate logos to airport signage. It was one of the first sans-serif fonts to remain identifiable in its various sizes and styles.

Nissan Laundry Soap silk-screen poster | **Hiroshi Ohchi**, 1954, Japan. Flat blocks of color are lightened by the fluid shapes and mass of carefully highlighted bubbles. The change of flesh tone above the wrists suggests water.

Bridlington poster | **Tom Eckersley**, 1955, UK. The vibrant colors and cheerful personification of the beach ball in this British Railways poster reflect the self-confidence of postwar Britain at its most optimistic.

The Man with the Golden Arm poster | **Saul Bass**, 1955, US. The jagged arm silhouette, uneven lettering, and irregular blocks of color in Bass's design combine to produce an unsettling effect, true to the atmosphere of the film.

Road safety poster | **Josef Müller-Brockmann**, 1957, **Switzerland**. The simple typography and the looming black vehicle that fills the poster's right-hand side convey its message instantly: "Passing? If in doubt, never!"

Propaganda poster | **Qinq Lingyu, Li Pingfan, Ping Ye, 1958, China**. Pitting China's steel industry against the UK's, this poster reads, "The industry of the Fatherland develops by leaps and bounds and frightens England so that it trembles with fear."

London Transport poster | **Abram Games**, 1947, **UK**. Games based his "At London's service" poster on London Transport's roundel device, bending it at the "waist" so that it bows, like a deferential servant, to passersby. This simple image makes its point immediately and works equally well from a distance or close up.

Script typeface for traditional slogan

MAX MIEDINGER

Helvetica

YEAR 1957 | **MANUFACTURER** Haas Type Foundry, Switzerland, licensed by Linotype, US | **DIMENSIONS** Variable | **MATERIALS** Originally type metal; now available as a digital font

On signs, posters, the printed page, and the computer screen, Helvetica is one of the most widely used fonts in the world, prized for its simplicity, elegance, and legibility. Its story began in the middle of the 20th century, when sans-serif typefaces (fonts without terminal strokes) were especially popular among printers and designers. At this time, typefaces were produced in metal by type foundries, and the Swiss Haas foundry wanted a sans-serif font of its own to rival the increasingly popular German typefaces.

Swiss typographer Max Miedinger responded with the 1957 design that became Helvetica—a simple, elegant typeface in which all the strokes end either vertically or horizontally, and the height of the lower-case "o" or "x" (known as the x-height) is relatively high, making the letters easily legible. Miedinger also specified that the letters should be set close together, giving them a strong impact and making them ideal for advertising and signage. Haas licensed the typeface to the American Linotype company, who named it Helvetica—part of the official Latin name for Switzerland (*Confoederatio Helvetica*)—in homage to the flair of Swiss typography.

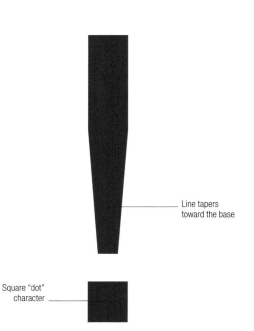

Line tapers toward the base

Square "dot" character

You have to breathe so you have to use Helvetica.

Erik **Spiekermann**
Typographer and designer

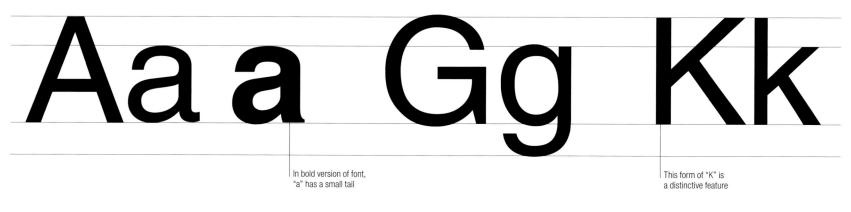

In bold version of font, "a" has a small tail

This form of "K" is a distinctive feature

Strokes of "c" terminate horizontally

Narrow spacing between letters

Aa a Gg Kk

abcdefghijklmnopqrs
tuvwxyz1234567890

EVOLUTION OF
CARS

After a slow beginning in the 1880s, when cars were made by hand and designed to look like carriages, the automobile industry was transformed by the development of mass production in the early 1900s. Since then, car design has broadened, with manufacturers making everything from economical, mass-produced family cars to carefully crafted luxury or high-performance vehicles.

The sleek, aerodynamic sports car and the sedan have since been joined by hatchbacks and completely innovative designs that remain classics, from the Austin Mini to the Citroën DS. More recently still, carmakers have taken up alternative engine systems, such as hybrid and electric motors, as customers become increasingly aware of the environmental and economic costs of gasoline.

Rack steering

Steel spoke wheel

1886 **Benz Patent-Motorwagen** | **Carl Benz, Germany**. The first production car had three wheels and a rear two-stroke gasoline engine. The spoked wheels, seat, springs, and other features were derived from those of the horse-drawn carriages of the period.

Hood enlarged only for 1970s 1302 model

Large wheels give a comfortable ride

Auxiliary headlights

Hydropneumatic suspension raises car when engine is turned on

Large body panels make the vehicle look virtually seamless

V8 engine

1939 **Volkswagen Beetle** | **Ferdinand Porsche, Germany**. Encouraged by Adolf Hitler, Ferdinand Porsche designed this inexpensive and simple "people's car." With its unusual shape and rear-mounted, air-cooled engine, the Beetle was instantly recognizable and eventually became the world's bestselling vehicle.

1955 **Citroën DS** | **Flaminio Bertoni, France**. The DS was one of the most innovative cars of all time. Its sleek, streamlined body instantly attracted attention, and its technical features included self-leveling suspension and hydraulically controlled brakes and clutch. Citroën made this convertible as well as a station wagon and a sedan version.

Silver bumper

V12 engine

Aircraft-grade aluminum

1965 **Ferrari 275GTB** | **Pininfarina for Ferrari, Italy**. Perfectly proportioned styling, a five-speed gearbox, and all-independent suspension showed that Ferrari was moving with the times. Six-carburetor versions reached speeds of 165 mph (265 km/h).

Speed lines mirror front diagonals

Signature scissor-type doors

1988 **Lamborghini Countach** | **Lamborghini and Bertone, Italy**. Bertone's star designer Marcello Gandini created a pronounced wedge shape for this car, named after the word *countach*, which expresses male approval of a beautiful woman in Piedmont dialect.

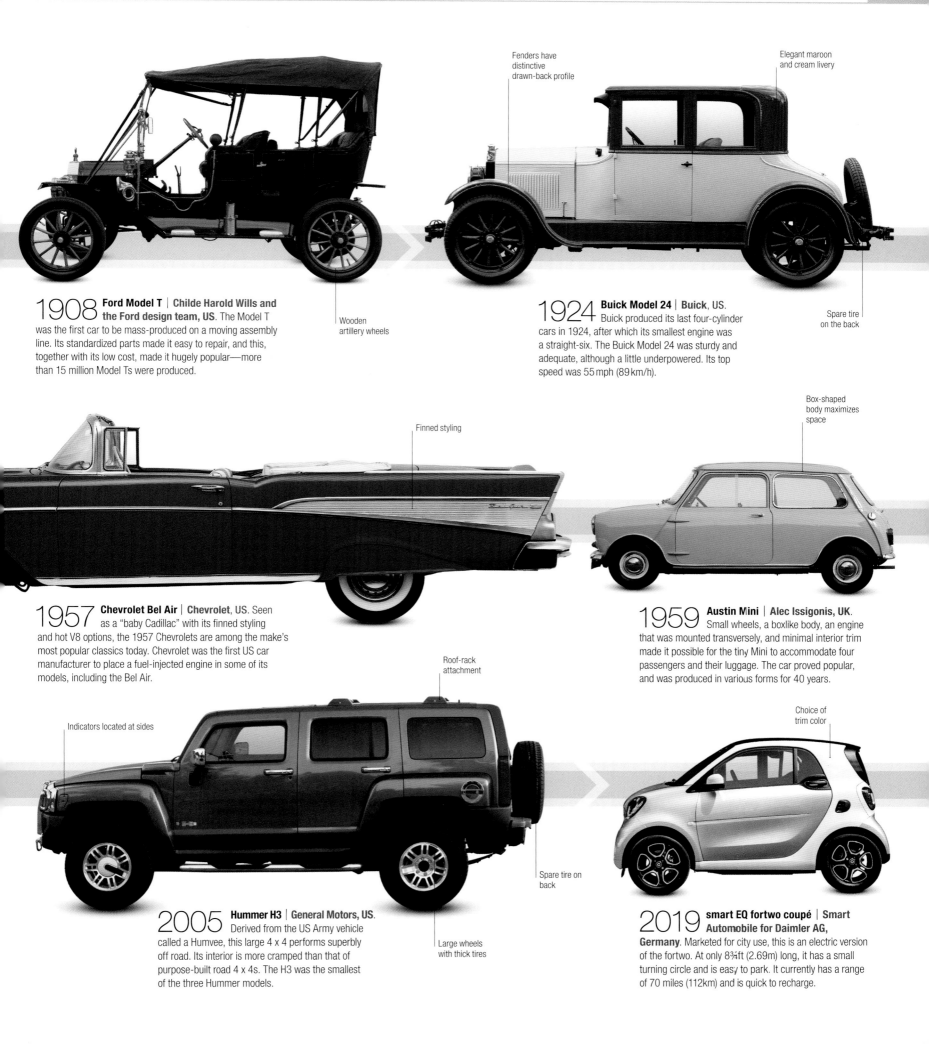

Fenders have distinctive drawn-back profile

Elegant maroon and cream livery

1908 **Ford Model T** | **Childe Harold Wills and the Ford design team, US**. The Model T was the first car to be mass-produced on a moving assembly line. Its standardized parts made it easy to repair, and this, together with its low cost, made it hugely popular—more than 15 million Model Ts were produced.

Wooden artillery wheels

1924 **Buick Model 24** | **Buick, US**. Buick produced its last four-cylinder cars in 1924, after which its smallest engine was a straight-six. The Buick Model 24 was sturdy and adequate, although a little underpowered. Its top speed was 55 mph (89 km/h).

Spare tire on the back

Finned styling

Box-shaped body maximizes space

1957 **Chevrolet Bel Air** | **Chevrolet, US**. Seen as a "baby Cadillac" with its finned styling and hot V8 options, the 1957 Chevrolets are among the make's most popular classics today. Chevrolet was the first US car manufacturer to place a fuel-injected engine in some of its models, including the Bel Air.

1959 **Austin Mini** | **Alec Issigonis, UK**. Small wheels, a boxlike body, an engine that was mounted transversely, and minimal interior trim made it possible for the tiny Mini to accommodate four passengers and their luggage. The car proved popular, and was produced in various forms for 40 years.

Roof-rack attachment

Indicators located at sides

Choice of trim color

2005 **Hummer H3** | **General Motors, US**. Derived from the US Army vehicle called a Humvee, this large 4 x 4 performs superbly off road. Its interior is more cramped than that of purpose-built road 4 x 4s. The H3 was the smallest of the three Hummer models.

Large wheels with thick tires

Spare tire on back

2019 **smart EQ fortwo coupé** | **Smart Automobile for Daimler AG, Germany**. Marketed for city use, this is an electric version of the fortwo. At only 8¾ft (2.69m) long, it has a small turning circle and is easy to park. It currently has a range of 70 miles (112km) and is quick to recharge.

CULTURAL REVOLUTION
1960–1979

Industry should be culture.

ETTORE SOTTSASS, ARCHITECT AND DESIGNER

CULTURAL REVOLUTION
Introduction

During the 1960s and 1970s, design became bolder and more sculptural, colorful, and brash, leavened with a touch of humor. After the austerity of the postwar years, the 1960s was a period of economic stability and relative prosperity. Many people lived in new homes built after the war, and, influenced by the layouts of Modernist buildings, these often had open-plan living rooms, larger kitchens, and picture windows. People were able to travel abroad more easily, thanks to organized tours, and this broadened their horizons. They also entertained more. Social change was in the air, and it created a boom in the market for affordable furnishings and homewares, leading to a wealth of new designs and products.

Pop culture

For the first time, the fashion-conscious young had their own spending power, so design became more democratic and was led to a large extent by street culture. From the Swinging London of the 1960s to 1970s punk, album covers, film posters, and advertisements targeted the young and reflected rebellion against traditional values.

Playful, ironic products, often made in brightly colored plastics and the other new synthetic materials, represented a clear break from the past and parodied the banality of consumer life. Pop Art, Op Art, and the fluorescent, psychedelic patterns associated with the hippie Flower Power movement influenced many areas of design.

PLASTICS

Injection-molded plastics gave designers new creative freedom, making it possible to mass-produce almost any shape (and color) quickly and cheaply. Plastic chairs could now be made in a single piece.

FLOWER POWER

The slogan "flower power" summed up the relaxed hippie ethos of the 1960s. It was reflected in bold textile and wallpaper designs featuring flattened, brightly colored, stylized flowers.

PLAYFUL FORMS

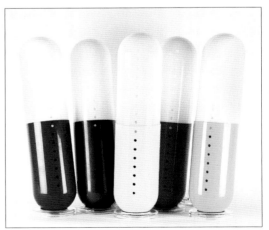

Designers defied expectation and created humorous, colorful products that parodied other forms, as in these Pillola lamps, which look like giant pills and can be tilted in different directions.

One sits more comfortably on a color that one likes.

Verner **Panton**

The fashion for bold visual statements was seen in pieces of furniture such as the scarlet Dalilips sofa by the Surrealist artist Salvador Dalí, and in sculptural molded chairs. The lighting specialists Flos and the furniture company Vitra had a huge impact, as did the British designer Terence Conran, a successful retailer with a mission to make good design accessible to all through his Habitat stores.

Designers and manufacturers did not all adhere to a single style but were eclectic in their approach. Furniture retailers stocked plastic chairs in vivid oranges or reds alongside items covered in more traditional fabrics, and Habitat sold everything from Modernist lamps to rustic pottery influenced by traditional French country wares.

Technological promise

Space exploration and the popularity of science fiction movies and novels sparked a move toward futuristic designs in sleek new forms. Designers no longer looked back to art for inspiration but forward to science. Technological advances opened up new horizons for product designers such as Dieter Rams and Kenneth Grange, and plastics and plastic-reinforced fiberglass gave furniture designers the chance to create the ambitious forms they had been working toward with plywood and sheet metal. New technologies gave designers a sense of endless possibility. From record players and phones to bus shelters and high-speed trains, they were shaping the modern world.

BRIGHT COLOR

Vivid, clashing colors were splashed across everything from furniture to textiles and posters. Neon greens and yellows were popular, as were fluorescent tones of scarlet, pink, and orange used together.

PICTOGRAMS

From road signs to product labels, pictograms came of age in the 1960s. They proved useful for international signage because they are easy for anyone to understand, whatever language they speak.

PRODUCT DESIGN

Products for the office and home were planned just as rigorously as other areas of design, to make them user-friendly, efficient, affordable, and attractive. Many came to be regarded as icons of good design.

CONCRETE CURVES

With its four soaring, intersecting vaults supported on unique Y-shaped buttresses, the TWA Terminal at John F. Kennedy International Airport in New York embodies the sculptural turn that modern architecture took in the early 1960s. The architect, Finnish-American Eero Saarinen, who was famous for thin-shell concrete structures, rejected the contemporary trend for uninspiring, shedlike airport buildings. With the TWA Terminal, he wanted to create a building that was as exciting as the latest jet airliners.

From the outside, the roofs of the terminal curve like aircraft wings. They cover spacious interiors that are beautifully lit because the roof shells do not quite meet, leaving glassed-covered gaps that let light flood in. Sweeping arches open up inviting vistas, and generous stairs ascend to the upper floor levels, their curving handrails leading the eye upward to the soaring ceilings.

The TWA Terminal showed how reinforced concrete could be molded to create structures with forms that were difficult or even impossible to achieve using more conventional materials, and it anticipated expressionist buildings like the Sydney Opera House.

The building represents a new idea in twentieth-century architecture.

Philip **Johnson**, 2001

TWA Terminal, New York City, Eero Saarinen, 1961 The terminal's concrete structure creates light, airy spaces with few straight lines and room for people to circulate. The landmark building has been restored by its owners, the Port Authority of New York and New Jersey, in conjunction with Beyer Blinder Belle.

EVOLUTION OF
TELEVISIONS

As with many electrical products, television design charts changes in both technology and taste. Displays have developed from bulky cathode-ray tubes to the crystal clarity of today's flat-screen displays. Television casings were originally made by cabinet-makers in traditional woods and shapes but have more recently incorporated plastics in everything from discreet black or gray forms to vivid colors and unconventional shapes, as designers respond to contemporary fashions or set trends of their own. Over the past century, the television has evolved from something to be disguised into a piece of furniture that takes pride of place.

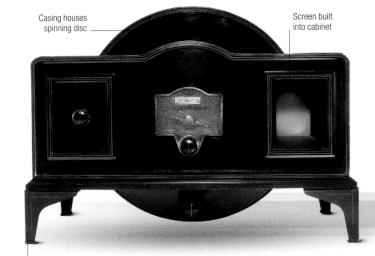

Casing houses spinning disc

Screen built into cabinet

Ornately carved legs

1926–1930 Televisor | John Logie Baird for Plessey, UK.
Baird's Televisor was the first commercially available television. It used Baird's own mechanical television system, which featured a huge spinning disc and a tiny screen.

Upper section swivels so that the user can find the best angle for viewing

Bracket allows screen to tilt

Shade to block out glare

Carrying handle

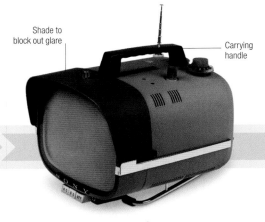

1957 Komet Combination Unit | Kuba Imperial, Germany.
Many early televisions also included a radio receiver; this one houses a radio and a record player in its exuberantly styled cabinet. The tapering design seems to mark the beginning of the Space Age.

1958 Tandem Predicta | Philco, US.
This television set has a screen that can be positioned separately from the loudspeaker unit. The screen also pivots, to give the best viewing angle. The colored, stripped-down screen points to the future of TV design.

1960 TV-8-301 | Sony Corporation, Japan.
At the end of the 1950s, manufacturers started to use transistors, making smaller and more reliable receivers. This Sony model had a carefully designed case, to make it truly portable.

Antenna built into carrying handle

Foldable antenna

Large speakers built into side of screen

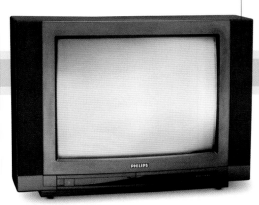

1970 National Commando 505 Portable Television | Matsushita, Japan.
This robust television set was encased in durable black plastic. Living up to its name, the Commando was designed to be used by the military, far from the comforts of home.

1980 Ferguson Portable Television Receiver | Thorn Industries, UK.
With a shiny black plastic case, this portable receiver occupied the midrange of the market. Its uncluttered design kept control dials and details to a minimum.

1992 Philips 21st Color Television Receiver | Philips, UK.
This popular television set was one of the last cathode-ray tube models to enjoy success before screen shapes began to change with the advent of wide-screen technology.

Cabinet and screen large enough to dominate a room

Tapered top makes the television look less bulky

1950s Cabinet television | Mullard, UK.
In the 1950s, people still saw large, upmarket TV receivers as furniture. This one, like many examples, concealed the screen behind a pair of doors, to make the unit look like a cupboard when closed.

1956 TV62 | Bush, UK. After the
war, televisions became cheaper, and smaller tabletop models like this were produced. The curved casing is made of Bakelite, with a loudspeaker grille incorporated between the two main controls.

1957 Pye CS17 | Robin Day, UK. A pale
wooden cabinet with the slimmest, most pared-down lines that were still workable, together with narrow, slightly splayed legs, mark Robin Day's design as one of the most refined receivers in the midcentury style.

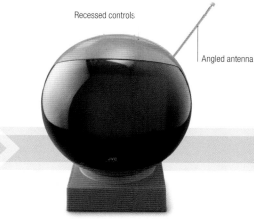

Fold-down carrying handle

Slimline casing

Recessed controls

Angled antenna

1964 Algol Portable Television | Marco
Zanuso and Richard Sapper for Brionvega, Italy. With its shiny finish, chrome handle, and upturned screen, the Algol was one of the most striking TVs of the time. It was available in a range of bright colors.

1968 Trinitron KV | Sony Corporation,
Japan. When color television became widespread at the end of the 1960s, Sony developed their impressive Trinitron system with clear controls and a screen that was flatter than those of earlier televisions.

1970 Videosphere | JVC, Japan. Breaking
away from the straight-edged designs of most TV receivers, JVC produced the Videosphere. Its plastic case and wraparound screen combined a Pop look with a shape reminiscent of an astronaut's helmet.

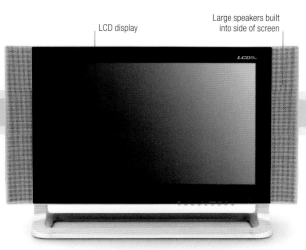

LCD display

Large speakers built into side of screen

Thin frame maximizes screen space

2000s LCD Television | Japan. Televisions
with conventional image tubes were bulky, so manufacturers and consumers alike welcomed receivers with flat-screen displays. Models like this dramatically reduced the space taken up by televisions.

2014 Curved-screen Television |
Samsung, South Korea.
Electronics manufacturers are now producing televisions with large, curved screens. The sweeping, concave display makes watching TV more cinematic and immersive, with improved depth and contrast.

EXPERIMENTAL
FURNITURE

Reflecting the experimental mood expressed by their counterparts in art and fashion, European furniture designers embraced a bold new look in the 1960s and 1970s, rejecting the simple, organic lines and sense of craft that had dominated the 1950s in favor of fun and novelty. Italian designers were at the forefront of innovation during this time, pioneering the avant-garde Radical Design movement. They based their designs on mundane, everyday objects but exaggerated their size and proportions, confounding previous ideas about what furniture should look like. The Italians' adventurous approach to plastics and industrial techniques had a profound influence on the work of designers elsewhere, especially in France, Germany, the UK, and Finland. Common themes for many European furniture innovators were a love of circular forms, imaginative design, and a youthful fashion for throwaway products.

Polyurethane foam covered in stretch fabric, with no supporting frame

Curved lines

Donna Up5 and Up6 | **Gaetano Pesce for C&B Italia (Cassina)**, 1969, Italy. A radical idea with innovative construction, Pesce's chair and ottoman represent a female fertility figure with a ball chained to her foot, like a prisoner. The pieces are made from foam with no supporting structure, allowing them to be sold compressed and vacuum-packed; upon opening, they expand to 10 times their packaged size.

Blow chair | Jonathan De Pas, Donato D'Urbino, Paolo Lommazo for Zanotta, 1967, Italy. Blow was the first mass-produced inflatable chair. It represented a youthful optimism in design and a desire for whimsical and inexpensive pieces.

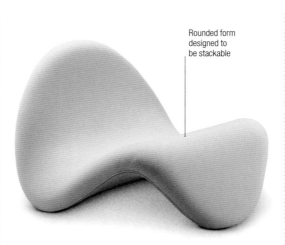

Rounded form designed to be stackable

Tongue chair | Pierre Paulin for Artifort, 1967, The Netherlands. While working for Artifort, Paris-born Paulin used his background in sculpture to design undulating chairs like this, in which the backrest flows seamlessly into the seat.

Weight of seated body pushes pellets into headrest area

Sacco chair | Piero Gatti, Cesare Paolini, Franco Teodoro for Zanotta, 1968, Italy. These three architect-designers used newly invented polystyrene pellets for the filling of their beanbag. Their idea was to make a hippie-style, squishy "non-chair."

My favorite design is the one to come.

Pierre **Paulin**

Seat holds two adults comfortably

"Finger" backrest

Joe armchair | Jonathan De Pas, Donato D'Urbino, and Paolo Lomazzi for Poltronova, 1970, Italy. Designed in Milan by three architects, Joe is named after baseball player Joe DiMaggio, the star center fielder of the New York Yankees.

Polyurethane covered in washable lacquer

Cactus coat rack | Guido Drocco and Franco Mello for Gufram, 1972, Italy. Drocco and Mello wanted this huge coat rack to blur the boundaries between interior and exterior, natural and synthetic, and to add a playful touch to the home.

Ottoman attached to chair

Integrated plastic seat and desk

Zocker chair | Luigi Colani for Top-System Burkhard Lübke, 1971–1972, Germany. An award-winning car designer for Fiat and BMW, Colani applied his knowledge of cars and aerodynamics to create quirky objects like this child's chair.

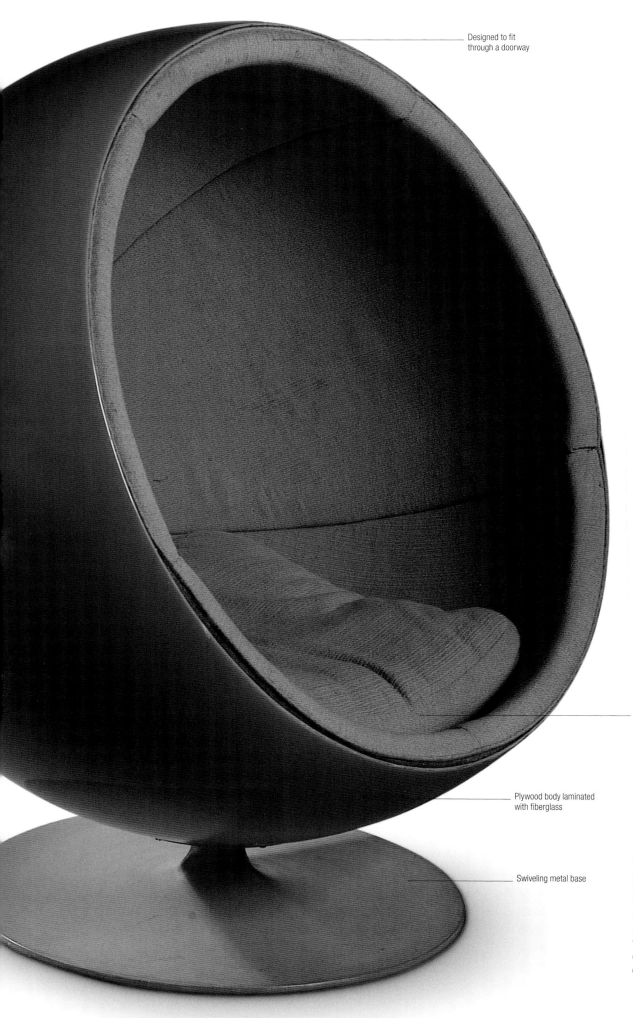

Designed to fit
through a doorway

Upholstered interior
and seat cushion

Plywood body laminated
with fiberglass

Swiveling metal base

Interior design

1850–present

Interior design as we know it developed in
the 19th century, when furniture makers
began to produce furnishings for the newly
affluent middle classes. Large retailers had
an effective monopoly on taste, as their wares
were bought to decorate entire houses from
top to bottom, following established styles.
At the beginning of the 20th century, this
state of affairs was challenged by designers,
who asserted that interior decor should be
a matter of personal taste.

Interior design became more established
as an area of design after World War II, but
today, as an increasing number of affordable
homeware and furniture stores proffer their
wares, homeowners have greater scope to
create their own styles of interiors.

A stripped-down white interior gives individual pieces of
furniture greater visual impact.

Ball (or Globe) chair | **Eero Aarnio for
Asko**, 1965, **Finland**. Aarnio's futuristic-
looking chair caused a sensation when
it was launched at the Cologne International
Furniture Fair in 1966. Aarnio had originally
designed it because he could not find a chair
that suited his new house. His original prototype
even included a red telephone, but this was
dropped for the production model.

INNOVATIVE FURNITURE

The social, technological, cultural, and political changes that unfolded during the 1960s and 1970s reinvigorated design. Although Europe was still perceived as the center of design, largely because of the powerful influence of Italian manufacturers, talent blossomed all around the world in the early 1960s, notably in Japan, Scandinavia, and the Americas, and the resulting cross-pollination of ideas led to innovative pieces of furniture being created for a more informal way of life. A key figure was Dino Gavina. In 1960, he formed the Gavina Group in Milan, which fostered artists and designers from Japan, Latin America, and Europe, commissioning furniture from them. Although Gavina was bought out by the US company Knoll in 1968, the new owners continued its policy of international collaboration, as did other furniture producers around the world.

Painted socklike protrusions filled with cotton stuffing

Ergonomic design

Foam-padded headrests and bolsters with fabric upholstery

Frame made from solid jacaranda wood

Accumulation No. 1 chair | **Yayoi Kusama**, 1962, US. A sculpture rather than a practical piece of furniture, this one-of-a-kind chair and later objects in the same series were created by the Japanese artist after she had moved to New York.

Shell chair | **Hans Wegner for Johannes Hansen**, 1963, Denmark. Wegner's background in architecture and cabinet-making is evident in the technical construction and graceful lines of this bent plywood piece, nicknamed "The Smiling Chair."

Tonico sofa | **Sergio Rodrigues**, 1963, Brazil. Architect Rodrigues adapted Bauhaus style to create furniture suited to Brazil's climate and relaxed way of life. He liked to work with hardwoods such as jacaranda that were native to his country.

Leather upholstery over a thin layer of foam for padding

Black bowler has fiberglass base with leather hatband

Cold-foam covered with stretch fabric

Around 60 layers of compressed, corrugated cardboard

Layers glued in alternate directions to give strength

Chair is hung from a metal frame so it rocks and swivels

Karuselli lounge chair and ottoman | **Yrjö Kukkapuro for Avarte**, 1964, Finland. Kukkapuro experimented for years to find the ideal ergonomic form for the Karuselli, hailed by the *New York Times* in 1974 as the world's most comfortable chair.

Magritte chair | **Roberto Matta for Gavina**, 1972, Italy. Chilean-born Matta was an architect and abstract expressionist painter. This chair looks like an apple in a hat and was an homage to *The Son of Man*, painted by René Magritte in 1964.

Wiggle chair | **Frank Gehry for Easy Edges**, 1972, US. Before finding acclaim as an architect, Canadian Gehry invented a cardboard strong enough to use for furniture. His successful line included side chairs, a dining table, and a chaise longue.

△ **The S-shaped design** of the Panton Chair (1968) was developed jointly with furniture maker Vitra. It was the world's first molded plastic chair.

Verner **Panton**

Born in Denmark in 1926, Verner Panton studied architecture in Copenhagen and worked for influential architect Arne Jacobsen before establishing his name as one of the most important furniture designers of the 1960s. This decade was undoubtedly his golden age—his futuristic designs in plastic embodied the pop culture aesthetic and were a mainstream success. Yet even before this, Panton had seen several of his designs go into production, including the Bachelor chair for Fritz Hansen in 1955 and the Cone Chair in 1959, which became the catalyst for his fame. He had designed the Cone Chair for his parents' restaurant on the Danish island of Fünen, where it was spotted by businessman Percy von Halling-Koch, who funded its production. Panton caused a furor by arranging naked mannequins on the chair for a photo shoot for Danish design magazine *Mobilia.* Later, in New York, the chair was removed by police from one shop window because it was attracting so many curious onlookers.

Panton's genius found a fresh audience in the 1990s, thanks to a growing appreciation of midcentury modern style. Vitra reissued his Panton Chair and IKEA commissioned the Vilbert chair, constructed from four sheets of medium-density fiberboard (MDF) in different colors. Cementing his revived success, a cover of British *Vogue* in 1995 featured a nude Kate Moss sitting on the Panton Chair.

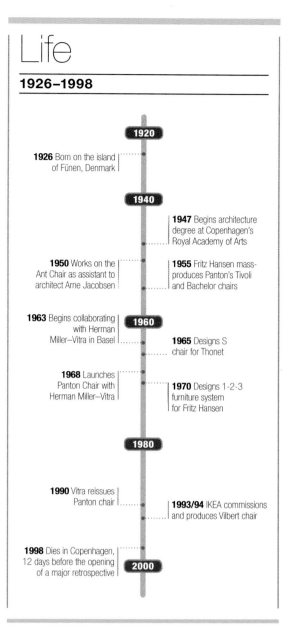

Life

1926–1998

1920

1926 Born on the island of Fünen, Denmark

1940

1947 Begins architecture degree at Copenhagen's Royal Academy of Arts

1950 Works on the Ant Chair as assistant to architect Arne Jacobsen

1955 Fritz Hansen mass-produces Panton's Tivoli and Bachelor chairs

1963 Begins collaborating with Herman Miller–Vitra in Basel

1960

1965 Designs S chair for Thonet

1968 Launches Panton Chair with Herman Miller–Vitra

1970 Designs 1-2-3 furniture system for Fritz Hansen

1980

1990 Vitra reissues Panton chair

1993/94 IKEA commissions and produces Vilbert chair

1998 Dies in Copenhagen, 12 days before the opening of a major retrospective

2000

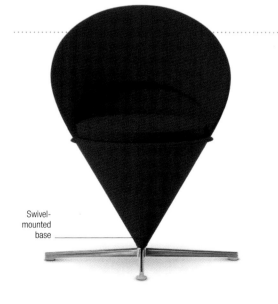

Swivel-mounted base

Cone Chair | **For Vitra**, 1959. This iconic chair is based on the simple geometric form of a cone and swivels on a stainless steel base. The top shell forms both the back and arm supports.

Flexible back shell

Amoebe | **For Vitra**, 1970. This chair was made for the Visiona II installation Panton created for the 1970 Cologne Furniture Fair. It has a laminated frame and foam upholstery.

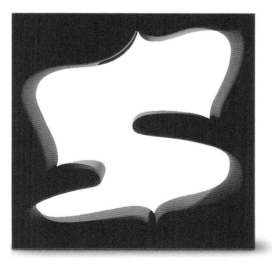

The Living Tower | **For Vitra**, 1969. Part sculpture, part furniture, and over six feet (two meters) high, this experimental form has seats inside the plywood and foam structure.

△ **Although Herman Miller** has specialized in office furniture since the 1940s, many of its products are used in homes.

Herman Miller

△ **Eames molded plywood chair** | **Ray and Charles Eames**, 1946–1957

The furniture manufacturer Herman Miller did not originally set out to create pieces that were modern and pioneering—in fact, the opposite was true. It began as the Star Furniture Company in Zeeland, Michigan, in 1905 and specialized in bedroom suites that replicated historical styles. Four years later, an ambitious young clerk named Dirk Jan De Pree joined the business, and by 1919, he was its director, buying out the majority share in 1923 together with his father-in-law Herman Miller, after whom he renamed the company.

However, it was only when sales dwindled during the Great Depression that Herman Miller warily ventured away from its traditional line of wood furniture and began to create Modernist designs, under the enthusiastic direction of the designer Gilbert Rohde. After Rohde's death in 1944, George Nelson took over as design director and, in what would prove a turning point, negotiated with Ray and Charles Eames for exclusive production rights to their plywood furniture. Nelson and De Pree later collaborated with other talented designers such as Isamu Noguchi and Alexander Girard, and the company also introduced Nelson's own designs and began to expand internationally. From the 1960s onward, Herman Miller developed innovative office furniture, including the world's first open-plan modular system, Action Office (AO), which revolutionized office design.

Key events

1923–

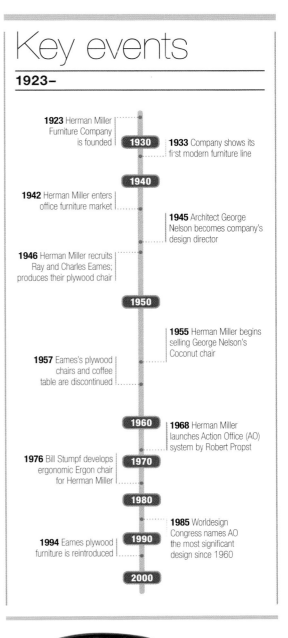

1923 Herman Miller Furniture Company is founded

1933 Company shows its first modern furniture line

1942 Herman Miller enters office furniture market

1945 Architect George Nelson becomes company's design director

1946 Herman Miller recruits Ray and Charles Eames; produces their plywood chair

1955 Herman Miller begins selling George Nelson's Coconut chair

1957 Eames's plywood chairs and coffee table are discontinued

1968 Herman Miller launches Action Office (AO) system by Robert Propst

1976 Bill Stumpf develops ergonomic Ergon chair for Herman Miller

1985 Worldesign Congress names AO the most significant design since 1960

1994 Eames plywood furniture is reintroduced

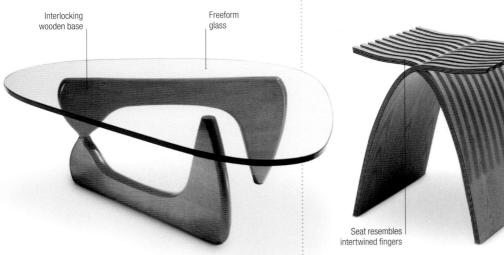

Interlocking wooden base

Freeform glass

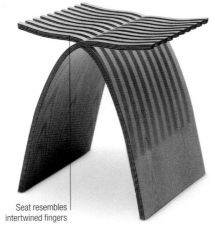

Seat resembles intertwined fingers

Woven material

Noguchi table | **Isamu Noguchi, 1947**. The prototype of this table was a rosewood and glass version, made in 1939. This 1947 model for Herman Miller was carved from walnut.

Capelli stool | **Carol Catalano, 1999**. Each half of this ergonomic stool is made from 11 layers of ash-veneered plywood. The two pieces slot together without fastenings.

Aeron chair | **Bill Stumpf and Don Chadwick**, 1994. This office chair classic was the result of a decade of research into ergonomic seating suitable for elderly people in long-term care.

WARREN PLATNER

Platner Coffee Table

YEAR 1966 | **MANUFACTURER** Knoll, US | **DIMENSIONS** *Height* 15 in (38.5 cm), *Diameter* 42 in (107 cm) | **MATERIALS** Plate glass top supported by nickel-plated steel rods

During the 1960s, the American architect Warren Platner, who had had extensive experience working with Modernist masters such as Eero Saarinen and I. M. Pei in both architectural and interior design, created a distinctive range of furniture supported on slender, nickel-plated steel rods. Platner developed his chairs, tables, and ottomans in collaboration with Knoll.

The range quickly established itself as an outstanding example of 1960s Modernism, combining curvaceous sculptural forms with a beautiful treatment of structural steel. The design of the circular tables may look simple, but they were meticulously constructed. Several hundred welds attached the many curving rods to the four reinforcing hoops, the steel was plated with nickel to create a shiny finish, and the glass top was immaculately polished. The result was a design that was of its time but also looked back to the purity of early Modernism and anticipated the high-tech designs of the 1970s.

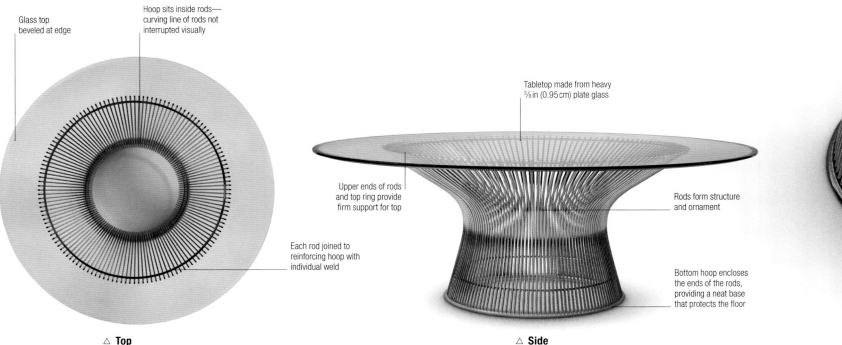

Glass top beveled at edge

Hoop sits inside rods—curving line of rods not interrupted visually

Tabletop made from heavy ³⁄₈ in (0.95 cm) plate glass

Upper ends of rods and top ring provide firm support for top

Each rod joined to reinforcing hoop with individual weld

Rods form structure and ornament

Bottom hoop encloses the ends of the rods, providing a neat base that protects the floor

△ **Top**

△ **Side**

... as a **designer**, I felt there was room for the kind of **decorative, gentle, graceful design** that appeared in period styles **like Louis XV.**

Warren **Platner**
1966

△ **The first Habitat mail-order catalog** was sent out in 1969. The cover of this 1974 edition depicts idealized Habitat rooms.

Habitat

From the beginning of his career, Terence Conran made his talent for business clear—he was as much an entrepreneur as a designer. Habitat—the chain of stores that Conran founded—created and marketed a lifestyle that appealed to a slowly recovering postwar Britain. Conran's talent for business was apparent early on, when he began selling textile prints while still a student at London's Central School of Arts and Crafts. After just two years of study, he left the course to take a more lucrative job assisting the architect Dennis Lennon on a commission for the 1951 Festival of Britain. Like other designers of the time, Conran was profoundly influenced by the Festival, which celebrated British design and projected an optimistic view of what the future might hold for the UK.

Conran's experiences of retail and design during the 1950s left him well-placed to open the first Habitat shop in 1964. The designer captured the mood of the times with his colorful, idealistic presentation of modern living. Habitat was more than just a stylish furniture shop; it was a meeting place, where customers could listen to music, leaf through the magazine-like catalog, eat, drink, and be seen. The London store soon became a fashionable venue, and the Habitat formula was repeated in dozens of stores around the UK. In 1973, an international Habitat store opened in Paris, the first of the chain's many outlets in Europe and beyond.

Key events

1964–

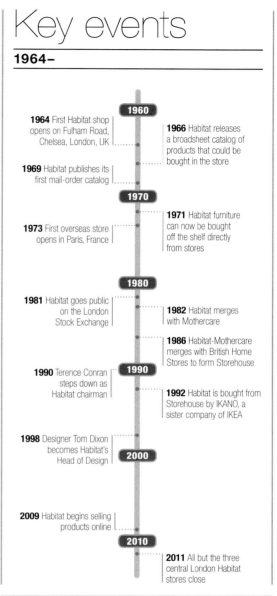

1964 First Habitat shop opens on Fulham Road, Chelsea, London, UK

1966 Habitat releases a broadsheet catalog of products that could be bought in the store

1969 Habitat publishes its first mail-order catalog

1971 Habitat furniture can now be bought off the shelf directly from stores

1973 First overseas store opens in Paris, France

1981 Habitat goes public on the London Stock Exchange

1982 Habitat merges with Mothercare

1986 Habitat-Mothercare merges with British Home Stores to form Storehouse

1990 Terence Conran steps down as Habitat chairman

1992 Habitat is bought from Storehouse by IKANO, a sister company of IKEA

1998 Designer Tom Dixon becomes Habitat's Head of Design

2009 Habitat begins selling products online

2011 All but the three central London Habitat stores close

Rough paintwork gives a rustic feel

Monaco creamer | 1970s. Habitat brought an earthy Provençal style into British homes, typified by the simple, bold, and rustically painted pattern on this porcelain creamer.

Tactile, ridged surface

Curved connection recalls natural forms

Chicken brick | 1968. This modern version of a primitive cooking tool allowed the chicken to cook in its own steam. The terra-cotta halves were made in a press mold.

High arms cradle sitter

Paler color offsets bright yellow details

Ella armchair | 1960s. Simple, Modernist lines, light, bright colors, and plain fabrics have been a hallmark of Habitat furniture such as this armchair since the 1960s.

CATHEDRAL OF LIGHT

Brasília Cathedral (dedicated in 1970) is one of the most striking architectural examples of the curvaceous, sculptural form of Modernism that emerged in the 1950s and 1960s. This masterpiece by Brazil's most famous architect, Oscar Niemeyer (1907–2012), has a very simple design based on a ring of 16 concrete columns that curve upward from the building's base, linking together to form a crown at the top of the cathedral. Between the columns are vast, glass-filled triangular areas that, together with the bright white columns, make the building shimmer in the sunlight.

The cathedral's unusual structure and unique shape stand out among the many landmark buildings, including the Congress, the Palace of Justice, and the President's residence, that Niemeyer created for Brazil's capital city. Inside, the glazed walls enclose a high, circular space flooded with light, in which the blue of the sky blends with the swirling patterns of the stained glass. As well as creating a modern Christian church, the architect's masterly handling of light is a poetic response to the bright sunshine and blue skies of Brazil.

> **I am not attracted to straight angles or to the straight line ... I am attracted to free-flowing, sensual curves.**

Oscar **Niemeyer**

Brasília Cathedral, Brasília, Brazil, Oscar Niemeyer, 1958–1970
The concrete columns of the cathedral, each of which weighs some 90 tons, rise up to create a shape that is often compared to a crown but also resembles arms stretching out toward the heavens.

△ **Vitra's flagship store, VitraHaus,** in Weil am Rhein, Germany, was designed by Dutch architects Herzog & de Meuron. It serves as both a showroom and an outlet for the company's full product line.

△ **Vitra ball clock** | **George Nelson**, 1948

Few design companies have had as much influence on contemporary European home and office environments as Vitra. Founders Willi and Erika Fehlbaum originally ran a business that outfitted stores before branching out into furniture in 1957. They had been inspired by the work of Ray and Charles Eames during a visit to New York four years earlier and negotiated with the Eames's American producer, Herman Miller, for a European manufacturing license. As the 1960s unfolded, the Fehlbaums forged relationships with other designers, including Isamu Noguchi and George Nelson, securing the European licensing rights to produce their furniture. Vitra also collaborated with local designers and began making pieces for Verner Panton, Antonio Citterio, and Jasper Morrison, among others.

Since then, Vitra has evolved and expanded beyond the scope of the typical furniture manufacturer. In 1984, it opened the doors of its production facility in Weil am Rhein, Germany, to the public in order to promote its culture and vision. Five years later, the company established the Vitra Design Museum, sealing its credentials. The Vitra campus is littered with the work of famous architects. Frank Gehry was commissioned for the Design Museum building itself, while Zaha Hadid designed the angular Fire Station (her first completed building), and Tadao Ando created the company's calm and restrained Conference Pavilion.

Key events

1950–

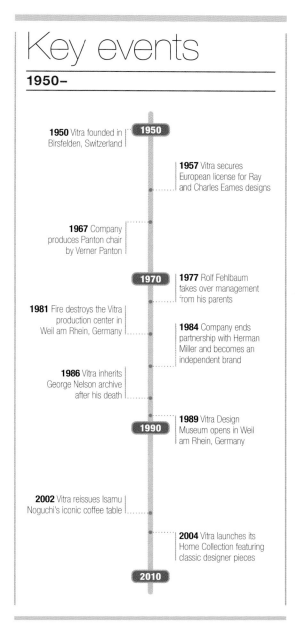

1950 Vitra founded in Birsfelden, Switzerland

1950

1957 Vitra secures European license for Ray and Charles Eames designs

1967 Company produces Panton chair by Verner Panton

1970

1977 Rolf Fehlbaum takes over management from his parents

1981 Fire destroys the Vitra production center in Weil am Rhein, Germany

1984 Company ends partnership with Herman Miller and becomes an independent brand

1986 Vitra inherits George Nelson archive after his death

1989 Vitra Design Museum opens in Weil am Rhein, Germany

1990

2002 Vitra reissues Isamu Noguchi's iconic coffee table

2004 Vitra launches its Home Collection featuring classic designer pieces

2010

Armrests made of oiled solid wood

Base made of molded sheet steel

Fauteuil de Salon armchair | **Jean Prouvé**, 1939. This design classic, with its innovative lightweight frame and thick padded upholstery, was updated for mass production by Vitra.

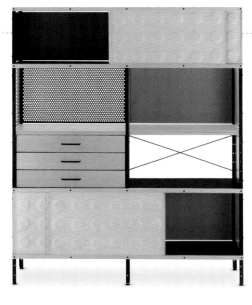

ESU bookcase | **Ray and Charles Eames**, 1949. This freestanding shelving with different-colored sliding doors and metal legs was inspired by industrial design and production.

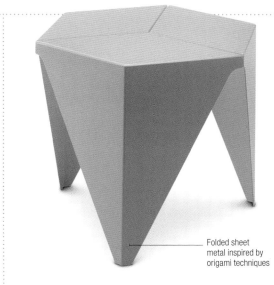

Folded sheet metal inspired by origami techniques

Prismatic table | **Isamu Noguchi**, 1957. Designed for US metal company Alcoa for an advertising campaign, the Prismatic side table is made from bent sheet aluminum.

Transfer-printed
pattern

Stylized, symmetrical
arrangement of leaves

Bersa tableware | **Stig Lindberg for Gustavsberg**, 1960, Sweden. This leaf design, Bersa, became one of Gustavsberg's most popular lines and remained in production from 1960 to 1974. Equally adept in ceramics, textiles, and illustration, Lindberg emerged as one of the most important and prolific designers in Scandinavia from the 1950s onward.

INVENTIVE CERAMICS

In the 1950s, the home was idealized as a place of domestic perfection and family harmony. Over the next two decades, however, a shift in attitudes meant that people had far more scope for self-expression, not only in terms of how they dressed but also in the way they decorated their homes. Living arrangements became more relaxed, and the resulting more informal style of dining led to a new concept called oven-to-table, with food cooked in the same dish in which it was served. Tableware and decorative ceramics became an important element in creating a stylish home. Meanwhile, artists and homeware designers were experimenting with color, pattern, and shape. Ceramicists in Japan and Scandinavia were particularly influential, often inspired by folk traditions. Many designers, from Ettore Sottsass in Italy to Susan Williams-Ellis, owner and head designer for the UK company Portmeirion, also looked farther afield to tribal cultures for inspiration.

Irregular, rectangular handle

Circular, folk-style pattern

Arabesque coffee pot | **Gill Pemberton for Denby**, 1964, UK. Denby lured top designers such as Pemberton to create its oven-to-table ranges—Arabesque, with its robust, chunky form and distinctive pattern, proved one of the most popular.

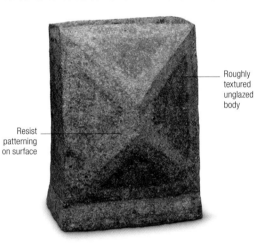

Roughly textured unglazed body

Resist patterning on surface

Stoneware vase | **Shoji Kamoda**, 1969, Japan. Kamoda's name is not well known outside art circles, but he was a major influence on the ceramics of the 1960s and 1970s. As here, his accomplished, earthy pieces emphasize the beauty of bare clay.

Decorated with symbols in relief

Matte glaze

Totem jug | **Susan Williams-Ellis for Portmeirion**, 1970s, UK. Totem was one of Williams-Ellis's most popular ranges. The design combined a modern, angular silhouette with symbols inspired by native American art.

Four stacking segments

Totem earthenware sculpture | **Ettore Sottsass for Bitossi Ceramiche**, c. 1965, Italy. Sottsass translated the totems (sacred objects) of native American and African culture into bold ceramics like this one, decorated with colored glazes.

Butterfly or insect in each design

Botanical Garden Citron plate | **Susan Williams-Ellis for Portmeirion**, 1972, UK. Portmeirion's most successful line, Botanical Garden reflected the casual dining trend of the 1970s. The botanical motifs were based on 19th-century engravings.

Holes for hooks

Signature turquoise glaze

Limited edition vase | **Aldo Londi for Bitossi Ceramiche**, 1973, Italy. After Londi joined Bitossi Ceramiche as art director, this family-run ceramics studio became renowned for its naïve folk-art style and brilliant glazes, as used in this vase.

Shallow, cylindrical cup

Izmir cup and saucer | **Villeroy & Boch**, c. 1973, Germany. Inspired by the Turkish port of Izmir, vivid patterning and tones made this a sought-after design, along with the related Acapulco and Cadiz wares. All three were based on cylindrical shapes.

Six holders at
different heights

Reflective surface

Tapering body

Brass candlesticks | **Tommi Parzinger for Dorlyn Silversmiths**, 1956, US. Known for using classical geometric shapes and restrained decoration, as here, Parzinger also made furniture, often incorporating his handcrafted metalware.

Teak
handles

Stainless steel
with satin finish

Campden coffee pourer for Old Hall | **Robert Welch**, 1957, UK. Welch studied and worked in Sweden, and the influence of Scandinavian metalware, with its precision lines and restrained sensibility, is evident in this coffee set.

Sol Lunaire candelabrum | **Tapio Wirkkala for Christofle**, *c.* 1959, Finland. As well as his more utilitarian work with cutlery and glassware, Wirkkala also created ornamental objects and jewelry in silver, bronze, and pewter. Functional but conceptual, his Sol Lunaire candelabrum in cast metal and silver plate fitted into both categories.

Base resembles
lunar landscape

SLEEK
METALWARE

Although new types of plastic were extremely fashionable for homeware and consumer products in the 1960s and 1970s, traditional materials were still popular. The creative atmosphere of the era, coupled with technological advances, stimulated the production of a new wave of metalware. On a practical level, much of this output was driven by improvements in machine tooling and the development of stainless steel, which had been pioneered in Sweden during World War II. Aesthetically, meanwhile, two forces were at play: a reappraisal of folk art and age-old craft traditions in which metalware featured prominently, combined with a fascination with the ultra-modern Space Age and the possibilities of a technology-driven future. The cool, sleek qualities of stainless steel and silver seemed the perfect means for expressing the spirit of the times.

Matte brushed stainless steel

Hook to clip spoon to fork

Salad serving set | Carl Auböck for Neuzeughammer Ambosswerk, 1967, **Austria**. Auböck's salad servers are ingenious: the pieces can be used separately or clipped together to become tongs.

Made from stainless steel and brass

Dramatically elongated spout

Single handle for water flow and mixing

Vola Spout mixer faucet | Arne Jacobsen for I. P. Lunds, 1968, **Denmark**. In this radical rethink of plumbing fixtures, only the faucet and handle are visible; the other components are hidden behind a wall or under a bench.

Inner coil can be removed for cleaning

Chunky curved bowl

Stainless steel Spirale ashtray | Achille Castiglioni for Alessi, 1970, **Italy**. Initially made in marble and silver plate for Bacci in Bologna, the Spirale was later produced by Alessi in stainless steel. The coil holds cigarettes in place.

Machine-edged steel blades

Handles made of resin

Chinese Ivory cutlery set | David Mellor, 1975, **UK**. Cutlery is a David Mellor specialty, ranging from exclusive pieces in sterling silver to steel sets like this. Chinese Ivory, and the related line Chinese Black, both won UK design awards in 1977.

Symmetrical form

Winged edges

Pendant | Henning Koppel for Georg Jensen, c. 1976, **Denmark**. Koppel's jewelry was considered groundbreaking for its combination of severe lines and organic, lifelike shapes, as here, reflecting his background in sculpture.

Sleek, severe form

Spring between handles

X&I scissors | Kazuo Kawasaki for Takefu Knife Village, 1983, **Japan**. Made by hand, these scissors were envisioned as a high-concept kitchen utensil. The lean design was named after the shapes the scissors make when they are opened and closed.

△ **Achille Castiglioni** sits beneath his Arco lamp of 1962, which was inspired by street lighting and curves about 8 ft (2.5 m) above the floor, an elegant alternative to ceiling lights.

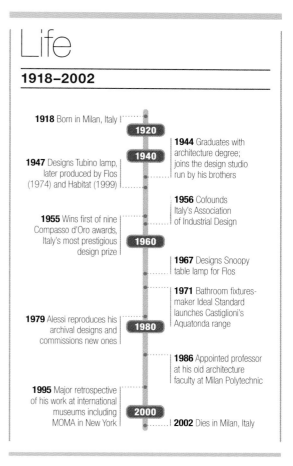

Achille
Castiglioni

△ **Taraxacum 88S pendant light** | **For Flos**, 1988

A prolific industrial designer throughout the second half of the 20th century, Castiglioni initially trained as an architect in Milan, graduating the year before World War II ended; however, since little work was available in architecture at the time, he joined his two brothers in the industrial design studio they had set up. They found no shortage of work for local manufacturers, who were relaunching their businesses after the war with help from Marshall Plan funding. New technologies and materials, many developed during the war, were also a stimulus to designers.

From 1961, Castiglioni forged enduring links with the lighting manufacturer Flos (see pp.292–293), for whom he designed the Arco and Tolo standing lamps. The Arco summed up Castiglioni's innovative approach—his irreverent but luxurious use of Carrara marble, the sculpting material favored by Michelangelo, solved the problem of finding a heavy enough counterweight to the arching steel arm and aluminum reflector—while the Tolo incorporated a transformer and a car headlight in its high-tech design. Castiglioni also worked for Zanotta and Driade from 1964, creating the witty yet functional San Carlo sofa and Mezzadro stool. Many of these pieces are still made or have been reissued. Castiglioni's common-sense attitude and his rapport with manufacturers, who consequently let him experiment, helped ensure his success.

Life

1918–2002

1918 Born in Milan, Italy
1920

1944 Graduates with architecture degree; joins the design studio run by his brothers
1940

1947 Designs Tubino lamp, later produced by Flos (1974) and Habitat (1999)

1956 Cofounds Italy's Association of Industrial Design

1955 Wins first of nine Compasso d'Oro awards, Italy's most prestigious design prize
1960

1967 Designs Snoopy table lamp for Flos

1971 Bathroom fixtures-maker Ideal Standard launches Castiglioni's Aquatonda range

1979 Alessi reproduces his archival designs and commissions new ones
1980

1986 Appointed professor at his old architecture faculty at Milan Polytechnic

1995 Major retrospective of his work at international museums including MOMA in New York
2000

2002 Dies in Milan, Italy

Stabilizing beech cross brace

Mezzadro stool | **For Zanotta**, 1970. Castiglioni often based his designs on everyday objects. Here, he combined a metal tractor seat with a strip steel bow leg.

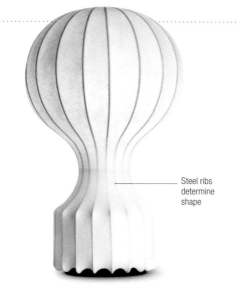

Steel ribs determine shape

Gatto table lamp | **For Flos**, 1960. For this lamp, made with his brother Pier Giacomo, Castiglioni used a new resin called Cocoon over a steel wire structure to generate a diffused light.

Enameled reflective metal

Snoopy table lamp | **For Flos**, 1967. Inspired by the Charles Schultz character, a marble stand supports an egg-shaped metal and glass shade.

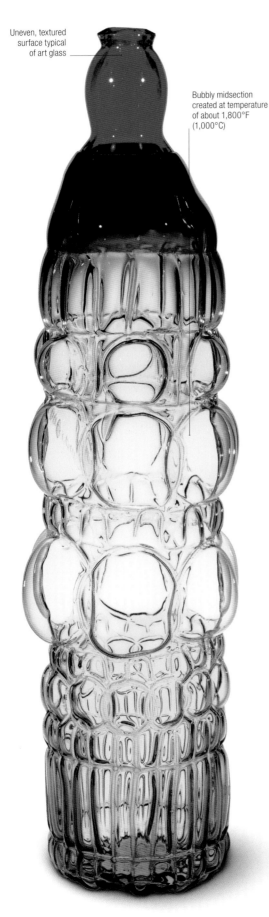

Uneven, textured surface typical of art glass

Bubbly midsection created at temperature of about 1,800°F (1,000°C)

Sculptural vessel | **Pavel Hlava**, 1965, Czechoslovakia. Hlava was used to the factory-dominated production of his native country but pioneered glass as a modern art form, as here, using a range of techniques including free-blowing.

Contrasting clear glass stopper

Stable bell shape

Decanter | **Viking Glass**, *c.* 1960, US. Viking's decorative and colorful bowls, figurines, and decanters, such as this unusual smoky violet example, were often seen on fashionable American sideboards and coffee tables in the 1960s.

Gently curving sides

Heavy base

Marja cocktail glasses | **Saara Hopea**, 1956, Finland. Also known for her jewelry and ceramics, Hopea designed a set of these unadorned, elegantly shaped glasses in several different rich colors.

Cylindrical neck with flat rim

Body almost spherical

Bottle-shaped vase | **Vladimír Kopecký**, 1965, Czechoslovakia. This mold-blown colorless vase is covered with enameled decoration like an abstract painting. Layers of color build up the intensity of blue.

Even coloring

New, inexpensive mass-production technique ensured smooth, consistent surface

Fuga bowl | **Sven Palmqvist for Orrefors**, 1960, Sweden. Palmqvist created a new glass production technique he called *Fuga* (force). The name refers to the centrifugal spin used to push molten glass up and out into a bowl shape.

Extreme elongated form

Emerald green was a favorite color of Myers

Bottle, Model 6937 | **Joel Philip Myers for Blenko Glass**, 1969, US. Typically, Blenko glassware was of a single vibrant color. Myers favored restrained designs in cylindrical shapes, interestingly stretched in this long, thin example.

Flared rim

Strong color contrast

Mold-blown vase | **František Vízner**, 1973, Czechoslovakia. Vízner used a range of techniques, including pressing and hand-grinding, to create this piece with classical proportions, crisp lines, and deep, luminous colors.

ARTISTIC GLASS

The age-old craft of glassmaking underwent a transformation in the 1960s and 1970s, while manufacturing technologies were revolutionizing home furnishings via the use of plastics and textiles. The studio glass movement, which championed the idea of glass as an artistic medium, developed in the US and spread to Europe, generating a revival characterized by vibrant color and experiments in form, scale, and texture. Scandinavia, already a leading producer of art glass, was at the forefront of this renaissance and, in the postwar years, it adapted easily to the needs of a new market. Companies such as Orrefors in Sweden produced Pop-art-inspired decorative pieces and colorful, inexpensive mix-and-match tableware, which was emulated internationally. Meanwhile, glassmakers in Czechoslovakia (now the Czech Republic) enjoyed a creative freedom rare among artists under a Communist regime.

Lollipop-shaped forms loosely resemble human figures

Transparent, heavy base

Lollipop Isle sculpture |
Oiva Toikka for Nuutajärvi Glassworks, 1969, Finland. Toikka's playful sculpture reached an international audience at an exhibition of Finnish arts and crafts held in London in 1969. The glass used in the sculpture is molded and free-blown.

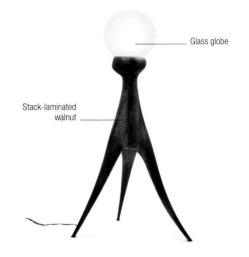

Glass globe

Stack-laminated walnut

Floor lamp | **Wendell Castle**, 1966, US. Although he taught industrial design, Castle was also inspired by traditional American craftsmanship and sleek modernity. Both influences can be seen in this hand-carved lamp.

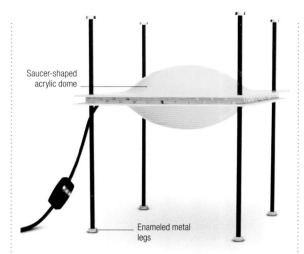

Saucer-shaped acrylic dome

Enameled metal legs

UFO table light | **Ettore Sottsass for Arredoluce**, 1957, **Italy**. The playful Sottsass tapped into popular enthusiasm for all things extraterrestrial with this statement piece, which subverts traditional forms by suspending the UFO lamp on elongated legs.

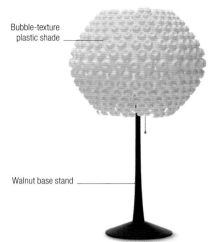

Bubble-texture plastic shade

Walnut base stand

Lantern series table lamp | **George Nelson**, 1962, US. The outlandish bubble plastic of this lampshade suggests the surface of an alien planet, creating a contrast in texture with the smooth walnut of the base stand.

Space Age

1957–1969

The Cold War entered its most dramatic phase as the US and the Soviet Union competed to prove their technological superiority with their space programs. The Soviets took an early lead in 1957 with the launch of Sputnik, the first artificial satellite, but the US triumphed in 1969, when Neil Armstrong became the first man on the moon.

The space race influenced a generation of confident and experimental designers. New technologies such as molded plastics were used alongside more traditional chrome and silver to suggest a spacecraft's living quarters or sleek exterior. The obsession with space also influenced pieces such as Sottsass's UFO light or the rocketlike lava lamp.

Buzz Aldrin's bulbous helmet inspired designers of everything from chairs to television sets.

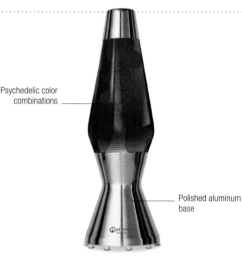

Psychedelic color combinations

Polished aluminum base

Astro lava lamp | **Edward Craven Walker**, 1963, UK. Advertised as an "exotic new conversation piece," the lava lamp was offered in a choice of five colors for the main fluid and four colors for the floating shapes.

Opaque white plastic shade

Stainless steel telescopic stand

Adjustable height

Pipistrello table lamp | **Gae Aulenti for Martinelli-Luce**, 1967, **Italy**. Pipistrello means "bat" in Italian and refers to the lampshade's winglike segments. Aulenti used subtle lighting to enhance, but not overpower, a room.

Handblown crystal glass

High-shine base of chromium-plated metal

Bulb table light | **Ingo Maurer for Ingo Maurer GmbH**, 1966, Germany. Part of the Pop Art and Radical Design movements that brought everyday objects to center stage, Maurer's design pays homage to the ordinary light bulb.

Polished steel

Lower sphere conceals bulb

Flowerpot pendant light | **Verner Panton**, 1968, **Denmark**. The classical proportions of this light are part of its appeal—the upper sphere is twice the size of the lower sphere. Together, they both conceal and reflect the light source.

Decoration can be a state of mind, an unusual perception, a ritual whisper.

Ettore **Sottsass**
Furniture designer

Multiple probes with
colored bulbs

Central metal
sphere

Sputnik chandelier | 1965. Named after the first artificial satellite, this type of chandelier was inspired by the advances in science and technology that were taking place in the 1960s. Sputnik's form is reminiscent of both the solar system and the structure of an atom, the smaller bulbs radiating from a central sun or nucleus. Sputnik was not the name of a specific lamp but of a generic style made in different colors, materials, and sizes throughout the 1960s. Despite its association with a particular time, the style is still popular today.

RADICAL LIGHTING

Not since the early 20th century had the idea of mood lighting flourished as it did during the 1960s and 1970s. While domestic and public lighting of the early 1950s had both attempted to create a sense of bright modernity to sweep away the memories of World War II, from the late 1950s onward, designers began to experiment with lighting that could create ambience.

By mimicking the atmosphere found in lounge bars, discos, and psychedelic parties, creative lighting could be used to transform an otherwise bland interior into a sultry retreat or futuristic pad, or simply to create a mood. Designers also drew inspiration from new materials and novel industrial techniques that helped them create radical new forms of conventional pendant and table lights.

△ **Taccia's transparent handblown lampshade, 1962,** cradles a reflective inner layer, providing both indirect and reflected light. It can be used as a table or floor lamp.

Flos

△ **Taraxacum lamp** | Achille Castiglioni, 1960

The Italian design visionary Dino Gavina was the initial force behind Flos, founding the company with Cesare Cassina in 1962 as part of his grand vision for a postwar Italy that would lead the world in interior design. Gavina already had a reputation for producing innovative pieces of furniture designed by Italian architects such as Achille and Pier Giacomo Castiglioni and Tobia Scarpa. The catalyst for his foray into lighting was his encounter with the Italian inventor Arturo Eisenkeil, who was trying out new uses for a spray-resin technology imported from the US called Cocoon. Cassina saw the potential of Cocoon for use in lighting and joined forces with Gavina to see how it could be used in lighting, also enrolling the Castiglionis and Scarpa.

The groundbreaking product line that Flos created paved the way for the company to collaborate with noted designers and use experimental processes to produce new residential and office lighting. This resulted in lights by Marc Newson (Australia), Philippe Starck (France), and Konstantin Grcic (Germany). All the company needed was a business brain to take the products global. Entrepreneur Sergio Gandini, who owned an influential furniture store in Brescia with his wife Piera Gandini, became the third partner in the business. He made the company commercially successful and, most significantly, launched it in the US.

Key dates

1959–2013

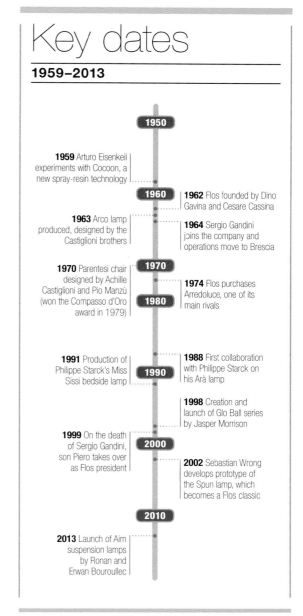

1950

1959 Arturo Eisenkeil experiments with Cocoon, a new spray-resin technology

1960

1962 Flos founded by Dino Gavina and Cesare Cassina

1963 Arco lamp produced, designed by the Castiglioni brothers

1964 Sergio Gandini joins the company and operations move to Brescia

1970 Parentesi chair designed by Achille Castiglioni and Pio Manzù (won the Compasso d'Oro award in 1979)

1970

1974 Flos purchases Arredoluce, one of its main rivals

1980

1991 Production of Philippe Starck's Miss Sissi bedside lamp

1988 First collaboration with Philippe Starck on his Arà lamp

1990

1998 Creation and launch of Glo Ball series by Jasper Morrison

1999 On the death of Sergio Gandini, son Piero takes over as Flos president

2000

2002 Sebastian Wrong develops prototype of the Spun lamp, which becomes a Flos classic

2010

2013 Launch of Aim suspension lamps by Ronan and Erwan Bouroullec

---

Partially sand-blasted bulb diffuses light

Lampadina | **Achille Castiglioni**, 1972. Designed for the opening of the Flos showroom in Turin, Castiglioni's oversized bulb sits on a reel that houses excess cord.

Shade comes in black or white

Upright is made from 18k gold-plated steel or chrome

Gun | **Philippe Starck**, 2005. Philippe Starck's witty approach to design is apparent in this bedside lamp, with its upright shaped like a machine gun and its switch like a trigger.

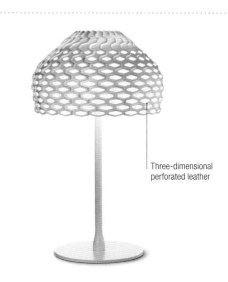

Three-dimensional perforated leather

Tatou T1 | **Patricia Urquiola**, 2012. Tatou, which means armadillo in French, was inspired by the animal's scaly skin. The lamp was the result of many production experiments.

SALVADOR DALÍ AND OSCAR TUSQUETS BLANCA

Dalilips Sofa

YEAR 1938 | **MANUFACTURER** BD (Barcelona Design), Spain | **DIMENSIONS** *Height* 28½ in (73 cm), *Width* 66¼ in (170 cm), *Depth* 39 in (100 cm) | **MATERIAL** Rotation-molded polyethylene

One of the most famous furniture designs of the 20th century, the Dalilips sofa was created by Spanish surrealist artist Salvador Dalí, and it reflects his obsession with American actress Mae West. Over the years, Dalí made various images based on West's face, including a painting using framed pictures for the actress's eyes, a fireplace for her nose, and a sofa for her lips. He designed his first bright red Mae West sofa in 1938, for his British patron Edward James. It was not designed primarily for comfort and was not mass-produced—the artist's intention was to produce a sculptural object that embodied glamour and sensuality. In 1972, Dalí and BD (Barcelona Design) designer Oscar Tusquets Blanca created another Lips Sofa, for the Mae West room in the Dalí Museum in Figueres, Spain. At the time, the technology did not exist to produce the sofa in large numbers, but 30 years later, BD began to produce it in polyethylene using the process of rotational molding, and it was possible, at last, for buyers to own this celebrated piece of 20th-century design.

Surrealism is destructive, but it destroys only what it considers to be shackles limiting our vision....

Salvador **Dalí**

Creases imitate
the texture of lips

Deep fissure
between seat
and back

△ **Side**

Sofa available in reds and
pinks, based on lipstick
colors; there are also
black and white versions

Artist's signature
incorporated into
front of sofa

△ **Side/front**

△ **These Kartell products** are all made of metallicized plastic, demonstrating how glamorous and luxurious plastic can look.

Kartell

△ **Dr. Yes chair** | **Philippe Starck with Eugeni Quitllet, 2009**

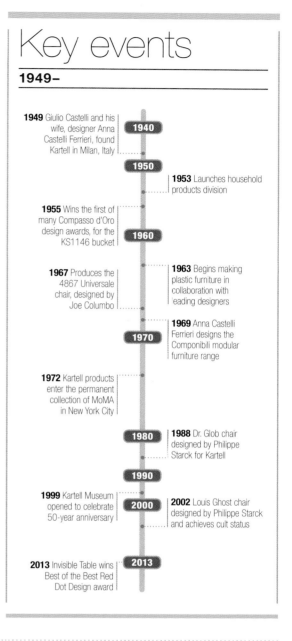

1949 Giulio Castelli and his wife, designer Anna Castelli Ferrieri, found Kartell in Milan, Italy

1940

1950

1953 Launches household products division

1955 Wins the first of many Compasso d'Oro design awards, for the KS1146 bucket

1960

1963 Begins making plastic furniture in collaboration with leading designers

1967 Produces the 4867 Universale chair, designed by Joe Columbo

1969 Anna Castelli Ferrieri designs the Componibili modular furniture range

1970

1972 Kartell products enter the permanent collection of MoMA in New York City

1980

1988 Dr. Glob chair designed by Philippe Starck for Kartell

1990

1999 Kartell Museum opened to celebrate 50-year anniversary

2000

2002 Louis Ghost chair designed by Philippe Starck and achieves cult status

2013 Invisible Table wins Best of the Best Red Dot Design award

2013

Famous for turning an unpopular material into something chic and desirable, Kartell has made designer plastic furniture a mass-market reality. Like many of the Italian home furnishing manufacturers that emerged after World War II, Kartell's origins were in industry. Chemical engineer Giulio Castelli started the company in 1949 to make car accessories, but his fascination with plastic led him to concentrate instead on household goods.

Kartell's range of imaginative pieces was popular with the pop culture generation, and by the 1960s, the company was beginning to grow in earnest. It continued to refine its style throughout the decade by commissioning out-of-house designers, including Joe Colombo and Giotto Stoppino, to create innovative new pieces, such as Colombo's 4867 Universale chair, which was internally printed by plastic injection.

In 1988, Castelli's son-in-law Claudio Luti took control of Kartell and inaugurated an era of experimentation. New construction methods were explored, creating lighter structures and detailed decoration that had not previously been used on plastic furniture. The weaving patterns of the Masters Chair by Philippe Starck or the undulating surface of Patricia Urquiola's Frilly would not have been possible without Kartell's research. This continuing collaboration with leading designers has helped cement its reputation and shows how much perceptions of plastic have changed.

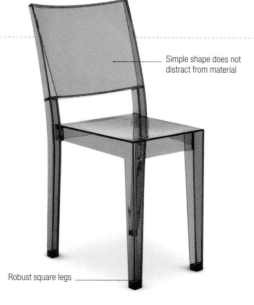

Simple shape does not distract from material

Robust square legs

Pleated lampshade

Scrolled stand

Componibili storage units | **Anna Castelli Ferrieri, 1969.** The modular units of this storage system, made from ABS plastic, have two or three sliding doors with finger-hole handles.

La Marie chair | **Philippe Starck, 1998.** Made from a single polycarbonate mold, La Marie was the world's first completely transparent chair, produced in a range of colors.

Bourgie table lamp | **Ferruccio Laviani, 2004.** A 21st-century take on 17th-century style, the baroque-inspired Bourgie table lamp is made from polycarbonate material.

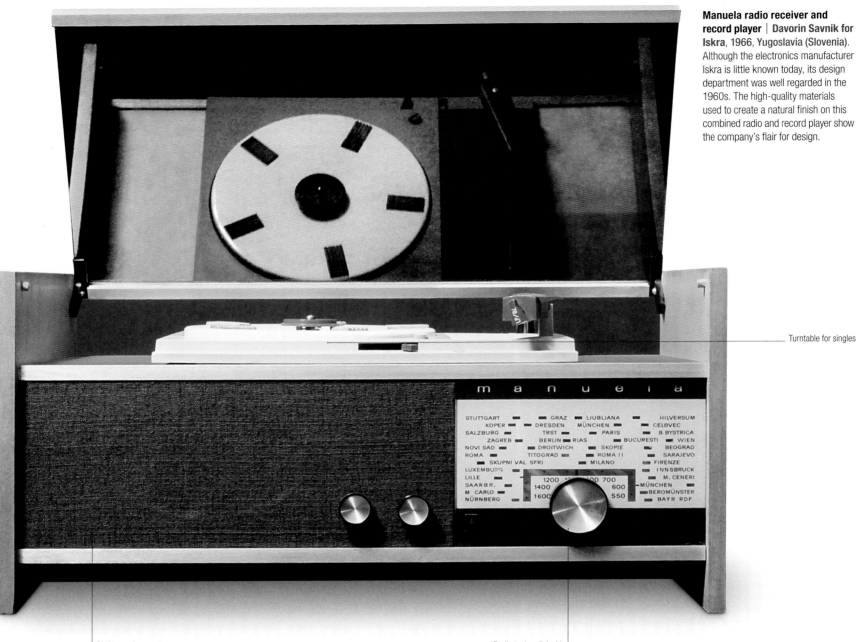

Manuela radio receiver and record player | **Davorin Savnik for Iskra**, 1966, Yugoslavia (Slovenia). Although the electronics manufacturer Iskra is little known today, its design department was well regarded in the 1960s. The high-quality materials used to create a natural finish on this combined radio and record player show the company's flair for design.

Turntable for singles

Cloth covering creates a natural finish

Radio tuning dial with stations marked on it

AUDIO-VISUAL
TECHNOLOGY

Although devices such as record players were already popular, it was during the 1960s that consumer electronics became de rigueur for the home. The change was driven by the growth of popular music and the development of technology on which to play it. By the late 1960s, users wanted stereo systems that incorporated a radio, a turntable, and a cassette player. Advanced electronics such as the integrated circuit made it possible for designers to make ever-smaller gadgets that were no longer bulky household fixtures but personal accessories. Meanwhile, photographic equipment became smaller and more sophisticated, and Kodak's Instamatic was the first series of point-and-shoot cameras. By the end of the 1970s, the optimistic modernism of the postwar years had been replaced by market-led design that catered to consumer taste. This was typified by the immensely popular Sony Walkman, which became as much a fashion item as a music player.

Light gray
top cover

Kodak
logo

Carousel-S slide projector | **Hans Gugelot and Reinhold Häcker for Kodak A/G**, 1963, Germany. The first fully automated slide projector that was guaranteed not to jam, the streamlined Carousel could hold up to 80 slides.

Integral
antenna

Casing designed
so screen tilts
upward

Algol 11 portable television | **Marco Zanuso and Richard Sapper for Brionvega**, 1964, Italy. Miniaturized circuitry made this the smallest 11-inch (28 cm) television on the market. It worked with a 12-volt power source or rechargeable battery.

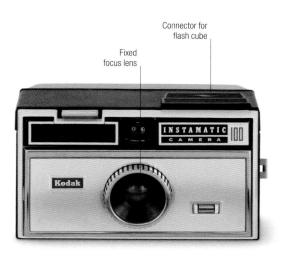

Connector for
flash cube

Fixed
focus lens

Instamatic camera | **Dean M. Peterson for Kodak**, 1960s, US. By the end of the 1960s, the Instamatic had become the world's most popular camera, with 50 million sold in seven years. It introduced a generation to casual point-and-shoot photography.

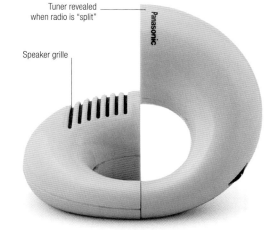

Tuner revealed
when radio is "split"

Speaker grille

R-72 radio | **Panasonic**, 1972, Japan. Designed to be wrapped around the wrist like a bangle, the R-72, or Toot-a-Loop, was a novelty AM radio. When twisted, the smaller section pivoted away from the main body to form an "S" shape.

The **job** of designing is as **old** as the **world.**

Hans **Gugelot**
Industrial designer

Red light flashes
for self-timer

Sliding cover
protects lens

XA camera | **Yoshihisa Maitani for Olympus Optical Co.**, 1979, Japan. Maitani worked with Olympus for more than 40 years. His XA was not merely the first small camera to feature a capsule design but also the first to use full-frame 35mm film.

Signature
metallic
blue case

Walkman personal cassette player | **Sony Corporation**, 1979, Japan. The world's first portable stereo, the Walkman was designed to fit into its owner's pocket. Its size, ease of use, and sound quality made it a worldwide success.

Sleek rosewood and
aluminum casing

Digital
display panel

Cordless
remote control

Beocenter 7000 music center | **Jacob Jensen for Bang & Olufsen**, 1979, Denmark. At the time of its release, Jensen's combination of radio, turntable, and cassette player was one of the most sophisticated stereo systems on the market. Its features included one-touch buttons, memory and timer settings, and an automated turntable.

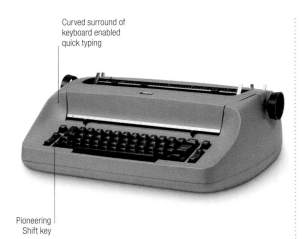

Curved surround of keyboard enabled quick typing

Pioneering Shift key

Selectric (golfball) typewriter | Eliot Noyes for IBM, **1961, US**. This innovative design replaced individual letter hammers with a single, ball-shaped type head that moved across the paper. The Selectric cornered the market.

Lids can be used as trays

Fanned rims serve as handles

Center Line cookware | Roberto Sambonet for Sambonet, **1964, Italy**. The four pots and four shallow pans of Sambonet's cookware could be stacked into one unit. The pieces could be used for storing and serving food as well as for cooking.

No visible seams on surface

Matte stainless steel finish

Cylinda corkscrew | Arne Jacobsen and Peter Holmblad for Stelton, **1964, Denmark**. The brushed stainless steel of the Cylinda line, which included tea and coffee sets and barware, was more sleek than the polished finish of other makes.

Clear typography

Base made of a single piece of plastic

Timor perpetual calendar | Enzo Mari for Danese, 1966, **Italy**. Rotating, interchangeable cards include the date, month, and day of the week so that the calendar can be used year after year. Available in several languages and colors, it is still popular.

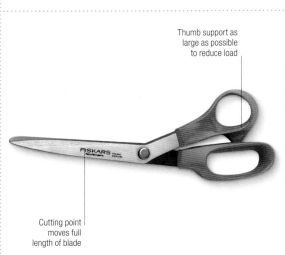

Thumb support as large as possible to reduce load

Cutting point moves full length of blade

Orange Handled Scissors | Olof Backstrom for Fiskars, **1967, Finland**. The invention of injection molding meant that plastic and steel could be merged. Backstrom took advantage of this with his ergonomic scissor grip that would work in plastic.

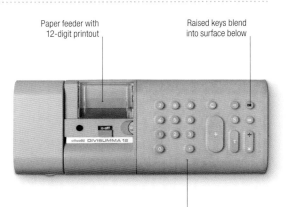

Paper feeder with 12-digit printout

Raised keys blend into surface below

Rubber membrane over keyboard

Divisumma 18 electronic printing calculator | Mario Bellini for Olivetti, 1972, **Italy**. This calculator was considered groundbreaking for its playful styling, vivid color, rubberized keyboard, integrated paper roll, and detachable charging unit.

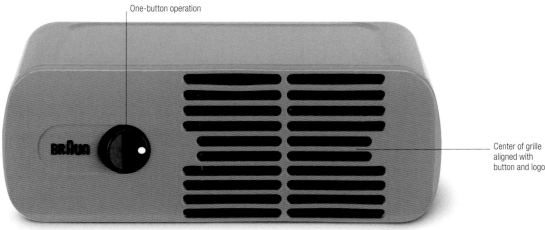

One-button operation

Center of grille aligned with button and logo

HLD4 hairdryer | Dieter Rams for Braun, 1970, **Germany**. An unconventional rectangular shape, bright colorways, and glossy finish made this hair dryer—aimed at men as well as women—something of a novelty. The device's compact size was made possible by the invention of improved electrical motors and lighter plastics.

Designing something new has always been ... a rare privilege.

Mario **Bellini**

HOME AND OFFICE

In the 1960s, there was a subtle but significant shift in the way people lived and worked, with a slew of products offering improved ways of performing mundane tasks. New industrial processes, materials, and technologies were a major catalyst, giving designers the impetus to create tools better suited to their purpose. Throughout the 1960s, small-scale inventions had a disproportionately large impact—even the humble pair of scissors was redesigned to make everyday life a little easier. In 1962 alone, the felt-tip pen, the first video game, and the audio cassette all first appeared. The remaining years of the decade yielded the video disc, BASIC computer language, acrylic paint, CDs, the first handheld calculator, the computer mouse, the first computer with integrated circuits, and RAM (random access memory).

Rounded corners

Carrying handle on back

Keyboard slides out

Valentine portable typewriter | **Ettore Sottsass and Perry King for Olivetti, 1969, Italy**. Inspired by Pop art, the Valentine shook perceptions of office equipment as conservative and lackluster and offered style-conscious consumers a functional yet attractive tool.

△ **Great Britain's first high-speed trains,** including British Rail's InterCity 125 train (1976), were given a futuristic look in molded plastic by Grange. Race cars inspired the train's streamlined nose.

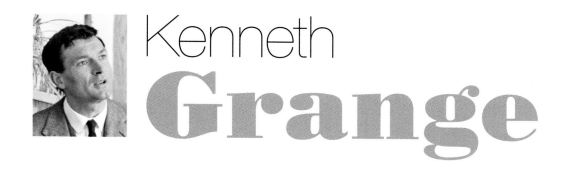

Kenneth Grange

With a career spanning more than 50 years, Kenneth Grange is Great Britain's foremost industrial designer. From the InterCity 125 train and the TX1 London taxi to mailboxes, parking meters, and benches, he has transformed the country's urban landscape. Although there are a number of furniture commissions to Grange's name, his focus is rarely on creating high-end, expensive pieces but on making everyday objects for ordinary people. His approach is to design products that are not just attractive but also a pleasure to use.

After working for several architects in the UK, including Jack Howe, Grange set up his own studio in 1956. Two years later, Howe commissioned him to design the interior of Kodak's stand at the Brussels World's Fair. The following year, Grange designed the company's replacement for the Box Brownie camera, the Brownie 44a. It was the first of many collaborations with Kodak, which included the phenomenally successful Instamatic 33 camera series of 1968.

For the rest of the century, Grange worked for a range of household names, designing small appliances for Kenwood, cigarette lighters for Ronson, pens for Parker, razors for Wilkinson Sword, and sewing machines for Maruzen in Japan. Over the decades, millions of consumers around the world have come in contact with Grange's functional and attractive products.

Life

1929–

- **1929** Born in the East End of London, UK | **1930**
- **1940** | **1947** Graduates from Willesden School of Arts and Crafts, London
- **1950**
- **1956** Sets up own design studio under the name Kenneth Grange
- **1958** Accepts the first of several Kodak commissions
- **1960** Designs the Kenwood Chef food mixer | **1960**
- **1970**
- **1972** Founds the influential Pentagram Design agency with four other partners
- **1976** Launch of Grange's train design, the High Speed InterCity 125
- **1983** Designs Retractor safety razor for Wilkinson Sword | **1980**
- **1997** Retires from Pentagram but continues to design under his own name | **1990**
- **2003** Commissioned by Anglepoise to create the Type 3 desk lamp | **2000**
- **2013** Knighted for services to design | **2010**

Ergonomically designed for back comfort

Turned ash legs on chromed steel skid base

hm82 (Edith) chair | For Hitch Mylius, 2011. Specially designed for the elderly, this chair comes with a high or low back and with or without arms.

Two exposure settings— sunny and cloudy

Instamatic 33 camera | For Kodak, 1960s. The Instamatic used cassette film, which was much easier to insert than normal film. This camera was hugely popular.

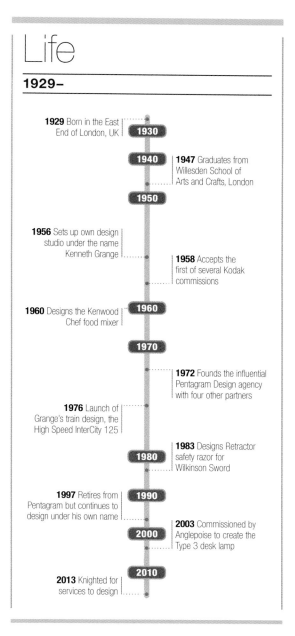

Shade comes in several bright colors

Tilting mechanism offers spotlight or ambient glow

Type 1228™ | For Anglepoise®, 2004. This desk lamp is as versatile and practical as the original Anglepoise® lamp but looks more contemporary.

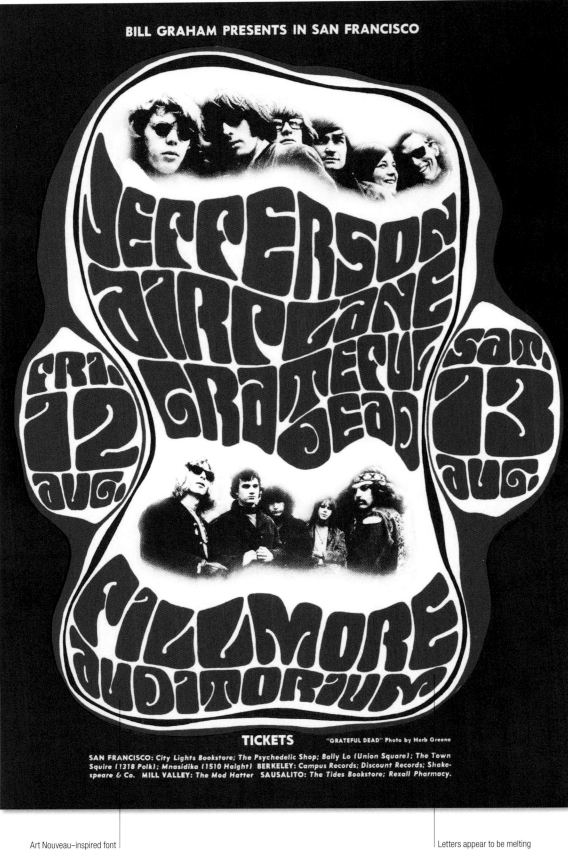

BILL GRAHAM PRESENTS IN SAN FRANCISCO

Art Nouveau–inspired font

Letters appear to be melting

Jefferson Airplane, Grateful Dead poster | Wes Wilson, 1966, US. Wilson specialized in psychedelic-style rock-concert posters and flyers for the San Francisco music scene. This was one of the first rock posters to feature band photographs. San Francisco was the focus for the "Summer of Love" in 1967, when students and hippies flocked to Golden Gate Park for the Human Be-In rally, where Jefferson Airplane played and LSD was handed out when a power outage stopped the music.

Turn on, *tune in,* drop out

Timothy **Leary**
San Francisco Summer of
Love Human Be-In rally, 1967

Horizontal Japanese text gives modern feel

Japanese poster for *Bonjour Tristesse* (Hello Sadness) |
Saul Bass, 1958, US. Evoking the movie's title, Bass used a few brushstrokes to suggest a face with a half smile punctuated by a tear. The poster was adapted for international audiences.

Characters in bright, alternating colors

***Kanze Noh Play* silk screen poster** | Ikko Tanaka, 1961, **Japan**. Tanaka was known for fusing traditional Japanese graphics (here in their normal vertical arrangement) with Western-style layouts.

PSYCHEDELIC POSTERS

Contemporary film, music, and theater were exciting and experimental during the 1960s and 1970s. Change was partly a response to a new, youth-oriented audience with more radical tastes, more open minds, and a heightened interest in politics, the arts, and cultural and sexual exploration. Filmmakers focused on fashionable themes and tried out novel techniques. Theater, dance, and opera, previously seen as a largely middle-class interest, charted fresh territory, often with ultra-modern sets, dynamic choreography, and confrontational themes, while music became more important than ever as a means of expression, both in itself and as a scene setter. These developments demanded a new visual language for the accompanying advertising, packaging, and other forms of promotion. Graphic designers helped lure audiences with compellingly styled posters and title sequences and seduced music lovers with psychedelic record sleeves.

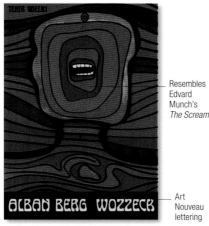

Resembles Edvard Munch's *The Scream*

Art Nouveau lettering

Poster for Polish National Opera production of Alban Berg's opera *Wozzeck* | **Jan Lenica**, 1964, Poland. Lenica's psychedelic colors and swirling lines mirrored the opera's theme of psychological pain and disorientation.

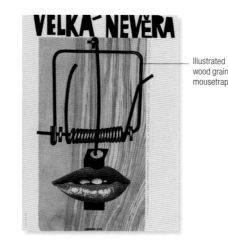

Illustrated wood grain mousetrap

Velká Nevĕra **(High Infidelity) film poster** | **Jiří Hilmar for director Franco Rossi**, 1965, Czechoslovakia. Advertising a film in which a cheese maker trades a night with his wife to clear his debts, this poster features glossy lips as the bait for a trap.

Anti-drug poster | **Public Health Service**, 1970, US. Using the language and counterculture imagery of the Be-In rally and its aftermath, this lithographic poster presented the message, "Will they turn you on or will they turn on you?".

Jan Lenica

1928–2001

Like many other designers of the 20th century, Lenica studied architecture before expressing his creative talents in other ways. Born in Poznań, Poland, he graduated from the architecture department of Warsaw Polytechnic in 1952. He built a multifaceted career as an acclaimed director of animated movies, poster artist, stamp designer for the German postal service, art editor, curator, and illustrator of children's books. His graphic work is characterized by flowing lines and a simplified lack of detail.

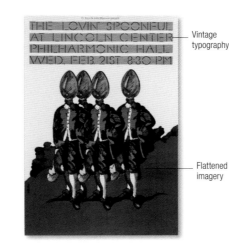

Vintage typography

Flattened imagery

Poster for The Lovin' Spoonful | **Milton Glaser**, 1967, US. Glaser, whose work was full of witty historical references, based this poster on the 18th-century British painting *The Blue Boy* by Gainsborough, multiplying it by four to represent the pop group.

Vivid, contrasting colors

Border of traditional woodblock prints

Poster for a Happening | **Tadanori Yokoo**, 1968, Japan. Inspired by the US psychedelic movement and Milton Glaser, Tadanori subverted traditional Japanese motifs, sexually explicit imagery, and graphic conventions to create this eclectic look.

TADANORI YOKOO

Exhibition Poster

YEAR *c.* 1956–1966 | **DIMENSIONS** *Height* 28 in (71.1 cm) *Width* 20¼ in (51.4 cm) | **MATERIALS** Photolithography on paper

Japanese artist and designer Tadanori Yokoo was interested in mysticism, Indian culture, and psychedelia, all of which he fused with motifs from Japanese art— the rising sun, waterfalls, and breaking waves—and images from his own life.

Because of its breadth of cultural reference and bright colors, his 1960s work became linked with Pop art. His bright, dynamic form of Pop imagery won Yokoo a large following, which grew further as a result of commissions for work from musicians such as the Beatles and Cat Stevens.

His poster for the 16th Exhibition of the Japan Advertising Artists Club (1968) combines several of his favorite motifs, arranging them with an artful combination of symmetry and asymmetry. The composition centers on a rising sun, seen by that time as an old-fashioned 19th- and early 20th-century symbol of imperial Japan but given new life in Yokoo's work. The leaping fish above it drips not with water but with colored paint—a vivid allusion to the artistic subject matter of the poster.

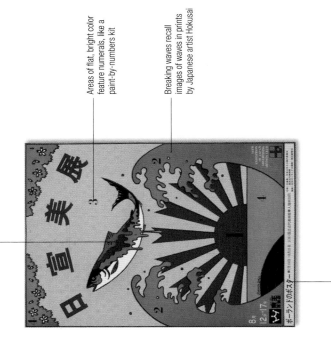

Fish is a traditional Japanese symbol of well-being and freedom

Areas of flat, bright color feature numerals, like a paint-by-numbers kit

Breaking waves recall images of waves in prints by Japanese artist Hokusai

Details of exhibition neatly arranged at bottom of poster

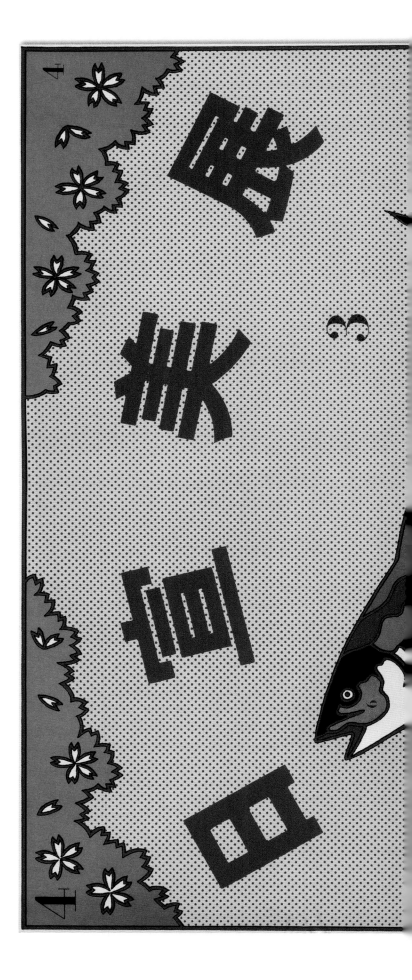

EVOLUTION OF
GUITARS

During the 20th century, the guitar evolved from an acoustic instrument used mainly in classical and folk music to an electric instrument, in which the vibrations of the strings are detected by a pickup and amplified. Both loud and expressive, the electric guitar became the central instrument in pop and rock music from the 1960s onward. Manufacturers responded to the instrument's popularity by creating different designs, varying the construction of the body, and developing the electronics and controls to produce a range of tones and styles.

c.1850s Classical guitar | Spain.
Early classical guitars such as this one evolved from five- to six-string instruments and had small bodies that produced a thinner sound than their later counterparts.

Decorated edges

1931–1932
Electro A-22 Frying pan | **George Beauchamp for Rickenbacker, US**. The first electric lap steel guitar, the A-22 was made to play the Hawaiian music that became popular in the 1930s.

Pickup containing horseshoe magnets

Signature Fender headstock design

1936 Gibson ES-150 | Gibson Guitar Corporation, US.
The Gibson ES-150 was popular among jazz players. They were used to Spanish-style acoustic guitars, and the Gibson was designed in a similar style but with an electric pickup to give it more volume in groups containing several instruments.

Violin-style tailpiece

1940 The Log | Les Paul, US.
Made from a standard piece of construction-grade wood, to which Paul attached strings, a pickup, and a bridge, the Log showed that electric guitars could be made very simply.

1954 Fender Stratocaster | Leo Fender, US.
With a distinctive horned body with cutaways that allow easy access to the upper register, the Stratocaster continues to appeal to players with its sleek looks and crisp sound. It is also extremely versatile, thanks to its three pickups and tremolo arm.

Bright, "twangy" bridge pickup

Contoured, ergonomic body

1958 Gibson Flying V | Ted McCarty for Gibson Guitar Corporation, US.
The appeal of the Flying V (together with its cousin the Explorer, shaped like a lightning bolt) lay in its radical, futuristic look and its solid mahogany body with excellent tonal properties.

Shape of scratch plate follows angular lines of body

Fingerboard

1982 Steinberger Bass | Ned Steinberger, US.
Steinberger adopted a minimalist approach to this bass guitar, with its "headless" neck and a slimmed-down, geometric body. This makes for a lightweight instrument but one that has a clear, smooth tone.

1860s **Acoustic classical guitar | Antonio Torres, Spain**. Torres added fan struts under his guitar's soundboards to boost their sound and stability. This, and their slightly larger size, set the blueprint for modern guitars.

Symmetrical wooden body

1908 **Gibson Style 0 | Orville Gibson, US**. This early instrument has a striking scroll decoration. Gibson originally made mandolins, and this scroll was based on the design of those instruments.

Oval sound hole

1930 **National Style 0 | John Dopyera, US**. Dopyera's resonator guitar has a metal body with an aluminum cone that picks up the strings' vibrations and amplifies them like a loudspeaker.

Perforations let sound escape from resonator

1950 **Fender Broadcaster | Leo Fender, US**. The solid-bodied Broadcaster is the result of Fender's project to create an electric Spanish-style guitar that could produce a high volume without the feedback that was common with hollow-bodied guitars. It is also the ancestor of the Telecaster.

Solid body

Plate metal bridge

1950s **Gibson Double-12 | Gibson Guitar Corporation, US**. This twin-neck guitar has 12 strings on one neck and six on the other, with separate controls for each neck. In effect, this arrangement gave guitarists two instruments in one, as they could switch instantly from one to the other.

Arm contour

1952 **Gibson Les Paul Goldtop | Gibson Guitar Corporation and Les Paul, US**. Two of the guitar's great innovators collaborated to produce Gibson's first solid-bodied instrument. A mahogany body and set (glued) neck help create its characteristically thick, heavy sound.

1990s **Ibanez 7-string | Ibanez, Japan**. Seven-string models offer an extended sonic range (usually at the low end) that has become popular in modern rock and fusion music. Ibanez manufactured the first mass-produced, electric seven-string guitars.

Les Paul–style switch

Bridge

2008 **Guitar Hero Controller | US**. Although not a real guitar, the controller enables players of Guitar Hero console games to simulate playing a real instrument. Controllers are modeled on various different electric guitars—this one is based on the Gibson Les Paul.

2009 **Gibson Dusk Tiger | Gibson Guitar Corporation, US**. Stretching the boundaries of guitar technology, players can edit the Dusk Tiger's sound profile by connecting the guitar to a computer. It can also tune itself automatically at the push of a button.

ADVERTISING AND SIGNS

Despite the rise of television news and advertising, print in the 1960s and 1970s was still crucial in many areas of life—in the form of subway maps and phone books, for example. Advertisers needed to appeal to a jaded market: the social and political awakening of the early 1960s meant that young consumers were wary of corporate messages. Posters increasingly used irony, creativity, and irreverence to target the new generation. The visually aware, counterculture audience responded readily to this new wave of graphics in print form, which was also partly triggered by dynamic developments in the art world that filtered through to illustrators and designers. This included Pop art, which harnessed bold forms, vivid color, and humor for impact, while surrealism and expressionism also influenced graphic artists.

Girl leads younger boy—previous signage showed boy leading girl

Triangular sign for warning conformed to European protocol

Highway signage system | **Jock Kinneir and Margaret Calvert for the British Ministry of Transport**, 1958, UK. This pictographic system unified British road signs in a model of efficient public design that instantly conveyed a message.

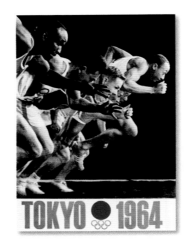

Tokyo 1964 poster for the Olympics | **Yusaku Kamekura**, 1962, Japan. Kamekura's lithograph stripped its message down to essentials, transcending language barriers. This was the first time photography was used to promote the Olympics.

SNCF advertisement | **Bernard Villemot for French National Railways**, 1962, France. The bright, cheerful colors are expressive, not realistic. Dynamic diagonals and minimal typography strengthen the impact of this color lithograph.

Sharp outlines

Stylized bubbles

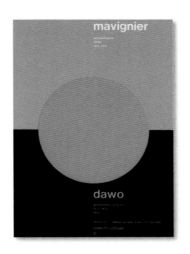

Dawo silk-screen poster | **Almir Mavignier**, 1963, Brazil. Mavignier identified with the Concrete art movement, advocating abstract art based on pure shapes and lines. This poster uses flat areas of color and geometric forms to provoke a reaction.

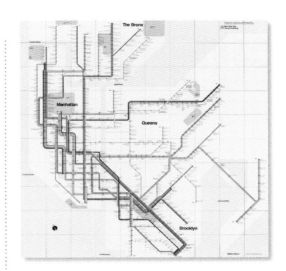

New York Subway map | **Massimo Vignelli for New York Metropolitan Transit Authority**, 1972, US. Vignelli used a grid of colors borrowed from the London Underground map to bring the New York subway map and signage up to date.

Orangina advertisement | **Bernard Villemot**, 1965, France. Villemot was considered the leading poster artist of his time, attracting major corporate clients, including Orangina, Perrier, Bally, and Air France. Here, he juxtaposed complementary blue and orange to make the colors look even brighter and more appetizing. Villemot followed a tradition in France of lithographic prints for advertising—Henri de Toulouse-Lautrec, Pablo Picasso, and Henri Matisse all designed such posters.

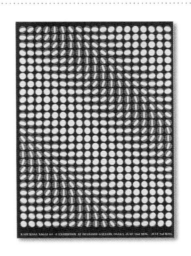

Silk-screen exhibition poster | **Kazumasa Nagai for Imbashi Gallery**, 1969, Japan. Nagai drew micropatterns by hand to create optical effects. Here, the pattern radiates from the central diagonal through the shape and fill-in of dots.

Olympic logo represents the five Olympic rings merged into a spiral

Blue and green palette evokes the German Alps

Manhattan Yellow Pages cover | **Peter Max**, 1970, US. Influenced by both Chinese design and his love of the comic book *Plastic Man*, Pop artist Max used warm, optimistic colors and cartoon-style imagery for this phone book cover.

Poster for Munich Olympics | **Otl Aicher**, 1972, Germany. The pictograms Aicher and his team developed for the 1972 Games have become the Olympic standard. Here, the Olympic logo is discreetly positioned above the sprinting athletes.

BRIGHT TEXTILES

Bold color was the hallmark of textiles in the 1960s and 1970s, which took their cue from the fashion world. The trend was driven in part by the counterculture of flower power, Pop art, drug use, and sexual and left-wing politics, all of which played their part in undermining the prevailing conservative taste of Western society. Rebellion was expressed with vivid colors, optical patterns, and swirling, fluid lines. New types of polyester fabric were perfected and mass produced, and they were not only cheap but could also take brilliantly colored dyes. Demographics were also a determining factor, as young people had more spending power and wanted to assert their independence in cultural and aesthetic terms. Using textiles, they could create fashionable homes with a limited budget, a vogue that continued into the 1970s.

Oversized poppies in the style of Pop art

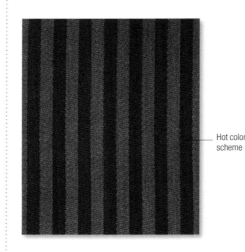

Hot color scheme

Art Nouveau–style swirls inspired by the 1920s Ballets Russes

Unikko | Maija Isola for Marimekko, 1964, Finland. In the spirit of flower-power rebellion, Isola flouted Marimekko's ban on floral prints to create this bestselling print, which was updated every decade in different colors.

Toostripe | Alexander Girard for Herman Miller, 1965, US. Based in Santa Fe, New Mexico, Girard was well known for his use of color and abstract geometric patterns, which were often striped, as here, and also for his interest in folk art.

Ballet Russes | Jack Lenor Larsen for Belle Fabrics, 1966–1969, US. Used first as a fashion fabric in stretch nylon, then for furnishings, the psychedelic pattern of this textile helped mask distortion when stretched over foam-molded furniture.

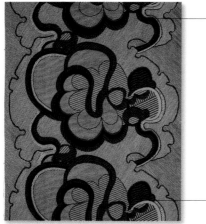

Overlapping, cloudlike shapes

Striated sections draw the eye in

Bold curves blend organic styling with symmetry

Checks countered by blocks and curves

Simple Solar | Shirley Craven for Hull Traders, 1968, UK. Craven made textiles look like works of art—she developed the Simple Solar pattern using paintings, drawings, and 3-D designs to create seemingly spontaneous, hand-drawn shapes.

Curve (Mira-X-SET) | Verner Panton for Mira-X, 1969, Denmark. Panton created a series of high-concept prints based on the number eight for the Swiss manufacturer Mira-X. Every curve has eight colors, each reproduced in one of eight shades.

Bauhaus | Susan Collier and Sarah Campbell for Liberty, 1972, UK. This design was adapted from a tapestry by Gunta Stölzl at the Bauhaus. Collier's admiration for the painter Matisse is also evident in the disciplined combination of line and color.

Pleasure sliding across the eye

Susan **Collier's** aim in her textile designs

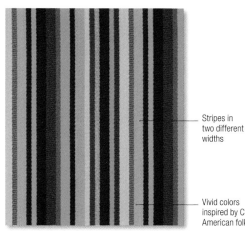

Stripes in two different widths

Vivid colors inspired by Central American folk art

Millerstripe | **Alexander Girard for Maharam**, 1973, US. Girard was inspired by folk art, an influence apparent in the 300 or more textiles he designed for modern American furniture maker Herman Miller, after whom this fabric was named.

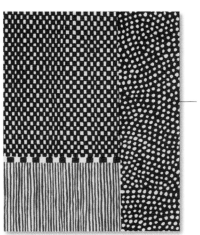

Irregular dot pattern creates a disorienting effect

Ma | **Katsuji Wakisaka for Wacoal Interior Fabrics**, 1977, **Japan**. In this design, Wakisaka combined the trademark bright colors of Marimekko, his former employer, with small geometric patterning inspired by the traditional cloth of Japan.

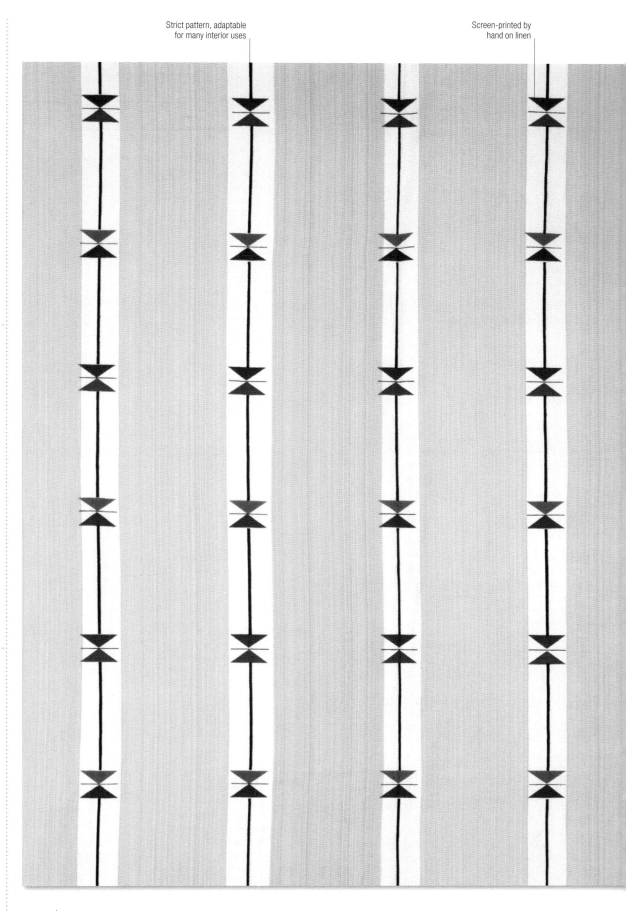

Strict pattern, adaptable for many interior uses

Screen-printed by hand on linen

Tattoo | **Astrid Sampe for Nordiska Kompaniet**, c. 1958, Sweden. With thin lines joining colored arrowheads and a sunny background, this pattern is typical of the optimism and simple purity of Sampe's work. For more than 30 years, Sampe was head of textiles at Stockholm department store Nordiska Kompaniet, commissioning designers such as Stig Lindberg and Hans Krondahl.

POSTMODERN & CONTEMPORARY

1980s onward

Less is a bore.

ROBERT VENTURI, ARCHITECT

POSTMODERN AND CONTEMPORARY
Introduction

ostmodernism was a movement in architecture and design that began in the 1970s but reached fruition in the 1980s. Designers rejected the Modernist drive for simplicity and purity and reveled instead in variety, complexity, and contradiction. Postmodernism was partly, therefore, a reaction against the straitjacket of the Modernist aesthetic still taught in design schools and partly a spirited response to the economic boom and the optimism of the 1980s. The resulting work was eclectic, witty, and often interpreted the styles of the past in an irreverent way. The movement began in architecture, with American architects such as Michael Graves and Philip Johnston adding brightly colored classical columns to skyscrapers and other obviously contemporary buildings. Individualistic designs like this created a sense of incongruity, but they were also intended to raise a smile.

Theatrical design
This anti-Modernist approach soon began to influence the design of everyday objects. At the forefront of the movement were Italian collectives such as the Memphis Group, who used bold colors, unconventional forms, and a touch of kitsch (bad taste) in furniture, ceramics, and other items, and Studio Alchimia, who reinterpreted traditional designs in bright colors. Their work struck a chord with designers because of its sheer theatricality and was

UNCONVENTIONAL FORMS

Postmodern architects distorted elements of their buildings to create something totally new, complex, and unconventional. Even more conventional-looking buildings were given unexpected ornamental details.

HISTORICAL INFLUENCES

Like designers before them, postmodernists looked back to the past for inspiration, but instead of following one style, they appropriated forms and motifs from different styles and merged them with a touch of irony.

ASYMMETRY

In defiance of Modernism, postmodern designers deliberately avoided symmetry in their use of form, structure, materials, and color. The results were often unconventional, childlike, and humorous.

An interest in ideas is a sign of human life.

Kenneth **Grange**

promoted by magazines such as *Domus*, which was sold internationally. The movement became fashionable and attracted both design enthusiasts and corporate clients, who commissioned postmodern buildings and furniture during the economic boom of the 1980s.

Although postmodernism, with its "anything goes" attitude, was a reaction against the idea that form should follow function, its influence is also evident in the work of engineers and industrial designers, such as James Dyson and Apple's design chief Jonathan Ive, whose colorful vacuum cleaners and computers with transparent casings and visible motors owe a debt to the irreverent, fun-loving creativity of postmodernism.

A new simplicity

The economic crash of 1987 signaled the end of the culture of excess that had dominated the 1980s. After almost 15 years of postmodernism and its rich, eclectic style, there was a move toward simpler, cleaner designs. From the late 1980s onward, the clashing colors, patterns, and surface decoration were increasingly replaced by clear glass and acrylics, exposed wood, and wicker, as designers began to revive the Modernist spirit of truth to materials. They have now reached a point where the lessons of both Modernism and postmodernism have been absorbed, leaving them free to follow their own paths and develop new approaches.

HUMOR

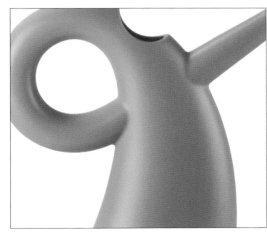

Witty references to animals and humans are a feature of postmodern style. Designers reinterpreted conventional forms, often adding humorous details to make them look like something else.

VIBRANT COLOR

Designers used strong colors and color contrasts to increase the impact of a piece, or to draw attention to how it worked. Even everyday household objects were given the same bold color treatment.

RECYCLING

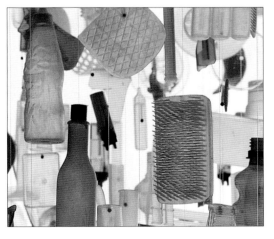

Awareness of the environment has played a significant part in design since the 1980s. Many designers make a statement by creating products that are energy-efficient or made from recycled components.

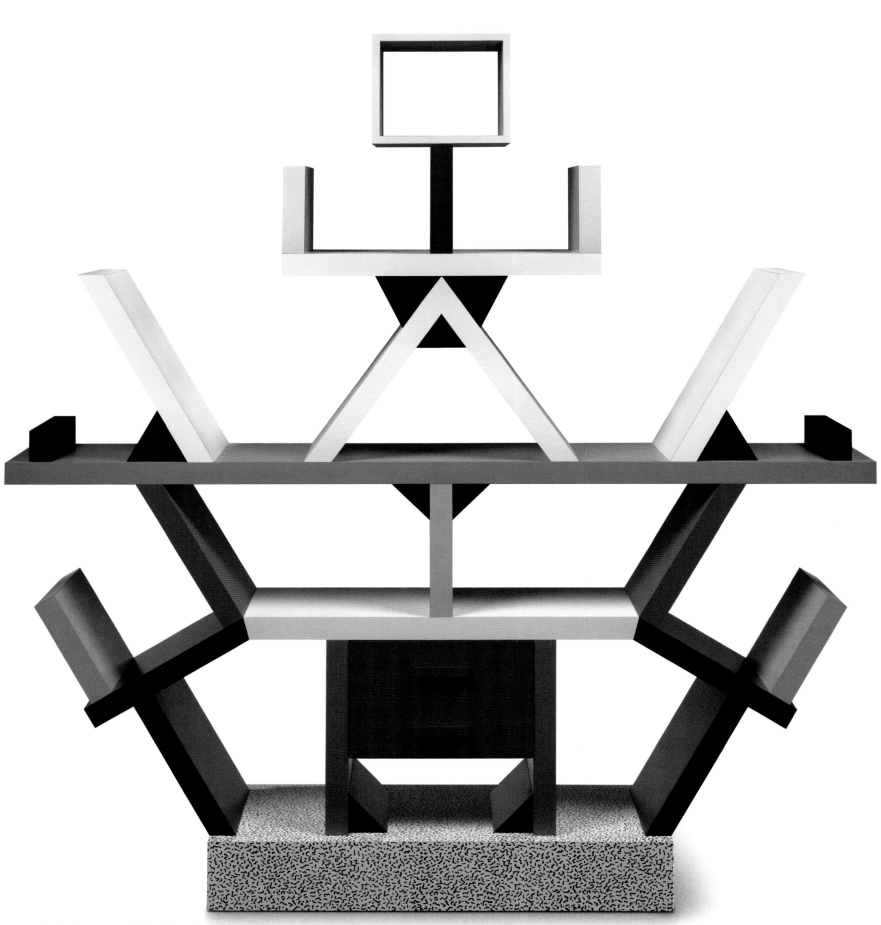

△ **Carlton bookcase,** 1981, with its bold geometrics, laminated surfaces, African symbols, and bright colors, encapsulated Memphis's audacious approach to design.

Ettore Sottsass

The name of Italian Ettore Sottsass is inseparable from that of Memphis, the design group he founded in Milan in reaction to what he saw as the restricting purity of Modernism. Sottsass began his career by following in his father's footsteps and studying architecture, but while Sottsass senior's approach was based solely on function, his son became intent on creating design that would separate an object from its purpose. "A table may need four legs to function," he said, "But no one can tell me that the four legs have to look the same." From the 1950s, he became a well-known figure in art and design, working for Olivetti on the red Valentine typewriter of 1970 (see p.301), producing ceramics, and launching a publishing house after meeting Allen Ginsberg and other Beat poets in California. In 1980, he established Sottsass Associati with several avant-garde architects; however, the following year, he began the project for which he would become best known—the Memphis Group.

Named after a Bob Dylan song, Memphis was a collaboration with young designers from around the world. It celebrated postmodern wit, ironically mixing expensive and throwaway materials and motifs from different eras and ethnicities in a colorful, kitsch, yet superbly constructed riot. The collective dominated interior design in the 1980s with their provocative, playful work. After five years, Sottsass left the group, focusing on architecture for the remainder of his career.

Life

1917–2007

1917 Born in Innsbruck, Austria

1920

1939 Graduates with architecture degree from Turin University

1940

1946 Sets up architecture practice in Milan

1956 Travels to New York to work with George Nelson for a month

1958 Becomes design consultant for Olivetti

1960

1965 Designs Totem ceramics, inspired by Pop art

1970 Valentine typewriter wins Compasso d'Oro award

1980 Forms Memphis design collective

1980

1985 Leaves Memphis and returns to architecture; designs Mandarin chairs for Knoll a year later

1989 Wins Compasso d'Oro award for Nuovo Milano cutlery for Alessi

2000

2000 Sottsass Associati design Malpensa Airport, Milan

2007 Dies in Milan

Totem 503 (left) and 502 (right) | For Bitossi Ceramics, 1965. Inspired by travels to India and the US, Sottsass collaborated with Aldo Londi on these ceramics.

Decorative rings emphasize height

Varying diameters

Westside lounge | For Knoll, 1983. The Westside collection was a radical departure from furniture styles of the 1980s, introducing primary colors and wedge-shaped armrests.

Components resemble a child's building blocks

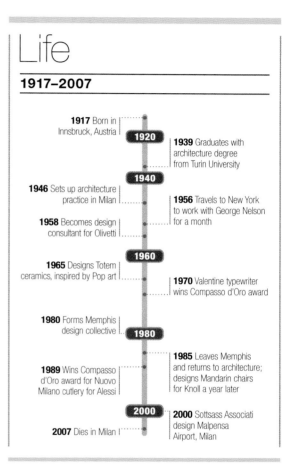

Sherezade vacuum flask | For Alessi, 1996. The Sherezade has a stainless-steel body with contrasting spout, lid, and handle in claret-colored plastic.

Hourglass shape

Tabletop inserted into striped support

Cylindrical footbar

Flamingo table | **Michele de Lucchi for Memphis**, 1983, **Italy**. De Lucchi designed the Flamingo as part of a series of four side tables. Each one had similar colors and motifs and came with a plaque bearing the designer's name.

Colors of the Italian flag

Cast resin with acrylic coating

Slanted table legs of varying diameters

Sansone table | **Gaetano Pesce**, 1980, **Italy**. The Sansone was made of polyester resin, poured by hand into molds for the legs, while each tabletop was a different shape, espousing Pesce's belief that every piece of furniture should have a personality.

Seat backs made of branches and log segments

Three legs in different shapes—straight, curved, and wavy

Two off-kilter rings steady the legs

Duplex stool | **Javier Mariscal for BD Barcelona Design**, 1986, Spain. Cobi, the mascot for the Barcelona 1992 Olympic Games, introduced Mariscal's work to the world, but he was already famous in design circles for this Duplex stool, conceived in 1980 for the interior of a bar in Valencia.

Animali Domestici seating | **Andrea Branzi for Zabro**, **1985, Italy**. Branzi cofounded the radical design group Archizoom to create furniture such as the Animali Domestici range that would question whether good taste was better than vulgarity.

POSTMODERN FURNITURE

During the late 20th century, southern Europe emerged as a powerful force in furniture design. Italy had always been at the forefront of the field, but now its neighbor Spain began to attract the attention of the international design community. Freed from the dictatorship of Franco in 1975, Spanish architects and designers began to flourish, also spurred by the Catalan independence movement based in Barcelona. At the 1986 Milan Furniture Fair, designers from Barcelona received great acclaim; six years later, the Barcelona Summer Olympics of 1992 fueled demand for Spanish designer products, from fashion to film, furniture, and homeware. In Italy, meanwhile, postmodernism and the Memphis movement (see pp.318–319) dominated furniture design. Architects Andrea Branzi and Gaetano Pesce, among others, challenged notions of good taste with their kitsch, colorful, humorous pieces.

Honeycomb texture on seat surface

Ultra-thin and lightweight

Light Light chair | **Alberto Meda for Alias**, 1987, Italy.
A mechanical engineer, Meda began experimenting with carbon fiber in the 1980s. His trials resulted in this chair, one of the first pieces of furniture made from a carbon-fiber composite.

> We have to **answer** people's needs, **create** something useful, **give joy and happiness.**
>
> Gaetano **Pesce**

Slatted back inspired by Samurai armor

Armrests cast separately from legs

Cushion over slatted seat

Toledo chair | **Jorge Pensi for Amat-3**, 1989, Spain.
Designed for Barcelona's outdoor cafés, this cast-aluminum chair is stackable and can withstand rain and sun. The gentle curves of its seat and backrest provide optimal comfort.

Top-stitched motif of leaves

Base resembles branches

Foliage sofa | **Patricia Urquiola for Kartell**, 2011, Spain.
Urquiola is known for the rich textures and curves of her furniture. The leaf patterns and twiglike base of this sofa were inspired by themes of nature and the idea of nesting.

Sofa back also functions as a screen

Turned wooden legs

Float sofa | **Karim Rashid for Sancal**, 2012, Spain. As its name implies, Rashid's sofa seat appears to float above the floor. Although apparently composed of separate elements, it looks unified overall because each part intersects and has the same rounded outline. A prolific industrial designer, Rashid was born in Egypt, raised in Canada, and now lives in the US, but he works for many southern European manufacturers, including Sancal.

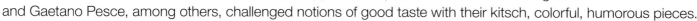

△ **In its catalogs** and retail displays, IKEA artfully presents practical solutions for small-space living on a budget.

△ **Storage table** | *c.* 2000s

Swedish company IKEA has the distinction of inventing flat-pack furniture. This simple idea has transformed homes around the world, challenging the assumption that furniture needs to be an expensive investment and forming the core of a business that generates more than 21 billion euros in sales each year.

Founder Ingvar Kamprad started IKEA in 1943, creating the name using his initials and the first letters of the farm (Elmtaryd) and village (Agunnaryd) where he was born. The company did not sell furniture at first but small items such as pens and picture frames. In 1948, it began to sell mail-order furniture. Legend has it that IKEA employee Gillis Lundgren was struggling to load a table into a car for delivery, so he removed its legs, and subsequently developed the idea of furniture that could be assembled at home. IKEA began producing flat-pack furniture in 1956 and opened a store soon after. In the 1970s, the company expanded dramatically overseas and introduced many of its classic designs, including the Billy bookcase and Klippan sofa. Over the years, IKEA—now a household name and a byword for affordable, compact furniture—has pioneered innovative designs such as magazine-style catalogs; removable, washable fabric covers; and the use of particleboard.

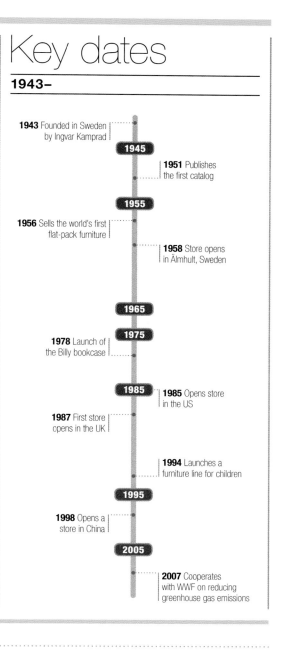

Key dates

1943–

1943 Founded in Sweden by Ingvar Kamprad

1945

1951 Publishes the first catalog

1955

1956 Sells the world's first flat-pack furniture

1958 Store opens in Älmhult, Sweden

1965

1975

1978 Launch of the Billy bookcase

1985

1985 Opens store in the US

1987 First store opens in the UK

1994 Launches a furniture line for children

1995

1998 Opens a store in China

2005

2007 Cooperates with WWF on reducing greenhouse gas emissions

Poem armchair | **Noboru Nakamura, 1976**. Later called Poäng, the Poem's classic Scandinavian lines are reminiscent of the designs of Alvar Aalto (see pp.194–195).

Lövbacken side table | 1960. The Lövbacken side table is based on the Lövet table, which was originally produced in 1960 and was one of IKEA's first flat-pack products.

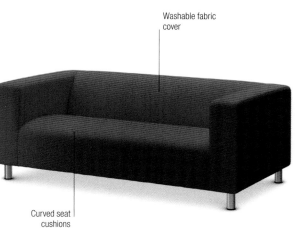

Washable fabric cover

Curved seat cushions

Klippan sofa | 1989. Launched in 1989, the Klippan sofa has become one of IKEA's most enduring and popular pieces. A flat-pack version was created in 2004.

Chair in sheet glass | Danny Lane, **1988, UK**. Lane's jagged glass chair caused a sensation in the 1980s, contrasting as it did with the sleek lines and glossy surfaces of much postmodern furniture of the time. Born in Illinois, Lane moved to London in the 1970s to study with one of Great Britain's leading stained-glass exponents. He is best known for his public sculptures and installations in glass but created this chair as a unique piece for his first solo show in London.

Back and sides threaded onto steel rods

Stacked sheet glass

Hammered finish on seat and back

Reflective stainless steel

Little Heavy chair | **Ron Arad for One Off Ltd.**, 1991, UK. Out of economic necessity, Arad initially made furniture from salvaged metal, which he welded by hand, as in this reflective stainless steel chair.

Flexible felt seat allows rocking movement

Sprung steel frame

Nomad chair | **Ilkka Suppanen**, 1994, **Finland**. Suppanen's interest in nomadic lifestyles led him to make this chair, which is easy to assemble or pack away. Its flexible, canopy-like seat is supported by slim metal rods that resemble tent poles.

Slim back contrasts with bulging seat

Natural imperfections in leather covering

Finely stitched seams

Daniela chair | **Jiří Pelcl for Atelier Pelcl**, 1995, **Czech Republic**. Pelcl transforms raw materials, including wood, metal, clay, and, for this chair, leather, into elegant and functional objects that project both warmth and wit.

EXPERIMENTAL FURNITURE

Postmodern furniture had its roots in the Memphis Group, founded by Ettore Sottsass in 1981 (see pp.318–319), and the color, wit, and irreverence of these Italian pioneers soon spread. Designers in northern Europe exploited advanced craft and industrial techniques to produce furniture that was both sophisticated and rugged, unlike the glossy Memphis style. Ilkka Suppanen, for example, fashioned wool felt into gravity-defying shapes that resembled bent plywood, while Danny Lane opted for jagged glass. Ron Arad and Tom Dixon engineered the most unyielding materials into curvaceous forms, and the Bouroullec brothers in France reenergized furniture design from the late 1990s onward with their streamlined and spirited designs. Philippe Starck shared the humor of his Italian counterparts, and both he and Michael Sodeau experimented with historical styles.

Alcove Highback Love Seat | **Ronan and Erwan Bouroullec for Vitra**, 2006, France. With its flexible, extended back and side panels connected by zippers, the Alcove is based on the idea that a sofa can be like a "room within a room."

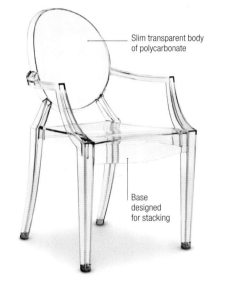

Slim transparent body of polycarbonate

Base designed for stacking

Louis Ghost chair | **Philippe Starck for Kartell**, 2002, France. The shape of the Louis Ghost is based on a classic late-18th-century Louis XVI armchair, but it is made of transparent resin rather than the traditional wood.

Library sofa | **Michael Sodeau for Modus**, 2012, UK. Although it looks contemporary, Sodeau's sleekly curved sofa recalls the wingback chairs of the Queen Anne style, which enclosed the sitter at the back and sides to keep out drafts.

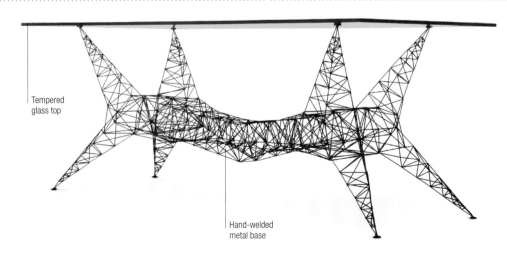

Tempered glass top

Hand-welded metal base

Pylon table | **Tom Dixon for Cappellini**, 1992, UK. The Pylon line of furniture began as a research project into structural engineering to produce the world's lightest chair. Dixon was inspired by bridges, towers, and space frames and used his welding skills to create the prototypes. The copper-plated steel rods of this table are lightweight but strong, and the X-frame of its legs looks both airy and stable.

Tom Dixon

1959–

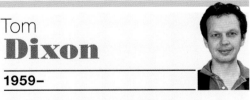

During the 1980s, Tunisian-born Dixon emerged as one of the most talked-about designers in Great Britain. With no formal design training, he began making furniture welded from salvage, but by 1990, he was working on commissions for Cappellini. In 1992, he set up a creative hub and shop called Space to showcase his work and that of other designers. Since then, he has gone on to consult, design interiors, and generate mass-production pieces for his own company and manufacturers such as Artek.

△ **Eero Saarinen's Tulip chair,** 1956, has become one of the most popular Knoll designs.

Knoll

△ **Bertoia Bird Chair** | **Harry Bertoia**, 1952

A dynamic force in modern and postmodern furniture, Knoll has helped shape the style of seating that has dominated offices and homes for much of the 20th century. For 80 years, it has commissioned and manufactured some of the most iconic—and most widely copied—chairs ever designed. Although the company's range of products now extends to tables, desks, lamps, textiles, and office accessories, it is still best known for its seating.

Knoll was founded in New York City in 1938 by Hans Knoll. Furniture making was in his blood—his grandfather started the family business in Stuttgart, Germany, in 1865, and Knoll's father took the company in a new direction in the 1920s, by focusing on Modernist interiors. When Hans moved to the US in 1938, he intended to import modern European furniture, but when World War II made shipping difficult, he decided to create his own line. He and his wife, Florence—who had attended the prestigious Cranbrook Academy of Arts in Detroit with Charles Eames, Ludwig Mies van der Rohe, and Eero Saarinen—subsequently commissioned some of the most creative minds of the second half of the 20th century, such as Frank Gehry, Ettore Sottsass, Piero Lissoni, Isamu Noguchi, and Robert Venturi, to design furniture and interiors.

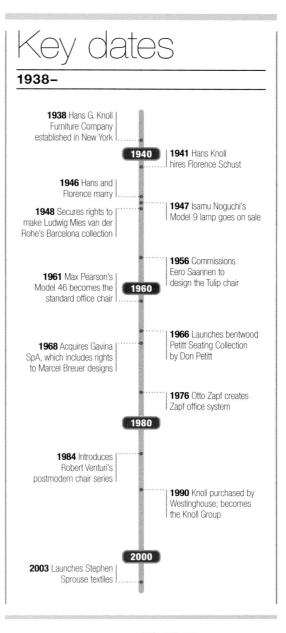

Key dates

1938–

1938 Hans G. Knoll Furniture Company established in New York

1940

1941 Hans Knoll hires Florence Schust

1946 Hans and Florence marry

1947 Isamu Noguchi's Model 9 lamp goes on sale

1948 Secures rights to make Ludwig Mies van der Rohe's Barcelona collection

1956 Commissions Eero Saarinen to design the Tulip chair

1961 Max Pearson's Model 46 becomes the standard office chair

1960

1966 Launches bentwood Petitt Seating Collection by Don Petitt

1968 Acquires Gavina SpA, which includes rights to Marcel Breuer designs

1976 Otto Zapf creates Zapf office system

1980

1984 Introduces Robert Venturi's postmodern chair series

1990 Knoll purchased by Westinghouse; becomes the Knoll Group

2000

2003 Launches Stephen Sprouse textiles

MR low table | **Ludwig Mies van der Rohe**, designed 1929, produced by Knoll 1977. A tubular stainless-steel frame and legs support the clear plate-glass top of this table.

Stainless steel legs

Florence Knoll lounge chair | **Florence Knoll**, 1954. The simple form of this chair recalls the minimalism of Mies van der Rohe, but the vibrant color and texture give the design warmth.

Cross Check chair | **Frank Gehry**, 1992. Inspired by the apple crates that Gehry played on when he was a child, this chair is made from interwoven ribbons of maplewood.

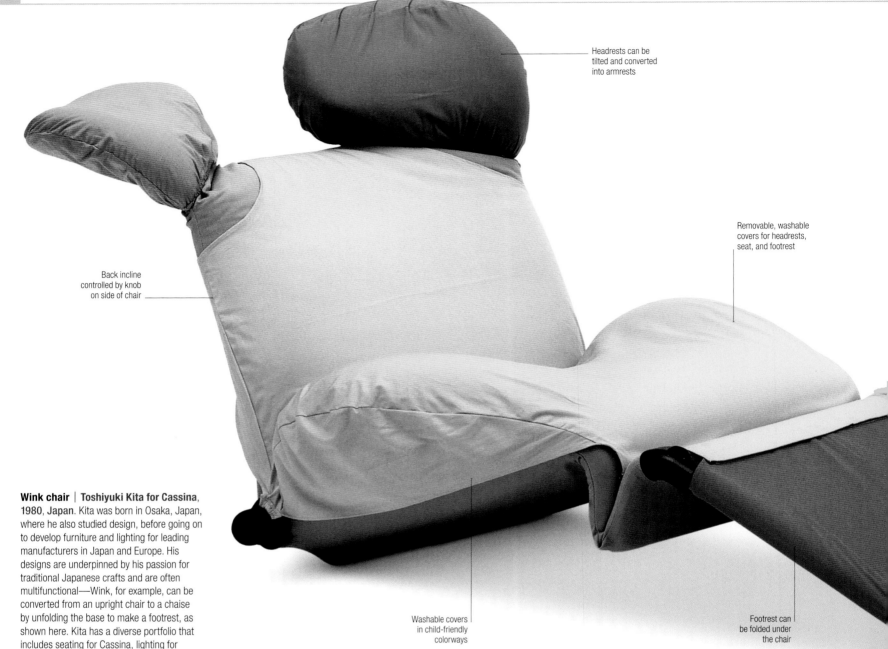

Headrests can be
tilted and converted
into armrests

Removable, washable
covers for headrests,
seat, and footrest

Back incline
controlled by knob
on side of chair

Wink chair | **Toshiyuki Kita for Cassina**,
1980, Japan. Kita was born in Osaka, Japan,
where he also studied design, before going on
to develop furniture and lighting for leading
manufacturers in Japan and Europe. His
designs are underpinned by his passion for
traditional Japanese crafts and are often
multifunctional—Wink, for example, can be
converted from an upright chair to a chaise
by unfolding the base to make a footrest, as
shown here. Kita has a diverse portfolio that
includes seating for Cassina, lighting for
Tecnolumen, and televisions for Mitsubishi.

Washable covers
in child-friendly
colorways

Footrest can
be folded under
the chair

THE SPREAD OF
POSTMODERNISM

One of the most controversial
design movements of the past century,
postmodernism reached its peak in the
1980s, influencing not only architecture and furniture but almost every aspect of popular culture. It began as a reaction to Modernism,
which had rejected historicism, and regarded technology and machinery as the route to a better future. Postmodernism reevaluated
elements of history and brought them back into design in ways that were often eclectic or experimental, and sometimes infused with
irony and humor. The postmodern Memphis Group was founded in Italy but made a deep impression on designers outside Europe,
including Marc Newson in Australia and Masanori Umeda in Japan. More recently, environmental issues have focused the attention
of furniture designers from all around the world on the theme of sustainability.

High, narrow back supports the length of the spine

Subtly curved seat

Bone-rest chair | **Toshiyuki Kita for Johoku Mokko Co. Ltd.**, 1983, Japan. This chair is pared down to show the beauty of its hinoki wood, which is prized in Japan for its light color and straight grain and used in palaces, temples, and shrines.

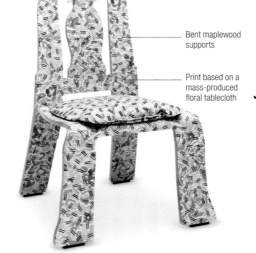

Bent maplewood supports

Print based on a mass-produced floral tablecloth

Queen Anne chair | **Robert Venturi and Denise Scott Brown for Knoll**, 1984, US. This flattened, patterned spoof of a Queen Anne–style chair is a witty comment on the popularity of historical furniture.

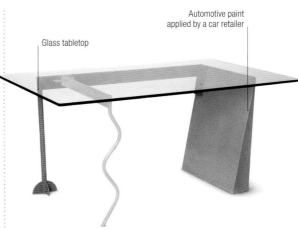

Automotive paint applied by a car retailer

Glass tabletop

Peninsula table | **Peter Shire**, 1982, US. Shire, an early member of the Memphis Group, drew on the exuberant car culture of his native Los Angeles in the design of this enameled metal and aluminum table.

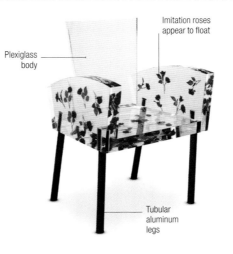

Imitation roses appear to float

Plexiglass body

Tubular aluminum legs

Miss Blanche chair | **Shiro Kuramata for Ishimaru Co.**, 1988, Japan. Kuramata's chair is named after Blanche DuBois from Tennessee Williams's play *A Streetcar Named Desire*. Her fading beauty is represented by the delicate rose motif.

Hand-filled petal cushions arranged in layers

Solid aluminum legs

Seat upholstered in thick velvet

Rose Chair | **Masanori Umeda for Edra**, 1990, Japan. Umeda's furniture is playful yet functional, like this romantic, luxurious flower-shaped chair. Based in Tokyo, he took part in the first Memphis show in Milan in 1981.

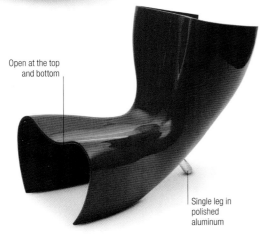

Open at the top and bottom

Single leg in polished aluminum

Felt chair | **Marc Newson for Cappellini**, 1993, Australia. Typically sleek and futuristic, this chair is formed from a sheet of reinforced fiberglass. Newson is renowned for his ability to engineer metal and plastic into fluid shapes.

Bundles of rolled textiles

Base and seat structure of iron rings

Sushi III chair | **Fernando and Humberto Campana for Estudio Campana**, 2002, Brazil. This chair is a witty interpretation by the Campana brothers of the Brazilian love of craftsmanship, vivid color, and thriftiness.

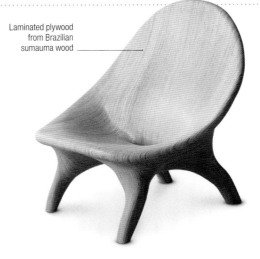

Laminated plywood from Brazilian sumauma wood

Poltrona Suave chair | **Julia Krantz**, 2008, Brazil. Driven by ecological concerns and her love of the Brazilian rain forest, Krantz handcrafts wooden furniture using lumber from suppliers who grow sustainably rather than felling trees in the wild.

△ **Newson's monochrome lobby bar** for the Puerta América hotel in Madrid features laser-cut aluminum panels on the walls and ceiling and a polished marble floor.

Marc **Newson**

An unconventional childhood—which included living in a beachfront hotel and traveling through Europe and Asia as a teenager—sowed the seeds for Marc Newson to blossom into one of the most exciting design talents of the 1990s. While growing up in Sydney, Australia, in the 1960s and early 1970s, Newson saw some of the iconic Italian designs of the era at the hotel where his mother worked as manager. He studied jewelry and sculpture design in his native Sydney and began experimenting with creating metal furniture. His first notable piece was the Lockheed Lounge, an industrial-style chaise longue, made with the help of a grant from the Australian Council for the Arts. Exhibited at a prominent Sydney gallery, it soon became a talking point in international design circles.

Commissions followed for a diverse range of products, including a concept car for Ford (the 021C); a perfume bottle for Shiseido; interiors for upscale restaurants and hotels around the world; sports shoes for Nike; homeware and furniture for prestigious European brands such as Flos, Moroso, Cappellini, and Alessi; the MN1 bicycle for Biomega; cookware for Tefal; and aircraft cabin interiors. Newson has since carved out a niche in the field of industrial design, with metalwork a recurring theme and vintage cars an ever-present influence. His style uses a sleek, industrial aesthetic to luxurious effect, with scale, ergonomics, and fluid forms adding emotional appeal.

Life

1963–

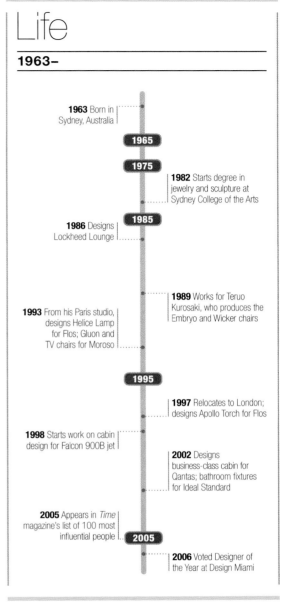

1963 Born in Sydney, Australia

1965

1975

1982 Starts degree in jewelry and sculpture at Sydney College of the Arts

1985

1986 Designs Lockheed Lounge

1989 Works for Teruo Kurosaki, who produces the Embryo and Wicker chairs

1993 From his Paris studio, designs Helice Lamp for Flos; Gluon and TV chairs for Moroso

1995

1997 Relocates to London; designs Apollo Torch for Flos

1998 Starts work on cabin design for Falcon 900B jet

2002 Designs business-class cabin for Qantas; bathroom fixtures for Ideal Standard

2005 Appears in *Time* magazine's list of 100 most influential people

2005

2006 Voted Designer of the Year at Design Miami

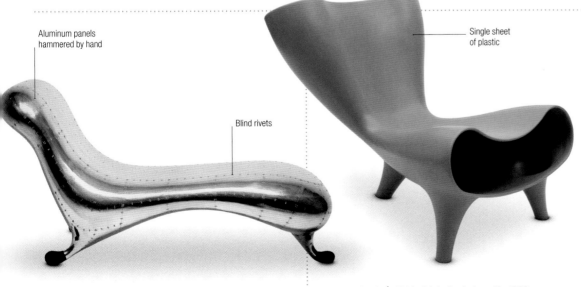

Aluminum panels hammered by hand

Blind rivets

Single sheet of plastic

Lockheed Lounge | 1986. Named after the American aircraft manufacturer, Lockheed Lounge is clad in aluminum and welded over a body of fiberglass-reinforced plastic.

Orgone Chair | 1998. Originally designed in 1993 as a limited edition in aluminum, Orgone was later produced as a mass-market chair made from colored polyethylene.

Backrest slats bent back to create seat

Wood Chair | **For Cappellini**, 1992. Fine strips of bent natural beechwood give this chair an impression of delicacy, although the overall effect is one of sturdiness.

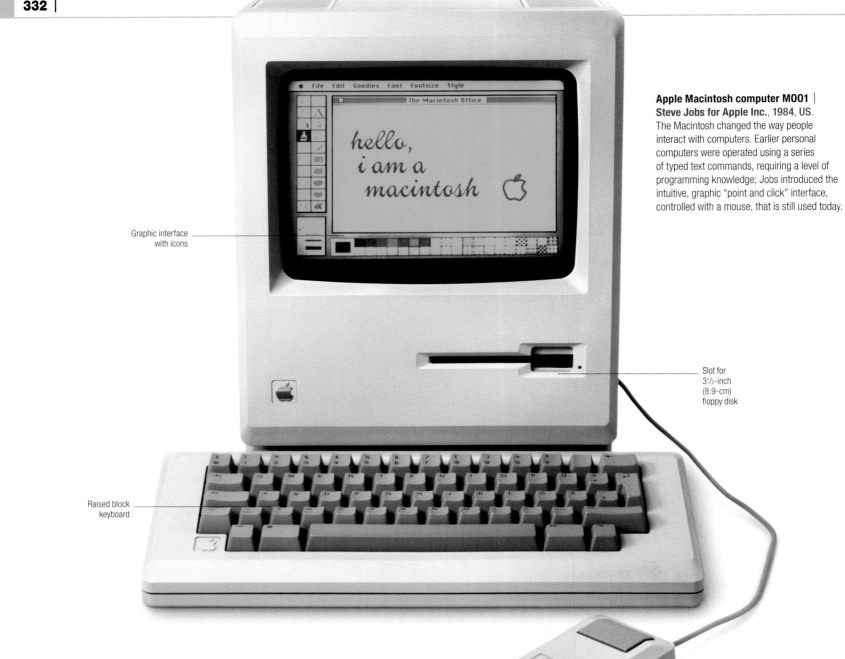

Graphic interface
with icons

Raised block
keyboard

**Apple Macintosh computer M001 |
Steve Jobs for Apple Inc.**, 1984, US.
The Macintosh changed the way people
interact with computers. Earlier personal
computers were operated using a series
of typed text commands, requiring a level of
programming knowledge; Jobs introduced the
intuitive, graphic "point and click" interface,
controlled with a mouse, that is still used today.

Slot for
3½-inch
(8.9-cm)
floppy disk

Rectangular,
block-shaped mouse

OFFICE EQUIPMENT
AND COMPUTERS

The competitive market conditions
of recent decades have led to significant
developments in office equipment—both
businesses and individuals want products that make work faster and smarter and are more connected. Technological milestones
have paved the way: the launch of Microsoft's Windows in 1983, the doubling of superconductor speeds in 1987, the creation of
the HTML coding language in 1990, public access to the internet in 1993, and the growing use of smartphones in the 2000s.

Product design has also kept pace with technological developments, as graphic interfaces have made electronics simple
and fun to use, and touch-screen smartphones make it possible to have instant contact with colleagues around the world. No
longer made of blocky, gray plastic, computers such as the sleek aluminum MacBook Pro have become objects of desire.

2647A Intelligent Graphics Terminal | Hewlett-Packard, 1978, US. Marketed as a graphics terminal because it did not have its own central processing unit, the boxy 2647A had built-in cartridge tapes offering 220k of memory storage.

Slim, lightweight handset

Diagonal keys maximize button surface area

BeoCom 1000 telephone | Gideon Loewy for Bang & Olufsen, 1986, Denmark. Bang & Olufsen introduced a splash of color to office phones with the BeoCom 1000, marketed on the basis of its sound quality and bright, youthful design.

Controls for video and audio

Angled handset features integrated keypad

BeoCom 1500 telephone | Bang & Olufsen, 1994, Denmark. The BeoCom 1500 was part of an entire Bang & Olufsen system. With its remote control buttons, users could raise or lower the volume of Bang & Olufsen stereos or TVs.

"Off" switch activates when not in use

Boxy shape with curved paper output path

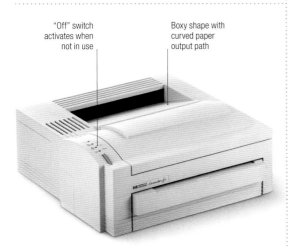

4L LaserJet printer | Hewlett-Packard, early 1990s, US. The 4L was a response to growing demand for home office equipment. Designed for personal use, it had an auto power-off feature and was both compact and reasonably priced.

Built-in iSight camera

LCD screen

MacBook Pro laptop | Jonathan Ive for Apple Inc., 2006, US. Although it was no lighter or slimmer than the PowerBook, Apple's original Macintosh laptop, the Pro had additional features such as a webcam and a magnetic power connector.

The modern office

1970–present

In recent years, the furniture and layout of the workplace has evolved almost as much as the technology used within it. Designers have been influenced by ergonomics, a field of study that emerged in the 1970s that examined the impact of regular office work on the human body. A greater appreciation of ergonomics produced Herman Miller's Aeron chair (see p.273). The comfortable mesh upholstery of this high-tech office seat adapts to any shape, keeping pressure even across the entire body and alleviating postural problems caused by prolonged computer use.

As devices and cables proliferate, desk space must now be carefully organized. Computers are elevated to a comfortable reading height, while cables are grouped together and concealed to reduce clutter.

VAIO Y series laptop | Sony, 2011, Japan. Sony's Y series was marketed as a netbook: a smaller, cheaper, and less power-hungry version of a conventional laptop. The screen was only 11³⁄₅ inches (29.5 cm) across.

Available in eight colors

Excellent image quality

Galaxy S20 | Samsung, 2020, South Korea. The latest Galaxy has a 6.2-inch screen with a fast refresh rate, 5G download speeds (where available), high-spec cameras on both sides of the phone, and a big battery.

Many offices are organized into small hubs like this. The ergonomic, mesh-upholstered chairs are based on the Aeron.

Vessels bowl for Next Interiors | **Janice Tchalenko**, early 1980s, UK. Award-winning potter Tchalenko mastered the art of throwing early on in her career, focusing on the form of the clay in her undecorated stoneware. In the late 1970s and early 1980s, however, she began to experiment with surface design, introducing bold patterns, as here, and bright colors. This change of direction helped invigorate the studio pottery movement and attracted a new audience to her work. In the 1980s, British chain store Next Interiors commissioned her to design a line of giftware, which included this Vessels bowl.

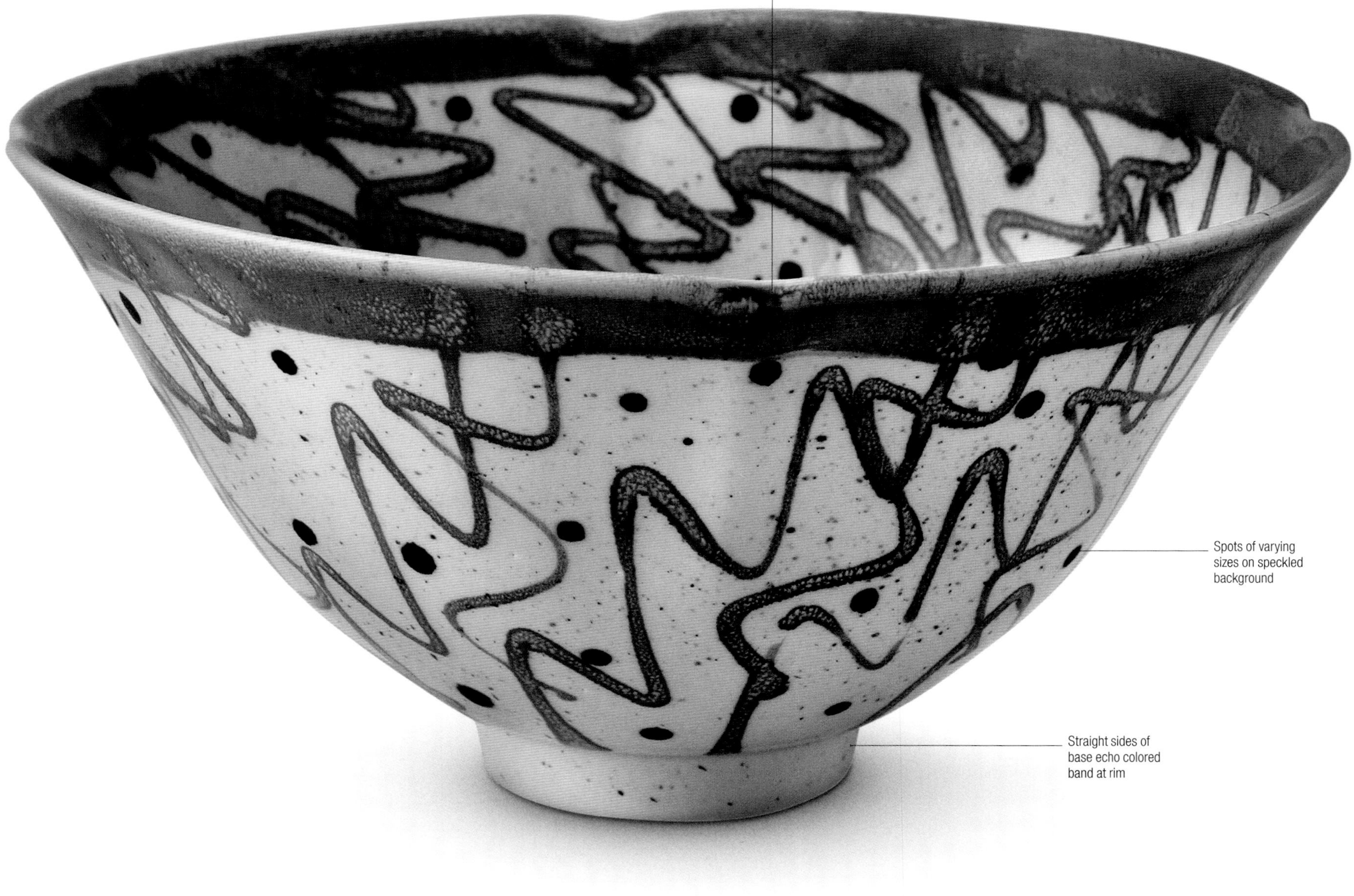

Notched edges
on rim of bowl

Spots of varying
sizes on speckled
background

Straight sides of
base echo colored
band at rim

THE ART OF
CERAMICS

From the 1980s onward, there was a new dynamism in the field of ceramics, with a move away from practical wares toward artistic and sculptural pieces. The role of the ceramicist was no longer seen as simply fulfilling the requirement for attractive tableware and cookware but as expressing personal creative impulses and appealing to a market that wanted to buy pottery purely for its inherent beauty. Ceramic pieces from studio potters were increasingly displayed on coffee tables and sideboards in homes and bought for collections as works of art in their own right, aside from any practical purpose. The lines between art and design, sculpture and craft, function and aesthetic became increasingly blurred, and as the appreciation of pottery as an art form spread globally in the late 20th century, the prices commanded by ceramics rose dramatically at art fairs and auction houses around the world.

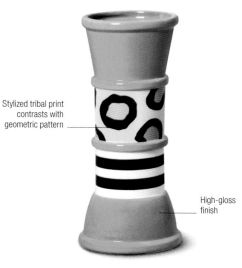

Stylized tribal print contrasts with geometric pattern

High-gloss finish

Carrot vase | **Nathalie du Pasquier for the Memphis Group**, 1985, **Italy**. The irreverent Memphis ethos is clear in du Pasquier's porcelain vase, with its lurid colors and seemingly random juxtaposition of decorative elements.

Gilded knob on lid

Integrated stand for pot

Big Dripper coffee pot | **Michael Graves for Swid Powell**, 1985–1987, **US**. The Big Dripper was part of a full coffee service of enameled porcelain. Its exaggerated proportions and lighthearted style reflect Graves's postmodern approach.

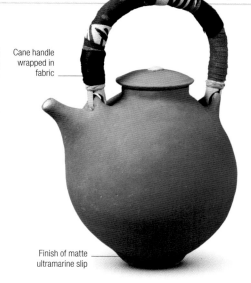

Cane handle wrapped in fabric

Finish of matte ultramarine slip

Earthenware teapot and lid | **Lisbeth Daehlin and Bente Saetrang**, 1988, **Norway**. Although it looks tribal, this teapot was designed in Frysja, near Oslo. Daehlin was the potter, using her signature blue slip, while Saetrang created the handle.

Stoneware plate | **Peter Voulkos**, 1989, **US**. Typical of Voulkos's vigorous approach, merging craft and art, this piece features an earthy palette, a sketch with a gouged surface, paint applied in uneven brushstrokes, and a ragged rim.

Elliptical form

Stoneware pitcher | **Emmanuel Cooper**, **UK**. Cooper viewed his pitchers as art forms rather than functional objects and was known for his glazes. This pitcher has a pitted glaze that gives an attractively speckled, matte appearance.

Transfer-printed images

Sgraffito figures

Matching Pair (detail) | **Grayson Perry**, 2017, **UK**. One of two ceramic vases created in response to the social division caused by Brexit, this depicts supporters of Remain. The vases were made by crowdsourcing images and ideas via social media.

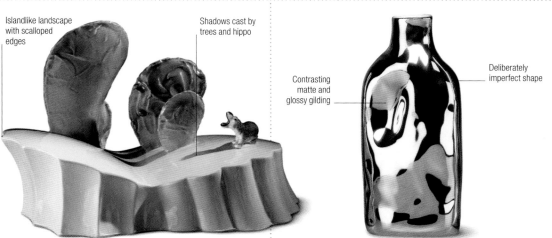

Islandlike landscape with scalloped edges

Shadows cast by trees and hippo

Landscape with Hippo | **Richard Slee**, 1997, **UK**. Slee's surreal creation is intended as a piece of art, commenting on a sentimental attachment to ornaments. It gives a factory-made hippo a new life by placing it in an unearthly landscape.

Contrasting matte and glossy gilding

Deliberately imperfect shape

Porcelain vase | **Maxim Velcovsky for Qubus**, 2008, **Czech Republic**. This gilded vase elevates an intentionally misshapen bottle to the status of a luxury ornament. Velcovsky has a talent for rethinking everyday objects.

EXPERIMENTAL
METALWARE

If the glint of silver conjured up a sense of Space Age chic in 1960s homes, by the 1980s, gold was the preferred metal, projecting an image of wealth and glamour. A decade later, white metals were once again in favor, especially utilitarian stainless steel. In a recessionary market, this offered an appealing compromise between cheap alloy cutlery and expensive silverware, so companies that had traditionally sold silver flatware began to introduce stainless steel alternatives.

Other newly introduced metals also inspired designers to find fresh ways of working; many rejected traditional forms altogether, creating sculptural statement pieces that made little concession to practicality. These stylized and often highly decorative pieces found a ready market among affluent buyers eager to own designer cutlery and flatware.

Tea set | **Daniel Libeskind for Sawaya & Moroni, 2008, Italy.** Libeskind used sharp and unexpected angles in this tea and coffee service. In a subversion typical of the Polish-American designer, each piece in the set merges with the tray underneath so that it looks more like a single, sculptural centerpiece or a futuristic cityscape than a set of functional objects.

> ## Cities are the greatest creations of humanity.
>
> Daniel **Libeskind**

Daniel Libeskind
1946–

A Polish-born American, Libeskind is renowned for his angular, idealistic, avant-garde architecture. His radical blueprint for the extension of London's Victoria and Albert Museum divided opinion, as did his designs for the Jewish Museum in Berlin, and the new World Trade Center in New York, for which he won the master plan competition but not the final commission. Libeskind has said he designs buildings as a metaphor, and that he is more interested in the language of architecture than its pure functionality.

Royal Ontario Museum, Toronto, Daniel Libeskind led the team in 2002 to renovate and expand the museum.

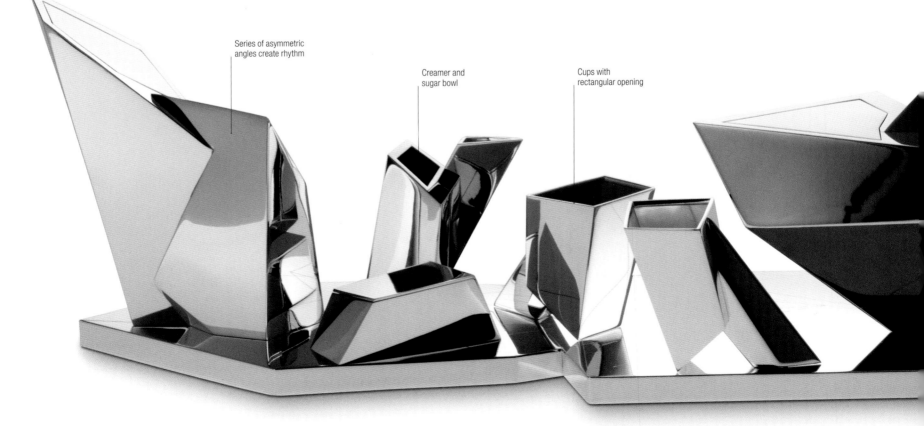

Series of asymmetric angles create rhythm

Creamer and sugar bowl

Cups with rectangular opening

Flatware | **Ward Bennett for Supreme Cutlery**, 1980, **Japan**. Bennett took advantage of Japan's traditional expertise in crafting swords and knives to produce this clean-lined, minimal flatware. The set is unified by the pieces' triangular handles.

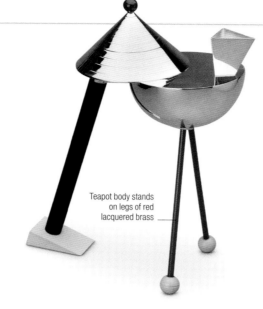

Teapot body stands on legs of red lacquered brass

Anchorage teapot | **Peter Shire for Rossi & Arcandi**, 1982, **Italy**. Shire's birdlike piece, made of electroplated nickel silver, was designed in collaboration with Memphis. Its colorful rejection of convention is typical of the group's work.

Murmansk fruit bowl | **Ettore Sottsass for Rossi & Arcandi**, 1982, **Italy**. One of the first products designed by Sottsass for the Memphis Group, this fruit bowl was inspired by the cold, isolated city of Murmansk in northwest Russia.

Hommage à Madonna cutlery | **Matteo Thun for WMF**, 1986, **Germany**. With handles recalling ring-bedecked fingers, this flatware was inspired by 1980s pop icon Madonna and her flamboyant fashion sense.

Spout looks like a continuation of the handle

Handle seems to pierce the teakettle's body

Matte cast aluminum with brushed finish

Hot Bertaa kettle | **Philippe Starck for Alessi**, 1987, **Italy**. Hot Bertaa transformed the traditional teakettle, but the bold styling, tilting body, and novel integration of handle and spout were not practical and the model was withdrawn.

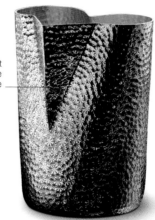

Folds catch light and accentuate surface texture

Silver carafe | **Afra and Tobia Scarpa for San Lorenzo**, 1990, **Italy**. The San Lorenzo studio was formed in 1970 to create high-quality designs in sterling silver, such as this crumple-topped carafe in parcel-gilt silver.

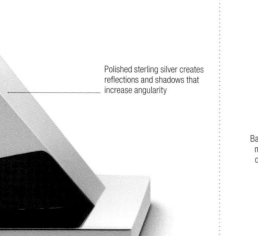

Polished sterling silver creates reflections and shadows that increase angularity

Base seems to melt from the candle's heat

Bronze cast from melted candle wax

Salvador candlestick | **Oscar Tusquets Blanca for Follies-Driade**, 1998, **Italy**. These bronze candlesticks are an homage to Tusquets Blanca's fellow Spaniard, Salvador Dalí, whose artworks often depict solid objects that appear to be melting.

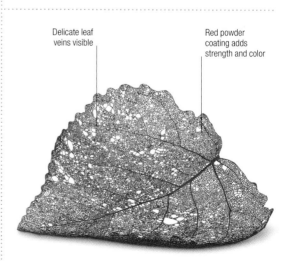

Delicate leaf veins visible

Red powder coating adds strength and color

Lehti fruit bowl | **Maria Jauhiainen**, 2004, **Finland**. Jauhiainen broke new ground with her choice of processes and materials. Here, she photo-etched a leaf onto a brass sheet then dissolved the metal with acid until only the leaf shape remained.

△ **Bookworm shelving,** one of Kartell's bestsellers in the 1990s, became a design icon because it was flexible, functional, and sculptural.

Ron Arad

The chairs that Ron Arad made from his studio in London first caught the attention of the design world in the 1980s. Arad made them by hand from rugged materials such as beaten steel and concrete, using techniques that he had taught himself. He chose this way of working partly because it was cheap and partly because it reflected the mood on the streets of post-punk London. Arad was also fascinated by the potential of these materials, which were unlikely choices for furniture, and by the beauty of worked and welded metal surfaces. Despite the chairs' lack of apparent luxury, design-conscious buyers took them up with enthusiasm, happy to pay well for pieces such as Arad's beaten-steel Tinker Chair of 1988.

It was not long before European manufacturers began to commission Arad. In 1986, he designed a springy metal lounge chair called Well-Tempered for Vitra in Switzerland. Moroso then approached him to develop a range of upholstered metal chairs. Working with metal remained a passion throughout the 1990s, when Arad became more involved in architectural and commercial interior projects. These have dominated his time for the past two decades: he installed the technology floor for Selfridges department store in London in 2001, created the Y's label Tokyo store for fashion designer Yohji Yamamoto in 2003, and designed a new headquarters for Magis in Treviso, Italy, in 2004.

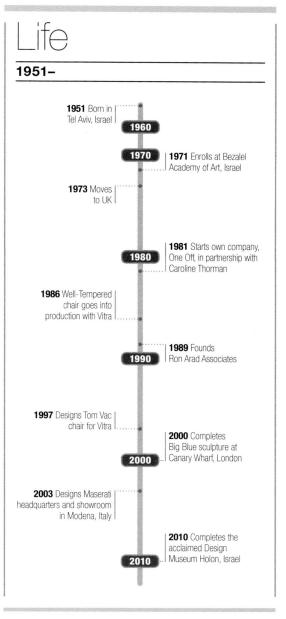

Life

1951–

1951 Born in Tel Aviv, Israel

1960

1970

1971 Enrolls at Bezalel Academy of Art, Israel

1973 Moves to UK

1980

1981 Starts own company, One Off, in partnership with Caroline Thorman

1986 Well-Tempered chair goes into production with Vitra

1989 Founds Ron Arad Associates

1990

1997 Designs Tom Vac chair for Vitra

2000 Completes Big Blue sculpture at Canary Wharf, London

2000

2003 Designs Maserati headquarters and showroom in Modena, Italy

2010 Completes the acclaimed Design Museum Holon, Israel

2010

Single sheet of plastic

Aluminum tube

Fantastic Plastic Elastic (FPE) chair | **For Kartell**, 1998. Named after its innate flexibility, FPE is engineered by attaching plastic to parallel metal tubes that form the chair's sides.

Tom Vac | **For Vitra**, 1997. Arad has experimented with plastics as well as his beloved metal. Tom Vac, with its ridged, ribbonlike structure, is made from injection-molded plastic.

Ridged sides

Voido | **For Magis**, 2006. Like his Bookworm shelving, Arad's Voido chair is a sculptural showpiece. It is ergonomically designed for people to recline on comfortably.

TANGLED ANGLES

When it was unveiled in 1989, the Vitra Design Museum, by Canadian architect Frank O. Gehry, amazed the world with its curving, jutting structure. It represented a new architectural style that became known as deconstructivism—a reaction against the postmodern buildings of the 1970s and 1980s. Whereas postmodernism had produced mostly formal, symmetrical buildings that often contained historical references, deconstructed buildings like the Vitra Design Museum are asymmetrical, fragmented, casual-looking, full of curves and odd angles, and often make use of unusual forms of siding or skin.

From the outside, the building is a fascinating tangle of elements. The walls are covered in white plaster, the roofs are clad in a titanium-zinc alloy, and different parts of the structure combine curves and sloping surfaces. Inside, the light, white spaces are ideal for displaying items of modern design. The success of this radical approach inspired even more daring structures from Gehry himself and other architects.

> Even though I often put as much **detail work into what I do as** anyone, it always **appears casual. That's the edge I'm after.**

Frank O. **Gehry**

Vitra Design Museum, Baden-Württemberg, Germany, Frank O. Gehry, 1989 The museum's exterior consists of towers, ramps, and cubes, with curved and sloping walls. However, these apparently disparate elements are unified by the careful composition and white walls.

STUDIO GLASS

The American studio glass movement began in the state of Ohio in the 1960s, where pioneering teacher Harvey Littleton taught glass art techniques to many aspiring artists at the University of Wisconsin, including Marvin Lipofsky. Later, the movement underwent a renaissance on the West Coast in the 1980s, where Seattle emerged as an important center. As studio glass grew in popularity and luminaries such as Lipofsky showed that it was possible for glass artists to find fame and fortune, a further generation, including Richard Marquis and William Morris, went on to establish their own studios. These developments, coupled with the international art market's reappraisal of the medium, helped invigorate glassmaking in China, Japan, and other parts of the world, where local traditions and themes came into play.

Asymmetric decoration

Orkney Island vessel | **William Morris**, 1984, US. Morris is inspired by indigenous cultures and uses complex techniques to decorate glass surfaces and create texture, achieving a deliberately aged look in this vessel.

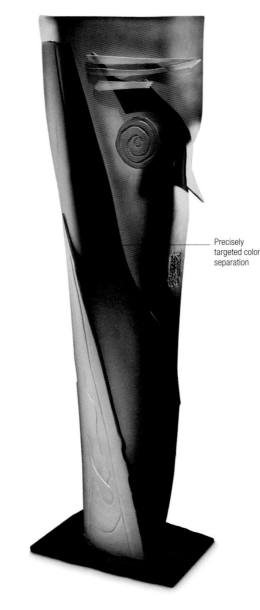

Precisely targeted color separation

Mold-blown glass box | **Fujita Kyohei**, 1988, Japan. This octagonal box draws on Japanese themes and traditions such as lacquerware. The red and white flakes represent plum blossom petals, and the box is decorated with gold leaf.

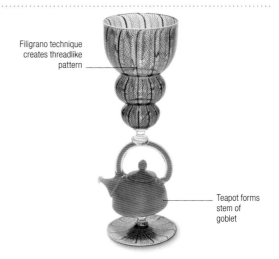

Filigrano technique creates threadlike pattern

Teapot forms stem of goblet

Skulls glass bowl | **Dante Marioni**, 1991, US. Marioni looks to ancient Etruscan and Greek pottery and Murano glass for inspiration, but his signatures are pristine forms and a simplified color palette. Here, he distorts the skull shapes in naive style.

Yellow on Purple | **Danny Perkins**, 1991, US. This glass form is an assemblage of separately mold-blown, slumped, cracked, and broken components, all sandblasted to create a uniform matt surface and then painted in oils.

Teapot with blown and applied glass goblet | **Richard Marquis**, 1990, US. Marquis is revered for his obsession with technical perfection, humor, and imagination. He strove for multiple layers of complexity in this mixed ornamental form.

You use a glass mirror to see your face; you use works of art to see your soul.

George Bernard **Shaw**

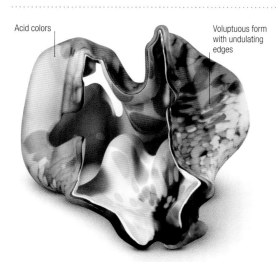

Acid colors

Voluptuous form with undulating edges

IGS VII 2000–2003 #9 | **Marvin Lipofsky**, 2000–2003, **US**. Lipofsky's sculptures are open, organic forms inspired by internal body parts such as brains and stomachs. Several layers of translucent glass are used to create a sense of depth.

Neon in Causeway Bay Hong Kong | **Lu Chi**, 2011, China. Lu Chi specializes in openwork sculptures, making models in clay before casting them in glass. Part of a series based on the artist's travels, this is a tribute to Hong Kong's neon lights.

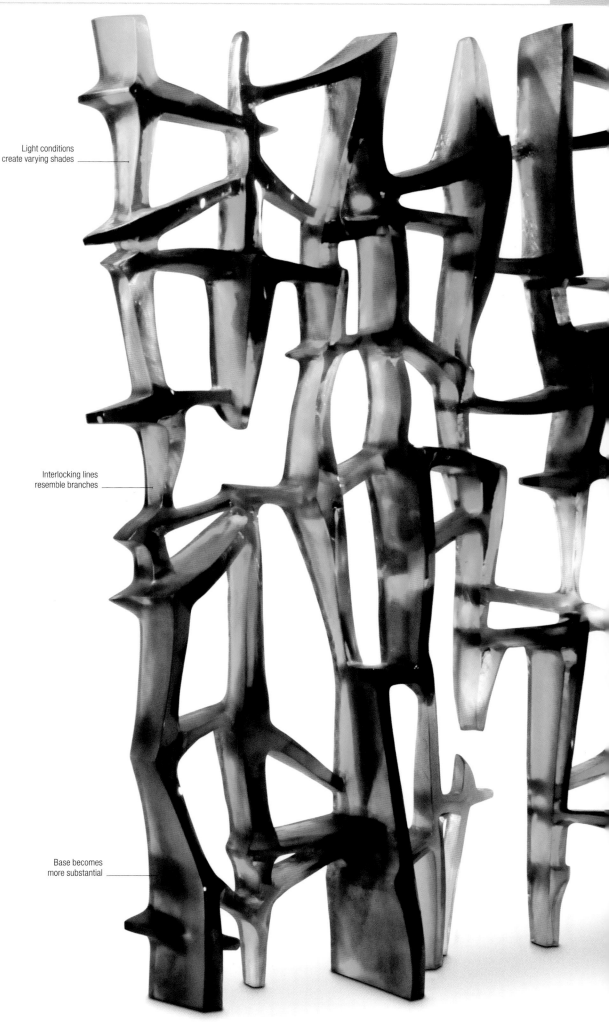

Light conditions create varying shades

Interlocking lines resemble branches

Base becomes more substantial

△ **Orrefors by Karl Lagerfeld Collection,** 2011, features elegant, geometric shapes and a neutral palette of clear, black, and white glass.

△ **Crystal carafe** | Simon Gate, 1924

stablished in Sweden in 1898, Orrefors began modestly, making glass for windows and bottles, but changed direction in 1913, when Johan Ekman bought the company with the aim of producing refined glassware and developing a design-driven business. He hired artists Simon Gate and Edvard Hald, as well as Eugen and Knut Bergkvist, who had worked at the nearby Kosta factory, and they transformed Orrefors into a company with an international reputation for finely engraved glass. At the Paris Exhibition of 1925, Orrefors and its design team won the Grand Prix for a goblet created by Simon Gate.

Employing artists was a novelty for a glassmaker and spurred Orrefors on to greater creativity and technical expertise, pioneering "art glass"—glassware designed primarily for its aesthetics. The company developed new techniques, such as graal, which integrated the design into the glass, and ariel, in which air bubbles were trapped in the glass, and attracted more artists because of its willingness to experiment. By 1939, when Orrefors exhibited at the New York World Fair, the glassworks was known as a producer of Swedish Modern, characterized by bold lines, color, and originality. Orrefors has pursued its culture of letting artists lead the way, for both domestic glassware and art glass, and when the art glass movement spread worldwide in the 1980s, the company continued to thrive.

Key dates

1898–

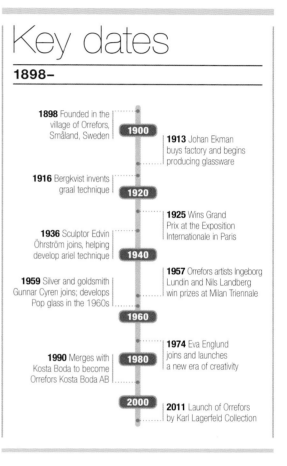

1898 Founded in the village of Orrefors, Småland, Sweden | **1900**

1913 Johan Ekman buys factory and begins producing glassware

1916 Bergkvist invents graal technique | **1920**

1925 Wins Grand Prix at the Exposition Internationale in Paris

1936 Sculptor Edvin Öhrström joins, helping develop ariel technique | **1940**

1957 Orrefors artists Ingeborg Lundin and Nils Landberg win prizes at Milan Triennale

1959 Silver and goldsmith Gunnar Cyren joins; develops Pop glass in the 1960s | **1960**

1974 Eva Englund joins and launches a new era of creativity

1990 Merges with Kosta Boda to become Orrefors Kosta Boda AB | **1980**

2000

2011 Launch of Orrefors by Karl Lagerfeld Collection

Ribbed glass catches the light

Triton vases | **Simon Gate**, 1916. The fluted glass of these vases emphasizes their graceful, curving forms. Their simplicity is enhanced by the use of a single color.

Rich, warm color

Long stem

Tulpan vases | **Nils Landberg**, 1957. Inspired by tulips, Landberg's vases were each blown as a single piece of glass. This design won a gold medal at the 1957 Milan Triennale.

Engraved fish and seaweed integrated into glass

Fish vase | **Edvard Hald**, 1930s. From the 1930s onward, Hald produced glassware that looked like miniature aquaria, using the graal technique.

EUROPEAN GLASS

As the art world became more international in the 1980s and 1990s, with residence programs and cultural exchanges taking some of the leading US glassmakers to Europe, enthusiasm about glass spread to a new generation of designers. Glassmakers from around the world still looked to Europe for technical and artistic inspiration: they traveled to Sweden to learn techniques such as graal decoration or to Murano, Italy, to study murrine, *millefiori*, and other techniques. Likewise, many European glassmakers welcomed the opportunity to work with Americans. As glassmakers of different nationalities exchanged ideas and perfected their skills, they pushed the boundaries of their craft, propelling it further into the realms of art. In the postmodern world, it was not just technique that gained glass artists a devoted following—the concept behind their work was increasingly valued, too.

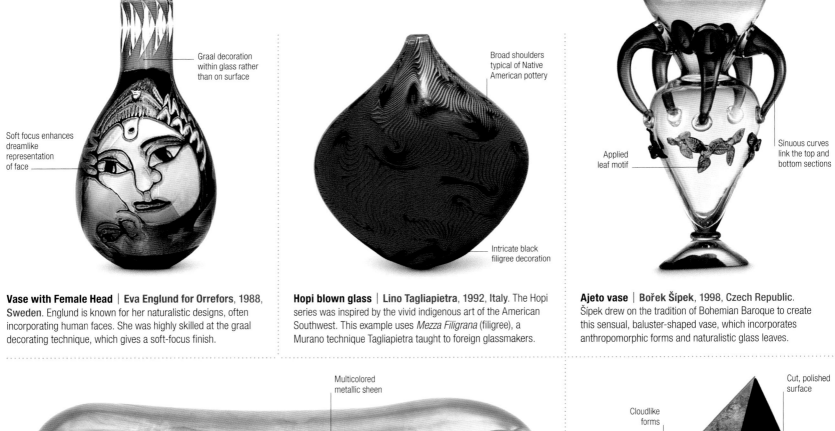

Graal decoration within glass rather than on surface

Soft focus enhances dreamlike representation of face

Vase with Female Head | **Eva Englund for Orrefors**, 1988, **Sweden**. Englund is known for her naturalistic designs, often incorporating human faces. She was highly skilled at the graal decorating technique, which gives a soft-focus finish.

Broad shoulders typical of Native American pottery

Intricate black filigree decoration

Hopi blown glass | **Lino Tagliapietra**, 1992, **Italy**. The Hopi series was inspired by the vivid indigenous art of the American Southwest. This example uses *Mezza Filigrana* (filigree), a Murano technique Tagliapietra taught to foreign glassmakers.

Applied leaf motif

Sinuous curves link the top and bottom sections

Ajeto vase | **Bořek Šípek**, 1998, **Czech Republic**. Šípek drew on the tradition of Bohemian Baroque to create this sensual, baluster-shaped vase, which incorporates anthropomorphic forms and naturalistic glass leaves.

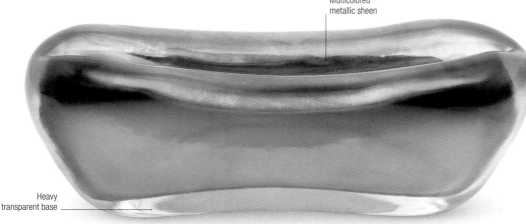

Multicolored metallic sheen

Heavy transparent base

Coupe (Sea Gold) | **Laura de Santillana**, 1997, **Italy**. The lustrous surface gives a sense of depth to this glass form. De Santillana belonged to the Venini glassware dynasty and was based in Venice, with her brother, Alessandro Diaz, also a glass artist. They created glass sculptures and installations as well as useful wares.

Cut, polished surface

Cloudlike forms

Pyramid form | **Colin Reid**, 1999, **UK**. This decorative piece was made by casting colored glass. The smooth surface and sharply cut diagonals contrast with the rough, jagged bottom edge, reflecting color around the interior of the pyramid.

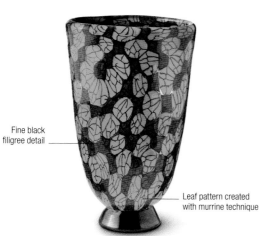

Fine black
filigree detail

Leaf pattern created
with murrine technique

Murrina vase | **Vittorio Ferro**, 2004, **Italy**. The son of
Murano maestro Giuseppe Ferro, Vittorio specializes in murrine,
a technique in which rods of glass are formed into a pattern,
fused under heat, and sliced into pieces that look like mosaics.

Large Ariel organic form | **Peter Layton**, 2004, **UK**.
Layton's abstract forms are inspired by the natural world. The
Ariel series was created in response to a client's request that
he make a version of chalcedony, emphasizing the blue hues.

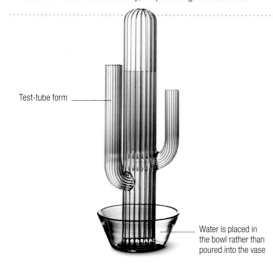

Test-tube form

Water is placed in
the bowl rather than
poured into the vase

Cactus vase | **Jiří Pelcl for Křehký**, 2007, **Czech Republic**.
Pelcl's travels in Peru inspired this vase. It is made from
borosilicate glass, which is normally used for test tubes,
and mimics their tubular shape.

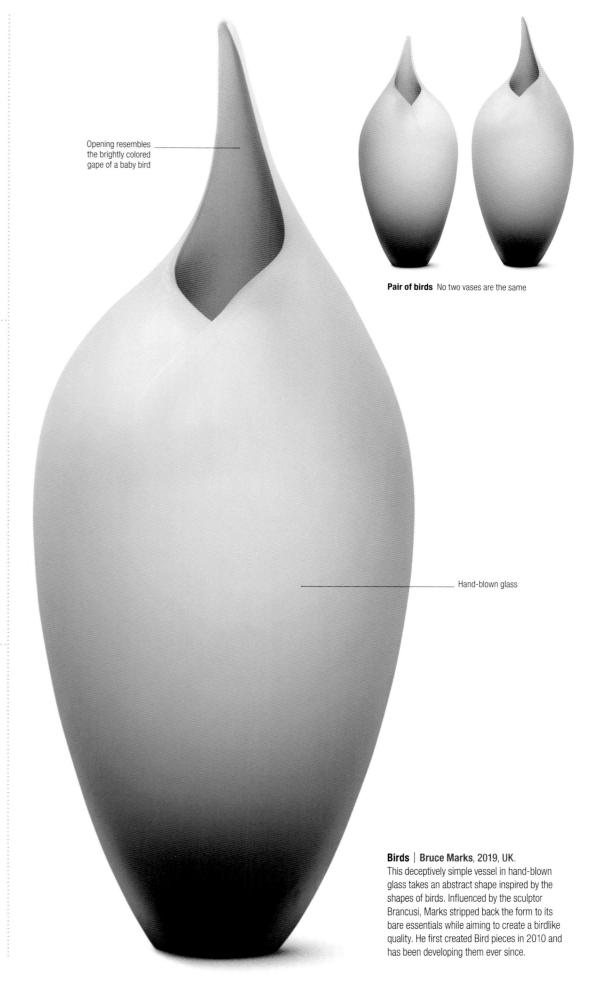

Opening resembles
the brightly colored
gape of a baby bird

Hand-blown glass

Pair of birds No two vases are the same

Birds | **Bruce Marks**, 2019, **UK**.
This deceptively simple vessel in hand-blown
glass takes an abstract shape inspired by the
shapes of birds. Influenced by the sculptor
Brancusi, Marks stripped back the form to its
bare essentials while aiming to create a birdlike
quality. He first created Bird pieces in 2010 and
has been developing them ever since.

Octo 4240 pendant light | **Seppo Koho for Secto Design**, *c.* 2000, Finland. Koho's background as an architect shows in this blend of structural precision and classic Scandinavian pale birchwood. Octo used the scale of the light, which is 21 in (54 cm) in diameter, to create impact.

Strips of laminated birch

Neck of lampshade is closely bound to diffuse light

NORTHERN LIGHTING

Interior lighting has always been important in northern Europe, where the long, dark winters plunge homes and cities into gloom for much of the day as well as through the night. The shifting seasonal light in Scandinavia has inspired the lamps of designers such as Andreas Engesvik and Tord Boontje, who created his iconic Midsummer light after observing sunlight filtering through leaves.

This fascination with lighting has led many northern European designers to make lamps in which the functional elements are clearly visible. Rody Graumans and Ingo Maurer, for example, have both stripped lighting back to its essentials, celebrating its basic component, the humble light bulb, with a sense of playfulness. There is humor, and beauty too, in Maurer's Lucellino lamp, which looks like a light-bulb bird with tiny feathered wings.

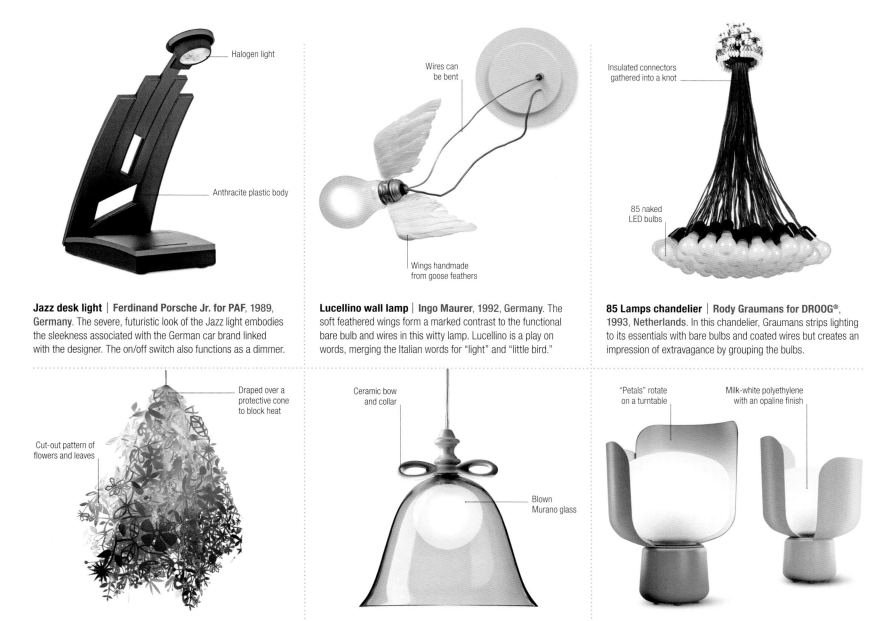

Halogen light

Anthracite plastic body

Wires can be bent

Wings handmade from goose feathers

Insulated connectors gathered into a knot

85 naked LED bulbs

Draped over a protective cone to block heat

Cut-out pattern of flowers and leaves

Ceramic bow and collar

Blown Murano glass

"Petals" rotate on a turntable

Milk-white polyethylene with an opaline finish

Jazz desk light | **Ferdinand Porsche Jr. for PAF**, 1989, **Germany**. The severe, futuristic look of the Jazz light embodies the sleekness associated with the German car brand linked with the designer. The on/off switch also functions as a dimmer.

Lucellino wall lamp | **Ingo Maurer**, 1992, **Germany**. The soft feathered wings form a marked contrast to the functional bare bulb and wires in this witty lamp. Lucellino is a play on words, merging the Italian words for "light" and "little bird."

85 Lamps chandelier | **Rody Graumans for DROOG®**, 1993, **Netherlands**. In this chandelier, Graumans strips lighting to its essentials with bare bulbs and coated wires but creates an impression of extravagance by grouping the bulbs.

Midsummer light | **Tord Boontje**, 2004, **Netherlands**. Boontje wanted to recreate the look of a paper lamp that was cut out by hand. He used a plastic called Tyvek, which is stronger than paper and can easily be cut, but not torn.

Small Bell lamp | **Marcel Wanders for Moooi**, 2013, **Netherlands**. This light was inspired by bells being used to summon a group of people—a recurring motif for Wanders. The festive bow is also reminiscent of a Christmas decoration.

Blom table lamp | **Andreas Engesvik for FontanaArte**, 2013, **Norway**. Engesvik designed this charming table lamp to look like a flower with "petals" that can be rotated to regulate the light. Its base is made of painted aluminum.

POSTMODERN LIGHTING

As part of their reaction against Modernism, postmodern designers began to reinterpret historical styles. Some lighting designers looked back to Art Nouveau lamps, as exemplified by Tiffany, to give their work a more organic feel. Albert Paley, for example, was captivated by Art Nouveau during its revival in the 1960s, but his designs of the 1980s and 1990s show his characteristic swirls and decorative flourishes constrained by industrial severity. On a more light-hearted level, the Memphis group drew upon Art Deco and Pop art and used everyday, often inexpensive materials, such as brightly patterned laminate, to add a touch of fun. Tom Dixon also made his designs humorous, experimenting with plastic and new technology to create his stackable Jack light.

Satin finish on colored glass

Each shape individually backlit

Paper shade diffuses light

Black steel frame

Kyo lamp | **Toshiyuki Kita for IDK Design Laboratory Ltd.**, **1983, Japan**. Kita's love of Japanese handicraft is expressed in this lamp, with its shade of handmade Mino washi paper that was traditionally used for lanterns.

Polyethylene works as opalescent light filter

Free-standing lights can be stacked together

Rounded edges

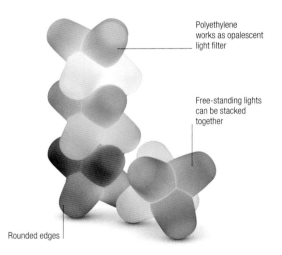

Jack light | **Tom Dixon for Eurolounge Ltd.**, **1997, UK**. While experimenting with plastics, Dixon came across the rotary molding used for traffic cones and adopted it to create this novel and inexpensive stackable light.

Aluminum shade with glass insert at top

Loops and ribbon detailing on base and stand

Fabricated steel base

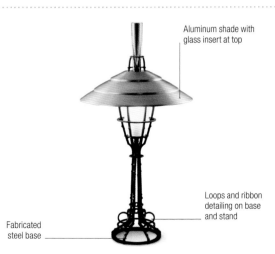

Clothing diffuses light source behind it

Fabric coated with resin

Orbital floor lamp | **Ferruccio Laviani for Foscarini**, **1992, Italy**. The Orbital lamp has a movable tripod of laser-cut steel, mounted with flat diffusers. Each diffuser is made from industrial glass, polished at the back to reflect the light source.

Corona table lamp | **Albert Paley**, **1999, US**. A metal sculptor and designer, Paley brings his love of decorative architectural elements to lighting. The shape and embellished swirls of this lamp are reminiscent of Art Nouveau.

Il Cestello lighting | **Gaetano Pesce**, **2003–2004, Italy**. This clothesline light was the focal point of Pesce's interior design for the Il Cestello restaurant in Florence, for which he created a surreal fantasy land akin to a children's playhouse.

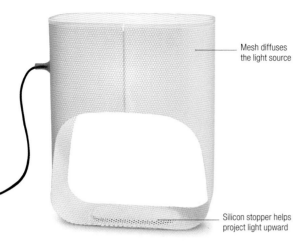

Mesh diffuses
the light source

Silicon stopper helps
project light upward

Bague table lamp | **Patricia Urquiola for Foscarini**, 2003,
Spain. Urquiola used a new technique for this lamp, based on
the shape of a ring—a perforated metal net was stretched to
create its form, then coated with silicon resin.

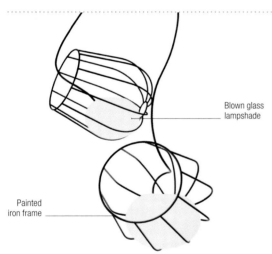

Blown glass
lampshade

Painted
iron frame

Light container | **Martín Azúa**, 2013, **Spain**. Deconstructing
conventional notions of lighting, Basque designer Azúa created
a flexible lighting system from wire baskets that can be hung or
put on a surface, each containing a globe of light.

Pinned to
stainless-steel wire

The length of the cables
can be adjusted

Mirror-polished gold
and acrylic disc

The spheres
were inspired by
celestial bodies

Eclipse chandelier | **Lee Broom**, 2018, UK.
A ring of LEDs is hidden within the circumference of
each acrylic disc, which emits light to create a halo
effect. Each circle of light interacts and dissects
with a polished gold disc that acts like a mirror. It
reflects the circle of light, which then disappears,
creates a halo, and reappears, creating a
contemporary yet playful design.

STUART HAYGARTH

Tide chandelier

YEAR 2005 | **DIMENSIONS** *Diameter of chandelier* 59 in (150 cm) *Width of square suspension platform* 60 in (152 cm) | **MATERIALS** Found translucent and transparent objects, mainly made of plastic, hung on monofilament line from suspension platform of MDF

The British designer Stuart Haygarth has produced an important body of work by gathering odds and ends washed up on the Kent coast in southeast England, sorting the objects, and using them to create sculptures, installations, and chandeliers. One of these is the Tide chandelier, which Haygarth produced by hanging a diverse range of mainly plastic objects on strands of clear fishing line from a suspension platform. The result is a large round form surrounding a 100-watt incandescent bulb. Initially, Haygarth made ten of these chandeliers, one of a number of similar commissions.

By juxtaposing eyeglasses, bottles, cups, toys, and other detritus, Haygarth gave these apparently random items new visual significance, both individually and as part of a larger whole. In addition, this sphere, with its pale-colored light, symbolizes the Moon, the force behind the tide that washed the objects up on the beach. With its focus on recycling, reevaluating the shapes and sculptural qualities of everyday objects, and arranging them in unusual combinations, Haygarth's work is surprising, ecologically aware, and aesthetically pleasing.

Suspension lines only visible close up

Individual items, many of them pale, transmit light

My work is about giving banal and overlooked objects new significance

Stuart **Haygarth**

△ **Stationery items** have been a mainstay of Muji since its inception. Its pens have a plain but distinctive transparent acrylic body, and many are refillable—reducing costs and helping the environment.

Muji

△ **Hakuji traditional teapot** | *c.* 2000s

The Japanese company Muji has succeeded in turning a line of unbranded, generic, everyday goods into a fashionable commodity, a feat few other retailers have even attempted. The full name, which in Japanese is read as Mujirushi Ryohin, can be translated as "no-brand quality goods." Despite this name, Muji now stands for clearly identifiable qualities and design criteria. Its products—well designed, with no frills, and at reasonable prices—were presented in such a chic way that they immediately appealed to consumers. One early success was its U-shaped spaghetti, made at low cost from the remnants left over from the manufacture of straight spaghetti and sold in simple but attractive packaging. Muji's rise is all the more remarkable because it took place against the backdrop of Japan in the 1980s, when the economy seemed unstoppable and spending on luxury brand goods—the opposite of Muji's ethos—reached new heights.

The brains behind Muji's "no-brand" branding was art director Ikko Tanaka, who developed a design strategy including the brown paper and clear cellophane packaging. Muji launched with a small range of 40 products, covering stationery, clothing, food staples, and kitchenware, then expanded its formula during the 1990s, when an economic recession in many countries enforced thrift. By the 2000s, Muji had broadened its range to more than 7,000 products, including a car developed with Nissan, and had 285 stores in Japan alone.

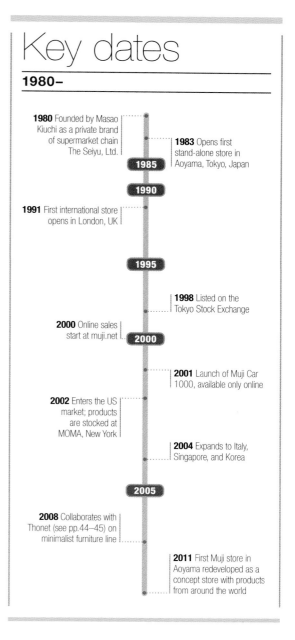

Key dates

1980–

1980 Founded by Masao Kiuchi as a private brand of supermarket chain The Seiyu, Ltd.

1983 Opens first stand-alone store in Aoyama, Tokyo, Japan

1985

1990

1991 First international store opens in London, UK

1995

1998 Listed on the Tokyo Stock Exchange

2000 Online sales start at muji.net

2000

2001 Launch of Muji Car 1000, available only online

2002 Enters the US market; products are stocked at MOMA, New York

2004 Expands to Italy, Singapore, and Korea

2005

2008 Collaborates with Thonet (see pp.44–45) on minimalist furniture line

2011 First Muji store in Aoyama redeveloped as a concept store with products from around the world

---

Removable trays

Office trays | *c.* **2000s**. Muji produces storage items such as this in clear plastic only—partly an aesthetic choice but also a cost-saving one, since colored plastic is more expensive.

USB desk fan | *c.* **2000s**. Designed by aerodynamics experts, this practical, low-emission desk fan can be plugged into any USB port to deliver a cooling breeze wherever it is needed.

Unit Sofa Corner | *c.* **2000s**. This unit is part of Muji's modular sofa system, which comprises three components that can be used alone or combined in different configurations.

PLASTIC HOMEWARES

In the late 20th and early 21st centuries, manufacturers such as Alessi and Kartell grasped the potential of cost-effective plastic homewares and enlisted an array of popular designers to create them. In contrast to many of their cheap and cheerful predecessors from the 1960s and 1970s, the latest items were technologically advanced and came with a celebrity name such as Philippe Starck or Michael Graves attached. The role of the product designer became more important than ever during the 1980s and 1990s. For consumers with high expectations and salaries and a growing appreciation of postmodern eclecticism and irony, a famous designer's touch was the ultimate sign of quality and value. Recycling symbols for plastic were introduced in 1988, which raised public concern for the environment and triggered efforts by designers and manufacturers to use materials with sustainable credentials, heralding a new era of "green" design.

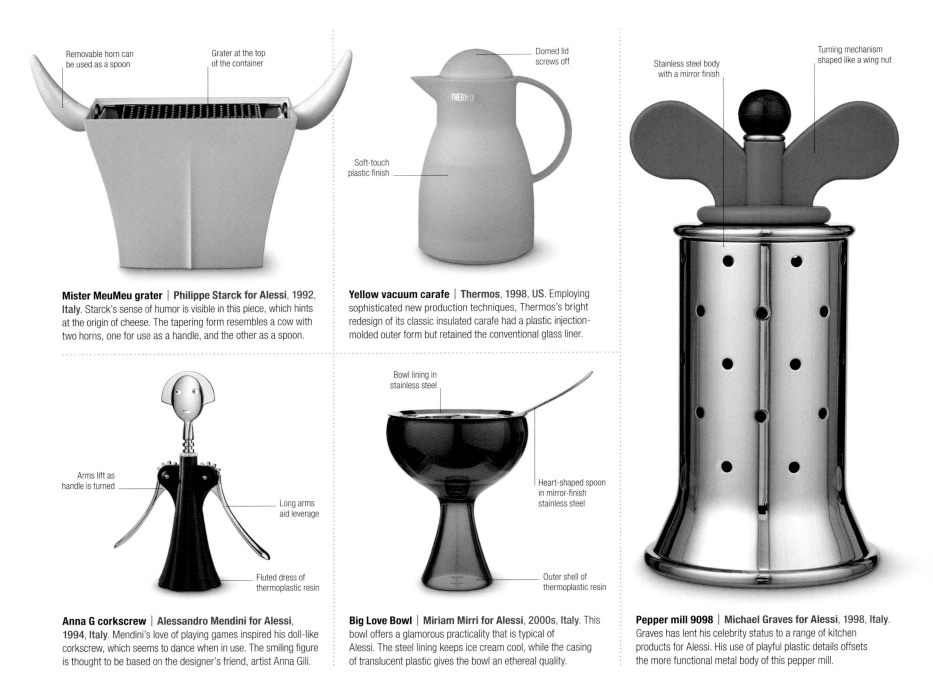

Removable horn can be used as a spoon

Grater at the top of the container

Domed lid screws off

Soft-touch plastic finish

Stainless steel body with a mirror finish

Turning mechanism shaped like a wing nut

Arms lift as handle is turned

Long arms aid leverage

Fluted dress of thermoplastic resin

Bowl lining in stainless steel

Heart-shaped spoon in mirror-finish stainless steel

Outer shell of thermoplastic resin

Mister MeuMeu grater | Philippe Starck for Alessi, 1992, **Italy.** Starck's sense of humor is visible in this piece, which hints at the origin of cheese. The tapering form resembles a cow with two horns, one for use as a handle, and the other as a spoon.

Yellow vacuum carafe | Thermos, 1998, **US.** Employing sophisticated new production techniques, Thermos's bright redesign of its classic insulated carafe had a plastic injection-molded outer form but retained the conventional glass liner.

Anna G corkscrew | Alessandro Mendini for Alessi, 1994, **Italy.** Mendini's love of playing games inspired his doll-like corkscrew, which seems to dance when in use. The smiling figure is thought to be based on the designer's friend, artist Anna Gili.

Big Love Bowl | Miriam Mirri for Alessi, 2000s, **Italy.** This bowl offers a glamorous practicality that is typical of Alessi. The steel lining keeps ice cream cool, while the casing of translucent plastic gives the bowl an ethereal quality.

Pepper mill 9098 | Michael Graves for Alessi, 1998, **Italy.** Graves has lent his celebrity status to a range of kitchen products for Alessi. His use of playful plastic details offsets the more functional metal body of this pepper mill.

DeLuxe cutlery set | **Fabio Bortolani and Donata Paruccini for Pandora Design**, 2004, Italy. A perfect example of homeware as designer object, this elegant and expensive cutlery set subverts the notion of disposable plastic.

Feet provide stability
and aid stacking

Distressed finish
highlights silver flecks

Biodegradable Eco-ware | **Tom Dixon**, 2007, UK. In response to public concern over the environment, and as an expression of his commitment to sustainability, Dixon's Eco-ware is made from a biodegradable bamboo fiber composite material.

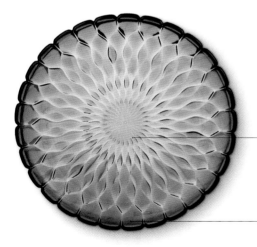

Translucent, colored plastic has a jellylike quality

Faceted surface mimics the look of cut crystal

Jelly | **Patricia Urquiola for Kartell**, 2013, Italy. Named for its translucent, patterned form, Jelly is made from recyclable clear plastic. Each of the entries in the line of dinnerware has a different pattern—Urquiola wanted the plates to mix and match.

△ **Starck's Louis Ghost chair** for Kartell is used as the seating for the interior of the restaurant Kong in Paris, echoing the surrounding expanse of glass.

Philippe Starck

Although Parisian designer Philippe Starck is associated with some of the most flamboyant buildings and interiors of the past few decades, his aim is simple—to make good design available to everyone and thereby improve the quality of people's lives. Part of this democratic ideal is affordability, and Starck often uses new processes or materials to make mass production possible, while maintaining quality and durability. Notably, he has designed stylish hotels and restaurants that are accessible to consumers on a budget (the Mama Shelter hotel chain, for example), while continuing to create interiors for the top end of the market.

Starck has cited inspiration from science fiction, Walt Disney, Italian Futurism, and American streamlining. His designs are aerodynamic, often with curvy lines and signature shapes such as the squiggle, horn, and teardrop, made in resins and soft plastics. Unexpected combinations are characteristic—traditional styles reinvented using cutting-edge materials and processes, idiosyncratic architectural features such as the giant golden flame atop his Asahi Beer Hall in Tokyo, and the use of incongruous juxtapositions such as velvet and chrome, or stone and glass. The designer's extraordinary output has included luggage for Samsonite; the Gun table lamp for Flos; the Louis Ghost chair for Kartell; Steve Jobs's yacht; the luxurious crystal Marie Coquine lamp for Baccarat; and a plastic flyswatter for Alessi.

Life

1949–

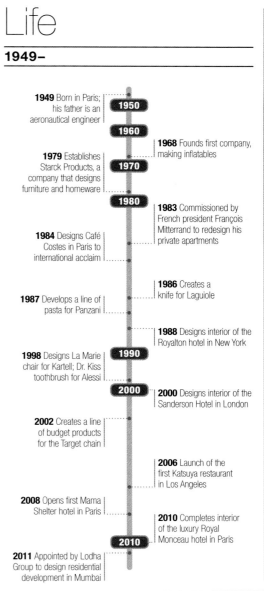

1949 Born in Paris; his father is an aeronautical engineer

1968 Founds first company, making inflatables

1979 Establishes Starck Products, a company that designs furniture and homeware

1983 Commissioned by French president François Mitterrand to redesign his private apartments

1984 Designs Café Costes in Paris to international acclaim

1986 Creates a knife for Laguiole

1987 Develops a line of pasta for Panzani

1988 Designs interior of the Royalton hotel in New York

1998 Designs La Marie chair for Kartell; Dr. Kiss toothbrush for Alessi

2000 Designs interior of the Sanderson Hotel in London

2002 Creates a line of budget products for the Target chain

2006 Launch of the first Katsuya restaurant in Los Angeles

2008 Opens first Mama Shelter hotel in Paris

2010 Completes interior of the luxury Royal Monceau hotel in Paris

2011 Appointed by Lodha Group to design residential development in Mumbai

Stands 11½ in (29 cm) high

Juicy Salif | **For Alessi**, 1990. Starck was inspired to base this futuristic-looking cast aluminum juicer on the shape of a squid when he was squeezing lemon over a dish of calamari.

Masters chair | **For Kartell**, 2009. The Masters pays homage to Modernist chair designs in a hybrid form that has a comfortable back of interlocking squiggles.

Base lead-weighted for stability

Miss Sissi table lamp | **For Flos**, 1991. This translucent bedside or shelf lamp, which also comes in a range of colors, is made from injection-molded polycarbonate.

△ **"The Wrong Garden,"** designed by James Dyson and Jim Honey for the 2003 Chelsea flower show in London, UK, featured water that appeared to flow uphill.

James
Dyson

British industrial designer, engineer, and manufacturer James Dyson has created some of the most successful products of the last four decades. He typically identifies problems with existing products and solves them with a combination of innovative engineering and a strong, colorful visual approach. Dyson's first commercial product was the Ballbarrow, a wheelbarrow with a plastic sphere instead of the usual wheel, but his first major success came in the form of his revolutionary vacuum cleaner and its dual cyclone mechanism, which uses the helical movement of air to extract dust and dirt. This system gave the vacuum cleaner much better suction than conventional cleaners, and it had the additional advantage of not requiring disposable bags. There was some initial resistance to the design in Europe, so in 1983 Dyson launched it as the G-Force in Japan. The western version, the DC01, subsequently sold in large numbers and was admired for its efficiency and unique appearance.

Dyson followed this success with a line of other vacuum cleaners, the Airblade hand dryer, the Air Multiplier bladeless fan, and a one-of-a-kind garden featuring a waterfall in which water seems to flow upward. His products continue to combine technical inventiveness with a strong visual aesthetic; as well as being commercially successful, they have influenced many other manufacturers and spawned imitations.

Life

1947–

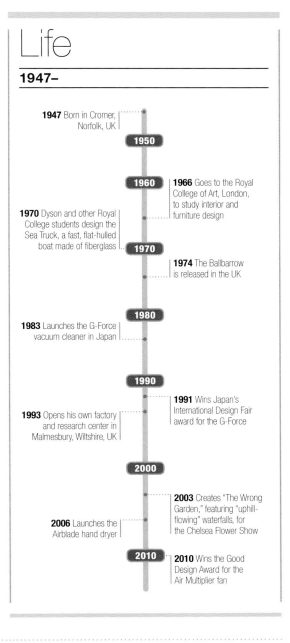

1947 Born in Cromer, Norfolk, UK

1950

1960

1966 Goes to the Royal College of Art, London, to study interior and furniture design

1970 Dyson and other Royal College students design the Sea Truck, a fast, flat-hulled boat made of fiberglass

1970

1974 The Ballbarrow is released in the UK

1980

1983 Launches the G-Force vacuum cleaner in Japan

1990

1991 Wins Japan's International Design Fair award for the G-Force

1993 Opens his own factory and research center in Malmesbury, Wiltshire, UK

2000

2003 Creates "The Wrong Garden," featuring "uphill-flowing" waterfalls, for the Chelsea Flower Show

2006 Launches the Airblade hand dryer

2010

2010 Wins the Good Design Award for the Air Multiplier fan

Onboard tool storage

Cleaning head works right up to the edge

DC01 vacuum cleaner | 1993. The tough ABS plastic design of the DC01 stands out with its bright colors. Its transparent body makes it possible to see the dust being collected.

Contrarotator washing machine | 2000. This washing machine has two drums with 5,000 perforations, to make it more efficient and remove water quickly during the spin cycle.

Curved air outlets follow shape of user's hands

Trough collects drips

Airblade hand dryer | 2006. By directing a high-speed jet of air over the user's hands, the Airblade dries them effectively in a few seconds. It has proved a success in public restrooms.

Bird-shaped whistle

9093 teakettle | **Michael Graves for Alessi**, 1985, **US**. Known as the "singing bird kettle" for its chirping spout cap, this teakettle was a hit with consumers in the mid-1980s, despite not being electric. The teakettle's design fused Graves's love of Art Deco, Pop art, and cartoon culture.

Magnetic steel bottom for induction cooking

PRODUCT
DESIGN

The advance in industrial processes that had been kick-started in the 1960s continued into the 1980s and beyond. This had two effects on product design: advances in circuitry meant that electrical goods could be smaller, and manufacturers began to experiment with unusual new forms for everyday products. The humble toothbrush, for example, was revamped. The Radius was the first departure in half a century from the standard shape, which had previously conformed to the designated slots of display stands in shops. A few years later, Philippe Starck designed a toothbrush that was the opposite in form—elongated, elegant, and with colored bristles that matched the handle. Both appealed to shoppers for their style rather than for any new dental hygiene feature. Likewise, new teakettles offered no notable benefit over traditional models other than their striking appearance and ability to whistle, but they were aggressively marketed as objects of desire. In Japan, meanwhile, this trend manifested itself in cute, playful products in friendly shapes and colors.

Brass whistle

Thermoplastic handle

Whistling teakettle | **Richard Sapper for Alessi**, 1982, **Germany**. Inspired by steamers on the Rhine River, the teakettle's whistle has two pipes in the keys of E and B, which play like a harmonica when steam passes through the spout.

5,500 ultra-fine bristles

Slender, tapered handle

Broad handle shaped for comfort

Toothbrushes | **Kevin Foley and James O'Halloran for Radius Toothbrush Company (left)**, 1984, **British Virgin Islands; Philippe Starck for Fluocaril**, 1989, **France**. These radical reinventions turned the toothbrush into a designer item.

Ceramic casing

Rounded form to match circular speaker

Bubble Boy loudspeakers | **Tomoyuki Sugiyama for NAX Corporation**, 1986, **Japan**. With their organic, egg-shaped silhouettes and mouthlike slots, Sugiyama's compact speakers resembled miniature robots.

Mahogany cap

Mirror-polished stainless steel

Pito teakettle | **Frank Gehry for Alessi**, 1988–1992, **US**. This teakettle's distinctive shape is intended to convey a sense of movement inspired by classical sculptures. The quirky, fish-shaped spout emits a melodic whistle.

Soft-touch handle dipped in rubber

Body of injection-molded acetal (a type of plastic)

TYPE HD 2001/A electric teakettle | **Alessi for Royal Philips Electronics**, 1994, **Italy**. The electric teakettle had been around since the 1970s, but Alessi came up with this streamlined alternative that used its design as a selling point.

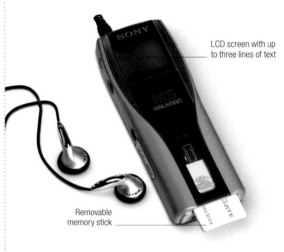

LCD screen with up to three lines of text

Removable memory stick

Memory Stick Walkman Model NW-MS7 personal stereo | **Sony**, 2000, **Japan**. Sony's compact, PC-compatible device could store 80 minutes of music and featured an anti-skip function to prevent music from stopping or jumping.

Whimsical handle and spout

Aio filter coffee maker | **Ronan and Erwan Bouroullec for Habitat**, 2000, **France**. Simple and slimline with a dash of wit, this coffee maker is part of a complete range of popular tableware that features interlocking pieces for stacking.

Clock face bare except for logo

Blank wall clock | **Martí Guixé for Alessi**, 2010, **Spain**. This clock face also functions as a whiteboard, on which the householder can write notes then wipe it clean and start again. The chunky hands can also be written on.

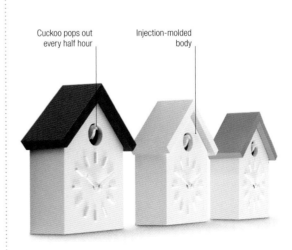

Cuckoo pops out every half hour

Injection-molded body

Cu-Clock | **Naoto Fukasawa for Magis**, 2011, **Japan**. In his modern interpretation of the cuckoo clock, Fukasawa strips away all the rich ornament of the traditional Swiss model, leaving only the pitched roof, a white bird, and a minimalist clock face.

△ **The iPhone 6,** released in 2014, demonstrates the love of elegant simplicity that underscores all of Ive's products.

Jonathan Ive

From a young age, British designer Jonathan Ive was fascinated by the way things worked, pulling apart objects he found around the house then trying to put them back together again. As a teenager, he was passionate about cars, and he thought about becoming a car designer before deciding on an industrial-design course. One of his first jobs after college was for a design agency in London, Tangerine, where he worked for a client called Apple. Eventually, Apple persuaded him to relocate to San Francisco and join their design team.

Ive's first solo design for Apple was the iMac G3 in 1998. It featured an egg-shaped back and translucent blue plastic outer casing (a color marketed as Bondi blue). Ive continued to evolve and redesign the iMac in a range of colors but also put his mind to new products that would help revive Apple's fortunes—the iPod, the original iPad, which was the first device to have a touch screen and sold more than 55 million units, the 2007 iPhone, the 2008 MacBook Air, and the 2011 Mac mini.

As the creative force behind some of Apple's biggest-selling products, Ive considers himself less a designer and more as someone who makes things. He has said, "I want to know what things are for, how they work, what they can or should be made of, before I even begin to think what they should look like." Engineering and branding go hand in hand—his finished products are easy to use and have a minimalist appeal. In 2019, Ive left Apple to start his own design company.

Life

1967–

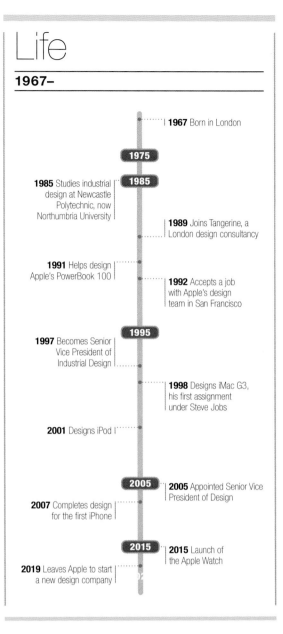

1967 Born in London

1975

1985 Studies industrial design at Newcastle Polytechnic, now Northumbria University

1985

1989 Joins Tangerine, a London design consultancy

1991 Helps design Apple's PowerBook 100

1992 Accepts a job with Apple's design team in San Francisco

1995

1997 Becomes Senior Vice President of Industrial Design

1998 Designs iMac G3, his first assignment under Steve Jobs

2001 Designs iPod

2005

2005 Appointed Senior Vice President of Design

2007 Completes design for the first iPhone

2015

2015 Launch of the Apple Watch

2019 Leaves Apple to start a new design company

iPod | For Apple Inc., 2001. Ive's groundbreaking music player was smaller, more intuitive, and had greater capacity than any music device that had been produced before it.

iMac G4 | For Apple Inc., 2002. With a thin, flat-panel LCD screen mounted on a cantilevered arm that could be angled to suit the user, the iMac G4 proved a serious rival to the PC.

Watch | For Apple Inc., 2015. Three years in the making, the Apple Watch features a thin, protective layer of sapphire crystal over the touch-screen display.

Visual pun on letter "I"

Black background makes colors stand out

Stripes on letter "M" repeat those on the bee's body

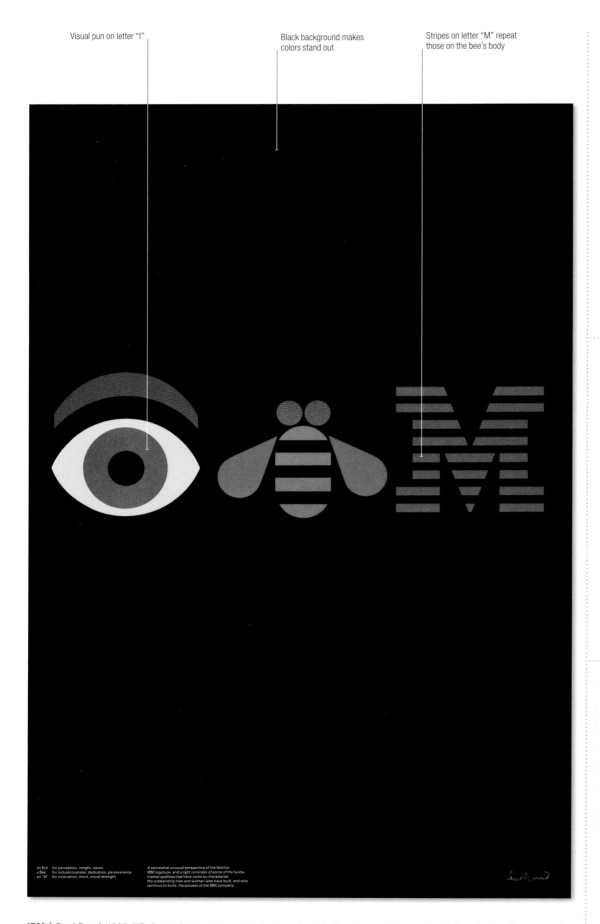

an Eye   for perception, insight, vision.
a Bee   for industriousness, dedication, perseverance.
an "M"   for motivation, merit, moral strength

A somewhat unusual perspective of the familiar IBM logotype, and a light reminder of some of the fundamental qualities that have come to characterize the outstanding men and women who have built, and who continue to build, the success of the IBM company.

IBM | **Paul Rand**, 1982, US. An art director and graphic designer, Rand designed some of the most iconic logos in American corporate history, such as this one for IBM, and he is also renowned for his advertising and poster designs. His approach to graphic commissions was often playful and he liked to improvise, as here, creating puzzles to stand for letters and inventing new ways with typography. His work was underscored by sincerity and thoughtfulness.

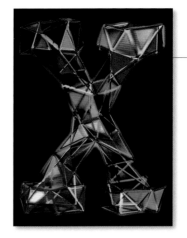

Letter "X" made to resemble scaffolding

X | **Toshifumi Kawahara for Morisawa & Co.**, 1993, Japan. Kawahara's silkscreen celebrating the 10th anniversary of the magazine *Tategumi Yokogumi* is one of several experimental posters commissioned by the typesetting company.

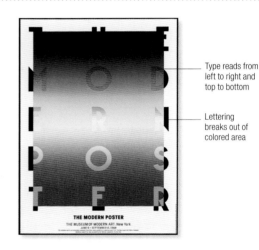

Type reads from left to right and top to bottom

Lettering breaks out of colored area

The Modern Poster | **Satō Kōichi**, 1988, Japan. Satō breaks convention by having the lettering intrude into the border of this poster. In this no-man's land, usually left as a visual breathing space, the Art Deco–style typography changes color.

Magnified detail of pixelation

Typography distorted to create underwater effect

Pacific Wave | **April Greiman for California Graphic Design exhibition**, 1989, US. Reflecting the rise of digital technology, Greiman takes a photograph as a starting point for her poster, then enlarges a pixelated segment into a feature.

POSTMODERN POSTERS

From the mid-20th century onward, a rational Modernist look had dominated typography, but in the 1980s and 1990s, new fonts were designed and type was used in more daring ways. Digital technology also transformed graphic design. The first desktop publishing computer program with a graphics card (hardware that enables an image to appear on the screen) was launched in the US in 1983, followed by the release of PageMaker in 1985, which soon became the standard graphics tool. As new software was developed, graphic designers began to exploit the digital techniques and processes available, especially to manipulate photographs and fonts. In Europe, the impact of political changes invigorated graphic design at grassroots level. In Poland, for example, posters played a vital role in garnering the public solidarity that ultimately led to the fall of Communism.

Stencil-style lettering breaks up typography

Additional block of vertical text balances top line

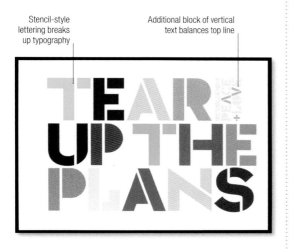

Tear up the Plans | **Neville Brody for V&A's 150th anniversary**, 2012, UK. Known for his radical styling of *The Face* magazine, Brody employed the stencil lettering associated with homemade protest posters and spray-painted slogans.

Solidarity logo represents a united mass of people

Pro-democracy elections | **Ewa Baluk-Zaborowska (poster) and Jerzy Janiszewski (logo)**, 1989, Poland. Janiszewski designed the Solidarity logo in 1980. It evolved into a full typeface called Solidaryca.

The response to coronavirus

2020

When the coronavirus spread and countries went into lockdown, governments put up billboards and posters providing guidance on what to do and where to go for help, but the pandemic also inspired vibrant messages of encouragement and gratitude. Children stuck rainbow pictures in their windows, and designers and artists created posters to raise awareness about social distancing and to thank key workers. Billboards were covered in imaginative, witty designs bringing color and heart-warming messages to the streets. In the US, grassroots movement Amplifier started an emergency campaign for artists to create works that communicated public health messages or promoted mental health during the pandemic.

Stylized stencil portrait of Obama in block colors

The words "progress" and "change" were also used

Barack Obama "Hope" | **Shepard Fairey**, *c.* 2008, US. This iconic poster came to represent Barack Obama's 2008 presidential campaign. Fairey created it in just one day, and it was originally printed as a street poster.

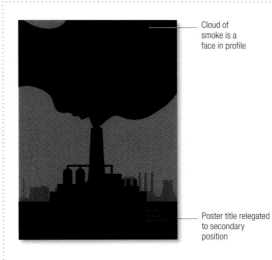

Cloud of smoke is a face in profile

Poster title relegated to secondary position

What Are We Breathing | **Wu Ouxiang**, *c.* 2013, Taiwan. Winner of the student category in the 2014 Red Dot Design Awards, Ouxiang deploys a cheerful, cartoonish style with little or no typography to convey this universal message.

Promotional poster (detail) for the Amplifier design contest, Thomas Wimberly, 2020, US

△ **The Seed Cathedral,** Heatherwick's UK Pavilion for the 2010 World Expo in Shanghai, is a large boxlike building, enshrining 250,000 seeds in clear acrylic rods that protrude from every surface.

Thomas
Heatherwick

British designer Thomas Heatherwick is an accomplished architect, sculptor, and urban planner. His rise to prominence began slowly with a number of small projects in the late 1990s and early 2000s. A window installation for the London department store Harvey Nichols, a handbag for the French luxury brand Longchamp, and a summerhouse in the Essex countryside all demonstrated his early versatility.

However, it was the Seed Cathedral, the UK Pavilion that Heatherwick designed for the 2010 World Expo in Shanghai, that brought him international acclaim. Resembling a giant pincushion of shimmering fibers, the Seed Cathedral was made from 60,000 acrylic rods, embedded with real seeds. Heatherwick's next major commission was the cauldron for the London 2012 Olympics. Made up of 204 petal-like copper objects, one for each competing country, it represented the coming together of nations.

Since 2012, Heatherwick has focused on architectural commissions for clients around the world. His projects include an educational hub for Nanyang Technological University in Singapore, a cluster of 12 tapered towers looking onto a central atrium. Heatherwick also designed Google's California campus, which has cycle paths and streams weaving between lightweight structures that can be moved and adapted as working practices change. Recent projects include a center for Maggie's, Leeds, UK, a charity that supports people with cancer. Constructed from natural, sustainable materials, the building incorporates plenty of green space and thousands of plants.

Life

1970–

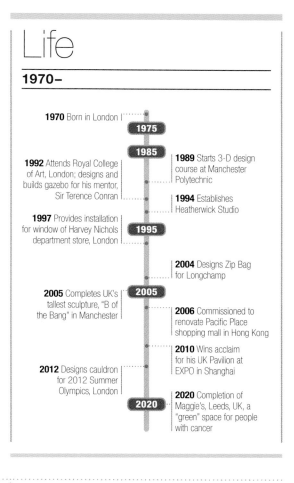

1970 Born in London

1975

1985

1989 Starts 3-D design course at Manchester Polytechnic

1992 Attends Royal College of Art, London; designs and builds gazebo for his mentor, Sir Terence Conran

1994 Establishes Heatherwick Studio

1997 Provides installation for window of Harvey Nichols department store, London

1995

2004 Designs Zip Bag for Longchamp

2005 Completes UK's tallest sculpture, "B of the Bang" in Manchester

2005

2006 Commissioned to renovate Pacific Place shopping mall in Hong Kong

2010 Wins acclaim for his UK Pavilion at EXPO in Shanghai

2012 Designs cauldron for 2012 Summer Olympics, London

2020 Completion of Maggie's, Leeds, UK, a "green" space for people with cancer

2020

Zip Bag | For Longchamp, 2004. Unzipping the single long zipper on the side of this handbag reveals a striking green material, creating a zigzag pattern and doubling the size of the bag.

Routemaster bus | For Transport for London, UK, 2012. Heatherwick's Routemaster redesign has a calm, coordinated interior and wraparound windows that fill the vehicle with light.

Sides act as chair's back and arms

Spun | For Magis, 2010. Evolving from Heatherwick's experiments in rotational plastic molding, Spun cradles the sitter while gently tilting and turning with their motion.

Clear, wide-screen display

Screen features either a map or oblique view

TomTom GPS unit | **TomTom**, 2002, Netherlands. Although satellite navigation has existed since the 1960s, commercial GPS units for use in cars are a recent development, and the technology is now packaged in a sleek, touch-screen unit.

iPod Shuffle | **Apple Inc.**, 2005 onward, US. The smallest in Apple's range of music players, the iPod Shuffle uses flash memory to store songs. Its metal case has clear, graphic controls as on larger iPods, but without the scroll wheel feature.

Beats by Dre headphones | **Beats Electronics**, 2008 onward, US. Record producer and rapper Dr. Dre (Andre Young) fronts this range of on-ear headphones for the fashion-conscious. All finishes have the distinctive Beats "b" symbol.

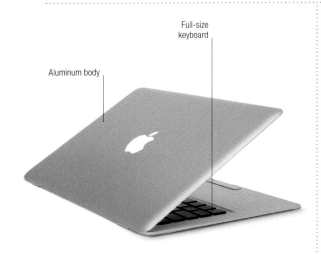

Full-size keyboard

Aluminum body

MacBook Air | **Apple Inc.**, 2008 onward, US. The world's thinnest laptop computer when it was launched, the MacBook Air combined lightweight, ultra-portable functionality with a distinctive, rounded form and a brushed aluminum finish.

Simple case harmonizes with existing TV and home theater equipment

PlayStation 4 | **Sony**, 2013–2014, Japan. The PS4 packs an impressive amount of processing power, plus facilities for social gaming. The unit's design is a simple combination of planes and contours, enabling it to sit unobtrusively in a modern living room.

iPad Air 2 | **Apple Inc.**, 2014, US. With their multi-touch screens, easy operating system, and sleek design, iPads are the most successful tablet computers. The iPad Air 2 has improved battery life, a high-resolution display, and a slimline body.

BlackBerry Passport | **BlackBerry**, 2014, Canada. BlackBerry specializes in mobile devices, mostly with physical keyboards and email, for business. The Passport combines smartphone and tablet, with a 4½in (11cm) HD screen.

E-Ink display works well in bright sunlight

Flush glass screen

Lightweight plastic body

Kindle Voyage | **Amazon**, 2014, US. Since launching its e-readers in 2007, Amazon has improved display, storage, and connectivity. The Kindle Voyage has a high-resolution adaptive LED display, which can adjust the screen illumination.

Charging case

Ear tips come in different sizes

Touch-sensitive surface

Momentum True Wireless 2 | **Sennheiser**, 2020, Germany. These are some of the best-sounding true wireless earbuds, with active noise canceling and a longer battery life. The metal cap of each earbud is a touch panel for the controls.

Apple Watch | **Apple Inc.**, **2015**, **US**. The Apple Watch brings the company's trademark pared-down, user-friendly design to the "smart watch." Functions such as messaging, email, calendar, telephone, mapping, and fitness monitoring are included. The face of the watch is customizable, and there is a range of cases and straps in different styles.

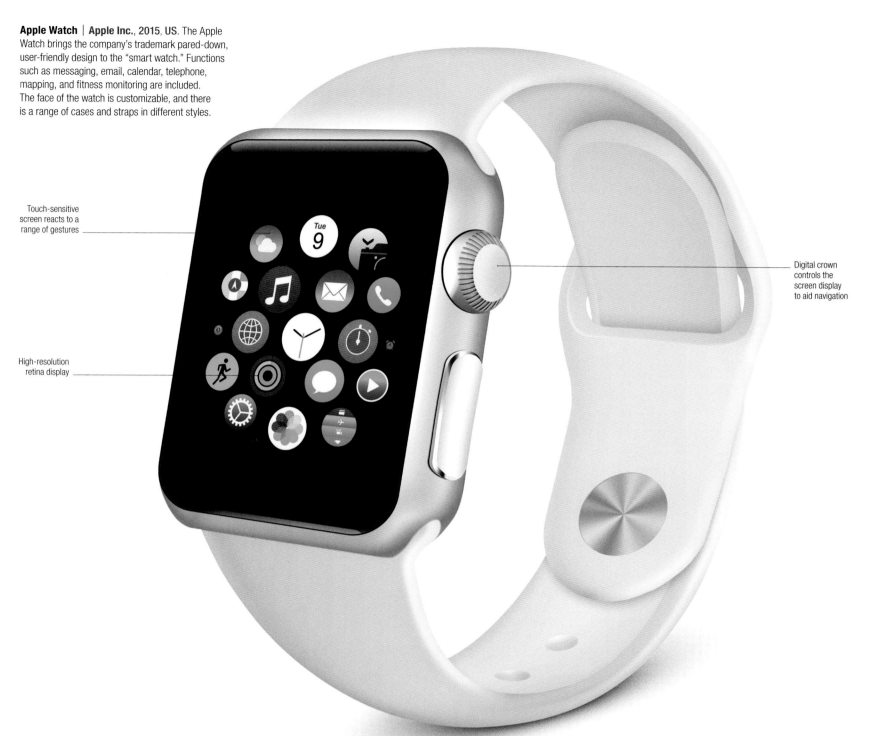

Touch-sensitive screen reacts to a range of gestures

Digital crown controls the screen display to aid navigation

High-resolution retina display

NEW TECHNOLOGY

Computers and associated technology now dominate many aspects of people's everyday lives, particularly the ways in which they communicate, listen to music, play games, and read. In the last few decades, designers have concentrated on making computers and similar devices easier to use, more compact, and better looking. The work of Apple, under Senior Vice President of Design Jonathan Ive (see pp.364–365), has led the way, with slimline laptops, iPads, iPods, and the Apple Watch all skillfully produced to fit seamlessly into the everyday lives of users. Other companies have followed, often creating more specialized items, such as Sony's game consoles or the handheld BlackBerry—a combined cell phone and email device. Just as inventive are the products that make use of technology in new ways, such as the Apple Watch, which offers users a revolutionary wearable display.

EVOLUTION OF
TELEPHONES

Since telephones were invented in the 1870s, they have gradually become smaller, easier to use, and more versatile. Before the invention of the dial—a major breakthrough—the first phones were connected by an operator working at a manual exchange. After World War II, the development of transistors and the increasing sophistication of plastics enabled designers to experiment with different shapes. Still more miniaturization, together with sophisticated programming and electronics, have enabled the smartphones of today, as manufacturers compete to combine advanced features with sleek, ergonomic designs.

Visible bell

Walnut case

Transmitter unit

c. 1900 **Ericsson wall phone** | **Ericsson, UK**. Early telephones were simply wall-mounted wooden boxes with handsets. There was no dial: turning the handle on the side connected users to the operator, who put calls through to the right line.

Strong Bakelite case

1931 **DHB 1001** | **Jean Heiberg and Christian Bjerknes for Ericsson, Sweden/Norway**. An enduring design, imitated around the world, the DBH 1001 was a robust Bakelite unit with enough space inside for a large, loud bell.

Heavy base keeps the phone upright

1949 **Ericofon** | **Ralph Lysell and Hugo Blomberg for Ericsson, Sweden**. With its dial hidden in the base and a curvaceous plastic body, the Ericofon was the first one-piece telephone. It combined ergonomic design with modern Scandinavian lines.

Dial concealed beneath handset when not in use

1960s **GTE telephone** | **General Telephone and Electric Corporation, US**. Newly developed plastics and transistorized electronics inspired the designers of the 1960s to experiment with colored plastics and smaller models, resulting in this compact phone.

Distinctive shape helps grip

Opaque plastic case

1994 **Swatch telephone** | **Swatch company, Switzerland**. The Swatch company, famous for inexpensive watches, used plastic with flair in this phone. The main decoration was provided by the accent color, picked up in the keys.

Recessed speaker

Dial with inset keys

1996 **StarTAC mobile phone** | **Motorola Inc., US**. The StarTAC was the first mobile flip-phone. The design, pioneered in the Grillo, proved ideal for compact mobiles. Folding had another advantage; it protected the keys and prevented accidental dialing.

Blue number keys

Handset displays gentle, harmonious curves

1990s **MG 1000** | **Michael Graves, US**. The leading postmodernist architect Michael Graves designed this push-button phone. Graves kept the layout simple, using contrasting colors and different sizes for the number and function buttons.

Handset

Mouthpiece

1929 **Neophone** | **Siemens Brothers, UK.** Improved technology meant that the Neophone's microphone could be built into the phone's handset, producing the one-piece receiver. To manufacture the new shape easily, this was the first phone to be made of plastic.

Receiver

Large antenna

c. **1900** **Candlestick phone** | **US.** As more telephone exchanges were built, phones with dials became more common. The most widely used model, which lasted for at least 40 years, was the candlestick phone.

Dial concealed when phone is folded

Individual push-button keys

Hinge attaches mouthpiece to body

Metal dial

1965 **Grillo** | **Richard Sapper and Marco Zanuso, Italy.** Developments in electronics made much smaller phones possible in the 1960s. One of the most ingenious designs was the Grillo (cricket), which folded to a clamshell shape that opened to reveal the mouthpiece and dial.

1984 **DynaTAC mobile telephone** | **Motorola Inc., US.** Early mobiles were life-changing devices, providing spoken communication on the move for the very first time. Although carefully designed, they were heavy, expensive, and had a limited battery life.

Monochromatic screen

Large, single-color LCD screen

Graphic icons represent apps

Buttons contoured for ease of use

Full QWERTY keyboard

Home button

2003 **Nokia 1100** | **Nokia, Finland.** A compact, curved-edged case, basic keypad, and small screen helped the Nokia 1100 become the world's bestselling mobile phone. Its simple design and robust construction mean it is still popular around the world.

2003 **BlackBerry 6200** | **Research in Motion Ltd., Canada.** Able to send and receive emails, the BlackBerry combined the functions of a mobile phone with those of a desktop computer. It was widely successful with business people.

2007 **iPhone** | **Jonathan Ive for Apple, US.** The iPhone transformed the mobile phone market. With its minimalist case, large, touch-sensitive screen, and navigation by means of specially designed icons, it was the ultimate user-friendly device.

FLUIDITY OF FORM

The Heydar Aliyev Cultural Center is a venue for concerts, exhibitions, and other events in the center of Baku, the capital of Azerbaijan. It was designed by the Iraqi British architect Zaha Hadid, who was well known for radical and original buildings that display innovative geometry and enthralling, fluid spaces. The Center takes a revolutionary form that is in total contrast to the dull high-rise architecture nearby, which dates from Baku's time as part of the Soviet Union.

The surrounding plaza seems to rise up, blending via a series of curves, undulations, and folds into the walls and roofs of the building itself. The resulting wavelike surface, clad with white fiberglass and reinforced concrete panels, envelops the building, leaving gaps at strategic places for entrances and windows. The flowing white walls are the same inside the Center, and the floors, steps, and other indoor surfaces are treated in a similar way. The building's unique curvilinear geometry encloses a 1,000-seat concert hall, a museum, a library, and other spaces, and it opened up new possibilities for future public buildings and cultural monuments.

> **It is an intoxicatingly beautiful building by the most brilliant architect at the height of her office's powers.**

Piers **Gough**

Heydar Aliyev Center, Baku, Azerbaijan, Zaha Hadid, 2012
The flowing shape and repeating patterns of glass and siding pay homage to Islamic architecture in western Asia. However, Hadid reinterpreted rather than copied earlier motifs for this new building.

A to Z Glossary

A

Acid-etching A technique in which a design is engraved into glass using hydrochloric acid. Areas not to be etched are protected with wax or varnish, then the glass is immersed in the acid, creating a design in relief. The technique is also used to remove areas of overlaid glass, to create designs in relief on cameo glass vessels.

Analogous colors Colors that are close to each other on the color wheel and look similar: red and orange, orange and yellow, or blue and purple, for example.

Anthropometrics The study of the size and proportions of people in relation to products, aimed at improving functionality; it is closely related to ergonomics.

Aesthetic movement A short-lived, late 19th-century artistic movement that advocated "art for art's sake." The cult of beauty in painting that it fostered was matched by a greater interest in interior design. The movement overlapped with Arts and Crafts, but its denial of any social or moral value in art set it apart from the views of William Morris.

Anthropomorphic Taking the form of a human being.

Argental Made of, containing, or resembling silver.

Ariel glass A technique developed by Orrefors, the Swedish glass manufacturer, in the late 1930s, in which air bubbles are trapped within layers of glass. The bubbles reflect and refract the light, creating a fluid, silvery appearance. *See also* Graal glass.

Art Deco A style of design characterized by bold colors and geometric shapes that spanned the 1920s and '30s and came to epitomize the glamour and luxury of the Jazz Age. It filtered into all areas of design, including photography, film, travel, and transportation.

Art Nouveau A style characterized by flowing, free-form imagery based on organic forms. It developed around 1890, influenced partly by the Arts and Crafts movement, and lasted until World War I.

Arts and Crafts A late 19th-century artistic movement that sought to reconcile the differences between artist and craftsman and aimed to create simple, well-made, functional furnishings for all levels of society.

B

Bakelite A robust, nonflammable synthetic plastic invented in 1909 and widely used for products for the home in the first half of the 20th century. Bakelite was popular because it can be molded, insulates electricity, and resists heat and chemical action.

Bauhaus A school of art, founded in Weimar, Germany, in 1919 by Walter Gropius, that sought to create total works of art by combining crafts and fine art. It had a defining influence on Modernist design and architecture. The Nazis closed the Bauhaus in 1933.

Bentwood A technique perfected in Austria by Michael Thonet in the mid-19th century that involves bending solid or laminated wood over steam to make curved sections for chair and table frames.

Biedermeier A restrained style of decorative arts popular in Germany, Austria, and Scandinavia in the first half of the 18th century. Biedermeier furniture is generally based on symmetrical, classical forms, with simple ornament such as shells, lyres, and urns.

Biomorphic A design based on a naturally occurring pattern or shape or on one that is reminiscent of a living organism.

Bone china A British porcelain that contains ox-bone ash, which makes it very white. It was first used in 1748 by Thomas Frye of Bow.

C

Cabinetmaking The craft of making fine furniture.

Cabochon A French term for a smooth, domed gem, also used to describe round or oval ornaments in carving, stonework, and furniture. The Arts and Crafts movement revived cabochon decoration of metalware.

Cameo glass Glass that is made of two or more separate colored layers. The top layer is wheel-carved or acid-etched to produce a relief image and to reveal the different, often contrasting, colored layer(s) of glass beneath.

Cantilever chair A chair without back legs; the seat is supported by the front legs and base alone.

1883 | Arts and Crafts
Strawberry Thief printed cotton, William Morris

c. 1895 | Acid-etching
Glass vase, Émile Gallé

Plique-à-jour butterfly wings with gold veining

c. 1900 | Art Nouveau Sylph
jewelry, René Lalique

Opal cabochon

c. 1900 | Cabochon
Silver and plique-à-jour brooch, Heinrich Levinger

c. 1910 | Leaded glass
Favrile glass chandelier, Tiffany Studios

Cased glass Layers of different-colored glass. The inner layer is blown and subsequent layers are added on top. The layers are then reheated so that they fuse.

Celluloid The first thermoplastic, originally called Parkesine. It was widely used from the mid-19th century, but because it was costly to produce and highly flammable, it had fallen out of favor by the mid-20th century.

Chaise longue A French term for an upholstered day bed that has a high support at one end.

Chamfer A cut on the corner of a surface, generally at a 45-degree angle to the adjacent faces.

Chrome Coated or plated with the metallic element chromium.

Classical orders In classical architecture, an order describes the way in which a column, capital (top of column), and entablature (above the column, supporting the roof) are arranged. Ancient Greek architecture used three orders: Doric (the plainest), Ionic (with two volutes on each capital), and Corinthian (the most ornamental, with scrolls and acanthus leaves). The forms and motifs of these orders were widely adopted by craftsmen and designers from the Renaissance onward and were used in combination in postmodern design.

Cloisonné A French term for "partitioned" that denotes a metalwork technique in which sections of a wire outline or pattern are filled with powdered enamel and then fired.

Color theory The study of colors and the effects that they create when combined in different ways.

Complementary colors Colors that are opposite each other on the color wheel, and make each other look brighter when placed close together. The complementary pairs are always a primary and secondary color: yellow and purple, blue and orange, red and green.

Constructivism An artistic movement that began in Russia after the 1917 October Revolution. It aimed to replace composition with construction and put modern materials to use in mass production to further a Communist society. The movement had a huge impact on art, architecture, graphic design, film, and theater design, and it influenced both the Bauhaus and the De Stijl movement.

Crystal glass Glass that has a high (at least 20 percent) lead oxide content, which makes it ideal for cut decoration. It is also known as crystal or leaded crystal glass.

Cubism A movement led by artists Pablo Picasso and Georges Braque from 1907 to 1914. Cubist pictures broke with the artistic convention of one-point perspective and showed different views of a still life or figure. The resulting fragmented, geometric abstraction filtered into Art Deco and Modernism.

Cut glass Glassware decorated with grooves and facets, usually cut by a rotating wheel.

D

Dado The lower part of a wall.

Deconstructivism A concept in architectural theory and practice from the 1980s onward, following on from postmodernism, relating to buildings in which the themes of dislocation, disruption, and distortion are explored.

Demi-lune A French term for a half-moon shape.

De Stijl A movement, named after the Dutch words for "the style," which lasted from 1917 to 1931. It was founded by avant-garde Dutch artists, architects, and designers who believed in reducing design to its essentials, using a geometry of straight lines and planes that did not intersect, and a restricted palette of black, white, and primary colors.

Dovetail A joint in which two pieces of wood are joined at right angles. Each piece of wood has a row of tenons (fan-shaped teeth), which interlock at the joint.

Dowel A small, headless, wooded pin used in furniture construction to join two pieces of wood.

E

Earthenware Pottery made from a porous clay body that has to be waterproofed with a glaze.

Ebonized wood Wood that has been stained black to look like ebony.

Embossing Metalware decoration made by punching out a relief (raised) or impressed pattern with a hammer. *See also* Repoussé.

1917 | De Stijl Red-Blue chair, Gerrit Rietveld

1928 | Art Deco Overlapping Triangles plate, Susie Cooper

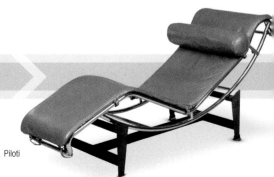

Piloti

1928–1929 | Pilotis Villa Savoye, Poissy, France, Le Corbusier

1928 | Chaise longue LC4 chaise longue, Charlotte Perriand, Le Corbusier, Pierre Jeanneret

Enamel Colored glass fused by heating it in a furnace to create a design or decorative finish on a metallic surface. Enamel can be produced in a wide range of translucent and opaque colors.

Engraving A technique that is used to decorate glass and metal, in which the design is cut with a sharp instrument such as a diamond point or wheel to create an image in small dots or relief. Also, a print made by cutting a picture into wood or metal, inking the surface, and pressing paper onto it.

Ergonomics The practice of designing objects to be comfortable, functional, and user-friendly, by taking into account the relation between the product and the people who will use it. The aim is to improve productivity and health.

F

Facade The front of a building or a piece of case furniture.

Femme-fleur A French term used to describe a hybrid of a woman and a flower. The motif was popular in Art Nouveau design.

Fiberglass A type of plastic that is reinforced with glass fibers, making it strong yet lightweight.

Figuring The natural markings and graining on wood that form a decorative pattern.

Finial A decorative element that is used as the top or terminal of an architectural spire, or on a piece of furniture, metalware, or ceramics, often in the form of an acorn, pine cone, or urn.

Flatware All flat tableware, such as plates, spoons, and forks, but excluding those with a cutting edge (which are classed as cutlery).

Foliate A term for decoration that resembles leaves.

Functionalism A principle of architecture decreeing that the design of a building should reflect its purpose. It was a central tenet of Modernism, and the same principle of utility over decoration was applied to Modernist designs.

Futurism An Italian avant-garde artistic and social movement of the early 20th century, influenced by Cubism, which celebrated advanced technology, the beauty of machinery, speed, and modernity.

G

Gesso A mixture of chalk, gypsum, or plaster with glue that was used as a base for carved and gilded decoration on wooden picture frames and furniture from the Middle Ages onward.

Gesamtkunstwerk A German term for "total work of art" that is applied in architecture to a design that includes all of the interior fixtures and furnishings that form part of a building, down to every last detail, including door handles, light switches, and sometimes tableware.

Gilding A decorative finish in which gold (or sometimes silver) leaf or powder is applied to the surface of wood, leather, silver, ceramics, or glass, usually onto a base, such as gesso.

Glossy A smooth, shiny, lustrous surface, as opposed to a matte one.

Golden ratio Also known as the golden section and as "phi" in Greek, this is a mathematical ratio of 1:1.618 that naturally occurs in objects such as nautilus shells and beehives, giving them proportions that people find harmonious and aesthetically pleasing. The ratio has been used in geometry, classical architecture, and Renaissance painting as well as design.

Gothic Revival (Neo-Gothic) A popular 19th-century revival of the medieval Gothic style, in which architectural elements, such as arches, tracery, quatrefoils, and carved motifs, were much replicated in design, especially on furniture.

Graal glass A technique developed by Orrefors, the Swedish glass manufacturer, in around 1916, in which an engraved layer of colored glass is enveloped within an outer shell of clear glass, refracting the original design and producing interesting optical effects. *See also* Ariel glass.

Grand Tour An educational journey around Europe, especially Italy, undertaken by young European, notably British, gentlemen in the late 18th century, to complete their education and collect works of art.

Grès A hard stoneware ceramic.

Ground A term used for the surface color of ceramics, onto which decoration can be applied. It can also refer to the background color of glass, textiles, or wallpaper.

1928 | Chrome
Teapot, Naum Slutzky

Ziggurat
1928 | Ziggurat
Silvered bronze and enamel clock, Jean Goulden

1929 | Modernism Barcelona chair, Ludwig Mies van der Rohe

1932 | Bakelite Ekco radio AD-65, Wells Coates

H

Hallmark A small mark stamped onto silverware that indicates the purity of the silver, the manufacturer, the date and place of manufacture, or other information.

Hue The name for a pure color, such as red.

I

Incalmo An Italian term describing a complex technique that is used by glassmakers on the Venetian island of Murano. Two separate gathers of differently colored glass are blown and carefully joined while still hot in order to create distinct bands of color in one vessel.

Inlay A decorative technique in which different-colored woods, stones, or exotic materials are inserted into the solid wood surface or veneer of furniture.

International Style A major architectural style, characterized by rectilinear forms, materials such as steel and concrete, and a lack of ornamentation that developed in Europe in the 1920s and spread to the US in the 1930s, where it dominated the skyline. It is often used as a synonym for Modernism.

Iridescence A lustrous rainbow-like surface that changes color depending on how the light hits it. In glassware, it is usually produced by spraying metallic salts on hot glass.

Isometric A shape, such as a pyramid, in which all the sides have equal dimensions.

J

Jacaranda A type of South American softwood, that is used particularly in turnery and for musical instruments, such as acoustic guitars.

Japonisme A style of European and American decorative arts inspired by Japanese design. Trade reopened between Japan and the West in the 1850s, stimulating Western interest in Japanese art objects.

Jazz Age A name for the exuberant, hedonistic 1920s, as captured in F. Scott Fitzgerald's *The Great Gatsby*, when jazz gained massive popularity in the US and Europe. Closely allied with Art Deco, it had a strong influence on popular culture but lost momentum during the Great Depression of the 1930s.

Jugendstil The German term for "youth style," this describes the German strand of Art Nouveau. The style was more rectilinear than its French and Belgian counterparts and derived its name from the art magazine *Jugend* (Youth), which was first published in 1896.

Jute A coarse vegetable fiber, often woven into mats and ropes.

K

Knop A decorative knob on a lid, used to lift it. Also, the decorative bulge halfway up a glass stem.

L

Lacquer A resin produced from the sap of the *Rhus verniciflua* tree. Once processed and dried, the resin forms a hard, smooth, and impermeable surface. Lacquer was used from the 6th century onward, particularly in Japan and China, and by Modernist designers.

Leaded glass A technique in which shaped pieces of cut glass are assembled into windows or lamps using narrow strips of lead. It is also known as stained glass.

Leaded crystal glass *See* Crystal glass.

Lithograph A printing technique developed around 1800 and much used for posters. An image is drawn on metal or stone with a greasy crayon, and the stone is treated with water and ink. The crayoned areas repel the water but retain the ink, which can then be transferred onto paper.

M

Machine Age A term coined in 1927 in *The New York Times Index* to describe the change after World War I from a largely rural society to a fast-paced urban lifestyle based around cars and machines. It led to a fashion for streamlining in design.

1934 | Bentwood
Armchair, Gerald Summers

1936 | Streamlining
Lincoln-Zephyr, John Tjaarda

1946 | Incalmo
Decanters, Gio Ponti

1948 | Fiberglass Rocking Armchair
Rod, Charles and Ray Eames

Magnalite A type of cast aluminum cookware first marketed in 1934.

Marquetry A decorative veneer made from shaped pieces of wood in different colors and sometimes also exotic materials such as ivory or mother-of-pearl, which are pieced together to form a pattern or picture.

Matte A dull or lusterless surface, as opposed to a glossy one.

Minimalism A style that pares designs down to their essential elements, characterized by simple geometric shapes, flat color or white, and no decoration. An offshoot of Modernism, it developed after World War II and was mainly associated with American artists in the 1960s and early 1970s.

Moderne A contemporary French term for Art Deco.

Modernism A term loosely describing a style of architecture and design characterized by geometry, abstraction, and mass production from about 1920 to the 1950s. Modernists consciously rejected the past, especially the decorative motifs of traditional styles and emphasized formal qualities of design.

Modernisme The Spanish word for Art Nouveau, as characterized in Spain by the work of the Catalan architect Antoni Gaudí.

Modular construction A method of construction in which factory-made units are assembled on site.

Murrine Slices of transparent or opaque, colored glass canes that have been fused together in bundles. Usually patterned, murrines can be pressed together to create a particular shape or picked up on a glass gather that is then blown into a vessel.

Neoplasticism *See* De Stijl.

New Typography A movement in 1920s and '30s design, named after the book of the same name by Jan Tschichold, that rejected traditional, symmetrical page layout and put typography at the forefront of poster and book design. It advocated asymmetrical layouts, the hierarchical organization of content, the use of white space as an important element in the design, and sans-serif typefaces.

Opalescent glass An opal-like, milky blue glass, in which opaque areas of thicker glass contrast with translucent areas of thinner glass. First made by Venetian glassmakers in the 16th century, it became popular again four centuries later in Art Deco pieces.

Organic A term used to describe design that is curved and free-form rather than linear, and inspired by shapes in nature.

Ormolu From the French phrase *or moulu*, meaning "ground gold," a process of gilding bronze for decorative mounts.

Parkesine The first synthetic plastic, which was later manufactured as Celluloid.

Pâte-de-verre From the French for "glass paste," a process in which ground glass is mixed with liquid to form paste, pressed into a mold, and heated to form a desired shape.

Patina A fine surface sheen and mellow appearance on silver and furniture, caused by years of handling, polishing, and wear.

Pattern Repeating, decorative design; the repeats can be regular or irregular.

Pavé set A method of mounting gemstones, in which the individual stones are set so close together that little or no setting is visible between them.

Photolithography A process by which electronic printed circuit boards (PCBs) and microprocessors are created, using light-sensitive materials to create paths between electronic components.

Photomontage The combination of multiple photographs to create a new composite image, often used in advertising.

Piloti In Modernist architecture, pilotis (also known as piers) are ground-level supporting columns. Reinforced concrete pilotis were used in place of structural walls in Le Corbusier's iconic Villa Savoye.

Plique-à-jour A highly skilled metalware technique in which translucent enamel is set in an

c. **1950** | **Organic**
Arabesco tea table, Carlo Mollino

Splat

1953 | **Splat** Valet chair,
Hans Wagner

1957 | **Cantilever** Paulistano chair,
Paolo Mendes da Rocha

1965 | **Enamel** Vase,
Vladimir Kopecký

unbacked framework to create an effect similar to that of light shining through a stained glass window.

Plywood A flexible wood made of several laminates (layers) of wood. Each layer is laid with the grain at right angles to that of the layer below, for additional strength.

Porcelain A hard, white ceramic first made in China in the late 6th century. It is translucent but strong and dense as well as watertight, and usually glazed. Soft-paste porcelain was developed in Europe in the 16th century in an attempt to compete with the highly valued hard-paste porcelain that was imported from China. Hard-paste porcelain was not made in Europe until 1709, when, after much trial and error, a formula was developed at Meissen in Germany.

Postmodernism An architectural movement that began in the late 1970s as a reaction against the austerity and functional emphasis of the Modernist style. Exemplified in design by Ettore Sottsass's Memphis group, the style was characterized by bright colors and exuberant decorative flourishes, witty references to styles and materials past and present, and mockery of notions of good taste.

Pre-Raphaelite Brotherhood An association of Victorian British painters founded in 1848, whose work emulated the style and ideals of Italian art before the High Renaissance painter Raphael. In its second phase, led by Dante Gabriel Rossetti, the Pre-Raphaelites idealized the medieval world, and both Rossetti and Edward Burne-Jones joined William Morris's design company. Their promotion of beauty for its own sake also chimed with the Aesthetic movement.

Primary colors The hues red, yellow and blue, which cannot be mixed from other colors.

Quartz crystal *See* Crystal glass.

Quatrefoil A Gothic motif that resembles a four-leaf clover.

Radical Design An avant-garde Italian design movement of the 1960s that glorified kitsch, bright

color and mass production. It prefigured the postmodernist period that began a decade later.

Radial symmetry A symmetrical arrangement of parts radiating out from a central point; often used in round objects such as plates.

Rattan Woven fibrous strips obtained from rattan palms and used to make furniture.

Relief Molded, carved, or stamped decoration that stands out from its surrounding.

Repoussé A French term for relief decoration on malleable metals, made by hand-hammering the design from the back or inside of the piece. *See also* Embossing.

Sans serif A typeface that does not have serifs—the small, terminal strokes at the top and bottom of the main strokes of letters in a Roman typeface.

Saturation The purity of a color; as soon as black or white is added, a color starts to lose its saturation.

Secondary color A color that is mixed from two primary colors: orange, from red and yellow; green, from yellow and blue; and purple, from blue and red.

Shibayama A type of decorative inlay, pioneered in Japan in the 18th century and later copied in the West, that used minutely carved pieces of inlay on a lacquer ground.

Skeuomorph A functional object or motif redesigned to be decorative, for example, linoleum designed to look like bark or marble.

Slag glass A type of inexpensive, opaque, colored glass with streaked patterns created by incorporating slag, a waste product from iron foundries.

Sommerso A glass technique developed on the Venetian island of Murano in the 1930s. The word comes from the Italian term for "submerged" and involves casing one or more layers of transparent, colored glass within a thick layer of colorless glass.

Splat The flat, central, vertical part of a chair back. It is sometimes shaped and can be left solid or decorated with carving, piercing, veneer, or inlay.

1970s | Organic Tootaloop bangle radio, Panasonic

1984 | Postmodernism Queen Anne chair, Robert Venturi

1988 | Graal glass Vase with Female Head, Eva Englund

1990 | Zoomorphic Juicy Salif, Philippe Starck

Knop

1990 | Knop Teapot, Richard Marquis

Stained glass *See* Leaded glass.

Stile Liberty The Italian term for Art Nouveau, named after the London department store.

Streamlining A term borrowed from engineering and used to describe American Art Deco furniture and other objects designed with smooth, clean-lined shapes in the 1920s and '30s.

Stoneware A type of ceramic that is similar to earthenware in appearance but has stone added to the clay mix, which makes it watertight and hard, like porcelain. Salt or lead glaze is often added to create a decorative effect.

Stretcher A horizontal rail or bar that joins the legs of tables, stools, and chairs to add strength to the construction of the furniture.

Studio glass The products made by independent glassmakers working in individual studies or with other like-minded glassmakers who wish to express their own artistry without commercial pressures. The studio movement of the 1960s, which began in the US, caused a revolution in the way glass was made and collected, raising its status and its commercial value.

Suprematism A Russian abstract art movement of the early 20th century, in which formal qualities reigned supreme. Its artists produced works with simple, geometric forms and a restricted palette of colors.

Symbolism A late-19th-century European artistic and literary movement that sought to express a deeper reality, representing images from dreams, the unconscious mind, and the imagination, with much use of symbols. Symbolist artists were influenced by religious mysticism and primitive art.

T

Teak A tropical hardwood with a density and oily composition that make it resistant to fungus and insects. It was widely used in the 18th century and then again in Danish furniture of the 1950s and 1960s.

Temperature Red is the hottest color, and the hues analogous to it are warm; blue is the coldest and the hues analogous to it are cool.

Terminal A decorative feature at the end of a structure or object.

Tertiary color A color mixed from a primary and a secondary color, or from two secondaries, such as red-orange or blue-green.

Texture The appearance and feel of a surface.

Thermoplastic A material that softens when it is heated and hardens when it is cooled.

Thermoset A polymer that is set hard, irreversibly, using heat.

Tone How dark or light a color is. Shades are dark tones; tints are light tones.

V

Veneer A thin layer of fine wood, ivory, or tortoiseshell applied to the surface of a piece of furniture that is usually constructed from an inferior wood.

Vienna Secession An alliance of artists, designers, and architects, including Josef Hoffmann and Koloman Moser, the founders of the Wiener Werkstätte. They broke away from the Viennese establishment in 1897 in favor of

Symbolism and Art Nouveau. The Austrian Art Nouveau style is often called Sezessionstil.

W

Webbing Strips of woven fabric that form the base of a chair seat.

Wiener Werkstätte Workshops founded in Vienna by Josef Hoffman, Koloman Moser, and Fritz Warndorfer as an association of craftsmen. The members of the workshops made a wide range of furniture, metalwork, and glass in a rectilinear Art Nouveau style, with the aim of merging architecture and interiors into total works of art.

Z

Ziggurat A stepped shape, based on the terraced temple towers of ancient Mesopotamia. It was a popular decorative outline in Art Deco architecture and design.

Zoomorphic A term used to describe ornament or shape that is based on animal forms.

Finial

1998 | Finial Pepper mill, Michael Graves

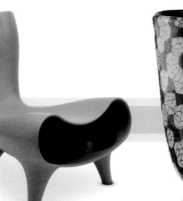

1998 | Biomorphic Orgone Chair, Marc Newson

2004 | Murrine Murrina vase, Vittorio Ferro

2010 | Stoneware Vase, Gustavo Pérez

2013 | Tone PlayStation 4, Sony

A

ALVAR AALTO

FINNISH, 1898–1976

One of the giants of Modernism, Aalto had a profound influence on the fields of architecture and furniture design. He studied at the Helsinki University of Technology before setting up his architectural practice in 1923. Early projects of note included the Viipuri Municipal Library (1927–1935) and the Paimio Tuberculosis Sanatorium (1929–1933). Aalto's furniture designs were closely related to his architectural work. His Paimio chair (Model No. 41, 1932) was specifically designed so that patients would sit in a position that aided their breathing. Similarly, his Stool 60 (1933) was made with Viipuri Library in mind—it was stackable and could be moved quietly.

Aalto's groundbreaking furniture designs stemmed from his experiments with bending and molding plywood. The results proved so popular that he and his wife formed a company, Artek (from the words "art" and "technology"), to market and manufacture the goods. Aalto's success earned him many awards, while MoMA, New York, devoted no fewer than three exhibitions to his achievements.

CAREER HIGHLIGHTS

1929 Begins work on the Paimio Tuberculosis Sanatorium

1935 Alvar and Aino Aalto set up their company, Artek

1838 Solo exhibition held at MoMA, New York

1939 Designs the Finnish pavilion at the Paris Exposition Internationale

EERO AARNIO

FINNISH, 1932–

Aarnio is celebrated for his playful and futuristic furniture designs, which encapsulate the exuberant spirit of the 1960s. He trained at the School of Industrial Design in Helsinki, where he set up his studio in 1962. Aarnio worked in interior design and graphics but is chiefly associated with seating. His first piece was a cane stool, though he preferred to work in fiberglass and plastic. The Ball or Globe chair, popularized in the cult television series *The Prisoner*, brought him international fame. Aarnio described it as a "room within a room," and even installed a telephone in some models. His transparent Bubble chair, designed to be suspended from the ceiling, was a variant on the theme.

CAREER HIGHLIGHTS

1963 Creates the Ball (Globe) chair

1968 Designs the Bubble chair

1994 Creates the Parabel table

FRIEDRICH ADLER

GERMAN, 1878–1942

A gifted metalware designer, Adler's work bridged the Art Nouveau and Art Deco styles. He studied in Munich, in a private applied arts studio run by Hermann Obrist and Wilhelm von Debschitz. This progressive workshop is often cited as a precursor of the Bauhaus. For much of his life, Adler taught at the School of Applied Art in Hamburg, but in 1897, he also began publishing designs in art journals. A commission to design the Württemberg pavilion at the Turin International Exhibition (1902) secured his reputation. Adler's finest designs were made in pewter, although he was also reputedly one of the first artists to use Bakelite. As a Jew, during World War II he was sent to Auschwitz, where, deemed too old for work, he was murdered by the Nazis.

OTL AICHER

GERMAN, 1922–1991

A graphic designer, typographer, and teacher. Aicher's early career was hampered by his opposition to the Nazis (he refused to join the Hitler Youth), but he set up his own studio in 1948 and cofounded the Hochschule für Gestaltung Ulm (Ulm College of Design) in the following year. He lectured there and later served as vice-chancellor (1962–1964). Aicher was a pioneer of corporate branding and is best known for designing the mascot, signage, uniforms, and sporting pictograms for the Munich Olympics (1972). He also created the famous Lufthansa logo (1969) and produced designs for Frankfurt Airport and the University of Konstanz.

▽ ANNI ALBERS

GERMAN, 1899–1994

A weaver, printmaker, and teacher, Albers was a student at the Bauhaus when she met and married the artist Josef Albers. Both taught there until 1933, when the rise of the Nazis forced them to flee to the US, taking up teaching posts at the newly founded Black Mountain College in North Carolina. Throughout her career, Anni Albers produced intricate, rectilinear textile designs and, in 1949, she became the first weaver to be honored with a solo exhibition at MoMA, New York. She was later awarded the Gold Medal of the American Craft Council for the superb quality of her work.

ALESSI

ITALIAN, 1921–

An Italian manufacturer of high-quality homewares, Alessi often creates products with a whimsical sense of humor. The company was founded in 1921 by Giovanni Alessi, operating initially as a foundry and metal workshop. In the late 1970s, it began to commission major designers, including such luminaries as Alessandro Mendini, Ron Arad, and Zaha Hadid. During the 1980s, Alessi became famous for its quirky postmodern designs. These were typified by Michael Graves's Whistling Bird kettle (1985), which featured a tiny plastic bird at the end of its spout. Its success encouraged the company to establish the Officina

DESIGN FOR A WALL HANGING, ANNI ALBERS, 1926

INTERIOR WITH BOOKWORM SHELVING, RON ARAD, 1993

Alessi line—a range of limited-edition products created by celebrity designers. Examples included the futuristic stainless-steel Fruitscape fruit holder by Stefano Giovannoni and an uneven, organically shaped shelf-stand, the Floating Earth étagère, by Ma Yan Song.

◁ RON ARAD

ISRAELI, 1951–

A self-confessed maverick, Arad has built up an enviable reputation for producing startling, innovative designs. He was educated at the Bezalel Academy of Art before completing his studies in London at the Architectural Association. In 1981, he founded his own company, One Off, with Caroline Thorman. At this stage, Arad was using unconventional "found" materials for his designs. His Rover chair, for example, combined a car seat with construction scaffolding.

In 1989, he founded Ron Arad Associates to cater to architectural and interior design clients. Through this agency, he gained commissions to work on two Belgo restaurants in London, a floor of Selfridges department store, and the foyer for the new Tel Aviv Opera House (1989–1994). Arad's furniture, in the meantime, was becoming more sculptural in appearance and increasingly successful commercially. His Big Easy armchair (1988) created an immediate impact and has been reproduced in numerous different materials, while his flexible Bookworm shelving (1993), marketed in colored PVC, was a huge bestseller.

EGMONT ARENS

AMERICAN, 1889–1966

Arens is best remembered as a prolific industrial designer. After studying at the universities of New Mexico and Chicago, he worked initially as a sports editor in Albuquerque. By 1917, he was in New York, where he ran a bookshop with a sideline in printing and publishing. Arens moved into design in 1929, when he joined the industrial styling division of Calkins & Holden. In 1935, he set up his own design company, where he was involved in projects ranging from furniture and toys to radios and boats. His most famous design was probably the Model K KitchenAid (1937), a food mixer that remained in production for many years.

JOSEPH-GABRIEL ARGY-ROUSSEAU

FRENCH, 1885–1953

An inventive glassmaker, Argy-Rousseau spearheaded the revival of *pâte-de-verre* (glass paste). This was an ancient technique combining powdered glass with striking coloring agents, which could then be molded in layers. After training at the École de Sèvres, Argy-Rousseau exhibited successfully at the Salon des Artistes Français before founding his own glassworks in 1921. Here, he produced a fine range of vases, lamps, and bowls in the fashionable Art Deco style. These were decorated with stylized flowers, animals, and insects, combined with geometrical motifs.

Occasionally, there were slight classical influences, which stemmed from his wife's Greek background. Gabriel adopted the first four letters of her name (Argyriadès), as a tribute to her influence.

▷ OTTO ARPKE

GERMAN, 1886–1943

A graphic designer, painter, and teacher, Arpke's earliest commercial designs were for Leunis & Chapman, a packaging firm, but in 1919, he set up his own company with Erich Ludwig Stahl. Together they produced a wide range of graphic material, ranging from banknotes and travel posters to the prospectus for the 1936 Olympic Games in Berlin.

Arpke and Stahl also created the decorations for two of the most famous German airships—the Hindenburg and the Graf Zeppelin II. Arpke's most celebrated design, though, was an eerie Expressionist poster for the horror movie *The Cabinet of Dr. Caligari* (1920).

CHARLES ROBERT ASHBEE

BRITISH, 1863–1942

A pioneering Arts and Crafts designer, Ashbee linked the movements in Great Britain and the US. He came from a wealthy background but was interested in social reform. In 1888, he became a cofounder of the Guild of Handicraft, an influential cooperative of craftsmen who participated in the Arts and Crafts exhibitions. Ashbee himself designed furniture and jewelry but is probably best remembered for his metalwork.

ADVERTISEMENT FOR LUFTHANSA AIRLINES, OTTO ARPKE, 1930

He specialized in elegant silver vessels, often decorated with cabochons, and with large, looped handles. Ashbee also became involved in printing. After William Morris's death, he acquired printing equipment from the Kelmscott Press and started up the Essex House Press (1898). He even designed a new typeface, called Endeavour, for it. Ashbee made an important contribution as an organizer. He was the dominant figure in the Guild of Handicraft, supervising its move to Chipping Campden in the Gloucestershire Cotswolds in 1902, and was also a key member of the Art Workers' Guild. In addition, his visits to the US in 1896 and 1900—when he met Frank Lloyd Wright in Chicago—helped raise the international profile of the movement. After the Guild of Handicraft closed, Ashbee worked as an architect and then lectured on English literature.

CAREER HIGHLIGHTS

1881 Cofounds the Guild of Handicraft
1902 Oversees the Guild's move to Chipping Campden

CARL AUBÖCK

AUSTRIAN, 1900–1957

Auböck was a designer of ingenious knickknacks. His father ran a workshop making small bronze figurines, and the young Auböck began his training there, before studying at the Academy of Fine Arts in Vienna. He spent two years at the Bauhaus in Weimar, supervised by Johannes Itten. Finally, in 1926, he took over his father's workshop. Auböck pursued a successful career as a painter,

but he continued making his whimsical—though also very useful—curios: a paperweight in the shape of a giant clothespin, a corkscrew attached to brass foot, a letter opener in the guise of a dolphin. Auböck's design won gold medals at the Milan Triennale of 1954.

GAE AULENTI

ITALIAN, 1927–2012

Trained as an architect, Aulenti specialized in creating highly original showrooms and museum spaces, most famously in her transformation of an old train station into the Musée d'Orsay in Paris. Her lighting and furniture designs were equally eye-catching and ingenious, typified by her Pipistrello (Bat) lamp, with its stylish combination of enameled black metal and white plastic. The shaft was telescopic, which meant that it could be used either as a desk lamp or as a floor lamp. Gae always took pride in this element of surprise: "When everyone reports that red is in fashion," she said, "I prefer to dress in green."

MARTÍN AZÚA

SPANISH/BASQUE, 1965–

An experimental designer and teacher, Azúa is best known for his highly inventive approach to ceramics, although he has also designed a backpack woven from chestnut wood, turning a rural Basque craft to urban use. He studied in Barcelona, specializing in architecture and installations. In 2004, he cofounded a design studio and combined this with teaching at the Elisava School of Design and Engineering.

In his experiments with ceramics, Azúa has explored the interaction between traditional crafts and nature. In 1998, he deposited porous white ceramics in a river, to endow the objects with a deep, natural stain and a thin coating of moss. Similarly, in his Vase with Stone project, simple clay vessels are shaped by the weight of large, smooth stones. The finished pieces exude an air of Zen-like tranquility.

CAREER HIGHLIGHTS

1999 Makes Rebotijo, a revamp of the traditional clay botijo water cooler
2004 Cofounds a design studio in Barcelona

POSTER FOR *VERTIGO*, SAUL BASS, 1958

B

OLOF BACKSTROM

FINNISH, 1922–1998

An industrial designer, Backstrom is best known for creating a very different take on a familiar household item—a pair of scissors. He began his career as an electrical engineer but changed course in the 1950s. He won two awards at the Milan Triennale (1957 and 1960), one for wooden kitchenware and the other for camping accessories. However, Backstrom's name is perhaps most closely associated with Fiskars, a Finnish company now based in Wisconsin. In the 1960s, he created a hugely successful range of tableware (Fiskamin), made out of brightly colored melamine. His most famous individual item, though, was an ergonomically designed pair of scissors with distinctive orange handles.

◁ SAUL BASS

AMERICAN, 1920–1996

Famed for his work in the movie industry, Bass was a successful graphic designer and art director. He trained as an animator at the Art Students League of New York, before moving to Los Angeles in 1946. There, he founded Saul Bass Associates, producing posters, trailers, and title sequences. His most important collaborations were with Otto Preminger, Billy Wilder, and Alfred Hitchcock. He acted as pictorial consultant for the latter, assisting with the famous shower scene in *Psycho*. Bass also created promotional material for Warner Communications, Continental Airlines, and the 1984 Los Angeles Olympics.

GEOFFREY BAXTER

BRITISH, 1922–1995

Baxter was an outstanding glass designer, representing the final flourish of the famous, old Whitefriars Glass firm. Precociously gifted, he entered Guildford School of Art at the age of 14. This was followed by a course at the new

Department of Industrial Glass at the Royal College of Art, in London. After graduating, Baxter was headhunted by Whitefriars Glass, joining it in 1954.

During this midcentury period, the market was dominated by sleek, Scandinavian styles, but by the 1960s, Baxter had developed a totally different approach. He created textured effects by lining glass molds with tree bark or nail heads. He also introduced zany new shapes, as in his iconic Banjo and Drunken Bricklayer vases.

HERBERT BAYER

AUSTRIAN, 1900–1985

A hugely versatile graphic designer, photographer, and painter, Bayer studied under Kandinsky at the Bauhaus and subsequently headed the Department of Typography and Advertising there. In 1923, he designed banknotes during Germany's period of hyperinflation. His plain, Constructivist style proved useful, as designs for new notes were required every few days.

Bayer emigrated to the US in 1938, spreading the gospel of the Bauhaus with a major exhibition at MoMA, New York. In 1946, he settled in Aspen, Colorado, teaching at the Aspen Institute and designing a number of buildings on the campus.

▷ LESTER BEALL

AMERICAN, 1903–1969

A graphic designer and photographer, Beall was noted for the clarity and strength of his images. He studied art in Chicago, producing murals for the 1934 World Fair, before setting up his design practice in New York. Beall incorporated avant-garde, European styles into his illustrations. Hints of Dada, Surrealism, and Constructivism can all be found in his work.

Beall's most memorable commission was a set of eight posters produced for the Rural Electrification Administration (1937–1941), one of the government's main initiatives during the Great Depression. In 1951, Beall transferred his design studio to a farm in Connecticut, but he remained as busy as ever. He became the first American graphic designer to be honored with an exhibition at MoMA.

MARTINE BEDIN

FRENCH, 1957–

Bedin made her name as a cofounder of the influential Memphis group, one of the early champions of postmodernism. She was trained as an architect but switched to design after moving to Italy. There, she exhibited an installation at the 1979 Milan Triennale and met Ettore Sottsass, who introduced her to the Memphis circle. Bedin produced her most famous design—her colorful Super Lamp—for their inaugural show in 1981. Consisting of six bulbs, mounted on a bright blue base with rubber wheels, it resembles a children's toy. This coincides with Bedin's aim of producing items of furniture "who were like friends."

CAREER HIGHLIGHTS

1979 Exhibits at the Milan Triennale
1981 Cofounds Memphis and creates Super Lamp for their first show

PETER BEHRENS

GERMAN, 1868–1940

A pioneering figure, Behrens is widely regarded as the first industrial designer. He was also a primary influence on Walter Gropius, Le Corbusier, and Ludwig Mies van der Rohe. He trained as a painter, joining the Munich Secession, but shifted toward applied art when he cofounded the United Workshops for Art and Craft in 1897. Two years later, Behrens joined an artists' colony in Darmstadt, where he designed and exhibited his first building. His Behrens House was a genuine *Gesamtkunstwerk*—he created all the furniture and accessories as well as the building itself.

Behrens took totality a stage further when he was employed by the electrical company, AEG, assuming responsibility for every aspect of their corporate identity. He designed their Turbine Factory (1908–1910) but also created individual products (clocks, fans, kettles) and a

POSTER FOR THE RURAL ELECTRIFICATION ADMINISTRATION, LESTER BEALL, 1937

broad range of promotional material (showrooms, brochures, store fronts). Toward the end of his career, Behrens taught architecture at the academies in Vienna and Berlin.

CAREER HIGHLIGHTS

1899 Designs the Behrens House inside and out, as a *Gesamtkunstwerk* (total work of art)
1906 Receives his first commission from AEG
1908 Starts designing the Turbine Factory

NORMAN BEL GEDDES

AMERICAN, 1893–1958

A flamboyant industrial and stage designer, Bel Geddes was fascinated by streamlining and visions of the future. He studied at the Art Institute of Chicago before establishing a reputation in the theater. Bel Geddes designed sets for the Metropolitan Opera in New York and costumes for Max Reinhardt but was also closely involved with the burgeoning movie industry, working with Cecil B. DeMille and D. W. Griffith. By the late 1920s, Bel Geddes's interest was shifting toward industrial design. He created furniture, radios, and stoves, while his chrome-plated Skyscraper cocktail service (1934) is an acknowledged classic of Art Deco design.

In the 1930s, Bel Geddes became increasingly interested in aerodynamic streamlining. He designed prototype cars for the Graham-Paige Company and lovingly created the Futurama exhibit in the General Motors Pavilion at the 1939 World's Fair in New York. Bel Geddes expanded upon this vision of the future in his books, *Horizons* (1932) and *Magic Motorways* (1940).

CAREER HIGHLIGHTS

1932 His book *Horizons* promotes streamlining as a design concept
1939 Shows the Futurama "building the world of tomorrow" installation at the New York World's Fair

MARIO BELLINI

ITALIAN, 1935–

With a phenomenally diverse career, Bellini has roamed from architecture to industrial and furniture design. He trained as an architect in Milan and is still based there. His numerous building projects include the Tokyo Design Center (1988–1992) and the Department of Islamic Arts at the Louvre (2005–2012), with its extraordinary golden canopy of tessellated glass triangles. In the interim, Bellini found time to design typewriters for Olivetti, lighting for Artemide and Flos, and the iconic CAB chairs for Cassina. As he remarked, "It feels natural to design a tray in the morning and to work on a huge building in the afternoon."

GERALD BENNEY

BRITISH, 1930–2008

A distinguished silversmith, Benney was the first British craftsman to hold four Royal Warrants simultaneously. He trained at the Royal College of Art in London and was initially influenced by the Arts and Crafts style. By the early 1960s, Benney had developed his trademark "bark finish"—a textured surface, achieved with the use of a bent hammer. He also added color to his work by reviving the almost-forgotten art of enameling. Benney had an impressive roster of royal and corporate clients, but he also worked for the mass market, producing a superb range of stainless steel cutlery (his Studio designs) for Viners.

LÉON BENOUVILLE

FRENCH, 1860–1903

An architectural engineer and furniture designer, Benouville worked in the Art Nouveau style. He came from an artistic background—his father was a successful academic painter and his brother was an architect. Trained under Anatole de Baudot, Benouville produced furniture that was designed to complement his building projects. He had his own company and exhibited regularly. His Artisan's Room caused a sensation at the Salon of 1903, and he was ranked among the greatest designers of the day at the Exposition Universelle of 1900 in Paris.

Benouville's furniture featured brass mounts and fruitwood marquetry inlays. He also had a taste for whimsical decoration, often adding carvings of praying mantises or beetles.

LUCIAN BERNHARD

GERMAN, 1883–1972

Active in many design fields, Bernhard is best known for his striking advertising posters. He was born Emil Kahn but adopted his working name in 1905. Influenced by the Beggarstaff Brothers,

Bernhard rapidly developed a distinctive style, using bright, contrasting colors and large, bold lettering. He also removed all extraneous details, creating the maximum impact for the object being advertised. Bernhard enhanced the effect even further by designing several new typefaces.

In 1923, Bernhard moved to New York, taking up teaching posts and cofounding the Contempora studio (1928), which produced designs for textiles, furniture, graphics, and interiors. In later life, Bernhard concentrated mainly on painting.

▽ HARRY BERTOIA

ITALIAN AMERICAN, 1915–1978

Bertoia enjoyed a successful career devoted to his two great passions—furniture and sculpture. Born in Italy, he moved to the US in 1930 and studied at the Cranbrook Academy of Art in Michigan. There, he met Charles Eames, collaborating with him on a series of chair designs from 1943 to 1946.

In 1950, Bertoia settled in Pennsylvania, where he worked for Knoll International. Here, he produced his most famous creation—the Diamond Chair, which won him the Designer of the Year award

(1955). Made out of wire mesh, the chair resembled a piece of sculpture, appearing different from every angle. Ironically, it proved so lucrative that Bertoia was able to give up furniture design and concentrate solely on his sculpture.

ALFONSO BIALETTI

ITALIAN, 1888–1970

The name of Bialetti will forever be linked with one of Italy's most famous products, an iconic coffee machine. Bialetti began his career as an engineer, opening a workshop making aluminum products in 1919. He switched to design in 1933, when he developed the Moka Express, a groundbreaking coffee maker that enabled Italians to enjoy real coffee at home. His inspiration came from the bathtubs used in steam laundries.

Assisted by the marketing skills of his son Renato, who introduced the company's mascot—a humorous, mustachioed man—Bialetti's business became a huge success. It is still mainly associated with coffee today, but it is also known for its Aeternum range of attractive kitchenware.

CAREER HIGHLIGHTS

1919 Starts a business making aluminum wares
1933 Produces the Moka Express stove-top coffee maker

FULVIO BIANCONI

ITALIAN, 1915–1996

Although he started his career as a prolific graphic artist, Bianconi is best remembered today as a designer of wonderfully imaginative glassware. His early aptitude for drawing cartoons led him to a career in graphic design. He produced hundreds of illustrations and book covers for major Italian publishers as well as advertising material for companies like Fiat and HMV. However, a meeting with the famous Murano glassmaker Paolo Venini offered him a new outlet for his talent. Bianconi's designs were both colorful and daring. He created figures from the Commedia dell'arte, such as Pezzato (spotted) glasses inspired by the Harlequin's costume, humorous pecking hens, and rippling Fazzoletto (handkerchief) vases.

LARGE DIAMOND CHAIR, HARRY BERTOIA, 1952

MAX BILL

SWISS, 1908–1994

In a varied career, Bill produced graphic and furniture designs, sculpture, and painting. He trained as a silversmith before a lecture by Le Corbusier prompted him to switch to architecture. He spent two years at the Dessau Bauhaus, where the teachings of Gropius had a profound influence on him, both in the clarity and simplicity of his designs, and in his role as an educator. Bill's somewhat austere approach is most evident from a famous series of watches that he designed for Junghans. He also cofounded the Ulm College of Design, serving as its first rector.

▷ PETER BLAKE

BRITISH, 1932–

Best known as a painter, Blake was a leading exponent of Pop art, but he is also a graphic designer and sculptor. He studied at Gravesend School of Art and the Royal College of Art in London. From the outset, he was fascinated by popular culture, particularly the burgeoning music scene in the Swinging Sixties. Blake was able to participate in this movement by designing a number of album covers. The iconic example was the Beatles' *Sergeant Pepper's Lonely Hearts Club Band*—for which he received a mere £200—but he has also produced covers for Paul Weller, Eric Clapton, Oasis, and The Who. Blake has equally been drawn to book illustration, most notably Dylan Thomas's *Under Milk Wood*.

THEODOR BOGLER

GERMAN, 1897–1968

A distinguished potter, Bogler was associated with the Bauhaus. He studied in the ceramics workshop there in the early 1920s and briefly managed the department. His best-known pieces from this period were combination teapots and coffee sets. These were modular designs, so they were eminently suitable for mass production.

Bogler left Weimar in 1924, to become director of the Velten-Vordamm Stoneware factory near Berlin. Always a devout man, he entered the Abbey of Maria Laach

ACADEMY, 1979, WATERCOLOR AND COLLAGE, PETER BLAKE, 1979

as a monk in 1927. He later ran the Ars Liturgica publishing company at the Abbey, although he also continued to produce ceramic designs for commercial concerns.

ANTONIO BONET

SPANISH, 1913–1989

This noted Catalan architect and furniture designer trained in Barcelona and also spent time in the offices of Josep Lluís Sert and Torres Clavé. Together, they joined GATCPAC, a group of Catalan architects who promoted Modernism. During the Spanish Civil War, Bonet moved to Paris, where he worked in the studio of Le Corbusier. There, he met

the Argentine architects Jorge Ferrari-Hardoy and Juan Kurchan. With political tensions in Europe mounting, Bonet decided to travel with them to Buenos Aires, where the trio worked together. Their most important furniture design was the BKF chair (named after their initials).

TORD BOONTJE

DUTCH, 1968–

A product designer, Boontje specializes in furniture, lighting, and glassware. He trained as an industrial designer at the Eindhoven Design Academy and the Royal College of Art in London. In 1996, he set up his first studio, working initially on glass vessels made from recycled

bottles and on his Rough-and-Ready furniture collection. There is a fairy-tale element in many of Boontje's designs. His Happy Ever After installation (2004) was full of romance, evoking a magical wonderland, although he did not entirely neglect the dark side. His Witches Kitchen range, for example, includes black, cauldron-like pots, ragged oven gloves, and serving forks that resemble wizened claws.

CAREER HIGHLIGHTS

1997 Creates Rough-and-Ready furniture

2001 Makes the Wednesday Collection of lights

2009 Appointed Professor and Head of Design Products at the Royal College of Art in London

▽ RONAN & ERWAN BOUROULLEC

FRENCH, 1971–, 1976–

The meteoric rise of the all-conquering Bouroullec brothers has transformed the design scene in France. Hailing from a sleepy village in Brittany, Ronan studied at the National School of Decorative Arts in Paris. One of his early ideas for a modular kitchen caught the eye of the president of Cappellini, who commissioned further designs. At this stage, Ronan enlisted the aid of his brother, who had just finished art school. "The user decides" has always been their motto. Their designs are highly adaptable, enabling the buyer to customize their purchases. This is typified by their ingenious Algae (2004), which consists of a series of plastic components

resembling seaweed. Available in various colors, these can be slotted together to form room dividers, curtains, canopies, or any other type of screen. Likewise, their double-faced Cloud shelving can be used horizontally or vertically, and clipped together to form "cloud lines."

▷ WILL BRADLEY

AMERICAN, 1868–1962

The son of a cartoonist, Bradley was an outstanding graphic artist, pioneering the Art Nouveau style in the US. He worked as a wood engraver in Michigan before opening a studio in Chicago. Here, he benefited from the poster craze that was sweeping the US. Bradley's style, with its flowing, sinuous lines, resembled the work of Aubrey Beardsley, but without the latter's decadent, sexual overtones. He exhibited at the World's Columbian Exposition and received commissions for book illustrations, magazine covers, and advertising posters. His designs for *The Chap Book* are typical examples. Later in his career, Bradley became an art director for William Randolph Hearst.

MARIANNE BRANDT

GERMAN, 1893–1983

Most women at the Bauhaus focused on pottery or textiles, but Brandt was one of the very few who excelled in the metalwork division. She entered the school in 1923, training under László Moholy-Nagy, and became deputy director of the metal workshop in 1928. Brandt briefly joined Walter Gropius in his Berlin practice, before her appointment as head of design at the Ruppelwerk Metalware Factory.

Brandt's most celebrated pieces are a starkly geometrical teapot and ashtray—masterpieces in the Bauhaus synthesis of functionalism and style—and her imaginative lighting designs, which were manufactured by Körting & Mathiesen. In her later years, Brandt also lectured on industrial design.

SIR FRANK BRANGWYN

BRITISH, 1867–1956

Probably best remembered today as a muralist, Brangwyn also designed furniture, ceramics, posters, and stained glass. Born in Belgium, the son of an architect who specialized in church furnishings, he was initially apprenticed to William Morris. In the 1890s, Brangwyn designed tapestries and carpets for Siegfried Bing's Art Nouveau gallery in Paris; during World War I, he produced recruitment posters that were so forceful that the Kaiser is said to have put a price on his head. Later in his career, Brangwyn designed pavilions for the Venice Biennale and dining rooms for the Canadian Pacific liner *Empress of Britain*.

ANDREA BRANZI

ITALIAN, 1938–

Branzi belongs to a generation of radical Italian theorists who challenged the values of modern design. He studied at the Florence School of Architecture and was a founding member of Archizoom Associates in 1966. This studio was run by an influential Anti-Design group, who rejected the elegance and conformism of Italian design. Instead, drawing on elements of Pop and kitsch, they demonstrated their experimental approach in projects like Dream Beds and No-Stop City. Branzi contributed to these and has since been involved with two other important, avant-garde groups, Studio Alchimia and Memphis. He has been awarded the Compasso d'Oro three times, in recognition of his achievements as a designer and theorist.

CLOUD SHELVING FOR CAPPELLINI,
RONAN & ERWAN BOUROULLEC, 2004

POSTER FOR VICTOR BICYCLES, WILL BRADLEY, 1896

PETER BREMERS

DUTCH, 1957–

Known for producing monumental cast-glass sculptures, Bremers sees them as his personal homage to "the awesome power and majesty of nature." He studied sculpture at the University of Fine Arts, Maastricht, followed by a course in three-dimensional design at the Jan van Eyck Akademie. Bremers decided to produce sculpted pieces that were suitable for either interior or exterior settings. He settled on glass as the best material for his purposes after watching the processes used by Andries Copier, a master glassmaker. Bremers's designs are especially effective when representing the extremes in nature. Accordingly, he based his Icebergs & Paraphernalia project on an expedition to Antarctica, while his Canyons and Deserts series reflects the searing temperatures he experienced in Arizona and New Mexico.

MARCEL BREUER

HUNGARIAN, 1902–1981

A leading member of the Bauhaus, Breuer was also a revolutionary figure in the field of furniture design. He was the son of a doctor, and he trained in the Weimar Bauhaus, later heading the furniture workshop, following the move to Dessau. Here, he achieved a major breakthrough with his Wassily chair (1925; named in honor of Wassily Kandinsky). Inspired by the handlebars on his bicycle, he tried using extruded tubular steel for the chair's frame. Light and easy to assemble, it proved an instant success and was much copied by other designers.

With the rise of the Nazis, Breuer emigrated to London in 1935. There, he designed the Isokon Long Chair—a remarkable recliner with no back legs—and the space-saving concept of nesting tables. With the outbreak of war, Breuer moved to the US, where he concentrated mainly on architecture. This included the UNESCO headquarters in Paris (1952–1958) and the Whitney Museum of American Art in New York (1963–1966).

CAREER HIGHLIGHTS

1925 Heads the Bauhaus furniture workshop and designs the iconic Wassily chair

1928 Opens an architectural studio in Berlin with Walter Gropius

1935 Emigrates to London and develops plywood furniture for Isokon

1952 Starts designing the UNESCO headquarters in Paris

ROGER BRODERS

FRENCH, 1883–1953

A talented graphic designer, Broders was best known for his delightful travel posters. He came from a Danish background (the family name was originally Brodersen), and both his parents were architects. After studying at the National School of the Decorative Arts in Paris, Broders began designing book illustrations and posters.

Aficionados of his work have focused in particular on a golden, 10-year period during the 1920s, when Broders was employed by the Paris-Lyon-Méditerranée (PLM) Railway Company. He produced 84 posters for them, extolling the virtues of the French Riviera. With their bright colors, simplified forms, and svelte figures in fashionable costumes, typically positioned in the left foreground, these carefree images epitomize the glamour of the Art Deco era.

CAREER HIGHLIGHTS

1920 Designs posters for Renault and Peugeot auto companies

1922 Meets the head of PLM and designs railroad advertising posters for the company for next 10 years

1928 Designs his best works, such as Saint Honoré les Bains

TEAR UP THE PLANS, CONTRIBUTION TO V&A'S 150TH ANNIVERSARY ALBUM, NEVILLE BRODY, 2007

◁ NEVILLE BRODY

BRITISH, 1957–

Frequently at the forefront of recent developments in graphic design and typography, Brody trained at the London College of Printing and began working on album covers and magazines. He produced artwork for Stiff Records and Rough Trade but made his name during his time at *The Face* (1981–1986). As art editor of this style magazine, Brody created a post-punk aesthetic that captured the mood of the times. He maximized its impact by designing a new typeface for the layouts. Since then, Brody has created many new fonts— he even produced one for the England soccer uniform, worn by the national team at the 2014 World Cup.

LEE BROOM

BRITISH, 1976–

A rising star in the field of product and interior design, Broom was born in Birmingham. He was a child actor with the Royal Shakespeare Company before training as a fashion designer at London's Central Saint Martins. While studying, Broom began designing bars and clubs with such success that interiors became the main focus of his interest. Here, his projects have ranged from the hospitality suites at Wembley Stadium to Louboutin's retail space at Harrods department store, while his first solo exhibition in Milan was set in a witty pastiche of a traditional British pub. Broom's initial furniture collections Neo Neon (2007) and Rough Diamond (2008) were received with great acclaim, while his showroom, Electra House in Shoreditch, London, has become a mecca for fashion seekers.

CARLO BUGATTI

ITALIAN, 1856–1940

A designer of silver, textiles, ceramics, and interiors, Bugatti is renowned above all for his extraordinarily original furniture. He studied fine art in Milan and Paris but developed his interest in furniture when designing a bedroom suite for his sister in 1880. Bugatti concocted a heady cocktail of different styles (Moorish, oriental, Gothic), combining them with unusual materials (vellum, ivory, copper) to produce his unique creations.

His undoubted masterpiece is the Cobra chair, which formed part of the Snail Room, a delightfully eccentric installation that he showed at the International Exhibition of Decorative Art in Turin (1902). Bugatti's son and grandson also found fame with their automobile designs.

RENÉ BUTHAUD

FRENCH, 1886–1986

A painter and graphic designer, Buthaud is mainly remembered for his superb Art Deco ceramics. He trained as an artist at the École des Beaux-Arts in Bordeaux, working initially as a painter and engraver before switching to ceramics.

Buthaud liked to create unusual surface effects, such as craquelure, lusters, and so-called snakeskin. His imagery was even more distinctive—he preferred to portray large, curvaceous nudes that were inspired partly by neoclassical models and partly by African sculpture. Buthaud found it easy to transfer his designs from one medium to another, and similar nudes can be found on his posters advertising Salon exhibitions or the local wine industry.

MARGARET CALVERT

BRITISH, 1936–

A highly regarded graphic designer, typographer, and teacher, Calvert, together with Jock Kinneir, is responsible for most of the signage still on Britain's roads today. Born in South Africa, she arrived in the UK in 1950. She was studying printmaking and illustration at Chelsea School of Art when Kinneir, a visiting instructor, recruited her to work as his assistant.

Among other creations, Calvert designed new pictograms for road signs, sometimes drawing on her own experiences. Her Schoolchildren Crossing sign, for example, was modeled on an old photograph of herself. She also designed the eponymous Calvert font, which is used on the metro system in Newcastle and, in her later years, taught at the Royal College of Art.

HUMBERTO & FERNANDO CAMPANA

BRAZILIAN, 1953–, 1961–

"Brazil is our great fountain of inspiration," proclaim the Campana brothers. Their furniture has caused a sensation wherever it has been shown, which is all the more impressive given that they fell into designing almost by accident. Humberto trained as a lawyer but gave it up to become a sculptor, while his younger brother Fernando studied to be an architect. They started experimenting with small objects, such as photo frames, in the early 1980s and held their first exhibition at the Museum in São Paolo in 1988. Both their inspiration and their materials come from the detritus of Brazilian street life. The Favela chair, composed of scraps of pinewood, echoes the shantytowns of Rio, while their Sushi chairs are made from strips of carpet underlay and remnants.

▷ PIERRE CARDIN

FRENCH, 1922–

One of France's most famous fashion designers, Cardin was born in Italy, but he was apprenticed to a tailor in Vichy at the age of 14. After World War II, he moved to Paris, working at the fashion houses of Paquin and Schiaparelli. Cardin's own designs were shown in Jean Cocteau's film *Beauty and the Beast* (1946) and, through the director, he was introduced to Christian Dior, assisting in the creation of his New Look.

Cardin launched his own fashion house in 1950. His bold creations have often caused a stir, none more so than his Space Age range in the 1960s, though the fashion world was equally shocked by his decision to make ready-to-wear lines. Over the years, Cardin's studio has grown into an empire, designing watches, perfume, luggage, and furniture.

MATTHEW CARTER

BRITISH, 1937–

The son of a typographer, book designer, and type historian, Carter has pioneered the design of fonts for use on screen. He spent a year in the type foundry at Enschedé in Haarlem, the Netherlands. Although making type by hand was becoming obsolete, the training imbued Carter with a sense of being an artisan so that he responds to the unique needs of each commission rather than imposing his personal stamp on a design.

With many typefaces to his name—Shelley Script (1972), Galliard and Bell Centennial (1978), and more recently, Miller (1997) and Yale (2004), to name but a few—Carter is distinguished by designing Verdana for Microsoft in 1994 in response to the need for a font that could be easily viewed on screen.

ACHILLE & PIER GIACOMO CASTIGLIONI

ITALIAN, 1918–2002, 1913–1968

The Castiglioni brothers were masters of the Italian Modernist movement, bringing a fresh approach to the design of furniture and lighting. All three brothers trained as architects at Milan Polytechnic. Pier Giacomo and Livio (1911–1979) set up a design studio in 1938, which Achille joined later. They achieved early success with a radio for Phonola, before Livio left the partnership in 1952. In the following years, the two remaining brothers built up a reputation for highly original, minimalist designs, which often had a humorous touch. This is typified by their most famous creation, the Mezzadro stool (1957), which consisted of a tractor seat perched on top of a cantilevered steel bar. This offered the same kind of springy support as for a bumpy tractor ride through a muddy field.

Achille continued the firm alone after Pier Giacomo's death. He was a founding member of the Association of Italian Designers and also taught industrial design at the Turin Polytechnic. His studio is now a museum.

CAREER HIGHLIGHTS

1957 Design the Mezzadro stool
1962 Create the Taccia table lamp and the Arco and Toio standard lamps
1988 Achille designs the Taraxacum hanging lamp

WENDELL CASTLE

AMERICAN, 1932–2018

The sumptuous creations of Wendell Castle have blurred the boundary between art and design. Regularly displayed in galleries, they resemble sculpture as much as furniture. Castle studied industrial design and sculpture at

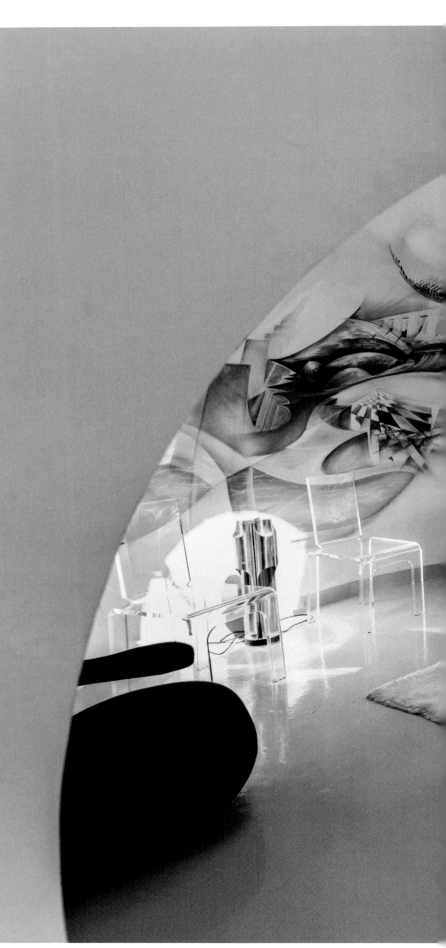

PIERRE CARDIN'S HOUSE IN SOUTHERN FRANCE, ANTTI LOVAG, 1990

CLOSE-UP OF FIORI DI COMO GLASS CHANDELIER INSTALLATION, BELLAGIO LOBBY CEILING, LAS VEGAS, DALE CHIHULY, 1998

the University of Kansas, before moving to New York to teach at the Rochester Institute of Technology. He developed new techniques for laminating wood, which gave his early pieces a quirky, organic appearance, though his work in molded plastic and fiberglass is probably even better known. Castle's celebrated Molar chairs and Cloud shelving have sold very well but could equally pass for Pop art sculpture. Over the years, Castle won many honors, the most apt perhaps being his Visionary of the American Craft Movement award (1994).

GEORGE CAWARDINE

BRITISH, 1887–1947

Cawardine was a car designer, though he is far better known for creating an iconic 20th-century item—the Anglepoise® lamp. He was born in Bath, serving his apprenticeship there at the Whiting Auto Works. Cawardine considered becoming a missionary in China but joined the Horstmann Car Company instead. By 1916, he was chief designer at this successful firm, which produced cars that raced at Brooklands. In 1924, Cawardine set up his own business, designing suspension systems, but the firm folded, and he became a freelance consulting engineer. He patented several versions of the lamp between 1931 and 1934 but eventually sold the rights to Jacob Jacobsen in 1937. The design went on to become a worldwide bestseller.

SERGE CHERMAYEFF

RUSSIAN, 1900–1996

A pivotal figure of Art Deco, Chermayeff was a prolific architect and furniture designer. He trained as a journalist but changed course and joined the furniture manufacturers Waring & Gillow. His designs featured the most fashionable materials—black glass, silver cellulose, and Macassar ebony. By the early 1930s, Chermayeff was a practicing architect, creating interiors for the BBC and, in partnership with Erich Mendelsohn, the De La Warr Pavilion in Bexhill (1934–1935), one of the landmark examples of Modernist architecture. In 1939, he emigrated to the US, where he taught architecture at Harvard and Yale and became president of the Chicago Institute of Design.

ALBERT CHEURET

FRENCH, 1884–1966

While Cheuret was a designer of furniture and clocks, he is chiefly known for his exotic Art Deco lighting. He trained as a sculptor under Jacques Perrin and Georges Lemaire and was already exhibiting at the Paris Salon by 1907. Cheuret made a particular splash at the 1925 Paris Exposition Internationale, when he displayed furniture, lighting, and small bronze sculptures.

Cheuret's modeling skills were certainly much in evidence in his sconces, lamps, and chandeliers, which often featured naturalistic representations of birds— usually swans, cranes, or herons. He was also swept up in the craze for Egyptian motifs that followed the discovery of Tutankhamen's tomb in 1922 and made several bronze clocks in the shape of a pharaoh's headdress.

◁ DALE CHIHULY

AMERICAN, 1941–

The most famous glass artist working today, Chihuly studied at the University of Washington and the Rhode Island School of Design, where he taught for several years. A visit to the Venini glass factory at Murano, near Venice, fired his enthusiasm still further. There, Chihuly witnessed the team system of blowing glass—a method he adopted after losing the sight in one eye. It also helped him create his huge, multipart glass sculptures. These are inspired by natural phenomena, such as icicles, plant forms, and sea anemones, as well as Navajo blanket patterns. Chihuly often designed his "chandeliers" as ceiling fixtures, although he also enjoys exhibiting them as installations in botanical settings. In 1996, he installed chandeliers around the city of Venice, lit by natural light, as well as glass forms that he floated along the canals, in an international collaboration.

▷ ROMAN CIESLEWICZ

POLISH-FRENCH, 1930–1996

A remarkable graphic designer, Cieslewicz worked in the West at the height of the Cold War. After studying at the Academy of Fine Arts in Cracow, he began producing posters for the movie industry and government agencies. In 1963,

Cieslewicz moved to Paris, where he divided his time between commercial work for *Vogue* and *Elle* and more challenging material for the arts magazine, *Opus International*. He described himself as a "visual journalist," anxious to use his disturbing images to provide wry commentaries on social and political issues. Cieslewicz was wary of relying on computers, preferring to use photomontage and bold, expressive lettering as the basis for his designs.

CLARICE CLIFF

BRITISH, 1899–1972

The most popular ceramics designer of her time, Cliff had a vibrant style that epitomizes the Jazz Age. At the age of 13, she began working as an apprentice enameler at a local pottery. Then, in 1916, she moved to Burslem, joining the firm of A. J. Wilkinson as a lithographer. Cliff's skills were soon noticed, and she was given her own studio within the company. In 1927, the first major collection of her designs was launched as Bizarre Ware. Salespeople were taken aback by the gaudy colors and the bold, geometric patterns, but the public loved them.

By 1930, Cliff had been promoted to art director, supervising more than a thousand workers, including her all-female team of painters, nicknamed the Bizarre Girls. Throughout the decade, Cliff produced delightful tableware with evocative names, such as Delicia, Biarritz, and Fantasque. She also designed ceramic wall masks and her charming Age of Jazz figurines—a set of five dancing couples, intended for display around a radio.

POSTER ADVERTISING *THE YEAR OF THE DANCE*, ROMAN CIESLEWICZ, 1988

WELLS WINTEMUTE COATES

CANADIAN, 1895–1958

A remarkable architect and designer, Coates was a pioneer of Modernism in Britain. He was born in Tokyo, the son of a Canadian missionary, and he trained as an engineer. Moving to London, he began designing store fixtures and interiors.

In 1931, Coates cofounded Isokon, a company devoted to housing and furniture design. This, in turn, spawned his crowning achievement, the Isokon Building (1934; also known as the Lawn Road Flats). The building was the British equivalent of Le Corbusier's "machine for living in": small, modular apartments with simple, built-in plywood furniture. In the early days, the Isokon Building's inhabitants included several Bauhaus exiles (Walter Gropius, Marcel Breuer, László Moholy-Nagy), a clutch of Soviet agents, and the crime novelist Agatha Christie. Coates also designed Bakelite radios for Ekco, including the famous circular Ekco AD65 (1934).

LUIGI COLANI

GERMAN, 1928–2019

A flamboyant industrial designer, Colani specialized in furniture and automobiles. He studied sculpture in Berlin before moving to Paris to take a course in aerodynamics at the Sorbonne. In the 1950s, Colani concentrated on car design, working mainly for Fiat and BMW. In the following decade, he extended his interest to furniture and household items. Here, Colani demonstrated his taste for sleek, biomorphic forms. This is particularly evident in the sensual outlines of his celebrated Drop teapot (1971), his space-age lamps, and his extraordinary Pegasus piano (1997), which resembles a section of one of his sports-car designs.

COTE D'AZURE FURNISHING FABRIC, SUSAN COLLIER, MADE 1983

◁ SUSAN COLLIER

BRITISH, 1938–2011

Working largely in partnership with her sister, Sarah Campbell, Collier was an inspirational textile designer. A self-taught painter, she launched her career in 1961, when Liberty bought six of her designs. By 1968, she was a permanent member of the company's staff, becoming its design and color consultant three years later. In 1977, the sisters formed Collier Campbell as an independent studio. Rather than relying on computers, both preferred to paint their patterns by hand, even leaving their brushstrokes visible in the finished designs. Ranging from the Matisse-inspired Cote d'Azure to the award-winning Six Views, these can be found on clothes, bed linen, and a variety of home furnishings.

EDWARD COLONNA

GERMAN, 1862–1948

With a varied career as a designer, Colonna is best known for creating fine Art Nouveau jewelry. He was born in Germany and trained as an architect in Brussels before moving to New York, where he worked for Louis Tiffany. While in the US, Colonna became caught up in the railroad boom and designed train cars for the Canadian Pacific Railway. He also wrote a small but influential book, *Essay on Broom Corn* (1887), explaining how his designs were inspired by a close observation of nature. This accords well with the sinuous, plantlike decoration on Colonna's metalwork and jewelry. He produced much of this for Siegfried Bing, culminating in his prestigious display at the 1900 Exposition Universelle in Paris.

SIR TERENCE CONRAN

BRITISH, 1931–2020

The most influential figure in modern British design, Conran's wide-ranging interests included architecture, publishing, restaurants, and interior design. He studied textile design at the Central School of Arts & Crafts, before founding the Conran Design Group in 1956. By this stage, he had already begun building his business empire. He had designed furniture with Eduardo Paolozzi, established Conran Fabrics, and opened his first restaurant. His most decisive step, though, came in 1964, when he launched his first Habitat shop. This proved an instant success, fulfilling Conran's mission to bring good design and styling into the British home.

Habitat expanded rapidly, becoming an international chain. Conran, meanwhile, looked for other ways to educate the public. He founded Octopus Books, showcasing his interest in cookery, gardening, and interior design and embarked on his longstanding ambition to create a permanent museum. The Boilerhouse Gallery (1981–1986) at the Victoria & Albert Museum provided an interim solution, before the Design Museum opened in 1989.

CAREER HIGHLIGHTS

1956 Founds the Conran Design Group

1964 Launches the first Habitat shop in London

1989 Opens Design Museum in London

▷ SUSIE COOPER

BRITISH, 1902–1995

A superb designer of ceramics, Cooper was one of the finest exponents of the Art Deco style. She studied at the Burslem School of Art and began working for a local potter, A. E. Gray. She established her own company in 1929, producing fine, hand-painted earthenware. Her brightly colored geometric patterns, typified by her Moon and Mountain range, were an instant hit.

Cooper also designed her own shapes, notably in her Curlew, Kestrel, and Quail ranges, and began to experiment with lithograph patterns. She produced tableware for Imperial Airways, and her Lion and Unicorn design was selected for the Royal Pavilion at the Festival of Britain, but her firm was eventually bought out by Wedgwood.

HANS CORAY

SWISS, 1906–1991

A sculptor, furniture designer, and teacher, Coray found fame with an award-winning chair. He was raised in an artistic environment in Zurich, gaining a doctorate in languages. Coray worked initially as a teacher but broadened his interests to include psychology, graphology, and astrology. From around 1930, he also began to design furniture. Although he was entirely self-taught, he won a prestigious competition in 1939 for a lightweight outdoor chair. Made from aluminum and perforated steel, and weighing a mere 6½ lb (3 kg), his Landi chair became a design classic (Landi was the nickname of the exhibition—the *Schweizerische Landesausstellung*). Coray continued to design furniture and trade-fair displays, but he never again reached these heights.

SUSIE COOPER PLATE, *c.* 1934

LE CORBUSIER

SWISS, 1887–1965

Probably the most influential architect of the 20th century, as well as a founding father of Modernism, Le Corbusier was born Charles-Édouard Jeanneret. He began training as a watch engraver then switched to architecture. He traveled widely in his youth, developing his radical theories about building and design.

Le Corbusier waged a war against style and decoration, developing his famous maxim: "A house is a machine for living in." He held similar ideas about the applied arts, setting these out in his publication, *L'Art Décoratif d'Aujourd'hui* (The Decorative Art of Today, 1925). Le Corbusier designed relatively little furniture, the most important pieces being three chairs, which he produced in collaboration with Charlotte Perriand— the B301 Grand Confort (Great Comfort) armchair, the B302 swivel chair, and the B306 chaise longue. These were exhibited in 1929 and have since become design classics. Perriand confirmed that their priority was to make the furniture "available to all, mass-produced and affordable."

LISBET DÆHLIN

DANISH, 1922–2012

A highly influential ceramics designer, Dæhlin raised the artistic profile of pottery in her adopted homeland. She studied at the School of Arts and Crafts (now the Danish Design School) in Copenhagen but spent most of her career in Norway. She settled there in 1949, working initially as an assistant to the sculptor Svein Visted.

Dæhlin experimented with new stoneware techniques, which were received enthusiastically when the pair exhibited together in 1950. She later moved to Oslo, concentrating on a repertoire of simple, everyday objects—

Batterie de Cuisine   designed by Lucienne Day®   twentytwentyone

Batterie de Cuisine

made in Ireland

BATTERIE DE CUISINE DISH TOWEL, LUCIENNE DAY, 1954

pitchers, vases, teapots—but endowing them with timeless elegance. Dæhlin also created large terra-cotta reliefs for public buildings, including the Norges Bank, the Aker Hospital, and the Parliament buildings in Oslo.

AUGUSTE & ANTONIN DAUM

FRENCH, 1853–1909, 1864–1930

Daum Frères became the leading art glass company in France after the death of Émile Gallé, enjoying its golden age during the Art Nouveau period. Based in Nancy, the firm was originally acquired in 1878 by the brothers' father, Jean Daum, a notary, as payment for an outstanding debt. Initially, it made functional tableware, but under the stewardship of Jean's sons, the emphasis shifted to decorative pieces. Gallé's success at the 1900 Exposition Universelle in Paris proved a genuine inspiration. The brothers formed Daum Frères in the same year, assembling an excellent team of artists, which included Henri Bergé, Jacques Gruber, and Amalric Walter.

Using a wide variety of techniques (cameo, acid-etching, engraving, molding, and enameling), Daum produced a stunning range of bowls, vases, and table lamps in soft, fall colors. These were decorated with swirling floral patterns and insects. The art department was forced to close during World War I but reopened afterward and adapted successfully to the chunkier Art Deco style.

CAREER HIGHLIGHTS

1889 Form Daum Frères
1900 Win the Grand Prix at the Exposition Universelle in Paris
1904 Émile Gallé dies, and Daum Frères dominates the glass industry until World War I

◁ LUCIENNE & ROBIN DAY

BRITISH, 1917–2010, 1915–2010

In their different ways, this celebrated couple revitalized British design after World War II. Robin studied initially at the art school in High Wycombe before moving on to the Royal College of Art in London. The couple met at a dance there in 1940 and married two years later. Throughout their working lives, they shared a studio, though they generally

POLAR TABLE, 1984; KRISTALL TABLE 1981; FLAMINGO TABLE, 1983, MICHELE DE LUCCHI

worked on separate projects. Robin specialized in furniture, making his mark with low-cost, functional seating and storage units. He explored the possibilities of modern materials, however, using tubular steel for his seats at the newly built Gatwick Airport (1958). He also pioneered the use of plastics, creating a polypropylene stacking chair (1963) that was a prodigious bestseller.

Lucienne, meanwhile, concentrated on textiles. She began by working on wallpaper and dress patterns but made her breakthrough with a design for furnishing fabrics. Calyx (1950)—so called because of its resemblance to spindly flower stems—was actually a colorful, abstract pattern. It created a sensation at the Festival of Britain, won a string of awards, and became the most popular textile design of the period.

CAREER HIGHLIGHTS

1950 Lucienne designs the Calyx pattern
1963 Robin designs his bestselling plastic stacking chair

△ MICHELE DE LUCCHI

ITALIAN, 1951–

An avant-garde furniture and lighting designer, De Lucchi has links to several influential anti-design groups. He trained as an architect at the University of Florence, working initially as a teacher. In 1973, he founded Cavart, a short-lived architectural association, but his links with two experimental groups—Studio Alchimia and Memphis—proved far more productive. For the latter, he created some of his most colorful and eye-catching designs. These include the Sinvola ceiling light (1979), which resembles a pincushion, and the extraordinary Kristall table (1981). Alongside these tours de force, De Lucchi produced more conventional designs, among them the Tolomeo office lamp (1986), which was a huge bestseller. He has also designed buildings, including the Milan Triennial Exhibition Palace in Rome and the Neues Museum in Berlin.

JONATHAN DE PAS

ITALIAN, 1932–1991

Together with Donato D'Urbino and Paolo Lomazzi, De Pas created a series of iconic pieces that are now regarded as prime examples of Pop culture. The trio met as students at Milan Polytechnic, forming their partnership in 1966. They operated as architects, town-planning consultants, and industrial designers but made their name with dramatic modular furniture. Their most celebrated creation was Blow (1967), the first inflatable chair to be mass-produced. Inspired by inflatable boats and made out of transparent PVC foil, it captured the fun, throwaway spirit of the times. It also forced trials for a new production process, since the foil had to be welded electronically to retain the transparency of the PVC. The group went on to make a splash with Joe (1970), an armchair in the shape of a giant baseball glove, designed as a tribute to Joe DiMaggio.

LAURA DE SANTILLANA

ITALIAN, 1955–2019

A highly talented glass designer, de Santillana carried on a proud family tradition in the field. She was born in Venice, the granddaughter of Paolo Venini, who established a celebrated glassworks in Murano in 1921. De Santillana studied at the School of Visual Arts in New York, while also working as a graphic designer in the studio of the Vignelli Associates (Massimo Vignelli had been a designer for the Venini company). She began creating glass from an early age. Her Four Seasons (1976)—a limited-edition set of blown glass plates—was acquired by the Corning Museum of Glass in New York.

CAREER HIGHLIGHTS

1976 Designs Four Seasons plates
2014 Exhibition of her and her brother Alessandro Diaz's work opens on the island of San Giorgio Maggiore in Venice

▽ SONIA DELAUNAY

RUSSIAN, 1885–1979

An avant-garde painter, graphic artist, and textile designer, Delaunay was born Sonia Stern. She married the artist Robert Delaunay in 1910, after settling in Paris. Both experimented with the latest trends in abstract painting and the notion of simultaneity, in which contrasting colors are thought to take on their own meaning and movement, and Sonia also explored these ideas in her fashion and textile designs. She created Simultaneous dresses and Poem dresses, which she sold through Casa Sonia, a shop that she opened in Madrid. She also had prestigious clients, such as Nancy Cunard and Gloria Swanson. Delaunay used her brightly colored, geometric designs for quilts, blankets, lampshades, curtains, advertising posters, and even her car (see below). She also displayed her wares in a Simultaneous boutique at the Paris Exposition Internationale of 1925.

CHRISTIAN DELL

GERMAN, 1893–1974

Dell trained as a silversmith and was master of the metal workshop at the Bauhaus during its early phase in Weimar. After leaving the Bauhaus in 1925, he ran the metalwork department at Frankfurt Art School, where he specialized in designing Bakelite lamps, many of which were mass-produced by local factories. Typical examples of his work include the Rondella-Polo table lamp (1927) and the Idell line of goods, which was produced by Kaiser & Co. Dell was later removed from his post by the Nazis and subsequently opened a jewelry shop in Wiesbaden (1948), which he managed until 1955.

DONALD DESKEY

AMERICAN, 1894–1989

A pioneering figure of industrial design, Deskey was one of the stars of American Art Deco. Trained as a painter and architect, he was strongly influenced by the designs exhibited at the 1925 Exposition Internationale in Paris. He began working in advertising and subsequently founded his own design company. Deskey secured his reputation with the opulent interiors he designed for the Radio City Music Hall in New York (1931–1934). With its sleek furnishings made out of aluminum, Bakelite, and cherry wood, this was the last word in modernity. Deskey's taste for ingenious, abstract designs is most evident in his desk lamps and textiles.

▷ TOM DIXON

BRITISH, 1959–

Once considered the *enfant terrible* of the British design scene, Dixon is now acknowledged as one of its leading lights. Born in Sfax, Tunisia, he studied briefly at the Chelsea School of Art but soon

SONIA DELAUNAY AND HER MATCHING CITROËN B12, 1925

dropped out, working initially as a musician and party planner. Dixon's switch to design was largely accidental. He taught himself welding, in order to fix his motorcycle, and started making furniture from scrap metal. An early kitchen chair, for example, was made from recycled frying pans. Encouraged by the positive reaction to these, he cofounded the Creative Salvage collective and later opened a shop called Space in London's Notting Hill.

Dixon's commercial breakthrough came in the late 1980s, when Cappellini marketed his S-chair and Bird lounger. His stock rose even further when he was appointed head of design at Habitat and creative director of Artek, the firm that Alvar Aalto had founded in 1935. Dixon continued to create his own designs while working at these prestigious companies.

CHRISTOPHER DRESSER

BRITISH, 1834–1904

A hugely influential figure, Dresser has often been described as Britain's first industrial designer. Born in Glasgow, he studied at the Government School of Design in London. He was an avid botanist, lecturing on this subject for a time and drawing inspiration from it for his own designs. Some of these were shown at the International Exhibition of 1862 in London. Here, Dresser was particularly impressed by the exhibits from Japan. He visited the country in 1876 and 1877 and subsequently set up a firm, Dresser & Holme, which traded in Oriental goods. In the meantime, he had expounded his own theories about design in a series of influential books, starting with *The Art of Decorative Design* (1862).

Dresser's designs were remarkably varied. He produced furniture, ceramics, wallpaper, glass, and textiles. His interest in botany and Japan is often reflected in these items, but it is his distinctive metalwork that has stood the test of time. Its stark, geometric forms prefigure the Bauhaus style and Modernism.

HENRY DREYFUSS

AMERICAN, 1903–1972

A versatile industrial designer and writer, Dreyfuss is best known for promoting the cause of ergonomics. He was born in New York and began an apprenticeship with Norman Bel Geddes, planning to

become a stage designer. By the late 1920s, he had switched to industrial design, opening his consultancy in 1929. In the same year, he won a Telephone of the Future competition, which earned him a lucrative contract with Bell Telephone Laboratories. Dreyfuss designed several telephones for them, most notably the revolutionary Model 300 (1937)—the first telephone to house the mouthpiece and receiver in a single unit. This paved the way for a phenomenal variety of commissions. Over the years, Dreyfuss designed tractors, alarm clocks, washing machines, vacuum cleaners, Polaroid cameras, and even two trains.

Dreyfuss ascribed his success to his commitment to ergonomics. In the first of his books, *Designing for People* (1955), he stressed the importance of using anthropometrics (human measurements) when creating designs. In 1965, he was made the first president of the Industrial Designers Society of America.

CAREER HIGHLIGHTS

1929 Opens an industrial design consultancy in New York
1937 Designs the Model 300 single-unit telephone
1955 Publishes *Designing for People*, making the case for ergonomics

RAOUL DUFY

FRENCH, 1877–1953

One of the Fauvist group of painters, who were known for their bright, pure colors, flattened perspective, and simplified detail, Dufy applied his artistic principles to lively theater designs, ceramics, and tapestries. He also worked as a printmaker and illustrator, creating vibrant sketches that he turned into etchings and lithographs in the 1920s and 1930s.

JAMES DYSON

BRITISH, 1947–

Inventive and original, Dyson's designs are so successful that his own name has become synonymous with one of them. He trained in London at the Byam Shaw School of Art and the Royal College of Art, codesigning his first product—the Sea Truck—while he was still a student. In 1970, Dyson made his name with the Ballbarrow (an upgraded wheelbarrow), but his most significant invention was the DC01, his revolutionary vacuum cleaner.

PYLON CHAIR, TOM DIXON, 1992

With its cyclonic suction process, dispensing with the need for a bag, the "Dyson" became an international bestseller. Nothing has stemmed his flow of inspiration. His more recent inventions have included the Dyson Airblade (a hand dryer), an Air Multiplier (a fan without blades), and a robotic vacuum cleaner.

Dyson is fully committed to the future of design in Britain. He is a member of the Design Council and a trustee of the Design Museum. He also set up the James Dyson Foundation and Award, to encourage and support the next generation of designers.

CAREER HIGHLIGHTS

1993 Releases the DC01 vacuum cleaner
2002 Sets up the James Dyson Foundation
2009 Launches the Air Multiplier fan
2015 Produces the DC50 Multi Floor vacuum cleaner

CHARLES & RAY EAMES

AMERICAN, 1907–1978, 1912–1988

A pundit at the *Washington Post* once remarked that this multitalented couple "changed how the 20th century sat down." Charles and Ray Eames achieved this with an impressive range of seating designs, which made pioneering use of new materials.

The pair met at the Cranbrook Academy of Art in 1940 and married the following year. Up until then, Charles had been a practicing architect, before heading the Experimental Design Department at Cranbrook. Ray, meanwhile, had trained as an artist. After marrying, the couple relocated to Los Angeles and began producing stretchers made of molded plywood for the US Navy. After the war, they designed furniture from the same material, fulfilling their ambition "to get the most of the best, to the greatest number of people, for the least."

Continuing to experiment, the couple produced their iconic DAR armchair (Dining Armchair Rod, c. 1948), made out of fiberglass-reinforced plastic. Hugely influential, this was the first plastic chair ever to go into mass production.

CAREER HIGHLIGHTS

1941   Charles and Ray marry
1945   Create the DCM (Dining Chair Metal) and the LCW (Lounge Chair Wood)
1949   Construct their home, Case Study House No. 8, a steel and glass cube on stilts
1953   Design the Hang-It-All-coat rack

EVA ENGLUND

SWEDISH, 1937–1998

One of the finest Swedish designers of the 20th century, Englund was best known for the dreamlike beauty of her Graal (Holy Grail) glassware. She trained initially at the Konstfackskolan (now the College of Arts) in Stockholm, continuing her studies at the Capellagården crafts school. In 1964, Englund produced the Carolina service and the colorful Malakit range for the Pukeberg Glassworks. Then, in 1974, she began designing for the long-established firm of Orrefors. Here, Englund produced her celebrated Graal vases. In these, mysterious faces seem to float inside a glass casing. Englund liked to depict mythical figures, such as Medea and the Sea Maid, as well as more enigmatic concepts, including Duality or Breathtaking.

▽ LUCIAN ERCOLANI

ITALIAN-BRITISH, 1888–1976

With his cost-conscious designs, Ercolani revitalized the British furniture industry in the drab postwar years. Born in Tuscany, he moved to London as a child and studied at the Shoreditch Technical Institute. Ercolani worked for a time in the joinery department of the Salvation Army, setting up his own firm only in 1920. Later known as Ercol, this company achieved its greatest success at the end of World War II, when Ercolani devised a method for mass-producing bentwood Windsor chairs that were affordable and attractive. The results were exhibited to acclaim at the Britain Can Make It exhibition (1946) and the Festival of Britain (1951).

GERMANO FACETTI

ITALIAN, 1926–2006

A remarkable graphic designer, Facetti was best known for transforming the appearance of Penguin Books. Born in Milan, he survived imprisonment in a Nazi concentration camp before joining BBPR, an architectural practice. There, he met and married the English architect Mary Crittall. In 1950, the couple settled in London, where Facetti studied typography and designed a showroom for Olivetti and a stage set for the Royal Court. Eventually, he specialized in publishing, becoming the art director of Penguin Books in 1960. Facetti overhauled the image of the company, altering the policy on book covers to create a much more contemporary, visual approach. He remained at Penguin until 1972, when he returned to work in Italy.

CAREER HIGHLIGHTS

1950   Moves to London
1960   Becomes art director of Penguin Books

JORGE FERRARI HARDOY

ARGENTINE, 1914–1977

A Modernist architect, town planner, and furniture designer, Ferrari Hardoy trained as an architect in Buenos Aires before traveling to Paris to study under Le Corbusier. On his return to Argentina in 1938, Ferrari Hardoy founded the Grupo Austral with Antonio Bonet and Juan Kurchan. They enjoyed their greatest success the same year with the Butterfly (BKF) chair. Made of two tubular steel rods and a detachable leather sling, this incredibly light chair was an instant success. It was shown at the third Salon de Artistas Decoradores (1940) in Buenos Aires, when one copy was acquired for MoMA in New York and another for Frank Lloyd Wright's Fallingwater.

VITTORIO FERRO

ITALIAN, 1932–2012

A master glassmaker, Ferro maintained a proud Venetian tradition that had flourished for centuries. He was born in Murano, into a long-established family of glass artists. At the age of 14, he was apprenticed to his uncles, Amleto and Armando Zuffi, at the Fratelli Toso factory. For much of his career, Ferro produced the standard items that the company

STUDIO COUCH, LUCIAN ERCOLANI, LATE 1950s

required, but he was able to give full rein to his imagination when he "retired." His specialty was murrine work—patterns composed of small tesserae, similar to a mosaic. This was a traditional format, but Ferro reinvigorated it by using brightly colored, abstract forms.

▷ PIERO FORNASETTI

ITALIAN, 1913–1988

Fornasetti created a witty and surreal repertoire of images, which he applied to a bewildering variety of designs, ranging from furniture and ceramics to fashion accessories and homeware.

The son of an accountant, Fornasetti studied briefly at the Brera Academy, but he was soon expelled and traveled around Africa instead. On his return, he designed some scarves, and they caught the attention of Gio Ponti, who became his lifelong collaborator. Fornasetti was drawn to the same themes again and again—owls, sunbursts, playing cards, and, above all, the face of a 19th-century opera singer named Lina Cavalieri. He used her in more than 350 designs, transforming her into a snake, a sheik, and even a hot-air balloon.

KAJ FRANCK

FINNISH, 1911–1989

A prominent industrial designer, Franck specialized in ceramics and glass. After studying at the Central School of Applied Arts in Helsinki, he worked in a variety of fields, designing lighting, textiles, and furniture. He found more permanent employment in 1945, when he became art director at the ceramics manufacturer Arabia. Franck overhauled its entire catalog, adding new lines of his own. His most popular creation was the Kilta range of tableware (1953), which was described at the time as "a revolution at the dinner table." Nothing could be more practical than this collection of colorful, stackable, mix-and-match items. Franck also enjoyed a lengthy association with Iittala, producing the Kartio range of pressed-glass wares for them.

CAREER HIGHLIGHTS

1953 Creates the Kilta tableware service
1960 Reforms the curriculum as artistic director of the Institute of Industrial Arts, Helsinki

PORCELAIN PLATES WITH CUPOLAS, PIERO FORNASETTI, c. 1950s

JOSEF FRANK

AUSTRIAN, 1885–1967

Although Austrian by birth, Frank is chiefly associated with developments in his adopted homeland. For many, he is the finest embodiment of the Swedish Modern aesthetic, which emerged in the 1930s. He trained as an architect in Vienna but, because of his Jewish background, emigrated to Sweden in 1933. There, Frank formed a fruitful association with the celebrated design company Svenskt Tenn. He played a major role for them at the Paris Exposition Internationale (1937), designing the Swedish pavilion, and again at the Warsaw International Exhibition (1938), as well as at the New York World's Fair of 1939–1940.

During World War II, Frank had to flee again, this time to the US. Here, he created marvelous wallpaper and textile designs, teeming with exotic birds and vegetation. Many people regard these as his most beautiful works.

ADRIAN FRUTIGER

SWISS, 1928–2015

A prolific typographer and typeface designer, Frutiger was an apprentice to a typesetter in Interlaken before studying sculpture and design at the College of Applied Arts in Zurich. In 1952, he moved to Paris to work for the type foundry Deberny & Peignot. There, he created his first major typefaces, Méridien (1955) and Univers (1957), which was intended for filmsetting. Frutiger set up his own studio in 1962, extending his activities to encompass corporate branding and logos, including designing typewriter fonts for IBM.

Frutiger designed new signage systems for several transportation bodies, including Charles de Gaulle Airport (for which he conceived the eponymous Frutiger typeface, 1974–1976), the Paris Métro, and French highways. In all, Frutiger developed well over 100 typefaces, and his books on the subject have become standard reference works.

NAOTO FUKASAWA

JAPANESE, 1956–

An award-winning industrial designer, Fukasawa trained in the product design department of Tama Art University and worked initially for Seiko Epson, where he specialized in microtechnology, designing wrist televisions and mini-printers. In 1989, he moved to San Francisco's Silicon Valley, before returning to Japan to set up his own company. Fukasawa's designs display elegant minimalism—he has professed his aim is "to reduce the object to its essence, but keep its poetry." He also likes his designs to be intuitive, removing the need for long-winded manuals. In 1996, he ran a series of Without Thought workshops expounding these notions. At one of them, Fukasawa had the idea for his most famous design—a wall-mounted CD player.

ÉMILE GALLÉ

FRENCH, 1846–1904

Together with René Lalique, Gallé was the greatest glass designer of the Art Nouveau era. His father ran a thriving glass and pottery studio, and as a youth, Emile used to produce floral decoration for these wares. He studied botany and mineralogy in Weimar, before following an apprenticeship in glassmaking at Meisenthal. Returning to Nancy, Gallé set up his own glass workshop in 1873, where he experimented constantly, developing complex new techniques. He created a different type of cameo glass and achieved novel, ornamental effects using metal foils, colored oxides, crazing, and air bubbles. The decoration of the glassware also revealed Gallé's profound love of nature and his poetic sensibility. His *verreries parlantes* (talking glass)—items inscribed with a line of verse—proved particularly popular.

Gallé also designed ornate furniture, using exotic woods, mother-of-pearl inlays, and exquisite marquetry. The decoration was often symbolic, as typified by his Dawn and Dusk bed. By 1900, Gallé's work had won international fame. He led a circle of designers now called the École de Nancy (School of Nancy).

USE SPADES NOT SHIPS

GROW YOUR OWN FOOD
AND SUPPLY YOUR OWN COOKHOUSE

POSTER FOR THE BRITISH WAR OFFICE, ABRAM GAMES, ISSUED 1941–1945

◁ ABRAM GAMES

BRITISH, 1914–1996

This influential graphic designer was best known for his wartime posters. The son of a Latvian photographer, Games studied briefly at Saint Martin's School of Art, but he left after two terms and was largely self-taught. Games worked as a freelancer for a time, designing colorful posters for London Transport and Shell, but his real opportunity came during the war. In 1941, he was employed by the Public Relations Department at the War Office to provide recruitment posters and public service messages. Games produced more than a hundred of these, adopting a simple Modernist style, leavened with a touch of humor. He used the same formula when producing the posters and souvenirs for the Festival of Britain (1951).

▷ ANTONI GAUDÍ

SPANISH, 1852–1926

Gaudí was a world-famous architect, and for many of his building projects, he also designed furniture, glass, and ceramics. He learned these techniques while studying in Barcelona, and, indeed, he designed an elaborate desk for himself as soon as he graduated (1878), decorating it with birds, snakes, and insects. Gaudí produced his most impressive furniture for the Güell Palace (1886–1888) and the Casa Calvet (1898–1900). The armchairs and benches in the latter have undulating contours that echo the forms of his architecture. In part, this is because Gaudí preferred to make clay models of his designs, rather than sketches. He used *trencadís (*mosaics made of broken ceramics) as a staple form of decoration on his buildings but also created ornamental ceramic details in his interiors. This is most evident in the Casa Vicens (1883–1888), which was commissioned by a tile maker.

FRANK GEHRY

CANADIAN-AMERICAN, 1929–

Chiefly known as an architect, Gehry is also a highly inventive furniture designer. Born in Toronto, he moved to Los Angeles in 1947 and studied architecture at the University of Southern California. He made his first foray into furniture design in the late 1960s with the Easy Edges line, made from corrugated cardboard. This proved very popular, winning plaudits from conservationists for the way that it recycled industrial packaging. Gehry was uneasy, though, feeling that it might detract from his reputation as an architect. He did not design furniture again until the 1980s, when he created the Bentwood Collection for Knoll International. These tables and chairs were made from the type of maple wood strips that were normally used for apple crates.

ERIC GILL

BRITISH, 1882–1940

Gill was an outstanding sculptor, letter-cutter, and typeface designer. He trained initially at Chichester Art School, before completing his studies at the Central School of Arts and Crafts in London. There, he was instructed by the master calligrapher Edward Johnston, who had a profound effect on his career. Gill worked mainly as a sculptor, but he also made a major contribution to book design. He created numerous initial letters and title pages for the Cranach Press (1905–1909) and was even more closely involved with the Golden Cockerel Press and illustrated several of its most lavish publications with fine wood engravings. Gill also devised some elegant new typefaces for the Monotype Corporation, among them Gill Sans-Serif (1928) and Perpetua (1930).

MILTON GLASER

AMERICAN, 1929–2020

A prolific graphic designer and illustrator, Glaser was the first to be honored with the National Medal of the Arts award. He studied illustration and typography at the Cooper Union art school in New York, followed by a year in Bologna, Italy, on a Fulbright scholarship, with the painter Giorgio Morandi. Returning in 1954, Glaser cofounded Push Pin Studios. The group published a highly eclectic magazine, combining Pop-influenced illustrations with vintage type styles, which had an enormous impact on advertising and packaging. Glaser, meanwhile, designed a plethora of posters, record covers, and magazine illustrations. His psychedelic poster of Bob Dylan (1967) is probably his best-known work. In 1968, he cofounded the *New York Magazine*.

EDWARD WILLIAM GODWIN

BRITISH, 1833–1886

A leading figure in the Aesthetic Movement, Godwin was a highly versatile architect and designer. Born in Bristol, he trained under a local architect and set up his own practice in 1854. As a furniture designer, he developed an Anglo-Japanese style, influenced by all the Japanese prints he saw at the 1862 International Exhibition in South Kensington. Many of his pieces are made of ebonized deal or mahogany with gilt decoration. Godwin's Japonisme was equally evident in his wallpaper designs and in the dresses that he created for Liberty & Co. During his affair with the actress Ellen Terry, he also became involved with theater and costume design.

JEAN GOULDEN

FRENCH, 1878–1947

Carving out a special niche for himself in the world of Art Deco, Goulden was an outstanding enameler. He was born in Alsace and was a doctor by profession. During World War I, he was stationed in Macedonia and, at the end of hostilities, lived with the monks on Mount Athos for several months. While there, Goulden became fascinated with Byzantine enamels and was determined to learn the techniques. After returning to France, he was taught these by Jean Dunand. Goulden made a number of exquisite items—mainly boxes and plaques—combining *champlevé* enameling with silver. He remained in Dunand's circle, exhibiting with them and marrying the daughter of one of the other artists.

MARCEL GOUPY

FRENCH, 1886–1954

A noted designer of ceramics and glass, Goupy was a fine exponent of Art Deco. He was born in Paris, where he studied architecture and interior design at the École Nationale des Arts Décoratifs. For much of his career, Goupy was employed as the artistic director of Maison Rouard (1909–1954), selling some of his own wares under its banner. He is best known for creating glass vases and bowls with brightly colored enamel decoration, usually depicting stylized birds, flowers, or mythological scenes. Goupy showed his work at the 1925 Paris Exposition Internationale, where he also served as vice president on the Glass Jury.

KENNETH GRANGE

BRITISH, 1929–

An award-winning product designer, Grange has an enviable track record of achievement. He studied at the Willesden School of Arts and Crafts in London, broadening his experience when he worked as an illustrator for the Royal Engineers.

In 1958, Grange set up his own design company and, in the same year, gained a key commission from Kodak. He went on to create several cameras for them, including the Brownie (1964) and the hugely popular Instamatic (1970). At the same time, he was also boosting the success of Kenwood with its Chefette hand mixer (1966) and its electric cordless knife (1968).

In 1972, Grange cofounded Pentagram, which has grown into the world's largest independent design consultancy. Originally, it had just five partners, but now there are 19. Grange remained with the group until 1997, undertaking a remarkably diverse array of projects. He has designed trains (the InterCity 125; 1976), revamped London's taxis (2000), and made sewing machines for Maruzen in Japan. At no stage has he ever allowed himself to be pigeonholed into a single area of design.

"EL DRAC" CERAMIC LIZARD, PARC GÜELL, ANTONI GAUDÍ, 1926

WENDINGEN RUG, EILEEN GRAY, *c.* 1930

MICHAEL GRAVES

AMERICAN, 1934–2015

Hailed as one of the pioneers of postmodernism, Graves brought color and fun into the worlds of architecture and product design. He studied at Harvard and was a practicing architect from 1964, but his postmodern designs date from the 1980s. In these, Graves was willfully eclectic, mixing historical styles and combining expensive veneers with cheap plastic laminates. He produced his most outrageous designs for the Memphis group and Alessi. His pieces often contained architectural references. His Plaza dressing table (1981) resembles an Art Deco skyscraper, while in his Tea & Coffee Piazza (1983) the pieces masquerade as miniature castles. In everything, irony was king: only Graves could have designed a coffeepot called The Big Dripper.

CAREER HIGHLIGHTS

1984 Creates the Bird kettle for Alessi
1985 Produces The Big Dripper coffeepot for Swid Powell; also the MG2 armchair and the MG3 club chair
1989 Designs the Walt Disney World Dolphin Hotel, Orlando, Florida
1994 Makes the Euclid thermos jug

◁ EILEEN GRAY

IRISH, 1878–1976

A pioneering architect and designer, Gray was best known for her inventive approach to furniture. The daughter of a landscape painter, she initially studied art in London and Paris, before developing an interest in Oriental lacquer. Gray was instructed in this unusual and painstaking process by a Japanese master, Seizo Sugawara. Together, they set up a workshop in Paris in 1910, and Eileen was soon producing remarkable pieces. Her allegorical screen, Le Destin (1914), and her extraordinary Dragon Chair (1917–1919) won her wide acclaim. Spurred on by this success, Gray opened her own shop, the Galerie Jean Désert, selling lacquer screens, rugs, and lighting.

Gray also produced architectural designs, most famously for her own seaside house (1926–1929), which she nicknamed E1027 (a code referring to herself and her partner). By this time, Gray had adopted a Modernist style in her furniture designs, making considerable use of tubular steel and chrome.

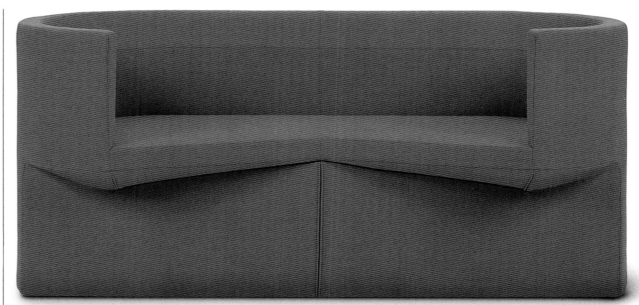

ODIN SOFA, KONSTANTIN GRCIC, 2005

△ KONSTANTIN GRCIC

GERMAN, 1965–

An award-winning industrial designer, Grcic has a special interest in furniture and lighting. He was born in Munich but studied at the Royal College of Art in London. In 1991, he set up his own design studio in Germany, winning commissions from a prestigious range of clients (Flos, Plank, Mattiazzi). Grcic's work is characterized by a taste for rigorous simplicity and a passion for technology. He has curated exhibitions at the Serpentine Gallery in London (2009) and the Istituto Svizzero in Rome (2010). Grcic's numerous awards include the Compasso d'Oro for his Mayday lamp (1999) and his Myto chair (2008).

WALTER GROPIUS

GERMAN, 1883–1969

A hugely influential architect, designer, and teacher, Gropius spread the gospel of Modernism. He trained as an architect in Munich and Berlin, before entering the studio of Peter Behrens. In 1910, Gropius formed his own architectural practice with Adolf Meyer, though he also designed furniture, interiors, and a diesel locomotive. After World War I, he took the momentous step of founding the Bauhaus, by amalgamating the schools of fine art and applied art in Weimar. Here, Gropius assembled an outstanding team of artists and designers, who would shape the future course of Modernism. Gropius left the Bauhaus in 1928, moving to London a few years later. There, he worked for Isokon, producing plywood furniture for its headquarters in the iconic Lawn Road Flats. Gropius became controller of design for the company in 1936, but, with another war approaching, he emigrated to the US, where he worked in partnership with Marcel Breuer, while also lecturing at Harvard University.

CAREER HIGHLIGHTS

1919 Founds the Bauhaus and becomes its first director
1926 Designs the Bauhaus building and director's house at Dessau
1937 Emigrates to US and becomes Professor of Architecture at Harvard University

HANS GUGELOT

DUTCH, 1920–1965

A gifted designer and architect, Gugelot epitomizes the rational, purist approach of the college at Ulm. He was born in Makassar, in present-day Indonesia, but grew up in Holland and Switzerland. After training as an architect in Zurich, he entered the workshop of Max Bill and joined him in his new venture at the Hochschule für Gestaltung (High School for Design) at Ulm. Gugelot followed its precepts, rejecting notions of style and individualism. This was most evident in the work he produced for Braun, which included radios, televisions, and shavers. Gugelot also helped develop the Hamburg U-Bahn (underground train) and a slide projector for Kodak.

LURELLE VAN ARSDALE GUILD

AMERICAN, 1898–1985

Guild was a prolific industrial designer and illustrator, best known for his Art Deco aluminum wares. He was born in Syracuse, New York, and studied painting at the local university. Guild had a salesman's eye for identifying and supplying the goods that the public wanted. In particular, he exploited the fashion for aluminum goods that blossomed in the 1930s. He developed a strong relationship with the Aluminum Company of America (Alcoa), designing more than 300 products for them, mostly in their Kensington Wares line of domestic items. Guild's most famous individual design, though, was his "facelift" for an Electrolux vacuum cleaner. He streamlined the old model, giving it a thoroughly modern look, and it remained in production for more than 20 years.

HECTOR GUIMARD

FRENCH, 1867–1942

Guimard was an architect and designer, one of the greatest exponents of the Art Nouveau style. He was born in Lyons and trained at the École des Arts Décoratifs in Paris. His first major commission was the Castel Béranger, where the decoration was so florid that one pundit dubbed it the Castel Dérangé (mad castle). This led to his most celebrated work—the entrances to the Paris Métro. Nothing epitomizes the Art Nouveau style more

GALAXY SOHO, BEIJING, ZAHA HADID, 2009–2012

beautifully than these gorgeous creations in wrought iron and glass, with their whiplash curves and their lamps that look like drooping, exotic flowers.

Guimard was an advocate of the *Gesamtkunstwerk* and paid equal attention to every aspect of his buildings, right down to the furnishings and door handles. Accordingly, he designed a wide range of furniture, lighting, and textiles. All of these exhibit his taste for flowing, sinuous lines. Sadly, though, Guimard's reputation faded as Art Nouveau went out of fashion, and he was a forgotten man by the time he emigrated to the US in 1938.

MARTÍ GUIXÉ

SPANISH, 1964–

A Catalan designer with a quirky sense of humor, Guixé describes himself as an ex-designer, meaning that his vision enables him to transcend the traditional boundaries of the role. He studied interior design at Elisava in Barcelona, followed by a course in industrial design at Milan Polytechnic. In 1994, he began work as a consultant in Seoul, South Korea, before returning to Spain to design shoe shops and lamps.

Guixé's humor is most evident in his food-related designs. These include edible jokes (cookies with tooth-mark decoration, freeway cakes with tire-print designs, "post-it" chips) and his charming Plant-me Pets (squeaky seed dispensers with legs, which can be used as toys before planting in the ground).

H

◁ ZAHA HADID

IRAQI BRITISH, 1950–2016

This world-famous architect also created furniture, lighting, and jewelry designs. She was born in Baghdad and grew up in a Bauhaus-inspired house. Moving to London in 1972, she trained at the Architectural Association before setting up her own practice in 1980. As an architect, she was linked with the Deconstructivists, and the same radical fluidity can be seen in her furniture designs. Working for companies such as Cassina and B&B Italia, Hadid created futuristic, amoeba-like sofas and tables. Her Moon System sofa is composed of interlocking, curvilinear units, while her Zephyr sofa was inspired by the effects of wind erosion on rock formations.

CAREER HIGHLIGHTS

1993 Completes the fire station for the Vitra furniture factory at Weil am Rhein, Germany

2012 Starts designing the 66-story One Thousand Museum, Miami

FRIDA HANSEN

NORWEGIAN, 1855–1931

A tapestry designer, Hansen trained as a painter, but her interest in textiles came from her family's financial troubles. Her husband went bankrupt and fled abroad, prompting Hansen to earn her own money. She began repairing embroideries, decided to learn the techniques, and was soon producing new tapestry designs. By 1892, she was running a weaving school and exhibiting her work. This culminated in her triumph at the 1900 Exposition Universelle in Paris, when she was awarded a gold medal. Hansen's style varied. Her most famous tapestry, *The Milky Way* (1898), is in a Symbolist vein, while her floral patterns are closer to Art Nouveau. Hansen's house in Stavanger has now opened as a museum.

KATE HARRIS

BRITISH, 19TH/20TH CENTURY

Disappointingly little is known about this superb silversmith. Harris studied art at the Hartley Institute in Southampton (the forerunner of the university). She then moved to the National Art Training School (later the Royal College of Art) in London, where she trained as a sculptor under Professor Lanteri. Harris won many awards, most notably at the 1900 Exposition Universelle in Paris. In 1898, she joined William Hutton & Sons as a staff designer. This firm had a high reputation and was a major supplier of Liberty & Co. Harris created a broad range of exquisite items for them, with flowing Art Nouveau decoration. Her style was extremely graceful, though without the eroticism that is often associated with the movement. Indeed, her most distinctive motif was a charming Puritan maid in a tight-fitting cap.

SEED CATHEDRAL, UK PAVILION, SHANGHAI EXPO, THOMAS HEATHERWICK, 2010

◁ THOMAS HEATHERWICK

BRITISH, 1970–

The most exciting designer on the British scene, Heatherwick has been operating his studio since 1994, but his public profile soared during the London Olympics, when international television audiences were stunned by the sight of his Cauldron during the opening ceremony. Born in London, Heatherwick has design in his genes. His mother was an enameler and jeweler, while his grandmother founded the Marks & Spencer textile studio. Heatherwick studied at Manchester Polytechnic and the Royal College of Art, in London. While at the latter, he met Terence Conran, who mentored the young man, later describing him as "the Leonardo da Vinci of our times."

Heatherwick first hit the headlines in 1997 with an eye-catching window display during London Fashion Week. This was followed by a succession of amazing designs, which include his extraordinary Seed Cathedral at Expo 2010, a futuristic beach café in Littlehampton, and the latest London Routemaster bus. Adventurous as ever, he is the creative force behind the controversial Garden Bridge over the Thames River.

CAREER HIGHLIGHTS

1994 Sets up the Heatherwick Studio in London
2012 Designs the Olympic Cauldron for the London Olympic Games

POUL HENNINGSEN

DANISH, 1894–1967

A multitalented designer, architect, and writer, Henningsen's main field of expertise was lighting. After studying at the Danish College of Technology in Copenhagen, he worked as both an architect and a journalist. As a critic, Henningsen deplored the unimaginative way that people lit their homes. He had grown up in the era of gas lighting, preferring this to the harsh glare of electricity. Henningsen's solution was to design his celebrated PH series of lamps. These were composed of several tiers of reflective metal "leaves," which diffused the light more softly and evenly. The best-known example is the Artichoke lamp (1958), so called because of its resemblance to the vegetable.

CHARLES HARRISON

AMERICAN, 1931–2018

Credited with silencing the metallic clang of early-morning trash collection, Chicago-based industrial designer Charles "Chuck" Harrison believed his best piece of work was the first plastic trash can. "When that can hit the market, it did so with the biggest bang you never heard," he wrote in his autobiography *A Life's Design* (2005).

Harrison led the team that designed the classic Model F View-Master photographic slide viewer in 1958, then joined Sears, Roebuck & Company in 1961. He spent 32 years there, until his retirement, designing household items as diverse as sewing machines, stereos, coffee percolators, hearing aids, power tools, and lawn mowers. He won a Lifetime Achievement Award from the Cooper Hewitt Smithsonian Design Museum in 2008.

STUART HAYGARTH

BRITISH, 1966–

Haygarth is a photographer and designer, with a particular talent for creating beauty out of recycled items. He studied graphic design at Exeter College of Art and Design and, in his early years, worked as a photographer and illustrator for clients such as Porsche and Sony. Haygarth's interest in design blossomed after 2000, when he began to create chandeliers and lamps out of discarded objects.

Haygarth's Millennium Chandelier (2005) was assembled from a thousand exploded party poppers, while the wittily named Twenty Twenty (2006) was composed of old prescription eyeglasses. His finest creation, perhaps, is the Tide Chandelier (2005), which was intricately constructed from human-made debris collected on a Kent beach. Beautiful to look at, it also carries an important message about sustainability.

▽ RENÉ HERBST

FRENCH, 1891–1982

This pioneering furniture designer was an early champion of Modernism between the two world wars. Herbst studied architecture in London and Frankfurt, but when he returned to France, he concentrated mainly on furniture and interior design. He made his mark with five exhibition stands at the 1925 Paris Exposition Internationale, but his real breakthrough was the revolutionary Sandows chair (1928). For this, he dispensed with upholstery and used exposed elastic stretchers hooked onto the tubular steel frame (*sandow* is French for a luggage stretcher). This elasticized creation caused a sensation at the 1929 Salon d'Automne—the same exhibition where Le Corbusier displayed his chairs. Herbst was a founding member of the UAM (Union des Artistes Modernes) and later became its chairman.

PAVEL HLAVA

CZECH, 1924–2003

Carrying on the Bohemian tradition of glassmaking during the Cold War era, Hlava trained at the State Professional Glassmaking School in Železný Brod, before completing his studies at the Academy of Applied Arts in Prague. At home, Hlava was best known for functional, mass-produced glassware, but he often exhibited abroad, particularly in Japan (where a prize is named after him) and the US. Hlava's studio glass was sculptural and experimental. He was especially fond of heat-sensitive glass, which enabled him to explore color. Much of his work was made by Exbor ("ex" for export and "bor" for the glassworks at Novy Bor).

JOSEF HOFFMANN

MORAVIAN, 1870–1956

Hoffmann was a hugely influential architect and designer, a founding member of both the Vienna Secession and the Wiener Werkstätte (Vienna Workshops). He trained as an architect at the Academy of Fine Arts in Vienna and, for many years, taught the subject at the Vienna School of Applied Art (1899–1941). In 1900, Hoffmann visited Britain, where he was influenced by Ashbee's Guild of Handicraft. Its ideals inspired him to cofound the Wiener Werkstätte (1903), for which he designed furniture, metalware, and jewelry.

Architecture was always a focus of Hoffmann's activities, and his architectural masterpiece was the Palais Stoclet in Brussels. Working in concert with Gustav Klimt and Carl Czeschka, he designed the entire ensemble, including the interiors and the furniture. Aside from architecture, Hoffmann is most famous for two chairs—his Sitting Machine (1908) was an adjustable seat, which he created as part

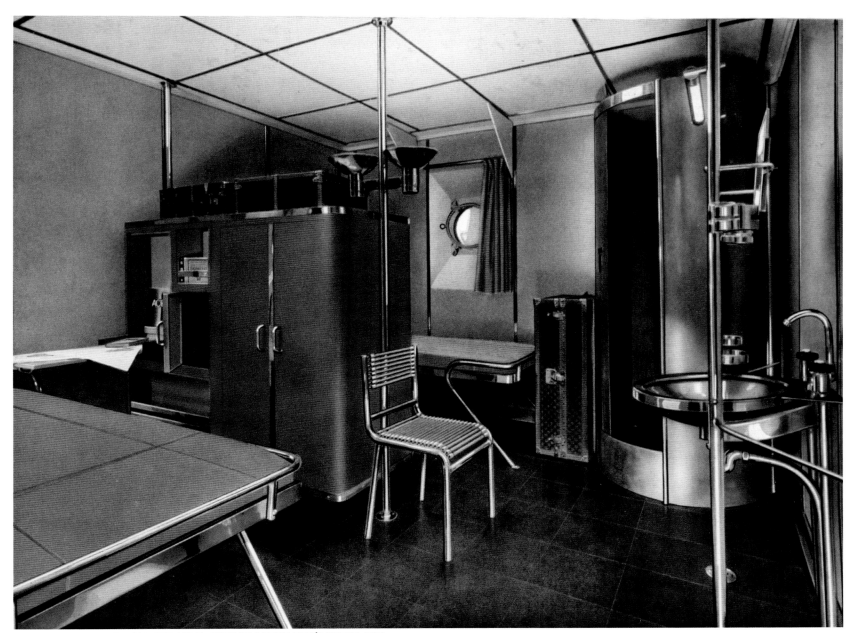

INTERIOR OF A FIRST-CLASS LINER CABIN, *ACIER* MAGAZINE, RENÉ HERBST, 1935

of his scheme for the Purkersdorf Sanatorium, while the Kubus (1910), as the name suggests, was based on the shape of a cube.

CAREER HIGHLIGHTS

1903 Cofounds the Wiener Werkstätte
1905 Starts designing the Palais Stoclet in Brussels
1908 Designs the Sitting Machine

PETER HOLMBLAD

DANISH, 1934–

A successful product designer and entrepreneur, Holmblad's interest in these fields was instilled at an early age, as his stepfather was Arne Jacobsen—one of Denmark's most famous designers. The pair worked together at Stelton, a firm specializing in stainless steel products. Holmblad joined the company as export manager in 1963, three years after it was founded. He immediately persuaded Jacobsen to collaborate on an exciting new project. This was the Cylinda-Line line of kitchenware and bar products. Simple but elegant, it proved highly popular and won awards. Holmblad took over Stelton in the late 1970s, remaining there until he sold the company in 2004.

SAARA HOPEA

FINNISH, 1925–1984

Best known for her jewelry and glassware, Hopea also designed furniture and lighting. She came from a family of goldsmiths but decided to study interior design at the Central School of Applied Arts in Helsinki.

Hopea began working for a furniture company until, in 1952, Kaj Franck—one of her old college instructors—persuaded her to design glassware for him at the Nuutajärvi glass factory. Her designs were extremely successful, winning a number of awards, but Hopea changed direction in 1958, when her father died and she had to return home to take over the family business. In her later years, she concentrated mainly on enamel and jewelry designs.

▽ VICTOR HORTA

BELGIAN, 1861–1947

Horta was one of the greatest masters of the Art Nouveau style, best known as an architect, but also an accomplished furniture designer, although he only ever designed objects to go with his own interior schemes. He studied drawing, textiles, and architecture at the Académie des Beaux-Arts, Ghent, before completing his studies in Brussels. From the outset, Horta took charge of every aspect of his buildings, right down to the light fixtures and the door handles. "I was not the first architect of my time to design furniture," he explained, "but I was the first to integrate it to my architecture."

Beginning with the townhouses called Maison Autrique (1893) in Schaerbeek and Hotel Tassel (1892–1893) in Brussels, all of Horta's interiors looked extremely light and decorative. They were some of the first private houses to be lit by electricity, and his signature whiplash curves were in evidence everywhere, from the grand, sweeping spiral staircases to the swirling ornamental details on his mirrors and clocks. Horta also designed interiors for public displays. He created a showroom for the Val Saint Lambert glass factory at the 1896 Brussels Exhibition, as well as the Belgian pavilion at the Turin International Exhibition in 1902.

CAREER HIGHLIGHTS

1892 Begins work on the Hotel Tassel, built for a Belgian scientist
1898 Completes the Maison & Atelier Horta, now the Horta Museum in Brussels
1902 Designs the Belgian pavilion for the Turin International Exhibition

ANTHONY INGOLIA

AMERICAN, 1921

Active in the field of lighting design, Ingolia studied at the Illinois Institute of Technology in Chicago, operating in the design department. His best-known creation was an adaptable desk lamp, which could also be mounted on a wall and used as a sconce. In 1951, Ingolia entered this in a competition for a modern lamp, which was sponsored by MoMA, New York, and the Heifetz Manufacturing Company. Made out of chrome-plated steel and enameled aluminum, it caught the eye of the judges and won a prize in the Low-Cost Lighting section of the competition. As part of the prize, Ingolia's lamp became part of MoMA's permanent collection.

▷ MAIJA ISOLA

FINNISH, 1927–2001

A major textile designer, Isola created bright, colorful patterns that helped shake Finland out of its postwar gloom. She studied at Helsinki Art School, graduating in 1949. In the same year, she joined Printex, a firm producing oil-cloth fabrics. This company failed two years later, but it was relaunched as Marimekko, a modern textiles firm, and Isola was taken on as a designer. This proved to be a marriage made in heaven, and in the end, she continued working there until 1987, producing more than 500 patterns for them. Isola's designs are striking with large, bold motifs, typified by her most famous creation—the Unikko (poppy) design, which was made in 1964 and is still in production.

JONATHAN IVE

BRITISH, 1967–

One of the most important product designers of the digital age, Ive is celebrated for his contribution to the meteoric rise of Apple. He was born in Chingford, on the fringes of London, and

STAIRCASE AT THE HORTA MUSEUM, BRUSSELS, VICTOR HORTA, 1898

studied industrial design at Newcastle Polytechnic. In 1989, he joined a design consultancy called Tangerine, working on a wide variety of projects, before moving to California three years later to take up a job with Apple. Success did not happen overnight, but Ive's fortunes rose when Steve Jobs returned to the company in 1997. The two men immediately found that they were on the same wavelength and their partnership produced a string of technological blockbusters.

Ive's candy-colored iMac appeared in 1998—a revelation in an age when computers were a drab gray or beige. This was followed by the iPod (2001), the iPhone (2007), and the iPad (2012). These have transformed Apple into one of the most successful companies on the planet and Ive into its star designer.

CAREER HIGHLIGHTS

1989 Co-founds industrial design consultancy Tangerine
1998 Completes design of the brightly colored, user-friendly iMac, transforming Apple's fortunes
2007 Apple launches iPhone

ARNE JACOBSEN

DANISH, 1902–1971

This major architect, textile, and furniture designer trained initially as a stonemason, before studying architecture at the Royal Danish Academy of Fine Arts. In 1930, he set up his own architectural practice, working in the International Modernist style. Jacobsen was a firm advocate of the *Gesamtkunstwerk*, preferring to design every aspect of his architectural projects, right down to the light fixtures. So it was natural that he should become involved in furniture design and, indeed, this is probably the aspect of his work that is now best known.

Jacobsen first exhibited a chair in 1925, but his golden period was in the 1950s, when he was collaborating with the manufacturer Fritz Hansen. Together, they produced three best-selling chairs—the Ant (1952), the Egg (1958), and the Swan (1958). The Ant, which was originally created for the cafeteria of a pharmaceuticals company, is now widely regarded as a classic.

APPELSIINI FURNISHING FABRIC, MAIJA ISOLA FOR MARIMEKKO, 1950

CAREER HIGHLIGHTS

1925 Wins a prize for chair design at Paris Exposition Internationale
1952 Designs the Ant chair
1958 Creates the Egg chair for the SAS Royal Hotel building, Copenhagen

PIERRE JEANNERET

SWISS, 1896–1967

Rather in the shadow of his famous relative Le Corbusier, Jeanneret was first and foremost an influential architect and a key figure in the spread of Modernism, but he was also a talented furniture designer. He studied at the École des Beaux-Arts in Geneva, then completed his training in the office of Auguste Perret.

For much of his career, Jeanneret worked in collaboration with his cousin Charles-Édouard Jeanneret, better known as Le Corbusier. Together with Charlotte Perriand, they created the groundbreaking furniture that was exhibited at the 1929 Salon d'Automne. Jeanneret also designed furniture for a major government project in Chandigarh, India, in the 1950s. These minimalist chairs, tables, and shelves, mostly made of teak or cane, were still firmly in the Modernist idiom.

GEORG JENSEN

DANISH, 1866–1935

A highly talented silversmith, Jensen became one of Denmark's most famous designers. Born in Raadvad, the son of a knife-grinder, he began work at the factory at the age of 13. A year later, the family moved to Copenhagen, where Georg was apprenticed to a goldsmith and later trained as a sculptor at the Royal Academy of Fine Arts. He worked briefly in a small pottery business, but by 1901, he was making silver again. Initially, he took a job with another silversmith, Mogens Ballin, but in 1904, he set up his own studio.

DRAWING FOR *THE GRAMMAR OF ORNAMENT*, PLATE XL MORESQUE NO. 2, OWEN JONES, 1856 (PUBLISHED)

Jensen's business was an immediate success. At first, he concentrated on jewelry, executed in the fashionable Art Nouveau style. He opened his first shop in Berlin in 1909, with others eventually following in Copenhagen, Paris, and London.

Soon, Jensen had expanded into flatware and hollow ware, much of it produced in collaboration with Johan Rohde. Jensen's designs were uncluttered, often embellished with simple fruit or flower motifs. His Magnolia and Acorn collections proved especially popular.

CAREER HIGHLIGHTS

1904 Establishes his own silversmithing workshop

1907 Persuades Johan Rohde to design for him

1924 Opens a showroom on New York's Fifth Avenue

1935 His son Jørgen takes over

BETTY JOEL

BRITISH, 1896–1985

Although largely self-taught, Joel was a highly successful furniture and textile designer. Born in Hong Kong, the daughter of a diplomat, she married a naval lieutenant. On their return to the UK, she set up a furniture workshop on Hayling Island, Hampshire. Joel's craftsmen came from the local shipbuilding trade, which explains the unusual carpentry style of her pieces. She sold her wares through a showroom in London's fashionable Chelsea, and the business rapidly expanded. Joel's designs were partly inspired by her father's collection of Chinese art—and many of her textiles were woven in China—though she was also in tune with the latest Art Deco trends. She retired in 1937, and her husband continued the business.

◁ OWEN JONES

BRITISH, 1809–1874

A seminal figure in the early history of British design, Jones trained as an architect before embarking on lengthy travels through Europe and the Middle East. He was particularly impressed by the Alhambra, in Spain, which inspired his designs for tiles, mosaics, and wallpaper. With his reputation growing, Jones was appointed joint architect of the Great Exhibition (1851) and was also given responsibility for the interior decoration of the Crystal Palace in Sydenham (1854). Here, he created a series of Courts, illustrating the international history of design. Jones supplemented this with his book, *The Grammar of Ornament* (1856), lavishly illustrated with designs from around the world. This became an essential reference for every Victorian designer.

▽ FINN JUHL

DANISH, 1912–1989

The first Danish designer to gain international acclaim for the quality of his furniture, Juhl more or less taught himself. He first trained as an architect at the Royal Academy in Copenhagen, and lectured on interior design at the Frederiksberg Technical School. Juhl began making furniture in the late 1930s, initially just for his own use. His distinctive style owed something to Modernism but was also influenced by abstract art and African sculpture.

Juhl's most celebrated piece is his Chieftain chair (so called because King Frederik IX of Denmark sat on it), its symbolism inspired by weaponry, which caused a stir when it was shown at the annual Cabinetmakers' Guild Exhibition in Copenhagen in 1949.

DESIGNS FOR AN ARMCHAIR AND SIDE CHAIR, FINN JUHL, c. 1955

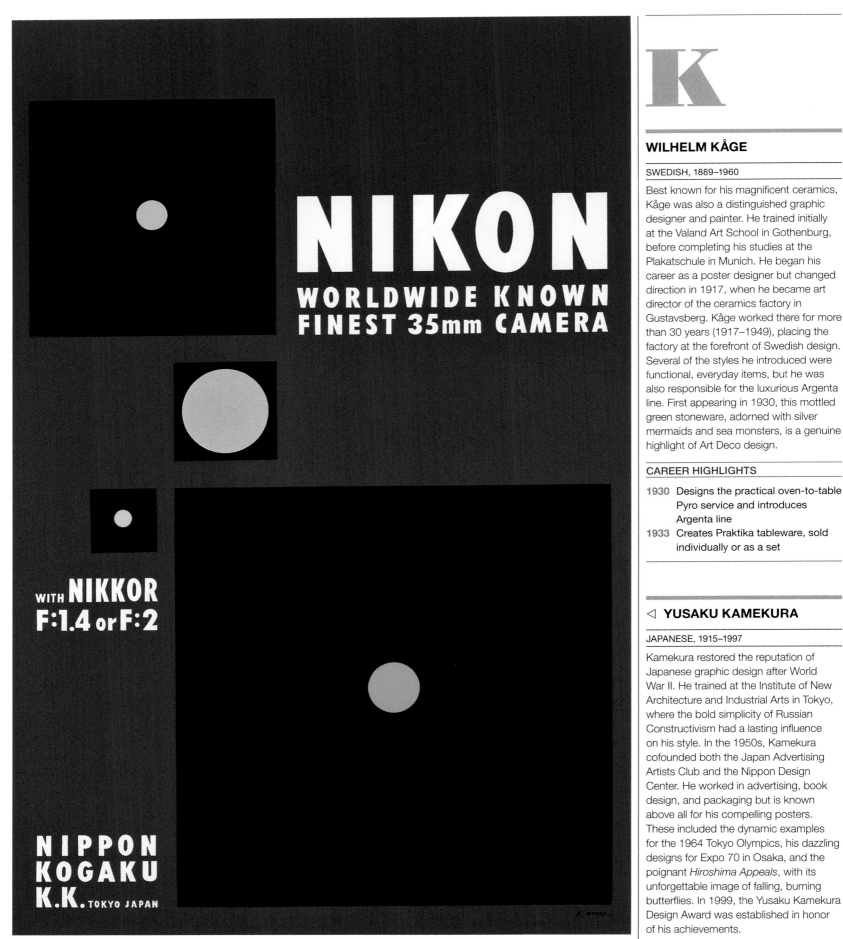

POSTER ADVERTISING NIKON CAMERA, YUSAKU KAMEKURA, *c.* 1955

K

WILHELM KÅGE

SWEDISH, 1889–1960

Best known for his magnificent ceramics, Kåge was also a distinguished graphic designer and painter. He trained initially at the Valand Art School in Gothenburg, before completing his studies at the Plakatschule in Munich. He began his career as a poster designer but changed direction in 1917, when he became art director of the ceramics factory in Gustavsberg. Kåge worked there for more than 30 years (1917–1949), placing the factory at the forefront of Swedish design. Several of the styles he introduced were functional, everyday items, but he was also responsible for the luxurious Argenta line. First appearing in 1930, this mottled green stoneware, adorned with silver mermaids and sea monsters, is a genuine highlight of Art Deco design.

CAREER HIGHLIGHTS

1930 Designs the practical oven-to-table Pyro service and introduces Argenta line

1933 Creates Praktika tableware, sold individually or as a set

◁ YUSAKU KAMEKURA

JAPANESE, 1915–1997

Kamekura restored the reputation of Japanese graphic design after World War II. He trained at the Institute of New Architecture and Industrial Arts in Tokyo, where the bold simplicity of Russian Constructivism had a lasting influence on his style. In the 1950s, Kamekura cofounded both the Japan Advertising Artists Club and the Nippon Design Center. He worked in advertising, book design, and packaging but is known above all for his compelling posters. These included the dynamic examples for the 1964 Tokyo Olympics, his dazzling designs for Expo 70 in Osaka, and the poignant *Hiroshima Appeals*, with its unforgettable image of falling, burning butterflies. In 1999, the Yusaku Kamekura Design Award was established in honor of his achievements.

SHOJI KAMODA

JAPANESE, 1933–1983

One of Japan's greatest potters, Shoji Kamoda was equally at home with modern and traditional styles. He trained in the Crafts Department of the Kyoto Municipal University of Art, studying under Tomimoto Kenkichi. Initially, he drew inspiration from wares produced in the Nara (710–794) and Heian (794–1185) periods. Then he set up his own kiln in Mashiko and, in 1965, held his first one-man show in Tokyo. From this time on, he was restlessly inventive, always seeking to create new, sculptural shapes and constantly experimenting with iron oxides or aluminum phosphate, in an attempt to create different surface effects on his pieces.

ILONKA KARASZ

HUNGARIAN AMERICAN, 1896–1981

An extraordinarily versatile artist, Karasz is probably best known for her graphic design and textiles. Born in Budapest, she studied at the Royal Academy of Arts and Crafts, before emigrating to the US in 1913. Once there, Karasz founded Design Group Inc., a company that worked in a bewildering variety of fields, ranging from metalwork and ceramics to toys and lamps.

Karasz's personal style was an unusual blend of traditional and modern. Her illustrations and textiles reflect her eastern European roots and have affinities with folk art, and her stark, geometric furniture could have been made at the Bauhaus. She is remembered, in particular, for the 186 covers that she illustrated for *The New Yorker*.

MITSUO KATSUI

JAPANESE, 1931–

An outstanding graphic designer, Katsui is renowned for his dazzling posters and calendars. He studied at Tokyo University, taking a postgraduate course in design and photography. Initially, Katsui worked for a food company, but he held his first exhibition, Fresh Eyes, in 1957 and went freelance four years later.

His early style was influenced by the bold, abstract forms and psychedelic coloring of Op art and Pop art, but Katsui has always kept abreast of the latest developments. In recent years, he has been at the forefront of experiments with computer graphics. Katsui was art director for Expo 70 in Osaka and for the Science Expo in 1985.

EDWARD McKNIGHT KAUFFER

AMERICAN, 1890–1954

Graphic designer Edward Kauffer was born in Great Falls, Montana. He took the middle name McKnight from a professor who sponsored him to study art in Paris in 1913. After moving to Britain, he was commissioned to design a poster for the London Underground in 1915. Over the following 25 years, he produced many posters for London Transport and Shell Oil, combining a wide range of artistic styles. He also designed textiles with his wife, Marion Dorn, exhibiting Cubist-inspired rugs in 1929. In 1940, he and Dorn returned to the US, where his career went into decline.

▷ KAZUO KAWASAKI

JAPANESE, 1949–

Kawasaki brings a passionate social conscience to his work as an industrial designer and teacher. He studied at the Kanazawa College of Art and began working on audio products for Toshiba. Then, at the age of 28, he suffered a serious car accident. Undismayed, Kawasaki designed a titanium wheelchair for himself and introduced a campaigning edge into his activities. "I want to change society through design," he declared. He undertook a number of medical projects, including designs for an artificial heart and for syringes that cannot be reused. Kawasaki has also worked on computers, domestic items, and robotics. Ironically, though, his most famous design is for eyeglass frames. Sarah Palin wore a pair of these during her bid for the US vice-presidential nomination, gaining worldwide publicity for Kawasaki.

CAREER HIGHLIGHTS

1983 Designs the Artus series of knives, each from a single piece of steel
1996 Creates the CRT FlexScan monitor for Eizo
1999 Receives a doctorate for his design of an artificial heart
2008 Sarah Palin popularizes his 704 Eyeglasses

ISAMU KENMOCHI

JAPANESE, 1912–1971

No one has done more to bridge the gap between eastern and western furniture styles than Kenmochi. He trained at the Tokyo College of Industrial Arts and broadened his knowledge through a study tour of the US. This focused his attention on western chairs—a bold move, as *tatami* mats had been more common in Japan until the 20th century. Kenmochi gained international renown with his round, body-hugging Rattan chair (1960), while his custom-made Kashiwado chair (1961)—named after a famous sumo wrestler—is admired for its sleek, sculptural appearance. Kenmochi's many awards include a gold medal at Expo 58 in Brussels and a Mainichi prize at Expo 70 in Osaka.

JOCK KINNEIR

BRITISH, 1917–1994

An influential writer, graphic designer, and typographer, Kinneir trained as an engraver at Chelsea School of Art in London before joining the Design Research Unit. In 1956, he set up his own practice, winning a contract to design new signage for Gatwick Airport. This proved so successful that Kinneir was asked to create standardized signs for Britain's road network. He tackled this monumental project with Margaret Calvert, who became a partner in his firm. The results were widely acclaimed and have been much copied around the world. Kinneir worked on similar projects for British Rail and the armed forces, before teaching at the Royal College of Art. He shared his theories in his book, *Words and Buildings: The Art and Practice of Public Lettering* (1980).

TOSHIYUKI KITA

JAPANESE, 1942–

Kita is a distinguished industrial designer, best known for his colorful furniture. He studied at the Naniwa Design College in Osaka, working initially as a product development officer for an aluminum company. In 1967, he set up his own studio, and two years later, he began his fruitful association with Italian companies. For Cassina, he created his versatile Wink chair (1980), which was selected for the

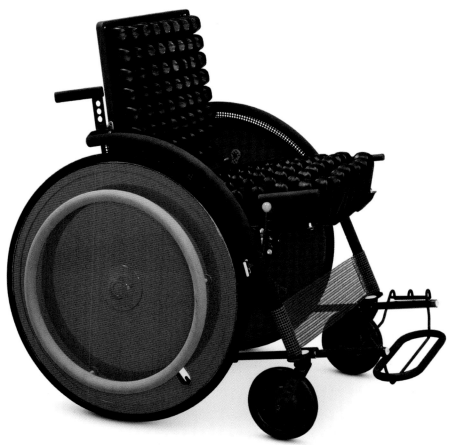

CARNA WHEELCHAIR, KAZUO KAWASAKI, 1989

CONTEMPORARY INTERIOR WITH FURNITURE MANUFACTURED BY KNOLL

permanent collection at MoMA, New York. Inspired by the bucket seats in cars, it can easily be turned into a recliner by adjusting the footrest. Although chiefly known for his furniture, Kita has also designed LCD television sets, as well as the extraordinary Wakamaru (2005), a bright yellow household robot.

KAARE KLINT

DANISH, 1888–1954

Regarded by many as the father of Danish furniture, Klint was the son of an architect, studying under him at the Copenhagen Academy. In 1914, he created furnishings for the Art Gallery at Faaborg, drawing inspiration from 18th–century English examples. Unlike Bauhaus designers, Klint was a firm believer in traditional materials and styles, though he was happy to update them using his knowledge of ergonomics. His best-known pieces are his Safari chair (1933) and the ingenious Propeller stool (1927). In addition, Klint was an influential teacher, lecturing at the Copenhagen Academy and also founding the Furniture School there.

◁ FLORENCE KNOLL

AMERICAN, 1917–2019

A leading furniture and textile designer, Knoll was initially drawn to architecture. She studied at the Cranbrook Academy of Art and worked for a time in the offices of Walter Gropius and Marcel Breuer. This gave her a thorough grounding in the principles of Modernism. By 1943, Florence was living in New York, where she met the furniture manufacturer Hans Knoll and took charge of the Planning Unit of his firm. The couple married in 1946, forming Knoll Associates.

Knoll immediately became the driving force behind the design team, using her Modernist contacts to commission work from Mies van der Rohe, Marcel Breuer, and Eero Saarinen. She also promoted her own vision of uncluttered, open-plan living, with simple but effective designs. The Florence Knoll sofa (1956) is now recognized as a modern classic. In 1947, Florence introduced Knoll Textiles, which created fabrics for offices, hospitals, and schools, in addition to the home. She became president of the company after her husband's death, retiring only in 1965.

CAREER HIGHLIGHTS

1943 Establishes the Knoll Planning Unit and becomes its director
1946 Marries Hans Knoll; the company becomes Knoll Associates
1956 Launches the Florence Knoll sofa

ARCHIBALD KNOX

BRITISH, 1864–1933

Specializing in metalware and jewelry, Knox was one of the finest designers working for Liberty & Co. He was born on the Isle of Man and studied at the Douglas School of Art there. He worked initially as a teacher but also began designing gravestones. Then, in 1897, Knox moved to London and started producing work for Liberty. He designed a variety of items, including carpets, textiles, wallpaper, and terra-cotta garden ornaments, but his most beautiful pieces were in silver (the Cymric line) or pewter (the Tudric line). Knox drew inspiration from the ancient Celtic stonework that he knew from the Isle of Man, but he modified the patterns to form a British variant of Art Nouveau. He continued working for the company until 1912 and later designed Arthur Liberty's headstone (1917).

Knox combined his design activities with teaching, holding posts at art schools in Redhill, Wimbledon, and Kingston. In his later years, he concentrated mainly on painting watercolors.

CAREER HIGHLIGHTS

1899 Cymric silverware and jewelry line sold at Liberty
1900 Tudric pewterware launched
1912 Designs carpets in the US

HENNING KOPPEL

DANISH, 1918–1981

A true innovator, Koppel was a silversmith, sculptor, and graphic designer. Born into a wealthy Jewish family, he trained as an artist at the Royal Danish Academy of Fine Arts and also the Académie Ranson in Paris. Koppel was forced to flee during the Nazi occupation of Denmark but joined the Georg Jensen firm on his return. Initially, he concentrated on jewelry, producing strange, biomorphic forms. His Amoeba necklaces and bracelets resemble whale vertebrae.

His flatware and hollow ware were equally sculptural, defying any notion that form should follow function. By contrast, though, Koppel's graceful New York line of cutlery was entirely practical and could be found in millions of homes.

JAN KOTIK

CZECH, 1916–2002

A painter, printmaker, and glass designer, Kotik was trained by his father, who was also a painter, and was exhibiting his work by the mid-1930s. His experimental style, however, fell foul of the authorities. It was classed as degenerate by the Nazis and was equally unacceptable during the Socialist Realist era under the Communists. Kotik's response was to design glass. The bulbous, sculptural shapes that were prohibited as paintings were perfectly acceptable when executed as glass vases. He did not blow or cut the glass himself but enlisted the aid of Emanuel Beránek at the Škrdlovice glass factory. Kotik's pieces are now much prized by collectors in the West.

YRJÖ KUKKAPURO

FINNISH, 1933–

A furniture designer and teacher, Kukkapuro was a leading exponent of functionalism. After training at the Imatra Art School and Institute of Industrial Art, he started work as an interior designer. In 1959, he set up his company, Design Studio Kukkapuro, though he always managed to combine these activities with his lecturing posts at various colleges in Helsinki.

As a designer, Kukkapuro's finest achievement was the Karuselli chair (Carousel; 1964). Composed of a fiberglass shell with a thin layer of foam, its genius lies in the steel spring base, which allows the sitter to swivel and rock. Terence Conran described it as the most comfortable chair he had ever sat in.

▷ SHIRO KURAMATA

JAPANESE, 1934–1991

Specializing in furniture design, Kuramata combined unusual, industrial materials with a poetic imagination. He studied architecture at the Tokyo Technical

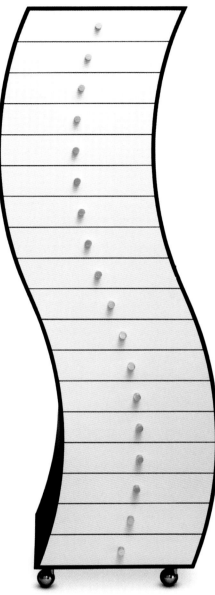

SIDE 2 IN LACQUERED WOOD AND ALUMINUM, SHIRO KURAMATA, 1970

College before training as a cabinetmaker at the Kuwasawa Institute for Design. After this, he carried out freelance work for department stores, eventually setting up the Kuramata Design Studio in 1965.

From the outset, Kuramata's furniture was light and minimalistic, in accordance with his stated ambition: "My strongest desire is to be free of gravity, free of bondage. I want to float." Kuramata's chests of drawers appeared to be dancing; his How High the Moon chair (1986, named after a Duke Ellington song) was made of nickel-plated steel mesh; while his undoubted masterpiece, the Miss Blanche chair (1988, named after a frail character in the play A Streetcar Named Desire) featured paper roses set within a transparent frame.

▽ RENÉ LALIQUE

FRENCH, 1860–1945

Acclaimed as the greatest Art Deco glassmaker, Lalique also excelled as an Art Nouveau jeweler and an interior designer. While he was apprenticed to the jeweler Louis Aucoc, he took evening classes at the École des Arts Décoratifs in Paris, then worked as a freelance artist, designing jewelry for Cartier, Boucheron, among others.

Lalique set up his own business in 1885 and opened his retail premises five years later. By then, he was creating jewelry—such as the celebrated brooch depicting a dragonfly with a woman's torso—for the actress Sarah Bernhardt, and his displays at the 1900 World's Fair were a triumph. Instead of using precious stones, Lalique favored employing semiprecious stones in organically inspired settings.

Gradually, Lalique's focus shifted to glassmaking. In 1908, he made the first of many perfume bottles for Coty, and the following year, he bought a glass factory. Soon he was making a wide range of objects, from vases and chandeliers to car hood ornaments. Lalique was also employed to create luxurious interiors with his glass furnishings, most famously for the *Normandie* ocean liner and the train cars of the Orient Express.

JACK LENOR LARSEN

AMERICAN, 1927–

Larsen is an influential textile designer, famed for spreading the popularity of ethnic styles. He studied architecture and furniture design at the University of Washington, also taking a course on weaving at the Cranbrook Academy of Art. In 1952, he established his studio in New York. Larsen's initial fabric designs were rejected by Florence Knoll for being "too individual," but Marcel Breuer liked them, and other furniture designers soon followed his lead. Larsen's company grew rapidly, appealing to large businesses such as Pan Am and Braniff Airways, as well as private clients, including Marilyn Monroe. Larsen's success stems from his openness to new ideas: he has traveled widely in Asia, Africa, and Latin America and is known for his enthusiasm for adopting new styles and materials.

WOLFGANG LAUBERSHEIMER

GERMAN, 1955–

Laubersheimer is an avant-garde industrial designer and teacher. He trained as a sculptor under Anton Berger in Cologne, Germany. In 1982, he joined forces with Reinhard Müller to launch the furniture company Unikate. In 1984, Laubersheimer produced the group's most iconic design, the Verspanntes Regal (Taut Shelf)—a radical reinvention of shelving. In 1985, he became a founding member of the influential design group Pentagon, which exhibited at a number of prestigious shows, such as Documenta 8 in Kassel, Germany, and the São Paulo Biennial in Brazil. He has maintained an academic career alongside his activities as a designer: since 1992, he has been a professor of production technology at the Köln International School of Design.

CAREER HIGHLIGHTS

1882 Founds the Unikate group, together with Reinhard Müller
1984 Creates his Taut Shelf design
1985 Cofounds the Pentagon group

FERRUCCIO LAVIANI

ITALIAN, 1960–

Born in Cremona, Laviani belongs to a fresh wave of exciting young designers who have emerged in Italy in recent years. He gained qualifications in architecture and design from Milan Polytechnic, Italy, graduating in 1986. By this stage, he had already begun to collaborate with Studio De Lucchi, where he eventually became a partner. Laviani also participated in the "12 Newcomers" and "Living on Earth" Memphis shows. As to be expected from a member of the Memphis circle, Laviani's designs are highly original and colorful and display a touch of postmodernist whimsy. These qualities are typified by his Taj LED table lamp, which was inspired by an elephant's tusk, and the Good Vibrations cabinet (2013).

PETER LAYTON

BRITISH, 1937–

Dubbed the "Grandmaster of Glass," Layton is a pioneer of the studio glass movement. Born in Prague, now in the Czech Republic, he studied ceramics at the Central School of Art and Design in London, UK, but switched to glass after taking up a temporary teaching post in Iowa. In 1969, Layton helped set up the Glasshouse in London; then, in 1976, he established his own London Glassblowing Workshop. This was one of the first hot-glass studios in Europe, and its influence has been immeasurable. Layton's own designs are richly colored and display subtle, painterly qualities. Indeed, in some of his works, he has drawn direct inspiration from the pictures of Van Gogh, Gauguin, and his childhood friend David Hockney.

JAN LENICA

POLISH, 1928–2001

Lenica was a versatile graphic designer and filmmaker, best known for his somewhat sinister posters. He trained as an architect at Warsaw Polytechnic, Poland, and, while still a student, began producing book illustrations and satirical cartoons. Lenica worked for a time with the film director Walerian Borowczyk and later made his own, highly acclaimed animated films. In 1963, he moved abroad, living initially in Paris and subsequently in Germany. Here, he designed postage stamps and posters for the 1972 Olympic Games in Munich. His greatest images, however, were reserved for stage and screen. In his posters and animations, Lenica created a potent mix of psychedelia and Expressionism. The most famous example is the Wozzeck poster (1964), in which a murderer's face is reduced to a screaming mouth, surrounded by ripples of blood.

ZDENĚK LHOTSKÝ

CZECH, 1956–

Lhotský is a major glass designer, maintaining the proud Czech tradition in this field. He trained at the University of Applied Arts in Prague, where his supervisor was Stanislav Libenský—a pioneer of studio glass in the East. In 1987, Lhotský became one of the

SOPHORA VASE, RENÉ LALIQUE, *c.* 1926

founding members of Tvrdohlaví (The Stubborn Ones), an influential association of contemporary Czech artists. Then, in 1994, he established the Lhotský Glass Studios at Pelechov, near Železný Brod in the Czech Republic, a traditional center of glass production. This rapidly achieved a superb reputation for the quality and design of its cast glass, which ranges from large vessels and sculptures to architectural reliefs.

▷ SIR ARTHUR LASENBY LIBERTY

BRITISH, 1843–1917

Through his celebrated department store, Liberty helped shape the course of modern British design. The son of a draper, he worked at Farmer and Rogers' Oriental Warehouse before opening his shop, Liberty & Co., in London, in 1875.

At first, Liberty specialized in selling silks and porcelain from East Asia, but he rapidly extended his range to include furniture and metalware. In 1883, he set up a furnishing and decorating studio to meet the demand for fashionable interiors by developing a style that merged Arts and Crafts design with commercial needs. Liberty was adept at identifying and exploiting new trends, and by 1900, his emporium was celebrated worldwide as a leader in the production of Arts and Crafts furniture. It also became an early champion of Art Nouveau. Indeed, in Italy, Art Nouveau became commonly known as the *Stile Liberty*.

FURNISHING FABRIC BY SIDNEY MAWSON, RETAILED BY LIBERTY, 1909

STIG LINDBERG

SWEDISH, 1916–1982

Whether working on ceramics, textiles, or book illustrations, Lindberg brought a genuine *joie de vivre* to all his designs. After graduating from the University College of Arts, Crafts, and Design in Konstfack, Sweden, he began his long association with the prestigious ceramics factory at Gustavsberg. Lindberg stayed there for most of his career, succeeding Wilhelm Kåge as Art Director in 1949. His output was diverse, ranging from leaf-shaped bowls to textured Reptil vases. Many of Lindberg's designs are biomorphic—they resemble living forms, but are actually abstract. This is also a feature of his superb creations for the NK Textile Design Studios.

OTTO LINDIG

GERMAN, 1895–1966

Born in Pössneck, Otto Lindig was a master potter. He studied at the Weimar Kunstgewerbeschule (Arts and Crafts School), then enrolled at the Bauhaus soon after it opened and studied at the ceramics workshop in Dornburg from 1920, later becoming a journeyman there.

Lindig was an influential figure at the Bauhaus. He became Technical Director of the workshop in 1924, and was eager to experiment with machine production, developing molds that could be used to mass-produce containers. He stayed in his post at Dornburg after the Bauhaus closed until 1930, and then worked in his own right as a master potter until 1947. Lindig finished his career at the Hamburg Academy of Fine Arts.

VICKE LINDSTRAND

SWEDISH, 1904–83

Born in Gothenburg, Lindstrand was a versatile talent who designed glass, ceramics, and textiles. He joined the glassware manufacturer Orrefors as artistic director in 1929 and first came to international attention with the enameled vases that he exhibited at the Stockholm World Fair in 1930. At Orrefors, Lindstrand worked on engraved glass and Graal vases. Together with the sculptor Edvin Öhrström, he also developed the Ariel technique, in which air is captured within the walls of a glass vessel. After working with the Upsala-Ekeby ceramics company from 1943 to 1950, he returned to glass as the artistic director at Kosta Glasbruk. Lindstrand also made several monumental glass sculptures.

EL LISSITZKY

RUSSIAN, 1890–1941

Lazar Markovich "El" Lissitzky was born in Pochinok, western Russia. He studied architecture in Darmstadt, Germany, then returned to Moscow in 1914 to become an architect. An ardent supporter of the Russian Revolution, Lissitzky applied Constructivist ideals to graphic design, aiming to create a form of art that was accessible to the proletariat. His graphic designs were bold, with asymmetrical layouts, changes of scale, and innovative use of typography. Sent as Soviet cultural ambassador to Germany in 1921, Lissitzky also had a profound influence on the Bauhaus. His wide-ranging work included posters, book designs, photomontages, and architectural projects.

▷ RAYMOND LOEWY

FRENCH AMERICAN, 1893–1986

The dominant figure in American industrial design in the mid-20th century, Loewy was born in Paris. He emigrated to New York after serving in the French army in World War I. Loewy set up his own design consultancy in the late 1920s, and his first major commission was a 1929 duplicator for Gestetner, but it was his styling of the Coldspot Super Six refrigerator (1934) that made his name. His streamlined designs, from steam locomotives for the Pennsylvania Railroad Company in the 1930s to the Greyhound Scenicruiser bus in 1951, helped to transform the image of American transportation.

Other Loewy classics included the Lucky Strike cigarette packet (1942), the Coca-Cola dispenser (1947) and the Shell Oil Company logo (1971). Loewy's consultancy also worked on the interior design of the Skylab space station for NASA in the late 1960s. He retired to his native France in 1980.

CAREER HIGHLIGHTS

1934 Designs the Coldspot Super Six refrigerator
1951 Publishes his autobiography, named after his motto, *Never Leave Well Enough Alone*

HEINRICH LÖFFELHARDT

GERMAN, 1901–1979

The most admired designer of porcelain and glassware in Germany in the 1950s and 1960s, Löffelhardt was born in Heilbronn. He began his career as a sculptor before taking up industrial design in the 1930s. He was drafted into the German army in 1941 and held in a Soviet prison camp after the war until 1947. From the 1950s, he designed porcelainware for the Arzberg company and glassware for Zwiesel.

ADOLF LOOS

SLOVAKIAN, 1870–1933

Born in Brno in what is now the Czech Republic, Loos studied architecture in Dresden, spent several years in the US, and worked as an architect in Austria and France. He is most famous for his essay *Ornament und Verbrechen* (Ornament and Crime, 1908), which he wrote in

EXHIBITION POSTER WITH RAYMOND LOEWY'S LUCKY STRIKE DESIGN OF 1942

turn-of-the-century Vienna at the same time as Sigmund Freud was developing his theories of psychoanalysis. In this essay, Loos vehemently opposed the ornamental Art Nouveau style, calling it degenerate, and linked morality and modernity with functional, plain forms. His designs for the Viennese Café Museum (1899), dubbed Café Nihilismus because it had no decoration, embodied his Modernist views.

ROSS LOVEGROVE

WELSH, 1958–

Cardiff-born Lovegrove is one of the most innovative contemporary product designers. A graduate of the Royal College of Art in London, he began his career at Frog Design in Germany in the 1980s, working on projects for Apple and

Sony. He established his own design studio, Studio X, in London's Notting Hill, in 1990. Although minimal and high-tech, his work is influenced by organic shapes drawn from nature. It ranges from the Coachline luggage collection for Connolly (1992) to the Go plastic chair he designed for Bernhardt Design (2001), and the Impronta ballpoint pen for Mandarina Duck (2004). Lovegrove won the World Technology Award for design in 2005.

HANS AND WASSILI LUCKHARDT

GERMAN, 1890–1954 AND 1889–1972

Born in Charlottenburg, Berlin, the Luckhardt brothers were architects who worked together for most of their lives. Participating in the ferment of aesthetic and political ideas in 1920s Germany,

they created innovative steel-framed buildings as part of a Modernist vision for the restructuring of society. They also made elegant tubular-steel furniture. The rise to power of the Nazi Party in the 1930s blighted their careers, and they never recovered their former prominence.

PER LÜTKEN

DANISH, 1916–1998

One of the great masters of Danish glass design, Lütken joined the country's long-established Holmegaard glass factory in 1942 and stayed there for the rest of his life, designing more than 3,000 items. His reputation blossomed when he created the Provence bowl in 1955 and the Selandia dish in 1957, both of which are regarded as modern classics. His other notable designs included the Carnaby line (1968), the Skibsglas range (1971), the Idéelle line (1978), and the Charlotte Amalie line (1981).

CHARLES RENNIE MACKINTOSH

SCOTTISH, 1868–1928

Mackintosh trained as an architect in his native Glasgow, while also studying at the city's school of art. His influences included Japanese art, and his mature work is highly geometric, as seen in his various chair designs, which are often high-backed with a rectilinear grid pattern, sometimes leavened with Celtic-style ornament. Contemporary with Arts and Crafts, he is also linked with European Art Nouveau and Modernism.

In 1896, Mackintosh began work on interiors for Glasgow tearooms and was commissioned to design a new building for the art school. Completed in 1909, the Glasgow Art School building was widely considered to be his masterpiece. Mackintosh exhibited at the Vienna Secession in 1900, and his furniture and decorative interiors were admired in Europe. He was overlooked at home, however, and in Britain his only other major commission was the Hill House at Helensburgh, overlooking the River Clyde, in 1904. He spent his later years painting.

VICO MAGISTRETTI

ITALIAN, 1920–2006

Born in Milan, Magistretti was originally an architect, and was prominent in idealistic projects for urban reconstruction in Italy after World War II. He became best known, however, as a designer of mass-produced furniture and lamps in the 1950s and 1960s.

Magistretti's most notable designs were the Carimate chair, commissioned by Cassina in 1959, the Eclisse lamp of 1967, and the fiberglass Selene chair manufactured by Artemide from 1968. All of his designs are characterized by understated elegance, practicality, and competitive pricing.

ERIK MAGNUSSEN (1)

DANISH, 1884–1961

An émigré silversmith, Magnussen is chiefly remembered for the Cubist, skyscraper-inspired coffee service he designed in 1927 after flying over New York and seeing that "the entire city made a picture of triangular patches of sun and shadow." Dubbed "The Lights and Shadows of Manhattan," its faceted silver panels, some gilded and others oxidized, glittered in the light, emphasizing its extreme angularity.

ERIK MAGNUSSEN (2)

DANISH, 1940–2014

Born in Copenhagen, Magnussen graduated from the School of Applied Arts and Design as a ceramicist. He worked for the Bing & Grøndahl ceramics firm before branching out to design furniture for Fritz Hansen, tableware for Stelton, kitchenware for Georg Jensen, and pewter for Royal Selangor. His elegant, functional designs, influenced by the work of Arne Jacobsen, included the Z chair, produced in 1965, and the 1977 cylindrical Stelton vacuum flask.

YOSHIHISA MAITANI

JAPANESE, 1933–2009

Born in the Shikoku region of Japan, camera designer Maitani made his first camera at the age of 10. He joined Olympus in 1956 and worked for the company for the following 40 years. He created small cameras with outstanding image quality and controls that were large enough to use comfortably. His classic innovative designs included the Olympus Pen in 1959, the 1963 Pen-F SLR, the OM-1 in 1973, and the XA in 1979.

LOUIS MAJORELLE

FRENCH, 1859–1926

Majorelle was the son of a furniture manufacturer in Nancy, eastern France. He originally intended to be an artist but took over the family business when his father died in 1879. In the 1890s, influenced by Émile Gallé, he adopted the Art Nouveau style, making furniture with organic forms and naturalistic motifs. He exhibited at the Paris Exposition Universelle of 1900, and the following year he helped found the École de Nancy association of Art Nouveau manufacturers. Majorelle made his elegant furniture relatively affordable by keeping production costs low. His factory was destroyed during World War I, but he resumed production in the 1920s, this time with Art Deco designs.

CAREER HIGHLIGHTS

1879	Takes over the family furniture business in Nancy
1901	Forms the École de Nancy with Émile Gallé
1916	Fire damages factory
1925	Designs the interior of the Nancy pavilion for the Paris Exposition Internationale

KASIMIR MALEVICH

RUSSIAN, 1878–1935

Born in Kursk, Ukraine, then part of the Russian Empire, Malevich was primarily an abstract artist. By 1915, influenced by Cubism, he had established his own Suprematist style and aesthetic philosophy in which simple geometric forms were more important than the subject matter.

After the Russian Revolution, bowing to political pressure to use art in a practical way only, Malevich experimented with product design, applying his Suprematist principles of form and color to ceramic tableware. He also undertook a number of architectural projects.

GERHARD MARCKS

GERMAN, 1889–1981

Born in Berlin, Marcks was an apprentice sculptor before serving in the German Army in World War I. After the armistice, he joined radical art movements in Berlin and, in 1919, he was one of the first artists invited to teach at the Bauhaus.

Marcks headed the Bauhaus ceramics workshop until 1925. When the Nazis rose to power in 1933, his sculpture was labeled degenerate and he was banned from teaching. He resumed teaching after the war then freelanced as a sculptor.

ENZO MARI

ITALIAN, 1932–

Born in Novara, Mari studied at the Brera Academy in Milan. Primarily a teacher and theoretician, he had his first commercial success as a designer with a children's puzzle in 1957. In the 1960s, he designed plastic containers and vases, and in the 1970s, he branched out into furniture with the Sof-Sof chair and self-assembly Box chair. Resisting what some saw as the excesses of postmodernism, he maintained a restrained functional style, which won him commissions from Muji in the 21st century.

▽ JAVIER MARISCAL

SPANISH, 1950–

An artist and designer, Mariscal was born in Valencia but has spent most of his life working in Barcelona. A wide-ranging designer, his work has included furniture, graphic design, interior design, and company branding. His Duplex barstool (1980) led to an invitation to exhibit with the postmodernist Memphis Group in Milan. Comic books have been a great influence on him, as seen in the Cobi mascot that he designed for the 1992 Barcelona Olympics. Mariscal has also styled interiors for several bars, hotels, and restaurants and was responsible for the integral design of the Gran Hotel Domine Bilbao in 2002.

ALESSANDRA CHAIR, JAVIER MARISCAL FOR MOROSO, 1995

RICHARD MARQUIS

AMERICAN, 1945–

Born in Arizona, Marquis is one of the most influential contemporary studio glassblowers. His work is characterized by wit, originality, and technical mastery, thanks in part to winning a Fulbright scholarship in 1969 to study glassmaking in the Venini factory in Murano. He was one of the first Americans to work under Venetian glass masters.

▽ DINO MARTENS

ITALIAN, 1894–1970

Born in Venice, Martens studied at the Accademia di Belle Arti and exhibited paintings in the 1920s at the Venice Biennale. He is best known, however, for his work as artistic director of the Murano glass company Aureliano Toso from 1939 to 1963. In his Oriente range of decorative glass, produced during the 1950s, he employed a variety of sophisticated, traditional techniques to create bold, colorful, abstract, and asymmetrical designs.

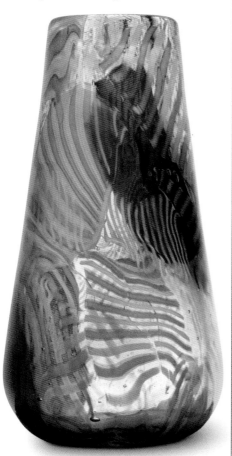

FRAMMENTATI VASE, DINO MARTENS FOR AURELIANO TOSO, 1952

CAREER HIGHLIGHTS

1924 First paintings exhibited at the Venice Biennale
1939 Becomes artistic director of Aureliano Toso
1948 His exuberant designs, the glass equivalent of Abstract Expressionist painting, cause a stir at the Venice Biennale

BRUNO MATHSSON

SWEDISH, 1907–1988

Mathsson was born the son of a cabinetmaker in the small town of Värnamo in rural Sweden. He learned to make traditional furniture in his father's workshop and taught himself about modern, functional design from books. In 1930, he began to create innovative chairs made from bent, laminated wood and braided webbing. Exhibiting at the 1937 Paris World Fair won him an international reputation. In the 1940s, Mathsson worked as an architect, but he returned to furniture design in the 1960s.

CAREER HIGHLIGHTS

1934 Designs the Eva chair with a seat of woven webbing, a material concealed in conventional furniture
1968 Designs the Superellipse Table Series with Piet Hein

ROBERTO MATTA

CHILEAN, 1911–2002

Born in Santiago, Chile, Roberto Sebastian Matta Echaurren was primarily a painter and sculptor, whose work developed from his involvement with the European Surrealist movement in the 1930s into a highly individual biomorphic style. In the 1950s, he worked with Asger Jorn and others at the Mazzotti ceramics workshop in Albisola, Italy, producing distinctive pottery that expressed his aesthetic and political radicalism.

ADOLF MATURA

CZECH, 1921–1979

Matura was a glass designer who worked for the Bohemian glassworks of the Czechoslovakian Sklo Union group—especially the Rosice, Libochovice, and Rudolfova glassworks. His retro designs for pressed glassware ranged from vases and bowls to ashtrays and jardinières. Especially prized are his Praha series for Rosice and his Head series for Libochovice, both of which date from the early 1970s. He also designed the internationally bestselling Kavalier teapot.

INGO MAURER

GERMAN, 1932–2019

Born on the island of Reichenau, Lake Constance, Maurer was initially a graphic designer. In 1966, he launched a lighting company, Design M, and made an immediate impact with the Pop art–influenced Bulb lamp. Many playful designs followed, including the Lucellino winged bulb (1992). Maurer also pursued technical innovation, from his YaYaHo halogen system of 1984 to OLEDs from 2006. His public lighting projects included lighting for the Westfriedhof Underground station in Munich, in 1998, and the Brussels Atomium, in 2006.

▷ PETER MAX

GERMAN AMERICAN, 1937–

Born Peter Max Finkelstein in Berlin, Max had a peripatetic childhood, moving from Germany to China, Israel, and France before settling in New York in 1953.

After studying at the Art Students League in Manhattan, Max set up a graphic design studio in 1961. His colorful, psychedelic style became one of the defining looks of the 1960s counterculture and was exploited in posters and in product branding, from clocks to soft drinks. His later work has included designs for major sports events, such as the 1994 FIFA World Cup.

CAREER HIGHLIGHTS

1961 Sets up a graphic design studio in New York
1967 Designs the poster for the Central Park Be-In student rally

ALBERTO MEDA

ITALIAN, 1945–

An industrial designer, Meda was born in Lenno on Lake Como and studied mechanical engineering at Milan Polytechnic. He became technical director at the plastic furniture company Kartell in 1973, and since 1979, he has worked as a consultant engineer and designer for Alfa Romeo, Alessi, Omron, Philips, Olivetti, and Vitra, among others. Since 1995, he has lectured at the Domus Academy, and he has won both Compasso d'Oro and Red Dot awards.

FRANCO MELLO

ITALIAN, 1945–

Mello was born in Genoa and educated at Turin Polytechnic. In 1972, with Guido Drocco, he designed the iconic Cactus clothes rack for Gufram. Made from polyurethane foam with a lacquered finish, the stand has been reissued in many different colors since then.

Mello's wide-ranging activities have included designing catalogs and posters, packaging, and photography. He teaches Industrial Design for Visual Communication at Turin Polytechnic.

DAVID MELLOR

BRITISH, 1930–2009

Born in Sheffield, Yorkshire, industrial designer Mellor was the most important British cutlery designer of the 20th century. He trained as a silversmith at his local art college before studying at the Royal College of Art in London from 1950. While still a student, he designed the elegant Pride line of cutlery, which is still in production today. Other flatware ranges he created include Provençal, Café, Savoy, and City. By the 1960s, he was designing street lighting, bus shelters, and traffic lights, as well as stainless steel cutlery.

From 1973, Mellor manufactured his own cutlery at Broom Hall in Sheffield and then, from 1990, in Hathersage in the Peak District. He opened the first of his kitchenware shops, called David Mellor Ironmonger, in London, in 1969. His son runs the business today.

CAREER HIGHLIGHTS

1953 Designs the Pride line of cutlery, which won a Design Council award in 1957
1966 Designs a mailbox for the British Post Office, and traffic lights
1969 Opens his first shop in London
2003 Designs Minimal range of cutlery

MEMPHIS

ITALIAN, 1981–1988

Started by the charismatic and outspoken Italian designer Ettore Sottsass, Memphis was a collective that grew out of Milanese avant-garde group Studio Alchimia, which itself stemmed from the Radical Design movement in Italy in the late 1960s.

The Memphis designers caused a furor when they exhibited their work at the 1981 Milan Furniture Fair. Their bold, colorful, irreverent, and often kitsch furniture, lighting, clocks, and ceramics set the tone for postmodern design in the 1980s, sending up historical styles and mixing luxurious materials with plastic laminates and Pop art.

PAOLO MENDES DA ROCHA

BRAZILIAN, 1928–

Architect Mendes da Rocha was born in Vitória, southeastern Brazil. He moved to São Paulo and, in the 1950s, became a member of the Paulista brutalist movement, creating uncompromising buildings in concrete and glass. In 1957, as part of his first commission—to design the Athletic Club of São Paulo—he created the Paulistano armchair, a single bent-steel bar with a leather cover. His architectural achievements include Brazil's pavilion at Expo 70 in Osaka, Japan, and the St. Peter Chapel in São Paulo (1987).

ALESSANDRO MENDINI

ITALIAN, 1931–2019

Postmodernist architect and designer Alessandro Mendini was born and educated in Milan. He worked for Marcello Nizzoli in the 1960s, before forming the radical Global Tools design group in 1973. Two of his most famous designs, the Proust armchair and the garish Sofa Kandissi, were made for Studio Alchimia in 1978–1979. The armchair was an example of "banal design," in which Mendini drew attention to the trite nature of existing objects with bright color and unexpected ornament, while the sofa poked fun at fine art with its Kandinsky-inspired wooden cutouts.

Mendini also created silverware and plastics for Alessi. He was head architect for the Groninger Museum in the Netherlands (completed in 1994), for which he designed a large yellow tower.

UNTITLED (BOB DYLAN), PETER MAX, 1967

CAREER HIGHLIGHTS

1973 Founding member of the Global Tools design group
1978 Designs the Proust and Vassilij armchairs for Studio Alchimia
1979 Wins the Compasso d'Oro award
1980 Organizes The Banal Object exhibition at the Venice Biennale

MAX MIEDINGER

SWISS, 1910–1980

As a young man, typeface designer Miedinger worked as a typesetter and typographer in his native Zurich. In 1946, he was taken on as a salesman by the Haas Typefoundry. He designed his first typeface, Pro Arte, in 1954.

In 1956, he went freelance and was commissioned by Haas director Eduard Hoffmann to design a new sans-serif typeface. Originally known as Neue Haas Grotesk, the Roman version was introduced in 1958 and a bold version in 1959. It was renamed Helvetica in 1960. Other Miedinger typefaces included Swiss 721 and Horizontal.

SEAGRAM BUILDING, LUDWIG MIES VAN DER ROHE, 1954–1958

◁ LUDWIG MIES VAN DER ROHE

GERMAN AMERICAN, 1886–1969

Mies was born in Aachen, the son of a stonemason. He received no formal art education but learned stone carving from his father. After moving to Berlin, he was apprenticed to Peter Behrens, then set up his own architecture studio in 1912. In the 1920s, he figured prominently in the German avant garde. Commissioned to design the German pavilion for the 1929 Barcelona International Exhibition, he created both an iconic Modernist building and the famous Barcelona chair.

From 1930, Mies was Bauhaus director. Throughout the 1930s, his steel furniture was manufactured by Thonet-Mundus. In 1937 Mies left the Bauhaus and emigrated to the US, basing himself in Chicago, where he became the leading exponent of the International Style in architecture. His projects included the Farnsworth House, Plano, Illinois (1946–1950), apartments on Lake Shore Drive, Chicago (1946–1959), the Mannheim Opera House (1954–1958), and the towering office block of the Seagram Building, New York (1954–1958), which Philip Johnson helped design.

CAREER HIGHLIGHTS

1926 Becomes Vice-President of the Deutscher Werkbund
1929 Designs the German national pavilion, including the Barcelona chair for use by the King of Spain, at the Barcelona Exhibition
1930 Becomes the last director of the Bauhaus
1937 Emigrates to the US and starts an architectural practice in Chicago

MIGUEL MILÁ

SPANISH, 1931–

Catalan industrial designer Milá was born into an artistic Barcelona family. He began designing furniture in the late 1950s, setting up his own manufacturing company, Tramo. Combining traditional materials with a Modernist aesthetic, he created durable classics such as the TMC lamp (1958) and the Cesta lamp (1964).

In the 1980s, Milá focused on designing interiors, but in the 1990s, he won acclaim for the furniture he designed for public spaces, notably his Neoromantico benches and tables. In 2008, he was awarded the Compasso d'Oro for his contribution to Spanish design.

HERMAN MILLER

AMERICAN, 1923–

The Star Furniture Company, founded in Michigan in 1905, was taken over by D. J. De Pree in 1923, and renamed Herman Miller, after De Pree's father-in-law. When George Nelson was appointed design director in 1947, the company became the leading American manufacturer of Modernist furniture, including Isamu Noguchi's Coffee table (1947) and the Eames' Lounge Chair 670 (1956). After employing Robert Propst from 1958, Herman Miller revolutionized office design with the cubicle system.

LÁSZLÓ MOHOLY-NAGY

HUNGARIAN, 1895–1946

Moholy-Nagy was a law student in Budapest when World War I broke out and started drawing and painting after he was wounded. When the war ended, he moved to Berlin and, from 1923 to 1928, he taught the preliminary course at the Bauhaus. He encouraged innovation in industrial design and typography, running a class on materials and space. With his wife, Lucia Moholy, he experimented with photomontages (combining photography and typography). He took over from Paul Klee as Master of Form of the metal workshop, teaching Marianne Brandt and Wilhelm Wagenfeld.

When the Nazis came to power in 1933, Moholy-Nagy had to leave Germany. In 1937, he settled in Chicago, where he established the New Bauhaus and, later, the Chicago School of Design.

▽ CARLO MOLLINO

ITALIAN, 1905–1973

The son of a wealthy Turin engineer, Mollino had an extravagant personality that found expression in skiing, auto racing, and erotic photography, as well as architecture and furniture design.

Working in his father's office, he designed his first house in 1930, followed by the Turin Riding School and the ski station at Lago Nero, which incorporated the swoops and curves that later came to feature in his furniture. He is perhaps best known for the biomorphic furniture he designed after World War II, such as the Arabesque Table (1950) and the Lattes Chair (1951). His late masterpiece was the reconstruction of the Teatro Regio in Turin, which began in 1967.

CAREER HIGHLIGHTS

1937 Designs the Società Ippica (Riding School) in Turin
1950 Designs the Arabesque Table, made from plywood and glass
1954 Osca 1100, a race car he designed, wins the Le Mans 24-hour race

MASAHIRO MORI

JAPANESE, 1927–2005

Born in Saga Prefecture on Kyushu island, Mori studied at the Tama College of Art and Design. From 1956 to 1978, he worked for the Hakusan Porcelain Company in Nagasaki. Bringing a refinement to the design of functional mass-produced ceramic tableware, Mori made his reputation with the G-type soy sauce bottle of 1958. He won Japan's Good Design Award in 1960, the first of 111 such awards. His last work was the 2004 Wa series for Muji.

STANLEY MORISON

BRITISH, 1889–1967

An influential typographer, Morison was raised in London and left school at 14. He taught himself typography by studying the history of printing and, from 1922, was typographic adviser to the British Monotype Corporation, where he revived historic typefaces, such as Baskerville and Bembo, and commissioned new ones, such as Gill Sans (1928).

In 1923, he became typographic advisor to Cambridge University Press, and in 1931, he commissioned Times New Roman for *The Times* newspaper. His book *First Principles of Typography* (1936) was hugely influential.

BISILURO (TWIN TORPEDO), CARLO MOLLINO, 1955

WILLIAM MORRIS (1)

BRITISH, 1834–1896

Designer, writer, and founder of the Arts and Crafts movement, Morris initially studied theology, but his love of medieval architecture inspired him to train instead as an architect. In 1861, he cofounded Morris, Marshall, Faulkner & Co. (later known as Morris & Co.) to design and manufacture fabrics, tapestries, furniture, stained glass, and other decorative items. All the furnishings were made of the finest natural materials, following traditional techniques, and Morris provided many of the designs himself, notably for the wallpapers and textiles.

Morris was also a prolific poet and polemical writer, promoting socialism and the value of traditional craftsmanship. From 1891, he ran his own publishing house, the Kelmscott Press, where many of his books were hand printed.

CAREER HIGHLIGHTS

1861　Starts the design company Morris, Marshall, Faulkner & Co.
1862　Creates his first wallpaper and textile designs
1866　Designs the Green Dining Room at the South Kensington Museum (now the Victoria and Albert Museum or V&A)
1891　Founds the Kelmscott Press

WILLIAM MORRIS (2)

AMERICAN, 1957–

Born in Carmel, California, Morris was educated at California State University and Central Washington University.

He learned glassmaking at the Pilchuck Glass School in Stanwood, Washington, where he arrived initially as a driver in 1978. He worked for glass sculptor Dale Chihuly at Pilchuck, before setting up his own studio in the late 1980s.

Morris's art glass often imitates stone or wood carving. Inspired by the work of ancient cultures, including classical sculpture and vases and prehistoric cave paintings, his forms are based on those of ritual vessels, such as rhytons and shamanic rattles, and are intended to convey the gulf between humans and their pagan roots. The inclusion of animals such as birds or deer references the increasing alienation of man from the natural world. Morris retired in 2007.

CAREER HIGHLIGHTS

1997　Receives New York Outstanding Achievement in Glass award
2007　Made a Fellow of the American Craft Council
2011　Releases documentary film "Creative Nature"

JASPER MORRISON

BRITISH, 1959–

London-born Morrison trained at the Royal College of Art and established a design agency in 1986. He first attracted attention with his minimalist, functional Ply Chair for Vitra in 1989, and the Series 1144 door handles for FSB the following year. As well as furniture, he has designed a range of home accessories, lamps, household goods, and electronic devices for companies such as Alessi, Magis, Flos, and Olivetti.

KOLOMAN MOSER

AUSTRIAN, 1868–1918

Viennese artist and designer Moser studied at the Vienna Academy of Fine Arts and the School of Applied Arts, supporting himself through commercial illustration. In 1897, he was one of the founders of the Vienna Secession, and he designed the Secession magazine *Ver Sacrum* from 1898.

In 1903, Moser established the Wiener Werkstätte (Vienna Workshops) with Josef Hoffmann and Fritz Wärndorfer. Moser designed furniture, ceramics, silver, and wallpaper for the Workshops and for private companies. In 1904, he created mosaics and stained glass for the Steinhof Church in Vienna. He left the Secession in 1905 and the Workshops in 1907. His later work included the design of postage stamps.

CAREER HIGHLIGHTS

1898　Becomes editor of *Ver Sacrum*, the Vienna Secession journal
1900　Exhibits furniture and glass at the Paris Exposition Universelle and the VIII Secessionist Exhibition in Vienna; becomes Professor of painting at the Kunstgewerbeschule in Vienna
1903　Cofounds the Wiener Werkstätte
1907　Leaves the Wiener Werkstätte

▽ PASCAL MOURGUE

FRENCH, 1943–2014

Parisian artist and designer Pascal Mourgue studied sculpture at the École Boulle and interior architecture at the École Nationale Supérieure des Arts Décoratifs. Primarily interested in fine art, he began designing furniture as a sideline from 1962. In the 1980s, he produced highly successful designs such as the Calin sofa (1984) and the Mourgue bed (1985). His later work included the Pas Si Classique sofa for Cinna (2007).

CAREER HIGHLIGHTS

1988　Exhibits at Victoria and Albert Museum (V&A), London
1994　Designs his first collection for Cinna, including the Calin armchair
1996　Awarded the Grand Prix National for industrial design

▷ ALPHONSE MUCHA

CZECH, 1860–1939

Art Nouveau decorative artist Mucha was born in Moravia, then part of the Austrian Empire, now in the Czech Republic. He learned his trade painting scenery for Viennese theaters before receiving a formal art education at the Munich Academy of Fine Arts and the Académie Julian in Paris. His breakthrough came in 1894, with an acclaimed poster of the actress Sarah Bernhardt in the play *Gismonda*. Over the following decade, Mucha produced a flood of advertising posters, magazine illustrations, and designs for packaging, postcards, bank notes, menus, jewelry, and textiles, all in quintessential Art Nouveau style. He also designed every detail of the interior of Georges Fouquet's jewelry shop in Paris, from the lighting to the door handles and stained glass. Fouquet also manufactured the jewelry that Mucha had designed for Bernhardt.

Mucha's decorative work featured prominently in the 1900 Paris Exposition Universelle. He spent most of his later life in Prague, celebrating Czech history in murals and stained glass.

CAREER HIGHLIGHTS

1879　Works as a theatrical painter in Vienna
1892　Creates his first poster
1894　Actress Sarah Bernhardt contracts him to make posters of her productions for next six years
1897　Exhibit of his work held in Paris; it travels abroad, sealing his international reputation
1900　Designs the Bosnia-Herzegovina pavilion at the Exposition Universelle in Paris.

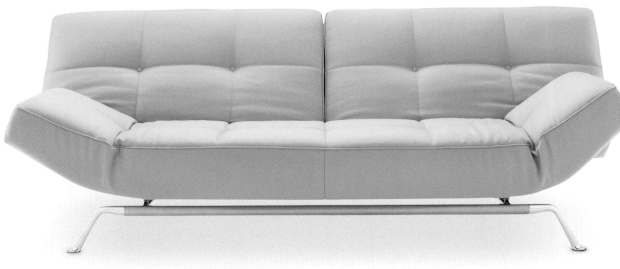

SMALA SOFA, PASCAL MOURGUE FOR LIGNE ROSET, 2000

STAINED GLASS PANEL OF *LA PLUME* POSTER, ALPHONSE MUCHA, 1899

MÜLLER FRÈRES

FRENCH, 1895–1936

The Müller Frères glassworks was established by a family of Alsatian origin in Lunéville, eastern France. Four of the nine Müller brothers had learned to produce art glass by working for Émile Gallé (1846–1904) in nearby Nancy. Like Gallé, they used the technique of fire polishing to melt away any surface imperfections caused by the acid-etching process. They produced stained glass, glass for electric lighting, and decorative wares.

The Müller brothers were renowned in the early 1900s for their wide range of Art Nouveau decorative glass. After World War I, they also produced an impressive line in Art Deco glass.

GERD ALFRED MÜLLER

GERMAN, 1932–1991

Born in Frankfurt am Main, Müller studied at the Wiesbaden School of Art from 1952. In 1955, he was employed by Braun, working alongside Dieter Rams, and his designs for Braun kitchen appliances and electric razors are considered classics. He established his own design studio in 1960. His clients included the writing instrument company Lamy, for whom he created the Lamy 2000 fountain pen in 1966.

CAREER HIGHLIGHTS

1955   Starts working for Braun
1957   Designs the KM3 kitchen mixer, exemplifying postwar efficiency
1966   Designs Lamy 2000 fountain pen

BUILT IN OUR TIME POSTER, JOSEF MÜLLER-BROCKMANN, 1958

△ JOSEF MÜLLER-BROCKMANN

SWISS, 1914–1996

Graphic designer Müller-Brockmann studied art and design in Zurich, where he set up his own office in 1936. Influenced by Bauhaus, Constructivism, and De Stijl, he favored sans-serif typefaces, grid layouts, and the use of photomontage. "Sans Serif as the Expression of our Age" was his motto.

He is most admired for his posters, especially those advertising concerts at the Zurich Tonhalle in the 1950s. Cofounder of the trilingual journal *Neue Grafik* (New Graphic Design) in 1958, he was a key figure in promoting the Swiss International Style. In 1967, he became the European design consultant for IBM. Müller-Brockmann wrote several books on graphic design, including *Grid Systems in Graphic Design* (1981).

BRUNO MUNARI

ITALIAN, 1907–1998

Born in Milan, Munari made a notable contribution to Italian culture, initially as an experimental Futurist artist in the 1930s. After World War II, he took up industrial and graphic design, producing the X Hour alarm clock in 1945. Some of his designs were practical, such as the Cube ashtray for Danese (1957), but many of them were playful, including The Chair for Very Short Visits (1945), The Unreadable Book (1951), and a knitted tubular lamp he created in 1964.

Munari also created many innovative children's books and toys, including Zizi, a flexible toy monkey that showcased Pirelli's new foam rubber (early 1950s), and the wire-form Flexy (1968). He published the treatise *Design as Art* in 1966. His motto was "lucidity, leanness, exactitude, and humor."

KEITH MURRAY

NEW ZEALANDER, 1892–1981

Born in Auckland, Murray moved to England at the age of 14 and trained as an architect in London. He worked as an illustrator at first, but in the 1930s, he began to design factory-made vases and tableware. He created more than 1,000 designs between 1932 and 1939, notably ceramics for Wedgwood and metalware for Mappin & Webb. His elegant and restrained earthenware vessels seemed to encapsulate British Modernism; their plain forms were minimally decorated, usually with a series of lathe-turned grooves, and a smooth, matte glaze.

CAREER HIGHLIGHTS

1933 Begins designing ceramics for Josiah Wedgwood & Sons

1936 One of the first of Royal Society of Arts' Royal Designers for Industry

KAZUMASA NAGAI

JAPANESE, 1929–

Born in Osaka, Nagai is a graphic artist and poster designer who first established his reputation in the 1960s. Since then, his posters and illustrations have evolved in a radical manner, mutating from abstract to figurative, and from painting to computer art. Examples of his work are held by several prominent museums, including MoMA, New York, and the National Museum of Contemporary Art in Tokyo.

HARRY NAPPER

BRITISH, 1860–1930

Napper was an influential textile designer whose work was informed by both the Arts and Crafts movement and European Art Nouveau styles. He began work for the Silver Studio textile design firm in 1893, before establishing his own studio in 1898. The floral patterns of his textiles and wallpaper were popular in the early 20th century and were sold by shops such as Liberty & Co. Napper was also an accomplished landscape painter.

GEORGE NELSON

AMERICAN, 1908–1986

Born in Hartford, Connecticut, Nelson graduated from the Yale School of Arts, and in 1932, visited Europe on a Prix de Rome bursary. He returned to the US fired with enthusiasm for Modernist architecture, which he promoted in the magazine *Architectural Forum*. Nelson worked as an architect, until his modular Storagewall was publicized in *Life* magazine in 1945. This led to his joining furniture company Herman Miller as design director from 1946 to 1966. His many innovative designs ranged from the Atomic clock (1949) to the Action Office furniture system (1962). Nelson was also an influential author and educator, promoting new concepts from pedestrian precincts to prefabricated buildings.

CAREER HIGHLIGHTS

1949 Designs the Atomic wall clock

1956 Creates the Marshmallow sofa, which anticipates Pop design

1965 Creates the Action Office, an early ergonomic workspace, for Herman Miller

1968 Designs the Editor 2 typewriter for Olivetti

▷ MARC NEWSON

AUSTRALIAN, 1963–

Born in Sydney, Newson studied jewelry design and sculpture at the Sydney College of the Arts. In 1986, he exhibited the iconic Lockheed Lounge aluminum-clad chaise longue, initiating a meteoric design career. He worked in Tokyo and Paris before establishing a design studio in London in 1997. His furniture designs have included the Orgone Lounge (1991), the Event Horizon table (1992), and the Embryo chair (1998).

Newson has also designed Ikepod wristwatches, lights for Flos, seating for Qantas airliners, champagne bottles for Dom Pérignon, alongside coat hangers and doorstops. His larger-scale projects include restaurant interiors, a concept car for Ford, and the styling for a Dassault business jet.

CAREER HIGHLIGHTS

1996 Designs the interior for the Syn recording studio, Tokyo

1997 Establishes a studio in London

1998 Designs the Embryo chair

INTERIOR WITH EMBRYO CHAIR, MARC NEWSON, 1998

MARCELLO NIZZOLI

ITALIAN, 1887–1969

Born in Emilia-Romagna, Nizzoli studied at the Parma Academy of Fine Arts. As a painter and architect, he was linked with the Futurist movement in the 1920s. Olivetti employed him in 1932 as a graphic designer and four years later made him head of product design. His Olivetti classics include the Summa calculating machine (1940) and the Lettera 22 portable typewriter (1950). He also designed the Mirella sewing machine for Necchi in 1957. His designs typically had sculpturally curved outer shells that concealed the mechanical components.

▽ ISAMU NOGUCHI

AMERICAN, 1904–1988

Sculptor and designer Noguchi was born in Los Angeles. He studied cabinetmaking in Japan, then worked as an assistant to the sculptor Constantin Brancusi in Paris, before returning to the US. From 1929, he was a set designer in New York, but he then applied his skills to a wide range of products, the first of which was the Radio Nurse intercom for Zenith (1937), which was designed to resembled a Japanese warrior's mask.

In the 1940s and 1950s, he designed sculptural furniture, notably for Herman Miller. In 1951, he designed the first of his Akari paper lanterns. Much of his later life was dedicated to garden design.

ELIOT NOYES

AMERICAN, 1910–1977

Architect and industrial designer Noyes was born in Boston, Massachusetts, and educated at Harvard, where he came under the Modernist influence of Walter Gropius. He set up his own design practice in 1947 and, from 1956, he masterminded a corporate design program for IBM, modernizing all aspects of the brand, from its products to its buildings, and marketing materials.

His designs include the IBM Selectric Golfball typewriter (1961) and several notable buildings for IBM. He also updated Mobil Oil's corporate image, redesigning their standard gas pumps in 1964. He championed the notion that good design is good business.

CAREER HIGHLIGHTS

1956 Appointed Corporate Design Director of IBM

1961 Designs the Executary dictating machine

1964 Becomes a consultant for Mobil Oil

ANTTI NURMESNIEMI

FINNISH, 1927–2003

After studying interior design in Helsinki, Nurmesniemi worked for architect Viljo Revell, designing the distinctive Sauna stool for the Helsinki Palace Hotel in 1952. He set up his own practice in 1956. His many successful kitchenware and furniture designs included the Finel enameled coffee pot (1957) and the Triennale chair, first shown at the 1960 Milan Triennale. He was married to textile designer Vuokko Eskolin-Nurmesniemi.

GUNNAR NYLUND

SWEDISH DANISH FINNISH, 1904–1997

Ceramic designer Nylund was the son of a Danish ceramicist mother and a Finnish sculptor. He trained as an architect but learned pottery in his mother's studio and began work at the Bing & Gröndahl porcelain factory in Copenhagen, in 1925. He set up his own workshop, Saxbo, in 1928, and in 1931 joined Swedish manufacturer Rörstand, chiefly in the role of design director, until 1955. Best known for his tableware, he also produced sculptures and reliefs for public spaces.

RED CUBE, ISAMU NOGUCHI, 1968

HERMANN OBRIST

SWISS GERMAN, 1862–1927

Born in Kilchberg near Zurich, Obrist studied science and medicine at German universities before transferring to the Karlsruhe School for the Applied Arts in 1888. In 1892, he began creating tapestry and embroidered textiles, establishing a workshop in Munich in 1894. Using his knowledge of botany, he produced elaborate floral designs, exemplified by the large 1895 tapestry Cyclamen. Embroidered by Berthe Ruchet, this introduced the sinuous whiplash motif for which Obrist is best known, especially after it was exhibited at the 1896 Arts and Crafts exhibition.

Established at the forefront of Munich Jugendstil (the German term for Art Nouveau), Obrist's prolific designs also included furniture, ceramics, metalware, and public sculptures. The house that he designed for himself in Munich, which was destroyed in 1944, was a showcase of the Jugendstil style.

CAREER HIGHLIGHTS

1892 Sets up an embroidery workshop with Berthe Ruchet in Florence
1895 Creates the Cyclamen tapestry
1897 Displays textiles at the VII International Art exhibition, Munich
1902 Cofounds a design school in Munich

▷ YOICHI OHIRA

JAPANESE, 1946–

Glass artist Ohira graduated from the Kuwasawa Design School in Tokyo in 1969. In 1973, he moved to Venice, where he remained for the next 38 years. While studying at the Venice Academy of Fine Arts, he created original designs for Vetreria de Majo, a Murano glassmaker, which won him international recognition in the early 1980s. In the 1990s, he began to produce one-of-a-kind art pieces in collaboration with Venetian glass maestros, merging traditional Japanese ideas with the techniques and skill of the Murano manufacturers.

MOSAIC-BLOWN MURRINO-STYLE
ASHANTI VASE, YOICHI OHIRA, 1993

GEORGE OHR

AMERICAN, 1857–1918

The son of a blacksmith of German origin, Ohr was a native of Biloxi, Mississippi. He learned the potter's craft in New Orleans and set up a workshop in Biloxi, in the early 1880s. Using local clay, he created art pottery in naturalistic but extravagant forms pinched paper thin, which he called his "mud babies," marketing himself as the Mad Potter of Biloxi. Having achieved little recognition and few sales, he retired in 1909. His work was unique in the US, although similar wares were designed in the UK. Rediscovered in the late 1960s, his ceramics have enjoyed a growing reputation since the 1980s.

CAREER HIGHLIGHTS

1879 Apprenticed to ceramicist Joseph Fortune Meyer in New Orleans
1884 Exhibits more than 600 ceramics in New Orleans
1900 Further exhibits at the Arts & Crafts Exhibition in Buffalo

JOSEPH MARIA OLBRICH

AUSTRIAN, 1867–1908

Born at Troppau in the Austro-Hungarian Empire, Olbrich studied architecture in Vienna and worked in the practice of the Viennese architect Otto Wagner before traveling to Italy and Tunisia. In 1897, he was a founding member of the Viennese Secession, designing the movement's exhibition hall. Like many of his buildings, the simple geometry of its construction was offset with elaborate decoration, in this case a glittering gilded globe of abstracted laurel leaves. The following year, Olbrich designed interiors for the Villa Friedmann and, in 1899, for Villa Stift. His use of rectilinear forms and stylized botanical decoration was greatly influenced by the work of Charles Rennie Mackintosh.

In 1899, Olbrich moved to Darmstadt, Germany, to join, build, and direct an artists' colony promoted by the Grand Duke Ernst Ludwig of Hesse. Olbrich created grounds complete with studios, exhibition rooms, and living quarters. As well as the buildings, he also designed the furniture, ceramics, cutlery, glass, and textiles. With other designers, including Peter Behrens, Olbrich cofounded the Deutscher Werkbund (German Association of Craftsmen) in 1907.

CAREER HIGHLIGHTS

1897 Cofounds the Vienna Secession
1898 Designs the Secession Building in Vienna
1899 Grand Duke of Hesse invites Olbrich and Peter Behrens to develop an art colony in Darmstadt
1907 Designs worker houses for the Opel Factory in Darmstadt

ORREFORS GLASSWORKS

SWEDISH, 1898–

The glassworks at the village of Orrefors in the Småland province of southern Sweden became a prominent producer of high-quality glassware and art glass from 1916, when it employed Simon Gate and Edvard Hald as designers. After winning acclaim at the 1925 Exposition Internationale in Paris, Orrefors continued its creative innovation through to the 1960s with designers such as Vicke Lindstrand, Nils Landberg, Sven Palmqvist, and Ingeborg Lundin.

J. J. P. OUD

DUTCH, 1890–1963

Architect Jacobus Johannes Pieter Oud was born in Purmerend, northern Holland. In 1917, he was a founding member of the De Stijl movement. In the 1920s, his Modernist designs included workers' housing in Rotterdam and the Hook of Holland, the Café de Unie in Rotterdam (1925), and parts of the Weissenhof exhibition estate in Stuttgart (1927). In the 1930s, he rejected the strict functionalism of the International Style. His later work included the 1956 Dutch National Monument in Amsterdam.

ALBERT PALEY

AMERICAN, 1944–

Born in Philadelphia, Pennsylvania, Paley studied fine arts at the city's Temple University. He then moved to Rochester, New York, where he created gold and silver jewelry before turning to metal sculpture in the 1970s. In 1972, he won a competition to design the Portal Gates for the Smithsonian's Renwick Gallery.

Paley has since created more than 50 site-specific metal works, many of them on a monumental scale, including Synergy (1987), a ceremonial archway in Philadelphia made out of forged and fabricated steel, and the Animals Always sculpture in St. Louis Zoo (2006). As well as sculptures, Paley designs architectural hardware such as door handles and also candlesticks and paperweights.

CAREER HIGHLIGHTS

1972 Designs the Portal Gates at the Renwick Gallery, Smithsonian
1995 Receives Institute Honors Award
2006 Creates the Animals Always sculpture for St. Louis Zoo

SVEN PALMQVIST

SWEDISH, 1906–1984

Palmqvist was born in Lenhovda, southern Sweden. An apprentice at the Orrefors glassworks from 1928, he learned his trade under Simon Gate. One of Orrefors' most technically audacious glassmakers, he introduced fishnet-patterned Kraka glass in 1944 and mosaic-effect Ravenna glass in 1948. In 1954, his acclaimed Fuga bowl series, made in a centrifuge, appeared, and won the Grand Prix at the Milan Triennale in 1957. Palmqvist retired in 1971.

INTERIOR WITH PANTON CHAIRS, VERNER PANTON, 1967

◁ **VERNER PANTON**

DANISH, 1926–1998

Born in Gentofte, eastern Denmark, Panton is famous for his one-piece stacking chairs in plastic or wood and for his extensive use of bright color. He studied at the Royal Danish Academy of Fine Arts in Copenhagen and worked for architect Arne Jacobsen before setting up his own studio in 1955. He first came to international attention with his Pop art Cone Chair (1959), which he designed to go with the all-red interior he created for an inn on a Danish island.

In 1963, Panton moved to Basel, Switzerland, developing a relationship with Swiss manufacturer Vitra. His designs included the first inflatable furniture, the Flying Chair (1964); the cantilevered plastic Panton Chair (1967), a reincarnation of the plywood S Chair he had made for Thonet the previous year; and the Living Tower (1969). He also designed lighting and Op art textiles, creating psychedelic "total environments," such as the one at the Varna Palace, Arhus, Denmark, made in 1969. Panton's Visiona 2 installation (1970) was a synthetic, futuristic environment that showed the Space Age influence of the Apollo moon landing the year before. Danish magazine *Mobilia* wrote that the extreme sensory experiences Panton aroused ranged "from claustrophobia to erotic desire." Panton himself was always bold, calling "a less successful experiment preferable to a beautiful platitude."

CAREER HIGHLIGHTS

1959 Designs the K2 Wire Cone Chair and the K3 Heart Wire Chair
1962 Moves to Basel, Switzerland
1969 Designs editorial office interiors for *Der Spiegel* magazine, Hamburg
1972 Creates Visiona 2 at International Furniture Fair, Cologne

CESARE PAOLINI

ITALIAN, 1937–1983

Born in Genoa, Paolini joined the young Turin architects Franco Teodoro and Pierro Gatti to establish the Gatti, Paolini, Teodoro design partnership in 1965. Their work included industrial design, interior design, architecture, and graphic design. In 1968, they launched the Sacco beanbag seats, manufactured by Zanotta, which were a worldwide success. The partnership lasted until Paolini's death.

WALLPAPER DESIGN, BRUNO PAUL, 1919

TOMMI PARZINGER

GERMAN AMERICAN, 1903–1981

Born in Munich, the son of a sculptor, Parzinger trained at the Munich School of Arts and Crafts. He moved to New York in 1935, initially making household ceramics and silverware. In 1939, he established a company to produce finely crafted furniture, including pieces customized for wealthy clients. Parzinger's furniture designs blended Bauhaus functionalism with luxurious ornamental detail. In the mid-1960s, he gave up design to concentrate on painting.

△ **BRUNO PAUL**

GERMAN, 1874–1968

Born in rural Saxony, Paul moved to Munich in 1894 and made his name as an illustrator for *Jugend* and *Simplicissimus* magazines. He also worked as an interior and furniture designer, and by 1900 he was recognized as a leading figure in the Jugendstil movement. In 1906, he took up a key role in the reform of art

education in Berlin, helping found the Deutscher Werkbund in 1907 and create the Vereinigte Staatschulen (United State Schools) in 1924. After World War I, Paul designed Modernist buildings, but his career as an architect and teacher ended when the Nazis rose to power in 1933.

CAREER HIGHLIGHTS

1892 Moves to Munich
1900 Wins Grand Prix at Paris Exposition Universelle for Bavarian-style huntsman's room
1907 Cofounds Deutscher Werkbund

PIERRE PAULIN

FRENCH, 1927–2009

Born in Paris, Paulin studied interior design and product design at the École Camondo. He worked for the Gascoin furniture company in Le Havre and for Thonet in Paris, before joining the Dutch manufacturer Artifort in 1958. While there, he created perhaps his best-known designs, including the Mushroom chair (1960) and the Tongue chair (1968).

In the 1970s, he was commissioned to decorate and furnish rooms at the Elysée presidential palace in Paris.

CAREER HIGHLIGHTS

1960 Designs the Oyster, Orange Slice, and Globe armchairs
1968 Creates the Tongue chair
1971 Designs the Elysée chair as part of a commission to furnish Georges Pompidou's private apartments

DAGOBERT PECHE

AUSTRIAN, 1887–1923

Born in Sankt Michael im Lungau near Salzburg, Peche studied architecture in Vienna, and established himself as a designer of textiles, wallpaper, metal jewelry, furniture, and ceramics. He exhibited with the Deutscher Werkbund in Cologne, in 1914, and joined the Wiener Werkstätte (Vienna Workshops) artists' community the following year. He developed a distinctive ornamental style, but his promising career was cut short by his death at the age of 36.

JIŘÍ PELCL

CZECH, 1950–

Born in Postrelmov in the Olomouc region of Czechoslovakia (now the Czech Republic), Pelcl studied design at the Royal College of Art in London. In 1987, he founded the Atika group of Czech postmodern designers, which radically challenged the official aesthetic of communist Czechoslovakia. His designs have included furniture, interiors, ceramics, and glassware. He was made Rector of the Prague Academy of Art, Architecture, and Design in 2002.

GILL PEMBERTON

BRITISH, c. 1940–

Trained at the Birmingham School of Art and the Royal College of Art in London, Gill Pemberton began working at Denby Pottery's Langley Mill site in 1960.

There she created definitive 1960s stoneware designs, notably the Chevron (1961) and the Arabesque (1962). Her later work for Denby included the 1970s Renaissance Collection and pieces designed in collaboration with Glyn Colledge. Freelance from 1981, Pemberton diversified into lights, cushions, and ceramic jewelry.

JORGE PENSI

ARGENTINIAN SPANISH, 1949–

Pensi studied architecture in his native Buenos Aires then moved to Barcelona in 1975. Two years later, he joined forces with several other designers to form the consultancy Grupo Berenguer. In 1984, he left and founded his own design studio, focusing on furniture and lighting. His acclaimed designs include the cast-aluminum stackable Toledo chair (1988), which became a familiar sight in outdoor cafés throughout Europe, the 1989 Orfilia chair for Thonet, and the Regina and Bluebird lamps for B.Lux. Pensi was awarded the Spanish National Design Prize in 1997. As well as working in Spain, he has extended his design consultancy to Italy, Germany, Finland, Singapore, South America, and the US.

CAREER HIGHLIGHTS

1977 Co-establishes a design consultancy in Barcelona
1986 Designs the Toledo chair for Knoll
1988 Creates the Olympia hanging lamp for B.Lux
2004 Designs the Tabasco chair and footstool for Perobell

GUSTAVO PÉREZ

MEXICAN, 1950–

Ceramicist Pérez was born in Mexico City and studied engineering before a first attempt at clay modeling in 1971 changed the course of his life. He studied ceramics at the School of Art and Design in Mexico City, graduating in 1973. He did not discover his own style as a potter, however, until two years of study at Breda in the Netherlands from 1981 immersed him in European art ceramics. His smooth, symmetrical, sand-colored stoneware vessels are decorated with subtly incised lines. Since 1992, Pérez

has been based in Zoncuantla, in Veracruz province. His work features in major collections, including the Los Angeles County Museum of Art and the Cultural Center of Contemporary Art in Mexico City.

CHARLOTTE PERRIAND

FRENCH, 1903–1999

Born in Paris, furniture designer and architect Charlotte Perriand studied at the École de l'Union Centrale des Arts Décoratifs from 1920 to 1925. Frustrated by the school's craft-based aesthetic, she found inspiration in the design theories of Le Corbusier.

In 1927, a Modernist rooftop bar that she had designed for the Paris Salon d'Automne won Le Corbusier's approval, and he invited her to join his studio. In collaboration with Le Corbusier and Pierre Jeanneret, she created Modernist furniture from chromium-plated tubular steel, including the Grand Confort chair and Chaise Longue (both 1928). In the 1930s, she designed furniture for Le Corbusier's buildings, as well as collaborating with artist Fernand Léger. She worked as a design consultant for Japan's Ministry of Trade and Industry in Tokyo from 1940 to 1942, and her later work shows both the influence of

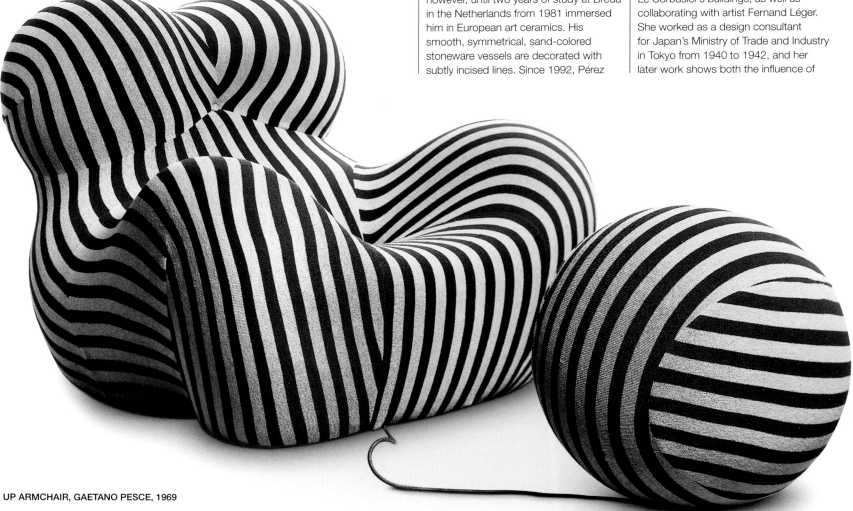

UP ARMCHAIR, GAETANO PESCE, 1969

Japanese art, as in her Synthèse des Arts chair (1955), and a return to the use of traditional materials, such as wood and cane, for her furniture.

CAREER HIGHLIGHTS

1928 Codesigns the LC3 Grand Confort chair and LC4 Chaise Longue
1931 Begins exhibiting under own name
1951 Designs a prototype kitchen for Le Corbusier's Unité d'Habitation in Marseilles

◁ GAETANO PESCE

ITALIAN, 1939–

Born in La Spezia, Pesce studied architecture and design at the University of Venice. In the 1960s, he was involved with the Gruppo N experimental group of artists and designers, working with light and kinetics. In 1969, he designed the Up series of polyurethane foam and stretch fabric chairs for C & B Italia.

In the 1970s, he worked for Cassina, creating extravagant designs such as the Tramonto a New York (Sunset in New York) sofa (1980) and the Feltri armchair (1987). Pesce has undertaken many architectural commissions worldwide, notably the plant-clad Organic building in Osaka (1993). He has lived in New York since the 1980s.

CAREER HIGHLIGHTS

1959 Cofounds Gruppo N
1971 Starts work for Cassina
2005 Retrospective of his work is held at the Triennale Museum, Milan

▷ GIOVANNI PINTORI

ITALIAN, 1912–1999

Graphic designer Pintori was born in Tresnuraghes on Sardinia. In 1936, after studying industrial design in Monza, Lombardy, he worked in the marketing department of Olivetti. The advertising posters he designed for them, with their vivid colors and repeating visual patterns, were internationally acclaimed, and exhibited at MoMA, New York, in 1952, and the Louvre in Paris, in 1955. In 1953, Pintori joined the elite graphic artists' association Alliance Graphique Internationale (AGI). In 1967, he began freelancing and completed a number of commissions for Pirelli and Gabbianelli among others.

LITHOGRAPHIC POSTER FOR OLIVETTI LETTERA 22 TYPEWRITER, GIOVANNI PINTORI, 1955

WARREN PLATNER

AMERICAN, 1909–2006

Born in Baltimore, Maryland, Platner graduated in architecture from Cornell University. He developed his talents working for Raymond Loewy and I. M. Pei, then, in 1960, joined the office of Finnish architect Eero Saarinen. He continued to work there under Kevin Roche after Saarinen's death. Platner's designs for Roche, including the 1967 interior of the Ford Foundation building in Manhattan, were notable for their restrained color schemes and informality. Platner is best known for the steel-wire chairs, tables, and ottomans with sculptural bases of nickel-plated steel rods that he created for Knoll in 1966. From 1967, Platner ran his own business in New Haven, Connecticut, designing interiors, lighting, textiles, and furniture. Together with Milton Glaser, he also designed the interior of the famous Windows on the World restaurant at the World Trade Center, which was completed in 1976.

CAREER HIGHLIGHTS

1945 Works for Raymond Loewy
1966 Creates wire furniture for Knoll
1967 Sets up own interior design studio

SPATIAL FORCE CONSTRUCTION, LYUBOV POPOVA, 1921

GIO PONTI

ITALIAN, 1891–1979

Often called the father of Italian design, Giovanni Ponti was born in Milan and studied architecture at the Polytechnic there. From the 1920s, he was associated with the Novecento style of architecture and design, which sought to marry old and new with neoclassical motifs and a return to the great Italian artistic tradition.

As well as designing buildings and furniture, Ponti established the magazine *Domus,* in 1928, to promote Novecento and worked as design director for the ceramics manufacturer Richard-Ginori. From 1936 to 1961, he taught at Milan Polytechnic. His most famous designs in a long and varied career were the streamlined chrome La Cornuta coffee machine, marketed by La Pavoni in 1948, and the iconic Superleggera chair (1957), hailed as "the world's lightest chair," for Cassina.

◁ LYUBOV POPOVA

RUSSIAN, 1889–1924

Artist and designer Lyubov Sergeyevna Popova was born into a wealthy, cultured family in Ivanovskoe near Moscow. Traveling widely in Russia and Western Europe, she became an avant-garde artist associated with Cubism, Futurism, and, from 1916, with Suprematism. After the Russian Revolution of 1917, she devoted her energies to the revolutionary cause, designing propaganda posters alongside her work as an abstract artist. In 1921, under the influence of Constructivism, she turned to theater and textile design.

In 1923, with Varvara Stepanova, Popova began to design textiles for mass production at the First State Textile Printing Factory in Moscow. She died of scarlet fever at age 35.

HENRI PRIVAT-LIVEMONT

BELGIAN, 1861–1936

Art Nouveau poster designer, decorative artist, and photographer Privat-Livemont was born in Brussels. He studied at the École des Art Décoratifs before moving to Paris. In 1883, he joined the studio of Lemaire, Lavastre & Duvignaud, taking part in the redecoration of the Hotel de Ville. He returned to Brussels in 1889. In the 1890s, he produced many poster designs, the most famous being for Absinthe Robette in 1896. He also provided decoration, such as ceramic tiles, for several buildings in Brussels. A talented photographer, he was one of the first people to create autochromes, an early type of color photograph.

JEAN PROUVÉ

FRENCH, 1901–1984

Born in Paris, Prouvé was a Modernist designer who made furniture from thin sheet steel. Describing himself as a "factory man," his main aim was to create furniture that was functional. Accordingly, he adopted the latest technology to make seating that could be supplied in kit form to hospitals, schools, and offices, some of it in collaboration with Charlotte Perriand.

OTTO PRUTSCHER

AUSTRIAN, 1880–1949

The son of a Viennese cabinetmaker, Prutscher studied at the Vienna School of Arts and Crafts, where he later taught for much of his life. He made his name in the early years of the 20th century, designing Jugendstil interiors in London and Paris with Erwin Puchinger. He went on to design buildings and interiors in Vienna and the surrounding area, including the Villa Rothberger in Baden bei Wien (1912) and the Flemmich House in Jägerndorf (1914). Prutscher also designed furniture, textiles, glass, jewelry, and ceramics, much of it in a rectilinear, geometric style. After World War I, he was the architect on several public housing projects in Vienna.

JEAN PUIFORCAT

FRENCH, 1897–1945

Puiforcat was born into a family of Parisian silversmiths and joined the family firm after military service in World War I. In the 1920s, he transformed the company into an avant-garde producer of Art Deco designs, using geometric forms and blending silver with precious stones and exotic woods. He was a founding member of the Union des Artistes Modernes (Union of Modern Artists) in 1929 and participated in the group's first exhibition the following year. In the

DIETER RAMS SURVEYS HIS 606 UNIVERSAL SHELVING SYSTEM FOR VITSŒ, 1960

1930s, Puiforcat created elegant sets of silver tableware and exhibited liturgical silverware at the Paris World Fair of 1937. He also worked as a sculptor.

R

ERNEST RACE

BRITISH, 1913–1964

Born in Newcastle-upon-Tyne, England, Race studied interior design at the Bartlett School of Architecture in London. He first made his reputation in the late 1930s, designing hand-woven textiles. In 1946, responding to the need for utility furniture in postwar Britain, he exhibited his BA series of aluminum chairs at the Victoria and Albert Museum's Britain Can Make It exhibition.

Race's metal furniture was commercially successful, and he followed up with the Antelope and Springbok steel-rod chairs, which were shown at the 1951 Festival of

Britain. His subsequent designs included Neptune deck chairs for the P&O shipping company (1953) and the Heron lounge chair (1955).

CAREER HIGHLIGHTS

1945 Designs BA Utility chairs
1951 The Antelope chair is displayed at the Festival of Britain
1955 Designs the Heron lounge chair

△ DIETER RAMS

GERMAN, 1932–

Dieter Rams was born in Wiesbaden. He trained as a carpenter—his grandfather's trade—but eventually graduated with a degree in architecture from the Wiesbaden Werkkunstschule (Art and Crafts school). He worked for Frankfurt-based architect Otto Appel from 1953, before joining the electrical appliance manufacturer Braun as an interior designer in 1955.

Rams soon moved to product design and, in 1956, he collaborated with Hans Gugelot of the Ulm School of Design to create the Phonosuper SK4 radio and record player. The SK4's streamlined,

white-painted metal body and plexiglass lid revolutionized the look of electrical goods. As Head of Design at Braun from 1961, and Director from 1988, Rams gave the company a consistent design philosophy, which was expressed in a wide range of products, from clocks and hairdryers to food mixers and shavers. Rams's minimalist, sculptural designs, with simple dials that were easy to use, made Braun a household name. They all demonstrated his 10 principles of good design, namely that products should be innovative, useful, aesthetically pleasing, and long-lasting, among other things. In 1959, Rams also began to design furniture, which was marketed by Vitsœ+Zapf, including the influential 606 Universal Shelving System (1960). Rams retired from Braun in 1997.

CAREER HIGHLIGHTS

1955 Starts working for Braun
1956 Designs the Phonosuper SK4 radio/record player with Hans Gugelot
1959 Creates the Studio 2 stereo system and T3 pocket radio receiver
1960 Produces the 606 shelf system
1987 Becomes President of German Design Council

the popularity of his lighthearted "blob" style, which combined bright colors with curvaceous forms. The range and quantity of his design work has been astonishing, from the Dirt Devil KONE vacuum cleaner to perfume bottles for Kenzo. He has produced restaurant interiors, manhole covers for the New York sewers, lighting for Artemide, and even a subway station in Naples (2011).

CAREER HIGHLIGHTS

1985 Starts working for KAN Industrial Designers in Canada
1993 Moves to New York
1996 Designs the Garbo Can
2012 Wins the Red Dot Design Award for his Ottawa Collection for BoConcept

RUTH REEVES

AMERICAN, 1892–1966

Textile designer Reeves studied at the Pratt Institute and the Art Students League in New York. She moved to Paris in 1921, studying painting under Fernand Léger. She returned to the US in 1928, where she began a career as a textile designer. Working with manufacturer W & J Sloane, she produced printed fabrics and wall hangings for a MoMA textile exhibition in 1930. In 1932, she designed the foyer carpet and a tapestry for the Radio City Music Hall in New York, and her Guatemalan-inspired patterns of 1935 were highly praised. For the last 10 years of her life, she lived in India.

CAREER HIGHLIGHTS

1928 Exhibited at a MoMA exhibition
1932 Designs textiles for the Radio City Music Hall in New York

COLIN REID

BRITISH, c. 1960–

Based in southwestern England, Reid works in glass on a large scale, often casting it in a kiln from natural forms. As well as sculptures for museums and gardens, he has cast a series of tables from giant tropical leaves, including one for the Devonshire Collection inspired by banana palm leaves in the conservatory at Chatsworth House, Derbyshire. In 2014, Reid won the Coburg Glass Prize Alexander Tutsek Award for his piece entitled Ring of Fire.

POSTER FOR ASPEN DESIGN CONFERENCE, PAUL RAND, 1966

△ PAUL RAND

AMERICAN, 1914–1996

Born Peretz Rosenbaum in Brooklyn, New York, graphic designer Paul Rand took various courses at the Pratt Institute, Parsons School of Design, and the Art Students League but learned most by studying the work of contemporary Modernist European designers. From 1936, he attracted attention with his design work on magazines such as Direction and Esquire. During the 1940s, he moved into advertising design, and, from the mid-1950s onward, he concentrated on creating company logos and corporate identities, his clients including IBM, Westinghouse, UPS, ABC television, Enron, and Next. Rand taught graphic design at Yale University from 1956 to 1969 and from 1974 to 1985.

CAREER HIGHLIGHTS

1956 Creates the IBM logo
1985 Redesigns the logo for Yale University Press

KARIM RASHID

EGYPTIAN AMERICAN, 1960–

Born in Cairo, Egypt, Rashid was raised in Canada and studied industrial design at Carleton University in Ottawa. He gained experience in Italy under Ettore Sottsass and Rodolfo Bonetto before opening his own design studio in New York in 1993. His breakthrough came with the Garbo Can wastebasket in 1996 and the Oh Chair in plastic for Umbra (1999). These two designs established

PAUL RENNER

GERMAN, 1878–1956

Born in Wernigerode, Saxony-Anhalt, Renner studied painting in Berlin, Munich, and Karlsruhe. In 1909, with Emil Preetorius, he founded a school of illustration and book production in Munich. He became an active member of the Deutscher Werkbund (German Association of Craftsmen) in 1910. During the 1920s, he taught graphics and typography in Frankfurt and Munich then designed the Futura sans-serif typeface (1927), for which he is famous. An active opponent of the Nazi Party, he was forced to flee to Switzerland after Adolf Hitler took power in 1933. He published two major texts, *Typography as Art* (1922) and *The Art of Typography* (1939).

CAREER HIGHLIGHTS

1922 Publishes *Typography as Art*
1927 Designs the Futura typeface
1939 Leaves Germany for Switzerland to escape the Nazi regime

FREDERICK ALFRED RHEAD

BRITISH, 1856–1933

Born into a family of pottery designers in Newcastle-under-Lyme, Staffordshire, Frederick Rhead learned his trade at Minton under Marc-Louis Solon, who taught him the *pâte-sur-pâte* decorative technique. As a designer and decorator for Wedgwood from 1878, he created highly praised exhibition pieces. He also worked as art director at other companies, including Wileman, before setting up as a freelancer in 1905. The failure of a tile factory he took on in 1908 caused him financial difficulties, but he found a safe haven as art director at Wood & Sons from 1912 to 1929, producing the popular Elers and Trellis lines.

LOUIS RHEAD

BRITISH AMERICAN, 1857–1926

Born in Etruria in the Staffordshire Potteries, Louis Rhead was sent to study painting in Paris at the age of 13. Like his brother Frederick Alfred Rhead (above), he then worked as a ceramic artist for Minton and Wedgwood. In 1879, Rhead won a scholarship to study at the National Art Training School in London, and in 1883, he took up a post with a New York publisher and soon gained American citizenship. In the 1890s, he became a fashionable poster artist and illustrator, with his work appearing in *Harper's Bazaar, Ladies' Home Journal,* and other magazines. From 1902, he worked primarily as a children's book illustrator for Harper Publishers.

GERRIT RIETVELD

DUTCH, 1888–1964

Rietveld was an architect and furniture designer associated with the De Stijl movement. The son of a carpenter in Utrecht, he learned how to make furniture from his father and studied architecture at evening classes beginning in 1906. In 1917, he set up a furniture workshop and designed his most celebrated piece, the Red-Blue chair. After joining the De Stijl group the following year, he started working as an architect and interior designer, and created the starkly Modernist Schröder House in Utrecht in 1924. In 1928, he became a founding member of the International Congress for Modern Architecture in 1928.

In the 1930s, Rietveld's innovative designs included the legless Zig-Zag chair (1934) and various social housing projects. Later in his life, he worked chiefly as an architect, designing the Dutch pavilion for the 1954 Venice Biennale and the Van Gogh Museum in Amsterdam, which was completed after his death.

CAREER HIGHLIGHTS

1917 Designs the Red-Blue chair
1918 Joins De Stijl
1924 Creates the Schröder House
1934 Designs the Zig-Zag chair

▷ ALEXANDER RODCHENKO

RUSSIAN, 1891–1956

Born in St. Petersburg, Rodchenko studied painting at the Kazan Art School and the Stroganov Institute in Moscow. Initially an abstract painter influenced by Suprematism, he adopted the ideals of the 1917 Bolshevik Revolution. In 1921, he abandoned painting for Productivism and Constructivism, movements that placed art at the service of the masses in an industrial society. His 1920s designs for books, posters, and magazines, using innovative typography, photomontage, and asymmetrical layouts, were immensely influential. He also designed furniture, ceramics, and textiles and produced set designs for film and theater. The advent of Soviet realism in the 1930s forced him to retreat from Modernism.

SERGIO RODRIGUES

BRAZILIAN, 1927–2014

Hailing from Rio de Janeiro, Rodrigues studied architecture before turning to furniture design. Using traditional materials such as tropical hardwood, cane, and leather, he sought to create furniture that would wed European Modernism with traditional Brazilian culture. Rodrigues first made a major impact in the 1950s, notably with his award-winning Poltrona Mole armchair (1957). His furniture was extensively used to furnish buildings designed for the new Brazilian capital, Brasília, between 1956 and 1960. His later designs included the Kilin chair (1973), made of wood with a leather slingback seat, and the Diz wooden lounge chair (2003).

GILBERT ROHDE

AMERICAN, 1894–1944

Born in the Bronx, New York, Rohde was the son of a cabinetmaker and learned his trade in his father's workshop. A trip to Europe in 1927 awakened his interest in modern design. In 1929, he opened an

SUN WORSHIPPERS, ALEXANDER RODCHENKO, 1933

TWA TERMINAL AT NEW YORK'S JOHN F. KENNEDY AIRPORT, ORIGINAL DESIGN BY EERO SAARINEN, 1955–1962

office in New York, creating unique pieces of furniture for wealthy clients. In the early 1930s, Rohde persuaded the Herman Miller furniture company to adopt a wide range of Modernist designs. He also designed furniture for companies such as Heywood-Wakefield and Widdicomb and is often credited with introducing Modernism to the American public at large. His innovative creations included the Plexiglass chair (1939) and the Executive Office Group modular furniture created for Herman Miller (1942).

JOHAN ROHDE

DANISH, 1856–1935

Born in Randers, Denmark, Rohde trained as a doctor before devoting himself to painting. He became a prominent figure in the Danish art world and was associated with the Free Exhibition movement after 1891. In 1897, he began to design furniture, showing some pieces at the Exposition Universelle in Paris, in 1900. In 1906, after designing some silverware for his own use, he began to work for the silversmith Georg Jensen. Rohde's sleek, restrained style was highly successful, and his collaboration with Jensen continued for the rest of his life, his reputation for elegant silverware eclipsing his acclaim as a painter.

JACQUES-ÉMILE RUHLMANN

FRENCH, 1879–1933

Art Deco furniture designer Ruhlmann was born in Paris, where his family had recently arrived from their native Alsace. As a young man, he worked in his father's painting and decorating firm, which he inherited in 1907. He then began designing furniture in the Art Nouveau style, which first attracted widespread attention at the Salon d'Automne in 1913. After World War I, he set up an interior design company, creating wallpaper, rugs, and lights as well as furniture. He employed the most skillful Parisian artisans and created luxury furniture made from expensive materials such as Macassar ebony, rosewood, amboyna burl, and ivory. It was formally elegant and sumptuous but restrained.

Together with architect Pierre Patout, Ruhlmann created the Hôtel d'un Collectioneur for the 1925 Paris Exposition Internationale. It was a sumptuous showcase for his interior

design and furniture. In his final years, his prestigious clients included the French government and the Maharajah of Indore.

CAREER HIGHLIGHTS

1913 Exhibits Art Nouveau furniture at the Salon d'Automne in Paris
1925 Creates Hôtel d'un Collectioneur for Paris Exposition Internationale
1932 Designs an ebony and chrome desk for the Maharajah of Indore

S

◁ EERO SAARINEN

FINNISH AMERICAN, 1910–1961

Son of the famous architect Eliel Saarinen, Eero Saarinen was born in Kirkkonummi, Finland, and emigrated to the US with his family at the age of 13. He studied architecture at Yale before joining his father's practice in Cranbrook, Michigan. Collaborating with Charles Eames, he designed prize-winning chairs for the Organic Design in Home Furnishings competition staged by MoMA in 1940. Saarinen went on to design furniture for Knoll International, notably the Womb chair (1946) and the classically Modernist Tulip chair (1955–1956).

Primarily an architect, Saarinen undertook major projects such as the TWA Terminal at New York's John F. Kennedy Airport and Dulles International Airport in Washington, DC, both of which were still under construction at the time of his death.

CAREER HIGHLIGHTS

1946 Designs the Womb chair
1955 Commissioned to design the TWA Terminal
1956 Knoll International produces his Tulip chair
1958 Receives a commission for Dulles International Airport

BENTE SAETRANG

NORWEGIAN, 1946–

Born in Oslo, textile artist Saetrang studied at the Academy of Art in Poznan, Poland, under Magdalena Abakanowicz (b. 1930). Saetrang established her reputation while working in Oslo in the 1980s, with tapestries such as Manhattan (1985) and Signal 1, 2 & 3 (1986), which she designed for the Norges Bank. Her later works included Transformation (1995) and Pink Madder Lake (2010). She was a professor at the Bergen National Academy of the Arts from 1988 to 1993.

▷ ASTRID SAMPE

SWEDISH, 1909–2002

Textile designer Sampe was born in Stockholm. She studied at Konstfack in her native city and at the Royal College of Art in London. In 1937, she began to work in the design studio of Stockholm's Nordiska Kompaniet (NK) department store. Her designs were prominently exhibited at the 1937 Paris Exposition Internationale and at the 1939 New York World's Fair. Sampe was head of textile design at NK from 1938 to 1971, where she promoted the use of new materials and techniques for textile production on an industrial scale. Some of her 1950s designs, made for other companies such as Knoll International, as well as for NK, were especially successful.

RICHARD SAPPER

GERMAN, 1932–2015

Born in Munich, Sapper studied engineering and business in college before becoming an industrial designer. Moving to Milan in the late 1950s, he formed a creative partnership with the Italian architect and designer Marco Zanuso. Their successful creations included a stackable plastic child's chair for Kartell (1964), the folding Grillo telephone for Siemens (1966), and numerous appliances for the Italian electronics company Brionvega, including the Doney portable television (1962).

Other Sapper designs include the iconic Tizio desk lamp for Artemide (1972) and the Bollitore kettle for Alessi (1984). In 1980, Sapper became principal design consultant for IBM, and he created the first ThinkPad in 1992.

CAREER HIGHLIGHTS

1966 With Marco Zanuso, designs the Grillo telephone for Siemens

1972 Designs the Tizio desk lamp for Artemide

1980 Becomes principal design consultant for IBM

PERSONS KRYDDSKÅP FABRIC DESIGN, ASTRID SAMPE, 1955

GINO SARFATTI

ITALIAN, 1912–1984

Born in Venice, Sarfatti studied aeronautical engineering at the University of Genoa but did not complete the course. He was working as a salesman when, in 1936, he created his first lamp for a friend. Entirely self-taught, by 1939 he had designed a range of lights and set up a company, Arteluce, to manufacture them. After World War II, Arteluce became the foremost lighting company in Italy. Sarfatti himself designed more than 400 lights and lamps as well as employed some of the leading Italian designers of the 1950s and 1960s. His last project before retirement in 1972 was lighting for the Teatro Regio in Turin.

TIMO SARPANEVA

FINNISH, 1926–2006

Glass designer Sarpaneva was born in Helsinki and graduated from the School of Art and Design at Aalto University in 1948. In the early 1950s, his skill at glass engraving won him a post at Iittala, with which he remained associated for most of his working life.

Sarpaneva created many award-winning tableware designs for Iittala, including the i-line series of plates and bottles (1956) and an iconic cast-iron pot (1960). His Finlandia glassware (1964) had a textural, wooden effect, achieved by casting glass in charred wooden molds. In his later years, he created glass sculptures inspired by the landscape and natural forms of Finland.

MUNETSUGU SATOMI

JAPANESE, 1904–1996

Born in Osaka, Satomi went to France in 1922 and studied at the École des Beaux Arts in Paris. He was influenced by Art Deco, particularly the poster artist Cassandre. In the 1930s, dividing his time between France and Japan, Satomi established himself as a leading poster designer. He was especially admired for his travel posters for clients, including Japanese Government Railways and the Dutch airline KLM. His career was halted by World War II, but his later work included the playful Golf poster (1960).

▷ RAYMOND SAVIGNAC

FRENCH, 1907–2002

Born in Paris, Savignac left school at the age of 15 and worked as a draftsman, drawing several cartoon characters for commercials. In 1935, he was taken on by poster artist Cassandre, but he did not make his breakthrough until 1949, with a provocatively witty poster for Monsavon soap. A flood of commissions followed for posters to advertise consumer products, ranging from pens to cigarettes, movies, and painkillers. By the 1970s, his style of visual humor was no longer fashionable, but he continued to work into the 1990s.

CARLO SCARPA

ITALIAN, 1906–1978

Born in Venice, Scarpa did not win renown as an architect and interior designer until after World War II. Like Frank Lloyd Wright, he blended craft skills with modern materials, in major projects such as the Castelvecchio Museum in Verona (1956), the Olivetti showroom in the Piazza San Marco in Venice (1957), and the Querini-Stampalia Foundation building, also in Venice (1962). On a smaller scale, Scarpa created vases and lighting for the Venini glassworks, Murano.

ARCHIMEDE SEGUSO

ITALIAN 1909–1999

Born into a family of glassworkers in Murano, Venice, Seguso was recognized as a master glassblower by the age of 17.

He founded his own art-glass company in 1933 and exhibited at the Venice Biennale for the first time three years later. In the 1950s, his technically adventurous glass, especially the Merletto series (1952) and the Piuma series (1956), were critically acclaimed. Seguso continued to produce innovative designs in the 1970s, including the Op art series (1972). His life's work was celebrated in solo shows at Tiffany's in New York in 1989 and at the Palazzo Ducale in Venice in 1991.

PETER SHIRE

AMERICAN, 1947–

Ceramicist and designer Peter Shire was born in the Echo Park suburb of Los Angeles and has remained there all his life. He trained at the Chouinard Art Institute in the 1960s and set up his own ceramics studio in 1972. The colorful geometric teapots that he created from 1974 onward attracted the attention of Ettore Sottsass, who invited him to join the Milan-based, postmodernist Memphis group in 1981.

While working with Memphis, Shire designed furniture in the same bright, angular mode, including the Bel Air armchair (1982) and the Big Sur couch (1986), as well as ceramics, silverware, and glassware. Since the 1980s, his work has included sculptures for Los Angeles and other California sites, tile murals, and paintings on ceramics.

CAREER HIGHLIGHTS

1972 Establishes a studio in his home city of Los Angeles
1981 Accepts Ettore Sottsass's invitation to join Memphis
1982 Designs the Bel Air armchair
1986 Creates the Big Sur couch

SILVER STUDIO

BRITISH, 1880–1963

In the last two decades of the 19th century, Arthur Silver built his London design studio, which made repeating patterns for textiles and wallpaper, into a creative center of British Art Nouveau. Employing designers such as Harry Napper, John Illingworth Kay, and Archibald Knox, as well as Silver's sons Rex and Harry, the Silver Studio marketed designs to retailers and to manufacturers. It found a responsive market in Europe and the US as well as in Britain.

The output of the studio ranged from furnishing fabrics and wallpapers to rugs, carpets, tablecloths, and metalwork. Led by Arthur's son Rex Silver from 1901, the studio maintained a high output right up until World War II, producing more than 20,000 designs in total.

BOŘEK ŠÍPEK

CZECH, 1949–2016

Born in Prague, then in Czechoslovakia, Šípek left for Germany after the failed Prague Spring uprising of 1968 and studied architecture in Hamburg. In 1983, he opened a design studio in Amsterdam, creating the Bambi chair from tubular steel and silk.

From the mid-1980s, his postmodernist designs for furniture, cutlery, porcelain, vases, and lamps achieved international renown, promoted by the Italian design company Driade and by Steltman in the Netherlands. Although remaining in his own view primarily an architect, he went on to produce designs for many major companies, including Alessi, Munari, Vitra, and Rosenthal. From 1990, he spent most of his time in his native country.

ADVERTISEMENT FOR DUNLOP, RAYMOND SAVIGNAC, 1956

NAUM SLUTZKY

RUSSIAN, 1894–1965

Born into a family of goldsmiths in Kiev, in the Russian Empire, Slutzky developed his craft at the Wiener Werkstätte in Vienna before joining the Bauhaus metal workshop at Weimar in 1919. He left the Bauhaus in 1923 to work as a freelance designer in Hamburg. He mostly created gold or silver jewelry, but he also made silver teapots, coffee pots, and lamps. In 1933, after the Nazis' rise to power in Germany, Slutzky moved to England. He became an influential teacher, notably at Dartington Hall in Devon, in the 1930s, and at the Royal College of Art in London, in the 1950s.

LUDVIKA SMRČKOVÁ

CZECH, 1903–1991

Born in Kročehlavy, then in Austria-Hungary, now in the Czech Republic, glass designer Smrčkova graduated from the Prague School of Decorative Arts. She first attracted attention when her work was shown at the 1925 Paris Exposition Internationale. Designing chiefly for the Moser glassworks, she created elegant, functional glassware such as the Breakfast Set (1936). Her work won a prize at the 1937 Paris Exposition Internationale. In the 1940s, her designs were also manufactured by the Rückl glassworks in Nizbor, and from 1948, she was chief designer for the nationalized Inwald glass manufacturers.

▽ MICHAEL SODEAU

BRITISH, 1969–

Born in London, Sodeau studied product design at the Central St. Martins College of Art and Design. After graduating in 1994, he cofounded Inflate, making inflatable versions of traditional products. He set up his own London-based company, Michael Sodeau Partnership, in 1997. His furniture designs have included the Wing line for Isokon Plus (1999), the Corallo coat stand for Gervasoni (2001), and the carbon-fiber Halo chair, exhibited in 2014. His celebrated Anything line of office stationery, which was developed for the Japanese company Suikosha, was launched in 2008. His other work has ranged from creating brand identities to designing restaurant interiors.

ETTORE SOTTSASS

ITALIAN, 1917–2007

Sottsass was born in Innsbruck, Austria, but grew up in Milan, Italy. He was the son of an architect and graduated in architecture from the Turin Polytechnic, but in the 1950s, he switched to industrial design. From 1958, he was design consultant to Olivetti, his bold styling of office equipment culminating in the celebrated, Pop art–influenced Valentine typewriter of 1969. By the 1970s, Sottsass had become a leading figure in the search for new approaches to architecture and design. In 1979, he joined the radical design studio Alchimia

and the following year founded his own company, Sottsass Associati, to take on larger-scale projects. In 1981, he set up Memphis, a Milan-based group of young furniture and product designers, whose postmodern style dominated early 1980s design. Sottsass's own work for Memphis included the Casablanca sideboard (1981), the Carlton sideboard (also 1981), and the Tartar table (1985). After leaving Memphis in 1985, Sottsass concentrated mainly on architectural projects.

CAREER HIGHLIGHTS

1969 Designs the Valentine typewriter
1981 Sets up the Memphis design group
1994 Has a solo exhibition at the Centre Pompidou in Paris

MART STAM

DUTCH, 1899–1986

Born in Purmerend, in northern Holland, Stam trained as a draftsman before working in architectural practices in Rotterdam, Berlin, and Zurich. In 1926, he designed the S43, the first tubular-steel cantilevered chair. The following year, he participated as an architect in the Weissenhof project in Stuttgart, coming in contact with Walter Gropius and Ludwig Mies van der Rohe. In 1930, he traveled to the Soviet Union with a group of German architects and planners to build new towns for the Communist state. He returned to the Netherlands in 1934 and continued his career as an architect and advocate of Modernism until his retirement in 1966.

ANTON STANKOWSKI

GERMAN, 1906–1998

Graphic designer Stankowski was born in Gelsenkirchen, Westphalia, and studied at the Folkwang University of the Arts. From 1929 to 1934, he worked at the Max Dalang advertising studio in Zurich, Switzerland, where he developed his concept of "constructive graphic art." After being a prisoner of war during World War II, he established his own studio in Stuttgart, in 1951. Over the next decades, he became a leading figure in graphic design, especially admired for his posters for Mercedes-Benz from 1955, his Berlin Layout logo and graphics (1968), and the Deutsche Bank logo (1974). Stankowski was also a painter and photographer.

▷ PHILIPPE STARCK

FRENCH, 1949–

Starck was born in Paris and studied design at the École Nissim de Camondo. A prodigy in his teens, he won a furniture design competition at age 16 and was appointed artistic director at the studio of fashion designer Pierre Cardin at the age of 20. In the 1970s, he became a fashionable interior designer, furnishing several bars and clubs in Paris. In 1982, French President François Mitterrand asked Starck to help refurbish his private rooms at the Élysée Palace. Two years later, Starck's furnishings for the Café Costes in Paris, including the three-legged Costes chair, confirmed his status as a design superstar.

Starck has continued to create innovative buildings and interiors, while also producing witty, inventive designs for products ranging from motorcycles to wind turbines and from shoes to candlesticks. Among his best-known designs are the Ara table lamp for Flos (1988), the iconic Juicy Salif lemon squeezer for Alessi (1990), and the Louis Ghost chair for Kartell (2002).

CAREER HIGHLIGHTS

1984 Designs the interior of Café Costes in Paris
1989 Designs La Flamme in Tokyo for the Asahi brewery
1990 Creates the Juicy Salif squeezer
2002 Designs the Louis Ghost chair
2007 Collaborates on the SLS luxury hotel in Beverly Hills
2009 Creates the wireless Zikmu speakers

THEOPHILE-STEINLEN

SWISS FRENCH, 1859–1923

Art Nouveau poster designer Steinlen was born in Lausanne, Switzerland. An aspiring artist with a mundane design job at a factory, he moved to Paris and settled in Montmartre around 1880. He frequented the cabaret Le Chat Noir, a favorite haunt of artists and poets, and, in 1883, he was commissioned to design publicity posters for the cabaret and illustrations for its magazine. Some of his prints, featuring the eponymous cat, were to achieve enduring fame. During his career, Steinlen produced hundreds of posters, and his illustrations appeared regularly in magazines such as *Le Rire* and *Gil Blas*. He also exhibited as a painter.

LIBRARY SOFA, MICHAEL SODEAU, 2014

RONALD STENNETT-WILLSON

BRITISH, 1915–2009

Born in Padgate, Cheshire, Stennett-Willson had no formal training in design. As a young man, he developed a passion for decorative glass and, in the 1950s, he became head of Wuidart glass importers. He promoted the products of Swedish glassmakers such as Orrefors and Kosta, then began to design Scandinavian-style vases, goblets, tankards, and pitchers, first for Wuidart and then, from 1959, for the Lemington Glassworks. In 1967, he set up his own manufacturer, the King's Lynn Glassworks, which was taken over by Wedgwood in 1969.

Among Stennett-Willson's most successful designs for Wedgwood were the Sheringham line and Sandringham candlesticks (1970s). He continued designing glassware until 1987.

VARVARA STEPANOVA

RUSSIAN, 1894–1958

Born in Lithuania, which was then in the Russian Empire, Stepanova trained at the Kazan Art School in Odessa and then at the Académie de la Palette in Paris. She belonged to the group of avant-garde artists in Moscow who welcomed the Russian Revolution of 1917. With her husband Alexander Rodchenko, she was a founder of the Constructivist movement in 1921. She created geometric textile designs for production by the First State Textile Printing Factory in 1922 and 1923. From 1925, she designed posters, some of them in collaboration with the poet Vladimir Mayakovsky. From the 1930s onward, she worked as a graphic designer for Soviet magazines.

GUSTAV STICKLEY

AMERICAN, 1858–1942

The child of first-generation German immigrants, Stickley was born Gustavus Stoeckel in Osceola, Wisconsin. From the age of 12, he worked as a stonemason. In 1875, he moved with his family to Brandt, Pennsylvania, where he was employed in an uncle's chair factory, and in 1883, he set up a furniture business with his brothers, soon moving to New York. In the mid-1890s, Stickley made two visits to Europe and was inspired by the ideas of the Arts and Crafts

ALHÓNDIGA CULTURAL AND LEISURE CENTER, BILBAO, SPAIN, PHILIPPE STARCK, 2010

movement. From 1898, he ran his own furniture factory in Syracuse, New York, and became a proselytizer for the Arts and Crafts philosophy. In 1900, he exhibited his New Furniture line, and the following year he launched *The Craftsman* magazine as a platform for his aesthetic and political beliefs. His business was renamed the Craftsman Workshops in 1903. As well as producing furniture, lighting, textiles, and metalware, Stickley also promoted self-build architecture.

CAREER HIGHLIGHTS

1898 Spreads the Arts and Crafts philosophy in the US
1901 Launches *The Craftsman* magazine

GUNTA STÖLZL

GERMAN SWISS, 1897–1983

Born in Munich, Stölzl's education at the Munich School of Applied Arts was interrupted by service as a nurse during World War I. She became a student at the Bauhaus in Weimar in 1919, and in 1921, she collaborated with Marcel Breuer on the wood-and-textile African Chair. From 1925 onward, Stölzl was the key figure in developing the weaving workshop at the Dessau Bauhaus. She experimented with new technology and synthetic materials and encouraged both hand-weaving and machine production of textiles. In 1931, she was forced out of the Bauhaus for political reasons. She then established herself in Zurich, where she continued to make textiles until 1967.

NIKOLAI SUETIN

RUSSIAN, 1897–1954

Suetin studied at the Vitebsk Higher Art Institute from 1918, where he came under the influence of the Suprematist artist Kasimir Malevich. In 1922, he followed Malevich to Petrograd (St. Petersburg), where he applied Suprematist principles of abstract art to porcelain decoration at the state-run Lomonossov ceramics factory. Despite the suppression of abstract art under Stalin, Suetin was made artistic director of the factory in 1932. He also worked as a book illustrator and an exhibition designer and was responsible for the interior of the Soviet pavilions at the Exposition Internationale in Paris in 1937 and the New York World's Fair in 1939.

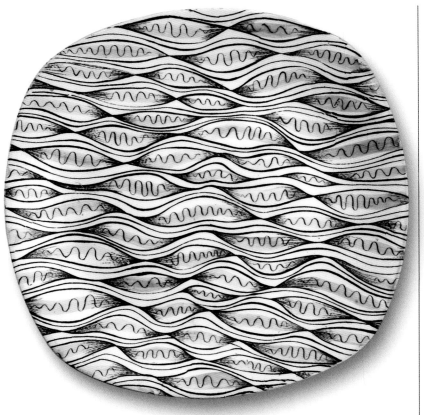

CARIBBEAN PATTERN PLATE, JESSIE TAIT FOR MIDWINTER POTTERY, *c.* 1955

ILKKA SUPPANEN

FINNISH, 1968–

Born in Kotka on the Gulf of Finland, Suppanen studied at the Helsinki University of Arts and Design and the Rietveld Academy in Amsterdam, Netherlands. He established his own studio in 1995 and, two years later, cofounded the Snowcrash design cooperative, which disbanded in 2002. Clients for Suppanen's clean-lined, user-friendly designs have included Artek, Cappellini, Lucente, Zanotta, Nokia, Marimekko, and Saab. His best-known works include the Rosebud chair for Vivero (2006), the Iittala Fireplace (2008), and the Everyday Holy mug for Muuto (2006). His work has been displayed around the world—for instance, at Venice Biennales and at MoMA in New York.

LADISLAV SUTNAR

CZECH, 1897–1976

Graphic designer Sutnar was born in Pilsen, now Plzeň in the Czech Republic, and studied painting and architecture in Prague. Working in Prague in the 1920s and 1930s, he designed books, magazines, exhibitions, and toys, while also teaching at the State School of Graphic Arts. In 1939, he moved to the US, where, as art director of Sweet's Catalog Service from 1941 to 1960, he led the development of information design, employing tabs, icons, and grids to make catalogs more user-friendly. He also clarified American telephone directories by putting area codes in parentheses. He wrote a number of influential books expounding the principles of visual design.

△ JESSIE TAIT

BRITISH, 1928–2010

Born in Stoke-on-Trent, in the area known as the Staffordshire Potteries, Tait was educated at the Burslem School of Art. At age 18, she was employed as a designer at the Midwinter Pottery, initially working under Charlotte Rhead. Tait produced her first distinctive designs for Midwinter's hand-painted Stylecraft line (from 1953), including Homeweave, Primavera, and Red Domino, and for the Fashion line (from 1954), including

Zambesi. Among her later Midwinter designs was Spanish Garden for the Fine range (1962). She also created patterns for the smaller Clayburn Pottery. In 1970, Midwinter was taken over by Wedgwood. Tait worked for Wedgwood and its subsidiaries until her retirement in 1993.

BRUCE TALBERT

BRITISH, 1838–1881

Born in Dundee, Talbert was a wood carver, architect, and interior designer but is best remembered for his furniture. He worked in the Reformed Gothic style championed by the Aesthetic Movement and applied ornate decorative carvings of chevrons, pierced and inlaid motifs such as quatrefoils, and chamfered edges to his elaborate pieces of furniture. He published several books on furniture promoting his style, including the influential *Gothic Forms Applied to Furniture, Metal Work and Decoration for Domestic Purposes* (1868).

ILMARI TAPIOVAARA

FINNISH, 1914–1999

Tapiovaara studied furniture design at the Central School of Applied Arts in Helsinki and became artistic director of Asko Oy, the largest furniture manufacturer in Finland, 1938. After World War II, together with his wife, Anniki Tapiovaara, he created furniture for the Domus Academica student housing in Helsinki, including the birch plywood Domus chair (1946).

In 1951, Tapiovaara set up a studio with Anniki, and they designed good-quality furniture at an affordable price, such as the Mademoiselle chair (1956), as well as interiors for banks, offices, and hotels. Tapiovaara was a professor at the Illinois Institute of Technology Chicago in 1962 and 1963 and designed furniture for UN projects in Paraguay and Mauritius.

JANICE TCHALENKO

BRITISH, 1942–2018

Pottery designer Tchalenko was born in Rugby, Warwickshire, and studied at the Putney and Harrow schools of art. She started as a studio potter making plain stoneware but introduced decoration into her work with vividly colored patterns in

NATIONAL CASH REGISTER BUILDING FOR NEW YORK WORLD'S FAIR, WALTER DORWIN TEAGUE, 1939

the late 1970s. In 1984, she became chief designer at Dartington Pottery in Devon, creating tableware for workshop production.

As well as her renowned designs for Dartington, Tchalenko created a ceramic collection for Next Interiors in 1986 and a series of ceramics illustrating the Seven Deadly Sins with the Spitting Image Workshop in 1993. She taught at Camberwell College of Arts in London and was a Fellow of the Royal College of Art from 1987.

△ WALTER DORWIN TEAGUE

AMERICAN, 1883–1960

A founding father of industrial design in the US, Teague was born in Indiana and studied painting at the Art Students League in New York. He initially worked in advertising, then set up an industrial design consultancy in 1926. His first and most loyal client was Eastman Kodak, for whom he designed cameras such as the Baby Brownie (1934) and Bantam Special (1936). In 1935, Teague also redesigned Texaco's gas stations. He was renowned for his exhibition design, especially his pavilions for the 1939 New York World's Fair. His business flourished after World War II, when he created corporate identities for clients such as Polaroid, Boeing, and NASA.

CAREER HIGHLIGHTS

1927 First commissioned by Kodak
1935 Designs the Blue Moon Radio
1954 Designs the interior of the Boeing 707 airliner

KAREL TEIGE

CZECH, 1900–1951

Teige was born in Prague, where his father was city archivist. Although he had no formal art training, he established himself as a key figure in Czechoslovakia's artistic avant-garde in 1920. He founded the Devětsil group of left-wing artists and, influenced by the Russian Constructivists, sought to promote socialism through architecture and book design. Between 1922 and 1938, he designed about 100

INTERIOR OF FORMER CASA DEL FASCIO, COMO, NORTHERN ITALY, GIUSEPPE TERRAGNI, 1932–1936

books and magazines, making radical use of typography and collage. Teige lectured at the Bauhaus in Dessau and worked with the French Surrealists from 1934. The German occupation of Prague in 1939 effectively ended his artistic career.

◁ GIUSEPPE TERRAGNI

ITALIAN, 1904–1943

Born in Meda, Lombardy, Terragni studied architecture at the Milan Polytechnic. In 1926, he became a founding member of Gruppo 7, a group of young architects committed to Rationalism, which they considered to be a middle way between classicism and industrial modernity. Terragni won commissions from Italy's Fascist authorities and contributed to the Exhibition of the Fascist Revolution in Rome, in 1932.

Terragni's major completed buildings were the Novocomum apartment building (1928–1929) and the Casa del Fascio (1932–1936), both in Como. He also designed furniture for the buildings' interiors, including the Novocomum table and the Follia chair (1934). In 1938, Mussolini's government commissioned the Danteum (see left), which Terragni regarded as an architectural equivalent of Dante's poem *The Divine Comedy*. The project was never built.

MICHAEL THONET

GERMAN AUSTRIAN, 1796–1871

Growing up in Boppard on the Rhine River, Thonet was apprenticed to a carpenter and opened his own furniture business in 1819. Around 1830, he began to experiment with bending laminated wood. The resulting bentwood furniture was exhibited at a trade fair in Koblenz in 1841 and attracted the attention of Prince von Metternich, the leading statesman of the Austrian Empire.

Under the patronage of the Austrian court, Thonet established a workshop in Vienna and created his Chair No. 1 (1849), shown at the Great Exhibition in London, in 1851. He set up Thonet Brothers in 1853, and, in 1856, he patented a process for bending solid wood. His chairs were ideal for mass production, and Thonet soon moved from workshop to factory production. The solid bentwood Chair No. 14 (1859) had sold more than 30 million units by 1930.

CAREER HIGHLIGHTS

1841 Exhibits the first examples of bentwood furniture
1849 Creates Chair No. 1
1853 Establishes Gerbruder Thonet
1856 Takes out a patent for bending solid wood

LOUIS COMFORT TIFFANY

AMERICAN, 1848–1933

The son of renowned jeweler Charles Tiffany, Louis Tiffany was born in New York City. He trained as a painter in the US and Europe, but around 1875, he became interested in glassmaking. In 1879, he cofounded a glassmaking and interior design business, which carried out a prestigious commission to redecorate the rooms of the White House in 1882.

In 1885, Tiffany set up a company on his own, which eventually became known as Tiffany Studios, to manufacture stained glass in the contemporary European Art Nouveau style for the US. From 1893, it also produced blown iridescent glass named Favrile that had color ingrained in the glass itself. The celebrated stained-glass Tiffany lamps were first introduced in 1895. The company employed hundreds of craftsmen and made many different decorative products, not only glassware but also ceramics, including tiles and mosaics. In 1902, Tiffany also became design director of the eponymous jewelry company founded by his father.

CAREER HIGHLIGHTS

1885 Sets up his own company
1893 Begins manufacturing blown Favrile glass
1895 Introduces Tiffany lamps
1902 Becomes design director of his father's jewelry company

OIVA TOIKKA

FINNISH, 1931–2019

Glass artist and designer Toikka was born on a farm near Viipuri in the Karelia region of Finland. He trained in ceramics at the Helsinki Institute of Industrial Arts and worked for the Arabia porcelain company from 1956. In 1963, he joined the littala glass factory at Nuutajärvi, and remained there for 50 years. In the 1960s, he designed mass-market products such as the Kastehelmi and Flora tableware lines, but his main interest was in blown art glass, from the Birds series begun in 1972 to the Art Works collection (2010). Toikka was also a prominent stage designer for Finnish theaters.

▷ **JAN TSCHICHOLD**

GERMAN, 1902–1974

Tschichold was born in Leipzig, the son of a signwriter, and trained as a calligrapher and typographer. In the 1920s, under the influence of Constructivism, he adopted sans-serif typefaces and photomontage, notably in posters for the Phoebus Palast cinema in Munich.

In 1928, Tschichold published his influential book *The New Typography*, arguing in favor of sans-serif fonts and unjustified (uneven right edge) type. In order to escape persecution by the Nazis, he moved to Switzerland in 1933. From 1947 to 1949, he lived in London, where he created a standardized layout for the jackets of Penguin paperbacks. His views on typography modified, and in 1966, he created Sabon, a serif typeface.

CAREER HIGHLIGHTS

1928 Publishes *Die Neue Typography* (The New Typography)
1947 Devises a standardized layout for Penguin paperback jackets
1966 Creates the Sabon typeface

OSCAR TUSQUETS BLANCA

SPANISH, 1941–

Tusquets Blanca was born in Barcelona and graduated from the Escuela Superior de Arquitectura. In 1965, he cofounded the radical architecture and design group Studio PER. In 1972, with Lluís Clotet, he designed the Belvedere Regas in Gerona, one of the first postmodernist buildings. Also in 1972, he cofounded BD Ediciones de Diseño (later known as BD Barcelona Design) to produce avant-garde furniture, tableware, and other objects. His own product designs include a tea and coffee set for Alessi (1983), the Alada table for Casas (1985), and the Perforano bench (1994).

CAREER HIGHLIGHTS

1972 Cofounds BD Ediciones de Diseño (now called BD Barcelona Design)
1985 Designs the Alada table for Casas

ADVERTISING POSTER FOR *NIGHT OF LOVE*, JAN TSCHICHOLD, 1927

MASANORI UMEDA

JAPANESE, 1941–

Born in Kanagawa, Umeda graduated from the Kuwasawa School of Design in Tokyo in 1962. In the late 1960s, he moved to Milan and worked in Achille Castiglioni's studio, before becoming design consultant for Olivetti in 1970. He left Olivetti in 1979 and was invited by Ettore Sottsass to join the postmodernist Memphis group, for which Umeda designed the celebrated Tawaraya boxing-ring bed (1981) and the Ginza robot-styled shelving system (1982).

Umeda returned to Japan in 1986 and opened his own studio, U-Metadesign, there. His later furniture designs included the Flower collection of armchairs for Edra (1990–1991).

PATRICIA URQUIOLA

SPANISH, 1961–

Born in Oviedo, Urquiola has described herself as an Asturian of Basque descent. She studied architecture in Madrid, then moved to Milan, graduating from the Polytechnic in 1989. She then taught at Milan Polytechnic as an assistant lecturer under Achille Castiglioni, while heading the De Padova furniture company's product development department. At De Padova, she collaborated with Vico Magistretti on designs including the Flower armchair (1996). After a spell

as head of the Lissoni Associati design group, she established her own studio in Milan in 2001.

Urquiola has also worked as an architect and interior designer, creating the striking Mandarin Oriental Hotel in Barcelona in 2010. Her many elegant and comfortable furniture designs include the Fjord armchair for Moroso (2002), the Night & Day sofa for Molteni (2009), and the Foliage sofa for Kartell (2011).

ARTUS VAN BRIGGLE

AMERICAN, 1869–1904

Born in Felicity, Ohio, Van Briggle studied painting at the Cincinnati Art School. After working as a decorator for Rookwood Pottery, he spent three years in Paris developing his artistic talent, then returned in 1896 to become Rookwood's head decorator. In 1899, after struggling with tuberculosis, he moved to the drier air of Colorado Springs, opening the Van Briggle Pottery in 1901. Aided by his wife Anne, he created ceramics that combined Art Nouveau style with innovative matte glazes. His Despondency vase won first place at the Paris Salon in 1903, and his work was much admired at the St. Louis Exposition of 1904, but he died later that year.

HENRY VAN DE VELDE

BELGIAN, 1863–1957

One of the founders of Art Nouveau, van de Velde studied painting in his native Antwerp and in Paris, but from 1892, after being inspired by the Arts and Crafts movement, he devoted himself to the decorative arts. His work included architecture, interior design, ceramics, textiles, and furniture.

In 1895, Van de Velde exhibited at the Maison de l'Art Nouveau gallery in Paris, and the following year, he completed the building of his own house in Brussels, the Bloemenwerf House, in the Art Nouveau style. By 1898, he had set up workshops in Brussels and Berlin to manufacture his designs and was creating posters and packaging for the German food company Tropon. Later, he moved to Germany and, in 1902, he founded the School of Arts and Crafts in Weimar, the predecessor of the Bauhaus. From 1907, he was active in the Deutscher Werkbund (German Association of Craftsmen). During World War I, he left Germany for Switzerland. He continued working into the 1940s but never regained his former prominence.

MAXIM VELCOVSKY

CZECH, 1976–

Porcelain and glass designer Velcovsky was born into a family of artists in Prague. He studied ceramics at the Prague Academy of Art, Architecture, and Design and, in 2002, set up the design studio Qubus with Jakub Berdych. Since 2011, Velcovsky has also been artistic director of Lasvit, the lighting firm.

Velcovsky's ceramics include the Waterproof series of vases shaped like gumboots (2001), a bowl in the shape of the Czech Republic (2003), and the Catastrophe vases (2007). In 2014, he presented the Frozen collection of glass lighting for Lasvit. Velcovsky has been Head of the ceramics workshop at the Prague Academy since 2011.

PAOLO VENINI

ITALIAN, 1895–1959

Glassmaker Venini was born in the small town of Cusano, outside Milan. He had been working as a lawyer in Milan when, in 1921, he joined with antique dealer Giacomo Cappelin to found a glass-making factory in Murano, Venice.

After Cappelin's departure in 1925, Venini & Co established a reputation as a leader in modern glass design. Venini personally contributed to the design of some of the firm's most famous lines, including the Diamante line of the mid-1930s, created with Carlo Scarpa, and the Fazzoletti vases he designed with Fulvio Bianconi after World War II.

▷ ROBERT VENTURI

AMERICAN, 1925–2018

Venturi was born into a Quaker family in Philadelphia, Pennsylvania. He studied architecture at Princeton University and worked under Eero Saarinen and Louis Kahn before setting up his own practice. He made his mark in 1964 with his design of the Vanna Venturi House for his mother,

VANNA VENTURI HOUSE, PHILADELPHIA, ROBERT VENTURI, 1964

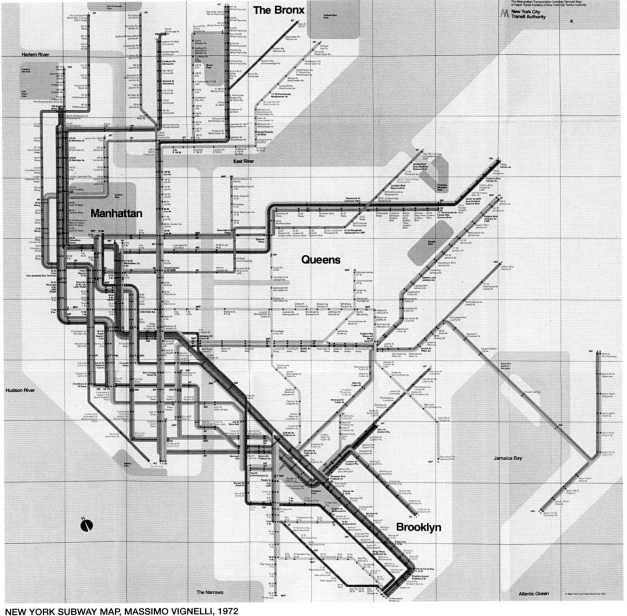

NEW YORK SUBWAY MAP, MASSIMO VIGNELLI, 1972

his first example of a postmodernist building, in which consistency was *not* a virtue, and the Guild House in Philadelphia. In 1966, Venturi published *Complexity and Contradiction in Architecture*, a seminal postmodernist text, which he followed with *Learning from Las Vegas* (1972).

Venturi's many architectural projects have included the Sainsbury Wing of the National Gallery in London (1991) and the Museum of Contemporary Art in San Diego (1996). He also designed furniture, notably nine chairs for Knoll (1979–1984), and ceramics, including a tea and coffee service for Alessi (1983) and the Grandmother Mug for Swid Powell (1984). Much of Venturi's work was carried out in collaboration with his wife, Denise Scott Brown.

CAREER HIGHLIGHTS

1966 Publishes *Complexity and Contradiction in Architecture*, a manifesto against Modernism
1976 Designs addition to Allen Memorial Art Museum, Oberlin, Ohio
1991 Designs the Seattle Art Museum and the Sainsbury Wing of London's National Gallery

△ MASSIMO VIGNELLI

ITALIAN AMERICAN, 1931–2014

Vignelli studied architecture at the polytechnic in his native Milan. With his wife, Lella Vignelli, he moved to New York in 1965 and founded the Unimark design consultancy. The Vignellis left Unimark in 1971 and set up Vignelli Associates.

Massimo Vignelli was primarily a graphic designer, best known for the signage and the controversially bold and colorful map he created for the New York subway in 1972. His other work included branding for American Airlines, shopping bags for Bloomingdale's, book design for Doubleday, and the signage for the Washington, DC, Metro. Vignelli Associates was also prominent in furniture, glassware, and product design.

CAREER HIGHLIGHTS

1967 Brands American Airlines with two bold "A"s on the airplane tails
1972 Redesigns New York subway map
1973 Designs Bloomingdale's Big Brown Bag

FRANTIŠEK VÍZNER

CZECH, 1936–2011

Born in Prague, Vízner trained as a glassmaker at schools in Novy Bor and Železný Brod, then finished his studies at the Prague Academy of Applied Arts, from which he graduated in 1962. He worked as a designer of mass-produced glassware for Sklo Union, and then, from 1967, created limited-edition, hot-shaped art glass for the Skrdlovice glassworks.

In 1975, Vízner set up his own studio, making one-of-a-kind, hand-cut pieces that established his international reputation. His work is in the collections of several major museums, including MoMA, New York, the V&A in London, and the Musée des Arts Décoratifs in Paris.

PETER VOULKOS

AMERICAN, 1924–2002

Born Panagiotis Voulkos, the son of Greek immigrant parents in Bozeman, Montana, the ceramicist served in World War II before studying pottery at Montana State College and the California College of Arts and Crafts.

In 1954, influenced by the Abstract Expressionist movement, Voulkos stopped making functional tableware and began to create ceramic art. He headed art ceramics departments, first at the Los Angeles County Art Institute and then, from 1959, at the University of California, Berkeley, where he continued teaching until 1985. Voulkos's influential ceramic sculptures are credited with breaking down the barrier between craft pottery and ceramic art.

▷ C. F. A. VOYSEY

BRITISH, 1857–1941

Architect and furniture and textile designer Charles Francis Annesley Voysey was born in Hessle, Yorkshire, the son of an Anglican vicar. Educated at home and then at Dulwich College, Voysey worked for various architectural practices, notably that of J. P. Seddon. In 1883, he began to design wallpaper. The following year, he joined the Art Workers' Guild, and in 1888, he exhibited textiles and wallpaper at the first Arts and Crafts Exhibition.

By the 1890s, Voysey had established himself as one of England's leading Arts and Crafts designers. He was best known for his wallpapers but also for his simple and elegant, furniture, metalwork, and carpets, all made from high-quality materials. A notable architect, Voysey designed several country houses with low, spreading lines in the Arts and Crafts style, including Broad Leys, Windermere (1888), and the Homestead, Essex (1905). He was elected Master of the Art Workers' Guild in 1924.

CAREER HIGHLIGHTS

1884 Joins the Art Workers' Guild
1888 Exhibits textile and wallpaper designs at the first Arts and Crafts Exhibition
1905 Designs the Homestead in Essex

WILHELM WAGENFELD

GERMAN, 1900–1990

Born in Bremen, industrial designer Wagenfeld served an apprenticeship in a silverware factory before joining the Bauhaus metal workshop in Weimar in 1923. In 1924, he designed the classic Bauhaus table lamp, in collaboration with Karl Jucker. Dedicated to functional design for mass production, Wagenfeld worked in the glass industry from 1931, first at the Schott glassworks in Jena and then at the Lausitzer glassworks in Weisswasser. His designs included a tea service for Schott (1934) and the Kubus modular storage containers for Lausitzer (1938). After World War II, he worked chiefly as a freelancer, designing many household products in glass, metal, plastic, and ceramics.

MARCEL WANDERS

DUTCH, 1963–

Avant-garde product designer Wanders was born in Boxtel, Netherlands, and graduated from the Institute of the Arts in Arnhem in 1988. He opened his own design studio in Amsterdam in 1995 and made an immediate impact with his Knotted Chair for DROOG® (1996), which combines a traditional form and the ancient technique of knotting with technologically advanced resin-coated carbon fiber, and the Egg Vase for Rosenthal (1997). Wanders has designed

BIRDS, STRAWBERRIES, AND LEAVES FABRIC, C. F. A. VOYSEY, 1897–1898

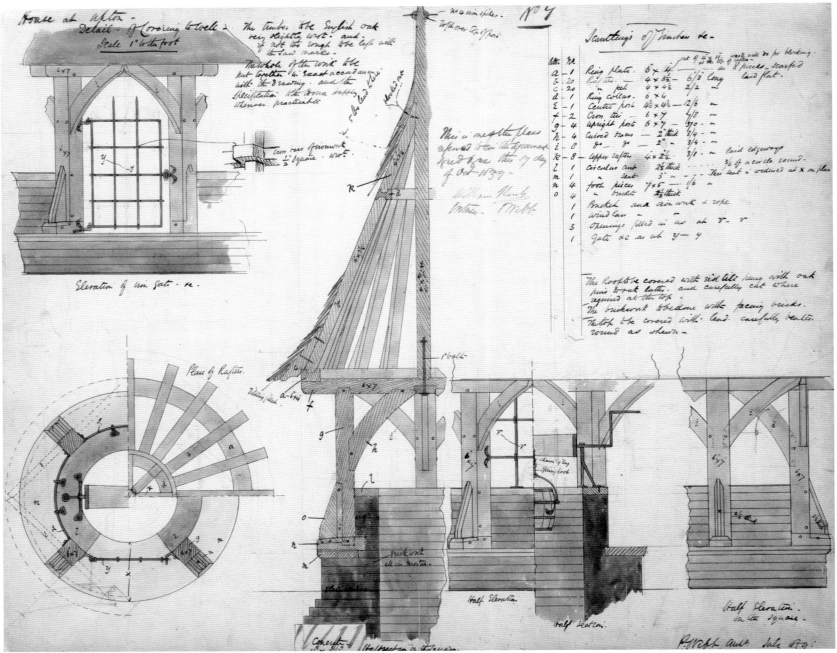

ARCHITECTURAL DRAWING FOR RED HOUSE, PHILIP WEBB FOR WILLIAM AND JANE MORRIS, 1859

a range of products for companies such as Alessi, Flos, Cappellini, Puma, and Target and founded the Marcel Wanders Studio design label in 2001. His designs typically give plain, traditional forms an unconventional twist. His architecture projects have included the Andaz Amsterdam Prinsengracht Hotel (2012).

RIKI WATANABE

JAPANESE 1911–2013

Industrial designer Watanabe was born in Shirogane, Tokyo, and trained in woodcraft at the Tokyo Higher School of Arts and Design. He worked under the German architect Bruno Taut in Gunma in the mid-1930s and absorbed the principles of Modernism. Watanabe established his own design studio in 1949, and the following year, he made his mark with the Himo Isu rope chair. Other popular designs included the Torii Stool (1956) and the Uni Tray (1976). Watanabe was a founding member of the Japan Industrial Design Association in 1952. He is also known for his watch and clock designs, and for his hotel interiors.

CAREER HIGHLIGHTS

1950 Designs the Himo Isu rope chair
1956 Creates the Torii Stool

SIDNEY WAUGH

AMERICAN, 1904–1963

Born in Amherst, Massachusetts, Waugh studied architecture in Massachusetts and art in Rome, then worked in Paris with sculptors Antoine Bourdelle and Henri Bouchard. In 1934, Waugh was commissioned by Steuben Glass to design engraved decoration that would raise their products to the level of art glass. Waugh came up with designs such as Gazelle (1935), in which Art Deco beasts bounded around the periphery of a bowl in a manner recalling ancient Greek red- and black-figure vases.

△ PHILIP WEBB

BRITISH, 1831–1915

Arts and Crafts architect Philip Speakman Webb was born in Oxford and worked as an assistant to G. E. Street before opening his own practice in 1858. In 1859, he designed the Red House, Bexleyheath, as a family home and studio for his friends William and Jane Morris. He subsequently became a partner in the furnishing and interior decoration company that Morris established in 1861.

As an architect, Webb designed St. Martin's Church in Brampton, Cumbria (1878), and Standen in West Sussex (1894). He also designed wallpaper, tiles, stained glass, and furniture, including the famous Morris Chair (1869). Webb founded the Society for the Protection of Ancient Buildings in 1877.

HANS J. WEGNER

DANISH, 1914–2007

Born in Tønder in southern Denmark, Wegner was apprenticed to a carpenter, then studied furniture design at the Copenhagen School of Applied Arts. After a spell working for the architect Arne Jacobsen in Aarhus, Wegner opened his own studio in 1943, forming a fruitful relationship with manufacturer Johannes Hansen.

Wegner's work was characterized by respect for natural materials, elegance, simplicity, and the finest craftsmanship. He designed more than 500 chairs in his long career, including the Peacock chair (1947) and the iconic Wishbone and Round chairs (1949), both of which were created for Johannes Hansen, and the Hoop Chair, designed in 1965. By 1968, he had been awarded 27 prizes by the Copenhagen Cabinetmakers' Guild.

ROBERT WELCH

BRITISH, 1929–2000

Silversmith and industrial designer Robert Welch was born in Hereford and studied at Birmingham College of Art and the Royal College of Art in London. After making extended visits to Norway and Sweden, he was heavily influenced by Scandinavian Modernism. In 1955, he set up a studio at Chipping Camden in the Cotswolds, while also becoming design consultant to J. & J. Wiggin, manufacturers of stainless steel tableware. His output ranged from handmade silverware to a range of industrial designs, including the Campden candelabrum (1957), the Alveston tableware range and Westclox Merlin alarm clock (both 1962), and the Chantry knife sharpener (1964).

SUSAN WILLIAMS-ELLIS

BRITISH, 1918–2007

Born in Guildford, Surrey, Susan Williams-Ellis was the daughter of the architect who created the Italianate village of Portmeirion in Wales. She was surrounded by artists from an early age and learned ceramics from the Leaches before attending Chelsea School of Art. In the 1950s, she ran the gift shop at Portmeirion, for which she commissioned pottery. In 1960, she took over one of her suppliers to found Portmeirion Pottery in Stoke-on-Trent. Among her successful tableware designs were the Totem line (1963) and the Botanic Garden line, which was introduced in 1972.

TAPIO WIRKKALA

FINNISH, 1915–1985

Born in Hanko, Finland, Wirkkala studied sculpture at the Central School of Arts and Crafts in Helsinki (he later became its director). In 1946, he designed the Kantarelli (Chanterelle) vases for Iittala, the beginning of a lifelong collaboration with the glass manufacturer. His work came to international attention at the 1951 and 1954 Milan Triennales, where he won several major awards. Wirkkala was astonishingly versatile—his designs ranged from the birch plywood Leaf Dish of 1951 (typical of the natural forms and the traditional craftsmanship he favored) to banknotes, and from plastic ketchup bottles to one-of-a-kind art pieces and knives.

From 1956 onward, Wirkkala designed ceramic vases, bowls, tableware services such as Variation and Composition (both 1963) and Polygon (1973), and cutlery for Rosenthal. He also designed glassware for Venini in Murano.

CAREER HIGHLIGHTS

1946 Wins joint first prize (with Kaj Franck) in the Iittala competition and becomes a glass designer

1951 Designs the Finnish pavilion at the Milan Triennale and wins three major awards

1952 Designs the Tapio glasses for Iittala, and Finnish banknotes

1966 Creates the Bolla bottle collection for Venini, Murano

KENWOOD CHEF, KENNETH WOOD, 1950 ONWARD

PHILIPPE WOLFERS

BELGIAN, 1858–1929

A jeweler, sculptor, and glassware designer, Wolfers learned his trade in his father's goldsmith firm. In 1892, Wolfers and his brothers Max and Robert took over the firm, and Philippe became design director. Using luxury materials from the Belgian Congo, Wolfers combined metal with ivory, enamel, opals, and pearls to create exquisite Symbolist and Art Nouveau pieces based on sinuous human, animal, and plant forms. He also worked for the Belgian Val Saint Lambert glassware company from 1893 to 1903, incorporating Symbolist metal mounts into glass.

▽ KENNETH WOOD

BRITISH, 1916–1997

London-born Kenneth Wood is best known for his food mixer, the Kenwood Chef. He set up business in 1947, selling domestic appliances such as toasters and the A200 food mixer. In 1950, he updated the A200 to the A700, called it the Kenwood Chef, and launched it at the Ideal Homes Exhibition. A whole range of products followed, including a mini-version of the mixer called the Chefette, a new toaster, and an electric cordless knife (1968). Wood was adept at identifying which chores were most arduous and developing machines to carry them out.

EDWARD WORMLEY

AMERICAN, 1907–1995

Born in Illinois, Wormley studied at the Art Institute of Chicago, then joined the design department of the Marshall Field department store in Chicago. In 1931, he was employed by the Indiana-based Dunbar Furniture Company. Dunbar's design director from the mid-1940s, he gave the company's traditional furniture a Modernist twist. The result was a commercial and aesthetic success, and Wormley's work was featured in the MoMA Good Design exhibitions from 1950 to 1952. In 1956 and 1957, he created Dunbar's popular Janus collection, which included tile-topped tables. Wormley also designed textiles, carpets, and lighting for other clients.

GUGGENHEIM MUSEUM, NEW YORK, FRANK LLOYD WRIGHT, 1943–1959

◁ FRANK LLOYD WRIGHT

AMERICAN, 1867–1949

Born in Wisconsin, Wright briefly studied engineering at the University of Wisconsin–Madison. He learned about architecture while he was working as a draftsman in Chicago, especially under architect Louis Sullivan, who became his mentor and allowed Wright to design his first buildings. In 1893, Wright set up his own architecture practice, producing houses in what became known as the Prairie style. Influenced by the Arts and Crafts movement, Wright considered furnishings to be an integral part of architecture and designed oak furniture with metal hardware, concealed lighting, vases, urns, rugs, and stained glass to match his buildings.

In the 1920s, Wright began to use reinforced concrete for his buildings, as in Fallingwater, the famous cantilevered house he built over a river in Pennsylvania in 1935, and the innovative Guggenheim Museum in New York, begun in 1943. Wright also had radical views on urban planning and put forward a proposal for a city composed of standardized, middle-income housing.

CAREER HIGHLIGHTS

1893 Sets up his own architecture practice on the outskirts of Chicago
1910 Completes Robie House, his masterpiece of Prairie style
1937 Completes Taliesin West, his winter home in Arizona
1935 Designs Fallingwater
1943 Begins designing the Guggenheim Museum, New York

RUSSEL WRIGHT

AMERICAN, 1904–1976

Born into a Quaker family in Lebanon, Ohio, Wright studied painting at the Art Academy of Cincinnati and sculpture at the Art Students League of New York. After working in theater design, he set up a studio in New York in 1930, initially to design novelty products, bar accessories, and kitchenware that was made out of spun aluminum.

Wright then expanded into wood and ceramics, creating the functional yet stylish American Modern furniture line (1935) and the bestselling American Modern dinnerware and flatware line (1937). His later successes included the Residential line of plastic dinnerware for Melmac (1953). Wright retired in 1955.

SORI YANAGI

JAPANESE, 1915–2011

Born in Tokyo, Yanagi was the son of a leading expert on Japanese folk art. He studied art and architecture at the Tokyo Academy of Fine Art before developing an interest in design. He worked as an assistant to Charlotte Perriand in the early 1940s, when she was in Japan, and by 1951, had become an award-winning industrial designer.

Yanagi established the Yanagi Industrial Design Institute in 1952 and created his most famous works, the Butterfly and Elephant stools, in 1954. Melding old and new, East and West, the Butterfly united a traditional form with plywood, while the Elephant was a softly rounded, plastic stacking stool. Yanagi went on to design a wide range of objects large and small, from bridges to motorcycles, and from subway stations to toys.

CAREER HIGHLIGHTS

1940 Assists in Charlotte Perriand's Tokyo design office until 1942
1954 Designs the Butterfly stool
1977 Becomes director of the Japan Folk Crafts Museum, Tokyo

LADISLAV ŽAK

CZECH, 1900–1973

Born in Prague, then in Austria-Hungary, now in the Czech Republic, Žak studied painting and architecture at the city's Academy of Fine Arts. Influenced by the Bauhaus, he became a successful architect in the 1930s, designing several villas in the Czech functionalist style. As well as buildings, Žak designed interiors and furniture. His tubular-steel Sessil Siesta of 1931 was an early example of a cantilever chair. In the late 1940s, after Czechoslovakia came under Communist rule, Žak fell out of favor with the regime and his career never quite recovered.

MARCO ZANUSO

ITALIAN, 1916–2001

Architect and designer Zanuso was born in Milan and studied at the Milan Polytechnic. After World War II, while editor of the magazine *Domus*, he was a key figure in debates about design in Italy. From 1945, he ran his own studio in Milan, creating foam rubber furniture for Arflex, including the Antropus chair (1949) and the Lady chair (1951). He also designed the iconic Borletti sewing machine (1956).

When German designer Richard Sapper joined Zanuso's studio in 1959, they collaborated on designs for Brionvega, Kartell, and Siemens. Zanuso's many architectural projects included the Olivetti factories in São Paulo and Buenos Aires in the mid-1950s and the Necchi office building in Pavia in 1961.

WALTER ZAPP

LATVIAN-GERMAN, 1905–2003

The inventor of the Minox subminiature camera, Zapp was born to German parents in Riga, Latvia, which was then part of the Russian Empire. He became interested in cameras as a young man, when he worked for an art photographer in Tallinn, Estonia. In 1936, after 14 years spent developing the concept, he created the first version of the Minox camera, which went into production in 1937 at the Valsts Elektrotechniske Fabrika (VEF) in Riga.

After the Soviet Union annexed Estonia in 1940, Zapp moved to Germany. He established the Minox company there after World War II and spent his later years in Switzerland.

EVA ZEISEL

HUNGARIAN AMERICAN, 1906–2011

Born into a highly cultured Jewish family in Budapest, Zeisel trained as a craft potter before moving to Germany, where she became a designer for ceramics manufacturers. In 1932, she moved to the Soviet Union, where her career flourished until she was arrested in a Stalinist purge. In 1938, she fled Europe's political troubles and settled in the US. There, she established her reputation with the Museum line of dishware, with its irregular geometry and exaggerated shapes, which was exhibited at MoMA, New York, in 1946 and later manufactured by Castleton. Another success was the Town and Country tableware line for Red Wing Pottery (1947). Its organic forms were easy to hold without handles. Zeisel also designed glassware, furniture, and lamps, continuing her career as an industrial designer into the 21st century.

PIET ZWART

DUTCH, 1885–1977

Born in Zaandijk, Zwart studied at the School of Applied Arts in Amsterdam. Originally drawn to the Arts and Crafts movement, he came under the influence of De Stijl and Constructivism after World War I. Also an architect and photographer, he is best known for his 1920s and 1930s graphic design work. His advertisements, brochures, and book designs, notably for the Nederlandsche Kabelfabriek (NKF) company and the Dutch post office, made use of photography and collage as well as innovative typography. After World War II, during which he was imprisoned by the Nazis, Zwart concentrated on his industrial design projects.

CAREER HIGHLIGHTS

1929 Organizes Dutch display at *Film and Foto* exhibition, Stuttgart
1938 Designs a revolutionary modular kitchen, composed of prefabricated self-contained units, for Bruynzeel

TOOTS ZYNSKY

AMERICAN, 1951–

Born in Boston, Massachusetts, studio glassmaker Mary Ann Toots Zynsky studied at the Rhode Island School of Design and learned glassblowing at the Pilchuck Glass Center in Stanwood, Washington. From 1980, she worked at the New York Experimental Glass Workshop in New York City, combining glass with barbed wire and making vessels with glass thread.

Zynsky moved to Europe in 1983, establishing studios in Amsterdam and, later, Paris. She also worked at Murano in Venice, designing the Folto vases for the Venini glassworks in 1984. Zynsky returned to the US in 1999 and settled in Providence, Rhode Island.

A to Z Index

H

Acknowledgments

The publishers would like to thank the following: Mark Hill for editorial advice; Pam Langdown and Katherine Pell, Museum of Design in Plastics, Arts University Bournemouth; Jan Van Den Bosch, Van Den Bosch silverware, London; Mark Gorringe, Gorringe Antiques, London; Benjamin Macklowe and Antonio Virardi, Macklowe Gallery, New York; Alioscia Re, Omar Barbati, and Federica Paleari, Knoll International; Gary Ombler for new photography; Margaret McCormack for indexing; Diane Kidd, Education Specialist, Department of Education, National Air and Space Museum, US, for consulting; Suhita Dharamjit, Harish Agarwal, and Saloni Singh for jacket design; Pooja Pipil for design assistance; Antara Moitra and Tejaswita Payal for editorial assistance; Kathryn Hennessy and Christine Stroyan for project management and editorial assistance.

For revised edition: DK would like to thank Suefa Lee (Senior Editor), Vikas Sachdeva (Senior Art Editor), Shipra Jain (Art Editor), Jaypal Chauhan and Syed Md Farhan (DTP Designers); and Suhita Dharamjit (Senior Jacket Designer), Harish Aggarwal (Senior DTP Designer), Priyanka Sharma (Jackets Editorial Coordinator), and Saloni Singh (Managing Jackets Editor) for help with the jacket.

The publisher would like to thank the following for their kind permission to reproduce their photographs:

Key: a-above; b-below/bottom; c-center; f-far; l-left; r-right; t-top

01 Cassina. 02–03 Courtesy of Marc Newson Ltd: Fabrice Gousset. **04 Corbis:** The Gallery Collection (tr). **Dorling Kindersley:** Quittenbaum / Judith Miller (tc). **05 Dorling Kindersley:** Judith Miller / Wallis and Wallis (tr); Von Zezschwitz / Judith Miller (ftr); Sloan's / Judith Miller (ftl). **V&A Images / Victoria and Albert Museum, London:** (tl). **06 Dorling Kindersley:** Freeman's / Judith Miller (tr); Judith Miller / Lyon and Turnbull Ltd. (ftl). **V&A Images / Victoria and Albert Museum, London:** (ftr). **www.classicon.com:** under licence from Aram Designs (tl). **07 Corbis:** Diego Lezama Orezzol (tl). **Stuart Haygarth:** (ftr). **Kartell Spa:** (tr). **Herman Miller:** (ftl). **08 Dorling Kindersley:** Museum of Design in Plastics, Bournemouth Arts University, UK. **12 Image courtesy of Anglepoise®. 13 Wright. 14 Photo Scala, Florence:** Museum of Modern Art (MoMA), New York, USA. **17 1stdibs. com:** (br). **Bridgeman Images:** Private Collection / Calmann & King Ltd / © Rodchenko & Stepanova Archive, DACS, RAO, 2015. / DACS, London 2015 (tr). **Dorling Kindersley:** Quittenbaum / Judith Miller (crb). **Marimekko:** (clb). **Photo Scala, Florence:** Museum of Modern Art (MoMA), New York, USA (tc). **V&A Images / Victoria and Albert Museum, London:** Shirley Craven (bc). **Wright:** (cra). **Dennis Zanone:** (cla). **18 Corbis:** (br). **iStockphoto.com:** Ministry Of Joy (bl). **19 Bridgeman Images:** Museum of Fine Arts, Houston, Texas, USA / Gift of the Houston Astros Baseball Club and Drayton McLane (tr); Tretyakov Gallery, Moscow, Russia (bl). **Cappellini Design Spa:** (tl). **Dorling Kindersley:** Museum of Design in Plastics, Bournemouth Arts University, UK (cl). **Herman Miller:** (br). **Photo Scala, Florence:** Museum of Modern Art (MoMA), New York, USA / DACS, London 2015 (cr). **21 Alessi (UK) Ltd:** (cl). **Dorling Kindersley:** Judith Miller / Design20c (tr). **Marvin Lipofsky: Photo:** M. Lee Fatherree (bc). **Photo Scala, Florence:** (bl). **V&A Images / Victoria and Albert Museum, London:** DACS, London 2015 (tl). **Dennis Zanone:** DACS, London 2015 (cr). **22 Dreamstime.com:** Halyna Kavun (13); Lorasutyagina (7); Pomah (11); Juris Sturainis (12); Vitaly Korovin (16); Daniil Peshkov (19). **Getty Images:** Kyoshino (17); RapidEye (10); malerapaso (15). **iStockphoto.com:** Bartosz Hadyniak (4); ivanastar (3); Frank van den Bergh (8); Stuart Renneberg (9, 14); Tortoon (18). **23 Bridgeman Images:** Private Collection / Christie's Images (tr). **Edra Spa:** (cr). **Flos S.p.A.:** (bl). **V&A Images / Victoria and Albert Museum, London:** (tl, br). **Wright:** (cl). **26 Dorling Kindersley:** Judith Miller / David Rago Auctions (bl); Judith Miller / Lyon and Turnbull Ltd. (bc, br). **27 Corbis:** Andreas von Einsiedel (bc). **Dorling Kindersley:** Judith Miller / Lyon and Turnbull Ltd. (bl, br). **28 Dorling Kindersley:** Judith Miller / Sloans & Kenyon (bc, br); Judith Miller / Lyon and Turnbull Ltd. (tl, bl); Judith Miller / Wallis and Wallis (tr); Judith Miller / Sloan's (fcl); Judith Miller / The Design Gallery (cl, cr); Dreweatt Neate / Judith Miller (fcr). **29 Dorling Kindersley:** Judith Miller / Lyon and Turnbull Ltd. (main). **30–31 Corbis:** Historical Picture Archive. **32 Cooper-Hewitt, Smithsonian Design Museum,:** Gift of Cowtan & Tout, Inc.. 1935-23-25. **33 Alamy Images:** V&A Images (bc). **Corbis:**

Bettmann (tl). **Dorling Kindersley:** Judith Miller (bl); Woolley and Wallis / Judith Miller (br). **34 akg-images:** A.F.Kersting (br). **Bonhams Auctioneers, London:** (l). **35 Dorling Kindersley:** Judith Miller / Gallery 532 (cl); Judith Miller / Wallis and Wallis (tl); Judith Miller / Geoffrey Diner Gallery (tr); Judith Miller / Lyon and Turnbull Ltd. (cr, bc); Quittenbaum / Judith Miller / © DACS, London 2015 (br). **Collection Paul Reeves:** (bl). **36 The Stickley Museum at Craftsman Farms, Parsippany, New Jersey:** photo by Ray Stubblebine. **37 Bridgeman Images:** Private Collection, Photo © Christie's Images (bl). **Dorling Kindersley:** Judith Miller (br). **Photo Scala, Florence:** Museum of Modern Art (MoMA), New York, USA (bc). **The Stickley Museum at Craftsman Farms, Parsippany, New Jersey:** (tl). **38 Corbis:** VIEW / Dennis Gilbert. **39 Corbis:** (tl). **Dorling Kindersley:** The Trustees of the British Museum (bl); Dreweatt Neate / Judith Miller (bc); Judith Miller (br). **40 Dorling Kindersley:** Dreweatt Neate / Judith Miller. **41 Dorling Kindersley:** Judith Miller / Puritan Values (tr, cl); Judith Miller / Lyon and Turnbull Ltd. (tl, tc, bc); Dreweatt Neate / Judith Miller (c, bl); Judith Miller / The Design Gallery (cr); Judith Miller / Sloan's (br). **43 Alamy Images:** Interfoto (bl). **Dorling Kindersley:** Judith Miller / Freeman's (tl, br); Judith Miller / Lyon and Turnbull Ltd. (bc). **44 Corbis:** Araldo de Luca. **45 akg-images:** (tl). **Dorling Kindersley:** Quittenbaum / Judith Miller (br); Von Zezschwitz / Judith Miller (bc). **Getty Images:** De Agostini Picture Library (bl). **46 Artek:** Tuomas Uusheimo (c). **Dorling Kindersley:** Judith Miller / Sloan's (tr); Judith Miller / Freeman's (br). **Fritz Hansen A/S:** (bc). **Photo Scala, Florence:** Museum of Modern Art (MoMA), New York, USA (cr). **Vitra Management AG:** (cl).**47 Alamy Images:** John Hammond (c); V&A Images (tc); Elizabeth Whiting & Associates (bc). **Bridgeman Images:** Saint Louis Art Museum, Missouri, USA (tr). **Dorling Kindersley:** Lyon and Turnbull Ltd. (bl). **Markus Johansson:** (br). **PP Møbler:** (cl). **Photo Scala, Florence:** Cooper-Hewitt, National Design Museum, Smithsonian Institution / Art Resource, NY (ftr); Museum of Modern Art (MoMA), New York, USA (tl). **48 Dorling Kindersley:** Judith Miller / Woolley and Wallis (bl, c); Judith Miller / Wallis and Wallis (cr, bc); Judith Miller / David Rago Auctions (br). **49 Dorling Kindersley:** Judith Miller / Wallis and Wallis (cl); Judith Miller / Woolley and Wallis (bl); Judith Miller / Geoffrey Diner Gallery (r). **50 Corbis:** Christie's Images. **51 Dorling Kindersley:** Judith Miller / Dawson & Nye Auctioneers & Appraisers (tl); Judith Miller / Wallis and Wallis (bl, bc, br, fbr). **52 Dorling Kindersley:** National Cycle Collection (tr, cl); Jonathan Sneath (c); Philip Gatward (br). **Science & Society Picture Library:** (cr, bl). **53 Cannondale © Cycling Sports Group, Inc. 2020:** (br). **Dorling Kindersley:** National Cycle Collection (tl); Jonathan Sneath (cl). **Photo Scala, Florence:** (cr). **Science & Society Picture Library:** (tc, tr, bc). **54 Dorling Kindersley:** Van Den Bosch (cr, bl); Judith Miller / Van Den Bosch (cl); Judith Miller / The Design Gallery (bc); Judith Miller / Style Gallery (br). **55 Dorling Kindersley:** Van Den Bosch (tl, cl, r); Judith Miller / The Design Gallery (bl). **56–57 Dorling Kindersley:** Van Den Bosch. **57 Dorling Kindersley:** Van Den Bosch (tl, tr, cra). **58 Dorling Kindersley:** Van Den Bosch. **59 Dorling Kindersley:** Van Den Bosch (tc); Dreweatt Neate / Judith Miller (tl); Judith Miller / Van Den Bosch (tr, bl); Judith Miller / Geoffrey Diner Gallery (cl, c); Judith Miller / Woolley and Wallis (bc). **Hart Silversmiths, Guild of Handicraft:** (br). **60 Cooper-Hewitt, Smithsonian Design Museum,:** Gift of Harry Lyons, 2004-11-1. **61 Dorling Kindersley:** Dreweatt Neate / Judith Miller (bc). **Maull & Polyblank:** (tl). **Photo Scala, Florence:** Art Resource / The Metropolitan Museum of Art (br). **V&A Images / Victoria and Albert Museum, London:** (bl). **62 Corbis:** The Gallery Collection. **63 Bridgeman Images:** Cleveland Museum of Art, OH, USA / The Severance and Greta Millikin Purchase Fund (br); Private Collection (tl). **Dorling Kindersley:** Judith Miller / Lyon and Turnbull Ltd. (tc); Judith Miller / John Nicholsons (bl). **Owen Jones:** The Grammar of Ornament, Publ Day & Son 1856 (cr). **Nazmiyal Antique Rugs http://nazmiyal.com:** (cl). **Photo Scala, Florence:** Art Resource / The Metropolitan Museum of Art (bc). **64 V&A Images / Victoria and Albert Museum, London:** Given by Rex Silver, Esq.. **65 Alamy Images:** Simon Curtis (bl). **Dorling Kindersley:** Judith Miller / Geoffrey Diner Gallery (tl); Judith Miller / Van Den Bosch (bc, br). **68 Dorling Kindersley:** Judith Miller / Mary Ann's Collectibles (bl); Judith Miller / Titus Omega (bc). **Getty Images:** DeAgostini (br). **69 Dorling Kindersley:** Judith Miller / Thomas Dreiling Collection (bl); Judith Miller / Sloan's (bc); Judith Miller / Mary Ann's Collectibles (br). **70 Bridgeman Images:** Detroit Institute of Arts, USA / Gift of Gilbert and Lila Silverman (c). **Dorling Kindersley:** Judith Miller / Mary Ann's Collectibles (cl); Quittenbaum / Judith Miller / © DACS, London 2015 (bl); Quittenbaum / Judith Miller (bc); Quittenbaum / Judith Miller / © DACS, London 2015 (br). **V&A Images / Victoria and Albert Museum, London:** (cr). **71 Mary Evans Picture Library:** Roger-Viollet / Petit Palais (br). **Photo Scala, Florence:** Christie's Images, London (l). **72 Alamy Images:** Hemis. **73 Alamy Images:**

Photos 12 (tl). **Dorling Kindersley:** Judith Miller / Mary Ann's Collectibles (bl, br). **Getty Images:** DeAgostini (bc). **74 Dorling Kindersley:** Quittenbaum / Judith Miller. **75 Dorling Kindersley:** Wiener Kunst Auktionen / Palais Kinsky / Judith Miller (cr); Quittenbaum / Judith Miller (tl, tc, tr); Palais Dorotheum / Judith Miller (c, bc); Dreweatt Neate / Judith Miller (br). **Wikipedia:** Koloman Moser, Plakatentwurf für die „Erste grosse Kunstaustellung" der Secession, 1897 (bl). **76 Corbis:** Paul Panayiotou. **77 Corbis:** Heritage Images (tl); Ramon Manent (br). **Photo Scala, Florence:** Museum of Modern Art (MoMA), New York, USA (bl, bc). **78–79 Corbis:** EPA. **80 Corbis:** Robert Harding World Imagery / Yadid Levy. **81 Alamy Images:** GL Archive (tl). **Bridgeman Images:** Art Gallery and Museum, Kelvingrove, Glasgow, Scotland, © Glasgow City Council (Museums) (br). **Dorling Kindersley:** Judith Miller / Lyon and Turnbull Ltd. (bc). **82 Dorling Kindersley:** Judith Miller / David Rago Auctions. **83 Bridgeman Images:** Indianapolis Museum of Art, USA / Robertine Daniels Art Fund in memory of her husband & son / Richard Monroe Fairbanks Sr. & Michael Fairbanks (br). **Dorling Kindersley:** Judith Miller / Mary Ann's Collectibles (tc, tr); Judith Miller / Freeman's (c); Quittenbaum / Judith Miller (bl); Judith Miller / Wallis and Wallis (bc); Quittenbaum / Judith Miller (tl). **84 Dorling Kindersley:** Courtesy of Van Den Bosch (bc, cr); Judith Miller / Mary Ann's Collectibles (cl, bl); Quittenbaum / Judith Miller (br). **85 Dorling Kindersley:** Courtesy of Van Den Bosch (bl, r); Quittenbaum / Judith Miller (cl). **86 Bridgeman Images:** Private Collection, Photo © Christie's Images. **87 Bridgeman Images:** Private Collection, Photo © Christie's Images (tl). **Dorling Kindersley:** Judith Miller / Lyon and Turnbull Ltd. (bl); Judith Miller / Style Gallery (bc); Judith Miller / The Design Gallery (br). **88 Alamy Images:** Interfoto (br). **Corbis Ramon Manent / DACS, London 2015:** (cr). **Tadema Gallery:** (cl, bl) / **DACS, London 2015:** (c). **89 Bridgeman Images:** Private Collection, Photo © Christie's Images (t). **Dorling Kindersley:** Judith Miller / Palais Dorotheum / © ADAGP, Paris and DACS, London 2015 (bl). **Tadema Gallery:** (bc, br). **90 akg-images:** Imagno / Josef Hoffmann. **91 akg-images:** Imagno (tl); Erich Lessing (br). **Dorling Kindersley:** Judith Miller / John Sollo / David Rago (Joint Sales) (bl). **Photo Scala, Florence:** Museum of Fine Arts, Boston / Bequest of the Estate of Mrs. Gertrude T. Taft, Gift of Edward Perry Warren, Gift of Alex Cochrane, Anonymous gift, Gift of Charles Loring, and Estate of Mrs. William Dorr Boardman through Gift of Mrs. Bernard C. Weld, by exchange. Inv. 1994.238 (bc). **94 Jean-Pierre Dalbéra:** Musée de l'Ecole de Nancy (bl). **Dorling Kindersley:** Gorringe Antiques (bc); Judith Miller / Mike Weedon (c); Quittenbaum / Judith Miller (cr). **Photo Scala, Florence:** Christie's Images, London (br). **95 Dorling Kindersley:** Judith Miller / David Rago Auctions (tl); Judith Miller / Titus Omega (bl); Judith Miller / Thomas Dreiling Collection (r). **96–97 Antonio Virardi of Macklowe Gallery, New York:** (all). **98 Dorling Kindersley:** Judith Miller / Mary Ann's Collectibles (c); Quittenbaum / Judith Miller (bl); Judith Miller / Sloan's (bc, br). **98–99 Dorling Kindersley:** James D Julia Inc / Judith Miller (t). **99 Bridgeman Images:** Private Collection, Photo © Christie's Images (bc). **Corbis:** Christie's Images (bl). **Dorling Kindersley:** Judith Miller / Sloan's (br). **100 Alamy Images:** Andrea Rescigno (bc). **Bridgeman Images:** Collection of the New-York Historical Society, USA (tr). **Dorling Kindersley:** Steve Shott (bl); Tecta / Judith Miller (c). **LE KLINT:** (cr). **Wright:** (br). **101 1stdibs.com:** (c). **Alamy Images:** Chris Brignell (tl). **Bridgeman Images:** The Israel Museum, Jerusalem, Israel / Gift of the manufacturer (bl). **Dorling Kindersley:** Judith Miller / Sloan's (tc); Judith Miller / Rosebery (cl). **Made.com:** (br). **Photo Scala, Florence:** Digital Image Museum Associates / LACMA / Art Resource NY (tr, cr). **V&A Images / Victoria and Albert Museum, London:** (bc). **102 Corbis:** James L Amos. **103 Dorling Kindersley:** Geoffrey Diner Gallery / Judith Miller (bc); James D Julia Inc / Judith Miller (bl); Sloan's / Judith Miller (br). **The Library of Congress, Washington DC:** LC-USZ62-115996 (tl). **104 Corbis:** Austrian Archives (br). **V&A Images / Victoria and Albert Museum, London:** (bl, c, cr, bc). **105 Münchner Stadtmuseum:** Sammlung Mode / Textilien / Kostümbibliothek (t). **V&A Images / Victoria and Albert Museum, London:** Given by G.P. & J. Baker Ltd (b). **106 Corbis:** Christie's Images (cl); Swim Ink 2, LLC (c); Found Image Press (cr, br); Leemage (bc). **Dorling Kindersley:** Woolley and Wallis / Judith Miller (bl). **107 Dorling Kindersley:** Lyon and Turnbull Ltd. / Judith Miller. **108 Alamy Images:** Positive image (bl). **Getty Images:** (br); George Rose (cl). **Science & Society Picture Library:** National Media Museum (cr). **109 Alamy Images:** Antiques & Collectables (tc). **Dorling Kindersley:** (tl); Museum of Design in Plastics, Bournemouth Arts University (cl); (cr). **Courtesy of Fujitsu Ltd:** (bl). **Getty Images:** Science & Society Picture Library (tr). **Courtesy of Nikon:** (bc). **© Panasonic Corporation:** (br). **Science & Society Picture Library:** Kodak Collection / NMeM (c). **112 Corbis:** Angelo Hornak (bc); Photononstop / Yves Talensac (br). **113 Corbis:** Norbert Eisele-Hein / JAI (bl). **V&A Images / Victoria and Albert Museum, London:** (bc, br). **114 Dorling Kindersley:** Alan Moss / Judith Miller. **115 Dorling Kindersley:** DeLorenzo Gallery / Judith Miller (tl); Jazzy Art Deco / Judith Miller (tc, tr); Eileen Lane Antiques / Judith Miller (cl); John Sollo / David rago (joint sales) / Judith Miller (c); High Style Deco / Judith Miller / **DACS, London 2015:** (bl, bc); Alan Moss / Judith Miller (br). **116 Dorling Kindersley:** DeLorenzo Gallery / Judith Miller. **117 Dorling Kindersley:** DeLorenzo Gallery / Judith Miller (tr); Quittenbaum / Judith Miller (tl); John Jesse / Judith Miller (tc); High Style Deco / Judith Miller (c); Freeman's / Judith Miller (bc); Jazzy Art Deco / Judith Miller (cl). **© MOURON. CASSANDRE. www.cassandre-france.com:** Lic 2015-17-03-02 (br). **118 RMN:** Jean-Gilles Berizzi, © ADAGP / DACS, London 2015. **119 Alamy Images:** The Art Archive (bc). **Bridgeman Images:** Private Collection, Photo © Christie's Images (br). **Dorling Kindersley:** DeLorenzo Gallery / Judith Miller (bl). **Getty Images:** Roger Viollet / Albin Guillot (tl). **120 Dorling Kindersley:** The Design Gallery / Judith Miller (cl); Moderne Gallery / Judith Miller (c); Gallery 1930 Susie Cooper / Judith Miller (bc); Woolley and Wallis / Judith Miller (bl, cr). **121 Cooper-Hewitt, Smithsonian Design Museum,:** Museum purchase from General Acquisitions Endowment. 1982-8-1 (cl). **Dorling Kindersley:** Gallery 1930 Susie Cooper / Judith Miller (tl). **V&A Images / Victoria and Albert Museum, London:** (r, bl). **122 Alamy Images:** James Jenkins – Visual Arts. **123 Dorling Kindersley:** Judith Miller / Lyon and Turnbull Ltd. (bl); Judith Miller / Gorringes (fbl); Judith Miller / Woolley and Wallis (bc, br). **Stoke-on-Trent City Archives:** (tl). **124 Cooper-Hewitt, Smithsonian Design Museum,:** Museum purchase from Friends of Applied Arts and Industrial Design, General Acquisitions Endowment, and Morrill Acquisitions Funds. 2002-3-2 (cl). **Dorling Kindersley:** Quittenbaum / Judith Miller (c, bc); Judith Miller / Sloans & Kenyon (bl). **125 Cooper-Hewitt, Smithsonian Design Museum,:** Museum purchase from Decorative Arts Association Acquisition and General Acquisitions Endowment Funds. 1993-111-3 (bl). **Dorling Kindersley:** Judith Miller / High Style Deco (bc). **Rhode Island School of Design:** (t). **Photo Scala, Florence:** Museum of Modern Art (MoMA), New York, USA (br). **126 Georg Jensen AS, Denmark**. **127 Dorling Kindersley:** Judith Miller / The Silver Fund / © DACS, London 2015 (br). Judith Miller / The Silver Fund (bl, bc). **Wikipedia:** Royal Library Copenhagen (tl). **128 Science & Society Picture Library:** National Railway Museum. **129 Getty Images:** Gamma-Keystone / Keystone-France (tl). **Photo Scala, Florence:** The Metropolitan Museum of Art, New York, Gift of David A. Hanks, 1986 (br). **V&A Images / Victoria and Albert Museum, London:** (bl, bc). **130 Corbis:** Bettmann (cr). **Dorling Kindersley:** Didcot Railway Centre (cl); The National Railway Museum, York / Science Museum Group (tr); Virginia Museum of Transportation (bl). **Science & Society Picture Library:** National Railway Museum (br). **131 colour-rail.com:** (bl). **Dorling Kindersley:** B&O Railroad Museum, Baltimore, Maryland, USA (tl); National Railway Museum, York (tr, c). **Vossloh AG:** (br). **132–133 Corbis:** William Manning. **134 Cooper-Hewitt, Smithsonian Design Museum,:** Gift of Paul F. Walter. 1991-30-4 / The Edith Lutyens and Norman Bel Geddes Foundation, Inc. (c). **Corbis:** Bettmann (br). **Dorling Kindersley:** Judith Miller / Edison Gallery (bl); Clive Streeter (tc). **Photo Scala, Florence:** Museum of Modern Art (MoMA), New York, USA (tl, cl, cr, tr). **135 Photo Scala, Florence:** Art Resource / The Metropolitan Museum of Art. **136 Dorling Kindersley:** Judith Miller / Ritzy (tc); Judith Miller / Atlantique City (c); Judith Miller / James Bridges Collection (cr, bc); Judith Miller / Sloan's (br). **Museum of Design in Plastics:** (bl); Kodak Hawkette Camera and trademarks are property of Kodak and are used with permission (tr). **138 Kelly Gallery, New York:** Jeffrey Apoian / © ADAGP, Paris and DACS, London 2015. **139 Alamy Images:** The Art Archive © ADAGP, Paris and DACS, London 2015 (br). **Bridgeman Images:** Private Collection, Photo © Christie's Images (tl). **Dorling Kindersley:** Judith Miller / Lyon and Turnbull Ltd. (tc); Judith Miller / Woolley and Wallis (cra); Judith Miller / Freeman's (bl); Dreweatt Neate / Judith Miller (bc). **Getty Images:** De Agostini Picture Library (cl). **140 Bridgeman Images:** Christie's Images (tl, bl); Saint Louis Art Museum, Missouri, USA / Gift of John Roslevich (cr). **Copyright P&G:** (br). **Dorling Kindersley:** Dave King (c); Museum of Design in Plastics, Bournemouth Arts University, UK (bc). **141 Alamy Images:** UAA (bc). **Bridgeman Images:** Dallas Museum of Art, Texas, USA / gift of the Alconda-Owsley Foundation in honor of Elizabeth Boeckman (cl). **Copyright P&G:** (bl). **Denhams:** (tl). **Dorling Kindersley:** (ftl); The Science Museum, London (tc). **IKEA UK Ltd:** (br). **Lorenz s.r.l.:** (r). **Photo Scala, Florence:** DeAgostini Picture Library (tr). **142 Design C20:** (bl, bc). **142–143 Design C20**. **144 akg-images:** Raymond Loewy™ by Loewy Design LLC. / www.RaymondLoewy.com / Cmg Worldwide. **145 Bridgeman Images:** Private Collection, Photo © Christie's Images / Cmg Worldwide (tl). **Getty Images:** Sylvain Grandadam (br). **Photo Scala, Florence:** Museum of Modern Art (MoMA), New York, USA (tc, tr, c, bl, bc). **Science & Society Picture Library:** Science Museum (cl). **146–147 Dorling Kindersley:** Courtesy of Colin Spong. **146 Dorling Kindersley:** Courtesy of Colin Spong (t). **147 Dorling Kindersley:** Courtesy of Colin Spong (tl, tr). **148 Dorling Kindersley:** Judith Miller / Bonny Yankauer (c); Quittenbaum / Judith Miller (bc); Judith Miller / John Jesse (br); Judith Miller / Cristobal (cr). **149 Dorling Kindersley:** Judith Miller / John Jesse (tl); Judith Miller / Freeman's (cl); Judith Miller / Macklowe Gallery (bl); Judith Miller / Somlo Antiques (r). **150 Dorling Kindersley:** Quittenbaum / Judith Miller. **151 Alamy Images:** The Art Archive (tl). **Bridgeman Images:** Indianapolis Museum of Art, USA / Carl H. Lieber Memorial Fund (bl). **Dorling Kindersley:** Mallett / Judith Miller (bc); Judith Miller / Macklowe Gallery (tc); **Bridgeman Images** / Private Collection / De Agostini Picture Library / A. Dagli Orti (tr); Judith Miller / Woolley and Wallis (c); Judith Miller / Mary Ann's Collectibles (br). **V&A Images / Victoria and Albert Museum, London:** (cl). **152 Getty Images:** Wolfgang Kaehler. **153 Dorling Kindersley:** Van Den Bosch (br); Judith Miller / David Rago Auctions (bc). **Musée Lalique:** S. Bandmann and R. Ooi Collection. Photo © Studio Y. Langlois, (bl). **TopFoto.co.uk:** Roger-Viollet (tl). **154 Photo Scala, Florence:** Museum of Modern Art (MoMA), New York, USA (l). **155 Dorling Kindersley:** James D Julia Inc / Judith Miller (l); Judith Miller / Mark Hill Collection (c); Judith Miller / Deco Etc (bc, tr); Judith Miller / Rosebery / © ADAGP, Paris and DACS, London 2015 (br). **Photo Scala, Florence:** Museum of Modern Art (MoMA), New York, USA (tc). **156 Alamy Images:** Lordprice Collection (cr). **Bridgeman Images:** Private Collection / DaTo Images (bc); Victoria & Albert Museum, London (c). **Corbis:** Found Image Press / ©

Dumbarton Arts, LLC/VAGA, NY/DACS, London 2015 (br); (cl); GraphicaArtis (bl). **157 © MOURON. CASSANDRE. www.cassandre-france.com:** Lic 2015-17-03-02. **158 Alamy Images:** Steve Vidler. **159 Bridgeman Images:** Pictures From History (tl). **By permission of The British Library:** ORB.40 / 404 (2) (br). **Shanghai Kaiming Book Store:** (bl). **Shiseido Corporate Museum:** (bc). **160 Photo Scala, Florence:** Museum of Modern Art (MoMA), New York, USA / © Succession Henri Matisse / DACS, London 2015. **161 Cooper-Hewitt, Smithsonian Design Museum,:** Gift of Cincinnati Art Museum; 1990-129-1 (tc); Museum purchase from Au Panier Fleuri Fund; 1934-14-4 / © ADAGP, Paris and DACS, London 2015 (c); Museum purchase through bequest of Ida C. McNeil in memory of Lincoln C. McNeil and Catherine McNeil; 1989-86-1. Courtesy Deskey Associates Inc. (cr); Museum purchase through gift of Frederick Rathbone; 1949-13-1 (br). **V&A Images / Victoria and Albert Museum, London:** (bl, bc); (tr, cl). **162–163 Corbis:** Photononstop / Yves Talensac. **166 Bridgeman Images:** The Fine Art Society, London, UK / DACS, London 2015 (br). **Dorling Kindersley:** Wiener Kunst Auktionen - Palais Kinsky / Judith Miller (bl). **www.classicon.com:** under licence from Aram Designs (bc). **167 Cassina:** (bc). **Dorling Kindersley:** Judith Miller / Woolley and Wallis (br); Wiener Kunst Auktionen – Palais Kinsky / Judith Miller (bl). **168 Corbis:** Hendrik Schmidt / Epa. **169 Alamy Images:** Universal Art Archive / DACS, London 2015 (bc). **Dorling Kindersley:** Herr Auctions / DACS, London 2015 (br); Judith Miller / Freeman's (tl). **1stdibs.com:** (bl). **170 akg-images:** Les Arts Décoratifs, Paris / Jean Tholance. **171 Alamy Images:** Andreas von Einsiedel (bl). **Courtesy Die Neue Sammlung – The International Design Courtesy Die Neue Sammlung - The International Design Museum Munich:** (tr). Dorling Kindersley: Judith Miller / Freeman's (tl). **Getty Images:** DeAgostini (c). **Photo Scala, Florence:** Museum of Modern Art (MoMA), New York, USA (tc, br). **Zanotta Spa:** (bc). **172 Alamy Images:** Julian Castle / DACS, London 2015 (bl). **Photo Scala, Florence:** Museum of Modern Art (MoMA), New York, USA / DACS, London 2015 (br). **173 Bridgeman Images:** Private Collection / Christie's Images (bl). **Designmuseum Danmark:** DACS, London 2015. **Photo Scala, Florence:** Museum of Modern Art (MoMA), New York, USA / DACS, London 2015 (tr); Museum of Modern Art (MoMA), New York, USA (cl, bc). **V&A Images / Victoria and Albert Museum, London:** (c, br).**174 Knoll Inc. 175 Corbis:** Arcaid / G. Jackson (bc). **Dorling Kindersley:** Wiener Kunst Auktionen / Palais Kinsky / Judith Miller (br). **Getty Images:** Fine Art Images / Heritage Images (tl). **Knoll Inc.:** (bl). **177 Dorling Kindersley:** Aram store: Stockist and photography location. **178 SuperStock:** Iain Masterton / age fotostock / © FLC/ ADAGP, Paris and DACS, London 2015. **179 Cassina:** (tl, br). **Dorling Kindersley:** Lyon and Turnbull Ltd. / Judith Miller / © ADAGP, Paris and DACS, London 2015 / © FLC/ ADAGP, Paris and DACS, London 2015 (bl). **Photo Scala, Florence:** Museum of Modern Art (MoMA), New York, USA (bc). **180–181 akg-images:** Bildarchiv Monheim / © ARS, Frank Lloyd Wright / DACS, London 2015.**182 Corbis:** Atlantide Phototravel / © ARS, NY, Frank Lloyd Wright / DACS, London 2015.**183 Alamy Images:** AF Fotografie (tl). **Dorling Kindersley:** Andrew Leyerle / © ARS, NY, Frank Lloyd Wright / DACS, London 2015 (bl). **Photo Scala, Florence:** Museum of Modern Art (MoMA), New York, USA / © ARS, NY, Frank Lloyd Wright / DACS, London 2015 (br). **184 Alamy Images:** Heritage Image Partnership Ltd. **185 Alamy Images:** Simon Curtis (tr). **Bridgeman Images:** Badisches Landesmuseum, Karlsruhe, Germany / DACS, London 2015 (cr); Tretyakov Gallery, Moscow, Russia / RIA Novosti (bl); Robert Bird Photography (br). **Dorling Kindersley:** Judith Miller / Woolley and Wallis (tl); Judith Miller / Freeman's (c). **V&A Images / Victoria and Albert Museum, London:** (bc). **186 www.classicon.com:** under licence from Aram Designs. **187 This image is reproduced with the kind permission of the National Museum of Ireland:** (tl). **www. classicon.com:** under licence from Aram Designs (bl, br, bc). **188 Bridgeman Images:** Minneapolis Institute of Arts, MN, USA / The Modernism Collection, gift of Norwest Bank Minnesota (bc). **National Museum of Fine Arts, Sweden:** (br). Rijksmuseum Amsterdam: (bl). **Photo Scala, Florence:** Art Resource / The Metropolitan Museum of Art (cl); Museum of Modern Art (MoMA), New York, USA (c). **189 Photo Scala, Florence:** Art Resource / The Metropolitan Museum of Art (cl). **V&A Images / Victoria and Albert Museum, London:** © ADAGP, Paris and DACS, London 2015 / DACS, London 2015 (r). **Vipp A/S:** (bl). **190 Photo Scala, Florence:** Museum of Modern Art (MoMA), New York, USA. **191 akg-images:** Interfoto (bl). **Alamy Images:** Heritage Image Partnership Ltd (bc). **Bridgeman Images:** Private Collection / Christie's Images (br). Corbis: Heritage Images (tl). **192 The Corning Museum of Glass, Corning, NY:** (tr). **Dorling Kindersley:** Judith Miller / Lyon and Turnbull Ltd. **193 Dorling Kindersley:** Judith Miller / Graham Cooley (tl). **LOBMEYR:** (bl). **Photo Scala, Florence:** (cl); Museum of Modern Art (MoMA), New York, USA (cr, br, bc). **194 akg-images:** Archives CDA / St-Genès. **195 Artek:** (bc, br). Corbis: Bettmann (tl). **Dorling Kindersley:** Judith Miller / Freeman's (bl). **196 akg-images:** (bl). Alamy Images: Givaga (c); Interfoto (bc). John Kratz: (br). **197 Bridgeman Images:** Dallas Museum of Art, Texas, USA / gift of John T. Howell and Thomas J. Howell in memory of their father John P. Howell (tr). **Cooper-Hewitt, Smithsonian Design Museum,:** (b). Getty Images: Science & Society Picture Library (tl). **198 Dorling Kindersley:** Judith Miller / Atlantique City (cl); The Science Museum, London (tr, tc); Museum of Design in Plastics, Bournemouth Arts University, UK (bl, cr). **199 © Amazon.com, Inc.:** Echo Devices & Alexa (br). **Dorling Kindersley:** The Museum of the Moving Image, London (tl). **200 Museum of Decorative Arts, Prague. 201 Alamy Images:** Universal Art Archive (bl). **Photo Scala, Florence:** Museum of Modern Art (MoMA), New York, USA (tl, cl, c, br). Wikipedia: (tr, bc). **202–202 Dorling Kindersley:** PENGUIN and the Penguin logo are trademarks of Penguin Books Ltd. **204 Alamy Images:** Heritage Image Partnership Ltd (br); Universal Art Archive (bc). **Bridgeman Images:** Private Collection / Calmann & King Ltd (bl); Tretyakov Gallery, Moscow, Russia (c). **Corbis:** Christie's Images (cl). **Photo Scala, Florence:** Museum of Modern Art (MoMA), New York, USA (cr). **205 Alamy Images:** AF Fotografie. **206 Dorling Kindersley:** Museum of Design in Plastics, Bournemouth Arts University, UK (c). **207 Dorling Kindersley:** Maidstone Museum and Bentliff Art Gallery (tr). **Reproduced with Permission of Dell COPYRIGHT © Dell 2020. ALL Rights Reserved.:** (br). **210 Dorling Kindersley:** Herr Auctions / Judith Miller / © DACS, London 2015 (bc). **Knoll Inc.:** (bl). **Orrefors Kosta Boda AB:** (br). **211 Dorling Kindersley:** Judith Miller / Bonhams, Bayswater (bl). **twentytwentyone shop:** Robin and Lucienne Day Foundation (original design for Thomas Somerset 1950s–1960s) (bc). **Vitra Management AG / © Eames Office LLC (eamesoffice.com)** (br). **212 V&A Images / Victoria and Albert Museum, London. 213 Estate of Abram Games** / © Estate of Abram Games (tl). Dorling Kindersley: Judith Miller / © Estate of Abram Games (br). **Race Furniture Limited:** (bc). **214 Bridgeman Images:** Dallas Museum of Art, Texas, USA / Gift of Herman Miller, Inc. Zeeland, Michigan (cl). **The Robin and Lucienne Day Foundation:** (bl). **Dorling Kindersley:** Judith Miller / Freeman's (cr). **Knoll Inc.:** (c). **twentytwentyone shop:** Robin and Lucienne Day Foundation (br). **215 Hayloft Mid Century (http://www.midcenturyhome. co.uk):** (br). **Photo Scala, Florence:** Museum of Modern Art (MoMA), New York, USA (bl). **Vitra Management AG:** (tr). **216 Corbis:** Arcaid / Richard Powers. **217 Artek:** (bl); Aino Huovio (tl). Orrefors Kosta Boda AB: (bc). Wirkkala archives: (br). **218 Bonacina Vittorio Design Srl:** (cr). **Photo Scala, Florence:** Museum of Modern Art (MoMA), New York, USA (bl, bc). **V&A Images / Victoria and Albert Museum, London:** (cl). **219 Artek:** Tuomas Uusheimo (bl). **Dorling Kindersley:** Judith Miller / Freeman's (r). **Photo Scala, Florence:** Museum of Modern Art (MoMA), New York, USA (cl). **220–221 Alamy Images:** Hemis. **222 akg-images** / © Eames Office LLC (eamesoffice.com). **223 Dorling Kindersley:** Judith Miller / Wallis and Wallis / © Eames Office LLC (eamesoffice.com) (bl) ; Judith Miller / Lyon and Turnbull Ltd / © Eames Office LLC (eamesoffice.com) (br). **Vitra Management AG:** (bc); (tl). **224 Onecollection A/S. Photo Scala, Florence:** Museum of Modern Art (MoMA), New York, USA (bl). **225 Dorling Kindersley:** Judith Miller / Lyon and Turnbull Ltd. (cl). **Knoll Inc.:** (tc, tr, cr). **Photo Scala, Florence:** Museum of Modern Art (MoMA), New York, USA (c, bc). **Tendo Co. Ltd:** (br). **Wright:** (tl). **226 Dorling Kindersley:** Judith Miller / Gary Grant (cl). **227 Dorling Kindersley:** Judith Miller / Gary Grant (cr, cl); Judith Miller / Freeman's (c); Judith Miller / Art Deco Etc (bl). **Maru:** (br). **© Rosenthal GmbH GERMANY:** (bc). **Photo Scala, Florence:** Museum of Modern Art (MoMA), New York, USA (tl, tr). **228 Bridgeman Images:** The Israel Museum, Jerusalem, Israel / Gift of the manufacturer (cr). **Dorling Kindersley:** The Silver Fund / Judith Miller (l). **Photo Scala, Florence:** Art Resource / The Metropolitan Museum of Art (br). **Yale University Art Gallery:** (tr). **229 Dorling Kindersley:** Judith Miller / Graham Cooley (bc). **Gateway Japan ApS:** (bl). **Photo Scala, Florence:** Museum of Modern Art (MoMA), New York, USA (cr). **V&A Images / Victoria and Albert Museum, London:** (cl, c, br). **230 V&A Images / Victoria and Albert Museum, London:** Robin and Lucienne Day Foundation. **231 Alamy Images:** V&A Images / Robin and Lucienne Day Foundation (bl, br). **The Robin and Lucienne Day Foundation:** (tl). **V&A Images / Victoria and Albert Museum, London:** Robin and Lucienne Day Foundation (bc). **232 The Advertising Archives. 233 Decophobia.com:** (bl). **Dorling Kindersley:** Museum of Design in Plastics, Bournemouth Arts University, UK (tl, bc, br). **234 Bridgeman Images:** Kunsthalle, Tubingen, Germany / © R. Hamilton. All Rights Reserved / DACS, London 2015 (bl). Dorling Kindersley: Judith Miller / Manic Attic (c); Judith Miller / Luna (br). **235 Alamy Images:** David Gee 4 (bc); Interfoto (br). das programm: (cr). **Photo Scala, Florence:** Museum of Modern Art (MoMA), New York, USA (tr). Smeg S.p.A: (l). **236 Dorling Kindersley:** Dyson Ltd (br). **Photo Scala, Florence:** Museum of Modern Art (MoMA), New York, USA (bc). **Science & Society Picture Library:** Science Museum (cl, c). **237 Alamy Images:** Huw Jones (cr). **Bridgeman Images:** Dallas Museum of Art, Texas, USA / gift of John T. Howell and Thomas J. Howell in memory of their father John P. Howell (c). **© Dyson 2020:** (br). **iRobot Corporation:** (bl). **Numatic:** (bc). **Science & Society Picture Library:** Science Museum (tl, tc, tr). **Vacuum Cleaner Museum / Tacony Corporation:** (cl). **238 Design Bibliotheque,** Photo Tom Brown. **239 Photo Scala, Florence:** bpk, Bildagentur fuer Kunst, Kultur und Geschichte, Berlin (tl); Museum of Modern Art (MoMA), New York, USA (bl, bc). **Science & Society Picture Library:** Science Museum (br). **240 Dorling Kindersley:** Museum of Design in Plastics, Bournemouth Arts University, UK (l, cr). **241 Dorling Kindersley:** Freeman's / Judith Miller (cl); Museum of Design in Plastics, Bournemouth Arts University, UK (bl, br). **Photo Scala, Florence:** DeAgostini Picture Library (cr); Museum of Modern Art (MoMA), New York, USA (bc, c). **242 Wright. 243 akg-images:** De Agostini Picture Lib. / A. Dagli Orti (tl). **Dorling Kindersley:** Judith Miller / Wallis and Wallis (tr); Judith Miller / Auktionhaus Dr Fischer / DACS, 2015 (ca); Judith Miller / Auktionhaus Dr Fischer (bc); Judith Miller / Quittenbaum (bl). **Museum of Decorative Arts, Prague:** Gabriel Urbanek (cl, br). **244–245 Wright. 245 Wright:** (br). **246 Bridgeman Images:** Private Collection / Christie's Images / Tapio Wirkkala Rut Bryk Foundation (br). **Dorling Kindersley:** Kim Thrower / Andy McConnell (l, tr). **V&A Images / Victoria and Albert Museum, London:** Nuutajarvi Glassworks (cr). **247 1stdibs.com:** (br). **Dorling Kindersley:** Judith

Miller / Mum Had That (cl, bl); Judith Miller / The Glass Merchant (c). **Photo Scala, Florence:** Museum of Modern Art (MoMA), New York, USA (bc). **248–249 Corbis:** Kenneth Johansson. **250 Photo Scala, Florence:** Museum of Modern Art (MoMA), New York, USA (cr). **Wright:** (tr). **251 Corbis:** G. Jackson / Arcaid (cr). **Louis Poulsen Lighting A/S:** (bc). **Santa & Cole:** (br). **Photo Scala, Florence:** (tr). **Vitra Management AG. Wright:** (c). **252 Bridgeman Images:** Private Collection / Christie's Images / Tapio Wirkkala Rut Bryk Foundation (cr); Private Collection / Christie's Images (bc, br). **Photo Scala, Florence:** Museum of Modern Art (MoMA), New York, USA (cl); © ADAGP, Paris / DACS, London 2015 (c). **Sherbyte:** Univers® (bl). **253 Getty Images:** Movie Poster Image Art / The Estate of Saul Bass (tl). **The International Institute of Social History (Amsterdam)**. **Photo Scala, Florence:** Museum of Modern Art (MoMA), New York, USA / DACS, London 2015 (cl); Museum of Modern Art (MoMA), New York, USA / © Estate of Abram Games and Transport for London (r). **256 Dorling Kindersley:** Peter Harris (br); Rodger Dudding (cr). **257 Barry Hayden:** Mercedes-Benz Cars UK Limited (br). **Dorling Kindersley:** R. Florio (tl). **James Mann:** (tr). **260 Marimekko:** (bc). **Photo Scala, Florence:** Christie's Images, London (br). **Vitra Management AG:** (bl). **261 Alamy Images:** Adrian Laschi (bc). **Bridgeman Images:** Private Collection / Christie's Images (bl). **Dorling Kindersley:** Museum of Design in Plastics, Bournemouth Arts University, UK (br). **262–263 Photograph courtesy of The Port Authority of New York and New Jersey:** John Bartelstone (Photographer). **264 Alamy Images:** Interfoto (cl, c, cr). **Dorling Kindersley:** Glasgow City Council (Museums) (tr); Judith Miller / Luna (bl). **Science & Society Picture Library:** National Museum of Photography, Film & Television (br); Science Museum (bc). **265 Alamy Images:** V&A Images / Robin and Lucienne Day Foundation (tr). **Dorling Kindersley:** Judith Miller / Lawrence's Fine Art Auctioneers (tl). **Dreamstime.com:** Kitchner Bain / Kitch (bl). Samsung: (br). **Photo Scala, Florence:** (cl). **Science & Society Picture Library:** National Museum of Photography, Film & Television (tc); (c); National Museum of Photography, Film & Television / JVC (cr). **266–267 Bridgeman Images:** Indianapolis Museum of Art, USA / Gift of Dr. Michael Sze (bl). **267 Bridgeman Images:** Museum of Fine Arts, Houston, Texas, USA / Gift of the Houston Astros Baseball Club and Drayton McLane (c). **Photo Scala, Florence:** Museum of Modern Art (MoMA), New York, USA (tc, tr, bc). **V&A Images / Victoria and Albert Museum, London:** Zanotta (tl). **Wright:** (br). **268 Dorling Kindersley:** Judith Miller / Lyon and Turnbull Ltd. (l). **The Interior Archive:** Edina Van Der Wyck (cr). **269 Carl Hansen & Søn Møbelfabrik A/S:** (c). **Photo Scala, Florence:** (br); Museum of Modern Art (MoMA), New York, USA (cl). **Wright:** (cr, bc). **270 Photoshot:** Red Cover / Anastasios Mentis. **271 Vitra Management AG:** (bc, br); (tl, bl). **272 Herman Miller. 273 Herman Miller** / © Eames Office LLC (eamesoffice.com) (tl); Herman Miller: (bl, bc, br). **276 Dorling Kindersley:** Judith Miller / VinMagCo. **277 Dorling Kindersley:** Judith Miller / China Search (bl). **Getty Images:** Hulton Archive / Jill Kennington (tl). **Habitat UK:** (bc, br). **278–279 Corbis:** Diego Lezama Orezzol / © NIEMEYER, Oscar / DACS, London 2015. **280 akg-images:** VIEW Pictures / Edmund Sumner. **281 Vitra Management AG:** (tl, bl, bc, br). **282 V&A Images / Victoria and Albert Museum, London. 283 Bitossi Ceramiche Srl:** (cr). **Dorling Kindersley:** Judith Miller / Festival (tl, tr); Judith Miller / China Search (br). **Getty Images:** DeAgostini (bl). **V&A Images / Victoria and Albert Museum, London:** (cl, bc). **284 Dorling Kindersley:** Judith Miller / Art Deco Etc (cr). **Wright:** Tapio Wirkkala (l); (tr). **285 Dorling Kindersley:** Judith Miller / Dreweatt Neate (bc). Photo Scala, Florence: Museum of Modern Art (MoMA), New York, USA (cl, c, cr, br). **V&A Images / Victoria and Albert Museum, London:** (bl). **286 © Foundation Achille Castiglioni. 287 Flos S.p.A.:** (tl, bc, br). Zanotta Spa: (bl). **288 The Corning Museum of Glass, Corning, NY:** gift of the Steinberg Foundation (l, bc). **Dorling Kindersley:** Judith Miller / Wallis and Wallis (tc, cr). **Photo Scala, Florence:** Museum of Modern Art (MoMA), New York, USA (c, tr). **František Vízner Collection:** (br). **289 V&A Images / Victoria and Albert Museum, London:** Nuutajärvi Glassworks. **290 Dorling Kindersley:** Judith Miller / Freeman's (bc). **Mathmos Ltd:** (c). **NASA:** (bl). **R & Company:** Sherry Griffin (tl). **Photo Scala, Florence:** Museum of Modern Art (MoMA), New York, USA (cr). **Wright:** (tc, tr, br). **291 Bridgeman Images:** Private Collection / Christie's Images. **292 Flos S.p.A. 293 Flos S.p.A.:** (bl, bc, br, tl). **294–295 BD Barcelona Design. 295 BD Barcelona Design:** (tl, tr). **296 Kartell Spa. 297 Kartell Spa:** (bc, bl); Ferruccio Laviani. **298 Documentation of Technical Museum of Slovenia. 299 Alamy Images:** Chris Willson (bl). **Dorling Kindersley:** Judith Miller / Design20c (cl). **Getty Images:** George Rose (tr). **Kev Z:** (cr). **Photo Scala, Florence:** Museum of Modern Art (MoMA), New York, USA (tl, tc, br). **300 Copyright P&G:** (bl). **Photo Scala, Florence:** Cooper-Hewitt, National Design Museum, Smithsonian Institution / Art Resource, NY (cr); Museum of Modern Art (MoMA), New York, USA (tc, cl, c). **Stelton A/S:** (tr). **V&A Images / Victoria and Albert Museum, London:** (tl). **302 Getty Images:** Central Press. **303 Alamy Images:** Kodak (bc). **Getty Images:** Popperfoto (tl). **hitchlmylius:** (bl). **Image courtesy of Anglepoise®:** (br). **304 Alamy Images:** Uber Bilder (l). **Dorling Kindersley:** Judith Miller / Posteritati (cr). **Photo Scala, Florence:** Museum of Modern Art (MoMA), New York, USA (br). **305 Alamy Images:** AF Fotografie / © ADAGP, Paris / DACS, London 2015 (cl). **Bridgeman Images:** Private Collection / Peter Newark Pictures (cr). **Lebrecht Music and Arts:** Jan Morek / Forum (bl). **Photo Scala, Florence:** (bc); Museum of Modern Art (MoMA), New York, USA / DACS, London 2015 (c); Museum of Modern Art (MoMA), New York, USA (br). **306–307 Photo Scala, Florence:** Museum of Modern Art (MoMA), New York, USA. **308 Dorling Kindersley:** The Bate Collection (tr). **309 Alamy Images:** David Lee (bc). **Lebrecht Music and Arts:** Museum of Fine Arts, Boston (tc); Private Collection (bl, br). **310 Alamy Images:** doti (clb); Peter Etchells (cl); Barrie Harwood Signs (bl); Universal Art Archive (c). **Bridgeman Images:** Private Collection / DaTo Images / © ADAGP, Paris / DACS, London 2015 (bc). **310–311 Photo Scala, Florence:** Christie's Images, London / © ADAGP, Paris / DACS, London 2015. **311 Dorling Kindersley:** Judith Miller / Wallis and Wallis (bc). **Photo Scala, Florence:** Museum of Modern Art (MoMA), New York, USA (tc, tr, c, br). **312 Bridgeman Images:** (cr). **Courtesy of Maharam:** (c). **Marimekko:** (cl). Verner Panton Design: (bc). **V&A Images / Victoria and Albert Museum, London:** Sarah Campbell Ltd (br); Shirley Craven (bl). **313 Courtesy of Maharam:** (cl). **Philadelphia Museum Of Art, Pennsylvania:** Gift of Wacoal Interior Fabrics, 1983 (bl). **V&A Images / Victoria and Albert Museum, London. 316 Corbis:** Topic Photo Agency (bl). **Kartell Spa:** (bc). **Dennis Zanone:** Memphis (br). **317 Alessi (UK) Ltd:** (bl). **Dyson Ltd:** (bc). **Stuart Haygarth:** (br). **318 Photo Scala, Florence:** Art Resource / The Metropolitan Museum of Art / Memphis. **319 Bitossi Ceramiche Srl:** (bl). **Dorling Kindersley:** Museum of Design in Plastics, Bournemouth Arts University, UK / Alessi (br). **Getty Images:** Keystone-France / Gamma-Keystone (tl). **Photo Scala, Florence:** Christie's Images, London / Knoll (bc). **320 akg-images:** BD Barcelona Design. **Bridgeman Images:** Private Collection / Christie's Images / Cassina (cr). **Wright:** Zabro (br). **Dennis Zanone:** Memphis (tr). **321 Kartell Spa:** (bl). **Knoll Inc.:** (cr). **Sancal Diseño S.L.:** (br). **Photo Scala, Florence:** Alias Design (cl). **322 IKEA UK Ltd. 323 IKEA UK Ltd:** (tl, bl, bc, br). **324 Atelier Pelcl:** (br). **Danny Lane Ltd. Studio Suppanen:** (cr). **V&A Images / Victoria and Albert Museum, London:** Ron Arad (tr). **325 Getty Images:** Stuart Wilson (br). Kartell Spa: (c). **Modus Furniture:** (cr). **Vitra Management AG:** (cl). **Wright:** Cappellini (bc). **326 Knoll Inc. 327 Knoll Inc.:** (tl, bc). **Photo Scala, Florence:** (bl, br). **328 Photo Scala, Florence:** Museum of Modern Art (MoMA), New York, USA / Cassina. **329 akg-images:** Les Arts Décoratifs, Paris / Béatrice Hatala (tl). **Edra Spa:** (cr). **Courtesy of Marc Newson Ltd:** Fabrice Gousset (bl). **R & Company:** © DACS 2015 (br). **Photo Scala, Florence:** Knoll (tc); Museum of Modern Art (MoMA), New York, USA (c). **Wright:** Estudio Campana (bc). **Dennis Zanone:** Memphis (tr). **330 Courtesy of Marc Newson Ltd:** Rafael Vargas. **331 Courtesy of Marc Newson Ltd:** Romeo Balancourt (tl); Carin Katt (bl); Fabrice Gousset (bc, br). **332 Dreamstime.com:** Alexander Kirch. **333 Alamy Images:** David J. Green (cl); Interfoto; VIEW Pictures Ltd (br). **Courtesy of Apple:** (c). **Bang & Olufsen:** (tc, tr). **Samsung Electronics:** (bc). **© Sony Corporation:** (bl). **334 Dorling Kindersley:** Mum Had That / Judith Miller. **335 Bridgeman Images:** (cl). **Dorling Kindersley:** Judith Miller / Woolley and Wallis (c). **Qubus Design:** (bc). **V&A Images / Victoria and Albert Museum, London:** Michael Graves (tc); Richard Slee (bl). **Dennis Zanone:** Memphis (tl). **Victoria Miro Gallery, London:** (br). **336 Corbis:** Rommel / Masterfile (cr); Bo Zaunders (tr). **Sawaya & Moroni, Milan:** Studio Libeskind / Photo Marirosa Toscani Ballo. **337 Archive Matteo Thun. Oscar Tusquets Blanca:** (bc). **San Lorenzo:** Alberto Parise (cr). **Photo Scala, Florence:** Alessi (c); Museum of Modern Art (MoMA), New York, USA (tl); Museum of Fine Arts, Boston / Memphis (tc, br). **Dennis Zanone:** Rossi & Arcandi (tr). **338 V&A Images / Victoria and Albert Museum, London:** Ron Arad. **339 Alamy Images:** Steve Speller (tl). **Dorling Kindersley:** Museum of Design in Plastics, Bournemouth Arts University, UK (bl). **Magis Spa:** Ron Arad (br). **Vitra Management AG:** Ron Arad (bc). **340–341 Alamy Images:** imageBROKER. **342 The Corning Museum of Glass, Corning, NY:** Dante Marioni (bl). **Photo Scala, Florence:** (cl). **V&A Images / Victoria and Albert Museum, London:** Fujita Kyohei (cr); Danny Perkins (bc). **Wright:** Richard Marquis (br). **343 Lu Chi:** (bc), (r). **Marvin Lipofsky:** Photo: M. Lee Fatherree (cl). **344 Orrefors Kosta Boda AB. 345 akg-images:** Les Arts Décoratifs, Paris / Jean Tholance (tl). **Dorling Kindersley:** Judith Miller / Auktionhaus Dr Fischer (br). **Orrefors Kosta Boda AB:** (bc). **346 1stdibs.com:** Orrefors (cl). **Adrian Sassoon:** Colin Reid (br). **akg-images:** De Agostini Picture Lib. (c); Les Arts Décoratifs , Paris / Jean Tholance (bl). **Borek Sipek:** (cr). **347 Atelier Pelcl:** (bl). **Bruce Marks Glass:** (r). **Dorling Kindersley:** Judith Miller / Wallis and Wallis (tl). London Glassblowing – Peter Layton www.londonglassblowing.co.uk (cl). **348 Secto Design Oy. 349 Cooper-Hewitt, Smithsonian Design Museum,:** Nemo S.r.l. (cl). **FontanaArte Spa:** Andreas Engesvik (br). **Moooi:** Marcel Wanders (bc). **Photo Scala, Florence:** Museum of Modern Art (MoMA), New York, USA (c). **Studio Tord Boontje:** (bl). **Wright:** DROOG® (cr). **350 Paley Studios Archive:** Albert Paley (bc). **Studio Laviani:** Photo archive Foscarini (l). **Toshiyuki Kita Design Laboratory Ltd. V&A Images / Victoria and Albert Museum, London:** Tom Dixon (cr). **350–351 Wright:** (b). **351 Designed by Martín Azúa, Barcelona 2013 | Produced by Martín Azúa / Numbered | Photography by Martín Azúa:** (cl). **Lee Broom Ltd:** (r).**Photo Scala, Florence:** Museum of Modern Art (MoMA), New York, USA / Foscarini (tl). **Dennis Zanone:** DACS, London 2015 (r). **352–353 Stuart Haygarth. 353 V&A Images / Victoria and Albert Museum, London:** Bente Sætrang (tr). **355 MUJI UK:** (bl, bc, bl/a). **356 Dorling Kindersley:** Museum of Design in Plastics, Bournemouth Arts University, UK / Alessi (cl, c, bl, bc, br). **357 Dorling Kindersley:** Museum of Design in Plastics, Bournemouth Arts University, UK / Pandora Design (tl, cl, bl, r). **358 Alamy Images:** Modern Design. **359 Alamy Images:** Hemis (tl). **Kartell Spa:** (bc). **360 Alamy Images:** David Sanger Photography. **361 Dyson Ltd:** (tl, bl, bc, br). **362 Dorling Kindersley:** Alessi. **363 akg-images:** Les Arts Décoratifs, Paris / Jean Tholance / Habitat (bl). **Alessi (UK) Ltd:** (cl, bc). **Dorling Kindersley:** Cooper-Hewitt, Smithsonian Design Museum, (tc); Museum of Design in Plastics, Bournemouth Arts

University, UK (c). **Magis Spa:** (br). **Photo Scala, Florence:** Museum of Modern Art (MoMA), New York, USA (tr). **V&A Images / Victoria and Albert Museum, London:** Alessi (tl); Sony (cr). **364 Alamy Images:** Stanca Sanda / Apple. **365 Alamy Images:** Chris Wilson / Apple (bl). **Courtesy of Apple:** (tl, bc, br). **366 Photo Scala, Florence:** Museum of Modern Art (MoMA), New York, USA / Paul Rand; Museum of Modern Art (MoMA), New York, USA (tr, cr). **V&A Images / Victoria and Albert Museum, London:** April Greiman (br). **367 Obeygiant.com:** Illustration courtesy of Shepard Fairey (bl). **Thomas Wimberly:** (br). **V&A Images / Victoria and Albert Museum, London:** Ewa Baluk-Zaborowska / Jerzy Janiszewski (c); Neville Brody (cl). **Wuouxiang:** (bc). **368 Getty Images:** View Pictures / UIG. **369 Alamy Images:** Justin Kase z12z (bc). **Getty Images:** John Stillwell / AFP (tl). **LONGCHAMP:** (bl). **Photo Scala, Florence:** Museum of Modern Art (MoMA), New York, USA (br). **370 © 2020 Sennheiser electronic GmbH & Co. KG:** (br). **Alamy Images:** Tony Cordoza / Sony (c); Adrian Lyon (cl). **Amazon.com, Inc.:** (bc). **Courtesy of Apple:** (tc, cr). **Beats Electronics:** (tr). **Blackberry:** (bl). **Getty Images:** Google (c). **TomTom:** (tl). **371 Alamy Images:** PG Pictures / Apple. **372 Courtesy of Michael Graves Design Group:** (br). **Photo Scala, Florence:** DeAgostini Picture Library (cr). **Science & Society Picture Library:** Science Museum (bc). **The Swatch Group (UK) Limited:** (bl). **373 akg-images:** De Agostini Picture Lib. / A. Dagli Orti (c). **Alamy Images:** Chris Willson (cr). **Courtesy of Apple:** (br). **Blackberry:** (bc). **Nokia Corporation:** (bl). **374–375 Corbis:** Jane Sweeney / JAI / Zaha Hadid Architects. **377 Bridgeman Images:** Private Collection, Photo © Christie's Images (bc). **Dorling Kindersley:** Judith Miller / Sloans & Kenyon (bl); Judith Miller / Lyon and Turnbull Ltd. (fbl); Judith Miller / Van Den Bosch (br); Judith Miller / Sloan's (fbr). **378 akg-images:** Bildarchiv Monheim (bc). **Dorling Kindersley:** Lyon and Turnbull Ltd. / Judith Miller (fbr); Judith Miller / Gallery 1930 Susie Cooper (bl). **Photo Scala, Florence:** Museum of Modern Art (MoMA), New York, USA (fbl). **379 Design C20:** (fbr). **Dorling Kindersley:** Aram store: Stockist and photography location (bc). **Kelly Gallery, New York:** Jeffrey Apoian (bl). **National Museum of Fine Arts, Sweden:** (fbl). **380 akg-images:** De Agostini Picture Lib. / A. Dagli Orti (bc). **Dorling Kindersley:** Judith Miller / Wallis and Wallis (fbr); Courtesy of Colin Spong (bl). **V&A Images / Victoria and Albert Museum, London:** (fbl). **381 The Corning Museum of Glass, Corning, NY:** gift of the Steinberg Foundation (fbr). **Photo Scala, Florence:** Museum of Modern Art (MoMA), New York, USA (bc, bl). **V&A Images / Victoria and Albert Museum, London:** (fbl). **382 1stdibs.com:** Orrefors (br). **Dorling Kindersley:** Judith Miller / Design20c (fbl). **Photo Scala, Florence:** Knoll (bl). **Wright:** Richard Marquis (fbr). **383 Alamy Images:** Tony Cordoza / Sony (fbr). **Dorling Kindersley:** Judith Miller / Wallis and Wallis (bc); Museum of Design in Plastics, Bournemouth Arts University, UK (fbl). **Image courtesy of Erskine, Hall & Coe Ltd:** Artwork by Gustavo Pérez / Photography by Michael Harvey (br). **Courtesy of Marc Newson Ltd:** Fabrice Gousset (bl). **385 Photo Scala, Florence:** Digital image, The Museum of Modern Art, New York / © Estate of Anni Albers; ARS, NY & DACS, 2015 / DACS, London 2015 (br). **386 GAP Interiors:** Douglas Gibb (l). **387 akg-images:** (tc). **388 Dorling Kindersley:** Judith Miller / Posteritati (l). **389 Photo Scala, Florence:** Digital image, The Museum of Modern Art, New York © DACS, London VAGA, New York / DACS, London 2015 (bc). **391 Bridgeman Images:** Christie's Images / DACS, London 2015 (tr). **392 Cappellini Design Spa:** (bl). **393 Bridgeman Images:** Collection Kharbine-Tapabor, Paris, France (tr). **394–395 V&A Images / Victoria and Albert Museum, London:** Neville Brody. **396–397 Alamy Images:** Hemis. **398 Dorling Kindersley:** Alan Keohane / Courtesy of the Bellagio, Las Vegas (l). **399 V&A Images / Victoria and Albert Museum, London:** DACS, London 2015 (bc). **400 V&A Images / Victoria and Albert Museum, London:** Sarah Campbell Limited. **401 Dorling Kindersley:** Judith Miller / Gallery 1930 Susie Cooper (tr). **402 twentytwentyone shop:** Robin and Lucienne Day Foundation. **403 Dennis Zanone:** Memphis. **404 Bridgeman Images:** Private Collection (b). **405 Cappellini Design Spa:** Tom Dixon. **406 ercol Furniture Ltd:** (b). **407 Fornasetti Immaginazione s.r.l.:** (tc, c). **408 Alamy Images:** Pictorial Press Ltd (l). **409 Alamy Images:** Steve Allen (br). **410 www.classicon.com:** under licence from Aram Designs. **411 www.classicon.com:** (tr). **412–413 Alamy Images:** VIEW Pictures Ltd / Zaha Hadid Architects. **414 Getty Images:** View Pictures (tl). **415 Bridgeman Images:** Bibliotheque des Arts Decoratifs, Paris, France / Archives Charmet (b). **416 Getty Images:** (bl). **417 Marimekko.** **418 V&A Images / Victoria and Albert Museum, London.** **419 Bridgeman Images:** Christie's Images (b). **420 Bridgeman Images:** Christie's Images (l). **421 Photo Scala, Florence:** Digital image, The Museum of Modern Art, New York (br). **422 Knoll Inc.. 423 Photo Scala, Florence:** Digital image, The Museum of Modern Art, New York (tr). **424 Dorling Kindersley:** Judith Miller / David Rago Auctions / DACS, London 2015 (bl). **425 V&A Images / Victoria and Albert Museum, London:** (tr). **426 akg-images:** Estate of Raymond Loewy (tc). **427 Moroso S.p.A. 428 Wright:** (bl). **429 Photo Scala, Florence:** Digital image, The Museum of Modern Art, New York (tr). **430 Photo Scala, Florence:** Digital image, The Museum of Modern Art, New York. **431 Museo Nazionale Della Scienza E Della Tecnica 'leonardo Da Vinci'. 432 Ligne Roset. 433 Dorling Kindersley:** Judith Miller / Lyon and Turnbull Ltd.. **434 Photo Scala, Florence:** Digital image, The Museum of Modern Art, New York / © DACS 2015 / DACS, London 2015 (tl). **435 Corbis:** Andreas von Einsiedel. **436 Alamy Images:** Norman Owen Tomalin (bl). **437 akg-images:** De Agostini Picture Library (bc). **438 Alamy Images:** Andreas von Einsiedel. **439 Bridgeman Images:** Museumslandschaft Hessen Kassel / Gabriele Boessert / DACS, London 2015 (tr). **440 Bridgeman Images:** Christie's Images (b). **441 Bridgeman Images:** Christie's Images (tr). **442 Bridgeman Images:** Christie's Images (l). **443 Courtesy of the Vitsœ Archive. 444 Photo Scala, Florence:** Digital image, The Museum of Modern Art, New York (tl). **445 Bridgeman Images:** Christie's Images / DACS, London 2015 (br). **446–447 David Leventi. 448 Hus & Hem Ltd. 449 Photo Scala, Florence:** White Images / DACS, London 2015 (br). **450 Modus Furniture:** (br). **451 Alamy Images:** VIEW Pictures Ltd (r). **452 Dorling Kindersley:** Judith Miller / Gary Grant (tc). **453 Corbis:** Underwood & Underwood (t). **454–455 Photo Scala, Florence:** Pediconi. **456 Bridgeman Images:** Christie's Images (tc). **457 VSBA:** Rollin La France. **458 Photo Scala, Florence:** Digital image, The Museum of Modern Art, New York (tl). **459 V&A Images / Victoria and Albert Museum, London. 460 V&A Images / Victoria and Albert Museum, London:** (t). **461 Frank C. Müller, Baden-Baden. 462 Getty Images:** Philipp Klinger / DACS, London 2015

All other images © Dorling Kindersley
For further information see: www.dkimages.com

The publishers would also like to thank the following companies, organizations, museums, and individuals for their generosity in allowing Dorling Kindersley access to their exhibits and private collections for photography:

Judith Miller
Miller's Antiques & Collectibles
www.millersantiquesguide.com

Dorotheum
www.dorotheum.com

Dreweatts and Bloomsbury
www.dreweatts.com

Im Kinsky
www.imkinsky.com

James D Julia Inc.
www.juliaauctions.com

Kunst & Auktionhaus W. G. Herr
www.herr-auktionen.de

Lyon and Turnbull Ltd
www.lyonandturnbull.com

Quittenbaum
www.quittenbaum.de

Rago Arts and Auction Center
www.ragoarts.com

Von Zezschwitz
www.von-zezschwitz.de

Museum of Design in Plastics, Arts University
Bournemouth, Wallisdown,
Poole, BH12 5HH, England
www.modip.ac.uk

Van Den Bosch
Specialist in fine silver and jewelry
123 Grays Antique Centre, 58 Davis Street,
London W1K 5LP, England
www.vandenbosch.co.uk

Gorringe Antiques
159/160 Grays Antique Centre, 58 Davis Street,
London W1K 5LP, England
www.gorringeantiques.co.uk

Macklowe Gallery
667 Madison Avenue, New York 10065,
United States
www.macklowegallery.com

Knoll International
91 Goswell Road, London, EC1V 7EX, England
www.knolleurope.com